The Open Classroom Reader

THE
OPEN
CLASSROOM
READER

Edited by

Charles E. Silberman

RANDOM HOUSE

New York

Library of Congress Cataloging in Publication Data

Silberman, Charles E   1925–   comp.
The open classroom reader.

1. Open plan schools. I. Title.
LB1029.06S49   1973   372.1'3   72–11430
ISBN 0–394–48221–2

Manufactured in the United States of America

First Edition

For Ellen
My First Daughter

Contents

Introduction

"To change long-established habits in the individual is a slow, difficult and complicated process," John Dewey wrote twenty years ago, in the disillusionment of old age. "To change long-established institutions," he added, "is a much slower, more difficult, and far more complicated process."

Few institutions have seemed so impervious to change as the public schools. The late 1950s and early 1960s, for example, saw one of the largest and most sustained (and certainly the best financed) educational reform movements in American history, an effort that many observers, myself included, thought would transform the schools. Yet nothing of the sort happened. The reforms of the Education Decade, as it was called, like those of the Progressive Movement of the 1920s and 1930s, produced innumerable changes—and left the schools themselves largely unchanged.

It would be a mistake, however, to conclude that reform is impossible, for educational reformers typically have made little attempt to understand the institution they were trying to change. The curriculum reform movement of the 1950s and 1960s failed, in particular, because its leaders tried to impose change from outside and above, without regard for what teachers and principals thought or felt. One of the hallmarks of that movement, in fact, was the curriculum reformers' thinly veiled contempt for classroom teachers. With academic hubris, the university scholars who were in the vanguard of the movement tried to bypass the classroom teacher altogether. Their goal—sometimes stated, sometimes implicit—was to construct "teacher-proof" packages that would work whether teachers liked or understood the materials or not. Treated like assembly-line workers, teachers understandably responded accordingly, in effect sabotaging the "great compositions" that the reformers tried to impose on them. (For a more detailed analysis of the failures of educational reform, see Chapter 5 of *Crisis in the Classroom* and Seymour B. Sarason's important but neglected volume, *The Culture of the School and the Problem of Change*.)

A new breed of reformers has emerged that is free of this myopia; they know that substantive change is impossible unless teachers and principals understand and accept the approach in question. The reformers know, too, that change can be terribly threatening unless it is voluntary and gradual. They are persuaded, however, that if teachers are free to choose and are given appropriate help and support, large numbers of them will be willing and able to change.

In contrast to the way things appeared just a few years ago, there is reason to think that we may be at the beginning of a period of substantive and substantial reform of the public schools. The emphasis is on the subjunctive; the time has been too short, and the evidence is still too scanty, to permit prophecy. I am not yet optimistic, only hopeful, and I should like to couch my hopefulness in careful terms.

And yet I do insist on being hopeful—more hopeful, certainly, than I dared to be two and a half years ago, when I finished writing *Crisis in the Classroom*. A profound shift seems to be taking place in the way Americans think about children and about schools. I know no other way of explaining the extraordinary acceptance of my critique of the public schools by parents, teachers, school administrators and superintendents, university educationists, leaders of teacher unions and professional associations of teachers and administrators, and even some state commissioners of education. As Joseph Featherstone has written of my complaint that American schools tend to be grim and joyless places, "What was once a point made by a handful of radical cultural critics is now very close to being official wisdom."

This change in attitude is being translated into a change in practice; the past two years have seen a remarkable upsurge of interest in what has come to be called "open education" or "the open classroom." Hardly a day has gone by since publication of *Crisis in the Classroom*, and certainly not a week, in which I have not heard of another teacher, or group of teachers, or school, or school system that is moving (or thinking about moving) in the directions I proposed and described.

I refer to a change in atmosphere—toward more humaneness and understanding, toward more encouragement and trust. I also refer to a change in learning style—away from the teacher as the source of all knowledge to the teacher as the facilitator of learning, away from the traditional whole-class orientation to more concern with individualized learning. These two changes, in atmosphere and in learning style, go hand in hand, for a focus on each individual learner can only occur if the classroom environment is transformed.

Since the changes are most visible and numerous on the elementary-school level, let me offer a thumbnail description of the kind of classroom I am talking about. Rows of desks and chairs, all facing the front of the classroom, where the teacher sits at her desk and talks—and talks, and talks—are being replaced by an entirely new arrangement, which converts classrooms into workshops, with a reading corner, stocked with books—"book-books" as well as readers; a math area; a science center; an art nook; and so on. Each "interest area" is richly stocked with *things,* not merely with paper and pencil materials. In the math area, for example, there will be scales and all sorts of things to weigh and measure, to add and subtract: bottle caps, pebbles, shells. There will be clocks and yardsticks and commercially manufactured math games, and whatever else the teacher and students choose to put in it. And so it goes from one interest area to another. A visitor will also notice that teachers and students are not ruled by the bell; the usual 40-minute period is replaced by longer stretches of time in which students may be free to choose from a number of possible activities.

I described classrooms of this sort in my book. The largest number were in primary schools my wife and I had visited in England, where informal education (another synonym for open education) has been developing since the end of the Second World War; but I also described a handful of open classrooms we had visited in North Dakota, New York City, Philadelphia, and Tucson, Arizona. Our problem then was to find enough good open classrooms to demonstrate that informal education can work in the United States as well as in England. One measure of the change is the fact that if I were writing today, my problem would be to decide which classrooms to describe.

It is important, of course, to keep these changes in perspective; against the broad backdrop of American public education, the classrooms I am talking about constitute a small handful. For all of Lillian Weber's work in New York City, for example, plus that of Ann Cook and Herb Mack and Vivian Windley and a host of others, and for all the encouragement given their work by Dr. Harvey Scribner during his tenure as Chancellor of the New York City Public Schools, and by New York State Commissioner of Education Ewald Nyquist, the overwhelming majority of New York City classrooms remain grim, joyless, and destructive. The same is true almost everywhere else.

And yet if change falls short of what I would like it to be—short of what it *needs* to be—it is useful to note that some students and practitioners of open education have been expressing the fear that change is proceeding *too* rapidly. Indeed, one of the main criticisms directed at me and some other advocates of informal education is that we have helped create a bandwagon atmosphere, whereby teachers and administrators are driven to adopt some of the rhetoric and some of the physical trappings of the open classroom because it is "the latest thing." Needless to say, when teachers and administrators change for this. reason, they tend to mistake form for substance.

I share some of this concern about faddism, but not all of it. Given the enormous resistance to innovation in public education, a certain amount of faddism may be a useful lubricant for the wheels of change. In any case, I find a certain irony in this concern that change is proceeding too rapidly; only two or three years ago, the question was whether change was even possible!

And I am bothered by an unstated yet implicit elitism in this concern over the rate of change. The purists who seem to be saying, "If we cannot provide complete and proper total training for a teacher who wants to change toward open education, we would prefer that the teacher not attempt the change at all" are suggesting, in effect, that they have a monopoly on wisdom. More important, they are overlooking the generation of children and youth who will be harmed or even destroyed if the schools do *not* change. It is one thing to warn teachers about the difficulties involved in opening a classroom; it is quite another to advise them not to change at all!

Hence this book, which has been designed for teachers, students, administrators, parents, school-board members—in a word, for anyone who is dissatisfied with the status quo in the elementary school and who wants to explore the alternative approaches that go under the rubric of informal education, open education, and the open classroom.

Some of the best practitioners and theorists of open education, I should add, object to the use of that term, or any other; to apply a label, they argue, is to imply that there is a specific model or package that can and should be taken over in its entirety. I find this view naive and obscurantist; *some* agreed-upon terminology is essential if interested people are to be able to communicate with one another. The purist shunning of labels is misleading as well. As Anne Bussis and Edward Chittenden have written of one such group of practitioners, their "apparent inarticulateness certainly does not stem from lack of beliefs or ideas about education." On the contrary, they have a common position, one that is "characterized by strong convictions regarding the *process* of educating children." * In this volume, therefore, the terms "informal education," "open education," and "the open classroom" will be used freely and more or less interchangeably.

There is a certain risk in using any label, of course, as there is in any

* Anne M. Bussis and Edward A. Chittenden, *Analysis of an Approach to Open Education* (Princeton: Educational Testing Service, 1970), p. 9.

attempt to communicate at all. Let me try to minimize the risk of mis-understanding by emphasizing here, as I shall at a number of points throughout the book, that open education (or informal education or the open classroom) is not a model, still less a set of techniques, to be slavishly imitated or followed. It is, rather, an approach to teaching and learning—a set of shared attitudes and convictions about the nature and purposes of teaching and learning, about the nature of childhood and adolescence and ultimately about the nature of man. Contrasting a description of a typical open classroom with a description of a typical traditional classroom, Charity James writes, "These are not differences simply of method. They are different ways in which lives are being spent. They represent fundamental differences of values between the two institutions."

What are these differences in values? What are the shared attitudes that lie at the heart of informal education?

Advocates of informal education generally agree that the major purpose of education should be to educate educators, which is to say, to turn out men and women who are able to educate themselves—men and women who have the desire and the capacity to take responsibility for their own education and who are likely, therefore, to be life-long, self-directed learners. "Being educated," Professor David Hawkins of the University of Colorado, a leading American exponent of informal education, writes, "means no longer needing a teacher." Or as Sir Alec Clegg, one of the great contemporary English educators, suggests, the object of education "is not so much to convey knowledge as it is to excite a determination in the child to acquire it for himself, and to teach him how to go about acquiring it." Jean Piaget, the most influential child psychologist of modern times, puts it in an even broader context. "The principal goal of education," he insists, "is to create men and women who are capable of doing new things, not simply of repeating what other generations have done—men and women who are creative, inventive, and discoverers," who "have minds which can be critical, can verify, and not accept everything they are offered."

Open educators share a conception of childhood as something to be cherished, a conception that leads, in turn, to a concern for the quality of the school experience in its own right, not merely as preparation for later schooling or later life. Classrooms must be decent, pleasant places in which to spend time; for childhood and adolescence are not simply corridors through which children should be rushed as rapidly as possible to get them to the next stage.

It is not enough merely to respect childhood; it is necessary to respect children as well, which means respecting students' individuality, their interests, their needs, their strengths, their weaknesses. This means valuing individual differences instead of seeing them as a problem. It means accepting the legitimacy of individual students' individual interests—understanding that students do have interests, indeed whole agendas, of their own that are not the same as the teacher's, but that are legitimate and worth recognizing. And this, in turn, means letting students' learning, at least part of the time, proceed from their interests; it means giving them freedom to explore and supporting them in their explorations.

For this to happen, trust is indispensable. Unless there is trust—trust in students' desire to learn, trust in their capacity to learn through their own explorations, trust in their capacity for growth and fulfillment—teachers will not feel able to allow students to make choices, to take responsibility, to make mistakes, and to learn from their own mistakes. By the same token, teachers will not feel able to proceed unless they, too, are trusted—by administrators, no less than by students.

While no two classrooms are (or should be) exactly alike—a good open classroom reflects its teacher's personality and interests as well as its students'—it is nonetheless true that open classrooms tend to have their own "look," as distinguished from that of traditional classrooms. This distinctive look is a direct outgrowth of the view informal educators take of the purposes of education and of the ways in which children learn.

• If a teacher wants to emphasize individualized learning more than whole-group instruction—if she wants to change her role from teller to facilitator of learning—the arrangement of space has to accommodate the change. That means moving away from the traditional room arrangement, in which the teacher sits in the front of the room and the students sit in rows facing the teacher instead of one another, toward more flexible use of space, in which students can learn individually in small groups and as a whole class.

• If a teacher wants to emphasize self-initiated and self-directed learning rather than teacher-directed learning, books and materials must be easily accessible and plainly marked. The room must be arranged to permit an easy flow of traffic and to accommodate children who need quiet or solitude as well as those who work in groups.

• If a teacher wants to promote active rather than passive learning, she needs an abundant supply of materials children can touch and manipulate.

In short, to talk about room arrangements is not simply to talk about whether the furniture should be placed this way or that, or the day organized this way or that; it is to talk about the educational purposes the teacher has in mind and the processes by which she hopes to achieve them. It may be useful, therefore, to suggest what the open classroom is *not*.

• Creating large open spaces does not, by itself, constitute open education.

• Replacing desks and chairs with "interest areas" does not, by itself, constitute open education.

• Filling the interest areas with concrete materials that children can manipulate and use does not, by itself, constitute open education.

• Individualizing instruction does not, by itself, constitute open education.

• Placing children in multiage groups does not, by itself, constitute open education.

All these techniques, it should be emphasized, can be useful, and some may be essential, in creating and running an open classroom. Technique *is* important; without a mastery of technique, all the understanding in the world can leave a teacher helpless when he or she comes face to face with thirty or forty children. But method alone, without serious, sustained, and systematic thought about education, will turn a teacher into a mere technician with a bag of sterile tricks. No technique should be used unless a teacher has thought about why it is being used, what he or she hopes to accomplish with it, and how it will affect the children in question. Throughout this Reader, therefore, practical descriptions of technique—how-to explanations and discussions of the nitty-gritty of classroom activity—are interspersed with theoretical discussions of why and what for.

Since informal educators take a holistic view of teaching and learning—the English generally prefer the term "the integrated day" to "the open classroom"—there is an inevitable overlap from one section of the Reader to another. It is impossible, for example, to talk about the teacher's role without talking about curriculum, and it is equally difficult to talk about either without referring to the aims of education or to the ways in which children learn and grow.

And yet distinctions do have to be made if we are to impose some kind of order on what might otherwise be chaos. There is an analogy, perhaps, to the classroom itself. While informal teachers like to see learning whole and are deeply concerned with the integration of the various parts of the curriculum, they nonetheless arrange their classrooms into separate interest areas. It may be useful, therefore, to explain how this volume is organized, and why.

1. In line with the approach to teaching and learning that informal educators take, the Reader will begin with the concrete before moving on to the abstract and the theoretical. Since most Americans have never seen an open classroom—their experience as students and as teachers having been confined to traditional, formal classrooms—Part One presents a number of selections describing what open classrooms look like

and sound like, how they are organized, what a typical student's day may be like, and what a typical teacher's day may be like.

2. Having described in Part One how open classrooms are organized and run, we proceed, in Part Two, to ask *why* they are organized and run that way. The answers fall into two broad categories: the view of the aims and purposes of education that informal educators tend to share; and their views of the nature of childhood and of the ways in which children learn and develop.

3. In Part Three we examine the teacher's role, about which there is a good deal of misunderstanding. Contrary to the view that some hold, and contrary to actual practice in so-called free schools, with which open classrooms are sometimes confused, the teacher plays a more active and creative role in an open classroom than in a traditional room. Hence the first chapter of this part is devoted to an overview of the teacher's role, with descriptive materials intermixed with more theoretical discussions of the nature of authority, the nature of choice, the ways in which the teacher intervenes, and the reasons why. Chapter II is devoted to discussions of how to manage time and space: how, and why, teachers organize and arrange the space and time at their disposal. Since concrete materials play a different and vastly more important role in the open classroom, Chapter III discusses the kinds of materials that are used, the places they can be obtained, and the criteria for choosing (and using) them. Chapter IV examines the process of change, with selections describing and explaining how teachers have made the transition from formal to informal education.

4. Part Four is concerned with the curriculum and the integration of its various component parts. In Chapter I, we examine the curriculum as a whole: how do informal educators think about curriculum, and why do they approach it the way they do. The remaining chapters are devoted to practical and theoretical discussions of some of the major curriculum areas: reading, writing, and language development; mathematics; science; and the arts.

The reader is entitled, too, to some explanation of the criteria I followed in choosing the particular selections that are represented here. In general, the choices were determined by the interplay between my desire to present as systematic a picture of open education as possible and the availability of useful materials. Some, I am sure, will disagree with the way I define "useful." I have omitted a number of important writers because of my prejudice against opaque and turgid prose; with few exceptions, I chose only books and articles written in reasonably clear and lucid English. Some authors whose writing *is* lucid are not represented, on the other hand, because their style makes it difficult to excerpt a relatively brief passage that can stand alone. Some useful material has been omitted, moreover, because of the limitations of space; I was eager to hold the Reader to some manageable size and price. And some valuable materials have been left out, I am sure, because of the limitations of my own knowledge.

Had I been limited to my own knowledge of the literature, this book would have been considerably thinner and weaker; in making the selections I have drawn upon the wisdom and advice of a number of valued friends whose assistance I should like to acknowledge. My largest debt is to Mrs. Celia Houghton, Director of The Teacher's Center at Greenwich, Greenwich, Connecticut, who opened her personal library to me and gave me the benefit of her encyclopedic knowledge of both the British and American literature. I am deeply indebted, too, to Professor Vincent Rogers of the University of Connecticut, who made a number of valuable suggestions, and to Professor Lillian Weber of City College, who, as always, gave me encouragement and support as well as the benefit of her wisdom and expertise.

I wish to express my gratitude, too, to Professor David Hawkins, Director of the Mountain View Center for Environmental Education at the University of Colorado, and Tony Kallet of the Mountain View Center staff, who called my attention to published and unpublished essays of their own that I might otherwise have missed. Thanks are due, too, to Henry Gallina, Curriculum Coordinator of the Lompoc, California Unified School District, who provided a number of valuable judgments and suggestions; to Sr. Voncile White of the Convent of the Sacred Heart School in Greenwich, Connecticut; Adeline Naiman, Director of Publications of the Education Development Center; Dr. Edward A. Chittenden of the Educational Testing Service; and Edward Yeomans, Director of the Greater Boston Teacher Center.

I wish to pay tribute, too, to my administrative assistant, Mrs. Doris Preisick, who deciphered my erratic typing and filing and, with unfailing good cheer, spent more hours than I care to remember at the typewriter and copying machine, all the while keeping track of my correspondence and appointments and administering a normally chaotic office.

I am indebted, too, to my editor and namesake, James H. Silberman, who conceived of this book and who accepted my missed deadlines with forbearance and humor.

I owe a debt of another sort to my wife, Arlene Silberman. With her, everything is possible; without her, nothing is possible. As always, she and our children, David, Ellen, Ricky, Jeff, and Steve gave me strength and support and, most important of all, reason for hope.

C.E.S.

Mount Vernon, N.Y.
March 1973

ONE

Overview of Practice:
What Do Open Classrooms
Look Like?

What is open education? What do open classrooms look like?
How do they differ from traditional formal classrooms?

In line with the approach to teaching and learning that informal educators tend to take, we begin with the concrete, i.e., descriptions of open classrooms in England and the United States, before moving on to the abstract and the theoretical. Most experienced teachers, after all, have never taught in anything but traditional, formal classrooms; most prospective teachers (and most parents and students) have never learned in anything but traditional, formal classrooms. The traditional classroom, with the teacher in the front of the room talking to students seated in rows of desks and chairs, is embedded so deeply in our mind's eye that it is a wrench for any of us to imagine, much less to believe, that classrooms can be organized and run successfully in radically different ways.

Before we can ask why and how, therefore, we need a reasonably clear picture of the "what" of open education. Subsequent chapters will be concerned with the goals of open education, its various techniques, and the theories of child development and of teaching and learning that underlie them. This part offers vivid descriptions of a number of open classrooms in England and the United States—descriptions that give the uninitiated reader some sense of the sound, appearance, and texture of good open classrooms, along with an appreciation of the enormous range and variety of practice that one can find from school to school, and even from classroom to classroom within the same school.

I

Portraits of English
Infant Schools

1. The Change Since 1931

It is to England, of course, that American educators have mainly turned for examples of what open education can be in a public school setting. And for good reason: England probably has more good informal primary schools than any other nation. More to the point, perhaps, the fact that open classrooms have sprung up in public schools in every part of England—in deteriorating slums and changing neighborhoods in London, Manchester, and Bristol; in the grimy coal-mining towns of the West Riding of Yorkshire; in industrialized Leicestershire and industrializing but still pastoral Oxfordshire—has demonstrated that approaches to teaching and learning that many Americans thought possible only in the hothouse atmosphere of a private school or university "laboratory school" can in fact flourish in a state-run system.

Curiously, given the enormous interest that now exists in English practice, the revolution in English primary education after the Second World War went largely unnoticed, in England as well as the United States, until 1967, when a Parliamentary Commission, the so-called Plowden Commission, called attention to the changes and urged their extension to all English primary schools. The twenty-five-member Central Advisory Council for Education (England), to use its official title, spent nearly four years in an intensive study of every aspect of primary education in England and in six foreign countries. The council's two-volume report, Children and Their Primary Schools, *more popularly known as "The Plowden Report" after the Council's chairwoman, Lady Bridget Plowden, is a document of extraordinary power and scope.*

*Written with clarity and grace, The Plowden Report has provided the
agenda for public and professional discussion and debate about education since its publication.*

*This selection from The Plowden Report, the first of several in this
Reader, takes a prototypical middle-aged visitor on a tour of several
"new" primary schools and attempts to explain how and why the
schools have changed from the ones the visitor attended.*

The general public is hardly aware of what a primary school run on
modern lines is like and of the extent as well as the profundity of the
changes that have taken place since the war. A middle-aged visitor,
educated in an ordinary elementary school at the time of the 1931
Report who visited a good primary school in 1966 would find much to
surprise him. If he arrived at the official opening hour, he would find
that many of the children had been there long before him, not penned
in the playground, but inside the school, caring for the livestock,
getting on with interesting occupations, reading or writing, painting,
carving or weaving or playing musical instruments. Probably some of
the teachers would also be early, but whether they were there or not,
would not affect what the children were doing. The visitor might be
surprised to learn that when the bell rang, if there was a bell, no very
obvious change took place. As the morning went on he would see various pieces of more organized activity, backward readers being taken as
a group, an assembly of the whole school for prayers and hymns, an
orchestra, some movement, some group instruction in mathematics,
some exploration outside and so on. During all this time he would hear
few commands and few raised voices. Children would be asked to do
things more often than told. They would move freely about the school,
fetching what they needed, books or material, without formality or interference. Teachers would be among the children, taking part in their
activities, helping and advising and discussing much more frequently
than standing before a class teaching. Mid-morning break and even
mid-day break for lunch would show little change and at the end of
the day there would be no sudden rush from school, leaving an
empty building, but a much more leisurely and individual departure,
so that important tasks could be finished and interesting questions answered. . . .

. . . We should like to accompany an imaginary visitor to three
schools run successfully on modern lines . . . The pictures given are
not imaginary, but the schools are composite.

From *Children and Their Primary Schools*, 2 vols. ("The Plowden Report").
Report of the Central Advisory Council for Education (England), (London: Her
Majesty's Stationery Office, 1967). Reprinted by permission of the Controller
of her Britannic Majesty's Stationery Office.

The first is an infant school occupying a seventy-year-old building, three stories high, near the station in a large city. The visitor, if he is a man, will attract a great deal of attention from the children . . . Children seem to be using every bit of the building (the top floor is sealed off) and surroundings. They spread into the hall, the corridors and the playground. The nursery class has its own quarters and the children are playing with sand, water, clay, paint, dolls, rocking horses and big push toys under the supervision of their teacher. This is how they learn. There is serenity in the room, belying the belief that happy children are always noisy. The children make rather a mess of themselves and their room, but this, with a little help, they clear up themselves. A dispute between two little boys about who is to play with what is resolved by the teacher and a first lesson in taking turns is learned. Learning is going on all the time, but there is not much direct teaching.

Going out into the playground, the visitor finds a group of children, with their teacher, clustered round a large square box full of earth. The excitement is all about an earthworm, which none of the children had ever seen before. Their classroom door opens on to the playground and inside are the rest of the class, seated at tables disposed informally about the room, some reading books that they have themselves chosen from the copious shelves along the side of the room and some measuring the quantities of water that different vessels will hold. Soon the teacher and worm watchers return except for two children who have gone to the library to find a book on worms and the class begins to tidy up in preparation for lunch. The visitor's attention is attracted by the paintings on the wall and, as he looks at them, he is soon joined by a number of children who volunteer information about them. In a moment the preparations for lunch are interrupted as the children press forward with things they have painted, or written, or constructed to show them to the visitor. The teacher allows this for a minute or two and then tells the children that they must really now get ready for lunch "and perhaps Mr. X. will come back afterwards and see what you have to show him." This is immediately accepted and a promise made. On the way out two of the children invite the visitor to join them at lunch and he finds that there is no difficulty about this. The head teacher and staff invariably lunch with the children and an extra adult is easily accommodated.

Later in the day, the visitor finds a small group of six and seven year olds who are writing about the music they have enjoyed with the headmistress. He picks up a home-made book entitled "My book of sounds" and reads the following, written on plain unlined paper:—

> The mandolin is made with lovely soft smooth wood and it has
> a pattern like tortoise shell on it. It has pearl on it and it is called

mother of pearl. It has eight strings and they are all together in
twos and all the pairs make a different noise. The ones with the
thickest strings make the lowest notes and the ones that have the
thinnest strings make the highest notes. When I put the mandolin
in my lap and I pulled the thickest string it kept on for a long time
and I pulled the thinnest wire and it did not last so long and I
stroked them all and they didn't go away for a long time.

Quite a number of these children write with equal fluency and ex-
pressiveness, and with concentration. The sound of music from the hall
attracts the visitor and there he finds a class who are making up and
performing a dance drama in which the forces of good are overcoming
the forces of evil to the accompaniment of drums and tambourines.

As he leaves the school and turns from the playground into the
grubby and unlovely street on which it abuts, the visitor passes a class
who, seated on boxes in a quiet, sunny corner, are listening to their
teacher telling them the story of Rumpelstiltskin.

The next school is a junior mixed school on the outskirts of the city
in an area that was not long since one of fields and copses and which
has been developed since 1950. The school building is light and spacious
with ample grass and hard paved areas around it and one of the old
copses along its borders. The children are well cared for and turned
out and a high proportion of them go on to grammar schools. The visitor
finds his way into a fourth year B class (the school is unstreamed in
the first three years) and finds a teacher who is a radio enthusiast. The
children, under his guidance, have made a lot of apparatus and have
set up a transmitting station. They have been in touch with another
school 80 miles away and sometimes talk to their teacher's friends who
are driving about in their cars in various parts of England. While the
visitor was present, part of the class disappeared into another classroom
and there broadcast through a home-made microphone a number of
poems chosen by themselves and all dealing with winter. "In a drear-
nighted December," "When icicles hang by the wall" and "This is the
weather the shepherd shuns" were clearly and sensitively spoken and
closely listened to. In another classroom the children had been asked
to make models at home which showed how things could be moved
without being touched. They had brought to school some extremely
ingenious constructions, using springs, pulleys, electromagnets, elastic
and levers and they came out before the class to demonstrate and explain them. When the visitor left they were preparing to describe their
ideas in their notebooks. A random sample of these books showed that
accuracy and careful presentation were as characteristic of the less able
children as of the obvious grammar school candidates.

During break some of the children went into the hall and listened to the headmaster's wife playing the C major prelude. In another room the chess club was meeting and the visitor saw a Ruy Lopez and a King's Pawn opening and the school champion lose his Queen. In yet another room the natural history club was meeting to discuss its programme for the coming year, while outside the school football team was having a short practice. The library was filled with children. The visitor was interested to notice that there was no contrast between this rich and varied out of school life and the life in school hours which offered just as much choice and stimulus. The library, for instance, was in constant use throughout the day, and at many different points in the school were to be found examples of good glass, pottery, turnery and silver, all of a standard higher than would be found in most of the children's homes. With all the children the visitor found conversation easy. They had much to tell him and many questions to ask him and they seemed to have every encouragement and no obstacles to learning.

The third school, a three teacher junior mixed and infant school, is in the country. It was built in 1878 by the squire and since 1951 it has been a Church of England voluntary controlled school. The church is a few yards away. The original building, with its high roof and window sills and its tiny infants' room, has been made over by the L.E.A., the infants' room being now a cloakroom and there is a big new infants' room at the back. This has encroached on the now very small playground, but there is a meadow just across the lane where the children play when it is dry enough. The village has grown and there are many commuters of varying social background who travel to the big country town nine miles away.

When the visitor arrived all the children in the first class were either on top of the church tower or standing in the churchyard and staring intently upwards. The headmaster appeared in the porch and explained what was happening. The children were making a study of the trees in the private park which lay 100 yards beyond the church. The tower party had taken up with them the seeds of various trees and were releasing these on the leeward side, and were measuring the wind speed with a homemade anemometer. The party down below had to watch each seed and measure the distance from the tower to the point where the seed landed. The children explained that ten of each kind were being released and that they would take the average distance and then compare the range of each species and calculate the actual distance travelled. When they had finished they went back to school to record their results, some in graph form, in the large folders which already contained many observations, photographs and sketches of the trees they were studying. The visitor was interested to notice a display of materials from which children were going to learn about their village, and social life generally, at the time the school was opened. They included photo-

stats of pages in the parish registers, the school log book and a diary
kept by the founder, as well as a collection of books and illustrations
lent by the county library.

The second class of sevens to nines were rather numerous for their
small room, but had spread out into the corridor and were engaged in
a variety of occupations. One group was gathered round their teacher
for some extra reading practice, another was at work on an extraordinary
structure of wood and metal which they said was a sputnik, a third was
collecting a number of objects and testing them to find out which could
be picked up by a magnet and two boys were at work on an immense
painting (six feet by four feet) of St. Michael defeating Satan. They
seemed to be working harmoniously according to an unfolding rather
than a preconceived plan. Conversation about the work that the children
were doing went on all the time.

In the large new infants' room, too, many different things were
going on. Some children were reading quietly to themselves; some were
using a recipe to make some buns, and were doubling the quantities
since they wanted to make twice the number; a few older children were
using commercial structural apparatus to consolidate their knowledge of
number relationships; some of the youngest children needed their
teacher's help in adding words and phrases to the pictures they had
painted. The teacher moved among individuals and groups doing these
and other things, and strove to make sure that all were learning.

These descriptions illustrate a point perhaps not often enough
stressed, that what goes on in primary schools cannot greatly differ from
one school to another, since there is only a limited range of material
within the capacity of primary school children. It is the approach, the
motivation, the emphasis and the outcome that are different. In these
schools, children's own interests direct their attention to many fields of
knowledge and the teacher is alert to provide material, books or experience for the development of their ideas.

2. A Typical Day in an Infant School

*Among the American teachers who have visited England to see for
themselves is a young couple, Casey and Liza Murrow. Unlike most of
us, however, the Murrows, both of them talented teachers with experience in open classrooms in the United States, were able to spend
an entire school year studying the informal English primary schools.
They visited some forty primary schools during the 1969–70 school
year, devoting the largest proportion of their time to classroom observation, but also interviewing the classroom teachers and head teachers in
each school as well as school administrators, government officials, and*

members of the faculty of a number of training institutions. Children
Come First *is a sensitive and highly readable account of what they discovered.* (*Mr. Murrow is now a teacher at the Wilmington Elementary
School, Wilmington, Vermont, and Mrs. Murrow is a member of the
faculty at the Antioch-Putney Graduate School of Education in Putney,
Vermont.*) *The selection that follows describes a typical day in an
infant school.*

————————

Six-year-old David runs up the walk, flings a farewell glance at his
mother and the baby, and disappears toward his school. He is pleased
with himself, the first one there. His friends will soon follow. With his
entry into the building, the day can begin; the school comes to life.

The visitor who arrives at a British school before its official nine
o'clock opening finds an atmosphere that differs radically from that of
many United States schools at the same time of day. Standing on the
grass, mothers talk with teachers or chat with friends. Children discuss
things that have happened since the close of school yesterday; they
hold hands, take a quick run around the playground, or swing on the
parallel bars. No lines are formed outside the school, and it is very
rare to hear a bell.

The noises are busy: a door opens and closes; the children talk
as they go into school to take up unfinished work from the day before.
Some go straight to the library corner and may read or look at pictures.
Others search for friends and teachers in nearby rooms. In one class,
a guinea pig escapes and is pursued from the paint corner to the
cupboard under the sink, where the children try to coax it out with a
piece of lettuce. There is much laughter and some singing. A child
calls to a friend next door, "Come quick, our guinea's got out!" Some
young volunteers arrive on the scene and plot a trap for their pet.

In the hallway, children move about purposefully or stand in small
groups. A few boys gather around David, who has brought a caterpillar
to school in a jar. His teacher comes through the door and approaches
the group. "What have you got, David?"

"A caterpillar. I'm going to make him a cage."

"Get on with it, then!"

Four girls help their teacher, a young woman with a warm smile, to
set up an exhibit of pottery just inside the front door. They are matching the browns and grays of the pots with bits of cloth dyed last week
by their class. "Look, Valerie," says the teacher, "here's what your
Mum finished in pottery class last night." Valerie smiles, takes the

bowl carefully, and holds it up for the others to see ("Ooh, that's lovely"). She finds a place for it on the table and agrees to work with her friend Helen on a sign that will explain the exhibit. They run off to their class to get started.

The door of the staff room opens, revealing a group of teachers waking up over a cup of coffee. The head teacher tells a story, and there is laughter and a general stirring as they leave each other for their class-rooms. The head teacher stops in the hall to greet a parent. "Mrs. Barnes, you must come in and see the decorations in the hall." They go off together, but stop to allow Mrs. Barnes to experiment with a xylophone left outside a classroom. She picks out a tune and then smiles at the head teacher. They continue down the corridor.

The beginning of the morning in infant schools sets the tone for the day. The visitor can sense an open and relaxed atmosphere that makes these schools remarkable places for everyone involved. In the first minutes spent in such a school, it is evident that the major concern is the development of relationships between child and child, teacher and child, and teacher and teacher. The sounds of children talking, work-ing, and singing throughout the building are themselves indications of the vibrant life of the school. The morning is soon under way.

In Bristol, a class of five-, six-, and seven-year-olds is gathered in the hall of an old building. A record player in one corner lets loose a rhythmical West Indian calypso, and the teacher, lost in the middle of her group of children, begins to dance. The children follow her and branch out on their own. Their bodies completely free, they interpret the happiness of the music with their arms, legs, torsos, and heads, and change their movements with shifts in the music. They are relaxed, aware of one another on the floor.

"That's lovely, Ian, lovely," says the teacher, her face flushed from the exercise. She stops the record, and the children gather around her or flop down on the floor. "Watch what Ian is doing," she says. The children make a space for the boy and watch as he moves to the calypso. As he dances, his face is open and smiling, yet intent on what he is doing.

Anyone who had seen Ian earlier that morning might have been amazed. He started off to school angry, having had little breakfast. Coal smoke sifted across rooftops and down into the street. A pale fog drifted across the chimneys. He crossed the remains of a river that carried garbage, old shoes, and sewage as it twisted past back yards filled with gray laundry. On the other side of the water his school sat waiting: a squat nineteenth-century building surrounded by an iron fence, its only playground a strip of asphalt at the rear.

Ian is West Indian, as are the majority of his classmates. His school has many characteristics of an impoverished school in a black neighborhood in the United States. Yet what goes on inside the building does not reflect the attitude of society which is evident in the building's rundown condition. When Ian came to school, he was not shouted at, or asked to line up, or expected to sit quietly through much of the morning. He was greeted by the head of the school, who gave him a hug, asked him how he was feeling, and said, "Hope you have a good day, Ian." Now he is deeply involved in the music, in the praise of his teacher, and in the expression of his feelings through movement.

As the record ends, the class moves across the hall. Small hands grip the waist of the child in front, and the snaking line follows the teacher into the classroom.

The teacher pauses at the door to take a little girl by the hand. Throughout the movement class this six-year-old child had been "hiding," secure in the fortress of an old sofa turned to the wall in a corner of the large hall. For some of the time she had been joined by a younger boy from another class. They had played a game that involved recognizing words on cards and then counting the cards to find the winner. Neither wanted to join his classmates. Instead, they sought out the soft cushions, the peace and privacy of the sofa. Teachers walked by and smiled at the pair, but never disturbed their sanctuary.

In a nearby classroom a small boy interrupts a story the teacher is reading to the class. Crouched on the floor, his head in his hands, Stephen breaks into a storm of tears. A sturdy boy slides over to him, touches his shoulder gently, and says to the teacher, "What's the matter with Stephen?" The teacher takes the small, crumpled Stephen into her lap. The older boy and the teacher learn that Stephen, still weak from a long illness, has bumped his head. Together they comfort him. The older boy pulls Stephen down beside him and the sobbing lessens and then stops as the teacher continues to read.

In Ian's classroom almost everyone has settled down to one task or another; they are relaxed and quiet after their dance—except Ian. Sometimes hostile and seldom able to concentrate for more than five minutes, he appears to be disturbing three or four others. He has refused two requests to come and read privately to his teacher. Knowing him well, she does not issue an order, but asks patiently.

A few moments later, Ian is ready to read—he demands to read—but the teacher is occupied with another child. He takes a friend (a better reader) by the hand and asks if he may read to him. They go into a corner and Ian begins. Another child comes near them, looking for something, and bumps into a chair and then into Ian's friend. Ian frowns at him and says, "Now if you weren't here that wouldn't happen, would it?" He starts to read again as the intruder departs quietly to return to his own work.

Ian dealt with this disturbance easily and without uproar because he was engaged in work he wanted to pursue. He had the help and support of a friend. He had no time for the disruptive response he would surely have made if he had been working on an assignment prescribed by the teacher.

Ian's infant school is in the port city of Bristol on the west coast of England. The slum area served by the school has yet to be recognized by the central government as eligible for additional Educational Priority Area money, although it meets the general standards. The teachers, however, do not assume that all is lost or hopeless. They firmly believe that many of the children have something special to offer; that their needs are different from those of children in other parts of the country, and that the school must respond to them individually. The children do not conform to standards set by some distant, abstract authority. Instead, the school adapts to the lives of its children.

In the same city there is a very different school located in a rather ordinary, middle-class area where row upon row of identical houses stand behind well-kept gardens. The head of this school expresses much the same philosophy with an entirely different group of children. In this school as well as in the one just described, the character of the children and the staff is evident throughout the building. As the children work at reading, writing, building, dressing up, or painting, one can watch the life of the school revolve around their interests.

In a classroom at one end of the corridor, children read aloud to each other and to the teacher. A child explains his painting to a girl who looks on over his shoulder. Nearby, a child asks a teacher's aide how to spell "angel." Two boys stand at a picture window, observing birds outside through a pair of binoculars. A third boy identifies the birds in a book and adds their names to a record he is keeping. Four or five children work out some mathematical problems using colored tiles, while others write stories, using words that are as vibrant and alive as the conversations around them. As in many infant schools, there are forty children in this class. Though the teacher certainly feels the group is too large, she has made the best of it. While many different projects are under way throughout the room, the group is unified by a sense of purpose and well-being.

In the midst of all this activity a boy picks out a tune on a xylophone in the corner, and suddenly, spontaneously, the class breaks into song. The teacher stops listening to a child read. She smiles and adds a bit of harmony while the boy at the instrument continues to play. Next to him a friend holds two paper cups at their bases and brings the open ends together in a strong, staccato rhythm that keeps the beat for the class. As the music dies away, work goes on as before, without a pause.

These two infant schools seem to be very different at first glance. Certainly, the children who attend them come from dissimilar backgrounds. The first school gives a great deal of attention to the immediate physical and emotional demands of the children. The second school appears more intent on encouraging the children to bring their emotions and thoughts into the open. Yet, in many ways, the children are similar.

The head of the second school believes that all normal children are equal in two important ways: first, their ability to move and use their bodies and, second, their capacity to communicate through speech. These are the natural resources that teachers must utilize and develop to the fullest extent, realizing that they are qualities that will enhance the child's learning. The entire school reflects this philosophy. The language of the children is the basic tool through which they come to read. The learning of mathematics, their use of poetry, music, drama, and art, all closely relate to the movement and character of individual children.

This philosophy is a dynamic ingredient in many good infant classrooms. As in Ian's school, children throughout England are encouraged to talk to one another while they work; they move around the room and the school freely. A teacher who believes that children learn through conversation with others and through deep involvement—whether physical, emotional, or intellectual—with the materials at hand will not be excessively occupied with maintaining "order," "silence," or "control."

Noise is a matter of concern only when there is too much of it for people to communicate easily or when it disturbs children working alone. Order is achieved because the children are totally immersed in their work.

The teacher in a good English school is primarily concerned with the full development of each child. She hopes to introduce him to experiences which will help him to think clearly and imaginatively, to discover the pleasure of learning, and to understand himself and others more fully. She encourages a creative approach to problem solving and opens his eyes to the world beyond the school. Above all, the child's personality is of prime importance. Because he takes an active role in learning—and in doing so, establishes a firm relationship with the teacher—issues of order and control are seldom spoken of in good infant classrooms.

While individual schools and classrooms are naturally very different, varying according to the interests of the people working within them, there are many similarities to be seen in a number of infant schools across England. Classrooms do not mark the boundaries of the child's experience in school. The curriculum is seldom compartmentalized into reading, writing, arithmetic, and other disciplines. One of the most subtle and important aspects of these classes is the way in which barriers between disciplines have come down, allowing the children to be involved in a broader view of learning.

First and foremost the schools and the classrooms belong to the children.

The appearance and arrangement of classrooms in many infant schools indicate how they are oriented to the children's needs. There are no desks in rows, no overwhelming blackboard toward which all eyes can be directed. Instead, there are these common features: small tables and chairs in groups; a sandbox on four legs, which can be moved outside in nice weather; a large, portable basin for water play; and a corner where painting and other messy activities take place. There is also a library corner. There is usually a counter or table covered with mathematics materials: objects for counting (buttons, shells, pebbles, tiles, pine cones), cards with math ideas on them, a small balancing scale. Much of the wall space is beautifully decorated with the children's work: paintings, poems, stories, descriptions of projects, puppets, collages—all representative of the children's interests. The room also reflects the talents of the teacher and contains, in corners and on tables, stimulative items and articles of interest that she has brought in.

In many classrooms the children make the curtains for the windows. They dye old sheets a solid color and then paint flowers and animals on the cloth. Or they may tie strings around bunches of the sheet and dip them in other dyes to create startling patterns through the process of tie dying. Thus, much of the classroom seems to vibrate with the things the children have made, as well as with the sounds and sights of work in progress.

The visitor familiar with American classrooms immediately notices that the teacher's desk is either nonexistent or pushed into a corner where it serves as another place to store papers, children's work, plants, and materials. When the children have a great deal of choice and freedom to move, the teacher's role is extremely dynamic. As she moves from one group to another, she engages in a variety of direct encounters with the children. She listens to three children read, starts others off on potato printing, observes a group working with numbers before talking with them about their work. She is constantly involved in eliciting responses from the children that tell her how much they understand about the material and how she can help them. Most of her work is extremely purposeful and structured.

The ways in which children learn in these circumstances are as varied as the children themselves. In order to talk about the process in greater detail, we must look at the arrangement of a child's day. It contains, within the changing activities and movements of the children, a very dynamic inner structure, established by the teacher and maintained by the children.

The morning usually begins with a meeting of the whole class. The children gather on the floor around the teacher and talk about what they want to do first. From past experience in the room and the school, they know the limits on their actions and, more important, the range of possible activities open to them.

Teacher and child know that some activities have specific places in the timetable. A period for physical education and perhaps a time for music are set aside. In addition, there are often tasks that the children must complete by lunch or by the close of school—drawing a picture and writing a story to accompany it, reading to the teacher or to a group, or working on a mathematics problem. This tacit understanding is essential to the successful operation of the classroom.

No teacher can keep track of up to forty children at every instant. In a classroom where children are seated passively and silently at their desks, the teacher can never tell what the children are thinking. In such situations—still the ideal for many English and American teachers eager to feel absolute control—it is impossible to ascertain whether the children are involved. They are asked to participate with only one sense at a time. They listen (or do they?); they answer a question (or try to). They watch as the blackboard is being filled and emptied, covered and erased. The whole child is rarely involved.

On the other hand, an infant-school teacher in many good English schools can glance around the room and discern whether her group is actively engaged in work. If not, there may be no need to scold—perhaps a child who appears idle is tired, in need of help, or lost in an important daydream. She trusts the children to take much of the initiative in their learning and she can watch them use every part of themselves as they do it.

Every class has its own manner of beginning. The early morning gathering provides a few moments for the teacher to be close to the children and for the children to be close to each other. Bodies touch; eyes and ears show eagerness to see and hear friends. Some children tell stories, while others listen to the teacher describe an evening spent with their parents or explain material they may use for a collage. It does not matter how the child communicates his plans, for the teacher usually understands him. He may say "I'll write," or "I'll be at the writing table," or just hold up his book and say "about the moon"—an idea he has for a picture. In any case, the teacher can see that he knows exactly where he is going, and a nod of her head and a smile of encouragement sends him on his way.

One by one, the children leave the group and spread out in the classroom. In these first moments, the teacher sees the individual rhythms of each child. Some are full of energy and need to move freely. Others want to sit down and work quietly. Because the structure that holds the day together is complex and sometimes difficult to discern amid all the activity, we will follow two infant-school children through a day to give a clearer picture of what takes place.

ANN

Ann is a five-year-old in her second term at an infant school in a suburban area. She is in a class of five-, six-, and seven-year-olds and is engaged in a number of activities which are leading her toward reading. Since she did not attend a nursery, her first term in school also involved a great deal of learning about how to get along with the other children in her class.

On her arrival in school in the morning, Ann's first concern is with some seeds she planted the day before. She finds her name on a flower pot and looks carefully into the dirt for signs of growth. She pokes the soil gently with one finger. Satisfied that nothing has happened, she joins the group seated on the floor and asks the teacher if she may do a painting. The teacher nods. Ann jumps up, puts on her smock, and goes to the corner of the room where a large easel and paints have already been set up. She fills the paper with vivid, colorful strokes and lines, stopping now and then to rinse her brush in the sink or to check on a friend's picture nearby. When the painting is done, her teacher comes over to talk about it.

"What a lovely painting. Can you tell me about it?"

"It's a pattern that the sun makes."

They talk for a few more minutes. An older child looks on and points out the painting to a friend. The teacher gets a pencil. Ann asks her to write on the picture, "My sun pattern. By Ann," and watches carefully as the teacher writes the bold letters beneath the painting.

"Let it dry a bit," says her teacher, "and then come to me. We'll see if you're ready to trace over the words with a crayon."

A crate of milk has arrived. Ann takes her picture off the easel, hangs it over the drying rack, and takes a small container of milk to a table where one of her friends is sitting. They talk about the pet hamster that belongs to the class and take a look at him. Ann fills his water jar and runs her finger down his back. "So soft, his fur." She goes back to check on her painting. She takes it to a table, where the teacher helps her to trace over the letters. A boy looks over her shoulder and reads "My sun pat—." "Pattern," says Ann. The teacher tells the class to leave what they are doing and go out to play. When Ann returns, she finds that her teacher has mounted the painting on the wall.

Ann joins a friend at the water table—a large, movable basin on legs. Using a funnel, they pour water from large containers into smaller ones. Their teacher looks on and talks with them about which container holds more. Ann spends the rest of the morning with her hands and arms deep in the water. She and her friend talk vividly about the water, what it feels like, and whether it will spill as they pour. Ann is totally absorbed in the activity and surprised when the teacher's voice rises above the others in the room.

"Time to clean up. When you have put things away, come and sit by me." The children protest: "But we're not finished yet!"

"Don't worry," says the teacher. "You can go on with it this afternoon." Ann and her friend find a rag and mop near the tub of water. In other parts of the room, math cards are put back in boxes. Paintings are hung over racks to dry. All is accomplished within minutes, with few directions from the teacher. She trusts her class to do this, and she may well continue working with a child on some writing completed that morning or help only the youngest children in the class to clean up. As the children come to sit round her once again, a girl whispers in her teacher's ear.

"Mary wants to read her story to the class," says the teacher. Ann and her classmates listen attentively while Mary reads a tale of adventure. A group of boys announce that they want to display their work. They have made a dragon, a prince, and a princess out of tissue paper, tinfoil, and bits of cloth to illustrate a poem the class likes. The figures are paraded in front of the group while the teacher and the class speak the words of the poem. Small bodies sway back and forth to the rhythm of the poetry.

When the poem is over, Ann washes for lunch and puts on her coat. She is one of the children in her class who go home for lunch. Her mother waits outside, near the classroom door. "Come in and see my painting," says Ann. They look at it together and then leave the school.

By the time Ann returns from lunch, everyone else has come in from the playground. Some of the children are already at work. Ann asks her teacher what she can do. "Would you like to join Sarah in the Wendy House? You haven't played there for a few days." Ann enters the little door and dresses herself in a long skirt, high heels, and a cloak. With the two other girls in the house, she agrees that she will be the "auntie," while they play "mum" and "granny." They troop out the door of the Wendy House, pushing a pram, parade through the classroom, and go to the playground, where they continue to act. When they come back in, a short while later, they do not go to the classroom, but search out the head teacher, who spends some time talking with them about their play.

After a few minutes, Ann returns to her classroom, where everyone is changing for physical education. She strips to pants and undershirt and joins the others in the hall. When the movement class ends, Ann spends the rest of the afternoon with Sheila, a seven-year-old from her class.

They collect the eggs from the chicken coop owned by the school. Sheila asks Ann to count them and then checks her answers. Ann watches as Sheila records the number on a chart, which is kept in the corridor so that all can see it. Children in other classes sometimes make graphs based on the information on the chart. The two girls rejoin their class for a story read by the teacher. As the children leave, Ann checks on her seeds—still no sign of growth—talks briefly with her teacher, and joins her mother at the front door.

NIGEL

Nigel lives on the top floor of a ten-story building in a rundown section of London. He arrives at school bursting with energy, and has trouble sitting still when the class gathers around the teacher. "Can I take the blocks and go outside?" he asks. His teacher agrees and opens the door, helping him to carry the wooden blocks out to the paved playground. Until the break at ten thirty, Nigel spends his time building a large roadway. He comes back inside once to find some toy cars to run on the road. His finished structure extends a third of the way across the playground and includes complexes of bridges and intersections as well as the necessary garage.

At ten thirty his teacher, who could see him from inside the classroom, joins him outside. "What a marvelous job you've done, Nigel. And isn't it long—will you measure it after the break and find out how long it is? Ask a friend to help you. But now tell me about it; what's this?" Nigel walks from one end to the other, talking, describing, pointing.

After the break, Nigel and Peter use a yardstick and discover that the roadway is twenty-six feet long. The teacher encourages him to draw a picture of the roadway and write what he discovered, pleased that from all she could see the boys had measured with great care. Nigel works quietly at a table, bent over a large sheet of paper. His time outside allowed him to work off steam, as well as to begin a project that he could happily carry on indoors.

At about eleven thirty, Nigel's teacher calls him over to join a small group seated around a table. Together they spend a few minutes working with math cards. Nigel shows his picture to the teacher. "After lunch I'm going to write about it," he says.

Rushing into the classroom in the afternoon, Nigel loses little time finding his picture book in his drawer. He writes, "I made a long road. Peter and I measured it. It was 26 feet." He takes the picture and the writing over to his teacher, reads what he has written, and talks with her a bit about it. When he leaves her, he joins a friend and they devote the rest of the afternoon until story time to fighting a severe "fire" that breaks out in the Wendy House. Fortunately, the classroom has two firemen's helmets and a few small fire-engine toys, which helps this game along.

While Nigel and Ann attend two very different schools, both their teachers believe firmly in the children's ability to make a number of decisions about the way they spend their time. This does not mean that the teachers avoid planning. On the contrary, classrooms that appear totally free are really skillfully engineered. They must be if they are to succeed. The teacher needs to be clear about what each child has accomplished and what sort of work he needs to become involved in during the coming days. She must watch him carefully, noticing the kinds of play in which he engages and the development of manual skills. She records what he has accomplished. Nigel's teacher knew that on this day he had done some writing, worked on two kinds of math, and done a great deal of building. On the following day, she may encourage him to devote more time to reading.

The atmosphere at the end of a day in a good English infant school implies a great deal about the life in the classrooms. As children gather around teachers to listen to a story, they show few of the tensions that one can see in children who have passed the school hours in a regimented classroom where tasks are assigned and work begins and ends at arbitrary intervals established by the teacher.

As they pull on their coats to go home, a number of six- and seven-year-olds may carry a book from the school library. Whether they read it or not is up to them. There is never any homework in an English infant school. Homework as we know it almost always consists of written work meant to reinforce a skill acquired in school. Infant-school teachers prefer to develop these skills in the classroom, where there is access to help of all sorts and less risk that a child will complete work mechanically without understanding it. The work the children do in school changes from moment to moment. Their levels of achievement naturally vary so that no two children go home in the afternoon needing the same sort of work.

Infant-school children often find a day in school exciting. Each day brings new discoveries; a child may show progress in reading or develop the insight that allows him to move on to more difficult math. There is none of the unnatural competition of a traditional classroom; there are no grades and no tests. The competition that does exist— between the two children playing a card game in their sofa hideout, or in a group racing to see who can most quickly represent the "four table" using small tiles—is induced by the children, and those who compete do so by their own choice.

There is little pressure of the sort remembered by the parents of today's infant-school child. If a child reads slowly or with difficulty, he has the time to work on it without pressure. If he cannot manage math on a given day, his teacher is likely to accept this fact and think of how she may be able to help him get around his difficulty tomorrow. In either of these situations, the child often receives help from a friend and does not approach the teacher for aid every time it is needed.

Flexibility is the most important single feature of a day in a good infant school. If something unusual crops up, it often enters naturally into the class activities. When a head teacher in one school was given some intriguing pieces of glass, she brought them into a class and the children became involved with the shape, color, and feel of different pieces. A number of children spent the morning talking with the teacher about them, classifying the glass in different ways and experimenting with refraction in different kinds of light. No one required that these six- and seven-year-olds sort the objects in any way. No one defined refraction or even mentioned the word. What the children accomplished was the result of their own curiosity and the interest and encouragement of their teacher.

The flexibility of the day and the lack of a rigid curriculum allow the teacher to reorganize a few days or a week around a special goal if it seems needed. One teacher we observed in Yorkshire was concerned that her class of predominantly five-year-olds grasp the concept of a number and its value. She knew that many of her children could count from one to ten, but they had little understanding of the meaning of the numbers. As one solution to this difficulty, she organized each of ten days around a number. On the fourth day, for instance, she asked the children to group themselves in fours for short periods of time. They sang four songs before lunch, counted out the milk bottles in fours, and drew four pictures on a sheet of paper. When we visited the class, the children were clear that the number 4 accurately described four beans, four chairs, or four days. They had also come to grasp more abstract groups of four, such as asking four questions.

Although there are certain patterns common to infant-school classes, the variety of formats used by English teachers in planning their days is vast. No two classes, even in the same school, are exactly alike because the teacher's skills and the children's interests are drawn upon to structure the day and the work that takes place.

3. Some Lasting Impressions of English Practice

No American visitor has studied English practice so carefully, or made so large an impact on American practice, as Lillian Weber, Professor of Early Childhood Education at New York's City College and Director of Advisory Services to the Open Corridor Reorganization of the New York City public schools. Professor Weber, a former nursery school director, was initially drawn to England by the discovery that while the "best" English and American nursery school practice looked quite similar, English practice occurred in large classes within the state school system, whereas American practice was limited to a relative handful of small private and laboratory or demonstration schools. "It had not been clear to me that 'good' education could exist under the conditions usually found in the public sector," she has written, "until I discovered that England had what I considered to be 'good' education, even with large classes, and that it provided this in the state framework." (*Emphasis hers*)

As a result of this discovery, Professor Weber went to England in September of 1966. Although her initial interest was to discover what in English preschool education was relevant to the American scene, her visits to infant schools led her to broaden her focus to the entire range of early childhood education, which is to say, the years from three to eight. Over a span of nearly eighteen months, during which she was also enrolled as a graduate student at the University of London Institute of Education, she visited fifty-six schools, fifty-three of them state (i.e. public) schools. The English Infant School and Informal Education *is based on an exhaustive analysis of forty-seven of these schools. The book, which originated as a thesis prepared under the guidance of the late Dorothy E. M. Gardner, for many years director of the Institute and one of the seminal figures in the reform of English primary education, is the definitive analysis of the theory and practice of informal education in English infant and nursery schools.*

In the selection that follows, Professor Weber offers a vivid picture of the richness and variety of individual and group activities that are going on at any given moment in an informal infant school. Her portrait makes clear, however, that for all the variety and all the individual choice, children are not simply "doing their own thing," nor are teachers neglecting cognitive learning. "The growth of skills is entwined with this life," Weber writes. "In the free, self-chosen movement of teachers and headmistress to children to help them in their activities, skills are not precluded; rather the activities seem to foster skills, giving the children something to talk about and to write about."

. . . an old stone building, a wall, a bare playground, but with large tubs for planting. Inside, suddenly all is light, movement, color. The first impression is of lovely things on the eye level of five-year-olds, in

From Lillian Weber, *The English Infant School and Informal Education* (Englewood Cliffs, N.J.: Prentice-Hall, Inc., 1971) (A Center for Urban Education Book) pp. 62–66. Copyright © 1971 by Lillian Weber. Reprinted by permission of Prentice-Hall, Inc., Englewood Cliffs, New Jersey.

corners that invite use and lingering—flowers and potted plants, easy chairs, books, paintings, shelves filled with china, a length of soft patterned fabric, a lovely bit of sea glass in the midst of an arrangement of blue pottery. The blue pottery is just one part of a total pattern of beauty—all for seeing and touching and arranging into new compositions. There are precious things, lovely things, colorful things where children can see them and handle them or, seated around a small table, enjoy quiet reading near them. Some of the corners display musical instruments, all laid out for children to see, to handle, to use. In fact, in all the corners all the objects seem to be set out with confidence that the children will handle beautiful things carefully and with respect. And also on view are things the children themselves have made with clay and wood, with paint and paper, with shells and stones.

An environment bursting with invitation, bursting with all the things children are producing right then and there. In the entry way is a paint table and three children at work painting. The hall itself is large, with five doors opening out on it. Six children are there, painting a large sheet, barefoot so they can get in on the painting. The teacher is right in there with them, offering them material. Three children are at a workbench. A couple are selling cakes they had made, making sales and change with real money. Another couple sit at a table writing; still another, quietly reading. Through an open door one catches a glimpse of three girls using weights, weighing flour, making some cakes; of others in a housekeeping corner; of two children building blocks on the floor; of a boy arranging number trays of nails, buttons and conkers (our American horse chestnuts); of another measuring with knotted string on the floor.

All over the classroom wall—under paintings, on shelves, in front of clay figures, attached to woodwork—are words. "I used three pieces of wood." "My boat is 11 and ¾ inches long." "This girl has a red dress." "It is a man." A little boy dictates to the teacher and watches while the teacher writes. Another writes his own sentence and asks for a word. A couple of children are absorbed at a water trolley with tubing, and with all shapes and sizes of plastic bottles, funnels, strainers, and a really fine collection of measuring cups. In the library are eight children, each one at his own task, which seems to be phonetics. The teacher helps each one separately in whatever way he needs. All during the day, groups or individuals, after asking permission, use the library, but book corners are in every room as well as in the corridor and in the big hall, often with easy chairs grouped around them and flowers on the table.

The classroom does not contain the class. The children spill all over in little groups going to use things in various areas of the room and hall. The teacher is not behind a desk but moving to all the children. The headmistress is in the midst of it all, too, knowing everyone, helping wherever needed. Talk is going on all the time. Words for activities are being sought all the time. The children seem to know just what they want to do, where to get material, how to go about it. The children move with self-assurance, *using* their school.

. . . In another infant school, also an old building, drab and gray, in one step I am in a gymnasium-sized room—the central hall—with five rooms leading off from it. I stop a child to ask for the headmistress. He takes me up to a lady in the center of a group around a workbench. They are cutting lino-prints. Another group nearby is printing for a book they are designing. Another is printing fabric. Two little girls are drawing thick wool threads through a standing pegboard, following a design they have drawn on the pegboard with colored chalk.

The room is full of activity. In one corner, two girls are marking what, on inquiry, I discover to be the register! Children collect milk money and sell snacks, using real money. Children are going in and out of a supply room that contains pieces of wood, different kinds of paper, thread and fabrics, buttons, boxes, animal supplies, wheels, paint—all sorted and labeled. A sign advertises: "Animal Grooming in Room C," and the cost; "Animal Food," and the cost. One little girl is weighing an amount of animal food. While a boy is giving out a circular describing the offerings of this animal clinic, another is making a sign needed for this. At a table six children and a teacher are cooking. An older child is helping a sewing group, and another is helping a child to read. Over in one corner two children are writing. Three little girls are walking about, holding and fondling guinea pigs, "loving them," they tell me. There seem to be no groups of more than six.

Even the old building poses no limits to possibilities of use. I begin to see that the use of the big hall and the corridor permits the breakthrough from classroom to use of *all* the school areas, thus creating a new unity of school life. Classroom doors are open to corridors or hall where children can go to acting boxes, to workbench, to musical instruments, to library corner. No child moves as part of a class; he moves as an individual to things he chooses to do and the teacher and the headmistress move to help him do these things. The classroom, the class, the teacher behind the desk—all are metamorphosed, all are changed.

Each classroom contains the standard equipment of blackboard, chairs, and tables. Though there are enough chairs to construct a large circle if desired, it is usually a few chairs around a number area, around a book corner, around an interest table, around a table covered with junk material or with clay, or around a table for children sitting writing. A good deal of empty space is left for block building, for floor projects, for all sorts of use. Children sit on the floor for storytelling, for group teaching, for a group reading. Children can always be seen writing, sprawled comfortably on the floor.

. . . There seems to be a plan of the day but few fixed periods. The fixed points tend to be the Morning Service, Music and Movement, and Physical Education (P.E.). These last two are class activities held in the big hall, and even these often break up into small groups where individual children may show their skill or make their own use of some of the P.E. apparatus. Sometimes children from the class having P.E. or Movement do not join with their class; sometimes children from other classes continue whatever they are doing in the big hall around the edges of the P.E. activity of the Music and Movement. Sometimes P.E. and Movement are the same activity.

At lunch, another fixed part of the day, there are eight children and a teacher or a "dinner-lady" at each table. Conversation is expected; a service that is orderly is expected, and some effort is made to make it attractive.

. . . There seems to be no syllabus controlling what work has to be covered nor at what time. The children come in one by one and start doing things. At any number of points in the day, an astonishing amount of writing is going on, an astonishing amount of measuring, of weighing, or exploration of shape and size. Writing and reading seem to be simultaneous, and standards of spelling seem to be relaxed. Children are not at all worried about whether they are right or not; they try. There seem to be no prescribed standards of achievement. A child is not competing. He is busy increasing his own growth.

. . . The growth of skills is entwined with this life. In the free, self-chosen movement of childen through all areas of the school, in the movement of teachers and headmistress to children to help them in their activities, skills are not precluded; rather the activities seem to foster skills, giving the children something to talk about and something to write about. The intense involvement of children in the running of the school—through errands, collecting of milk money and dinner money, marking of the register, helping prepare material—itself becomes a steady stream keeping fresh and vital the ways and means of communication.

. . . The headmistress in this old school tries "to have something in the environment which will fire off the child." This interest, she says, "must then be kept going." The notebooks the teachers keep of some of the casual conversations with children indicate a possible interest, a starting point they can follow up. As I sit near a child fingering the shape-board and talk with him about it, the teacher looks up and suggests, "He isn't up to that yet. He's just looking," and tells me at what point he is and encourages me to become even more involved. I am free to talk to the children: children read to me, show me their books, ask me questions—always as individuals, not as a class instigated by the teacher.

. . . Teachers take time to read poetry, and children have favorite poems and ask for these during almost every one of my visits. Children create poetry. Poems, their own as well as their favorites, are written large on display boards next to paintings or in other places. Poetry is also part of the Morning Service.

. . . The headmistress seems to know every child, to know things about a child: that his grandmother is sick; that his dog had run away; that he is going with his daddy on holiday; that he has an "aunty" in Australia. If, in a rare moment, the headmistress sits down and talks to me in her office, situated sometimes on a half-floor above the central hall and from which she can see all that is going on, children are soon knocking, asking would she like to see their building, their painting, their junk invention, or read their poem or story. There seems to be complete free access to the headmistress. A word or two to this one or that one is part of her progress though the school. Incidental learning flows from her. A small sample: A child tells her, "I want to be a teacher in this school when I grow up." The time of growing up is calculated. The head asks how old would she (the head) be then, and would she then still be the head? "Oh no, my granny is that old and she has the rheumatism." The children write her notes, receive answers, write back. I recall a child asking the headmistress was she aware that he is this height? Her answer is prompt: No, she appreciates knowing that he is that height, and is he aware that she is this height? In quick response he writes, telling her how much taller she is. . . .

4. One Morning in an Infant School

To encourage the spread of good informal practice in both England and the United States, the Anglo-American Primary School Project commissioned a series of twenty-three pamphlets on various aspects of informal education. Published in this country by Citation Press and in Great Britain by Macmillan Education Ltd., the series was prepared under the general guidance of the Schools Council, a quasi-governmental English body that sponsors research, coordinates reform efforts, and acts as a clearinghouse for new ideas; financial support for the project came from the Ford Foundation.

David and Elizabeth Grugeon, who have had experience teaching adolescents, college students, and adults as well as young children, believe that the flexibility and sensitivity with which infant-school teachers respond to individual children's individual needs can and should have their counterpart in the education of older children and adults. In the excerpt that follows, the Grugeons' observations of a classroom in a large London infant school are interspersed with written and oral reports by the teacher herself.

This is a description of a fairly large infant school on the outskirts of London, near London Airport. . . . The difficulty of providing an accurate portrait of an infant school was precisely described by one teacher as its "multi-dimensional complexity." This is particularly true of a vertically grouped infant school where the children in each class are a mixture of five-, six- and seven-year-olds and where the day is an integrated day with no artificial splitting of the time into divisions for subjects or activities. The same teacher went on to give an account of a morning in her classroom which makes the best possible opening to this study. As the morning proceeds, we sense the many roles of the infant teacher: provider of materials and encouragement, listener, guide, peacemaker, sounding board, approver, controller, extender, observer, friend, provoker, surrogate parent, adult.

> Carlo (seven) tells me he saw a harp last night—someone was carrying it—not quite like the harp I had in my cupboard but the same sort of thing. I ask if he could paint it and show me what he means. He paints this and we discuss the way the strings work. Would he like to try to make one? I find a couple of boxes and some rubber bands of different lengths and thicknesses and he goes away with them. He comes back about ten minutes later— some of the bands make a better noise than others. He then goes away with them again, and comes back a little later with a piece of canvas material tucked in and out of the rubber bands. He says he has turned his harp into a trampoline! He and Michael take it down to the bottom of the concrete steps outside the class and find different things to drop on it. Carlo comes back to tell me (it's his own idea) which things bounce highest and farthest. At my suggestion, they take a ruler and try to measure these differences.
>
> Beverley (five-plus) wants some cotton-wool; she is dressed up as a nurse and is playing at hospitals. An extended search fails to find any—I remember afterwards that I used the last of it when someone urgently wanted it to represent smoke! I give her

some paper hankies. She says she will use them as nappies. I notice later that she has macerated them with water in a plastic cup and is feeding this as medicine to the dolls.

Andrew (seven) and Kerry (six) have been out looking for insects and come back very excited as they *nearly* caught a bee. However, they're a bit cautious about handling one, and have decided they need a net. Having discussed with them what they think they'll need for one, I find an old broom handle, and part of a net curtain (rather heavily embroidered but Andrew considers that there are enough small holes left to make it all right really), and they ask the schoolkeeper and another teacher for some wire. The practical problems involved in actually constructing the net (and fixing two rather bendy pieces of wire together) are not inconsiderable. Andrew hammers two nails into the wood, and twists the wire round them. Kerry tries to sew the bag together—it's the first time she has ever used a needle and thread, she says. Andrew helps her to finish it and they set off in pursuit of the bee.

Jimmy (six-plus) is busy making something at the woodwork bench, and comes up to tell me what it is when he has finished— a windmill with a cover over it.

Alan (seven) has spent about twenty minutes painting an "underwater" picture. One of a family of eleven children, a boy of cheerful nature and limited vocabulary, he has never actually been to the sea. The picture, as he describes it, has a lady swimming and a baby swimming and two rocks and a tortoise with eight legs (up in the far left corner) which reminds one suspiciously of a sun. Further conversation elicits that in fact the "tortoise" had started life as a sun, but Alan had changed his mind.

Franco (five-plus) has asked me for a container for his marbles (a current craze). Having been told to look for one in the scrap materials, he returns with an orange-juice tin which appears to satisfy him. Five minutes later, he has come back to show me that when he blows down the tin the marbles all rattle and make an unusual noise. He's delighted with this discovery and takes it round the class, showing people. Then he gets a yoghourt carton and fixes it onto the other end: the marbles now rattle to and fro. He taps one end with his fingers, and there's a rattle and he suddenly gets the idea of putting string through both ends, tying it round his neck and using it like a drum. He finds he's able to make a hole through it with a pair of scissors. Much pleased, he then finds two pieces of wood to act as drumsticks and continues to wear his "drum" for the remainder of the morning.

Martina (seven-plus), who is a fluent reader, is helping some of the less able readers to read (from their reading books). This

is her own idea—she has often said she would like to be a teacher
—and she is patient with the slower ones. She spends about an
hour doing this, and then takes a book from the reading corner
and reads several children a story.

Ian (five) and Lee (seven) have made a "hide-out" in the
large bricks, using a couple of old army blankets. Ian says he is a
bandit and is watching everybody through a peephole.

Tracey (six) and Sophie (six) are washing some of the clothes
from the home corner, hanging them on the pipes outside to dry.
Sophie is surprised later on in the day to find that the things really
do look cleaner. "I like doing this work," says Tracey. "I often
help my Mum at home like this." She often asks to do this job.

June (six) and Ashley (six) spend some time with the guinea
pigs. To their request to be allowed to go and get some grass for
them, I make the alternative suggestion that they clean the cage
out first. Neither of them has done this before, and it involves
going over to the main school building and asking a teacher over
there where the sawdust and hay are kept. They divide the various
jobs between them quite well, and don't forget to give the guinea
pigs food and water. They throw away the old paper and food
in the right places, but aren't so keen on sweeping up the generous
allocation of hay and sawdust that the floor has received.

Malcolm (five) has drawn a picture to which he would like me
to add the writing. He's able enough to begin to work with a
dictionary and I ask him if he'd like one. After a moment's inward
debate, he tells me he will when he's in the middle group (ie, in
the following term when he will be six). Usually I've written
words for him and he has either gone over the top of my writing
or written underneath. Today I suggest a change: that I should
write what he wants on a separate piece of paper, and that he
can copy from that. He agrees to this, and describes how in his
picture there's an Indian being chased by a boat and there's another boat chasing that one.

Martin (seven) and Michael (seven) bring me some leaves
that they collected yesterday, because they want me to see how
they've shrunk since then. Out come the rulers. Martin is sure that
one is at least three centimeters shorter than it was. At my suggestion, they go out and make another collection of similar leaves
and measure them when they bring them back; if they measure
them tomorrow they can see (a) if they always shrink and (b) by
how much. Actually they come back with more than just leaves,
managing to find two stalks of horse chestnut buds. Martin says
he has found some conkers and looks disbelieving when I try to
explain that they're flower buds. However, he agrees that if they

are flower heads they'll come out, so he finds a jar and puts them in it.

The stick insects need some fresh privet. Carlo (seven), Franco (five) and Andrew (seven) are given directions (by me) about where to find the leaves. Andrew is particular over the exact *kind* of leaf to bring back, the dark green or the "new" green as he calls it. When they're given the new leaves, Martina (seven-plus), to whom the insects seem particularly alarming, wants to know what would happen if she picked one up? She can try, I tell her, so she comes back wearing an old black rubber glove that I'd put in the water trolley equipment. She puts her hand out but withdraws it the moment she sees the insect move, and says she's "changed her mind!"

Carlo (seven) has found two cardboard toilet rolls and is making a pair of binoculars from them. He has tried tying them together but it isn't working—they keep slipping about so he comes to ask if he can have some sellotape.

Stewart (six) is playing "war-games" he informs me: he has some number apparatus, and he and Malcolm (five) have built identical forts on the table and are "firing" small sticks at each other's construction. A slight fracas develops when one building is demolished more than was intended—which appears to demand retaliatory action. I attempt to resolve the situation by suggesting that they rebuild each other's constructions.

I hear Michael B (seven) read. It's an uphill struggle—this is the second book of the third reading scheme he has attempted, and it takes a good ten minutes to hear him read two pages at the most.

A shriek from Deirdre (seven); her sister Annette (six) has pinched her. They are doing a play in the home corner. Deirdre looks concerned that I've noticed the noise but makes no complaint against Annette, just records the fact that that's what made her make the noise.

Kevin (five), Sean (five) and Rosalind (five) are playing in the dry sand. They've got practically all the sand toys, e.g., cars, people, trees and houses, all crammed into one small tray. Kevin says they're playing cowboys. They're all chattering away but they don't seem to be taking much notice of one another's conversation.

Beverley (five-plus) wants me to hear her read again. She's very anxious to learn but finds it very difficult to retain any words. In the last couple of days she has been persevering at her book, walking round with it and trying to catch me (when I don't seem otherwise occupied!) to ask me if she has got the next word right. She has only just come to the class and although she says she hasn't had a book before, she often mistakes a phrase in the book

she has at present for one that's in another book (of a different
reading series).

Debbie (seven) first stands by the door, watching the others
at woodwork, then wanders about the room, has her milk, and
starts to pester the children who are making up a play. I tell her
to leave them alone if she can't join in sensibly with them. She
sulks and rushes off across the room. Five minutes later, she says
she doesn't know what to do. I give her five minutes to look
round the room or follow up some suggestions I give her. None
seem to appeal so I give her something definite to do. She goes to
it in a desultory fashion but doesn't really concentrate.

Muna (seven) says he almost knows how to play the theme
tune of Z Cars on the xylophone, and gets as far as the first
couple of bars. It is recognized by Kerry (six) who says she'll
come and help him play the next bit. They practise for about ten
minutes and then Muna returns to *We Three Kings* his perennial
favorite.

Lee (seven) wants an opportunity to go outside—and makes
several dud suggestions as to why he should (there's an inevitable
restriction on the number who can do so at any one time and
certain criteria to be fulfilled, i.e., that they are able to tell me
exactly why they want to go outside and what kind of work it
is they hope to do). Lee has seen Carlo and Jimmy measuring the
class "garden" yesterday—idea! Perhaps he could do the same. He
takes the measure with him and does the work quite accurately
but is obviously puzzled when I suggest that he could also measure
the "width"—"how wide" it is. I try the phrase "across—you
know, from side to side." That seems to mean something, and off
he goes.

Mark (five) is wearing a hat from the dressing-up clothes. It
covers his head but not his ears. "Look, it's to keep my ears
warm!" he says. Ian (five), standing by him, who tells me it's a
"Stetson" hat, disagrees (as I do) but Mark insists it's to keep his
ears warm, even when I tell him to feel where his ears are and to
look in the mirror.

Rumpus with Ashley (six) and June (six) because the latter has
been thumped by the former. "She wouldn't listen to me—*so!*"
says Ashley in explanation. June is understandably upset. Ashley
says her Mum has told her she has got to fight (so she does, endlessly). This is about the third time she's had someone in tears this
morning. I lift her bodily and with some feeling, and leave her to
cool off on a chair by herself.

Sophie has painted a picture—very similar to one she did
yesterday, except that today there's no eagle and yesterday there

was no wigwam. She falls in with the suggestion that she put a label underneath and writes it out quite quickly.

I'm requested by a child, sent on a message from the head, to find out certain numbers from the register. Martin (seven) is interested in the way the marks are put down on the page (divided by thick lines). He thinks the divisions are the days, and I show him the initial letters at the top of each section. He picks up the idea and follows through the weeks, telling the days of the week as he does so (the answer to the head's request being delayed somewhat!).

"Tuck" time. Beverley thinks she might have change from 3p after buying a packet of crisps for 3p. The older ones nearby disabuse her of any such idea. Rosalind is very insistent that I don't forget *her* change.

Class discussion: I found an onion sprouting in my vegetable rack at home, and show it. They seem quite intrigued. Martin (seven) asks if it's a bulb. Quite a number can say the names of several other bulbs, though Alan suggests a potato. Jimmy says the curved leaves (an odd shape as they grew towards a thin crack of light) make him think of toenails. Afterwards I put it resting on the rim of a jar of water; several children come up to tell me that the water has changed colour (to bright yellow). I also show the children the seeds I told them I would bring for the garden. They like looking at the pictures on the front of the packets which seem to be mostly categorized by them as chrysanthemums, roses, and pansies (in fact, marigolds, nasturtiums, sweet peas, godetia, and cornflowers). I also found at home some wrapping paper with children's faces on it, which they take to—the faces being of a "comic" type—and they point out resemblances to each other's faces on it. Lee (seven) and Kerry (six) want to count the different sorts.

June has heard that tadpoles grow legs, and comes up to me very excited—"they've got one leg now," she says, and points out their tails! She is not altogether convinced when I show her a book illustration of the various stages.

Ashley (six) is now looking at a box of shells, and is turning over the ones she likes best (the smallest ones). She tells me that shells sometimes grow in gardens, as well as at the seaside, because you see them in people's gardens. A tulip petal has fallen into the box: "Look how dark and felty—no, I mean velvety, it is! I'll put it on the interest table." I ask her what sort of things go on an interest table. "Oh, things people like to look at, you know" . . . What sort of things then would one *not* put on an interest table? "Oh, things that aren't interesting—you know, things you've seen before and things like that." Also apropos of nothing in particular, she tells me her dad lived in a bus when he was a little boy, and he hadn't any TV so he'd had to listen to records all the time.

John (seven), Jimmy (six-plus) and Alan (seven) have been brought back after playtime by the head, who has had to talk to them after they'd been caught throwing stones at each other and fighting in the playground. Heads cast down, they listen to their final reprimand before she returns to the main school. Once she has gone, they all solemnly, silently and spontaneously shake hands with each other, and then go their separate ways grinning like hyenas.

The writer describes this as "an account of *some* of a morning's happenings—please may it be noted that there were many things that happened/didn't happen that morning which may/may not have happened on other mornings. For instance, there was no movement, PE (physical education), poetry, or story. Fewer children read or wrote than might have been usual, and so on."

Even so, the account is impressive, both for its detail and for the evidence of flexible and thoughtful response by the teacher to the twenty-eight children she has mentioned during the morning (two were away that morning, from a full roll of thirty). We see how the children she has known for several months have confidence in her and tell her some of their most pressing thoughts and interests. These are the starting points for suggestions from the teacher which enlarge a sketchy idea into a hypothesis for testing. And the teacher has to be on hand to provide further practical stimulus that will elicit the right questions to lead to a sensible way of testing the hypothesis, with materials that will furnish results that can be talked about so that the children can draw conclusions from the test. Infinite flexibility and patience, listening to successes and failures, sympathizing, approving, allowing for alternative procedures to encourage the child's enquiry to become fruitful; all these demand skills in relation to young human beings that one supposes are demanded of a scientist on the frontiers of research.

Each child has to be adapted to: Alan, who has ten brothers and sisters and who has a special need for *extra* conversation; Franco, who has a craze for marbles; younger children who chatter away to themselves in the dry sand; an older sister who can objectively record the reason for her shriek without recriminations. There is no doubt that the teacher is tested by the open structure of the school day and the composition of the class, but she is able to turn this to advantage. Older children help younger ones; older children who feel very young can be with younger ones when they want (and vice versa). Children are encouraged to make use of human resources other than their own teacher (during the morning described, another teacher, the schoolkeeper and the headteacher all became involved). The teacher has trained the children to be sufficiently independent to allow her time to concentrate on individual children (she hears two children who are finding reading difficult—one for ten minutes); and she can spend time with small groups, and occasionally has the whole class together to share ideas. Each child's rhythm of work is different.

II

Portraits of American Open Classrooms

1. Learning in the Open Corridor

Lillian Weber's impact on practice has stemmed less from her writing than from her work in the public school classrooms of New York City. On her return from England in the winter of 1968, Mrs. Weber found herself increasingly dissatisfied with the fact that she was sending her City College students into conventional classrooms to do their student teaching. It made no sense, she felt, to give her students an understanding of the psychology of learning and the nature of child development, only to have them do their student teaching in classrooms that controverted everything she had tried to teach them. Such an arrangement was not only senseless but self-defeating, since a large body of research suggests that the classroom teacher with whom students do their practice teaching exerts a decisive influence on the development of their teaching style.

Placing the students in the hothouse atmosphere of a private school or university laboratory school, on the other hand, seemed equally unsatisfactory; it would not, Professor Weber felt, prepare her students for the harsh realities of the classrooms and schools in which, in all probability, they would be working. If they were to be able to exert any influence for change, she reasoned, the students would have to learn how to deal with schools as they are, and how to handle all the obstacles, frustrations, and petty irritations that change usually evokes. And change was possible, in Professor Weber's view; what had sent her to England in the first place was the discovery that approaches that American nursery educators had assumed were possible only in private schools were widely used in the English state system.

The solution was to carve out a small section of P.S. 123, a Central Harlem elementary school, where Mrs. Weber served as consultant, and which was affiliated with City College's School of Education. In the course of her close study of informal English schools, Professor Weber had come to regard their use of the halls and corridors—what she likes to call "in and outness"—as one of the keys to the schools' success. Her program at P.S. 123 began, therefore, by using only the corridor outside a group of five participating classrooms located around the L at one end of the school's first floor.

Setting up the "stuff" for informal teaching in the corridor—initially, for just an hour a day three days a week—had the further advantage of giving the five teachers access to the new approach without forcing it upon them. Professor Weber feels strongly that voluntarism is essential if change is to be successful; she was determined, therefore, to avoid any direct challenge to the teachers or to the autonomy of their classrooms. Her object, in addition to providing an informal teaching experience for her own students, was to explore how far one could go toward freeing the classroom structure and developing more intimate, humane settings, starting with the base of the existing curriculum and grade organization. (For Professor Weber's own account of her initial goals and the ways in which they have been modified as a result of her experience, see Chapter III below.)

The first selection describes the early days of the open corridor program at P.S. 123. Arthur J. Tobier has been following Professor Weber's work since it began, initially as a staff member of the Center for Urban Education and now as a staff member of Professor Weber's Advisory Services—Open Corridor Reorganization of the New York Public Schools.

At 9:30 A.M. teacher aides and student teachers begin to line the small, L-shaped section of the corridor with tables and chairs. Out of a storage room they bring out boxes full of materials and spread the contents on the tables. There are scales, Cuisenaire rods, water vessels, musical instruments, a dozen different kinds of math puzzles, counting devices, hexagons, trapezoids, animals, clay, all manner of measuring devices. Singly, and in pairs, threes, and fours, children filter into the corridor from five classrooms, the doors of which are open and inside of which teachers are conducting lessons. Outside, the corridor has become another kind of place. Some children move directly to activities, having learned the corridor's offerings. Others, sometimes with a friend in tow,

From Arthur J. Tobier, "The Open Classroom: Humanizing the Coldness of Public Places," *The Center Forum*, May 16, 1969, pp. 19–23.

shop around before settling down to one thing. And others, perhaps first or second graders, after staying awhile, move through the corridor into one of the classrooms, perhaps a kindergarten or prekindergarten, to listen to a story or play a piano, or to play with animals or with the workbench. At one table a four year old girl is manipulating a game about people, identifying relationships. Behind, a six year old has spread herself on a piece of newsprint on the floor while a student teacher traces her form in crayon, which she will then measure in blocks, and hang on the wall. Other children are pacing off distances, measuring with string. At another table a five year old boy, who until the previous week had been disruptive, doing nothing in the corridor but running back and forth, has just put together, with an effort of intense concentration, a puzzle consisting of triangular and rectangular shapes. Encouraged to show his teacher what he's done, ("Show her, Paul, she doesn't know you can do this"), he brings her into the corridor. Lillian Weber, who set up the corridor, comes by and suggests that the boy record his feat. A second grader is called over to write what he describes. Another second grader who has just entered the corridor stops Mrs. Weber and announces she is about to write a story about the educator. Mrs. Weber stands absolutely still as the girl counts the 114 stripes on her dress. In a minute, both stories are completed, passed around, read and re-read, and posted on a bulletin board already 12 deep in stories and records of activity. A few feet away a group of four has been working steadily for an hour weighing shoes and discussing relationships with the corridor teacher, a young graduate student hired for the job. Two kindergarten boys come by, full of themselves and of being on their own, puffing hard from running. A visitor holds one boy, tells him how fast his heart is beating, and gets him to listen to his friend's heart beat. Now the movement in the corridor is fluid. There is a lot of doing and a lot of telling. Questions are investigated in many ways. Nothing that is said or done is left unexamined. Children return to their classes, others come out, work continues in all the rooms. A child pauses at the entrance of one room before going in to show her teacher a paper flower she has just made. Inside the room, run along formal lines, there is a striking absence of restlessness. Children are hard at work despite the sounds and movement from the corridor. In sharp contrast, a second grade class next door operates informally in small clusters of children. A teacher comes to the doorway of her room, watches the activity in the corridor for a time, and returns to her work. By 11 A.M. the corridor begins to clear. Materials, tables, and chairs have been returned to their storeroom. Left on the corridor walls are the paper cutouts of children's figures. It is only then, when the corridor is empty, that a visitor notices how dark it is inside the school.

* * *

*The "open corridor" came into being at P.S. 123 in the spring of 1968.
Before that first semester was over, a group of parents and teachers
from P.S. 84, an elementary school in a racially mixed neighborhood of
low-income to high-income families, came to observe the program in
action. They were sufficiently impressed to invite Professor Weber to
introduce the open corridor the following year in P.S. 84. The following
selection describes the operation of the program two years later. (Walter
and Miriam Schneir, free-lance writers and journalists, have been active
in encouraging the creation of open classrooms in Westchester County,
New York, where they live.)*

The underlying assumption of "informal" schools, both British and
American, is that in an enriched and carefully planned environment that
supports *the natural drive toward learning* children are able to learn
mostly by themselves, from each other and from books. They learn in
encounters with the things and people around them, and they do so at
their own irregular and individual pace. They learn most intensely when
they are interested and see the pertinence of what they are doing. The
role of the teacher is important, but quite untraditional: there are few,
if any, whole-class lessons, no standardized tests, no meticulously detailed
and rigidly enforced curriculum.

Informal methods are being tried in New York City and in the Westchester communities of New Rochelle, Greenburgh and Irvington, and
across the country in such cities as Washington, Detroit, New Haven,
Newark and Berkeley, as well as such states as North Dakota, Vermont,
Maine and Arizona.

One of the most interesting experiments singled out for mention by
the Carnegie report is taking place at P.S. 84, a school in a racially and
economically varied neighborhood along Manhattan's Upper West Side.
The school, with 900 children in pre-kindergarten through sixth grade,
has an enrollment that is about one-third black, one-third white and
one-third Spanish-American.

Today at P.S. 84, the visitor can see in operation the most dramatic
physical innovation of the British primary schools: the use of hallways
as extensions of the classroom. The British were forced to adopt this
plan because of overcrowded schools. But necessity proved to be a virtue
when classroom doors were thrown open and the children were allowed
free access to the corridors. The arrangement made possible a sense of
community among students and staff, a spirit of mutual help and learning.

From Walter Schneir and Miriam Schneir, "The Joy of Learning—In the Open
Corridor," *The New York Times Magazine*, April 4, 1971, pp. 30–31, 72–80, 92–97.
Copyright © 1971 by The New York Times Company. Reprinted by permission.

The educator who has promoted this particular approach in New York, Mrs. Lillian Weber, describes it as the "open corridor" program.

The sight of a small boy sliding down a bannister greets the two visitors to P.S. 84, situated at 92d Street between Columbus Avenue and Central Park West. The sliding boy and a companion, who is taking the more conventional route down a short flight of stairs from a first floor landing, are conversing animatedly.

Walking up a half dozen steps, we come upon a first floor corridor that is the connecting passage between four primary classrooms that open off it. At 10 A.M. in the corridor, four kindergarten girls, seated cross-legged on some cushions with a pile of magazines, a paste pot and a very large sheet of brown paper, are cutting and pasting. Nearby, a third grader is reading a story to a younger child; both are giggling at the antics of "Curious George." Two girls sitting side by side on the corridor floor are each absorbed in a book, as is a boy leaning against the opposite wall. Several youngsters are writing in notebooks or on loose sheets of paper. A large, bright yellow wooden tub on wheels, with two children and an oversized stuffed dog crowded into it, is being pushed along the corridor by a highly energetic boy.

The children who are working do not look up as the cart rolls by. No adult is present in the corridor aside from the visitors. From time to time, a child gets up and goes into one of the classrooms to ask some available adult a question; occasionally, a child turns to us for help. One asks, "How do you spell Morison?," the name of the school's principal to whom she is writing a letter. Presently, a teacher comes out of a classroom and offers the four kindergarten girls a few more illustrated magazines. The girls speak English to their teacher, and converse quietly in Spanish together.

The institutional tile walls of the corridor are covered with a variety of art work and posters. Any child who wants to can tape up his work. It is not long past Halloween and a group of highly individualistic jack-o'-lanterns leer down. A poster, one of many, provides the following information: "We guessed how much our pumpkin would weigh. Risa thought it weighed 21 pounds. She weighed it and it weighed 20 pounds. After we took out the seeds and pulp, it weighed 16 pounds." In the corridor we are nearly surrounded by words, words of songs, poems, stories, announcements, news items—all placed at a convenient height for children to read.

A third-grade classroom opens off the corridor. At first our eyes are assailed by the apparent chaos of the scene—a profusion of movement, sounds, colors, shapes. Gradually, however, the organization of the class reveals itself. The room is perhaps a little smaller than is standard and has a class register of 30 children, a few of whom are in the corridor or visiting other classes. What is most striking is that there are no desks for pupils or teachers. Instead, the room is arranged as a workshop.

Carelessly draped over the seat, arm and back of a big old easy chair are three children, each reading to himself. Several other children nearby sprawl comfortably on a covered mattress on the floor, rehearsing a song they have written and copied neatly into a song folio.

One grouping of tables is a science area with equipment ranging from magnets, mirrors, a prism, magnifying glasses, a microscope, a kaleidoscope, batteries, wires, an electric bell, to various natural objects (shells, seeds, feathers, bones and a bird's nest). Also on nearby shelves are a cage with gerbils, a turtle tank and plants grown by the children. Several other tables placed together and surrounded by chairs hold a great variety of math materials such as shaped blocks known as "geo blocks," combination locks and Cuisenaire rods, rulers and graph paper. A separate balance table contains four scales.

The teacher sits down at a small, round table for a few minutes with two boys, and they work together on vocabulary with word cards; her paraprofessional assistant is at the blackboard with several children who are writing. A student teacher (available in the mornings only) praises a drawing a girl has brought over to show her; other children display their work to the visitors with obvious pride.

Children move in and out of the classroom constantly. The teacher seems alert to the nuances of all the activity. To a boy trying to explain to a classmate how to construct a rather complex paper fan, she suggests, "As a game, see if you can describe it to her with your hands behind your back." To a child who has produced a collection of ink-blot pictures, she casually introduces the idea of "symmetry." She keeps a record book handy in which she jots notations on each of the children. Seeing a child filling and emptying different sized plastic containers at the sink, she stops for a moment and talks about pints and quarts. Weighing, measuring and graph-making appear to be favorite activities.

In spite of all that is happening—the constant conversation, the singing—the noise level is quite subdued. The children look engaged, bright-eyed, happy. A little boy breaks into an impromptu rock 'n' roll dance; nobody takes any particular notice. Apparently satisfied, he returns to the math area.

In the corridor on the second floor of P.S. 84, a tumbling mat is taken out for the first time this year. Children from classrooms off this hallway line up and take turns: handstands, cartwheels, but mostly somersaults. They are good. One boy does a headstand and holds the pose. After a few moments, the "corridor teacher" begins to count and the children chime in. They get up to 47 before the child stands again and proudly struts to the end of the line.

In a first-grade classroom a prominent sign suggests: "Things to Do. Play at the math table. Paint a picture. Make a book. Play with sand. Use the typewriter. Use the chalk board. Play a reading game. Listen to a record. Read a book. Play checkers." Most of these activities are being sampled. The level of noise and movement, though noticeably higher than in the older third grade, is not overpowering. As in the other class visited, the teacher has a record book in which she makes notes about individual children, such as: "Speaks in monosyllables," "Counts to 15, recognizes number symbols to 8," "Built huge bridge out of blocks —I promised to bring book on bridges."

A box labeled "story starters" contains pictures that are employed to suggest narrative. On a wall is a collection of such stories dictated by the children and copied down by an adult. A Chagall print adorns one wall and beneath it is a story by a child named Rachel:

> This bird is playing in the water. The flying horse is watching it play. The bird is having fun playing in the water. Now the bird is chasing its tail while the flying horse is shaking the weeds. The flying horse is getting closer to the river while the bird is getting dizzier and dizzier. The flying horse is getting closer and closer to the bird near the river. Then the bird sees the flying horse and then the bird paddles away.

2. Excitement in North Dakota

The burgeoning interest in open education reflects some deep-rooted and extensive currents in American life and thought. Witness the fact that at the same time that Lillian Weber was beginning her attempt to open up the elementary schools of New York City, a similar reform effort was getting underway some 1,500 miles to the west, in hamlets and towns with such unlikely names as Starkweather and Devils Lake. It would be hard to imagine more dissimilar elementary school environments than those of Harlem or Manhattan's Upper West Side and the cities, towns, and villages of North Dakota. If open classrooms can work effectively in both New York City and North Dakota, it is reasonable to assume that they can work almost anywhere.

The following selection describes how North Dakota's open classrooms looked several years ago to an experienced observer. Arlene Silberman, a widely published free-lance writer, served as Chief of Research for the Carnegie Study of the Education of Educators; her study of informal classrooms in North Dakota, New York, Philadelphia, and Tucson formed the basis for Chapter 7 of Crisis in the Classroom. (*For an account of how the North Dakota reforms originated, see* Crisis in the Classroom, *pp. 284 ff.*)

A new kind of education is beginning to sweep across the plains of North Dakota and shows signs of finding its way into schools across the nation. Children who used to be the last to trickle in to class each morning and the first to bound out, are arriving early and lingering late. Parents who once tried to drill multiplication tables into unwilling minds, now report that their children regard mathematics as a fascinating game. And veteran teachers exclaim that they are realizing the full satisfaction of their profession for the first time.

Tributes have come from many distinguished educators, including former U.S. Commissioner of Education, Harold Howe, but the ultimate testimonial came from a tear-streaked eight year old tow-head. "I just realized," she sobbed one January afternoon, "the year is half over already. And when it's all over," her chin quivered, "I can't come back 'til next year."

The schools that are earning this devotion are vastly different from traditional public schools. Gone is the familiar classroom where the teacher stands up front, expecting all eyes to face her and all ears to listen as she pours identical information into rows of silent children. Gone are the rigid lines of forward facing desks, so arranged that the teacher can keep her eye on every child at the same time. In their stead are scatterings of lightweight desks or tables and chairs and home-made room dividers which create unexpected nooks and crannies where children can slip away for independent work.

At first glance it may seem as if the teacher herself is gone, for she no longer dominates the room; the children and their activities do. But a second look will spot the teacher. She may be helping a few students in the math center, listening to a small group discussion in the social studies center or observing a youngster's experiment in the science center.

Having divided her room into a number of interest centers, so richly equipped that even six year olds can proceed on their own, the teacher can devote herself to a few students at a time or arrange frequent individual conferences without having to assign "busy-work" to keep the rest of the class occupied.

Occupied they are! Some boys are likely to be stretched out comfortably on the scraps of carpet that cover the floor of the reading center, engrossed in a variety of books, while a few girls snuggle into easy chairs and rockers to read. Another cluster may be signing up at the "Book Sharing" wall, selecting the date each will be ready to report on his reading. Some may read a favorite portion aloud, some may dramatize a section, while others prefer to impersonate the main characters or tell the story by way of a puppet show or a movie. The emphasis has changed from offering proof of having done an assignment to sharing the delight of having enjoyed a book. Small wonder that children become such avid readers!

Several more students are likely to be gathered in the writing center where a typewriter and a tape recorder entice reluctant writers while film strips offer fresh possibilities for the child who is "stuck" for an idea. Most youngsters, however, are neither reluctant nor lacking in ideas because they have so much to write about in rooms that burst with interest and activity. Their outpouring of poems, plays, stories, letters and diaries is astonishing.

Although the emphasis is on creativity, basic skills are not neglected. It is common practice to see a child in the writing center administering a weekly spelling test to a classmate, for youngsters sign up to be tested as each feels prepared. In some schools each student has an individualized spelling list, culled from the mistakes he has made in his own writing.

Elsewhere in the room, music lovers may be plugged into a record player, earphones dimming the sound, while young artists complete a mural. Even upper elementary classrooms have art centers because a child's native creativity does not end in first or second grade—unless the school brings it to an abrupt halt.

Meanwhile, future scientists and mathematicians are learning important concepts in the carefully planned centers that the teacher has set up to promote self-directed work. Yet the hum of all this activity disturbs neither the teacher nor the student who are conferring, because sound and movement are expected parts of classroom life.

Creating such classrooms, where each child pursues learning independently, is no easy task, for the teacher must find the delicate balance that encourages student initiative without abdicating her own responsibility.

"You have to be careful not to 'cop-out,' " explained a recent graduate of New School, the special division of the University of North Dakota that is pioneering in this way of teaching. "The kids are having such a ball that it's easy to convince yourself that anything they do is educational. But if a teacher forgets *her* role, she becomes a baby sitter."

Instead of abandoning the teacher's role, which was a fatal flaw in progressive education, New School has redefined it, blending the traditional American emphasis on basic skills with the latest practices in British elementary education. The teacher is no longer concerned with instructing an entire class, which the British slyly label "talk and chalk," nor even with "individualizing" the identical material to enable each child to cover the same content at his own pace. Instead, the teacher fosters truly individualized learning which develops out of each child's particular interests. It follows, then, that *how* a child goes about learning concerns the teacher as much as *what* he learns. And the ultimate test of a teacher becomes not what she pours into her students, but what she gets out of them.

"It's almost like starting a new profession," an experienced teacher declared following her year at New School. "After twenty years of being a giver of information, I've finally become a teacher! Teaching," she went on to explain, "means offering each student opportunities for his own learning. That's what New School offered me and that's what I'm now offering my children. New School," she concluded, "is the most important thing that ever happened to me."

New School may also be the most important thing that has happened to American education in thirty years because its approach can be applied in any classroom, urban or rural, and with any group of children from the most privileged Caucasians to the most deprived minority groups. Sensing this potential, educators from a dozen states from New York to California have been turning to North Dakota for the bold leadership that the most prestigious, long established Schools of Education have failed to provide. As a result, the first New School style classrooms have spread to Minnesota, Pennsylvania, and South Dakota.

Founded in the spring of 1968 after a state-wide study revealed that fifty-nine percent of North Dakota's elementary school teachers lacked a college degree, New School refused to become a stop-gap provider of hurried sheepskins. Instead, it created a unique program to develop teachers who would teach in a dramatically different way. Old-timers with thirty years experience and college juniors and seniors who have yet to teach their first year are now studying together without either group feeling that the content is repetitious or irrelevant.

"We're all inexperienced teachers now," a gray-haired veteran said, "because none of us has ever taught this way."

"None of us has ever learned this way, either," a college junior added.

To Dr. Vito Perrone, gifted young Dean of New School, having university students learn mathematics by manipulating buttons and blocks, abacus beads and Cuisenaire rods makes perfect sense. "We can't logically spend a year or two giving lecture courses to our students," he commented, "and then caution, 'Now don't *you* do that much talking when you teach.' We want our students to do as we do. And," he added with undisguised pleasure, "judging by our Masters candidates, they do!"

New School's Masters candidates have been manning classrooms in the state's largest cities and towns and its smallest villages and hamlets while experienced teachers take temporary leave to study for their degree at New School. Initially, fifty-five such replacements covered classrooms in fourteen school districts; within a year 103 more replacements were teaching in thirty districts, reaching some five thousand children. As a bonus, particularly in a state that has been losing population, all but three of the original fifty-five are continuing to teach in North Dakota. By 1975 it is expected that every elementary school teacher in the state will have a college degree—more often than not from New School or one of the State Teachers Colleges with an affiliated program. Equally gratifying, New School graduates are already proving to be missionaries, converting traditional teachers who have not come directly under New School's impact.

Teaching in this new manner requires talents that go beyond the ability to create interest centers that will evoke youngsters' independent explorations. Teachers must also know how to extend those explorations into further learning.

When some children found a wounded bird on their school grounds, they were eager to know what kind of bird they had and what food he would need. Unbound by a formal lesson plan, their teacher was able to use the opportunity to enlarge these interests. Four girls began studying the habits of a variety of birds, keeping notebooks of their observations; three others took photographs which they learned to develop and enlarge, while a pair of artists sketched pictures to accompany the notebooks. A number of boys built bird houses; one enterprising team "bugged" its bird house to tape record bird songs. When a particularly shy child learned to imitate bird calls, he became sound-effects man for a skit another group wrote about the wounded bird's recovery. Thus, the narrow lines that strait-jacket one subject from another were broken down as spelling, writing, art, drama, mathematics and science became a united whole. And all because of a wounded bird and a teacher who knew how to develop learning out of an unexpected happening.

Clearly, the teacher's role is a demanding one. Although no two children are necessarily reading the same book, or even reading at the same time, she must be certain that every child is reading regularly and progressing well. If some are not improving, she must serve as diagnostician, analyzing the reason in each case. The teacher must provide similar individualization in the other areas of the curriculum, yet she must be certain that her self-reliant youngsters are progressing steadily in all of them. Although learning develops out of individual interests, it cannot be left to chance. A New School program is not to be confused with a haphazard one. "Purposeful activity," one teacher noted, "is not chaos any more than freedom is license."

At times it may seem as if the teacher needs eyes in the back of her head and more than the normal allotment of arms and legs. Quite often she has them! New School has encouraged what the English call "family" or "vertical" grouping, which places six to eight year olds in one class, nine to elevens in another, and twelve to fourteens in a third. In this way older children serve as mini-teachers for younger ones, and the more skillful assist the less skillful. Professional educators label this "new" arrangement "peer teaching," but graduates of one-room school houses know there is nothing new about it except the terminology.

Everyone benefits under this arrangement: The teacher because of the assistance she gets, the younger children because they have more than one person to whom they can turn for help, and the older children who learn more as a result of the role they play. Take eight-year-old Ian who would have been considered a poor reader in any conventional second grade. He doesn't feel at the bottom of the heap, however, because now six year olds often turn to him for help. The extra practice Ian gets while helping younger ones, combined with a new sense of esteem, have resulted in significant gains in his own reading.

Reading has not been the only skill to improve, of course. For many students the entire level of work has risen. "In these lively classrooms," an enthusiastic principal explained, "learning isn't something children 'get' if they have a good instructor. It's something they *do* if they have a New School teacher."

Not every child was immediately ready to become a do-er. Some were confused when their teacher didn't give specific directions all day long, and self-conscious when they realized that each was regarded as a distinct individual personality. Some were uncertain. Could they really move about the interest centers and talk as they worked in small groups without winding up in the principal's office? Surprisingly few tested the limits.

Curiously, when New School ran a one-week Summer Workshop for the principals of schools that were entering the program in 1969, it encountered similar confusion and self-consciousness—this time on the part of the principals! By the end of the workshop, however, twenty-four of the twenty-five principals had become so enthusiastic that they requested a series of two-day workshops throughout the year.

The children have become equally enthusiastic. One teacher tells of having been absent for half a day during which time a conventional teacher served as substitute. "The next day my children were mad as hops," she said. "Little Julie put it bluntly when she said, 'Don't *ever* do that to us again!' "

Many parents were won over by their children's enthusiasm. Others remained to be convinced. As Lois Trapp, editorial writer for the weekly *Enderlin Independent* put it in her column, "North Dakotans are strangely hung up about that word 'new.' We like new and improved soap or breakfast cereal, new cars, new clothes and new machinery, but we want no part of new ideas, new education, or new religion." Yet the very people who resist innovation found themselves in the midst of the newest ideas in education; understandably, some were bewildered. Recalling their own school days, they assumed that education had to be tedious to be worthwhile, but their children seemed to spend much of their time "playing." Not realizing that play is a child's work through which he does a good bit of learning, they worried that their children were wasting time. Were these New School teachers neglecting the three Rs? Were they failing to prepare youngsters for later life?

Ultimately, most came to see that the New School not only taught the basic skills, but also prepared children for adult life in the fullest sense of the term. By fostering individual initiative, school was developing independent minds that would continue to seek and to learn on their own long after school days were over.

At first, however, some adults had a very different perspective. One mother recalled how she scoffed when her first grade daughter asked for an apple or a potato to bring to school. "I figured we were in for a year of seeing Wanda play house and store, and I pitied the poor second-grade teacher who would have my daughter next year." To her astonishment, Wanda began showing a genuine grasp of fractions. "And not only the easy ones," her mother boasted, "but even one like 1/28."

By dividing apples, carrots and such into increasingly smaller pieces, which Wanda regarded as play, she had gained a concrete understanding of fractions, which adults call school "work."

"Her brother didn't have fractions until fifth grade," the mother added, "and even then he simply memorized whatever the teacher told him. But Wanda seems to understand the concepts. At age six!"

Parents of older children were even more doubtful at first. "Can you imagine my feelings," the father of a ten-year-old boy asked, "when I walked into Eric's room and saw a lot of buttons and spools and even golf tees in that math center of theirs? I saw everything but sensible math workbooks. I was ready to go raise Cain with the principal." His work-hardened hands tightened into fists. "Then I spotted Eric with a bunch of kids playing some game they called 'Tower of Hanoi,' of all things. There they sat, six husky kids—two of 'em taller than the teacher—with a little wooden board that had three sticks jutting out of it and about five different sized discs stacked on the first stick. Instead of doing their work, they were trying to move those fool discs from one stick to another so that they landed in the same order.

" 'Watch this, Pa,' my kid said, not the least ashamed that I caught him playing behind the teacher's back, 'and remember, you can't put a bigger one on top of a smaller one.' "

What Eric's father saw was not a game in the usual sense of the word. Like every other game his teacher had selected for the math center, it was designed to lead students to specific concepts. Accompanying each game is an Exercise Card the teacher prepared to guide his students' thinking. The card for the "Tower of Hanoi" reads:

"1. Three discs require seven moves. Is there a way to tell you the least number of moves for two discs? four discs? five?

"2. Find the rule for this game. Let x be the number of discs and y be the number of moves.

$$
\begin{array}{c|c}
x & y \\
\hline
1. & \\
2. & \\
3. & \\
4. & \\
5. & \\
6. & \\
\end{array}
$$

"3. Graph your equation using the ordered pairs you found in No. 2."

Students are not confined to proceeding alone, however. Eric's teacher knows when to ask critical questions to redirect youngsters' thinking if it starts to veer too far off course; equally important, he knows when to leave them alone.

After Eric's father watched the class and teacher in action, he realized that his ten-year-old son was figuring out algebraic functions, a technique usually taught in high school.

"I'm sold," he admitted. "These kids are learning more than I ever did, and they're having fun in the bargain."

Once parents saw their children's academic achievements, they could allow themselves to enjoy their children's delight. The groans at wrong moves and shouts at right ones no longer seemed inappropriate because they reflected the thrill that comes from figuring something out independently. Furthermore, having figured out the answers themselves with discs and spools, buttons and boards, and all sorts of material that they can manipulate, these students *know* when they are right and can prove it. They no longer need the teacher or the textbook to confirm their answers.

The individualized program was another innovation that required explanation. Some parents saw its merit from the outset. "I was a sickly child," one said, "and I dreaded returning to school after each absence because of all the work I had to catch up with. If I had been permitted to pick up where I had left off, without the pressure of catching up with the rest of the class, I wouldn't have been the little nervous wreck I was."

Other parents were less sympathetic. "Either Lars is on the fifth grade level or he isn't," his mother stated flatly, not realising that fifth graders typically differ by as much as five years in achievement, just as fourth graders show a four-year span and sixth graders a six-year range. "If Lars is on grade level," his mother went on, "why can't he read the same book as every other child? And if he isn't—what's he doing in fifth grade?"

Knowing that parents had these concerns, teachers offered to explain the program during their evening hours. On many a winter's day, they stayed in school until after dark preparing material for their interest centers, stopped for hurried suppers, and drove long miles over icy roads to talk at local gatherings where they explained the wide range in ability and achievement that every teacher invariably faces.

When parents asked why some children weren't retained and others skipped so that the teacher could teach to a single level, they learned that most children do not progress evenly; they spurt ahead in some areas and lag in others. "Where shall I put the child who reads her brother's eighth-grade literature book but who is still struggling with long division?" a sixth-grade teacher asked. "Or the boy who's ready for high school chemistry but who can't write a clear paragraph? I doubt if I have a single 'sixth grader' in my sixth-grade class," she concluded.

With parental understanding came parental support. Instead of irritation at the teacher who permitted sets of basal readers in good condition to remain stacked in the closet, they expressed annoyance at teachers who continued to rely on them. Similarly, after hearing a third grade teacher report that her twenty five children tested out to fifteen different reading levels, parents favored replacing the three conventional reading groups of slow, average and gifted, with the individualized program they had previously deplored.

The community meetings also enabled teachers to resolve doubt about so-called "frills" such as drama, dancing, music and painting.

"Two years ago when my students were studying American History," a seventh grade teacher confessed, "they wanted to write and stage a play about Abraham Lincoln. I said we didn't have time to waste." She blushed. "How mistaken I was! Think of the experience in reading, writing, research, drama, art and history that I denied them by droning on with dates and battlefields instead."

The arts often serve as tools for aiding learning. They also serve as important outlets in their own right, releasing the native ability that children seem to possess until school stifles it. When parents viewed slides, they were amazed to see a talented and tender painting done by a rough and tumble farm boy whose only previous interest seemed to have been ice hockey. When they listened to tapes, they heard the voice of a particularly shy little girl coming across as a confident and gifted puppeteer. "I never would have believed it!" her incredulous mother said.

New School puts strong emphasis on awakening and nurturing creativity in children—and in teachers. While there, teachers take courses in Creative Expression in which they compose operettas, sculpt, act in original skits, write poetry, create collages and generally engage in all of the arts.

"If we can't make every teacher personally creative," Dean Perrone notes, "we can make every teacher sensitive to the creativity in her children so that she will nourish their attempts. Teachers who have done something as 'simple' as making a collage, for example, are less likely to reject their children's offerings on the grounds of neatness once they have personally discovered how easily paint drips and paste oozes. And teachers who have experienced stage fright themselves are not likely to boom out 'LOUDER' at some terrified little actress. It's funny," he mused, "how many things we insist that our children do that we haven't done ourselves in years."

The emphasis on creativity, however, in no way turns classrooms into hot-houses for little girls. Probably no public schools in the country offer so many opportunities for boys to be boys.

Visit a bustling upper elementary science center and you'll see three boys putting an internal combustion engine in working order while two others restore a rusty motor from an ancient washing machine. Another group is repairing an old radio while a ten year old, working on his own, assembles an intercom system. Another enterprising boy is completing a project demonstrating how an automobile's ignition system works, down to the last spark plug. To accommodate this activity the teachers had to have the wall between two rooms removed to create one huge work area.

Nor is science the only area where there are clearly masculine appeals. The magazines heaped on the tables of the reading centers show that sports fans, mechanics, and would-be hot rodders have not been neglected, and the selection of books confirms the fact.

Indeed, North Dakota may have found a solution to a problem that plagues the nation's schools, where boys are less successful learners than girls. Two-thirds of the children who are not promoted each year are boys, and the ratio of boys to girls in remedial reading classes and speech clinics runs anywhere from three to one to ten to one. Why the imbalance? Perhaps because schools are excessively feminine places. Docile girls who sit quietly and line up politely wind up as teachers' pets, whereas wiggling, squirming, active boys wind up having to "stay after"—a practice which suggests that school is so undesirable a place that the best punishment is to make someone remain there! Neat little girls who keep careful margins are singled out for praise, whereas messy little boys who get smudges on their papers are also singled out, but not for praise. And motivated little girls who enjoy reading about Dick, Jane and Sally become good readers, whereas young boys who would rather read about Willie Mays and Wilt Chamberlain than Puff and Spot become the main tenants of remedial reading classes.

In these North Dakota classrooms, however, every child, boy or girl, gifted or otherwise, is a distinct individual whose learning is rooted in his own interests and who follows through on his own initiative.

"I can't wait to see those kids grow up," a father commented after visiting school for a day. "If Newton figured out the Law of Gravity after watching an apple fall and Ben Franklin invented the lightning rod after flying his kite in a storm," he smiled, "heaven knows what those independent spirits will come up with. One thing I'll wager: they'll never stop learning."

3. Learning in Vermont

Like North Dakotans, residents of Vermont often take pride in their conservatism and commitment to traditional values. Yet Vermont is also one of the states where open education has flourished. The Prospect School, a quasi-public, quasi-private school founded by some Bennington College faculty members in 1965, has been developing its own indigenous approach to open education, developing an approach to evaluation of open education, and training teachers for public school systems in Vermont and elsewhere, including New York City.

This is a story about children. About gifted children like Carol and slower children like Andy, and just plain "ordinary" children like— well, what child is just plain "ordinary"? This is a story about silent children like Jeanie and jabberers like Ronnie and stutterers like Linda. Except Linda doesn't stutter any more and Jeanie is no longer mute. Nor is Andy quite so slow.

This is also a story about a white clapboard house with blue shutters, perched on a hilltop in North Bennington, Vt. Once upon a time it was a typical New England home, the kind you see in picture books, with autumn leaves falling or spring flowers blossoming. Today it is a school-house, known far and wide as The Prospect School. Flowers still blossom here, of course, but, even more important, children blossom too. It is

Arlene Silberman, "The School of Your Child's Dreams," *Good Housekeeping,* March 1971, pp. 69, 196–199. Copyright © 1971 by the Hearst Corporation. Reprinted by permission.

here that Carol's remarkable intelligence continues to develop and Jeanie's speech to expand. It is here that ten-year-old Tom learned to read for the first time, while ten-year-old Nick learned to take his head out of his books and discover a wider world. It is here that learning becomes an adventure, and children become explorers, each pursuing his individual course.

Let me tell you about Tom. He was a wiry nine-year-old with a pinched, scared look on his face when he first entered The Prospect School, carrying a lunch box in his hands and a burden on his shoulders —the burden of knowing that he had been considered a failure in first grade, again in second grade, and still again in third grade at the traditional elementary school he had been attending. Anyone who doesn't learn to read "on schedule" (on the *school's* schedule, that is) gets labeled "failure" by the end of first grade. For Tom the label seemed to have been written in indelible ink. In spite of his keen intelligence, in spite of all the drills and all the flash cards, he could neither read nor write.

Tom inched his way into the building, dreading the moment when he would be seated at a desk, given a reader, and classified as a "Redbird" or a "Daisy" or a "Jet." The name of the reading group varies from one school to another, but children are not easily deceived. They know which is the "smart" group, which the "so-so" group and, worst of all, which the "dumb" group. Tom was always at the bottom of the heap.

This time he didn't see the rows of desks he had been expecting, much less the reading groups. In fact, he didn't see anything that looked like a classroom. True, some kids were reading, but they were stretched out on a big, braided rug with floppy pillows for comfort. Besides, there were plenty of guys doing other things. A few of them were grouped around a cage, examining the school's new baby mice at the same time that a bunch of girls were sewing puppets and some other kids were playing chess. One girl was curled up in the fireplace with a dictionary, a pad and a pencil. Tom saw children scattered in all parts of the school, going from one room to another as they wished. Everyone seemed busy even though no bell had sounded for school to begin.

Of course, Tom had never been to London or Oxfordshire or Yorkshire, so he had no way of knowing that his new school was an American version of the famous British Infant and Junior Schools. He only knew that some irresistible urge was attracting him to a table that was heaped with pencils, crayons, inks, paints and charcoals. Forgetting his fears for the moment, he began sketching a picture. Being a gifted little artist, Tom spent the entire day drawing one picture after another, stopping only to eat and to play in the wonderful outdoor "gymnasium"—acres and acres of land and trees.

Toward afternoon, he suddenly realized that something strange was happening. "When is the bell gonna ring?" he asked another boy who was also working in the art center.

"We don't have bells here," he answered.

"Well, how do you know when it's time to leave one subject and start another?"

"We don't have subjects either," came the reply.

"No bells?" Tom asked. "No subjects? Well, what do you do here?"

"We learn."

Tom watched more carefully and discovered that children simply worked at something as long as they were interested, and then went on to something else. Finally, unable to believe that the pressure was really off, Tom asked timidly, "Isn't anyone gonna *make* me read?"

Patricia Carini, who was one of the three founders of The Prospect School in 1965 and who has remained as one of its psychologists ever since, happened to be standing nearby. (There always seems to be a staff member in close range.) She put her arm around Tom's narrow little shoulders and felt his whole taut body trembling. "You seem to be enjoying drawing right now, Tom, and I can see why. You're a real artist!"

"But when you're nine years old, you're *supposed* to read." Tom parroted the words and the actual tone of voice he had heard so many times as one well-meaning teacher after another had prodded and coaxed and nagged and goaded and punished and humiliated him into reading—or, rather, into not reading.

"When you're ready to read, we'll help you," Mrs. Carini assured him, with the easy confidence that comes from years of having watched children unfold like flowers, each at his own time and season, assuming he receives proper nurture. And proper nurture is what The Prospect School is all about.

For many days and weeks Tom's crayons and charcoals were his most important nurture. He was doing something that interested him, and he was experiencing success for the first time. Before this, Tom's paintings and portraits had gone unnoticed because art was regarded as unimportant in the school he'd gone to before. Instead of being known as the boy who could draw such unusual pictures, he was known as the unusual boy who *still* couldn't read or write. At The Prospect School, however, things were different.

"Hey, Tom, I like the way you made that ghost," one boy commented.

"Gee, could you show me how to draw a ball player with his arm up like that?" another asked.

Equally important, perhaps even more important, the teachers admired his work with real appreciation. Tom's face began to brighten and the pinched, scared look showed signs of disappearing. Day by day he produced his remarkable pictures. And week by week his teacher jotted down notes about Tom's activities, as she does for every child.

"We only meet as a group a few times a day, and then not for more than ten or 15 minutes at a time," she explained, "because children begin to lose interest after that. But I have to be aware of what each of my 27 youngsters is doing the rest of the time, so I can guide the learning. Look," she motioned, "Frank just went into the library on his own for the first time." Automatically, she pulled out her pad and scribbled a swift note about Frank's progress. Then she excused herself and left to join him.

Here are a few excerpts from her pages about Tom:

Sept. 25: Tom leaves his painting whenever I read a story to the group. He listens eagerly.

Oct. 2: Tom has begun joining in during class discussions. He has good ideas and expresses them well.

Oct. 9: Tom's interest in colors has gotten him to join Carl and Joe in a project on autumn leaves.

Oct. 16: Tom is now putting several pictures together in book form. Each picture has an obvious connection with the one that went before it.

Oct. 23: Carl asked Tom to explain his latest book, and Tom made up a complicated ghost story to go with the pictures, page by page.

Having kept close tabs on Tom's comings and goings, his teacher sensed when the time was ripe to help him translate his stories into written words. Her entry for November 2 begins: "Tom wrote his first sentence today!"

"It was all quite natural," she told me. "I simply said, 'Tom, do you think you'd like to write the story you were just telling Joe?' Very matter-of-factly, he opened the book he had been making and asked, 'How do I write: This is a three-headed giraffe'? I wrote the words under the picture and Tom copied them, writing each word under mine. From then on, we were off and running. By the way," she added with a broad smile, "you might like to know that Tom's giraffe was named Horace-Homer-Harold Smith."

Tom finished his three-headed-giraffe book that week. So many children wanted to read it that he went on to make a special copy for the school library the following week. Then he began a longer book that wound up being the second in a whole series of "Animal Stories by Tom."

He didn't have to rely on his teacher all this time, however. At The Prospect School, nine-, ten- and 11-year-olds are grouped together, and they are accustomed to helping each other. Even the seven- and eight-year-olds turn to them for help, as well as turning to each other. It was in this spirit of cooperation that three boys signed a project, "By Mike,

Neal & Joe, with a little help from some of their friends." It was in the same spirit that Tom showed Nancy how to draw a three-dimensional table, and Nancy showed Tom how to spell t-a-b-l-e. Ideally, every child at Prospect is a teacher some of the time and a learner all of the time.

The climax of Tom's story came the morning he looked up from a book he was writing and suddenly shouted, "Hey, you know what? I can *read!* I can really-truly read. And I'm not dumb any more." The pinched, scared look was gone forever.

Tom began to blossom as Pat Carini had predicted he would. The entire schoolhouse became his workshop. When he wasn't devising science experiments in one room, he was building wooden ships in another; or figuring out how many seconds it takes the earth to revolve around the sun; or sculpting clay animals; or tending plants and animals; or doing a dozen other things that his stimulating environment suggested.

The Prospect School is a treasure house of magnets and prisms, looms and wool, sand and stones, hourglasses and stopwatches. Every room tends to resemble what most of us think of as a kindergarten room. There are balance scales and metronomes, pots and pans, twigs, and leaves, blocks and more blocks, and, of course, musical instruments of every kind.

"Some people look at all these things and wonder what's going on, especially with our oldest children, our 11-year-olds," says psychologist Joan Blake, another of the founders of The Prospect School. "They think that playing has replaced learning. But after they spend a little time here, they see that it's quite the opposite: playing *produces* learning—when teachers know how to link them together. Ours do," she adds in her gentle voice with its quiet assurance.

What's more, playing produces joyful learning, and The Prospect School cares deeply about joy, unlike most schools that often seem downright suspicious of it. That's why grim little Nick caused so much concern at Prospect, in spite of his academic achievements.

Nick was already a good reader when he entered Prospect at age five and a half, and he went on to become an excellent one. Nonetheless, his first teacher remarked after a few months, "Nick learns to read as if someone were paying him a nickel for every word he learns. He doesn't seem to find delight in reading." His mathematical ability was equally impressive, but, this same teacher worried, "There does not seem to be much that makes Nick laugh." Laughter and delight matter at The Prospect School. Nick had problems with both.

Nevertheless, he probably would have collected a string of gold stars and a great many "A" report cards at any ordinary school. To its great credit, Prospect isn't "any ordinary school." It doesn't go in for gold stars and "A's" in the first place. "I don't want my kids working for a gold star the way a horse works for a lump of sugar," one teacher told me.

"I want them working for the satisfaction that comes from accomplishing something they set out to do. That's the best reward of all—and no one can give it to you. It comes from within." (I knew what he meant, incidentally, because I can still recall the thrill I felt the day I finished making my first dress. What a sense of achievement!)

In any event, Prospect is convinced that academic achievement is only one measure of a human being, important as it may be. The school wants to develop inventive youngsters with creative ways of approaching their work as well as their play—if such a distinction can be made. In many ways, as Joan Blake suggested, play *is* a child's work; similarly, work is a child's play.

"We don't brush math and reading aside," Pat Carini emphasizes. "Far from it. In fact, if Nick had been enjoying his academic work, I wouldn't have felt quite distressed that he avoided every activity where imagination and originality have free rein. But," she sighed, "Nick viewed every problem solved and every book read as another hurdle crossed. The poor child was so rigid and so terrified of exploring new materials!"

The entire staff celebrated the day Nick baked an apple pie. He felt able to attempt baking because he had a recipe that he could follow step by step for security. "I've never seen anyone consult a recipe as many times as Nick did to make certain he was doing the right thing," his teacher recalls. "It was in such contrast to his friend, Roger, who loves to whip up his own personal concoctions." But at the same time that his teacher noticed this, he also noticed that Nick enjoyed slapping the dough around. This led him to ask Nick if he would like to mess around with clay. The boy began cautiously, in true Nick-style, but with time and encouragement, he became a little freer.

From there it was an easier step to get him to try his hand in the art corner. At first he preferred copying diagrams of the human anatomy from a high school textbook. He also enjoyed copying maps. Neither maps nor diagrams forced him to use his imagination, of course. But one day, after making a trip to a greenhouse, Nick made a charming painting of the flowers he had seen.

"Better yet," his teacher remembers, "he painted a great tiger—and we hadn't made a trip to the zoo. That tiger was the first painting to come right out of Nick's imagination!"

Nick is ten and a half now and the folder of things he has produced is beginning to swell. His parents, both lawyers who once thought that reading, writing and arithmetic were all that mattered, are delighted with their creative young scholar. So is Joan Blake, who will plop every child's folder on your lap at the slightest indication of interest. "These paintings and writings tell us more about our children's growth than the usual standardized tests," she explains. Nonetheless, she smilingly admits that the school has resigned itself to administering standardized tests as well.

"Some people feel the need of so-called 'objective evidence' of learning, so we oblige. If only they realized how misleading those tests can be!" To prove her point, Mrs. Blake told me about nine-year-old Janie's experience with a standardized math test.

It seems that Janie encountered a question about fractions, and she had not yet experienced fractions in school. She raised her hand. "I don't know how to do this one," she said. Her teacher told her to forget it and move on to the next question. But Janie, accustomed to puzzling things out independently, was not willing to "forget it." Instead, she drew little boxes in the margin until she finally figured out how to answer the question. Having lingered so long over one item, her total score was dismal, needless to say. But, as her teacher put it, "That child taught herself a whole new concept! Isn't the ability to approach a problem with the thought, 'I can figure out a way to work this thing through,' more valuable than achieving a higher score by following my advice to 'forget it'?"

Nevertheless, in spite of the Janies—and Prospect is proud to have produced quite a number like her—who score poorly because they are more inventive and thoughtful than the tests desire, the school's test average is comfortably above the national average. Yet its children are no different in background or ability from children in any average school. Because of some Ford Foundation help at the beginning and some government funding all the way through, Prospect has always been able to insist upon accepting as high a proportion of disadvantaged children as the local public schools have.

"It's the children of professional parents who have trouble getting in here; this school discriminates—in reverse," one father pretended to grumble.

"It's not quite that bad," Mrs. Carini protests laughingly, "but it is true that we refuse to become an elite school for privileged, talented children. Twenty-five percent of our children are on full scholarship, and slightly more than another 25 percent are on partial scholarship. Even the families who pay full tuition only pay $400 a year. You see," she says earnestly, "the day that Prospect has a different group of children from our local public schools will be the day we stop doing what we set out to do."

What The Prospect School set out to do was demonstrated by its own example that there is a better way for every school to help children learn. The proof of the pudding is in the eating, of course, and—in one sense—Prospect's pudding can't be eaten until September. At that time its first graduating class will enter the seventh grade in various local public-school systems to learn side by side with youngsters who have spent their first six years of schooling in conventional classrooms. How will Prospect's children fare? It is too soon to be certain, of course, but judging by the successful experiences of occasional boys and girls who have transferred out of Prospect these past few years, the answer is likely to be, "Very, very well."

Indeed, Prospect's early success prompted other schools to try its informal approach long before the pudding was finished. First, Montpelier, the state capital, asked if Prospect could spare its first head teacher (who was also the third member of the trio that founded the school back in 1965), so that she could introduce playful open classrooms there.

"We were only two years old at the time," Pat Carini recalls, "and we really needed Marian Stroud very much, but—how could we say no when our goal is to help schools change?"

Two years later, New Rochelle, N.Y. (a suburban city of some 75,000 people), wooed away Prospect's second head teacher. Again, the white clapboard school on the hilltop smiled through its tears.

Then, Lebanon, N.H., asked if it could "borrow" a teacher for a year, to help retrain its teachers.

Losing and lending staff to public schools was a "happy problem." Finding the time to welcome the flocks of teachers and principals who kept trekking to North Bennington to observe Prospect's teachers in action was another. "But with too many 'happy problems' we could run the risk of being loved to death," one teacher observed sagely.

Fortunately, for Prospect's sake, there are like-minded schools in other parts of the country that are also serving as centers for change. Many, like Prospect, originally borrowed their ideas from the English Infant and Junior Schools, and then went on to adapt them to American needs. Other informal, child-centered programs began right here in the United States in cities 3,000 miles apart: Tucson, Ariz., and Philadelphia, Pa., without either knowing anything about the English schools. (They have since found out, of course.)

You can find classrooms that resemble Prospect's in many ways throughout the state of North Dakota, in its four mini-sized cities—Fargo, Grand Forks, Minot and Bismarck—and in tiny hamlets with names like Starkweather and Lakota. You can also find such classrooms in large cities like New York, Chicago and Los Angeles . . . and in medium-sized cities like Fort Worth, Texas; Newark, N.J.; and Wichita, Kan. . . . and in small cities like Durham, N.C.; Santa Fe, N.M.; and Lincoln, Neb. . . . and even in rural outposts like Hoonah, Alaska; Pikeville, Ky.; and Rosebud, Texas. There's hardly a state in the Union that doesn't have some classrooms that are similar to Prospect's. The children may be black or Appalachian white, American Indian or Mexican-American—or, as is the case in North Dakota and Vermont, predominantly majority-culture white.

Clearly, The Prospect School is part of a whole new movement. It is a movement that is being encouraged and supported by the U.S. Office of Education and by private foundations, by several colleges and by at least five large state universities: Arizona, New Mexico, North Dakota, Connecticut and Massachusetts.

"I sometimes think we ought to install a direct telephone wire between our school and the University of Massachusetts," Joan Blake jokes. "Every time another public school turns to them for help in changing its approach, their College of Education seems to turn to us. We're flattered, delighted and," she says with a smile, "exhausted."

In spite of its "exhaustion," Prospect is busy developing still another scheme so that it can send a staff member to consult, on site, with any school that asks for help. Prospect's reasoning is simple and direct: "If teachers and principals can't get to us, we'll have to find ways of getting to them." Like a mother who knows how important it is to be ready when her child has a problem, Prospect also wants to be ready when the need arises. So don't be surprised if you meet Pat Carini or Joan Blake in your own child's school one of these days—assuming that your PTA or your principal has asked for assistance.

It's sometimes hard to believe that Pat and Joan, each no bigger than a minute, head up so important and influential a school that Vermont's State Department of Education classifies it as both an official "demonstration center" and an official "teacher-training center." Blue-eyed Pat and red-headed Joan may look like schoolgirls themselves, but between them, they have enormous know-how. That's why so many schools outside of Vermont keep turning to The Prospect School for advice. That's why schools within the state lean ever more heavily toward them. And that's why the school has earned the many compliments it receives. Perhaps the nicest one of all came from a happily bewildered mother. "Who ever heard of an eight-year-old boy crying because he can't go to school for a day or two?" she asked. "Isn't that ridiculous—and marvelous!"

TWO

The Reason Why

Having described what open classrooms look like and sound like—
having given the reader unfamiliar with open classrooms verbal images of
a number of classrooms in England and the United States—we turn, in
Part Two, to an examination of why informal educators arrange their
classrooms the way they do. The reasons fall into two broad categories,
corresponding to the shared assumptions that lie at the heart of open
education. As we have pointed out in the Introduction, informal educators tend to share certain assumptions about (1) the aims and purposes of education; and (2) the ways in which children learn and grow.

I

The Aims of Education

1. Why Did We Change?

We were still very American, my wife and I, when we first met Sir Alec Clegg, Education Officer of the West Riding of Yorkshire. Early in the conversation, therefore, we asked that inevitable American question: "Do you have any statistics?"—statistics that might permit us to compare the achievement of students in informal and formal schools. Sir Alec hoisted an enormous leather portfolio onto his conference table and opened it. "Here are the statistics," he said, as he began to show us the contents: samples of the extraordinary paintings, drawings, collages, embroideries, stories, poems, and essays produced by students in his district. Lest we be misled, he added a cautionary note: "All these things are the by-products; the children are the products."

It would be hard to imagine a better introduction to the fundamental difference in the way formal and informal educators view the purposes of education. "It is a matter of intense interest to me," Sir Alec writes in the booklet from which this selection is taken, "to watch, over a 20-year span, the development of the fundamentals of education as seen, not in intelligence tests or reading techniques or history syllabuses, but in the way children dance and paint and write and behave toward one another." If American principals and superintendents—and school-board members and parents—evaluated their work in this way, we would not be reeling from crisis to crisis.

Small wonder that Sir Alec Clegg is widely acknowledged as one of the giants of British education, or that he has been one of the leaders of the quiet revolution that has transformed British primary education since

World War II. The selection that follows bears reading and rereading, so crammed is it with insights and suggestions, sometimes presented directly, sometimes almost in passing. Sir Alec's approach is so self-effacing and his style so understated that it takes several readings to catch all the nuances of what he is saying.

Sir Alec's diffidence should not be confused with lack of leadership. Quite the contrary; Revolution in the British Primary Schools is, among other things, a clear and persuasive account of how schools can be transformed through leadership—nonauthoritarian leadership. Posing the question, "How is this best done?" Sir Alec answers it by describing how he himself did it.

In the last analysis leadership of the Clegg variety is an attempt to help everyone concerned with children's education—teachers, principals, administrators, and advisers—to get first things first, which is to say, to think about what they are doing, why they are doing it, and what the consequences will be.

Much of the earlier, more formal way of teaching was based on aims that were wrongly conceived and on assumptions that were erroneous. The work children did tended to matter more than what happened to the child as a consequence of his doing it. What a child "knew" tended to matter more than the kind of person he was growing into. The work was a by-product of teaching and was more important than the child, who was the product. Again, the shadow was mistaken for the substance.

Authority was often misused, and children were hemmed in by admonitions: Don't talk. Don't move around. Don't get out of line. Don't ask questions. Don't fidget. Don't make a noise. Listen to me. Look at me. Do as I do. Do as I say.

We denied children their right to learn by choosing and discriminating and forming judgments themselves. We created conditions in which it was impossible for children to make mistakes and then we congratulated ourselves because they didn't make them. It was as if a herdsman drove his herd down a long and narrow alley with six-foot walls on either side and then remarked what intelligent beasts they were for going in a dead-straight line.

As a system of education it "worked," but it tended to work best with the most gifted. Those for whom it worked least were often improperly judged dull, ill endowed, and incapable. Teachers didn't know how to use success as an educational tool, and they were unaware of the great

From Sir Alec Clegg, *Revolution in the British Primary Schools* (Washington, D.C.: National Association of Elementary School Principals, National Education Association, 1971), p. 14–28, 46–48. Copyright © 1971 by National Association of Elementary School Principals. All rights reserved.

significance of failure. We all know now that the child whose parents love him and support him in his endeavors may be safely challenged by failure. We also know that if a child is unloved or regarded with indifference at home and is allowed to fall into a learning situation at school in which he is bound to fail, then home and school are accomplices in distorting his growth as a human being.

The aims and assumptions of our earlier ways of teaching were clear enough to those who pursued them. They can be summed up in part as follows:

• Children have to master the skills of reading, writing, and arithmetic. In order to read, they must pursue a carefully graded course of activity. In order to write correctly, they have to learn the rules of grammar that govern the correct use of English.

• There are basic facts of history and geography that all educated persons should possess, and these should be set out in syllabuses graded according to the age of the children who are to learn them.

• Scripture must be learned and understood because it forms the basis of morality.

• Children should be obedient and honest, and it is a task of the school to make them so. The best way of doing this is by judicious use of rewards and punishments.

• In order to do all these things economically, children should be organized into "homogeneous" ability groups so that all may perform the same task at the same time.

• The main motivation should be competition. Marks should be allotted, and children should be graded according to their marks and encouraged to work hard and improve their marks.

• The general pedagogical principle is: "This is what you have to do; this is how you have to do it; do it and I will mark it to see if you have done it correctly; then I will reward you or punish you accordingly."

In recent years, the validity of these practices and beliefs has been drastically questioned by gifted teachers who have found newer ways. These teachers are saying, for example, that skills are acquired for a purpose. If we become obsessed with the acquisition of skills, we tend to lose sight of the purposes for which they were meant to be used. It is important, for instance, that a child should learn to read, but it is also very important that he should want to read what is worth reading. Once a start has been made, generous provision of well-written and carefully graded books that tap a wide range of interests and a wide range of reading difficulty will generally do the rest.

Teachers are saying that learning to write is important—but to write *what?* To record what one has seen or heard is important, but to be able to express one's ideas personally, cogently, and, on occasion, imaginatively is equally important. And what evidence is there for believing that a knowledge of the rules of grammar leads to more expressive writing? If a man knows he is using an expletive, is what he says likely to be more expressive because of this knowledge? As Whitehead said, "There is no necessary connection between literature and grammar."

In the teaching of arithmetic—and of so much else—why do we so often put the cart before the horse? When we learn to play a field game, we play it and we learn the rules as we go along. If we had to study the rules and master them mechanically before we were allowed to play, what would happen to our enthusiasm for the game? But this is how many of us were taught arithmetic, and this is probably why only the adept survived such teaching.

And what about the "body of knowledge everyone should have?" Should everyone know how many states there are in Australia, or that New York is south of Rome? Should everyone be able to name the constituents of the air we breathe? If so, at what age and at what IQ levels should these facts be known?

Furthermore, since knowledge is doubling every ten years or less, what sense is there in believing that the scraps of it that were used to stimulate *our* juvenile minds will serve equally well to stimulate the minds of our children and our grandchildren? How much of the knowledge crammed into us was fruitful and how much was sterile? How much of it moved our minds to activity and how much was merely acquired for the moment in order that we might make the grade or pass the examination?

And what have we done to children by the way in which we have used art and craft in our school program? When we tell the child what to do and how to do it, when we provide him with patterns to be followed without deviation, all we do is traffic in measurable techniques. Actually, we do more than that: We sever connection with common sense *and* with the principles of pedagogy. Surely, the main purpose of the arts and crafts is to help the child find some creative outlet in which he can succeed and find satisfaction. A child should express his own rather than his teacher's ideas, and he should express them in his own rather than in his teacher's way. *His* imagination and *his* initiative and *his* spontaneity and *his* love of beauty should be given full rein.

As for a knowledge of the Scriptures, does such knowledge really make us more moral or honest? Are atheists or Mohammedans less honest than Christians?

And what about discipline? What, in fact, is the value of discipline enforced by fear? What evidence do we have that a child who acts in a certain way because he fears to do otherwise will continue to act in that way once the fear has been removed? It is like being honest because "honesty is the best policy," because it pays off, rather than being honest because one believes that this is the right way of behaving toward one's fellowmen.

What about the teaching of "homogeneous" groups of children? This surely is nonsense; such groups cannot exist. The learning processes of all children are affected by all kinds of extraneous matters. In any group of children, one will be the most timid and one the most bold; one will come from a home that gives most, another from a home that gives least; one will be the most intelligent, one the least; one the most imaginative, one the least—and so on. To think that somehow or other we can erase these supports or these impediments and arrive at a clean —and uniform—foundation for each child on which progress can be built is pedagogically stupid. And when, knowing of these supports and these impediments, we nevertheless grade children according to their so-called ability in order to what we call in our jargon, "motivate" them, this is surely pedagogical folly of a very high order indeed. But we still do it.

And how wise is it to try to teach the same thing to 30 children at the same time? Is it not inevitable that the bright and the interested will to some extent mark time, that the dull and the bored will to some extent fail to keep up, and that the pace will be set by the average? The folly of trying to teach the same thing at the same time to a group of children comes home to us if we look at what happens when a group of 30 children are asked to tackle the same physical objective—say a high jump or a vault. The first half-dozen or so will succeed because of the way God Almighty or their physical inheritance has endowed them—but the teacher takes the credit. The middle group may improve under instruction. The last half-dozen are likely to prove wretchedly clumsy. When that happens, as it will, they and their inheritance *and* the Almighty— but not the teacher—take the blame.

What damage have we done by indiscriminate use of external examinations and tests? We have allowed control of the curriculum to be handed over to the examiners, people who never see the children to whom their tests are applied. Since some things can be measured more readily than others, we have tended to emphasize what can be measured and to undervalue what cannot. And yet, perhaps the things that are most worthwhile are those that cannot be measured. We have looked at IQ tests and aptitude tests, and we have led ourselves to believe that we can make an exact diagnosis of a child's potential. This we certainly cannot do. We have encouraged teachers to expend energy in thwarting the examiner rather than in teaching the child as he should be taught. And when we have looked at the results of an examination, we have exalted those who are "above the line" and disregarded—or even despised—those below it.

And, finally, what matters most in education—what one "knows" or the sort of person he becomes?

These, then, are some of the points that gifted teachers of young children tend to raise as they look at the practices we have followed in English primary schools until recent years and which, unfortunately, we still practice in many of them to this day.

What Have We Changed To?

The outward signs of changes that have taken place in the primary schools are obvious enough. These are some of them:

• Children no longer sit in rows facing the chalkboard; they work in groups or as individuals and arrange their desks accordingly.

• The teacher less frequently gives a formal lesson to the whole class by standing in front of the chalkboard and expounding on a preselected topic. In short, there are far fewer history "lessons" or geography "lessons."

• The whole basis of learning depends less on the facts of a "subject" and far more on an experience of some kind or another that results in either the class going out of the school or in someone or something of interest being brought into it. Such experiences provide material for expression in speech, in writing, in painting, in modeling with clay, and in using many other materials—including material for calculation.

• It follows that the day is no longer broken up as it once was into "lessons" but is "integrated" as the current jargon has it. This means that children work at their own pace on a topic chosen by them from a range carefully prepared by the teacher and that the school bell plays an ever-diminishing part in the organization of the day. But it cannot be too strongly emphasized that the success of this so-called "integrated day" depends upon the wisdom of the teacher in handling the material and not in merely abolishing the bell. It is also true that a young and inexperienced teacher might need to rely on the structured situation which separate lessons provide.

• Spelling lists, formal exercises in English, and mechanical sums in arithmetic are more rarely used than in the past.

• The teacher tends to conceal or withhold his knowledge rather than reveal it. He does this in the hope that the child will seek knowledge elsewhere and that child and teacher will find out together.

• There are fewer "sets" of books and more individual books. This is true of reference materials and of fiction and poetry as well.

It cannot be too strongly stated, however, that outward signs of change can be most lamentably misleading and deceptive. They should not be accepted as a guarantee of quality in the work produced or, indeed, of understanding on the part of the teacher or the administration. No judgment on the value and quality of any change should be made until appropriate criteria have been applied. For example: What are the standards of achievement? What is the evidence of progress? What do the children do when left on their own? How do the strong among them behave to the weak?

Having said this, I must make it clear that in my experience, and judged by the criteria I have mentioned, there is no doubt that the change in English primary schools is a momentous one. And it carries an educational message that we earnestly hope our secondary schools, our universities, and indeed the population at large will receive. Our primary schools, at their best, are models of the kind of social communities in which we would all wish to live.

Well before the last war, we had grasped the value of nursery schools and classes. These were places where children learned to behave socially and sociably together, to give and take, to live and let live, to help others and to share, as well as places in which they began to learn to do up their buttons and attend to life's little necessities. Each child got to know new adults outside his family circle—adults who would listen and who would talk an understandable language all the time. He learned to handle bricks and sand and water, and the resultant mess was not the catastrophe that it was in some homes. There were books to look at and books from which stories were read, and all this whetted the appetite for reading. There were colors and pencils and clay which tempted the child to take the first steps in painting and drawing and modeling. There was much encouragement; there was time for confidence to grow; and the child became "ready" for school.

Also before the war, many infant schools had begun to forge ahead, although most of these still put the cart before the horse. More often than not, reading began with the alphabet, just as history in the schools invariably began with the ancient Britons. There was much matching of letters and words in isolation—C A T spelled *cat,* and, of course, "the cat sat on the mat," "Tom got his cap wet," and "the pot was on the hob." "Phonics" was the order of the day. And, when the child was ready for them, there were well-known and carefully graded "readers" about nice little middle-class boys and girls.

Writing followed reading, and it tended to begin with pot hooks, followed by letters written in four lines. This was done in order that, as a Yorkshire schoolmaster had said 400 years earlier, they might "write all their words in an even line, with the tops, bellies, and bottoms of the letters of an even size." There followed much writing from copybooks, and writing in those days meant handwriting, whereas today it tends to mean the quality of the English that the child uses. This change in itself is significant.

In painting and drawing, children were taught to "do" houses and trees and men so that they could all be put together into a picture. And while they were being taught in these ways, the children sat in rows at desks facing the teacher who stood before the chalkboard and instructed them.

But the ways have changed. Today, from the start, the child is given an urge to write. He will draw a picture and explain to his interested teacher that he has drawn "our car." The teacher writes underneath it, "This is our car," and the child copies it. The difference between copying this and copying from a copybook is that the child starts with a sentence that is not only meaningful to him but emotionally charged. It is a sentence in which both he and his teacher are interested. Gradually, the child realizes that if he wants to tell his fellows about his affairs and to learn about theirs, reading, writing, and painting are important ways of doing it and they are ways in which his teacher is interested. He must, therefore, master the skills of handwriting and of reading. As he takes these first steps, he comes to see that this word is like that one and that this sound is heard in this word and also in that one. All the time, it is the horse of meaningful expression that pulls the cart of writing and spelling—and not the other way round.

And so with the beginnings of mathematics. In the nursery school or class, children have already learned the meaning of "big" and "little," "bigger" and "smaller," "lighter" and "heavier." This continues in the early days of the infant schools, when they count and match and group and learn that "three" applies equally to three elephants and to three pins. Here again the horse is before the cart. The desire to do what he wants to be able to do provides the child with the drive to master the mechanical skills that he needs in order to be able to do it.

Once a start has been made in these skills, the object of the teacher is to concentrate on the urge to use the newly acquired skills as a means of expressing personal ideas. The standard lessons in history and geography were no more conducive to this than were the routine compositions on the life of a penny. What has taken their place?

Since World War II, one of the most popular sayings about the learning of young people has been: "What I hear, I forget. What I see, I remember. What I do, I understand." The first two of these propositions may be open to debate, but there is very little doubt about the third and this is what the teachers have seized on. If you have actually done something—grown a plant, taken a simple piece of machinery to pieces, or investigated an old building—the urge to write about it or draw it or read more about it is so much stronger than if you had merely been told about it, and this urge may provide work for a considerable span of time, not only hours but days. There is thus much more drawing, more painting, more modeling than there used to be. And, provided that its purpose is understood, all of it serves to establish the success that gives rise to the confidence on which educational progress is built.

Formal lessons have become far less frequent than they used to be, and the object of teaching is not, for example, to give the child a systematic chronological account of history from its storybook beginnings but to provide worthwhile experiences for further investigation. Grandfather probably knows what the area was like 60 years ago, and, what is more, he knows what *his* grandfather told him. Grandfather's possessions are history. The objects of these early days, collected and brought to school, provide endless opportunity for discussion, for painting, writing, modeling, and calculating. So, of course, do visits to the railway station, the canal lock, the power station, the farm, the church, and the nearest factory. If the child is fortunate enough to attend a school that is supplied by an imaginative resources center, he will benefit from all kinds of objects that can be brought into the school. These will range from collections of butterflies to a model of a coal mine or a penny farthing bicycle. Then there are pets of all kinds in the schools, and these can be drawn and painted and their ways and habits recorded in paint and writing. One of the minor mysteries of life is the way a guinea pig will stand motionless on a table and allow itself to be drawn and modeled and painted.

The children work individually or in groups, as the need strikes them. Those who are quick to learn use easily the generous supply of material available, and the teacher thus has time to help the slow over their difficulties. Some children write, some paint, some make music, and some calculate. The task of the teacher is to see that no child overlooks any worthwhile medium of expression.

The day is much less rigidly scheduled than it used to be, although physical education may make some scheduling of time necessary if the hall with its physical education apparatus has to be used. And it is perhaps in the use of this apparatus that the greatest change has come about. Routine exercises have disappeared and team competitions are fewer than they once were. The subject of physical education has been widened to include not only gymnastics and games but also dance and drama. Far less is imposed on the children and far more drawn from them. I shall not readily forget the alarm of an American superintendent of schools when I took him into a school hall where 6-year-olds were swarming up ropes to the ceiling and climbing about on beams only a few feet below it. The aim of the teacher was to see that each child should achieve success and the confidence that it brings—a confidence that can be transferred to the three R's which are still as important as they ever were, although the learning of them has so radically changed.

The results of writing and of painting show this change. Let us consider for a moment two pieces of writing from an 8-year-old girl in a village school.

The first piece is the kind of thing that we have come to expect from a bright little 8-year-old. This girl is interested in a cat; she has, no doubt, been encouraged to examine one carefully, and she has read about cats and mastered words like *sensitive, fang, carnivorous, mammals,* and *retractable.* A book she read has played an obvious part in what she has written:

> A cat is a mammal. The eyes are very good for seeing at night because the pupil opens up more so that more light goes in. Their whiskers are very sensitive. The whiskers are the same length as the fattest part of their body, so when they go through a hole if the whiskers can not fit through the hole they can not. The two very long and sharp teeth in the mouth of a cat are called fangs. Cats are carnivorous mammals. Also the eyes are on the front of the head which means he is an animal of prey. When the eyes are on the side of the head it is an animal that is hunted. A cat is always warm because it has soft cuddly fur. The claws of a cat are retractable so that when he walks out he does not break them. His ears are also movable.

True enough. But one of the main purposes of writing is to be able not merely to record but also to convey one's sensitive, imaginative, and personal feelings. Such writing may take the form of prose or it may take the form of verse, rhymed or unrhymed.

The piece that follows was written by the same child who wrote about cats. It was written after the village school had been visited by a theatre group that had produced a play called *From Sea to Sky.* Following this play, one corner of the classroom had been turned into a kind of under-water kingdom, and much that the children then did was connected with the sea.

STILL AND LONELY
(by Louise Holmes, age 8)

Wading in the sea
so cold, so alone.
I stumble and fall
to the bottom of a strange new kingdom.
Everything is so still and lonely.
Sometimes I see melancholy fish swimming
slowly by.
The lonely, still sea all around my gliding
body moves gently,

Wrecked ships from long ago,
Oysters with hidden pearls,
Waving seaweed, seen once in a lifetime.
All so marvellous it must be a dream.
My hair floating in the calm, gentle sea.
Waving seaweed, or lines of colour
all so wonderful it must be a dream.
Floating along go mermaids and mermen
With long golden hair drifting in the
cloud of water
Endless water
All so still and beautiful.
Nets catching fish.
Goodbye fish!
Crawling creatures
Still creatures
Youth creatures playing
Pink, yellow, red, blue, black.
All so colourful.
The deep sea kingdom is so wonderful
so glorious
Shells lying on the bottom of the sea
all colours,
smooth to my touch.
Crabs moving from side to side
blowing bubbles.
Stones and shells,
rocks,
all to be seen,
but no human beings ever will.
This kingdom is so lovely,
yet still and lonely.
So quiet.
So noisy above.
Nothing disturbs the silence.
They all keep quiet,
hiding as I swim by,
watching my slow moving body
so different from theirs.

What an adventure for
a plain person
like me!

This second, imaginative, expressive piece would have been very rare 30 years ago, and the likelihood is that it would have been a "sport" —something written for personal diversion, not a part of a school program, and not the product of wise and inspired teaching. The intentions of the teachers have indeed changed. A teacher who was teaching 30 years ago has described the way in which he encouraged children to write a composition on lighting a fire. These are his notes:

1. The teacher discusses the material required—sticks, newspaper, coal, matches. He "teaches" the difference between "thorough" and "through."
2. He discusses the laying of the fire and teaches the difference between "lay" and "lie," "laid" and "lied." He mentions cleaning the grate (difference between "grate" and "great"), crumple, and the placing of sticks and coal.
3. He discusses lighting the newspaper, where to light, how to strike a match to avoid danger.

This kind of preparation led to 40 grammatically accurate, correctly spelled, but somewhat sterile compositions, and if this was the result the teacher wanted, then his preparation was sound enough. Here is one of the compositions:

Before you light the fire you must prepare thoroughly. You have to get the sticks, the coal and some newspapers before you begin. When you have got these things or you can call them materials, you have to take out the ashes from the grate. When you have raked out the ashes from the grate, you put the newspaper in. Then you put some sticks on. Then you put some coal on. When you have put these things or materials on, you light a match.
You must know how to light a match before you strike it. You must hold the box in one hand and hold the match in the other and pull the match away from you so as to avoid danger.
You then light the paper.

Twenty years later, the teacher had changed his aims. He was as concerned with the personal expression of the child and the development of his individuality as he was with spelling and handwriting. Moreover, he had realized the value of Locke's words: "Never trouble yourself about those Faults in them, which you know Age will cure."
The village fish and chip shop had caught fire and the teacher seized on the excitement of the occasion to get from each child a description of

a particular fire which he had lit. Only one boy wrote about lighting a domestic fire, and this is what he wrote:

> When my Mam and Dad won't get up me and our Alan get up and light the fire. I rake out the deadness from the grate and our Alan chops some of my Dad's shed-wood. We put the newspaper in the grate but don't squash it too tight or it won't burn so good. Put the sticks in and then some nice pieces of best Barnsley seam coal. This is the best coal in the world my Dad says. Then we put the shovel on the bars and a big piece of newspaper over that to blow it up. Now its all ready to light the paper. If it won't go I get some of my Dad's paraffin in a pop bottle and throw it on. This makes it go smashing. If the blow up paper catches fire I have to shout my Dad and he comes down in his shirt swearing and clips us. I like lighting fires.

The preceding examples illustrate clearly the change of emphasis that has taken place in the teaching of writing in recent years.

There has been a similar change in the teaching of arithmetic. When I was young, my arithmetic consisted of "doing sums." Recently, I was talking with an inspector colleague of mine about how changes had occurred and how the child's surroundings were now used to give him an understanding that I never had. My colleague told me, for example, how teachers will use the tiles of a hall floor to help them in their teaching. First of all, a child would find the number by counting. Then the question would be asked: Is there an easier and quicker way? Perhaps 37 rows of 19 tiles (or 19 rows of 37 tiles)? How do we do this? Add nineteen 37's together—or thirty-seven 19's?

Such investigations lead to an understanding of long multiplication as repeated addition. What is the most economical way of doing this? The conventional way of thirty-seven 10's and thirty-seven 9's? Or perhaps, in this case, thirty-seven 20's minus 37 would be quicker. But the important thing is that the children have a chance to think about different ways and to compare methods, and their own experience will provide the urge to do so. Eventually, of course, they will need to know an economic method that always works, and this is often, although not always, the traditional method.

Another example that suggests the same approach is that of measurement, where a child will pass through various stages:

1a. Measuring length (or weight or capacity) by arbitrary units; for example, handspans, strides, foot lengths, and so forth, leading on to:

b. Standardized units, yardsticks, metre sticks, and so forth, and statements like "this room is 10 yards and a bit long."

c. Refining measurement so that you can say more exactly how many feet and how many inches long.

One hopes that the child will also develop an appreciation of the suitability of certain measures and an awareness of approximation and degrees of accuracy. For example, one needs to contrast the degree of accuracy in measuring, on the one hand, the distance from the earth to the sun, and, on the other, the distance between the point of the gap of a spark plug.

2. The measurement of height offers interesting material for the mind to work on. It is important that children use their measuring not just to develop arithmetic but also to think about different ways of tackling a job.

In finding the height of a building, for example, they might:

a. Estimate—a process traditionally neglected.

b. Compare with the height of a friend.

c. Count the number of bricks.

d. Investigate the length of the shadow.

e. Use simple apparatus—even a cardboard, right-angled triangle can provide a good result after a scale drawing is made.

f. Eventually some children may well devise an accurate trigonometrical method.

After my colleague had explained all this to me, he told me about Jeremy, a boy who forged ahead after having been introduced to new methods, whereas he probably would not have made anything like the same progress if he had been kept on with the old methods.

Jeremy had transferred from a formal school to one where practical activities and individual approaches to mathematics were encouraged. During his two years of very formal work in his first school, he had derived satisfaction from habitually obtaining full marks for all his sums. On arriving at his new school at the age of 9, he was at first somewhat bewildered by the different emphasis. After an initial period where he was allowed to maintain his security by continuing familiar work, he was gradually encouraged to strike off in new directions on his own. He was soon able to talk about what he had been doing. Shortly after his tenth birthday, he described his work as follows:

"I saw in a book about there being a relationship between the squares of whole numbers so I wrote down the cubes of all the numbers from 1 to 20 and decided to see if I could find a similar relationship. First I found the differences between them, and then the differences between the differences. I found I got part of a six times table. So I thought that I ought to be able to work back from this and I carried on the table starting with the differences between the differences and so got the cube of 21, the cube of 22, and so on."

He set out his work:

DIFFERENCE

DIFFERENCE

1^3	1		
		7	
2^3	8		12
		19	
3^3	27		18
		37	
4^3	64		24
		61	
5^3	125		.
.			.
.			.
.			.

He eventually went on to generalize his answer, and said: "I thought that this showed that there was a way of working out the cube of any number from the cube of the previous number and I found that if any number was called 'n' the cube of the next number would be

$$\text{'}n^3 + 3n^2 + 3n + 1.\text{'}\text{''}$$

Jeremy had also developed his own work on "Magic Square," finally constructing his own square of 16 or 17 rows and columns and explaining to a visitor: "It is very easy to work out once you've understood the pattern."

In Jeremy's case, one must, of course, make allowances for exceptional brilliance, but even so, one cannot help contrasting the way in which he had been allowed to think along his own lines and develop his own mathematical ideas with the way in which his previous mathematical education had been restricted to routine work with arithmetical processes. And one should also contrast the demands made on him in his new way of working with the demands of the former situation where he always obtained full marks without really being asked to exert any mathematical "thinking" as he worked.

A Summing Up

What, overall, can we expect to find in an English primary school today that reflects changes that have been made? Let me put it this way: When I go into what I would call "a good school" today, whether the building is new or whether it was built in the last century, I would expect to find light, colorful classrooms with a broad band of pin-up board around the walls on which examples of work from *all* the children in the group are carefully and lovingly displayed at one time or another. In the main, this work would be painting and drawing, but there would also be some mathematics and some written expression—poetry and prose. In all like-lihood, I would be discreetly invited to admire the work of some pupils who, at that moment, stood most in need of a word of praise.

Desks and tables would be arranged in groups rather than in rows. Somewhere in the room there would most certainly be a table on which were set out natural objects that were both beautiful and scientifically interesting. Elsewhere in the room there might be a well-arranged display of fabrics and other objects of interest and beauty, designed to emphasize textures, colors, and shapes. There might be some small animals kept as pets in the room. And there would certainly be a generous and easily accessible supply of books of reference and fiction.

Some children would be standing, some sitting, some talking, some walking, some working intently. One child might be painting; another might be arranging flowers. Two children with a stopwatch might be observing ball bearings rolling down a plank, while a third child tabulates the results. One group might be potato printing on fabric; others would be reading, writing, measuring, modeling, or calculating.

After the initial activities period, it is likely that the class might settle down to pursue a piece of work resulting from a recent visit to a water canal lock, a post office, a sewage works, a power station, or some other place of interest and excitement. Under the stimulus of this experience, some would paint, some write, some calculate, some read and investigate. Other children might be pursuing a completely different topic. But, under the stimulus of a first-hand experience, and with abundant inter-est, all children would be engaged in something that in other, more formal schools would fall into the often arid compartments of history, geography, English, and mathematics.

In the school I am talking about, such technical matters as spelling would be dealt with as adults would deal with them—by looking up in small dictionaries the word that is needed in the context of the moment.

In a classroom in this school, I might have some momentary difficulty in locating the teacher. He would be acting more as a consultant, and would speak when spoken to. But his main task—and this is a profes-sional task of the highest order that I, as a schoolmaster, didn't exert because I taught the whole class at once—would be to keep a watchful eye on what each pupil was doing in order to be certain that the child did not forego or neglect any important area of learning. There would, of course, be times when the whole class was called to attention to deal with a teaching point of common concern, but the teacher would be spending much of his time giving individual help, particularly to slow learners.

When a child raises a question and the teacher does not know the an-swer, he would not hesitate to admit it. Often, if he *knew* the answer, he would be reluctant to give it lest an opportunity for drawing out the child's initiative be lost.

There would, of course, be activities shared by the whole class as, for instance, when they sang together, or went into the hall for what we call, unfortunately perhaps, a "movement lesson." This is a physical activity —sometimes gymnastic, sometimes dramatic—based very largely on the inspiration from Rudolf von Laban, a refugee from Hitler, who introduced this work and modern dance into England and whose most distinguished disciple is probably Martha Graham.

In a school such as I am describing, I should expect pupils to start work first thing in the morning, whether the teacher was there or not. Indeed, on the previous evening, many of the pupils would have been able to say what they intended to do first thing in the morning. The number able to do this would be an indication of the responsibility that the school successfully laid on its pupils. And I have seen not only children of 10 or 11 settle down to a day's work with no teacher present but also tiny children no more than 5 or 6 years old.

These, then, are some of the things we can expect to find in a good English primary school today.

What Have We Gained From the Revolution in the Primary Schools?

When we seek to answer this question, we must keep clearly in mind just what we want. If what we want is the learning of the basic skills and the ability to acquire information from books, we have gained something —but not all that much. If we broaden our goals, however, to include freedom to learn by exploring, choosing, and making judgments; an eager interest in nature and in human society; the ability to express personal ideas and feelings fluently, forcefully, and, as occasion demands, imaginatively; the development of self-respect and of compassionate regard for others; and the capacity to enjoy those great aspects of civilization designed to be enjoyed—such as music, art, and literature —then there is no doubt at all that the newer ways are vastly superior to those that preceded them.

Perhaps the first and most important gain derives from the fact that because the child learns from his own explorations, he's *eager* in his learning. Artificial goals, such as the competitive lists, merit marks, and examination results, then tend to be redundant. Once this situation comes about, the well-endowed child is no longer exalted beyond his deserts; the endeavors of the least able are more easily cherished; the self-aggrandizement of the quick in the presence of the slow and the envy of the slow for the quick are both reduced. Each child makes his mark and receives "that recognition which our natures crave and acknowledge with renewed endeavor." This is a quotation from a statement made a hundred years ago by a school inspector who knew then what we must continue to keep in mind: We all crave recognition; it is the spur to nearly all our endeavors.

In the "new" schools, the individual can't be lost in the mass. The talking and listening that go on in the early years are part of the love that is the start of life for all pupils. Painting, drawing, acting, modeling, singing, and dancing offer to our children the beginnings of an enjoyment of beauty that later enriches adult life. The opportunity pupils have to learn from natural phenomena gives them their first acquaintance with scientific truth. Thus it is that love and beauty and truth are changing our schools, and we are moving away from the obedience that is so important in the Old Testament law to the truths of the New Testament which affirm "that knowledge puffeth up, that charity edifyeth, and that love is the fulfilling of the law."

One of the interesting aspects of the changes that are taking place in my own county, the West Riding, is that they are completely spontaneous, as far as I can determine. I know the schools in which the changes began and I know something about how the ideas spread—and what has happened had nothing at all to do with "educational philosophy." I don't believe that the people who started the changes had ever heard of Caldwell Cook or Dewey. They owed nothing to the progressive school movement of the 1920's and 1930's. What is most interesting, however, is that the good educational theorists and philosophers of the past would have given full support to the people who are making today's changes.

Support would have come also from many other people, because the newer ways lean heavily toward the aesthetic and moral convictions of many thoughtful and sensitive and compassionate persons. The new ways, for example, agree with Plutarch that the soul is not a vase to be filled but rather a hearth that is to be made to glow. They agree with Erasmus and his love of the liberal arts; with Rabelais in taking Gargantua through the meadows and over grassy places to observe all that grows; with Montaigne in urging that the child observe the curious in his surroundings; with Locke in his opinion that learning must be had but as subservient only to the greater qualities; with Rousseau in his avoidance of verbal lessons; with Goethe who said that to digest knowledge, one must have swallowed with a good appetite; with Ruskin who held that the spirit needs several sorts of food, of which knowledge is only one; with Whitehead in his condemnation of inert ideas and his conviction that every child should experience the joy of discovery; with John Dewey in much that he said in *Experience and Education*; and certainly with a great deal that is set out in *The Humanities in the Schools,* a little book published in the United States in 1968.

To be a bit more specific about our gains, I would say that children certainly express themselves in painting and writing and dramatic movement as they never did in the days of formal instruction. In mathematics, they may not manage the grotesque calculations of our grandfathers, but their understanding of the whys and wherefores of mathematics is far greater than it used to be. In one of the schools that I know best, the quality of teaching is completely upsetting the national norms. The really significant gain, however, is the dramatic change in children's behavior, and how this has come about is something that I cannot readily explain.

One thing I know is that the changes in our primary schools are affecting the human spirit just as much as they are affecting the human mind, despite the endless succession of pressures that conspire to focus our attention on what can be measured to the neglect of what cannot. Perhaps I had better explain what I mean by "spirit," an archaic word that has dropped out of fashion in this age of measurement. My spirit deals with my loves and my hates and my hopes and my fears and my ambitions and my enthusiasms and my enjoyment of what is beautiful. My mind tells me that six times seven is forty-two; my spirit responds to the kindness of my friends. As I see it, when the human spirit is wrong, it makes for evil and cruelty and strife and warfare. When it is right, it makes for generosity and compassion and nobility.

The education of the mind is relatively easy. We bring it about by the processes of mathematics and science, by manipulating the facts of history and geography, and by all our school programs where measurement is so important. We bring in effective gadgetry to make these programs more efficient, we build splendid buildings, and we write textbooks. Education officers and superintendents of schools evolve new systems of organization. And 90 percent of all this business is aimed at the mind. We overvalue the mind and extol its products—from the two times table to the technicalities of the space program. We let these things take on more importance than the actual growth and development of the child himself.

And since the things of the spirit are impalpable and cannot be measured, they are difficult to deal with and are conveniently put aside. As we all know, the result is that the growth of knowledge and mental acuity has far outstripped the growth of humanity and compassion and other manifestations of the qualities of the spirit.

The kind of teaching and learning that is developing in our best elementary schools does not exalt mind over spirit; it starts and ends with the individual. From the outset, the child is thrown on his own resources. Once this happens, initiative and sensitivity and determination and many other qualities emerge as by-products of the learning process. The child learns to recognize and value his power of expression, and this power of expression is central to the new forms of learning. Sensitivity to beauty in a variety of forms is deliberately cultivated. And more and more, the

teacher comes to realize that what really matters is not the quality of the
picture that the child has drawn or the excellence of the writing he has
produced but what has happened to the child during the process.

2. Preparing Children for a Changing World

*As it did in so many other areas, the Plowden Committee provided as
clear and succinct a statement of the aims of informal education as can
be found anywhere. Although the Committee heard the testimony of
a number of distinguished educationists and philosophers, it concluded
that its most useful role would be to draw its own conclusions of what
the aims of education are, and should be, from its own examination of
the ways in which the best primary schools actually functioned.*

*One objective, the Committee argued, should be what it has always
been: to prepare students for the society in which they will live. Indeed,
the Committee took what in many ways is a traditional view of the
aims of education, attaching considerable importance, for example, to
"the older virtues . . . of neatness, accuracy, care, and perseverance."
"These are genuine virtues," the group wrote, "and an education which
does not foster them is faulty." It is not the traditional aims of education
that the Plowden Committee rejected, in short, but rather the assumption that these aims were achieved automatically by traditional formal
schooling and that they would be neglected by informal schools. The
reverse is closer to the truth, the Committee believed.*

All schools reflect the views of society, or of some section of society,
about the way children should be brought up, whether or not these views
are consciously held or defined. The old English elementary school derived, in part at least, from the National Society for the Education of the
Poorer Classes in the principles of the Established Church founded in
1811, the aim of which was to provide for what were then thought to be
the educational needs of the working class. The effects of the hierarchical
view of society which this title implied persisted long after the view itself
became unacceptable and out of date. American schools have had, as
an avowed purpose, the Americanization of children from diverse cultures, races and climates. Russian education is strictly geared to particular political and social beliefs. Our society is in a state of transition
and there is controversy about the relative rights of society and the in-

From *Children and Their Primary Schools* ("The Plowden Report"), vol. 1,
paragraphs 493–497, 501–507. Reprinted by permission of the Controller of Her
Britannic Majesty's Stationery Office.

dividual. But agreement can be reached in the midst of this uncertainty about the objectives of English education, and in particular of English primary schools, in the last third of the twentieth century.

One obvious purpose is to fit children for the society into which they will grow up. To do this successfully it is necessary to predict what that society will be like. It will certainly be one marked by rapid and far-reaching economic and social change. It is likely to be richer than now, with even more choice of goods, with tastes dominated by majorities and with more leisure for all; more people will be called upon to change their occupation.

About such a society we can be both hopeful and fearful. We can hope it will care for all its members, for the old as well as the young, for the handicapped as well as the gifted, for the deviant as well as the conformer, and that it will create an environment that is stimulating, honest and tolerant. We can fear that it will be much engrossed with the pursuit of material wealth, too hostile to minorities, too dominated by mass opinion, too uncertain of its values.

For such a society, children, and the adults they will become, will need above all to be adaptable and capable of adjusting to their changing environment. They will need as always to be able to live with their fellows, appreciating and respecting their differences, understanding and sympathizing with their feelings. They will need the power of discrimination and, when necessary, to be able to withstand mass pressures. They will need to be well balanced, with neither emotions nor intellect giving ground to each other. They will need throughout their adult life to be capable of being taught, and of learning, the new skills called for by the changing economic scene. They will need to understand that in a democratic society each individual has obligations to the community, as well as rights within it.

When we asked our witnesses for their views on the aims of primary education we found a wide general measure of agreement, though many of the replies seemed to have as much relevance to other phases of education as to primary. The heads of both junior and infant schools laid emphasis upon the all-round development of the individual and upon the acquisition of the basic skills necessary in contemporary society. Many added a third aim, that of the religious and moral development of the child, and some a fourth, that of children's physical development and acquisition of motor skills. Phrases such as "whole personality," "happy atmosphere," "full and satisfying life," "full development of powers," "satisfaction of curiosity," "confidence," "perseverance" and "alertness" occurred again and again. This list shows that general statements of aims, even by those engaged in teaching, tend to be little more than expressions of benevolent aspiration which may provide a rough guide to the general climate of the school, but which may have a rather tenuous relationship to the educational practices that actually go on there. It was interesting that some of the head teachers who were considered by H.M.I. inspectors to be most successful in practice were least able to formulate their aims clearly and convincingly. . . .

It is difficult to reach agreement on the aims of primary education if anything but the broadest terms are used, but formulations of that kind are little more than platitudes. We invited the help of a number of distinguished educationists and professors of educational philosophy, and enjoyed a lengthy and interesting discussion with them. They all confirmed the view that general statements of aims were of limited value, and that a pragmatic approach to the purposes of education was more likely to be fruitful. We now turn to the implications of this conclusion.

An individual as distinct from a general statement of aims may be more worth making. It clears the writer's mind and compels him to examine what he is doing and why. This is a useful professional exercise for all teachers. Head teachers have for long written statements of this kind to help their staffs. They are useful in so far as they promote real thought and are not confined to a mere set of directions. They should encourage class teachers to look specifically at their day to day work, relating it to guiding principles and not simply to short-term objectives. One of our witnesses gives such a list: "Physical health, intellectual development, emotional and moral health, aesthetic awareness, a valid perspective, practical skills, social skills, personal fulfillment," and so on, with each main heading divided into appropriate subheadings. But it goes on to say: "Such an itemized statement of purposes has doubtful value, except as an academic exercise or as a check list." Check lists, however, have their uses and the items on the lists should be double-checked against current practices. What practices in my school develop these qualities? Which of these qualities are developed by this particular practice? Rather commonplace little exercises such as these encourage the staff of the school to keep thinking about what they are doing. Because statements of aims of this kind are written for a small and intimate circle, there is less risk of disagreement about the underlying assumptions than with documents intended for a wider public.

Another approach might be to draw up a list of danger signs, which would indicate that something has gone wrong in a school: fragmented knowledge, no changes in past decade, creative work very limited, much time spent on teaching, few questions from children, many exercises, too many rules, frequent punishments, and concentration on tests. Such a list, of course, involves value judgments at the outset, but it is an invitation to thought and argument and not simply to compliance. Then it could be asked what aims are implicit in, for example, play activity, painting, free writing, "movement," games, the new mathematics, learning by heart, grammar, and so on. To subject all educational practices to this kind of questioning might be healthy. Habit is an immensely strong influence in schools and it is one that should be weakened though it is never likely to be removed. These words are particularly addressed to practicing teachers and especially to head teachers, rather than to educational theorists, who seldom fear innovation, but whose ideas may flounder because of their ignorance of what schools (and sometimes teachers) are really like.

If these methods were applied to all primary schools it would be apparent that the trend of their practices and outlook corresponds to a recognizable philosophy of education, and to a view of society, which may be summarized as follows.

A school is not merely a teaching shop, it must transmit values and attitudes. It is a community in which children learn to live first and foremost as children and not as future adults. In family life, children learn to live with people of all ages. The school sets out deliberately to devise the right environment for children, to allow them to be themselves and to develop in the way and at the pace appropriate to them. It tries to equalize opportunities and to compensate for handicaps. It lays special stress on individual discovery, on first-hand experience and on opportunities for creative work. It insists that knowledge does not fall into neatly separate compartments and that work and play are not opposite but complementary. A child brought up in such an atmosphere at all stages of his education has some help of becoming a balanced and mature adult and of being able to live in, to contribute to, and to look critically at the society of which he forms a part. Not all primary schools correspond to this picture, but it does represent a general and quickening trend.

Some people, while conceding that children are happier under the modern regime and perhaps more versatile, question whether they are being fitted to grapple with the world which they will enter when they leave school. This view is worth examining because it is widely held, but we think it rests on a misconception. It isolates the long-term objective, that of living in and serving society, and regards education as being at all stages recognizably and specifically a preparation for this. It fails to understand that the best preparation for being a happy and useful man or woman is to live fully as a child. Finally, it assumes, quite wrongly, that the older virtues, as they are usually called, of neatness, accuracy, care and perseverance, and the sheer knowledge which is an essential of being educated, will decline. These are genuine virtues and an education which does not foster them is faulty.

Society is right to expect that importance will be attached to these virtues in all schools. Children need them, and need knowledge, if they are to gain satisfaction from their education. What we repudiate is the view that they were automatically fostered by the old kind of elementary education. Patently they were not, for enormous numbers of the products of that education do not possess them. Still more, we repudiate the fear that the modern primary approach leads to their neglect. On the contrary it can, and when properly understood, does lay a much firmer foundation for their development and it is more in the interests of the children. But those interests are complex. Children need to be themselves, to live with other children and with grownups, to learn from their environment, to enjoy the present, to get ready for the future, to create and to love, to learn to face adversity, to behave responsibly, in a word, to be human beings. Decisions about the influences and situations that ought to be contrived to these ends must be left to individual schools, teachers and parents. What must be ensured is that the decisions taken in schools spring from the best available knowledge and are not simply dictated by habit or convention.

3. Education for a Well-Spent Youth

One of the key convictions shared by informal educators is that since childhood and adolescence are important in their own right, not merely as preparation for later schooling and later life, the quality of the school experience is also important in its own right. Children have a right to a rich and happy school experience; there is no inherent contradiction between this goal of education and the equally important goal of preparing children for life as adults. On the contrary, part of the preparation for life as an adult is to live fully and happily as a child.

Few English educators have argued this thesis as persuasively as Charity James, the founder and first director of the Curriculum Laboratory at the University of London's Goldsmiths' College. Radical reform is necessary, she argues, because the stakes are so high. If schools fail, the cost is not failed examinations but "failed humanity"; and if they succeed, the consequences are "new possibilities of richly enjoyable living by people who are more fully, generously, and diversely persons than we with our long training in parsimony can even imagine. We must not miss this moment," Mrs. James, who now lives in the United States, insists. "Young lives are at stake." While Charity James's book is about the junior high school years, it applies equally well to elementary education.

. . . There is an urgent need to seek an education that is appropriate for adolescence, since this is in modern societies a vitally important

From Charity James, *Young Lives at Stake* (London: Collins, 1968, published in the United States by Agathon Press, 1972), pp. 7–9, 13–15, 17–18, 52–53. Copyright © 1968, 1972 by Charity James. Reprinted by permission of Agathon Press, Inc.

period of growth, when new ranges of personal development can be explored and new qualities of personal relationships established. At present there is no model of secondary schooling that is remotely in line with our growing understanding of what human living might become or is relevant to our context of continuing change. To make school a good place to live in has been the task we have set ourselves . . .

That the need for change is urgent we can hardly doubt. A teacher bounded by the present lives in the past. Rather as a creative artist cannot permit himself to be the mouthpiece of commonly understood social consensus, but has to discover a new vision through patiently working with his material, so the creative teacher contributes fully to the making of tomorrow's culture not by enslaving himself to the current demands of today's society but by being open to the needs and potential of the young.

Today's teachers are perhaps uniquely fortunate, if they have the faith to see it. . . . They must seek to make education fully human, drawing out the strengths and talents of all young people so that they can acquire the intellectual, practical, and social skills they need, but above all helping them to find within themselves the resources that alone can help them to live at ease with a changing world.

For discovering, accepting, and confirming the self, adolescence is a critical period. And the stakes are higher than they have ever been: on the one hand, not "failed O-level" or "failed B.A.," but "failed humanity," and on the other, new possibilities of richly enjoyable living by people who are more fully, generously, and diversely persons than we with our long training in parsimony can even imagine. We must not miss this moment. Young lives are at stake. . . .

During the present century there has been a quiet revolution in our treatment of young children, a gradual removal of physical restraint and a withdrawal from judgmental attitudes. Demand feeding, gentle weaning, a more permissive attitude towards toilet training, sandpits to get dirty in, water for sensual delight, these early experiences are followed at best by an interest-centered, creative primary education, which is officially sanctioned if not always practised.

All this is evidence of a major cultural change. The rationale may not always be widely understood and the deeper motivation is open to different interpretations. We may choose to attribute the change, for instance, to a late flowering of 19th century romanticism; or to a vulgarization (usually in the good sense of that word, but sometimes indeed an oversimplification as in regard to repression) of psychoanalytic theories; or we may look to economic causes, to a gradual weakening of the insistence on postponed gratifications as thrift loses its moral grip or as parents begin to sense that an affluent society can afford golden days for children. Perhaps it is simply that having fewer we value them more and observe them more closely. Whatever the explanation may be, the facts are clear: prevailing attitudes to childhood are increasingly child-centered and increasingly child-trusting. Modern primary education has greatly benefited by this change. It has also greatly contributed to it. We have an admirable model for primary education, one that is respected all over the world, and it is based on perceiving and trusting children.

The harsh world of the adolescent, in school at any rate, still awaits its spring. . . . Certainly there is no justification in terms of human development for the sharp discontinuity in social experience to which we subject young people in the years embracing or preceding puberty. We have some consensus of opinion as to how childhood might be well spent, in school and out of it, and the opinion is coherent. Yet it seems that although individually many teachers and most parents are increasingly humane and relaxed in their relationships with adolescents, and observant of their needs, the demands that society makes on young people through its secondary schools are neither.

If for a moment we forget our preconceptions about secondary schooling and imagine ourselves able to start afresh, can we really be content with the way in which our young people's days are spent? Would we allow them, if we had the choice, to spend this time in squads (groups is too rich a word) being addressed or grilled by adults, one adult after another, and in a totally incoherent order? Would we not wish them, at an age apt for what Allport has called "propriate striving" (the development of a momentum towards personally recognized goals) to have the chance to undertake some major task during a school day, or week, or year? Would we not like them to learn to work cooperatively rather than in a moral climate so competitive that sharing is denigrated as "cheating" and actually punished? Would we really wish them to find much of their satisfaction in having some others to be better than? Animals, we are told, rescue their wounded. Who rescues the children at the bottom of the heap, the bottom children in the bottom stream? Sometimes a kindly, occasionally a superbly imaginative remedial teacher; certainly, never their peers in higher streams.

If we really thought of young people as people, would we go on playing Bingo with their lives, demanding that they should be able to produce all the necessary pieces to match the standardized pre-ordained picture of what a satisfactory young person would be? At breakfast they seem to be quite different from one another, and again at tea, and we are well satisfied. Why ask them all to do the same things (or as nearly so as possible) in the time between? Are there so few things to know and to do that we must insist on these and no others?

If we were once again to look at adolescents with innocent eyes, unblinkered by tradition, would we not want them to spend this time in part at least in discovering themselves, and enabling them to communicate their findings to others, using the many windows on to themselves that our culture can provide—not only speaking up in the occasional "class discussion" but working in cooperative groups, seeking and exploring materials which at that moment seem supremely interesting, drawing on phantasy to enrich self-understanding and the perception of others, using the behavioral sciences to study the behavior of human beings?

And would we not be seeking to help them now (and ourselves also) to understand better what it is like to live in a technological society? Would we not be trying to help them to become the kinds of people who will be able to solve the appalling problems of the human misery that is part—to some young people perhaps the most noticeable part—of the culture that we transmit? Could anyone claim that our secondary education as it is today is one which will help them to meet collaboratively and with courage the problems that will crowd in on them?

Is my description of the school day a caricature, or is the school day in many schools a caricature of living? Secondary education is so strange a process, one without parallel among other creatures, and the change from our model of primary schooling represents so sharp a slashing of the growing human being's experience, that we have to ask on what grounds, psychological or sociological, we can explain it, and whether we can defend it at all. Are we allowing millions of people in schools, children and adults, to spend their time disagreeably when it is quite unnecessary that they should do so? . . .

If you close your eyes and picture a good infant school, you will probably visualize children immersed in a whole diversity of pursuits, some dressing up, some collected together to have a story read to them, some in the shop, some literally immersed or partly so in complicated experiments with water. They are working but it looks like play. If you close your eyes and picture a good typical secondary school your second picture may well be of young people engaged in craft, or singing, or acting or dancing, but your first will surely be of passing through long corridors, and glancing in at rows of children sometimes being questioned, sometimes writing, sometimes being addressed, but all in any one room the same thing, and always sitting nose to nape, behind their desks, eyes down to book or front to teacher. They are working. It does not look at all like play.

These are not differences simply of method. They are different ways in which lives are being spent. They represent fundamental differences of values between the two institutions. It is not superficial to start by looking at such externals. Our best primary education is based on a belief that we should observe children with care and expertise, allowing them to reveal their interests and their potential through individual or group

work, as far as possible programming their own learning by drawing
what they need, with the teacher's direct help at times, from a very rich
and stimulating environment. . . .

4. Is There Any Knowledge That a Man *Must* Have?

*One of the central dilemmas of open education is the tension between the
desire to respond to individual interests and the desire to bring students
into possession of their culture. (We will return to this problem in both
Part Three, on The Role of the Teacher, and Part Four, on The Curriculum.) The dilemma is made more acute by the fact that many
thoughtful educators have begun to question whether, given the ex-
ponential growth of information and knowledge, the notion of a common learning is still tenable.*

*Interestingly enough, university educators are struggling with the same
problem. For them, the question is whether—or how—a liberal education is possible in the absence of an agreed-upon common curriculum.
In the selection that follows, Wayne C. Booth, professor of English and
former dean of the undergraduate College of the University of Chicago,
argues that liberal education is possible: while there is no set body of
courses that all students need to master, there is a body of knowledge
that all men must have if they are to be fully educated, which is to say,
if they are to be fully human. Professor Booth defines that knowledge in
terms of ways of thinking rather than bodies of fact. Although the substance of his essay is addressed to the problem of undergraduate education, his arguments apply equally well to elementary and secondary
education.*

As you have no doubt already recognized, my topic is simply a more
exasperating form of the general topic of this conference.[1] All of the
ambiguities and annoyances that are stirred up when we ask what is
most worth knowing are brought to the boiling point when we ask
whether some things really *must* be known.

Such questions are not faced cheerfully by most of us in this empirical
generation. It is true, of course, that we regularly make choices that are

[1] A Liberal Arts Conference sponsored by the undergraduate College of the
University of Chicago upon University's seventy-fifth anniversary, general topic
being "The Knowledge Most Worth Having."

based on implied standards of what is worth knowing. We set degree requirements, we organize courses, we give examinations, and we would scarcely want to say that what we do is entirely arbitrary. We conduct research on this rather than that subject, and we urge our students in this rather than that direction; though we may profess a happy relativism of goals, as if all knowledge were equally valuable, we cannot and do not run our lives or our universities on entirely relativistic assumptions. And yet we seem to be radically unwilling to discuss the ground for our choices; it is almost as if we expected that a close look would reveal a scandal at the heart of our academic endeavor. The journals are full, true enough, of breast-beating and soul-searching, especially since "Berkeley." But you will look a long while before you find any discussion of what is worth knowing. You will look even longer before you find anything written in the past ten years worthy of being entered into the great debate on liberal education,[2] as it is represented by the selections in the "syllabus" prepared for this conference. When Herbert Spencer, for example, wrote the essay from which we paraphrased our title, he knew that he addressed a public steeped in a tradition of careful argument about "What Knowledge Is of Most Worth." Though he disagreed with the traditional practice of placing classical studies at the center of liberal education, he knew that he could not defend scientific education simply by asserting its superiority. The very tradition he was attacking had educated an audience that required him to argue his case as cogently as possible, and, at the same time, it gave him confidence that his readers would think his question both important and amenable to productive discussion.

We were able to feel no such confidence in calling for a similar debate within a major university in 1966. Even at the University of Chicago, which has been more hospitable than most universities to serious controversy about the aims of education, we expected that the threat of hierarchical judgment implied by our topic would make men nervous. And we were right. "You will simply stir up meaningless controversy," one faculty member complained. "Since nobody can say what is most worth knowing, you'll get as many opinions as there are people, and the debate will be pointless." One bright fourth-year student said, "In choosing my major I've already chosen the knowledge which *for me* is most worth having. Each man chooses his own answers to this question, and the right choice for you is not the right choice for me." And then—curiously enough—he repeated what I had heard earlier from the faculty member: "You'll get as many answers as there are men discussing."

Well, first of all, even if we think of knowledge as inert information,

[2] Since the conference, one fine exception has appeared, Daniel Bell's *The Reforming of General Education* (New York: Columbia University Press, 1966).

something that we can *have,* this simply is not so. There are not enough opinions about what is worth knowing to provide each of us with a custom-built model of his own. In the past few months, I have heard hundreds of defenses of this or that body of information or pattern of skills as worth learning, but there have been nothing like hundreds of different views. I suspect that a bit of logical sorting would reveal no more than twenty or thirty distinct views in this community, and perhaps no more than a good round dozen.

I raise what may seem like little more than a quibble because I think it is important at the beginning of this conference to recognize what our topic asks of us. Taken seriously, it not only asks us to affirm what we think is educationally important; we're all ready enough to do that at the drop of a hat. What is troublesome is that it asks us to reason to-gether about our various preferences, and it assumes that some answers to the question will be better than others—not just preferable to you or to me, because of the way we have been educated, but better, period (or as men used to say, better, absolutely). It does not, of course, as-sume that finding answers will be easy; we cannot, like some non-academics, discover an indictment of the "knowledge factories" simply by ferreting out thesis topics that sound ridiculous. But it does assume that there is something irrational in our contemporary neglect of system-atic thought about educational goals. Scholars in the middle ages are often accused of having automatically assumed hierarchies in every subject. Many of us as automatically assume that value judgments among types or bits of knowledge are irrelevant. Yet we cannot escape implying, by our practice, that though all "knowledges" are equal, some are more equal than others. Our choice of topic asks us to attempt, during this conference, to think seriously about the ground for the hierarchies that our practical choices imply.

Everyone lives on the assumption that a great deal of knowledge is not worth bothering about; though we all know that what looks trivial in one man's hands may turn out to be earth-shaking in another's, we simply cannot know very much, compared with what might be known, and we must therefore choose. What is shocking is not the act of choice which we all commit openly but the claim that some choices are wrong. Especially shocking is the claim implied by my title: There is some knowledge that a man *must* have.

There clearly is no such thing, if by knowledge we mean mere ac-quaintance with this or that thing, fact, concept, literary work, or scientific law. When C. P. Snow and F. R. Leavis exchanged blows on whether knowledge of Shakespeare is more important than knowledge of the second law of thermodynamics, they were both, it seemed to me, much too ready to assume as indispensable what a great many wise and good men have quite obviously got along without. And it is not only nonprofessionals who can survive in happy ignorance of this or that bit of lore. I suspect that many successful scientists (in biology, say) have lost whatever hold they might once have had on the second law; I know that a great many literary scholars survive and even flourish without knowing certain "indispensable" classics. We all get along without vast loads of learning that other men take as necessary marks of an educated man. If we once begin to "reason the need" we will find, like Lear, that "our basest beggars/Are in the poorest thing superfluous." Indeed, we can survive, in a manner of speaking, even in the modern world, with little more than the bare literacy necessary to tell the "off" buttons from the "on."

Herbert Spencer would remind us at this point that we are interpreting *need* as if it were entirely a question of private survival. Though he talks about what a man must know to stay alive, he is more interested, in his defense of science, in what a *society* must know to survive: "Is there any knowledge that *man* must have?"—not *a* man, but *man*. This question is put to us much more acutely in our time than it was in Spencer's, and it is by no means as easy to argue now as it was then that the knowledge needed for man's survival is scientific knowledge. The threats of atomic annihilation, of engulfing population growth, of depleted air, water, and food must obviously be met, if man is to survive, and in meeting them man will, it is true, need more and more scientific knowledge; but it is not at all clear that more and more scientific knowledge will by itself suffice. Even so, a modern Herbert Spencer might well argue that a conference like this one, with its emphasis on the individual and his cognitive needs, is simply repeating the mistakes of the classical tradition. The knowledge most worth having would be, from his point of view, that of how to pull mankind through the next century or so without absolute self-destruction. The precise proportions of different kinds of knowledge—physical, biological, political, ethical, psychological, historical, or whatever—would be different from those prescribed in Spencer's essay, but the nature of the search would be precisely the same.

We can admit the relevance of this emphasis on social utility and at the same time argue that our business here is with other matters entirely. If the only knowledge a man *must* have is how to cross the street without getting knocked down—or, in other words, how to navigate the centuries without blowing himself up—then we may as well close the conference and go home. We may as well also roll up the college and mail it to a research institute, because almost any place that is not cluttered up with notions of liberal education will be able to discover and transmit practical bits of survival-lore better than we can.

Our problem of survival is a rather different one, thrust at us as soon as
we change our title slightly once again to "Is there any knowledge
(other than the knowledge for survival) that *a* man must have?" That
slight shift opens a new perspective on the problem, because the question of what it is to be a man, of what it is to be fully human, is the
question at the heart of liberal education.

To be human, to be human, to be fully human. What does it mean?
What is required? Immediately, we start feeling nervous again. Is the
speaker suggesting that some of us are not fully human *yet?* Here come
those hierarchies again. Surely in our pluralistic society we can admit
an unlimited number of legitimate ways to be a man, without prescribing some outmoded aristocratic code!

Who—or what—is the creature we would educate? Our answer will
determine our answers to educational questions, and it is therefore, I
think, worth far more vigorous effort than it usually receives. I find it
convenient, and only slightly unfair, to classify the educational talk I
encounter these days under four notions of man, three of them metaphorical, only one literal. Though nobody's position, I suppose, fits my
types neatly, some educators talk as if they were programming machines,
some talk as if they were conditioning rats, some talk as if they were
training ants to take a position in the anthill, and some—precious few
—talk as if they thought of themselves as men dealing with men. . . .

But it is long past time for me to turn from these negative, truncated
portraits of what man really is not and attempt to say what he is. And
here we encounter a difficulty that I find very curious. You will note
that each of these metaphors has reduced man to something less than
man, or at least to a partial aspect of man. It is easy to say that man
is not a machine, though he is in some limited respects organized like a
machine and even to some degree "programmable." It is also easy to
say that man is not simply a complicated rat or monkey, though he is
in some ways like rats and monkeys. Nor is man an ant, though he
lives and must function in a complicated social milieu. All these metaphors break down not because they are flatly false but because they *are*
metaphors, and any metaphorical definition is inevitably misleading. The
ones I have been dealing with are especially misleading, because in
every case they have reduced something more complex to something
much less complex. But even if we were to analogize man to something
more complex, say, the universe, we would be dissatisfied. What we want
is some notion of what man really *is,* so that we will know what or whom
we are trying to educate.

And here it is that we discover something very important about man,
something that even the least religious person must find himself mysti-
fied by: man is the one "thing" we know that is completely resistant
to our efforts at metaphor or analogy or image-making. What seems to

be the most important literal characteristic of man is his resistance to definitions in terms of anything else. If you call me a machine, even a very complicated machine, I know that you deny what I care most about, my selfhood, my sense of being a person, my consciousness, my conviction of freedom and dignity, my awareness of love, my laughter. Machines have none of these things, and even if we were generous to their prospects, and imagined machines immeasurably superior to the most complicated ones now in existence, we would still feel an infinite gap between them and what we know to be a basic truth about ourselves: machines are expendable, ultimately expendable, and men are mysteriously ends in themselves.

I hear people deny this, but when they do they always argue for their position by claiming marvelous feats of super-machine calculation that machines can now do or will someday be able to do. But that is not the point; of course machines can outcalculate us. The question to ask is entirely a different one: Will they ever outlove us, outlive us, outvalue us? Do we build machines because machines are good things in themselves? Do we nurture them for their own good, as we nurture our children? An obvious way to test our sense of worth in men and machines is to ask ourselves whether we would ever campaign to liberate the poor downtrodden machines who have been enslaved. Shall we form a National Association for the Advancement of Machinery? Will anyone ever feel a smidgeon of moral indignation because this or that piece of machinery is not given equal rights before the law? Or put it another way: Does anyone value Gemini more than the twins? There may be men now alive who would rather "destruct," as we say, the pilot than the experimental rocket, but most of us still believe that the human being in the space ship is more important than the space ship.

When college students protest the so-called depersonalization of education, what they mean, finally, is not simply that they want to meet their professors socially or that they want small classes or that they do not want to be dealt with by IBM machines. All these things are but symptoms of a deeper sense of a violation of their literal reality as persons, ends in themselves rather than mere expendable things. Similarly, the current deep-spirited revolt against racial and economic injustice seems to me best explained as a sudden assertion that people, of whatever color or class, are not reducible to social conveniences. When you organize your labor force or your educational system as if men were mere social conveniences, "human resources," as we say, contributors to the gross national product, you violate something that we all know, in a form of knowledge much deeper than our knowledge of the times tables or the second law of thermodynamics: those field hands, those children crowded into the deadening classroom, those men laboring without dignity in the city anthills are *men,* creatures whose worth is mysteriously more than any description of it we might make in justifying what we do to them.

Ants, rats, and machines can all learn a great deal. Taken together, they "know" a very great part of what our schools and colleges are now designed to teach. But is there any kind of knowledge that a creature must have to qualify as a man? Is there any part of the educational task that is demanded of us by virture of our claim to educate this curious entity, this *person* that cannot be reduced to mechanism or animality alone?

You will not be surprised, by now, to have me sound, in my answer, terribly traditional, not to say square: the education that a *man* must have is what has traditionally been called liberal education. The knowledge it yields is the knowledge or capacity or power of how to act freely as a man. That's why we call liberal education liberal: it is intended to liberate from whatever it is that makes animals act like animals and machines act like machines.

I'll return in a moment to what it means to act freely as a man. But we are already in a position to say something about what knowledge a man must have—he must first of all be able to learn for himself. If he cannot learn for himself, he is enslaved by his teachers' ideas, or by the ideas of his more persuasive contemporaries, or by machines programmed by other men. He may have what we call a good formal education, yet still be totally bound by whatever opinions happen to have come his way in attractive garb. One wonders how many of our graduates have learned how to take hold of a subject and "work it up," so that they can make themselves experts on what other men have concluded. In some ways this is not a very demanding goal, and it is certainly not very exciting. It says nothing about that popular concept, creativity, or about imagination or originality. All it says is that anyone who is dependent on his teachers *is* dependent, not free, and that anyone who knows how to learn for himself is less like animals and machines than anyone who does not know how to learn for himself.

We see already that a college is not being merely capricious or arbitrary when it insists that some kinds of learning are more important than some others. The world is overflowing with interesting subjects and valuable skills, but surely any college worth the name will put first things first: it will try to insure, as one inescapable goal, that every graduate can dig out from the printed page what he needs to know. And it will not let the desire to tamp in additional tidbits of knowledge, however delicious, interfere with training minds for whom a formal teacher is no longer required.

To put our first goal in this way raises some real problems—perhaps even problems that we cannot solve. Obviously no college can produce self-learners in very many subjects. Are we not lucky if a graduate can learn for himself even in one field, now that knowledge in all areas has advanced as far as it has? Surely we cannot expect our graduates to reach a stage of independence in mathematics and physics, in political science and psychology, in philosophy and English, *and* in all the other nice subjects that one would like to master.

Rather than answer this objection right away, let me make things even more difficult by saying that it is not enough to learn how to learn. The man who cannot *think* for himself, going beyond what other men have learned or thought, is still enslaved to other men's ideas. Obviously the goal of learning to think is even more difficult than the goal of learning to learn. But difficult as it is we must add it to our list. It is simply not enough to be able to get up a subject on one's own, like a good encyclopedia employee, even though any college would take pride if all its graduates could do so. To be fully human means in part to think one's own thoughts, to reach a point at which, whether one's ideas are different from or similar to other men's, they are truly one's own.

The art of asking oneself critical questions that lead either to new answers or to genuine revitalizing of old answers, the art of making thought live anew in each new generation, may not be entirely amenable to instruction. But it is a necessary art nonetheless, for any man who wants to be free. It is an art that all philosophers have tried to pursue, and many of them have given direct guidance in how to pursue it. Needless to say, it is an art the pursuit of which is never fully completed. No one thinks for himself very much of the time or in very many subjects. Yet the habitual effort to ask the right critical questions and to apply rigorous tests to our hunches is a clearer mark than any other of an educated man.

But again we stumble upon the question, "Learn to think about *what?*" The modern world presents us with innumerable subjects to think about. Does it matter whether anyone achieves this rare and difficult point in more than one subject? And if not, won't the best education simply be the one that brings a man into mastery of a narrow specialty as soon as possible, so that he can learn to think for himself as soon as possible? Even at best most of us are enslaved to opinions provided for us by experts in *most* fields. So far, it might be argued, I still have not shown that there is any kind of knowledge that a man must have, only that there are certain skills that he must be able to exercise in at least one field.

To provide a proper grounding for my answer to that objection would require far more time than I have left, and I'm not at all sure that I could do so even with all the time in the world. The question of whether it is possible to maintain a human stance toward any more than a tiny fraction of modern knowledge is not clearly answerable at this stage in our history. It will be answered, if at all, only when men have learned how to store and retrieve all "machinable" knowledge, freeing themselves for distinctively human tasks. But in the meantime, I find myself unable to surrender, as it were, three distinct kinds of knowledge that seem to me indispensable to being human.

To be a man, a man must first know something about his own nature and his place in Nature, with a capital N—something about the truth of things, as men used to say in the old-fashioned days before the word "truth" was banned from academia. Machines are not curious, so far as I can judge; animals are, but presumably they never go, in their philosophies, even at the furthest, beyond a kind of solipsistic existentialism. But in science, in philosophy (ancient and modern), in theology, in psychology and anthropology, and in literature (of some kinds), we are presented with accounts of our universe and of our place in it that as men we can respond to in only one manly way: by thinking about them, by speculating and testing our speculations.

We know before we start that our thought is doomed to incompleteness and error and downright chanciness. Even the most rigorously scientific view will be changed, we know, within a decade, or perhaps even by tomorrow. But to refuse the effort to understand is to resign from the human race; the unexamined life can no doubt be worth living in other respects—after all, it is no mean thing to be a vegetable, an oak tree, an elephant or a lion. But a man, a man will want to see, in this speculative domain, beyond his next dinner.

By putting it in this way, I think we can avoid the claim that to be a man I must have studied any one field—philosophy, science, theology. But to be a man, *I must speculate,* and I must learn how to test my speculations so that they are not simply capricious, unchecked by other men's speculations. A college education, surely, should throw every student into a regular torrent of speculation, and it should school him to recognize the different standards of validation proper to different kinds of claims to truth. You cannot distinguish a man who in this respect is educated from other men by whether or not he believes in God, or in UFOs. But you can tell an educated man by the way he takes hold of the question of whether God exists, or whether UFOs are from Mars. Do you know your own reasons for your beliefs, or do you absorb your beliefs from whatever happens to be in your environment, like plankton taking in nourishment?

Second, the man who has not learned how to make the great human achievements in the arts his own, who does not know what it means to *earn* a great novel or symphony or painting for himself, is enslaved either to caprice or to other men's testimony or to a life of ugliness. You will notice that as I turn thus to "beauty"—another old-fashioned term—I do not say that a man must know how to prove what is beautiful or how to discourse on aesthetics. Such speculative activities are pleasant and worthwhile in themselves, but they belong in my first domain. Here we are asking that a man be educated to the experience of beauty; speculation about it can then follow. My point is simply that a man is less than a man if he cannot respond to the art made by his fellow man.

Again I have tried to put the standard in a way that allows for the impossibility of any one man's achieving independent responses in very many arts. Some would argue that education should insure some minimal human competence in all of the arts, or at least in music, painting, and literature. I suppose I would be satisfied if all of our graduates had been "hooked" by at least one art, hooked so deeply that they could never get free. As in the domain of speculation, we could say that the more types of distinctively human activity a man can master, the better, but we are today talking about floors, not ceilings, and I shall simply rest content with saying that to be a man, a man must know artistic beauty, in some form, and know it in the way that beauty can be known. (The distinction between natural and man-made beauty might give me trouble if you pushed me on it here, but let me just say, dogmatically, that I would not be satisfied simply to know natural beauty—women and sunsets, say—as a substitute for art.)

Finally, the man who has not learned anything about how to understand his own intentions and to make them effective in the world, who has not, through experience and books, learned something about what is possible and what impossible, what desirable and what undesirable, will be enslaved by the political and social intentions of other men, benign or malign. The domain of practical wisdom is at least as complex and troublesome as the other two, and at the same time it is even more self-evidently indispensable. How should a man live? How should a society be run? What direction should a university take in 1966? For that matter what should be the proportion, in a good university, of inquiry into truth, beauty, and "goodness"? What kind of knowledge of self or of society is pertinent to living the life proper to a man? In short, the very question of this conference falls within this final domain: What knowledge, if any, is most worthy of pursuit? You cannot distinguish the men from the boys according to any one set of conclusions, but you *can* recognize a man, in this domain, simply by discovering whether he can think for himself about practical questions, with some degree of freedom from blind psychological or political or economic compulsions. Ernest Hemingway tells somewhere of a man who had "moved one dollar's width to the [political] right for every dollar that he'd ever earned." Perhaps no man ever achieves the opposite extreme, complete freedom in his choices from irrelevant compulsions. But all of us who believe in education believe that it is possible for any man, through study and conscientious thought, to school his choices—that is, to free them through coming to understand the forces working on them.

Even from this brief discussion of the three domains, I think we are put in a position to see how it can be said that there is some knowledge that a man must have. The line I have been pursuing will not lead to a list of great books, or even to a list of indispensable departments in a university. Nor will it lead, in any clear-cut fashion, to a pattern of requirements in each of the divisions. Truth, beauty, and goodness (or "right choice") are relevant to study in every division within the university; the humanities, for example, have no corner on beauty or imagination or art, and the sciences have no corner on speculative truth. What is more, a man can be ignorant even of Shakespeare, Aristotle, Beethoven, and Einstein, and be a man for a' that—*if* he has learned how to think his own thoughts, experience beauty for himself, and choose his own actions.

It is not the business of a college to determine or limit what a man will know; if it tries to, he will properly resent its impositions, perhaps immediately, perhaps ten years later when the imposed information is outmoded. But I think that it *is* the business of a college to help teach a man how to use his mind for himself, in at least the three directions I have suggested. There has been a splendid tradition in the College of the University of Chicago of honoring these goals with hard planning and devoted teaching. To think for oneself is, as we all know, hard enough. To design a program and assemble faculty to assist rather than hinder students in their efforts to think for themselves is even harder. But in an age that is oppressed by huge accumulations of unassimilated knowledge, the task of discovering what it means to educate a man is perhaps more important than ever before.

5. A Goal Toward Which to Move

"It is one of the complaints of the schoolmaster that the public does not defer to his professional opinion as completely as it does to that of practitioners in other professions," John Dewey wrote in one of his last published works. While this might appear to be a defect in the way education is organized, he argued, it in fact is not, for the relation between professionals and the public is different in education than in any other profession. "Education is a public business with us, in a sense that the protection and restoration of personal health or legal rights are not." The reason is simple: "To an extent characteristic of no other institution, save that of the state itself, the school has the power to

modify the social order. And under our political system, it is the right of each individual to have a voice in the making of social policies as, indeed, he has a vote in the determination of political affairs. If this be true," Dewey concluded, "education is primarily a public business, and only secondarily a specialized vocation. The layman, then, will always have his right to some utterance on the operation of public schools."

Few state departments of education have recognized the truth of Dewey's argument as fully as the Vermont Department of Education. Under the leadership first of Dr. Harvey Scribner, the former Vermont Commissioner of Education, and then of his successor, Joseph H. Oakey, the Vermont Department has been trying to engage the citizens of Vermont in a public dialogue over how public schools should be organized, and to what end. Wide circulation of The Vermont Design for Education, *an attractive twenty-five-page pamphlet from which the following selection is taken, has been one of the principal means of stimulating that dialogue.*

———

Education in Vermont, if it is to move forward, must have a goal toward which to move, a basic philosophy which combines the best which is known about learning, children, development, and human relations with the unique and general needs and desires of Vermont communities. It is entirely possible to discuss goals and ideals in terms of more and better classrooms, expanded library facilities, health services, audio-visual equipment, and such. The Vermont Design for Education takes the position that, although these are certainly justifiable concerns, an educational philosophy should center around and focus upon the individual, his learning process, and his relationship and interaction with the teacher. Toward these ends, the following premises are offered which, taken in summation, constitute a goal, an ideal, a student-centered philosophy for the process of education in Vermont.

1. The emphasis must be upon learning, rather than teaching. Education is a process conceived to benefit the learner. Central to any focus is the individual and how his learning process may be maximized. This idea is basic and provides the foundation of all other elements of quality education.

2. A student must be accepted as a person. His feelings and ideas deserve consideration and his inquiries an honest response. He should have the right to doubt—he should even be encouraged to doubt with responsibility, to question, to discuss with teachers, textbooks authors, and other authorities. He must, however, do more than doubt; he must

From *The Vermont Design for Education* (Montpelier, Vermont: The Vermont Department of Education, 1968), pp. 1–19.

strive to seek solutions to those issues which he questions. Each individual must be free to determine whether a position being advocated by an authority or another student is justifiable and rational.

3. Education should be based upon the individual's strong, inherent desire to learn and to make sense of his environment. Desire to learn is accentuated when the experiences are stimulating and non-threatening. Learning about things is a natural part of a child's life, and in the process of growing up, the better part of learning is done independently.

The inherent motivation basic to this natural learning experience is internal, based upon a child's desire to answer a question, solve a problem, fill a gap in his knowledge, make things fit together, glimpse a pattern, or discover an order. When a child thus extends his knowledge, it is sufficiently rewarding in itself to make him happy to have learned and eager to learn more. This internal motivation must also become the basis for learning in the school situation. If school work is to absorb his interest, he must know something of its purpose. Involvement in planning and true decision making will help retain the initial enthusiasm with which a child enters school. The structure of the school must complement the natural way in which children learn.

4. All people need success to prosper. Youth is no exception. A continual series of failures, if experienced in the school, can lead to a negative self-image, loss of face, loss of desire to continue to participate, and an urge to seek this needed success outside of the school situation. A school situation should be flexible and divergent enough to allow each person regularly to find some measure of success.

5. Education should strive to maintain the individuality and originality of the learner. The school's function is to expand the differences between individuals and create a respect for those differences.

6. Emphasis should be upon a child's own way of learning—through discovery and exploration—through real rather than abstract experiences. At no time in a person's life does one learn more or better than during early childhood. It is most revealing to watch a young child in this learning process—exploring, testing through trial and error, manipulating his environment, questioning, repeating.

The opportunity for this type of natural learning should be provided in schools. How much more meaningful for a pupil to be able to see the relationships in a numerical system expressed in concrete objects which he can manipulate to discover their interactions, rather than being faced with a set of numbers in an arithmetic textbook.

Compare the learning which can take place if a student can study trees in a wood lot, discover the interdependency of life in a pond, collect and analyze rocks, minerals, and soil from the surrounding area, rather than struggle through a series of charts and exercises in a workbook. Compare the meaning a student derives from involvement in the actions of a legislative committee with a textbook account of the same process.

7. The development of an individual's thought process should be primary. Rote learning of facts should be de-emphasized—facts should become the building blocks for generalities and processes. The ability to solve problems, whether social, mathematical, or economic must be given preference.

A person equipped to function adequately is able to relate his knowledge to new situations in order to solve new problems. He can use judgment and forethought—he is able to reason and imagine. Such a person can perceive problems as well as solve them.

8. People should perceive the learning process as related to their own sense of reality. There must be a conscientious effort to make the readings, discussions and issues faced in school relate to the world which people experience—to what they see when they look about and read the newspaper.

Schools cannot expect the trust and understanding of their students if agriculture is discussed in terms of the stereotype family farm, when these same students perceive around them huge agriculture combines and underpaid migrant labor.

9. An individual must be allowed to work according to his own abilities. Students are as diverse intellectually as they are physically, having different backgrounds and experiences, feelings, ways of thinking, personalities, and ways of working and learning. In order to be effective, schools must allow and encourage students to work at their own rate, to develop their own unique style of learning, conceptualizing and piecing together the parts to form coherent patterns. Learning experiences must be geared to individual needs rather than group norms.

10. The teacher's role must be that of a partner and guide in the learning process. The role of the teacher must not be one of an imparter of knowledge, someone who knows all the answers and is never wrong, but rather one who possesses those skills necessary to establish an appropriate learning climate, both in atmosphere as well as equipment and materials. The teacher must constantly be aware of each person's abilities and accomplishments, lead that person from one level of conceptualizing to the next, from his immediate interests to a logical learning process, involve him in the planning and decision making process and allow him the freedom and responsibility of becoming deeply involved. The teacher must extend the student's horizons beyond the limitations of the interests and abilities of the student, or even beyond those of the teacher. The teacher must help the individual realize what he has learned, and channel random discoveries into systematized learning.

The role of the teacher might be illustrated by the following example.

Consider a child who expresses interests in whales through a freely created clay model. The teacher must be aware of the great number of learning experiences in which the child might become involved deriving directly from his self-expressed interest in whales.

These experiences might include numerical work through measuring, weighing, and developing of the ratios of various parts of the model to each other or in comparison to the real animal. Science, prediction and logical thinking can be involved through forecasting the model's daily loss in weight, questioning why this loss, what is lost, where it goes and in what form. Language development can be furthered through writing stories about one's own whale, or reading stories involving other whales, and research through exploration of different types of whales, their culture, classifications, habits and environment. The teacher must help the child determine which of these experiences would be most appropriate to move toward an individualized set of expectancies.

Consideration should be given to allowing students to set up their own course of study in a subject-matter field if it is not relevant to a particular learning situation. For example, in the pursuit of knowledge in the field of chemistry, a student's needs might be better met through the development of a program acceptable to him and the teacher-counselor rather than the existing textbook-laboratory course.

The teacher does not abdicate his leadership role in the student-centered approach, but indeed assumes a far more important role of leadership, one responding to the individualized needs of each person with whom he works.

11. The development of a personal philosophy, a basic set of values, is perhaps one of the most important of human achievements. The school must assume an active role in helping each individual to evolve a set of personal values which will be most meaningful in helping him meet the challenges of life as a student and later as an adult. The teacher must not dictate a particular set of values or try to impose his own, but rather must help each person sort out his own experiences and seek a set of truths which can provide a tentative philosophy, one which can be re-evaluated in terms of further experiences and knowledge.

12. We must seek to individualize our expectations of a person's progress as we strive to individualize the learning experiences for each person. Evaluations, based upon standardized expectancies, force students to adopt standardized learning in order to compete. Many of today's expectancies are influenced by publishing concerns and hardware vendors. We must develop personalized ways of assessing an individual's progress, his strengths and weaknesses, keeping in mind that the ultimate purpose of evaluation is to strengthen the learning process.

13. The environment within which students are encouraged to learn must be greatly expanded. The classroom, or even the school, is an

extremely limited learning environment. The total culture surrounding each individual should become his learning environment. The surrounding parks, forests, lakes, homes, businesses, museums, factories should be as widely used as the resources of classrooms and libraries. The wealth of personal talent in the community should be utilized. The talents, crafts, hobbies, travel experiences of persons of all walks of life should become resources for the learning process. Students should be encouraged to taste life, to become actively involved in the activities and the decision making processes of the community.

14. The school should provide a structure in which students can learn from each other. Much learning takes place naturally through association with peers or older siblings, and much of the motivation to learn and explore comes from this association. Students who have developed certain abilities can provide models for those less developed. Those engaged in some activity often provide the needed stimulus to interest others in becoming involved in that learning activity. Schools should encourage students to work together cooperatively, to realize that individual efforts can often be improved through the combined effect of what each has to contribute to the common project.

15. To provide a maximum learning experience for all students requires the involvement and support of the entire community. In order to make maximum use of available learning opportunities, students need the support and understanding of teachers, who in turn need the support of the school administration to allow students to operate effectively. The administration is responsible to the community and the State. If any of the links' in this chain operate independently and resist efforts to maximize learning for students through lack of understanding, the students themselves suffer. All parties must work cooperatively toward a common set of concepts and goals if students are to reap maximum benefit from the learning opportunities which should be theirs.

16. Schools should be compatible with reality. Learning which is compartmentalized into artificial subject fields by teachers and administrators is contrary to what is known about the learning process. The interdependencies of real life which involve the combined use of a number of skills, should suggest a direction for school activities such as math, reading, science, social studies. It is unrealistic that math, or any subject, be limited to a certain period during the day, to be turned on and off by a bell.

How much more meaningful if math can be explored as one of a series of factors necessary to solving real problems as they arise during the course of the day. If we again look to the natural learning of preschool children as a model, it is apparent that they do not compartmentalize learning into neat little packages.

17. Individuals should be encouraged to develop a sense of respon-

sibility. A student's school should be HIS school, one to be proud of. He should be actively involved in its direction, its maintenance, and its care. The attitude of belonging and being an important contributor can do much toward establishing a spirit of cooperation and respect. This sense of responsibility should be further developed to include peers and adults. It is vital that students realize other people are individuals with feelings, ideas which may conflict with their own, strengths, weaknesses, and problems. A sense of responsibility and respect for the individuality of each person is necessary for better understanding and cooperation.

6. What Should Parents Look for in Their Children's School?

While the following article was addressed to parents, teachers and administrators have found it equally useful, reprinting it by the thousands. In suggesting what parents should look for in evaluating their children's school, Arlene Silberman suggests a set of criteria with which most informal educators will agree.

Four years and 50,000 miles ago, I first began to learn what good schools can and should be like. As the mother of four school-age sons, with a master's degree from Teachers College, Columbia University, and years of teaching experience, I thought I already knew. . . . Three continents and countless classrooms later, I can finally answer all the parents who ask, "How can I tell if my child's school is doing a good job?" I can also answer those mothers who add, "And how can I make things better?" Some of my discoveries may surprise you—as they surprised me.

The first thing you may have to do is scrap some of your preconceptions. I was halfway through my travels, for example, before I could admit that small classes aren't as essential as I had always thought; some of the best schools I visited had 40 children to one teacher! Modern buildings aren't essential, either. I visited some schools in Victorian structures that I wish my sons could attend, and some up-to-the-minute schools with all the things that matter least and few that matter most. So don't worry if your school doesn't have a television set in every room—and don't be unduly impressed if it does.

From Arlene Silberman, "How to Rate Your Child's School," *Ladies Home Journal*, February 1971, pp. 39, 40, 48.

There are only three requirements for a good elementary school:

1. a pleasant atmosphere in which every child feels valued and successful

2. a faculty concerned with developing youngsters who delight in learning

3. programs that respond to each child's individual needs.

Let's visit a school together so you'll know how to spot the clues that tell you if the combination is working.

We'll start early because you'll get your first inkling in the school yard as the children arrive. Do they enter the building freely, as they do at home, or must they line up like soldiers awaiting orders? Too many schools forget that they are a child's home for most of the day, not a military base. If we see youngsters locked out in an icy wind, we'll know to look for other signs of insensitivity in this school.

You may wonder if a pleasant atmosphere really matters. I am convinced it does, for if a child's early experiences are distasteful, he may decide that learning, like medicine, is only to be taken in small doses when absolutely necessary. In that case, his school has failed. I can say flatly that I have never seen a good school within a harsh environment.

We'll find our next clue in the hallways. Bare walls suggest a school that is barren in other ways, too. Good schools typically burst with paintings, posters and murals because they know that children are creative creatures whose talents and love of beauty will grow, if properly nurtured. They also know that children can express feelings through art that they may not yet be able to put into words. What's more, even the least able student feels successful when he sees his painting on display. Art, in sum, is essential to a good elementary school.

Our next stop is the outer office. While we're there, notice if the principal keeps his door open (except during private conferences) so that he can hear the pulsebeat of his school. Later we'll see if he remains closeted away or if he visits classes and chats with children in the halls. You'll know he doesn't emerge often if he calls every girl "Sweetheart" and every boy "Son." I always like the principal who asks Ida (by name) about her baby sister and Bill (by name) about his latest Scout badge.

If a string of children starts trickling down to the office for punishment almost as soon as the day begins, we're in a school that creates its own discipline problems by insisting that pupils bottle up all their energies. "Nine times out of ten the child who has been sent to me hasn't done anything worse than talk when the teacher wanted silence," a veteran principal told me, "but it happened to be the straw that broke the teacher's back. The teacher needs time to regain her composure, but the child doesn't have to be treated like a criminal." Consequently, this principal keeps a supply of books and puppets stashed away and "nine times out of ten" invites the child to read or play for a while. "When I think the teacher is ready to receive him, I send the child back," she explained.

Your principal is the key to your school. If he views himself as an administrator, wrapped up in lunch schedules and absence notes, the school may be efficient, but don't expect much more. But if he views himself as an educator—a teacher of teachers and children—chances are he runs a good school.

The tip-off to whether you're with an administrator or an educator is to ask, "What do you see as your goals?" If he replies with the curriculum he wants "covered," grade by grade, you're not talking with an educator; if he talks about the attitudes and abilities he tries to foster in his children, you probably are, for educators know that *how* a child learns may be as important as *what* he learns. Repeating what the teacher and textbooks say is one thing; having the initiative to raise questions and the know-how to explore new areas independently is quite another. The first is memorizing; the second, learning. It's important not to confuse the two.

While we're in the office, let's ask to see a sample report card, because that's another clue to the school's values. Most cards have a category called "Ability to Follow Directions." Good schools are also likely to have report card categories such as "Intellectual Curiosity" and "Resourcefulness." Does yours?

Let's also ask to see schoolwide scores on standardized reading and math tests so we can compare them with national norms. If the achievement is low, why? If it's above average, how has the school achieved its success? But remember, children who come from homes full of books, magazines and dinner-table conversation *should* score higher. Something's wrong if they don't.

Don't make the mistake of thinking that reading scores tell the whole story, however. I did, until a London headmistress set me straight. "I'll gladly show you our reading scores," she replied to my request, "but first I must point out that *what* my children read concerns me as much as how well they read. Too many competent readers develop into adults who read trash. I want my youngsters to enjoy poetry and drama, fiction and biography—and you won't discover that from test scores." How right she was!

Since we'll make most of our discoveries in the classroom, let's visit as many as we can. We may be given a list of rooms that are open to us, with an explanation that the teachers in these rooms have been told (warned?) to expect us, but most good schools open all their classrooms to visitors.

Does the teacher greet us as we enter, or does she pretend that we are phantoms, silent and invisible? Do the children glance at us furtively, not daring to let their eyes meet ours, much less risking to say "hello" or to have us greet them? These are all signs of a tense, unnatural environment where normal sociability is forbidden. A similar sign is the requirement that children ask permission to sharpen a pencil or throw a piece of paper away.

Keep listening to the sounds of the room. In a good classroom you may hear laughing and squeals of delight as children suddenly grasp a new idea or make an unexpected discovery; you may hear groans of disappointment if an experiment doesn't work out. And you may hear conversation as children help one another. But you won't encounter long periods of silence, except during a test. Nor will you hear the teacher doing 70 to 80 percent of the talking (which is about average, according to research studies), because the children will be participating more.

As you listen, count the number of times the teacher says "no" or an equivalent put-down. Teachers who hear tape recordings of themselves are often shocked to learn how negative they sound. "No wonder half my class never volunteers," a young teacher confessed after listening to herself. "I've crushed them!"

The best teacher I ever saw spent an entire day without once rejecting a child's answer, even though her Mexican-American youngsters needed many corrections because they had not yet mastered the English language. When Juan gave the answer "shirt," for example, instead of "apron," this teacher said, "The material does feel like a shirt, doesn't it? I wonder who wears something like this in your home?" From this she elicited the word "mother," and next, "apron."

Be alert to what happens if a child gives a correct answer that doesn't happen to be the one the teacher wanted. Does the teacher brush it aside because she is determined to follow her lesson plan? Or does she accept the unexpected learning opportunity?

Look around the room. The little towhead, squirming in his seat, has zipped through six pages in his math workbook while the boy sitting next to him is still struggling with the first page. And the pale child biting her nails is frantically trying to catch up because she was absent when her class learned long division. Unusual circumstances? Definitely not. There's not a classroom in any public school where every child performs at the same level. Even when the school separates children into "ability groups," there are wide differences in performance.

Consequently, a good school finds ways of individualizing the program. At least a thousand classrooms have completely abandoned the usual approach of having a teacher instruct the entire class as a unit. Instead, students work individually or in small groups, according to their interests and skills, while the teacher circulates about the room, helping a few children at a time, knowing that the others are proceeding independently or helping one another. In the same class Sally may still be learning to write simple sentences while Jill is already composing intricate stories. Neither has to be skipped or left back. And any child who has been absent simply picks up where he left off.

What's more, children learn by following their individual interests. Tim may be becoming an expert on rocks at the same time that Sam is delving into rocketry. There's no reason why they must both read the same books, or even take the same spelling test. Each child's spelling list is composed of words he needs for the reading and writing *he* happens to be doing, and no two are alike.

Look for Clues

There's hardly a state in the union that doesn't have some classrooms of this sort, with North Dakota and Vermont leading the way, and their numbers are growing rapidly. But even if we visit a more conventional classroom, we can still look for clues that tell us whether each child is regarded as a distinct individual. Notice the books. Is there only one set of readers, riveting every youngster to the same reading level regardless of his skill? A good third-grade room, for example, should have primers and sixth-grade readers as well as all stops in-between. Look for other kinds of books, too, to see whether the children are being taught, in the words of the London headmistress, to enjoy "poetry and drama, fiction and biography." A magazine table is also a good sign; it indicates a teacher who knows that sports, fashions, mechanics and recipes also offer ways to reach the child who "hates" reading.

We can form an opinion about whether children enjoy reading by watching what happens when the teacher steps into the hall to talk with us. Do they sit numbly, waiting for her to return and redirect them, or do they seize the unexpected opportunity to read? Notice, too, if a child is ever so engrossed in his reading, social studies project, science experiment, or original short story that he skips recess or lingers late.

Watching children is always revealing because their faces are so open that you can detect delight as easily as disinterest. Since children are naturally inquisitive, you may suspect that a bored child is the product of a boring classroom. Whenever I visit a room, I take rapid-fire notes about everything that's on the bulletin boards and about all the materials and equipment I see. Some classrooms are so bland I can write them up in five minutes; others are so rich it takes an hour to capture everything. You might try the same test yourself.

A good classroom shows many signs of interest in national and local affairs, in music, art and poetry, in science—and, of course, in the children themselves. To use the current term, such classrooms are "relevant." You'll notice as you read the children's work that when they write about things that interest them, they show a verve and style that is missing from those required reports on "Mining in Iceland." Even their spelling improves!

Many rooms have a gold star chart. Too many, for the stars are not merely a way of rewarding the successful but also a way of labeling the failures. "I don't have a lot of stars because I'm dumb in arithmetic" (or spelling or reading—I've heard them all). And the tearful child who whispers this confession uses a very different tone of voice from the youngster who is eager for me to see his impressive collection of gold stars. Since we know that the child who senses he has been labeled a failure often lives up to that expectation, it's essential to build his self-esteem, not chip away at it.

Top Prizes

Good schools provide ways for every child to feel successful. I still remember the reply that a New York City principal gave me when I mentioned how proud she must feel because her school had the highest reading scores in the district. "Of course I'm pleased," she said. "The scores indicate that we're doing a good job in an essential area. But I'm also delighted that our children won top prizes in the Harlem Hospital art show and in the citywide garden contest. And I'm thrilled with the Black History Museum that they assembled." She went on to express pleasure over the grace and skill that her sixth-grade boys had displayed in a recent karate exhibit and wound up inviting me to a forthcoming musical production. "The children made the scenery, sewed the costumes and built some of the props," she beamed. "Besides, they sing like angels." Clearly, success is not limited to paper-and-pencil achievement.

Nevertheless, we shouldn't overlook that paper-and-pencil work. Let's ask to look at some tests that different teachers have given, to ascertain the level of the children's work—and the level of the teacher's questions. "What is the capital of Arizona?" won't evoke the same quality of thinking as, "What would happen if Arizona's deserts had water?" Good teachers know how to pose questions that prompt children to think on their own, and to enjoy the challenge.

No school can measure up in every way, of course, but every school can be helped to do a better job. You can begin to help your child's school by getting to know it well. Don't limit your visits to one or two classrooms during Open School Week. And go with an open mind— and with open eyes and ears.

There is something worthwhile in every school, and you would do well to compliment people on the things that please you. They will appreciate the fact that you have not come to debunk all of their efforts. Then single out two or three things that trouble you most.

Undaunted Mother

Try to begin with a problem to which you see a solution—preferably an inexpensive one so that you won't be rebuffed with "That's a fine idea, but we haven't got the money." Some school administrators believe that nothing can be changed without large expenditures, but that simply isn't so. I think of one mother, for example, who was distressed when she visited school and discovered that the children, by and large, did not enjoy reading. But she also discovered a small, unused library, housed in an extra supply room that was shrouded in darkness and cobwebs; yet the library had some good books left over from the days when the school had a part-time librarian.

Fired with enthusiasm, the mother asked the principal if the school couldn't reopen its library. "They took the librarian out of my budget," he said glumly. "Couldn't our PTA run it?" the mother persisted. The principal offered no encouragement, but neither did he deny permission. Undaunted, this mother enlisted eight more parents to scrub and paint the room and arrange books in tempting displays. Finally, they hung an inviting poster on the door and provided mothers to serve as librarians and story-readers each afternoon. Predictably, children started flocking to the most inviting nook in the school. Overcome by success, the PTA next ran a book drive to enrich its supply.

As you spend more time in your child's school, you will get to know the principal and teachers better, and will feel free to question more things. Why don't the lower grades have music? Why doesn't the social studies program include present-day concerns? Why must children walk through the halls in silent lines? You may discover, as I often have, that no one has raised these questions before. Once people start thinking about things they have taken for granted, you stand some chance of effecting change. Be on the lookout for little changes at first, as teachers start to realize that they can do things differently in their classrooms without any official "edict" from higher-ups.

If you want to bring about major reform, however, you'll want to meet those higher-ups. And you can if you go to school board meetings. The school board hires and fires, sets the budget, and votes on countless decisions that either liberate or hamstring your school. At a time when government has become increasingly removed from the people, control of the schools still remains a local matter. And school board meetings are, typically, one of the last remaining examples of the old "town meeting," where every citizen has the right to ask questions and present his viewpoint. *You* can be heard at your school board meetings. *You* can make a difference—if you care enough. It takes work, for there is no magic wand you can wave. But if there's one thing I've learned in my travels, it's that most communities have the schools they deserve. Does yours?

7. The Acquisition of the Art of the Utilization of Knowledge

While the informal English primary schools have enjoyed their greatest growth since the end of World War II, their roots are deep in English life and thought. One of the wellsprings is the work of Alfred North Whitehead, the great philosopher, mathematician, and educator, who died in 1947 at the age of eighty-six. Whitehead's influence on contemporary educational reform movements is more profound than has generally been acknowledged. His essay on "The Aims of Education," from which this selection is taken, was delivered in 1916, as Whitehead's presidential address to the Mathematical Association of England. His plea for relevance—his demand that teachers ask why they are teaching what they are teaching and how pupils can use their knowledge—and his insistence that educators "eradicate the fatal disconnection of subjects which kills the vitality of our modern curriculum" expresses a view of education that most informal educators share.

Culture is activity of thought, and receptiveness to beauty and humane feeling. Scraps of information have nothing to do with it. A merely well-informed man is the most useless bore on God's earth. What we should aim at producing is men who possess both culture and expert knowledge in some special direction. Their expert knowledge will give them the ground to start from, and their culture will lead them as deep as philosophy and as high as art. We have to remember that the valuable intellectual development is self-development, and that it mostly takes place between the ages of sixteen and thirty. As to training, the most important part is given by mothers before the age of twelve. A saying due to Archbishop Temple illustrates my meaning. Surprise was expressed at the success in after-life of a man, who as a boy at Rugby had been somewhat undistinguished. He answered, "It is not what they are at eighteen, it is what they become afterwards that matters."

In training a child to activity of thought, above all things we must

From Alfred North Whitehead, "The Aims of Education" in A. N. Whitehead, *The Aims of Education and other Essays* (New York: *New American Library,* Mentor Books, 1949), pp. 13–26.

beware of what I will call "inert ideas"—that is to say, ideas that are merely received into the mind without being utilised, or tested, or thrown into fresh combinations.

In the history of education, the most striking phenomenon is that schools of learning, which at one epoch are alive with a ferment of genius, in a succeeding generation exhibit merely pedantry and routine. The reason is, that they are overladen with inert ideas. Education with inert ideas is not only useless: it is, above all things, harmful—*Corruptio optimi, pessima*. Except at rare intervals of intellectual ferment, education in the past has been radically infected with inert ideas. That is the reason why uneducated clever women, who have seen much of the world, are in middle life so much the most cultured part of the community. They have been saved from this horrible burden of inert ideas. Every intellectual revolution which has ever stirred humanity into greatness has been a passionate protest against inert ideas. Then, alas, with pathetic ignorance of human psychology, it has proceeded by some education scheme to bind humanity afresh with inert ideas of its own fashioning.

Let us now ask how in our system of education we are to guard against this mental dryrot. We enunciate two educational commandments, "Do not teach too many subjects," and again, "What you teach, teach thoroughly."

The result of teaching small parts of a large number of subjects is the passive reception of disconnected ideas, not illumined with any spark of vitality. Let the main ideas which are introduced into a child's education be few and important, and let them be thrown into every combination possible. The child should make them his own, and should understand their application here and now in the circumstances of his actual life. From the very beginning of his education, the child should experience the joy of discovery. The discovery which he has to make, is that general ideas give an understanding of that stream of events which pours through his life, which is his life. By understanding I mean more than a mere logical analysis, though that is included. I mean "understanding" in the sense in which it is used in the French proverb, "To understand all, is to forgive all." Pedants sneer at an education which is useful. But if education is not useful, what is it? Is it a talent, to be hidden away in a napkin? Of course, education should be useful, whatever your aim in life. It was useful to Saint Augustine and it was useful to Napoleon. It is useful, because understanding is useful.

I pass lightly over that understanding which should be given by the literary side of education. Nor do I wish to be supposed to pronounce on the relative merits of a classical or modern curriculum. I would only remark that the understanding which we want is an understanding of an insistent present. The only use of a knowledge of the past is to equip us for the present. No more deadly harm can be done to young minds than by depreciation of the present. The present contains all that there is. It is holy ground; for it is the past, and it is the future. At the same time it must be observed that an age is no less past if it existed two hundred years ago than if it existed two thousand years ago. Do not be deceived by the pedantry of dates. The ages of Shakespeare and of Moliére are no less past than are the ages of Sophocles and of Virgil. The communion of saints is a great and inspiring assemblage, but it has only one possible hall of meeting, and that is, the present; and the mere lapse of time through which any particular group of saints must travel to reach that meeting place, makes very little difference.

Passing now to the scientific and logical side of education, we remember that here also ideas which are not utilized are positively harmful. By utilizing an idea, I mean relating it to that stream, compounded of sense perceptions, feelings, hopes, desires, and of mental activities adjusting thought to thought, which forms our life. I can imagine a set of beings which might fortify their souls by passively reviewing disconnected ideas. Humanity is not built that way—except perhaps some editors of newspapers.

In scientific training, the first thing to do with an idea is to prove it. But allow me for one moment to extend the meaning of "prove"; I mean —to prove its worth. Now an idea is not worth much unless the propositions in which it is embodied are true. Accordingly an essential part of the proof of an idea is the proof, either by experiment or by logic, of the truth of the propositions. But it is not essential that this proof of the truth should constitute the first introduction to the idea. After all, its assertion by the authority of respectable teachers is sufficient evidence to begin with. In our first contact with a set of propositions, we commence by appreciating their importance. That is what we all do in after-life. We do not attempt, in the strict sense, to prove or to disprove anything, unless its importance makes it worthy of that honour. These two processes of proof, in the narrow sense, and of appreciation, do not require a rigid separation in time. Both can be proceeded with nearly concurrently. But in so far as either process must have the priority, it should be that of appreciation by use.

Furthermore, we should not endeavour to use propositions in isolation. Emphatically I do not mean, a neat little set of experiments to illustrate Proposition I and then the proof of Proposition I, a neat little set of experiments to illustrate Proposition II and then the proof of Proposition II, and so on to the end of the book. Nothing could be more boring. Interrelated truths are utilized *en bloc,* and the various propositions are employed in any order, and with any reiteration. Choose some important applications of your theoretical subject; and study them concurrently with the systematic theoretical exposition. Keep the theoretical exposition short and simple, but let it be strict and rigid so far as it goes. It should not be too long for it to be easily known with thoroughness and accuracy. The consequences of a plethora of half-digested theoretical knowledge are deplorable. Also the theory should not be muddled up with the practice. The child should have no doubt when it is proving and when it is utilizing. My point is that what is proved should be utilized, and that what is utilized should—so far as is practicable—be proved. I am far from asserting that proof and utilization are the same thing.

At this point of my discourse, I can most directly carry forward my argument in the outward form of a digression. We are only just realising that the art and science of education require a genius and a study of their own; and that this genius and this science are more than a bare knowledge of some branch of science or of literature. This truth was partially perceived in the past generation; and headmasters, somewhat crudely, were apt to supersede learning in their colleagues by requiring left-hand bowling and a taste for football. But culture is more than cricket, and more than football, and more than extent of knowledge.

Education is the acquisition of the art of the utilization of knowledge. This is an art very difficult to impart. Whenever a textbook is written of real educational worth, you may be quite certain that some reviewer will say that it will be difficult to teach from it. Of course it will be difficult to teach from it. If it were easy, the book ought to be burned; for it cannot be educational. In education, as elsewhere, the broad prim-rose path leads to a nasty place. This evil path is represented by a book or a set of lectures which will practically enable the student to learn by heart all the questions likely to be asked at the next external examina-tion. And I may say in passing that no educational system is possible unless every question directly asked of a pupil at any examination is either framed or modified by the actual teacher of that pupil in that subject. The external accessor may report on the curriculum or on the performance of the pupils, but never should be allowed to ask the pupil a question which has not been strictly supervised by the actual teacher, or at least inspired by a long conference with him. There are a few exceptions to this rule, but they are exceptions, and could easily be allowed for under the general rule.

We now return to my previous point, that theoretical ideas should always find important applications within the pupil's curriculum. This is not an easy doctrine to apply, but a very hard one. It contains within itself the problem of keeping knowledge alive, of preventing it from becoming inert, which is the central problem of all education.

The best procedure will depend on several factors, none of which can be neglected, namely, the genius of the teacher, the intellectual type of the pupils, their prospects in life, the opportunities offered by the immediate surroundings of the school, and allied factors of this sort. It is for this reason that the uniform external examination is to deadly. We do not denounce it because we are cranks, and like denouncing established things. We are not so childish. Also, of course, such examinations have their use in testing slackness. Our reason for dislike is very definite and very practical. It kills the best part of culture. When you analyse in the light of experience the central task of education, you find that its successful accomplishment depends on a delicate adjustment of many variable factors. The reason is that we are dealing with human minds, and not with dead matter. The evocation of curiosity, of judgment, of the power of mastering a complicated tangle of circumstances, the use of theory in giving foresight in special cases—all these powers are not to be imparted by a set rule embodied in one schedule of examination subjects.

I appeal to you, as practical teachers. With good discipline, it is always possible to pump into the minds of a class a certain quantity of inert knowledge. You take a textbook and make them learn it. So far, so good. The child then knows how to solve a quadratic equation. But what is the point of teaching a child to solve a quadratic equation? There is a traditional answer to this question. It runs thus: The mind is an instrument, you first sharpen it, and then use it; the acquisition of the power of solving a quadratic equation is part of the process of sharpening the mind. Now there is just enough truth in this answer to have made it live through the ages. But for all its half-truth, it embodies a radical error which bids fair to stifle the genius of the modern world. I do not know who was first responsible for this analogy of the mind to a dead instrument. For aught I know, it may have been one of the seven wise men of Greece, or a committee of the whole lot of them. Whoever was the originator, there can be no doubt of the authority which it has acquired by the continuous approval bestowed upon it by eminent persons. But whatever its weight of authority, whatever the high approval which it can quote, I have no hesitation in denouncing it as one of the most fatal, erroneous, and dangerous conceptions ever introduced into the theory of education. The mind is never passive; it is a perpetual activity, delicate, receptive, responsive to stimulus. Whatever interest attaches to your subject-matter must be evoked here and now. That is the golden rule of education, and a very difficult rule to follow.

The difficulty is just this: the apprehension of general ideas, intellectual habits of mind, and pleasurable interest in mental achievement can be evoked by no form of words, however accurately adjusted. All practical teachers know that education is a patient process of the mastery of details, minute by minute, hour by hour, day by day. There is no royal road to learning through an airy path of brilliant generalisations. There is a proverb about the difficulty of seeing the wood because of the trees. That difficulty is exactly the point which I am enforcing. The problem of education is to make the pupil see the wood by means of the trees.

The solution which I am urging, is to eradicate the fatal disconnection of subjects which kills the vitality of our modern curriculum. There is only one subject-matter for education, and that is Life in all its manifestations. Instead of this single unity, we offer children—Algebra, from which nothing follows; Geometry, from which nothing follows; Science, from which nothing follows; History, from which nothing follows; a Couple of Languages, never mastered; and lastly, most dreary of all, Literature, represented by plays of Shakespeare, with philological notes and short analyses of plot and character to be in substance committed to memory. Can such a list be said to represent Life, as it is known in the midst of the living of it? The best that can be said of it is, that it is a rapid table of contents which a deity might run over in his mind while he was thinking of creating a world, and had not yet determined how to put it together.

Let us now return to quadratic equations. We still have on hand the unanswered question. Why should children be taught their solution? Unless quadratic equations fit into a connected curriculum, of course, there is no reason to teach anything about them. Furthermore, extensive as should be the place of mathematics in a complete culture, I am a little doubtful whether for many types of boys algebraic solutions of quadratic equations do not lie on the specialist side of mathematics. I may here remind you that as yet I have not said anything of the psychology or the content of the specialism, which is so necessary a part of an ideal education. But all that is an evasion of our real question, and I merely state it in order to avoid being misunderstood in my answer.

Quadratic equations are part of algebra, and algebra is the intellectual instrument which has been created for rendering clear the quantitative aspects of the world. There is no getting out of it. Through and through the world is infected with quantity. To talk sense, is to talk in quantities. It is no use saying that the nation is large,—How large? It is no use saying that radium is scarce,—How scarce? You cannot evade quantity. You may fly to poetry and to music, and quantity and number will face you in your rhythms and your octaves. Elegant intellects which despise the theory of quantity, are but half developed. They are more to be pitied than blamed. The scraps of gibberish, which in their school-days were taught to them in the name of algebra, deserve some contempt.

This question of the degeneration of algebra into gibberish, both in word and in fact, affords a pathetic instance of the uselessness of reforming educational schedules without a clear conception of the attributes which you wish to evoke in the living minds of the children.

A few years ago there was an outcry that school algebra was in need of reform, but there was a general agreement that graphs would put everything right. So all sorts of things were extruded, and graphs were introduced. So far as I can see, with no sort of idea behind them, but just graphs. Now every examination paper has one or two questions on graphs. Personally, I am an enthusiastic adherent of graphs. But I wonder whether as yet we have gained very much. You cannot put life into any schedule of general education unless you succeed in exhibiting its relation to some essential characteristic of all intelligent or emotional perception. It is a hard saying, but it is true; and I do not see how to make it any easier. In making these little formal alterations you are beaten by the very nature of things. You are pitted against too skilful an adversary, who will see to it that the pea is always under the other thimble.

Reformation must begin at the other end. First, you must make up your mind as to those quantitative aspects of the world which are simple enough to be introduced into general education; then a schedule of algebra should be framed which will about find its exemplification in these applications. We need not fear for our pet graphs, they will be there in plenty when we once begin to treat algebra as a serious means of studying the world. Some of the simplest applications will be found in the quantities which occur in the simplest study of society. The curves of history are more vivid and more informing than the dry catalogues of names and dates which comprise the greater part of that arid school study. What purpose is effected by a catalogue of undistinguished kings and queens? Tom, Dick, or Harry, they are all dead. General resurrections are failures, and are better postponed. The quantitative flux of the forces of modern society is capable of very simple exhibition. Meanwhile, the ideas of the variable, of the function, of rate of change, of equations and their solution, of elimination, are being studied as an abstract science for their own sake. Not, of course, in the pompous phrases with which I am alluding to them, here, but with that iteration of simple special cases proper to teaching.

If this course be followed, the route from Chaucer to the Black Death, from the Black Death to modern Labour troubles, will connect the tales of the medieval pilgrims with the abstract science of algebra, both yielding diverse aspects of that single theme, Life. I know what most of you are thinking at this point. It is that the exact course which I have sketched out is not the particular one which you would have chosen, or even see how to work. I quite agree. I am not claiming that I could do it myself. But your objection is the precise reason why a common external examination system is fatal to education. The process of exhibiting the applications of knowledge must, for its success, essentially depend on the character of the pupils and the genius of the teacher.

Of course I have left out the easiest applications with which most of us are more at home. I mean the quantitative sides of sciences, such as mechanics and physics.

Again, in the same connection we plot the statistics of social phenomena against the time. We then eliminate the time between suitable pairs. We can speculate how far we have exhibited a real causal connection, or how far a mere temporal coincidence. We notice that we might have plotted against the time one set of statistics for one country and another set for another country, and thus, with suitable choice of subjects, have obtained graphs which certainly exhibited mere coincidence. Also other graphs exhibit obvious causal connections. We wonder how to discriminate. And so are drawn on as far as we will.

But in considering this description, I must beg you to remember what I have been insisting on above. In the first place, one train of thought will not suit all groups of children. For example, I should expect that artisan children will want something more concrete and, in a sense, swifter than I have set down here. Perhaps I am wrong, but that is what I should guess. In the second place, I am not contemplating one beautiful lecture stimulating, once and for all, an admiring class. That is not the way in which education proceeds. No; all the time the pupils are hard at work solving examples, drawing graphs, and making experiments, until they have a thorough hold on the whole subject. I am describing the interspersed explanations, the directions which should be given to their thoughts. The pupils have got to be made to feel that they are studying something, and are not merely executing intellectual minuets.

Finally, if you are teaching pupils for some general examination, the problem of sound teaching is greatly complicated. Have you ever noticed the zig-zag moulding round a Norman arch? The ancient work is beautiful, the modern work is hideous. The reason is, that the modern work is done to exact measure, the ancient work is varied according to the idiosyncrasy of the workman. Here it is crowded, and there it is expanded. Now the essence of getting pupils through examinations is to give equal weight to all parts of the schedule. But mankind is naturally specialist. One man sees a whole subject, where another can find only a few detached examples. I know that it seems contradictory to allow for specialism in a curriculum especially designed for a broad culture. Without contradictions the world would be simpler, and perhaps duller. But I am certain that in education wherever you exclude specialism you destroy life.

We now come to the other great branch of a general mathematical education, namely Geometry. The same principles apply. The theoretical part should be clear-cut, rigid, short, and important. Every proposition not absolutely necessary to exhibit the main connection of ideas should be cut out, but the great fundamental ideas should be all there. No omission of concepts, such as those of Similarity and Proportion. We must remember that, owing to the aid rendered by the visual presence of a figure, Geometry is a field of unequalled excellence for the exercise of the deductive faculties of reasoning. Then, of course, there follows Geometrical Drawing, with its training for the hand and eye.

But, like Algebra, Geometry and Geometrical Drawing must be extended beyond the mere circle of geometric ideas. In an industrial neighborhood, machinery and workshop practice form the appropriate extension. For example, in the London Polytechnics this has been achieved with conspicuous success. For many secondary schools I suggest that surveying and maps are the natural applications. In particular, plane-table surveying should lead pupils to a vivid apprehension of the immediate application of geometric truths. Simple drawing apparatus, a surveyor's chain, and a surveyor's compass, should enable the pupils to rise from the survey and mensuration of a field to the construction of the map of a small district. The best education is to be found in gaining the utmost information from the simplest apparatus. The provision of elaborate instruments is greatly to be deprecated. To have constructed the map of a small district, to have considered its roads, its contours, its geology, its climate, its relation to other districts, the effects on the status of its inhabitants, will teach more history and geography than any knowledge of Perkin Warbeck or of Behren's Straits. I mean not a nebulous lecture on the subject, but a serious investigation in which the real facts are definitely ascertained by the aid of accurate theoretical knowledge. A typical mathematical problem should be: Survey such and such a field, draw a plan of it to such and such a scale, and find the area. It would be quite a good procedure to impart the necessary geometrical propositions without their proofs. Then, concurrently in the same term, the proofs of the propositions would be learnt while the survey was being made.

Fortunately, the specialist side of education presents an easier problem than does the provision of a general culture. For this there are many reasons. One is that many of the principles of procedure to be observed are the same in both cases, and it is unnecessary to recapitulate. Another reason is that specialist training takes place—or should take place—at a more advanced stage of the pupil's course, and thus there is easier material to work upon. But undoubtedly the chief reason is that the specialist study is normally a study of peculiar interest to the student. He is studying it because, for some reason, he wants to know it. This makes all the difference. The general culture is designed to foster an activity of mind; the specialist course utilises this activity. But it does not do to lay too much stress on these neat antitheses. As we have already seen, in the general course foci of special interest will arise; and similarly in the special study, the external connections of the subject drag thought outwards.

Again, there is not one course of study which merely gives general culture, and another which gives special knowledge. The subjects pursued for the sake of a general education are special subjects specially studied; and, on the other hand, one of the ways of encouraging general mental activity is to foster a special devotion. You may not divide the seamless coat of learning. What education has to impart is an intimate sense for the power of ideas, for the beauty of ideas, and for the structure of ideas, together with a particular body of knowledge which has peculiar reference to the life of the being possessing it.

The appreciation of the structure of ideas is that side of a cultured mind which can only grow under the influence of a special study. I mean that eye for the whole chessboard, for the bearing of one set of ideas on another. Nothing but a special study can give any appreciation for the exact formulation of general ideas, for their relations when formulated, for their service in the comprehension of life. A mind so disciplined should be both more abstract and more concrete. It has been trained in the comprehension of abstract thought and in the analysis of facts.

Finally, there should grow the most austere of all mental qualities; I mean the sense for style. It is an aesthetic sense, based on admiration for the direct attainment of a foreseen end, simply and without waste. Style in art, style in literature, style in science, style in logic, style in practical execution have fundamentally the same aesthetic qualities, namely, attainment and restraint. The love of a subject in itself and for itself, where it is not the sleepy pleasure of pacing a mental quarterdeck, is the love of style as manifested in that study.

Here we are brought back to the position from which we started, the utility of education. Style, in its finest sense, is the last acquirement of the educated mind; it is also the most useful. It pervades the whole being. The administrator with a sense for style hates waste; the engineer with a sense for style economises his material; the artisan with a sense for style prefers good work. Style is the ultimate morality of mind.

But above style, and above knowledge, there is something, a vague shape like fate above the Greek gods. That something is Power. Style is the fashioning of power, the restraining of power. But, after all, the power of attainment of the desired end is fundamental. The first thing is to get there. Do not bother about your style, but solve your problem, justify the ways of God to man, administer your province, or do whatever else is set before you.

Where, then, does style help? In this, with style the end is attained without side issues, without raising undesirable inflammations. With style you attain your end and nothing but your end. With style the effect of your activity is calculable, and foresight is the last gift of the gods to men. With style your power is increased, for your mind is not distracted with irrelevancies, and you are more likely to attain your object. Now style is the exclusive privilege of the expert. Whoever heard of the style of an amateur painter, of the style of an amateur poet? Style is always the product of specialist study, the peculiar contribution of specialism to culture.

English education in its present phase suffers from a lack of definite aim, and from an external machinery which kills its vitality. Hitherto in this address I have been considering the aims which should govern education. In this respect England halts between two opinions. It has not decided whether to produce amateurs or experts. The profound change in the world which the nineteenth century has produced is that the growth of knowledge has given foresight. The amateur is essentially a man with appreciation and with immense versatility in mastering a given routine. But he lacks the foresight which comes from special knowledge. The object of this address is to suggest how to produce the expert without loss of the essential virtues of the amateur. The machinery of our secondary education is rigid where it should be yielding, and lax where it should be rigid. Every school is bound on pain of extinction to train its boys for a small set of definite examinations. No headmaster has a free hand to develop his general education or his specialist studies in accordance with the opportunities of his school, which are created by its staff, its environment, its class of boys, and its endowments. I suggest that no system of external tests which aims primarily at examining individual scholars can result in anything but educational waste.

Primarily it is the schools and not the scholars which should be inspected. Each school should grant its own leaving certificates, based on its own curriculum. The standards of these schools should be sampled and corrected. But the first requisite for educational reform is the school as a unit, with its approved curriculum based on its own needs, and evolved by its own staff. If we fail to secure that, we simply fall from one formalism into another, from one dung-hill of inert ideas into another.

In stating that the school is the true educational unit in any national system for the safeguarding of efficiency, I have conceived the alternative system as being the external examination of the individual scholar. But every Scylla is faced by its Charybdis—or, in more homely language, there is a ditch on both sides of the road. It will be equally fatal to education if we fall into the hands of a supervising department which is under the impression that it can divide all schools into two or three rigid categories, each type being forced to adopt a rigid curriculum. When I say that the school is the educational unit, I mean exactly what I say, no larger unit, no smaller unit. Each school must have the claim to be considered in relation to its special circumstances. The classifying of schools for some purposes is necessary. But no absolutely rigid curriculum, not modified by its own staff, should be permissible. Exactly the same principles apply, with the proper modifications, to universities and to technical colleges.

When one considers in its length and in its breadth the importance of this question of the education of a nation's young, the broken lives, the defeated hopes, the national failures, which result from the frivolous inertia with which it is treated, it is difficult to restrain within oneself a savage rage. In the conditions of modern life the rule is absolute, the race which does not value trained intelligence is doomed. Not all your heroism, not all your social charm, not all your wit, not all your victories on land or at sea, can move back the finger of fate. Today we maintain ourselves. Tomorrow science will have moved forward yet one more step, and there will be no appeal from the judgment which will then be pronounced on the uneducated.

We can be content with no less than the old summary of educational ideal which has been current at any time from the dawn of our civilisation. The essence of education is that it be religious.

Pray, what is religious education?

A religious education is an education which inculcates duty and reverence. Duty arises from our potential control over the course of events. Where attainable knowledge could have changed the issue, ignorance has the guilt of vice. And the foundation of reverence is this perception, that the present holds within itself the complete sum of existence, backwards and forwards, that whole amplitude of time, which is eternity.

8. Education as Growth

One of the happy by-products of the new interest in open education in the United States is the rediscovery of the work of John Dewey, perhaps the greatest (and certainly the most maligned and misunderstood) educational philosopher this country has produced. Curiously, Dewey has been more widely read, and has had a more profound impact on practice, in England than in the United States. His discussion of education as growth remains fresh and perceptive.

It is sometimes supposed that it is the business of the philosophy of education to tell what education *should* be. But the only way of deciding what education should be, at least, the only way which does not lead us into the clouds, is discovery of what actually takes place when education really occurs. And before we can formulate a philosophy of education we must know how human nature is constituted in the concrete; we must know about the working of actual social forces; we must know about the operations through which the basic raw materials are modified into something of greater value. The need for a philosophy of education is thus fundamentally the need for finding out what education really *is*. . . .

What then is education when we find actual satisfactory specimens of it in existence? In the first place, it is a process of development, of growth. And it is the *process* and not merely the result that is important. A truly healthy person is not something fixed and completed. He is a person whose processes and activities go on in such a way that he will continue to be healthy. Similarly, an educated person is a person who has the power to go on and get more education. . . . Nothing would be more extraordinary if we had a proper system of education than the assumption, now so commonly made, that the mind of the individual is naturally averse to learning, and has to be either browbeaten or coaxed into action. Every mind, even of the youngest, is naturally or inherently seeking for those modes of active operation that are within the limits of his capacity. . . .

While the raw material and the starting point of growth are found in native capacities, the environing conditions which it is the duty of the educator to furnish are the indispensable means by which intrinsic possibilities are developed. Native capacities are the beginning, the starting point. They are not the end, and they do not of themselves decide the end. . . . The great problem of the adult who has to deal with the young is to see, and to feel deeply as well as merely to see intellectually, the forces that are moving in the young; but it is to see them as possibilities, as signs and promises; to interpret them, in short, in the light of what they may come to be. . . .

The essential weakness of the old and traditional education was not just that it emphasized the necessity for provision of definite subject matter and activities. These things *are* necessities for anything that can rightly be called education. The weakness and evil was that the imagination of educators did not go beyond provision of a fixed and rigid environment of subject matter, one drawn moreover from sources al-

From John Dewey, "The Need for a Philosophy of Education," in Reginald D. Archambault, *John Dewey on Education* (New York: Random House, 1964), pp. 3, 4, 5, 6, 8–14.

together too remote from the experiences of their pupil. What is needed in the new education is more attention, not less, to subject matter and to progress and technique. But when I say more, I do not mean more in quantity of the same old kind. I mean an imaginative vision that sees that no prescribed and ready-made scheme can possibly determine the exact subject matter that will best promote the educative growth of every individual young person; that every new individual sets a new problem; that he calls for at least a somewhat different emphasis in subject matter presented. There is nothing more blindly obtuse than the convention which supposes that the matter actually contained in textbooks of arithmetic, history, geography, etc. is just what will further the educational development of all children.

But withdrawal from the hard and fast and narrow contents of the old curriculum is only the negative side of the matter . . . complete isolation is impossible in nature. The young live in some environment whether we intend it or not, and this environment is constantly inter-acting with what children and youth bring to it, and the result is the shaping of their interests, minds and character—either educatively or mis-educatively. If the professed educator abdicates his responsibility for judging and selecting the kind of environment that his best under-standing leads him to think will be conducive to growth, then the young are left at the mercy of all the unorganized and casual forces of the modern social environment that inevitably play upon them as long as they live. In the educative environment, the knowledge, judgment and experience of the teacher is a greater, not a smaller, factor, than it is in the traditional school. The difference is that the teacher operates not as a magistrate set on high and marked by arbitrary authority but as a friendly co-partner and guide in a common enterprise. . . . Indeed, the new educational processes require much more planning ahead on the part of teachers than did the old—for there the planning was all done in advance by the fixed curriculum. . . .

. . . The acquisition of skills is not an end in itself. They are things to be put to use, and that use is their contribution to a common and shared life. They are intended, indeed, to make an individual more capable of self-support and of self-respecting independence. But unless this end is placed in the context of services rendered to others, skills gained will be put to an egoistic and selfish use, and may be employed as means of a trained shrewdness in which one person gets the better of others . . .

What is true of the skills acquired in school, is true also of the knowledge gained there. The educational end and the ultimate test of the value of what is learned is its use and application in carrying on and improving the common life of all. . . .

There are two outstanding reasons why in the conditions of the world at present the philosophy of education must make the social aim of education the central article in its creed. . . . It is necessary to prepare the coming generation for a new and more just and humane society which is sure to come, and which, unless hearts and minds are prepared by education, is likely to come attended with all the evils that result from social changes effected by violence.

The other need especially urgent at the present time is connected with the unprecedented wave of nationalistic sentiment, of racial and national prejudice, of readiness to resort to the ordeal of arms to settle questions that animate the world at the present time. The schools of the world must have somehow failed grievously or the rise of this evil spirit on so vast a scale would not have been possible. . . . Unless the schools of the world can engage in a common effort to rebuild the spirit of common understanding, of mutual sympathy and good will among all peoples and races, to exorcise the demon of prejudice, isolation and hatred, the schools themselves are likely to be submerged by the general return to barbarism, which is the sure outcome of present tendencies if they go on unchecked by the forces which education alone can evoke and fortify.

* * *

What is Progressive Education? . . . All of the [progressive] schools . . . exhibit as compared with traditional schools a common emphasis upon respect for individuality and for increased freedom; a common disposition to build upon the nature and experience of the boys and girls that come to them, instead of imposing from without external subject-matter and standards. They all display a certain atmosphere of informality, because experience has proved that formalization is hostile to genuine mental activity and to sincere emotional expression and growth. Emphasis upon activity as distinct from passivity is one of the common factors. And again I assume that there is in all of these schools a common unusual attention to the human factors, to normal social relations, to communication and intercourse which is like in kind to that which is found in the great world beyond the school doors; that all alike believe that these normal human contacts of child with child and of child with teacher are of supreme educational importance, and that all alike disbelieve in those artificial personal relations which have been the chief factor in isolation of schools from life. So much at least of common spirit and purpose we may assume to exist. And in so far

From John Dewey, "Progressive Education and the Science of Education," *Progressive Education,* vol. 5 (1928), reprinted in Martin S. Dworkin, ed., *Dewey on Education* (New York: Teachers College Press, Classics in Education, No. 3, 1965).

we already have the elements of a distinctive contribution to the body
of educational theory: respect for individual capacities, interests and
experience; enough external freedom and informality at least to enable teachers to become acquainted with children as they really are;
respect for self-initiated and self-conducted learning; respect for activity as the stimulus and center of learning; and perhaps above all
belief in social contact, communication, and cooperation upon a normal
human plane . . .

. . . Even if it be true that everything which exists could be measured—if only we knew how—that which does *not* exist cannot be
measured. And it is no paradox to say that the teacher is deeply concerned with what does not exist. For a progressive school is primarily
concerned with growth, with a moving and changing process, with *transforming* existing capacities and experiences; what already exists by way
of native endowment and past achievement is subordinate to what it
may become. Possibilities are more important than what already exists,
and knowledge of the latter counts only in its bearing upon possibilities. . . .

Organization and administration are words associated together in
the traditional scheme, hence organization conveys the idea of something external and set. But reaction from this sort of organization only
creates a demand for another sort. Any genuine intellectual organization is flexible and moving, but it does not lack its own internal principles of order and continuity. An experimental school is under the
temptation to improvise its subject matter. It must take advantage of
unexpected events and turn to account unexpected questions and interests. Yet if it permits improvisation to dictate its course, the result
is a jerky, discontinuous movement which works against the possibility
of making any important contribution to educational subject matter.
Incidents are momentary, but the use made of them should not be
momentary or short-lived. They're to be brought within the scope of a
developing whole of content and purpose, which is a whole because it
has continuity and consecutiveness in its parts. There is no single subject matter which all schools must adopt, but in every school there
should be some significant subject matters undergoing growth and
formulation.

An illustration may help make clearer what is meant. Progressive
schools set store by individuality, and sometimes it seems to be thought
that orderly organization of subject matter is hostile to the needs of
students in their individual character. But individuality is something
developing and to be continuously attained, not something given all
at once and ready-made. . . . A child's individuality cannot be found
in what he does or in what he consciously likes at a given moment; it
can be found only in the connected course of his actions. Consciousness

of desire and purpose can be genuinely attained only toward the close of some fairly prolonged sequence of activities. Consequently some organization of subject matter reached through a serial or consecutive course of doings, held together within the unity of progressively growing occupational projects, is the only means which corresponds to real individuality. So far is organization from being hostile to the principle of individuality.

II

How Children Learn
and Grow

The trend toward open education in England and the United States is not a sudden departure from the past. In England, in particular, the trend has developed gradually over the last half century, out of the insights and experiments of innumerable teachers, "heads" (principals), local and national school inspectors and advisers, and college and university professors. "I should love to be able to believe that the primary teachers who in the past three decades have brought about such important changes in outlook did so from a base of deeply considered educational policy coupled with splendid practical foresight concerning the needs of society in the future," Sybil Marshall of the University of Sussex, herself an important figure in the change, has written; "but looking back myself over thirty-plus years of teaching I cannot honestly do so." Like Kanga in Winnie-the-Pooh, *these teachers, out of simple concern for the children in their care, "did a Good Thing without knowing it." The revolution came about, as Miss Marshall puts it, because "teachers in infant classes everywhere began to act on a professional instinct that told them a happy child actively involved in something he wanted to do was getting more out of his educational opportunities than a passive, bored child politely resisting most of the instruction dished out to him in 30-minute parcels."*

That "professional instinct" gained official encouragement in 1934 with the publication of the "Hadow Committee" Report on Infant and Nursery Schools, *which some advocates of informal education regard as the best piece of educational writing of the century. The "instinct" was heightened again during the Second World War, when urban teachers and their pupils were evacuated because of the bombing raids.*

"Teachers who had taught the same stuff in the same city classrooms for fifteen years found themselves in the fens, or the hills, or the farmlands," John Blackie recalls, where they were "the only link with the children's background, and they simply had to re-think what they were doing."

The rethinking was made all the more necessary by the fact that the teachers found themselves with the children twenty-four hours a day; forced into a new relationship with their students, they began to see them in a different light. Learning was clearly something that went on all the time, not just during school hours; hence the teachers were persuaded that it is fruitless to try to segment and compartmentalize children or learning. They were even more persuaded when the war ended. Back in their traditional classrooms, teachers found themselves confronting a roomful of children who had been dispersed all over England, some of whom, consequently, could read fluently, some poorly, and some not at all. Faced with a range of background, knowledge, and ability several times the prewar norm, teachers once again found it necessary to improvise.

While the change in primary education has grown out of the pragmatic responses of a great many teachers, it is backed by a substantial body of theory about the nature of children and the ways in which they grow and learn, as well as about the nature of knowledge, the processes of instruction, and the aims of education. Like Molière's bourgeois gentilhomme, *the teachers discovered after the fact that they had been speaking prose all along. Their intuitive responses have strong theoretical support in the writings and work of Rousseau, Friedrich Froebel, the nineteenth-century "inventor" of the kindergarten, Maria Montessori, John Dewey, Rachel Macmillan, Susan Isaacs, Jerome Bruner, and most important, the Swiss biologist-psychologist-epistemologist, Jean Piaget—the "giant of the nursery," as he has been called—whose forty-odd years of study of the development of children's mental processes are just beginning to be appreciated in the United States.*

Chapter II of this part, therefore, is devoted to a number of statements of the theories of learning, teaching, and child development that underlie, and provide a theoretical justification for, open education.

1. A Unified Approach to Learning

Joseph Featherstone, a contributing editor of The New Republic *and lecturer at Harvard University's John F. Kennedy School of Government, was the first American journalist to describe the revolution in English primary education. A series of three articles which he wrote in*

The New Republic in 1967 (August 19, September 2, and September 9)
played a major role in calling the attention of American teachers, edu-
cationists, and writers to the growth of informal English primary schools.

In the selection that follows, Featherstone describes what he calls
"the initial, tentative outline of what may one day be fully articulated
as a unified approach to children's learning"—an outline drawn from
his careful study of informal English primary schools. The selection is
drawn from the long essay Featherstone wrote introducing the series of
booklets, Informal Schools in Britain Today, *produced by the Anglo-*
American Primary School Project.

Since for some time it has seemed quite natural for good English teachers
to relate their teaching practice to basic theories of child development, the influence of developmental psychology has been important—
which is, of course, not to say that ordinary teachers spend a great
deal of their time boning up on Jean Piaget and other developmental
theorists. The ideas are more or less in the air. In recent years, the
fusion of developmental theory and practice has been easiest to see in
the area of mathematics, where certain assumptions, such as Piaget's
idea that young children need to build up a store of experience before
they can evolve abstractions, are beginning to pervade good classrooms
and shape the direction of further innovation.

Part Two of The Plowden Report, *The Growth of the Child,* shows
this broad developmental influence at work, in its cogent arguments
that each child develops at a separate pace, and that, therefore, teaching
practice ought to work from individual differences. Behind practices in
good schools, the report points out, there is a definite view of teaching:
"It lays special stress on individual discovery, on first-hand experience,
and on opportunities for creative work. It insists that knowledge does
not fall neatly into separate compartments, and that work and play are
not opposite, but complementary."

Yet, while developmental theory plays a role, and while a body of
intertwined theory and pedagogical practice is slowly emerging from
the work of good British schools, it is important for Americans to note
that the headteachers most successful in practice are sometimes unable
to formulate their aims clearly . . . What teachers do, however, is
essentially the result of personal experience, worked out in classrooms
over time. Another way of saying this is to admit that we still know little
about children's learning or the art of teaching. The best educational

From Joseph Featherstone, *An Introduction: Informal Schools in Britain Today,*
Anglo-American Primary School Project (New York: Citation Press, 1917), pp.
21–24, 50, 54, 55–57. Copyright © 1971 by School's Council Publication. Used by
permission of Citation Press, a division of Scholastic Magazines, Inc.

practice outstrips the best theory; the lesson of good English primary schools is not that theory is unimportant, but that it can only be of practical use when it has a living relationship to teachers and children. Without an intimate connection to the realm of practice, theory grows abstract and sterile, academic in the bad sense of the word.

Emerging slowly and unevenly from work in good schools is the initial, tentative outline of what may one day be fully articulated as a unified approach to children's learning. It has been developed by teachers and specialists working together with children in actual classrooms, not handed down, full-blown by curriculum planners and outside experts. Common sense indicates that curricula should, in general, follow, not precede, theories of the nature of learning, and, indeed in much work with young children this has been the case. Yet, in work with children of all ages in good British schools, one keeps coming across instances where practice has led the way, where the internal momentum of work in one subject area—maths, say, or music—has carried teachers and children to a point that one could not have anticipated.

Good practitioners in Britain, as in the US, are, nonetheless, operating on general principles that seem to be confirmed both by theory and by the work of outstanding schools. Each would no doubt emphasize something different, but a bald summary which many might agree with would run something like this: Teachers should assume that childhood is something to be cherished, which does not mean, sentimentalized; good teachers start with the lives of children here and now, and proceed from their experiences toward more disciplined inquiry. Teaching is more effective if teachers can find out where the learner is, by watching him in action and talking with him; learning is more effective if it grows out of the interests of the learner. (And of course interests are not just there, like flowers waiting to bud: they are formed and cultivated by good teaching.) Both experience and theory suggest that active learning is better than passive rote. Giving children choices within a planned environment helps them develop initiative, competence, and an ability to think for themselves. A good curriculum offers children knowledge worth learning: it is essential that children learn reading skills, for example, but they must also see the point of being literate, taking an interest in books and knowing how to use them. Teaching practice ought to reflect the enormous diversities among children, treating them as individuals, and proceeding, when possible, from their strengths, rather than from their weaknesses. For this reason, and not for any intrinsic merit in informality, teachers ought to be able to set informal schedules, physical arrangements, and patterns of grouping and instruction. No technique or organizational change is as important as the social and emotional context of learning; the ordinary relationships among children, and between adults and children, are of supreme educational importance. This is why much learning in a good educational setting receives direction and takes shape in the course of ordinary conversation.

The aim of education expressed in this primary school movement is to influence children to become thinking, autonomous, sensitive people. The need for a wholeness of approach does not absolve schools from a particular responsibility for cultivating the power of children's minds. Teachers ought to work with a mental picture of the qualities of a good thinker: confidence, concentration, and an ability to make informed, rather than haphazard, guesses and estimates; mental habits of synthesizing ideas and making analogies; the capacity to communicate thoughts and feelings in various forms of expression.

Put in these bare terms, all this is familiar, perhaps too familiar, to Americans. This is the theory still preached in certain lecture halls in American education colleges. To practitioners in many US schools it must seem a counsel of perfection, and therefore of despair. Administrators and teachers in US schools often agree with these principles, but they seldom feel able to convert understanding into practice. A host of what are seen as necessary evils overwhelms them: "tracking" (equivalent of the British "streaming"); IQ and standard tests; formal lessons; a specified curriculum; set hours for set subjects; emphasis on reading skills, with no concern for literacy; discipline; fixed ages for entering school and for promotion; the imperatives of administration. The work of good British primary schools invites us to ponder these supposed necessities . . .

It is clear that word of British schools reaches America at a time of great cultural, as well as political ferment. Indeed, the American vogue for the British reforms must be seen as one element in a complex and many-sided cultural movement. Within the schools, there is nearly a pedagogical vacuum. Few reformers have suggested practical alternatives to existing approaches, and even fewer have deigned to address themselves to working teachers. The slow, grass-roots nature of the British reforms, with their emphasis on the central importance of good teaching, has a great appeal for people in US schools, who are, too often, victims of the "general-staff" mentality of school reformers and managers. Blacks and other minorities are interested in new approaches simply because they reject all the workings of the schools as they stand; some of the best of the community control ventures, such as the East Harlem Block Schools, have been promoting informal methods, as have some of the parent-controlled Headstart programmes. And there are growing numbers of middle- and upper-middle-class parents in favour of "open" and "informal," not to mention "free" schooling, even though they are vague about the pedagogical implications of these terms. . . .

. . . It would be essential, in order to promote good practice today, to abandon many old and fruitless ideological debates . . . Take the issue of freedom, for example. Informality, letting children talk and move about, is helpful in establishing a setting in which a teacher can find out about pupils; it helps children to learn actively, to get into the habit of framing purposes independently, and of using their own judgment. But this sort of freedom is a means to an end, not a goal in itself. As a goal, freedom is meaningless; as e e cummings once put it, "freedom is a breakfast food."

There is a long philosophic debate concerning the nature of freedom. There are always those who argue that freedom is something negative —freedom *from*—and those who argue, on the contrary, that freedom is a positive thing. From Plato to libertarians like Kant, the second line of argument has linked freedom with knowledge—the free use of reason or intelligence—and, sometimes, action with knowledge. Whatever the merits of the positions in this fascinating, perpetual debate, it seems much more appropriate for educators of children to conceive of freedom in the second sense, not a momentary thing at all, but the result of a process of discipline and learning. Informality is pointless unless it leads to intellectual stimulation. Too many children in US "free" schools are not happy, and one suspects that part of the reason is that they are bored with their own lack of intellectual progress. As William Hull remarks in the course of a trenchant critique of the current fad for "open" education: "Children are not going to be happy for very long in schools in which they realize they are not accomplishing very much."

Or take the issue of Authority. That it even *is* an issue is a mark of deep cultural confusion, as well as a reflection of the frequent misuse of legitimate authority in America. Whatever their politics, good practitioners assume as a matter of course that teachers have a responsibility to create a decent learning environment, that there is what might be called a natural, legitimate basis for the authority of an adult working with children. In his profound little book, *The Lives of Children,* George Dennison outlines the nature of this legitimate authority:

> Its attributes are obvious: adults are larger, more experienced, possess more words, have entered into prior agreement with themselves. When all this takes on a positive instead of a merely negative, character, the children see the adults as protectors and as sources of certitude, approval, novelty, skills. In the fact that adults have entered into prior agreements, children intuit a seriousness and a web of relations in the life that surrounds them. If it is a bit mysterious, it is also impressive and somewhat attractive; they see it quite correctly as the way of the world, and they are not indifferent to its benefits and demands . . . (for a child) the adult

is his ally, his model—and his obstacle (for there are natural conflicts, too, and they must be given their due).

This ought to be self-evident, but isn't. Disciplinary matters and the
rest of the structure of authority in many US schools work against the
exercise of legitimate authority. And thus, in reaction against the schools,
people foolishly assume that all adult guidance is an invasion of children's freedom. Actually, in a proper informal setting, as John Dewey
once pointed out, adults ought to become more important: ". . . basing
education upon personal experience may mean more multiplied and
more intimate contacts between the mature and the immature than ever
existed in the traditional schools, and consequently more rather than
less guidance."

It ought to be obvious that if you remove adult authority from a
group of children, you are not necessarily giving them freedom; often,
you are sentencing them to the tyranny of their peers, as David Riesman
pointed out in *The Lonely Crowd*'s criticism of the "progressive"
schools. Unacknowledged adult authority has a way of creeping back in
subtle and manipulative ways that can be more arbitrary than its formal
exercise.

Another false issue in the debates on "open" education is the distinction between education as something formed from without, the
question of whether to have a child-centered or an adult-directed classroom. There are, to be sure, certain respects in which the best informal
practice is child-centered. The basic conception of learning, after all,
reflects the image of Piaget's child-inventor, fashioning an orderly model
of the universe from his varied encounters with experience. Plainly, the
child's experience is the starting point of all good informal teaching. But
passive teaching has no more place in a good informal setting than have
passive children. Active teaching is essential. Indeed, one of the appeals of this sort of approach, to experienced teachers, is that it transforms the teacher's role: from enacting somebody else's text or curriculum, the teacher moves towards working out his own responses to
children's learning.

Still another confusion on the American scene is the notion that
liberalizing the repressive atmosphere of the schools—which is of course
worth doing for its own sake—will automatically promote children's
intellectual development. America needs more humane schools, but she
also needs a steady concern for intellectual progress and workmanship.
Without this concern, it is unlikely that any sort of cumulative development will be achieved or that standards will ever be established by which
to judge good and bad work.

2. "At the heart of the educational process lies the child."

The Plowden Committee's approach to education is reflected in the way the Committee chose to title its report. It did not call the document "English Primary Education" or "The Education of Primary School Children," but rather "Children and Their Primary Schools." In the title, as in the schools the Committee admired most, the children come first, and the schools are defined as theirs—not the teachers', nor the local education authorities', nor the taxpayers'.

The orientation is made explicit in the body of the report itself. "At the heart of the educational process lies the child," the Committee flatly states in its opening paragraphs. "No advances in policy, no acquisitions of new equipment have their desired effect unless they are in harmony with the nature of the child. . . ." It follows, therefore, that the clearer their understanding of how children learn and grow, the more effective teachers are likely to be. In the selection that follows, the Plowden Committee sets forth its view of what is known about learning and child development.

At the heart of the educational process lies the child. No advances in policy, no acquisitions of new equipment have their desired effect unless they are in harmony with the nature of the child, unless they are fundamentally acceptable to him. We know a little about what happens to the child who is deprived of the stimuli of pictures, books and spoken words; we know much less about what happens to a child who is exposed to stimuli which are perceptually, intellectually or emotionally inappropriate to his age, his state of development, or the sort of individual he is. We are still far from knowing how best to identify in an individual child the first flicker of a new intellectual or emotional awareness, the first readiness to embrace new sets of concepts or to enter into new relations.

Knowledge of the manner in which children develop, therefore, is of prime importance, both in avoiding educationally harmful practices and in introducing effective ones. In the last 50 years much work has been done on the physical, emotional and intellectual growth of children. There is a vast array of facts, and a number of general principles have been established. This chapter is confined to those facts which have

From *Children and Their Primary Schools* ("The Plowden Report"), vol. 1, Para. 9–11, 73–75, 518–535. Reprinted by permission of the Controller of Her Britannic Majesty's Stationery Office.

greatest educational significance and those principles which have a direct bearing on educational practice and planning.

Among the relevant facts are the early growth of the brain, compared with most of the rest of the body; the earlier development of girls compared with boys; the enormously wide variability in physical and intellectual maturity amongst children of the same age, particularly at adolescence, and the tendency nowadays for children to mature physically earlier than they used to. Among the principles are present-day concepts about critical or sensitive periods, about developmental "sequence" (that is, events which are fixed in their order but varying in the age at which the sequence begins); about the poorer resilience of boys than girls under adverse conditions; and, above all, about the complex and continuous interaction between the developing organism and its environment. Under this last rather cumbersome phrase lies the coffin of the old nature-versus-nurture controversy. A better understanding of genetics and human biology has ended the general argument, and provided a clearer picture of what is implied when we talk of changes in measured intelligence during a child's development.

. . . Moral development is closely associated with emotional and social development. The child forms his sense of personal worth and his moral sense from early experiences of acceptance, approval, and disapproval. Out of an externally imposed rule of what is permitted arises a sense of what ought to be done and an internal system of control: in everyday terms, a conscience. The very young child, limited in understanding, acts according to strict rules, even though he often breaks them. What is right and wrong relates closely to what his parents say and to the situation arising in the home. Later, as the child develops intellectually and lives with others, his sense of right and wrong derives from a wider circle and becomes more qualified; the rules of a game are seen to be arrived at by a consensus, and therefore modifiable by common agreement. Even so, the 11 year old still has a fairly crude and concrete sense of justice. It appears doubtful whether an autonomous conscience is established before adolescence.

Although much work has been done on physical growth during puberty, little study has been made of the progress towards emotional maturity and stability. The subject is important not only because it might be relevant to the age of transfer from primary to secondary education, but also because of the increasing number of children who begin to enter puberty before they leave the primary school. Psychological changes at adolescence centre on the search for personal identity, for independence arising out of increasing competence and self-esteem, and on the development of maturer sexual attitudes and behaviour. The emotional changeability of some adolescent children is well recognised, and may sometimes lead to quite bewildering and contradictory behaviour. But opinion differs widely as to whether it is the majority or a minority of adolescents who behave in this way. Both biological and cultural factors affect adolescent behaviour, and physical and psychological changes do not necessarily coincide. There is also conflicting evidence as to whether the transition from primary to secondary school, selective or unselective, is a cause of distress. What seems most likely is that it brings to the surface psychological difficulties in vulnerable children.

This chapter has been concerned with some aspects of the growth and development of children on which sound educational theory and practice must be built. We have taken them into account in making our recommendations on the issues discussed in the Report. It is not possible to summarise further this material but the more obvious implications of it can be stated baldly as follows:

(a) Individual differences between children of the same age are so great that any class, however homogeneous it seems, must always be treated as a body of children needing individual and different attention.

(b) Until a child is ready to take a particular step forward, it is a waste of time to try to teach him to take it.

(c) Even at the ages with which we are concerned, boys and girls develop at different rates and react in different ways—a fact which needs particular attention because we have co-educational schools. Boys are more vulnerable to adverse environmental circumstances than girls. Both reach maturity earlier than they did.

(d) Though I.Q. scores are a useful rough indication of potential ability, they should not be treated as infallible predictors. Judgments which determine careers should be deferred as long as possible.

(e) Since a child grows up intellectually, emotionally and physically at different rates, his teachers need to know and take account of his "developmental age" in all three respects. The child's physique, personality, and capacity to learn develop as a result of continuous interaction between his environmental and genetical inheritance. Unlike the genetic factors, the environmental factors are, or ought to be, largely within our control. . . .

. . . Towards the end of the nineteenth century, research began to supplement general observation of children's methods of learning, though even now it would be difficult to find many teachers who could relate what they are doing in the classroom to any particular piece of research. Here, as in other fields, the pace has recently quickened. Many teachers, for example, are following research on various methods of teaching children to read. More fundamentally, an encouraging number of teachers are beginning to concern themselves with theories of learning. By their practical work in the classroom, teachers have perhaps as much to contribute to psychology as the psychologists to educational practice.

Research into the ways in which children learn has produced, broadly, two interpretations of the learning process. One, which is still dominant in the United States, and is associated with the names of Thorndike, Hull, Pavlov and Skinner among others, is essentially behaviourist. It is concerned with simple and complex operant conditioning, the place of reinforcement in learning, habit formation and the measurement of various kinds of stimulus-response behaviour. Much of the more recent work derives from animal studies and its main relevance is to motor learning, though some work has been done on the learning of information, concepts and skills by children and adults. It does not offer very much direct help to teachers since, for the most part, the motives and sequence of children's learning are too complicated for analysis in terms of simple models. A recent review of programmed learning suggests that even simple segments of learning do not always conform closely to models of learning theory such as Skinner's. It is in a whole situation with a history behind it that a child or adult learns. Success in using a machine may be due as much to relaxation from anxiety or to a feeling of self-importance as to the small steps used in linear programming on the Skinner system. Most teachers of young children have seen the value of a gradual build-up of vocabulary in the teaching of reading. But they have also had evidence of the rapid strides that children can make when a particular book holds such interest for them that they are determined to read it quickly.

Some of the experiments of the behaviourists confirm that prolonged periods of routine practice in, for example, computation or handwriting reduce rather than improve accuracy. This is a lesson which is particularly relevant to schools working on traditional lines.

A second school of research, which is dominant in Great Britain and apparently gaining ground in the United States, is associated with the names of Baldwin, Isaacs, Luria, Bruner, and in particular Jean Piaget. This school is interested in discovering the ground plan of the growth of intellectual powers and the order in which they are acquired. One of its most important conclusions is that the great majority of primary school children can only learn efficiently from concrete situations, as lived or described. From these situations, children acquire concepts in every area of the curriculum. According to Piaget, all learning calls for organisation of material or of behaviour on the part of the learner, and the learner has to adapt himself and is altered in the process. Learning takes place through a continuous process of interaction between the learner and his environment, which results in the building up of consistent and stable patterns of behaviour, physical and mental. Each new experience reorganises, however slightly, the structure of the mind and contributes to the child's world picture.

Piaget's thought, which influenced the 1931 Report and our own, is not easy to understand. It is almost impossible to express in other than technical terms. Although he is not primarily an educationalist, his work has important implications for teachers. His observations of the sequence in the development of children's concepts are being tested on samples of children in many countries and these tests are tending to confirm his main findings. Much more investigation is needed on the extent to which the school environment and the guidance and teaching provided by teachers can accelerate children's progress. The effect of social expectations on the way children learn also calls for study. Nevertheless Piaget's explanations appear to most educationalists in this country to fit the observed facts of children's learning more satisfactorily than any other. It is in accord with previous research by genetic psychologists and with what is generally regarded as the most effective primary school practice, as it has been worked out empirically. The main implications of that practice are described in the following paragraphs and, where relevant, reference is made to the support given them by the Piagetian school of thought.

Play is the central activity in all nursery schools and in many infant schools. This sometimes leads to accusations that children are wasting their time in school: they should be "working." But this distinction between work and play is false, possibly throughout life, certainly in the primary school. Its essence lies in past notions of what is done in school hours (work) and what is done out of school (play). We know now that, play—in the sense of "messing" about either with material objects or with other children, and of creating fantasies—is vital to children's learning and therefore vital in school. Adults who criticise teachers for allowing children to play are unaware that play is the principal means of learning in early childhood. It is the way through which children reconcile their inner lives with external reality. In play, children gradually develop concepts of causal relationships, the power to discriminate, to make judgements, to analyse and synthesise, to imagine and to formulate. Children become absorbed in their play and the satisfaction of bringing it to a satisfactory conclusion fixes habits of concentration which can be transferred to other learning.

From infancy, children investigate the material world. Their interest is not wholly scientific but arises from a desire to control or use the things about them. Pleasure in "being a cause" seems to permeate children's earliest contact with materials. To destroy and construct involves learning the properties of things and in this way children can build up concepts of weight, height, size, volume and texture.

Primitive materials such as sand, water, clay and wood attract young

children and evoke concentration and inventiveness. Children are also
stimulated by natural or manufactured materials of many shapes, colours
and textures. Their imagination seizes on particular facets of objects
and leads them to invent as well as to create. All kinds of causal connections are discovered, illustrated and used. Children also use objects
as symbols for things, feelings and experiences, for which they may lack
words. A small girl may use a piece of material in slightly different ways
to make herself into a bride, a queen or a nurse. When teachers enter
into the play activity of children, they can help by watching the connections and relationships which children are making and by introducing,
almost incidentally, the words for the concepts and feelings that are
being expressed. Some symbolism is unconscious and may be the means
by which children come to terms with actions or thoughts which are not
acceptable to adults or are too frightening for the children themselves.
In play are the roots of drama, expressive movement and art. In this
way too children learn to understand other people. The earliest play of
this kind probably emerges from play with materials. A child playing
with a toy aeroplane can be seen to take the role of both the aeroplane
and the pilot apparently simultaneously. All the important people of
his world figure in this play: he imitates, he becomes, he symbolises.
He works off aggression or compensates himself for lack of love by
"being" one or other of the people who impinge on his life. By acting
as he conceives they do, he tries to understand them. Since children tend
to have inflexible roles thrust on them by adults, they need opportunities
to explore different roles and to make a freer choice of their own. Early
exploration of the actions, motives and feelings of themselves and of
others is likely to be an important factor in the ability to form right
relationships, which in its turn seems to be a crucial element in mental
health. The difficulties of blind and deaf children whose play is restricted
show how much play enriches the lives of ordinary children. Adults can
help children in this form of play, and in their social development, by
references to the thoughts, feelings and needs of other people. Through
stories told to them, children enter into different ways of behaving and of
looking at the world, and play new parts.

Just as adults relive experience in thought or words, so children play
over and over the important happenings of their lives. The repetition is
usually selective. Children who re-enact a painful scene repeatedly are
not doing it to preserve the pain but to make it bearable and understandable. They incorporate those parts of the difficult situation which are
endurable and add others as their courage and confidence grows. This
is one of the ways in which they bring under control the feelings of
frustration which must be experienced by those who are dependent on
the will and love of adults. This kind of play can preserve self esteem

by reducing unpleasant experiences to size, and reinforce confidence by dwelling on success.

Much of children's play is "cultural" play as opposed to the "natural" play of animals which mainly practices physical and survival skills. It often needs adult participation so that cultural facts and their significance can be communicated to children. The introduction into the classroom of objects for hospital play provides opportunities for coming to terms with one of the most common fears. Similarly the arrival of a new baby in the family, the death of someone important to the child, the invention of space rockets or new weapons may all call for the provision of materials for dramatic play which will help children to give expression to their feelings as a preliminary to understanding and controlling them. Sensitivity and observation are called for rather than intervention from the teacher. The knowledge of children gained from "active" observation is invaluable to teachers. It gives common ground for conversation and exchange of ideas which it is among the most important duties of teachers to initiate and foster.

A child's play at any given moment contains many elements. The layers of meaning may include a highly conscious organisation of the environment, exploration of physical and social relationships and an expression of the deepest levels of fantasy. Wide ranging and satisfying play is a means of learning, a powerful stimulus to learning, and a way to free learning from distortion by the emotions. Several writers have recently emphasised the importance of a period of play and exploration in new learning as, for example, in mathematics and science. Adults as well as children approach new learning in this way. The child is the agent in his own learning. This was the message of the often quoted comment from the 1931 Report: "The curriculum is to be thought of in terms of activity and experience rather than of knowledge to be acquired and facts to be stored." Read in isolation, the passage has sometimes been taken to imply that children could not learn from imaginative experience and that activity and experience did not lead to the acquisition of knowledge. The context makes it plain that the actual implication is almost the opposite of this. It is that activity and experience, both physical and mental, are often the best means of gaining knowledge and acquiring facts. This is more generally recognised today but still needs to be said. We certainly would not wish to undervalue knowledge and facts, but facts are best retained when they are used and understood, when right attitudes to learning are created, when children learn to learn. Instruction in many primary schools continues to bewilder children because it outruns their experience. Even in infant schools, where innovation has gone furthest, time is sometimes wasted in teaching written "sums" before children are able to understand what they are doing. The N.C.D.S.

Survey shows that 17 per cent of children start doing sums in infant schools before the age of five and a half.

The intense interest shown by young children in the world about them, their powers of concentration on whatever is occupying their attention, or serving their immediate purposes, are apparent to both teachers and parents. Skills of reading and writing or the techniques used in art and craft can best be taught when the need for them is evident to children. A child who has no immediate incentive for learning to read is unlikely to succeed because of warnings about the disadvantages of illiteracy in adult life. There is, therefore, good reason for allowing young children to choose within a carefully prepared environment in which choices and interest are supported by their teachers, who will have in mind the potentialities for further learning. Piaget's observations support the belief that children have a natural urge to explore and discover, that they find pleasure in satisfying it and that it is therefore self-perpetuating. When children are learning new patterns of behaviour or new concepts they tend both to practise them spontaneously and to seek out relevant experience, as can be seen from the way they acquire skills in movement. It takes much longer than teachers have previously realised for children to master through experience new concepts or new levels of complex concepts. When understanding has been achieved, consolidation should follow. At this stage children profit from various types of practice devised by their teachers, and from direct instruction. Children will of course vary in the degree of interest that they show and their urge to learn will be strengthened or weakened, as we have suggested in Chapter 3, by the attitudes of parents, teachers and others with whom they identify themselves. Apathy may result when parents show no interest, clamp down on children's curiosity and enterprise, tell them constantly not to touch and do not answer their questions. Children can also learn to be passive from a teacher who allows them little scope in managing their own affairs and in learning. A teacher who relies only on instruction, who forestalls children's questions or who answers them too quickly, instead of asking the further questions which will set children on the way to their own solution, will disincline children to learn. A new teacher with time and patience can usually help children who have learnt from their teachers to be too dependent. Those who have been deprived at home need more than that. Their self-confidence can only be restored by affection, stability and order. They must have special attention from adults who can discover, by observing their responses, what experiences awaken interest, and can seize on them to reinforce the desire to learn.

External incentives such as marks and stars, and other rewards and punishments, influence children's learning mainly by evoking or representing parents' or teachers' approval. Although children vary temperamentally in their response to rewards and punishments, positive incentives are generally more effective than punishment, and neither is as damaging as neglect. But the children who most need the incentive of good marks are least likely to gain them, even when, as in many primary schools, they are given for effort rather than for achievement. In any case, one of the main educational tasks of the primary school is to build on and strengthen children's intrinsic interest in learning and lead them to learn for themselves rather than from fear of disapproval or desire for praise.

Learning is a continuous process from birth. The teacher's task is to provide an environment and opportunities which are sufficiently challenging for children and yet not so difficult as to be outside their reach. There has to be the right mixture of the familiar and the novel, the right match to the stage of learning the child has reached. If the material is too familiar or the learning skills too easy, children will become inattentive and bored. If too great maturity is demanded of them, they fall back on half remembered formulae and become concerned only to give the reply the teacher wants. Children can think and form concepts, so long as they work at their own level, and are not made to feel that they are failures.

Teachers must rely both on their general knowledge of child development and on detailed observation of individual children for matching their demands to children's stages of development. This concept of "readiness" was first applied to reading. It has sometimes been thought of in too negative a way. Children can . . . be led to want to read, provided that they are sufficiently mature. Learning can be undertaken too late as well as too early. Piaget's work can help teachers in diagnosing children's readiness in mathematics, and gives some pointers as to how it can be encouraged.

At every stage of learning children need rich and varied materials and situations, though the pace at which they should be introduced may vary according to the children. If children are limited in materials, they tend to solve problems in isolation and fail to see their relevance to other similar situations. This stands out particularly clearly in young children's learning of mathematics. Similarly, children need to accumulate much experience of human behaviour before they can develop moral concepts. If teachers or parents are inconsistent in their attitudes or contradict by their behaviour what they preach, it becomes difficult for children to develop stable and mature concepts. Verbal explanation, in advance of understanding based on experience, may be an obstacle to learning, and children's knowledge of the right words may conceal from teachers their lack of understanding. Yet it is inevitable that children will pick up words which outstrip their understanding. Discussion with other children and with adults is one of the principal ways in which children check their concepts against those of others and build up an objective view of reality. There is every justification for the conversation which is a characteristic feature of the contemporary primary school. One of the most important responsibilities of teachers is to help children to see order and pattern in experience, and to extend their ideas by analogies and by the provision of suitable vocabulary. Rigid division of the curriculum into subjects tends to interrupt children's trains of thought and of interest and to hinder them from realising the common elements in problem solving. These are among the many reasons why some work, at least, should cut across subject divisions at all stages in the primary school.

3. The Rationale of Informal Education

The power of Lillian Weber's insights into the nature of informal education stems from the fact that she combines the instincts and experience of a classroom teacher with a scholar's concern for theory. In Chapter 4 of her book, The English Infant School and Informal Education, *from which the following excerpt is taken, Professor Weber traces the eclectic, theoretical roots of open education, with particular attention to the influence of Jean Piaget, Susan Isaacs, a great English child psychiatrist and educator, and her husband, Nathan Isaacs, an important educator and writer in his own right, who popularized and reconciled the work of Piaget and Susan Isaacs.*

The literature that synthesizes a description of the infant school entity, including the multiplicity of illustrations and case studies, the Hadow Report, The Plowden Report, and the Nuffield case histories, had as its touchstone a view of how children grow and learn. Each report put itself into the context of a common voice by presenting this view in its initial section—as rationale for practice. It was an analysis common to all and accounted for the infant school entity: the similarity within a nonprescriptive system. It underlay the *idea* of informal education.

The idea was indeed one of the conditions of informal education— even the key condition. As I came to comprehend this, the idea could no longer be dismissed as the "background of common premises" presupposed at the outset of this study. My observations had added facets that did not entirely fit my previous premises, and so the idea had to be found by dissection. Such dissection started with my observations, continued with gleanings from conversations with heads, and concluded with analysis of the literature that confirmed and sharpened my recall.

Central to the conversations was always a child: What does he need? What is he *interested* in? What is he *ready* for? What are his *purposes?* How does *he* follow them? What are *his questions?* What is he *playing?* These questions about children *seemed* to be uppermost in developing plans for the classroom, for plans were made not from the vantage point of a syllabus of demands which a child had to meet, but with relevance to children in the most immediate way. A plan fitted itself *to* a child. It was developed in response to the pace and internal pattern of his own growth and in support of his own purposes. It was developed through watching a child, studying him at his moments of deepest involvement in play.

Play was important to headmistresses. They often talked of curiosity. They seemed to trust curiosity as a motive force. They seemed to trust that the forces of a child's development had a forward propulsion— "how else would he adapt at all?" Their job was to keep this momentum going, to maintain it. But it was a *child* who learned and so he had to be *allowed* to do so. A free situation, activity, movement, a rich environment were just the implements, the ways of unimpeding a child's own propulsion. The prototype of a teacher as controller, or "giver-out," and a child as "taker-in" inevitably gave way to a different concept, still developing in England. With such an analysis as base, *teaching* gives way to *helping* learning. It is a difficult concept and its implications are still being explored and reached for in the real test of actual practice. The first part of the idea, however—the centrality of a child's development and school as a support for continuation of this development—is certainly accepted.

The idea had long roots, its present unique integration and character being an offshoot strand, woven from many such strands, of the main root of the history of education—from Montaigne, Rousseau, Owen, Pestalozzi, Froebel, Montessori, McMillan, Dewey. Rereading the English formulations of educational ideas and practice that were familiar to me in another way in the United States, I understood for the first time the controversies, the intellectual probing, the relationship of each part to the whole. Respect for play and spontaneous activity as a child's natural way of learning, respect for natural development, came from these early roots. From Montessori came the technique of individual work, of a child's own pace and progression, and the introduction into the classroom of more concrete materials to add to the already existent influence of the Froebelian "gifts." From Dewey came the emphasis on the experiencing of social relationships and community, on learning generated from a child's activities and his experiences. The English continued to stress individual work stemming from individual interests, but the sharing of communal functions and responsibilities in school was added to the accumulating implications of an educational method supportive of natural development.

Susan and Nathan Isaacs

Out of this background of eclecticism, too, grew the ideas of Susan Isaacs. Examining and questioning the research and researchers of her time—from Freud to Piaget—she searched for clarity. Her context of English educational history and thought and the realities of the developing English educational organization modified all ideas and practices, American or otherwise, as she absorbed them. With the way paved by a climate of opinion supporting education as implementing the natural development of children, her work found a receptive audience. She joined this conscious continuity of English development without resting her ideas solely and separately on her psychoanalytic insights, using the combined insights of past and current thinking, her self-awareness as teacher and human being and, most of all, her careful observation and study of children. From this study, Susan Isaacs produced solid evidence to bolster what had been largely a philosophic belief, and English ideas on education were thereby deepened. She gave an objective base, in the context of genetic psychology, to previous generalities on natural development, on the deep connections linking inner and outer reality, emotional and intellectual life.

The connections between Susan Isaacs's developmental descriptions of children and actual school practice were still further spelled out in the writings of Nathan Isaacs. Isaacs developed the implications in his wife's work on intellectual development and reconciled these with Piaget's analyses of the development of the mental structures in a child. The slight differences between Susan Isaacs's and Piaget's analysis, probed in a mutually respectful exchange of letters, were made compatible. Nathan Isaacs accepted as corrective to previous estimates of developmental time Piaget's descriptions of the long process of constant accommodation and reaccommodation before the formation of logical relations. Susan Isaacs had considered Piaget's description an *inflexible* doctrine of stages in this time process. This she called a "pseudo-biological sequence, totally independent of experience." Her own view was that stages were *broadly* descriptive of levels of development and sequence. It was not hard for Nathan Isaacs to reconcile these positions. And with this reconciliation, Nathan Isaacs demonstrated to English teachers the reinforcement to their own beliefs that could come from an understanding of Piaget. His contribution is considered monumental.

From the Froebel Institute, from the Nuffield Foundation, from other analyzers of informal education, have come writings which accept the formulations of the two Isaacs as core for the continuing development and extension of the definition and application of informal education. These formulations confirmed the conclusions of their own systematic observation of children, and made clear the continuity in the thinking of English informal educators on how children learn, as well as the consensus on the informal organization of the infant school.

The Plowden Report, absorbing all of this past, reaffirmed this common context of idea basic to English infant education. A child, the Report affirmed, is active agent in his own learning, and the internal processes of mental structuring and restructuring contain their own self-perpetuating propulsion. The Plowden Report defined the school role in terms that follow this analysis: provision of environment to support a child's individual and unsegmentalized development; inclusion of the play life that is vital to a child's reconciliation of inner and outer reality and that is vital to his development of judgment and discrimination; allowance to each child for the time necessary for his own individual mental synthesizing.

The Plowden summary is only a summary. Presented in more full-bodied detail filtered through all these roots and the more recent contributions, the English idea based itself on the knowledge of the child's development gained from study, much of it a kind of "watching," a systematic observation of a child acting spontaneously in a natural situation. The attempt is to understand the meaning of each piece of a child's development in a total context. While all research was used, Susan Isaacs's critique of research methods was certainly accepted.

> Without such a background of the total responses of children to whole situations, partial studies of this or that response to limited experimental problems may be no more than sterile and misleading artifacts.
>
> One could take point after point of those appearing on the various rating scales or developmental schedules, and show how far they are from being single trends which can be measured in themselves apart from specified total situations.

Most important, about children under five years she noted, *"what a child does for one person under certain conditions is not a reliable index of what he may do for another person in another situation."* (Italics in original) Elsewhere she continued:

> For our own convenience in study, we may pick out now one, now another of the aspects of growth, but they are never separate in fact. Nor can we ever say that one dominates the rest. It is always the whole child who plays and laughs, who quarrels and loves, who

thinks and asks questions, through all the hours of his day and all the years of his childhood.

It is in this frame that The Plowden Report criticizes behaviorist learning theory and any analysis based on the theories of segmentalized learning.

A Child: Active, Unique, Whole

The students of child development in England see each child as unique and active in all aspects of his individual development. No one of these aspects can be separated, they reason, because development rests within the whole that is a child. These three characterizations of a child—as active, individual, and whole—are focal to English analyses. It is only for purposes of definition that the characterizations, always intertwined in English discussion, are separated.

Recognition of a child's *active* thrust, described also as curiosity, is in the English view unavoidable, for "without some native drive towards active growth normality would not have been achieved at all." It is this active growth, a child's active construction and reconstruction of his own development, that is described in Nathan Isaacs's explication of Piaget:

> Piaget's work as a whole has made plain all the vital education that goes on in the child quite independently of the set educational processes, and above all in his first few years, before those processes have even begun. Indeed, by far the most important portion of his intellectual growth is achieved by himself, through the direct working of the interchange cycle by which he actively learns to take in all the main features and the general make-up of the physical and social world around him.
>
> This process of absorbing and organizing experiences round the activities that produce them Piaget calls *"assimilation."* He regards it as our most fundamental process of learning and growth, which indeed goes on for the rest of our lives. However, assimilation is always being modified by an accompanying process of *accommodation.* Many situations or objects resist the activity patterns the child tries on them, and in so doing impose some changes on these patterns themselves. Still others yield *new* results which go to enrich the range or scope of the patterns.

This active thrust, this assimilative, accommodative process is always individual. A child is born a unique individual, and development is *in* this individual. His world of inner needs and meanings is personal, lived out in the human relationships into which he is born and with people whose world has been equally individually determined. He has particular, specific bits of experiences and particular, specific expectations, and it is these that he brings to his relationships—meeting people with differing experiences and expectations. His development is individual and uneven in pattern and pace and made even more individual by the personal route of his interests. Having made these observations, the English do not *strive for* or seek to *produce* individuality. They *recognize* it, and the individuality of learning—in process and in product— underlies all discussion of theory and practice in English education.

The active and individual process of assimilation-accommodation- reaccommodation occurs within a *child* who is a whole—uncompart- mentalized, unsegmentalized—with his social, emotional, and intellectual development inextricably linked. The links are forged from the very nature of a child's existence in the world with others. The English description of these links gives additional meaning to the accommodative and reaccommodative process, to the restructuring and correction of the first learning. All familiar education components are reexamined in this context.

The wholeness, the inextricable links, long predate school. There can be no separation of inner needs and outer adaptations. A child is born into the human relationship and thereby immediately into adaptation with another who is separate.

> It is the child's first experience of instinctual frustration, or un- satisfied longing for food and love in the intervals between satis- faction, which provides the first stimulus to his appreciation of the external world. When he wants the breast and it is not there, he cries out for it and eventually it comes to him. When he wants warmth and comfort and sheltering arms, he can obtain these by his cries directed to those who will bring him what he wants. But some gap between desire and satisfaction there must inevitably be, and since it is persons who bring the child relief, he appre- hends his dissatisfactions in personal terms.

But while his world is personal, it is never separate.

> . . . his external world, as soon as knowledge of it begins to awaken, is understood very largely in terms of that with which he is already familiar—himself and his own feelings.

His inner needs are the *force* for his outer adaptations, but they are *necessarily* exercised in a context that makes for adaptation and develop- ment. From the very beginning his unique development, both emotional and intellectual, is affected by the reality of his environment and the reality of his relationships with the people in that environment.

As with all mammalian young, the child's first relations are with his kind rather than directly with the physical world. . . . But whilst recognising this . . . one cannot shut one's eyes to the influence of direct contact with the physical world. The child makes a partial discovery of the limits which the physical world sets to his activities surely almost as early as he comes to know other human beings as persons.

Reaccommodation: Fantasy and Play

The discrepancies between what children expect of the world and of people and what they actually meet in interaction with these are an impetus for the reaccommodation that is *also* one of expectancies. Susan Isaacs discusses the corrective to fantasy that children derive from real experience:

> . . . phantasy itself more and more takes up reality into its own tissue . . . there is a progressive penetration of feeling and phantasy by experience. . . .
>
> What imaginative play does . . . is to create practical *situations*. . . .
>
> Whilst it is certainly true that the *first* value which the physical world has for the child is as a canvas upon which to project his personal wishes and anxieties, and that his first form of interest in it is one of dramatic representation, yet, as I have already urged, this does not prevent him from getting direct actual experience of physical processes. Physical events become, in fact, the test and measure of reality. There is no wheedling or cajoling or bullying or deceiving *them*. Their answer is *yes* or *no*, and remains the same to-day as yesterday. It is surely they that wean the child from personal schemas, and give content to "objectivity."

Ruth Griffiths similarly speaks of fantasy and its necessary role in intellectual development:

> Imagination is, in fact, the child's method not so much of avoiding the problems presented by environment, but of overcoming those difficulties in a piecemeal and indirect fashion, returning again and again in imagination to the problem, and gradually developing a socialized attitude which finally finds expression at the level of overt action and adapted behaviour.

The importance of the external environment, of play, of a free situation in which a child *can use* the environment *and* play, all are implied

in these analyses of reaccommodation, these analyses of how expectancies are corrected.

At no point was play conceived by these thinkers as an "extra," without bearing on intellectual development. Even in its important function
of pleasure and release it was always related to learning. As Susan
Isaacs stated:

> Play is the child's means of living, and of understanding life.
> . . . it helps him to achieve inner balance and harmony through
> the active expression of his inner world of feelings and impulses,
> and of the people that dwell in his inner world.

Play was related to reworkings:

> The child *re-creates* selectively those elements in past situations
> which can embody his emotional or intellectual need of the
> present. . . .

Thus, though the first impetus to re-creation was the inner pressure of
feeling and fantasy, the re-creation was made in an external world, with
children using external things, being forced to adapt, and thus led to
correcting themselves by the encounter. And sometimes the re-creation,
which implied a remembering of past feeling, implied also an ability to
see what cohered, what went with what, what future was implied in the
past.

Peel sums this up, restating it in Piagetian terms:

> Play also has an important role in the intellectual growth of the
> child, being at once the cause and expression of changes from
> egocentric to objective judgments and of growth of language and of
> reversible action and judgment.

Reaccommodation: Social Interchange and the Adult

It is not only a child's play but his relations to other people, even as
he plays, that lead to corrections, reaccommodations, better adaptation
to reality, and finally, learning. The intense egocentricity of a child,
intellectually and emotionally, is corrected through companionship with
children and interaction with their different purposes and points of view.
From his companionship with other children he gains perspective about
adults in his life, and can find allies against their pressures. Since social
interchange, discussion, and differing points of view are essentials for
this operation of the challenge of discrepancies, a *free* social situation is
necessary. This free social interchange is "fed" best in a challenging
atmosphere, rich in possible activities that can provide the "stuff" of

discussion. The need for the free social interchange is expressed by
Susan Isaacs:

> . . . if we deprive him of free speech with his fellows, we take
> away from him one of the most valuable means of intellectual and
> social growth.

> It is not the mere presence of other children but active participa-
> tion with them, doing real things together, an active interchange of
> feeling and experience, which educates the child.

The correctives to discrepancies that result from the *actual* relationships help define the adult role. That role was spelled out in the basic
biological relationship of care and the basic obligation to allow a child's
growing away from his need for adult care. It was spelled out, too, in
the adult's obligation to provide and to extend the environment as
necessary for each child's learning, and in the adult's obligation to offer
the correctives of reality and discussions of additional and alternate
possibilities that might encourage and support a child's own restruc-
turings of his first reference frames. Much of Susan Isaacs' *Intellectual
Growth in Young Children* is an account of such discussions and the
resulting corrections and self-corrections.

> . . . we tried to use our parental powers in such a way as to reduce
> the children's need for them.

> To shirk or evade the responsibility for satisfying his emotional
> and social requirements is for society's representatives to act as
> bad parents themselves.

> . . . the educator cannot teach the child, nor can he learn for him.
> All that he can do is to create such situations as will give the child
> opportunities to learn for himself. In this regard he has to control
> the social environment of the child as well as the physical, in order
> to make it possible for the child to learn. The child can, however,
> learn only by his own real experience, whether social or physical,
> and the educator must not stand between the child and his ex-
> perience.

Because the *actual* reality in which a child lives is the corrective
impelling him to new accommodations, the adult's role should be mild,
sane, but strong enough to support a child's growth, strong enough to
help him to further reaccommodations.

Words, verbal commandments, abstract principles, have no significance except in so far as they are embodied in the actions and the personalities of the people upon whom he is dependent. What parents and teachers are, and his real experience of them, is infinitely more important than what they profess or claim to be, or tell him he ought to be.

If he neither finds fulfilment of his phantastic dreads in the outer world, nor is left at their mercy in his inner world by having no external support, but is slowly educated by a tempered, real control, mild and understanding, appropriate to each situation as it arises, he is led forward on the path of reality and towards all those indirect satisfactions in the real world, the sublimatory activities.

All of these—real experiences in play, in social life, and in companionship with other children and adults—are the avenues of correctives to a child's inner fantasies, necessarily played out in an external world. They are the avenues of correctives to the discrepancies of a child's first structurings, and the process of learning in these many ways can be subsumed under the infant assimilative-accommodative-reaccommodative drive. This drive is the bedrock on which the English rest their belief in the active thrust of development, in curiosity. It is on this that they rest belief in play, in experience, in the wholeness of children as emotional, social, and intellectual beings, their belief in a child's active individuality.

Language and Experience

The English analysis of this prior-to-school learning also permeates their discussion of the relationships of language and experience. Susan Isaacs emphasized in all her books the importance of the mother's early talk to her child, the stimulation to language from ordinary living. The stimulation as the English see it occurs in an active relationship of interaction and experiencing, not only in a verbal relationship.

Obviously, the argument has never been about the importance of language. The English are a literate people.

It is only as [a child] learns to use words that he can effectively draw upon the experience of other people and deal with problems less immediate and concrete than those involved in actual handling of material.

Equally, the argument is certainly not about the importance of adults to a child's development of language.

> [A child] has little power for sustaining conversation as such, and
> needs the opportunity to talk with people who talk well. Grown-ups
> or older children who will listen to what he has to say and respond
> appropriately are of far more value to him than specific lessons in
> clear speech.

But, the impulse to speech and the development of speech involve more.
"It is under the stimulus of wishes and emotions that language develops
most freely and fully." And this stimulus, these drives, are exerted in
interaction with an external world. "It is only in the most intimate contact with activity and actual experience that he begins to talk freely and
to exchange ideas." Thus, on verbalism as a mode of teaching a child
new material, Susan Isaacs writes:

> . . . words are only tokens of experience, and are either empty or
> confusing to the children until they have had enough immediate
> experience to give the words content. With young children, words
> are valueless unless they are backed by the true coin of things and
> doings. They have their own place as aids to experience, and to
> clear thought about experience.

> The evidence . . . shows . . . that one of the main stimuli to
> the expression of reasoning in words comes to young children from
> their practical interests in play, and from the discussions and argu-
> ments which these play interests give rise to. When occasion calls
> for it, they break into theoretical statement, although they cannot
> yet *sustain* verbal thinking.

> Verbal reasoning and the clear formulation of judgments are no
> more than wave-crests upon the flow of young children's thought.
> . . . Verbal thinking can hardly yet be *sustained in its own right,*
> in the earlier years. It draws its vitality from the actual problems of
> concrete understanding and of manipulation in which it takes its
> rise, and the solution of which it furthers.

Verbal Reasoning and Preverbal Logic

The earliest learning, the prior-to-school learning, could not be taken
for granted in order to concentrate on what came later. Study of coherent thinking, for one thing, could not *begin* with verbal reasoning;
the earliest learning was, in effect, a preview of the later verbal reasoning, which would be inexplicable on its own. A child's manipulations
and actions had a coherence, a sense not matched by his unstable, feeble
verbal reasoning. This coherence revealed the whole network of his
earlier learnings, his adaptations. The preverbal working logic of a child
—the frame of the first accommodations he made from his engagement

with outer reality—was the base for the later development of his ability to *formulate* logically, to think in language about experience.

> Right from the start we build up in our minds a kind of working model of the world around us; in other words, a model of a world of persisting and moving objects and recurring happenings set in a framework of space and time and showing a regular order.

> . . . though he starts from practically nothing but the familiar "blooming, buzzing confusion" of his first few weeks, there is formed in his mind, by the age of 5–6 years, a far-reaching *functional working model* of his surrounding world.

> His verbal thinking, however, lags far behind his practical logic. He can deal with the problems of right and left, of degree and order, and of social relations, *in practice,* long before he can handle the same issues in words, and in thought divorced from action.

The discussion of verbal thinking in the context of its prehistory had its parallel for all forms of learning. Susan Isaacs stressed that *all* complicated ways of functioning had beginnings in prior growth, psychologically and physically. They were not independent, separate, newly appeared qualities, but had a history of implication and of possibility. The mental process as it unfolded was propelled by its own prehistory. The beginnings may have been momentary and unstable, unmaintained in the balance of forces and meanings in which they appared. But their appearance at all, the conditions under which they appeared and what happened to them as they appeared, was part of the history of their new function in a new stage of development. New "stages" were descriptive of a major balance of drives and major functions. In between the stages the lines were blurred and unstable. Susan Isaacs described the unevenness of the pattern of learning in the individual, or the "many disparate types of behaviour coexisting in the same children":

> Thus any final theory of development must allow for the fact that these different levels of functioning may occur alongside each other, and that the presence of one type of behaviour under certain conditions does not justify us in assuming that no other would be found at the same age, in different circumstances. Intellectual growth certainly shows a psychological coherence; but this coherence has the elasticity and vital movement of a living process, not the rigid formality of a logical system. It is most fully expressed in the *continuity* of development in noetic synthesis, and in the

way in which the later and more highly integrated forms draw their life from the simpler and earlier.

The Case for Continuity

Unevenness and individuality of patterning in the learning process make even stronger the case for continuity. Nathan Isaacs quite explicitly urged the educator to intervene only in ways "continuous with the real structure that is already there." He stated that the educator *must* be aware of this real structure because the learning that predates school, that is, the prehistory of school learning, is the *base* for school learning.

> Certainly outward teaching which is not related to inward growth, and to the stage which this has already reached, becomes peculiarly futile and meaningless—as meaningless as progressive educationists have long contended it to be. By the same token any approach which is not based on *clear and full understanding* of that growth must inevitably fail, even if the utmost will to educate from within is there.

It was inherent in the obligations of the adult role and therefore of the school that the individual, unsegmentalized character of the assimilative-accommodative process should be understood, its continuity fostered.

The adult has the obligation not only to provide continuity, but also to provide extension. A child's prehistory of development propels him and readies him for further experience. The adult and the school provide experiences that a child can use to extend and correct his previous conclusions, whereupon new possibilities are posed. But a child's use of all new material is dependent on his own ability to make connections from new to old.

The same was felt to be true of the adult's and the school's obligation to allow *time*. Piaget's research indicated that a child needed time for all his very gradual adaptation to reality, a prolonged time of active engagement with the many concrete situations in the environment. The school's obligation was to allow *more* time than had previously been thought necessary, to allow whatever time was needed by an individual child.

The School Environment

Following from such an analysis of the primary process of interaction, the provision of rich environment is not just as supplemental enrichment or as "aids to teaching," but as the material of action, the material on which accommodation, and therefore further reordering and rebuilding and stretching of the frame of reference, happens. It is the rich environment experienced in differing ways that is the "stuff" or material of discussion. As expressed by Nathan Isaacs in an analysis derived from Piaget, because human mental growth "springs essentially out of the interaction between the child and the world he finds around him, . . . [and] the character of that world must be constantly affecting his growth," the quality of the environment becomes important. Growth will, to some extent, turn on the "helping or hindering features of the world." Fitting Piaget's view to his own linking of inner and outer growth and the importance of the environment, Nathan Isaacs says:

> Piaget's basic view of the very process of inward growth is . . . pivoted on the continual cycle of interchanges between the child and the outward world: his action on that world and its reaction on him. It is this cycle that is the very motor of the child's mental advance, which proceeds by a constant rhythm of in turn assimilating outward reality and accommodating to it. . . . Thus outward reality is as all-important for inward growth as the inward impetus in the child himself.

In this analysis, people, the social world, are included in the term "outward reality." The educator, meanwhile, is responsible for ensuring the quality of the environment and he takes the primary process of interaction as guide. He prepares the environment after familiarizing himself, as best he can, with the world that surrounds a child.

Curiosity and A Child's Own Question

If a setting is prepared that allows engagement with the world to continue, then curiosity—the active thrust of a child as agent of his own development—can be trusted to extend his engagement. "A really rich and stimulating school environment engenders interests which in turn engender the energy to pursue them."

And so the implications of believing and trusting in the description of a child's active thrust of development, the active and independent nature of the assimilative-accommodative process, become clear. The school must *allow* a child to *be* the active agent. It must be aware of and use a *child's* question, a *child's* purpose. A child's own question arising through *his own* experience is what will forward the next step in learning. The Nuffield *Teacher's Guide,* in fact, insists on the necessity for a child's own question:

> . . . however little we know of children's questions, we may be sure that, although they will often accept problems other people put to them, their own mean more to them. When they are allowed

to exchange other people's problems for their own, it is striking how much more enthusiastic and ready to apply themselves they are. *Their own questions seem to be the most significant and to result most often in careful investigations.*

It is however not only the active thrust that is stressed in this discussion, it is the *individual* patterning of a child's integration of his learning. A child helps determine the direction of his development by the experiences he chooses to pursue and the questions he asks of these.

Susan Isaacs applies this analysis in another context when she discusses how we can help fatherless children.

> Moreover, the child has to find his *own* way out. Just as children show their difficulties in different ways, so they will find different ways of overcoming them, whatever sort of help we give. We cannot determine the ultimate effect of his experience upon the child's character and social attitudes. We cannot say that his development shall take this line rather than that, nor decide what sort of person he shall become in the end.

A child can be the active agent only in the free situation. The free situation allows the expectancies of a child to interact with reality. He finds discrepancies and makes corrections. A child must find a solution for the problem *he* was searching to understand, a solution that makes sense of the observations *he* has made. Discussion may help a child locate his problem more clearly but the adult cannot decide in advance on the suitable solution or even the path to a solution.

> *And if the next most relevant piece of understanding is the bit which dovetails into the pattern already existing in the child's mind, it is almost impossible for a teacher to predict what it will be. It will certainly be different for every child in the group, and only the individual child is able to ask the question which will be most significant for himself.* (Italics in original)

This formulation—a child's "own questions," his "own purpose"— is a combining of activity and individual interest, but in a more sophisticated way. Nathan Isaacs speaks of this as an in-depth application of Dewey's concepts of democracy to a child's psychological development.

> The integrity of a human person is one and indivisible, and if we mean to respect it, the time to begin is when he first begins. And that holds all the more because for so long his integrity depends

utterly on those in natural authority over him. They claim, indeed, not only the right but the duty to rule and mould him, and up to a point this is quite incontrovertible; but the real question is whether it shall be deliberately restricted to the unavoidable minimum. . . . For those who fully accept the principle of respect for each person's integrity the answer is not in doubt. For them the future individuality of every child is a trust, to be honoured to the utmost attainable extent from his earliest years.

It follows . . . that he must do his own growing. . . . We must understand . . . how dependent it is on the child's own positive assimilative and integrative activity; and how much it needs to be continuous and of one piece.

A child can even correct his very poor image of himself as weak or helpless by finding out all he can *do* in being active. A necessity for a child's future growth, in fact, is that he be allowed decision and responsibility so that he *conceive* of himself as active agent in his own learning and growth, experiencing the outcome and integrating the fruits and consequences of his choices.

If he has the chance to develop manipulative and creative skills, to share in the social and practical life of his home, to be *active* in learning at school, he gradually comes to believe that he can contribute to others as well as take from them, can make a real return for what has been done for him when he was weak and helpless. Only *active* learning, however, and active social participation and interchange with those who love him and give him responsibility can build up in him a confidence in his own future.

These are the ideas basic to English infant education—summarized for the most part from formulations of Susan Isaacs and from Nathan Isaacs's use of Piagetian formulations. They are ideas of the wholeness, the continuity, the cumulative nature of development, of the need for time. They are ideas of individual and actively independent development, a development propelled further by its own prehistory and by the active thrust of curiosity and individual purpose. In this analysis, development results from each child's constant unique interactions—his integrations and reintegrations and the constructions and reconstructions of his understanding—within the human relationship into which he is born, in an outer reality that is social as well as physical.

Nathan Isaacs applied these formulations to the defense of English "activity" methods, to infant school practice.

It can, I think, be fairly said that Piaget's fundamental psychology of mental growth not merely supports such methods, but decisively demands them. A radical "activity" approach over virtually the whole front of education is in fact now shown to be the only one that *makes psychological sense*. . . .

This was a real stiffening of the past formulations of the English informal tradition which had interpreted the school's role as one of nurturance and the simple implementation of a child's development. It demanded further extension of "activity" methods over "the whole front of education," not only experiments or even only infant school.

The Formal School

The old way, the formal way, was analyzed and discarded as inconsistent with the facts of development. Peel says:

Up to this stage [of formal schooling] their intellectual development has marched in line with a "natural" environment from which they take just what is required for their particular stage of thought-growth. But now the environment is no longer "natural," instructions are given, skills are developed and verbal and numerical habits formed that may outstrip the level of thinking reached.

But what, in fact, is this formal school, this usual concept of "teaching"? Nathan Isaacs sums this up unforgettably, in words whose aptness goes far beyond the English scene.

. . . the teaching situation so conceived involves lifting the child right out of the context of his living learning—with its own motive-springs and starting-points, its active stretching-out and all its rewarding own achievements—and setting him down in a sort of "looking-glass" world where things virtually go by opposites. Here he must acquire a new way of life (oddly known as "learning"), which is essentially behaving to order, under continuous verbal direction. Nowadays, of course, this no longer starts abruptly and in full force; most children are allowed quite a long period of transition. But in the end they must fall in with the *real* aims and rules for which they are being sent to school.

For [children] are in effect put there to be taught, which means expressly clearing out of their minds all that ordinarily fills these and handing them over to the teacher with, as it were, "vacant possession." Their task is to co-operate faithfully with his attempt to furnish their minds, compartment by compartment, as they ought to be furnished. They must make every effort to *take in* what he offers, as he offers it; they must listen as directed, look where directed, act when directed. Of these various demands on them, listening is the most crucial, because it is both so difficult to keep up, and so essential. For language can alone provide the necessary connecting links, give the teaching continuity and cohesion, and build up organisation. Therefore, children must above all follow the spoken word, lesson by lesson—and thus allow themselves to be slowly led, according to some master plan of which they know nothing, to various labelled but otherwise unknown destinations. These they must patiently wait to learn more about when they begin to get there.

It is a shattering formulation but one's experience underlines its undeniable truth.

Naturally most children will obediently try, as far as in them lies, to comply with what is expected of them. In their varying degrees they will endeavour to "learn" at least some part of what they are taught. A number of them will indeed get fired with real interest in this or that "subject" and put active energy into mastering it. But even then it will often remain a "school" interest, and a transitory one. Whilst in far too many cases no spark will pass at all. Something will be "learnt," but it will not begin to *mean* anything to the child, and most of his own dutiful efforts as well as those of the teacher will in the long run just go to waste. In other words, the foregoing account of the way the teaching situation operates is not the travesty it might look, but a description of the way it actually works out, psychologically, for quite a large proportion of children.

Where the education is half-successful, Isaacs attributes the success to the out-of-school learning which has fused with some of the school learning.

Of course in a number of cases . . . true mental growth will continue outside school, strong interests will get formed, and . . . these self-educative processes may eventually pick up, and fuse with the more congenial parts of school education.

In 1932, in *The Children We Teach,* Susan Isaacs offered specific applications of this theory of how children learn in order to encourage change in the schools. Moreover, the aims of her Malting House School and her description of its activities were not so far from the aims and activities of today's infant schools. Thus, it was never *only* theory.

Susan Isaacs identified herself with teachers, she worked for the British Nursery Association, she taught a whole generation of advanced students at the Institute of Education, University of London. She linked herself to application in the schools. She said:

> I was a trained teacher of young children and a student of Dewey's educational theories long before I knew anything about Freud. . . .

> . . . I do not hold that any entirely new or innovatory educational principle emerges from this deeper understanding of the child's relation with his parents or fellows. Such is hardly to be expected, since wise mothers and gifted teachers have long known how to treat little children satisfactorily.

She wrote out of a commitment to make schools better, and out of concern. She and all the forementioned English educators felt the responsibility to *apply* all the results of their study to the service of all children.

And how long should a child be helped with this kind of learning? And how continuous should it be? The Nuffield group, speaking for the junior education that now in some cases goes up to age 13, contends that the answer is indeterminate.

> The time this process takes and the extent of the experience required will vary from child to child. How long it will take is unpredictable, but it will certainly be much longer than most people imagine. *The evidence suggests that it is not possible to hasten the forming of concepts, but that schools can make it easier by providing suitable materials and situations.*

Nathan Isaacs also answers broadly.

> Direct learning—always through exploration, experimentation and the striving for fresh achievement—must in fact be steadily restimulated and aided to advance further and further, until the help of planned teaching becomes its own next need and active demand.

This active learning, if continued, "at least over the whole vital period of the foundation-building primary years," will provide the broadest framework for the phase of systematic teaching to come.

Granted their analysis of the ways of development, the English answers and the choices of the ways of education were not niceties or kindnesses. They seemed necessities that were consonant with the evidence and, presented as such, provided the rationale for the infant school entity.

4. The Importance of Experience

For nearly a decade, the Education Development Center of Newton, Massachusetts, a nonprofit educational research and development organization, has been an important source of interest in, and expertise about, open education. EDC has bolstered the movement toward open education in a number of ways: through the films it has produced of open classrooms in England and the United States; through the Elementary Science Study, a federally funded reform of the elementary school science curriculum which has become a major source of materials for teachers interested in opening up their classrooms; through the EDC Open Education Follow Through Program, in which EDC has worked with ten school systems around the country that are part of the U.S. Office of Education's Follow Through program; and through the EDC Open Education Advisory, whereby EDC is using the advisory approach that has grown out of the Follow Through program to assist other communities interested in fostering open education.

The selection that follows is the outgrowth of a study, funded by the U.S. Office of Education and carried out by members of the Early Education Research Group at the Educational Testing Service in Princeton, New Jersey, in cooperation with the EDC Follow Through advisory group. The study, which is still in process, was designed to develop criteria of evaluation for the open classrooms in the EDC Follow Through Program. The project director, Dr. Edward A. Chittenden of ETS, decided that he and his colleagues had to understand the EDC approach before they could work on evaluation; they spent their first year, therefore, observing the EDC classrooms and talking to both the classroom teachers and the EDC advisers.

The educational approach sponsored by EDC is patterned to some extent on current reforms in the British Primary Schools and represents a broadly conceived position with respect both to teaching methods and instructional goals. By its very nature, however, this "open" approach defies easy translation into behavioral objectives or prescribed techniques—characteristics which have generally been regarded by the psychometric profession as essential for scientific evaluation. . . . It does not propose a set of instructional objectives and procedures for attain-

From Anne M. Bussis and Edward A. Chittenden, *Analysis of an Approach to Open Education* (Princeton, N.J.: Educational Testing Service, 1970), pp. 1, 8–10, 12–17, 17–19.

ing them which are the characteristic earmarks of a "model" in educational research today.

. . . In its extreme form, the shunning of labels and instructional
objectives gives the approach espoused by EDC a reputation of inarticulateness which critics call "mystic" and friends describe as "intuitive." In the case of EDC, however, it seems apparent that regardless
of difficulties in stating objectives, their position is characterized by strong
convictions regarding the *process* of educating children. In other words,
any apparent inarticulateness certainly does not stem from lack of belief
or ideas about education. . . . The question of whether or not to state
objectives in behavioral terms is more than just a question of taste or
technique. "The differences between individuals regarding the nature
and the use of educational objectives spring from differences in their
conceptions of education; under the rug of technique lies an image of
man" . . . In summary, EDC seeks to promote a philosophy of education—not a particular set of educational prescriptions. . . .

Throughout EDC philosophy, there is a marked and pervasive emphasis on the importance of experience for human development and
change. This proposition holds for the development of understanding in
a mature adult, as well as for the development of basic skills and abilities in children. In other words, the verbalization of correct answers or
theoretical postulates may indicate that a person "knows" something,
but it is not sufficient evidence that he understands it.

EDC's stress on the importance of an experiential foundation for understanding seems most obvious in terms of the individual child. Here,
one can quickly perceive compatibility with Piaget's conception of assimilation and accommodation—that the child organizes information
and constructs ideas through action upon the physical environment and
interaction with the social environment. Such an emphasis on action and
experience is certainly not unique to EDC nor new in the history of
educational thinking.

When we focus on the teacher, however, the role of experience in
understanding presents a somewhat more complex picture. For one thing,
this principle means that abstract knowledge of child development and
of the learning properties of various materials—while essential—is not
sufficient in itself to produce the understanding required of good teaching. Personal involvement and "messing about" with materials, as well
as the exercise of imagination, are also critical. When understanding is
bolstered by both kinds of components the teacher is best prepared for
the task of guiding children's learning with sensitivity.

Numerous examples could be given to illustrate this premise, but one
should suffice to make the point. Consider first the teacher who conceives of mathematics as a given amount of rather elementary subject
matter "to be covered" over the year—from "subtraction with borrow-

ing through basic operations of long division," or whatever. Now contrast that image with the teacher who conceives of mathematics as a way of thinking; who has herself experimented with cuisenaire rods or dominos and perhaps discovered some property of the number system; and who has given serious thought to what the formalized and arbitrary world of numbers must look like to a child. The latter teacher, to be sure, also has a list of skills that should presumably be mastered by her students over the course of the year. But the latter teacher will have richer resources to draw upon in helping students learn not only the skills, but an understanding and appreciation of mathematics that goes beyond the acquisition of skills alone. To summarize, it is the experiential component of understanding that makes up a substantial part of what might be called the "craft" of teaching.

There is a second implication for the teacher once experience is promoted to a consequential role in understanding. From the EDC viewpoint, good teaching means giving credence to the legitimacy of children's emotional experience. Adults often hold an attitude toward childhood that serves to nullify much of the significance and human quality of a child's emotional life. If another adult should show signs of anger, fear, joy, resentment, or intense interest, the nature and motivational impact of his feelings is understood. When it comes to a child's emotions, however, adult empathy is often dulled. We tend to strip the child of acute feeling and may attribute quite inaccurate motivations to him. Thus, boredom becomes "inattentiveness"; anger becomes "acting out"; fear becomes "insecurity" or "lack of experience"; resentment becomes "resistance" to adult authority; joy is often entirely divested of emotion and seen simply as "cute" behavior; and intense interest may even be read as "obstinacy" or "dawdling." It is only natural in some respects for the adult to adopt a "this too shall pass" attitude toward children's feelings. Sometimes such an attitude is quite necessary and lends perspective to the situation. But when perspective begins to blind a teacher to the immediacy and reality of children's emotions—and to the important consequences of those emotions for learning—then the EDC position would argue that it no longer serves the aims of teaching.

Finally, the importance-of-experience premise suggests that the teacher recognize and accept the legitimacy of her own feelings. This is certainly not to imply that she become an emotional barometer, but many teachers tend to the opposite extreme and stamp out every vestige of personal feeling and expression as they pass through the classroom door. They don a "teaching face" and become something of a robot in the midst of children. Soon they get across the message that the children, too, would do well to dampen their spontaneity and become more mechanical in response. It is argued that a more healthy environment for learning is one in which children experience their teacher as a unique feeling individual, with mature interests of her own, capable of expressing genuine emotion and of manifesting weaknesses as well as strengths.

Perhaps one of the most distinguishing assumptions of the EDC approach is that children constitute the basic resources of the educational process. In contrast to those educational theories which *assume* the presence of a child during instruction, an EDC approach *requires* the presence of a child to define instruction. Teaching begins with the assumption that the children coming into a classroom come with capabilities and experiences—shared and unique—and it is the teacher's job to see that those resources give a direction and meaning to learning.

It is important to distinguish this EDC position from other child-centered viewpoints which have become prominent in practice or in the literature. In all their various forms, these approaches stress the importance of understanding children—but for slightly different reasons and purposes. Perhaps the most obvious distinction to be made is between EDC philosophy and the view which says that the teacher must understand what kinds of capabilities the child possesses, and to what degree, for the purpose of helping him contend with the curriculum. Such a viewpoint is often accompanied by an emphasis on the use of standardized tests. Educators holding the EDC philosophy, however, assume that all children have resources of human intelligence, creativity, and constructive action. They are puzzled, if not angered, at the psychometric paradigm of ordering children according to more or less intelligence, more or less readiness, and so on. Their animosity to such differentiation stems not so much from an animosity to tests *per se* as from the fact that test results tend to turn the educator's attention away from individual resources toward an attempt to categorize pupils, "waterdown" instruction, or other similar efforts to fit the child to the curriculum. Individual differences are prized, not denied, by EDC and they see the opening of education as an excellent way of meeting each child's learning requirements. Suspicion of tests, therefore, springs from the fact that they are often used to rank children, thus portraying individual differences in terms of a deficiency model. To the extent that teachers focus on such a model and teaching is based on it, the very real resources of children will be neglected.

A second distinction between EDC and other child-centered positions concerns the issue of motivating children and stimulating their interests. One common approach is to try to understand the child's interests in order to attach these to subject matter that ordinarily might not interest him. Using batting averages of baseball players in the service of mathematics instruction might be one trivial example. An approach more characteristic of what EDC seeks to foster is taking the interests of the child for what they are and encouraging their extension in any of several directions. An interest in batting averages, for example, undoubtedly reflects a broader interest in baseball—and a more natural and significant extension of such interest might be in the direction of biographies of players, history of the sport, or geometry of the field. In the first example, the teacher uses the child's interest to capture attention regarding an uninteresting topic; while in the second example, interest is not only the starting point of an activity but is the sustaining and directing sustenance of that activity. Thus, EDC advisors are less impressed with the teacher who understands and can capture interest for periods of time than they are with the teacher who brings out in children the sort of interests that underlie sustained involvement in learning. In a good classroom the observer would undoubtedly see both the "captured" and the sustaining interest, but the emphasis would be on the latter . . .

Assuming that teaching begins with children's resourcefulness, the question nonetheless remains as to what an open classroom strives to accomplish. What does the teacher want to "do" with the inherent resources of children? Certainly there are many who argue along with EDC that the ultimate goal of education is to help extend intellectual and emotional resources so that the child becomes an integrated adult, capable of bringing rational consideration and personal value to bear in the life processes of making decisions, organizing experience, and utilizing knowledge. The extension of learning in this manner is an extremely complex subject, however, and beyond the scope of this particular discussion. The more modest but critical point to be made here is that any extension of individual resources is not possible until the child is both *willing* and *able* to draw upon those resources. This, then, is one crucial goal of an open classroom.

A number of recent books have offered the products of children as evidence of what can be accomplished when individual resources have received encouragement and support. John Blackie, in reference to a rather remarkable poem written by a 9 year old, says, "You cannot teach children to write poetry like that, but you can create conditions in school in which a child who has that particular thing to say can say it. A child only writes a poem like that for someone whom he trusts." Such writers, together with the EDC advisors, propose that the teacher must create a situation in which the child is willing to project himself into an activity if his resources are to be brought into play. The opening of a classroom, in itself, is no guarantee that this will happen. Putting oneself into an activity of the classroom, whether in writing a poem or constructing a graph, depends upon the relationship that has gradually been established between the teacher and children. It also depends upon past experiences in school. It is argued that the basic lesson learned by many children in the first years of traditional schools is that they should *not* look to themselves as originators—that they should *not* be in touch with their own interests as sources and origins of learning. Such children, even though they are perhaps willing to put themselves into some effort, may find it difficult to proceed in this way. The ability (the "ableness") to draw upon personal resources must be recultivated for these children.

In summary, the EDC position appears to argue that the best way to help a child utilize his capabilities is to create a climate in which there is both support and appeal for him to do so. Thus, to contribute to his capabilities as an author and to his skills in writing, the teacher should strive for an environment in which he will have something to say; to promote ability as a reader, create an environment in which he will find personal value in books; to contribute to his capabilities as a thinker, establish room and reason for thought.

5. The Sources of Pleasure

Perhaps the most striking impression someone visiting a good open classroom for the first time receives is that the children are having a marvelous time. Roland S. Barth, who has been an elementary school principal in New Haven, Connecticut and Newton, Massachusetts, identifies the classroom characteristics that determine whether or not children enjoy school.

What distinguishes the child who is enjoying school from one who is not? Should children enjoy school? Is enjoyment positively related to learning, negatively related, or not related at all? To what extent is children's enjoyment a priority of teachers, of parents, of children?

The vagueness surrounding the subject of children's enjoyment of school suggests that perhaps its importance has been taken for granted. More likely, however, this topic has not been seen as legitimate, academic, or tangible enough to warrant serious discussion and investigation. Whatever the answers to the above questions, it is quite clear that many students in American schools do not presently enjoy their educational experience.

Reports from Britain indicate that such a condition need not prevail. The scores of educators who are visiting infant schools (ages five to seven) and junior schools (ages eight to eleven) in England return with

From Roland S. Barth, "When Children Enjoy School—Some Lessons from Britain," *Childhood Education*, Vol. 46, No. 4, January 1970. Reprinted by permission Roland S. Barth and the Association for Childhood Education International, 3615 Wisconsin Avenue N.W., Washington, D.C. Copyright © 1970 by the Association.

many different and often contradictory impressions. But on one observation they agree: children in a large number of these schools seem to enjoy what they are doing most of the time. Having reviewed a large number of verbal and written reports of these visitors and having made firsthand observations of my own, I would like to identify some characteristics of these British schools and a few in this country that appear to be associated with children's enjoyment of their experience in formal education. For convenience, I shall refer to these schools as "open schools" and what goes on in them as "open education."

In England the schools of Leicestershire have most often been associated with the movement toward open education, but those of other British education authorities (such as Bristol, Oxfordshire, and The West Riding) deserve equal attention. Though proponents of the movement seem at first view to have in common little more than humanism and acceptance of diversity, what binds them together is a way of thinking and similar beliefs about children, learning and knowledge.

Children's Enjoyment of School

1. A child's enjoyment of school is related to the number of significant options available to him each day.

In open schools legitimate classroom pursuits cover a wide range of possibilities: children engage in physical activities involving manipulative materials (sand, tools, clay animals, blocks, nature study), as well as more abstract, symbolic activities (involving books, maps, numbers). Children may work alone in numerous nooks and crannies into which some areas of the classroom are divided or in groups. They work outside in the woods, at water tables, on the playing field, and inside at "interest tables" (cooking; making constructions out of wood, clay and metal). Available are task-oriented options (checkers, sums, workbooks, memorizing a poem) and more open-ended, ambiguous kinds of experiences (modelling with clay, painting, putting on skits).

Appearance in junior school classrooms of sand, blocks, water tables and clay elicits strong reactions on the part of many visitors concerned with academic excellence and high intellectual standards, for such materials connote childish, or at best childlike activities, hardly appropriate for ten- and eleven-year-olds who are "capable of so much more." The difference between infant schools and junior schools is not that the former contain sand, wood, water and the latter do not—in many cases both do—but rather in what children at each level do with these same materials. Older children, using blocks of different sizes, shapes, angles, investigate problems concerning such concepts as volume, different bases, square, square root, complementary and supplementary angles, and the like. They might use a sand table to make a 3-D topographical map, to study erosion, friction or solubility. A tub of water might become a laboratory in which to explore density, specific gravity, buoyancy, conductivity of electricity, oxidation or evaporation.

In short, the very same simple materials may be found in classrooms of children of all ages. Important exploration and learning with these and other similar materials is not confined to kindergarten, as any engineer, artist, scientist, mathematician, craftsman, or poet will attest. Children, like adults, seem to enjoy situations that offer a full representation of the objects and opportunities of the real world.

2. A child's enjoyment of school is related to his having significant choice in determining the activity in which he will be engaged.

In some schools the names of activities are posted on a large bulletin board: "paper construction," "clay," "puzzles," "math corner," "book corner," "water table," etc. Every morning each child places his namecard beside the activity in which he would like to work that day (the teacher can limit the number of children in each as he wishes). Choices are not idle; the child makes a deliberate, conscious commitment that affects not only what he will be doing that day but what the teacher and other children may be doing as well.

With significant choice goes physical mobility. Being engaged in "woodwork" a child will find he needs to run out to the woods and find an old tree root, search in the art corner to find some paints, ask the teacher about some nails, or borrow chisels from another classroom. So with all of the children—as interest and need dictate, they move freely and frequently to all parts of the room, the school and even the neighborhood.

Significant choice for children also implies recognition by the teacher that he must respect a child's choices, no matter how frivolous these appear to the adult at the moment. The bright eleven-year-old, playing with blocks in a corner, may be daydreaming or may be developing a concept of center of gravity. If children are going to exercise considerable choice, teachers must exercise considerable restraint in censoring or passing judgments—and hold in abeyance the notion of wasted time.

3. A child's enjoyment of school is related to his being able to pose his own problems and determine the manner in which he will pursue them . . . with respect to the materials and activities available to him.

In open classrooms, problems are more likely to be suggested by materials than teachers' prescriptions. A pendulum may suggest to a child the questions, "How much weight can I put on it before the string breaks?" or "How do I make it swing faster?" or "Could I hand some sand leaking out of a paper cup and make some pretty designs?" or . . . nothing at all. Once a problem has been suggested to a child by the materials and he becomes active in its formulation, it becomes his problem. It has dignity and he is likely to invest all of himself in finding ways to pursue it. The British experience indicates clearly that children are capable of posing problems for themselves—legitimate, difficult, important, instructive problems—and if encouraged and permitted to do so they will marshal all of their imagination and energy toward their solution.

What of the teacher? If he does not pose problems for the children to solve, what does he do? Teachers who become aware of temptations to step in and show the right way, give the right answer and prevent mistakes soon recognize that these kinds of interventions often serve their own needs more than those of the child. Such teachers pose a problem for themselves: "How little can I intervene and yet have the child continue his involvement in an activity?" The teacher's role in this kind of situation then, although no less important than in conventional classrooms, is quite different: he provides the conditions that will make children's exploration likely and fruitful—that will encourage children to ask and pursue their own questions. In open classrooms, a teacher more likely will be responding helpfully to the initiatives of children—supplying equipment, answering a question, helping hold a wire—than forcing children to respond to his directions.

4. A child's enjoyment of school is related to the extent he is permitted to collaborate with his peers.

Children want to share their experiences with those around them. In some schools this social behavior might be seen as "talking" or even as "cheating." In open schools it is viewed as valuable learning experience for the child and his peers. Children's own ideas and enthusiasms are infectious. The child who, with only a battery, a bulb and a wire, discovers he can make it "light" runs to others to show them, to instruct them, to lead them through the experience he has had. Together, by combining their resources, two children may decide to try and make a brighter light or a blinker.

The quite natural desire for a child to make overt what has been a private learning experience is always leading to another.

5. A child's enjoyment of school is related to the extent to which he is trusted by adults.

Out of teachers' distrust of children many repressive and unpleasant classroom practices arise: "One at a time out of your seat." "No working together." In short, no overt behavior.

Few teachers in English open schools are foolish or naive enough to suppose that whatever a child wants he gets, whatever a child says is true, whatever a child does is acceptable. Teachers in these schools more likely operate on the principle, "I can trust this child until he gives me reason not to, and then I will be more cautious about trusting or entrusting him in that particular area," than on the principle, "I can't trust any child until he gives me ample evidence that he deserves to be trusted."

Many visitors of open classrooms express surprise at seeing the number and variety of situations in which children prove themselves worthy of the teacher's trust—working with expensive equipment, alone, together; working unsupervised, inside and outside of school. Children tend to respond to lack of trust and confidence with destructive, hostile, surreptitious, immature behavior. They tend to respond to genuine expressions of trust with positive, mature, productive, constructive and enjoyable behavior.

6. A child is likely to enjoy school to the extent that it has a climate of consistent order.

British open schools are not laissez-faire places where anything goes. The teacher knows and the child knows that an authority is in charge, that the adult—no matter how personal and supportive he may be—is that authority. Teachers believe that, although a child may contribute to disorder and appear to work for it, no child enjoys disorder, at school or at home. Children in these classes soon recognize that unless someone is in charge they will not be able to move freely, explore freely or choose freely.

In many classrooms only two rules exist: no destroying equipment; no destroying or interfering with the work, play and activities of other children. These rules seem sufficient for establishing and maintaining a climate in which learning can flourish. Fewer rules may threaten the minimum order necessary for children to fully explore and enjoy what they are doing. But a larger number of rules suggests that an authoritarian rather than an authority is in charge.

7. A child's enjoyment of school is associated with the extent to which explicit and implicit comparisons between his performance and the performance of other children are minimized.

Differences between children in a classroom are of course, many. Some differences such as artistic expression in painting, music, dance are important for the teacher to acknowledge. Others, children find out for themselves. A great many distinctions commonly used to categorize children serve no useful purpose, however, and are played down in open classrooms:

Age. A common practice in British open schools is "family grouping," placing children of ages five to seven in one classroom and those eight to eleven in another. A child is not seen as a second-grader or a fifth-grader, or primarily as a six-year-old or an eleven-year-old. He is to teachers and administrators (and therefore to other children and himself) a member of the classroom family—one who, in terms of materials, privileges and rules, enjoys the same first-class citizenship as every other child.

Sex. Sex-appropriate behavior is not established or reinforced by most teachers or children in open schools. Girls frequently engage in woodworking and tinker with electric motors just as boys often enjoy cooking, poetry, and art. A child's choice of an activity seems determined more by his intrinsic interest and perhaps competence than by the gender the activity connotes.

Ability. Though "streaming," as ability grouping is called in England, is uncommon in open schools, grouping per se is not. Children, rather than being placed by the teacher into groups according to a judgment of their ability (top, middle, bottom reading groups, etc.), choose to work together in ad hoc groups when they share a common interest or difficulty. When interest in cooperative efforts wanes or need no longer exist, a group disbands. Thus grouping is not a rigidly routinized contrivance but a flexible, natural practice, employed when it serves a useful purpose for children.

Teachers also minimize distinctions by the ways they evaluate children. Rather than ascribing to each child letter or number grades, which lend themselves so readily to comparison by children and parents, many teachers believe that a sample of the child's work is the best measure of his achievement. Consequently they commonly maintain extensive folders to which examples of each child's work are regularly added. Periodically the teachers bring out these folders to discuss with parents and the child his development in different areas, his strengths and weaknesses. Use of these primary source materials helps keep evaluations specific to both the child and to what he is or is not learning.

The presence of error is not seen as behavior to be avoided or concealed at any cost; neither is its absence something to strive for as an objective of education. Rather, errors in open schools are seen as providing information necessary to subsequent learning, much as they help the scientist redirect and refine his investigations. When mistakes come to be seen as helpful rather than as moral wrongs, they are less likely to become sources of anxiety or to be used as yardsticks with which to compare one child against another.

The Price of Enjoying School

Lest one begin to think that schools where these conditions prevail are necessarily blissful and serene, let me mention some of the more apparent problems associated with children's enjoyment of school.

I have spoken with parents of children in open schools who were angry and resentful. "He used to obey and respect me and now he doesn't even listen to me. He only tells me that at school his teacher lets him do . . ." "He used to run home from school glad to see me. Now he stays there until dark." Some parents appear to depend for their children's affection on their children's not liking school, on the teacher's being an ogre, in which case the parents, by comparison, come out ahead. When school becomes pleasant, when the teacher is humane, when children enjoy school, these parents feel they become the ogres.

Another response of parents of children who enjoy school is, "That's fine, I'm glad that he's happy, but . . .", seemingly expressing the feeling that if a child is enjoying school, discipline and the three R's must necessarily be shortchanged. "If they are happy, they can't be learning very much." These parents feel that happiness is important enough to permit their child to enjoy school by day but, having little confidence that he is learning enough, often tutor him in traditional ways in the three R's by night.

In one highly regarded junior school I visited in England, most classrooms were quite traditional. Children looked rather bored and uninterested in what they were doing—except one class tucked away behind the building. The children in this classroom were doing things that seemed to involve them totally: wiring electric circuits, drawing pictures and making clay models of the fish in their aquarium, and putting on plays. They appeared to be both learning and enjoying themselves. Quite to my surprise, this was a class for the mentally retarded. In this school, enjoying themselves appeared legitimate for children only when the possibility of their learning anything of "significance" had been written off.

Finally I have often noticed that in a situation where an open classroom exists next to one where children are accorded little trust and choice, the teacher in the latter becomes resentful. She is likely to express annoyance for the increased noise, movement, laughter and the general distraction they cause for her own class. But one might suspect that the teacher's real resentment is in having to constantly witness a neighboring environment more pleasant than her own. In this case, she becomes the ogre.

The price of children's enjoying school is dear. Not only are the sources of resistance many and intense, but the magnitude of the change implied for child, teacher, and the nature of school is profound. The reason more children don't enjoy school is probably not that adults don't want them to enjoy it but rather that, if children are to enjoy school, what children and adults do in school must be of a significantly different order.

Byproduct, Not Pre-Condition

The conditions I have suggested as associated with children's enjoyment of school are not pre-conditions. No assurance exists that, if a teacher or an administrator were to deliberately attempt to implement one of these conditions, children would enjoy school. Few open-school educators state as a central goal, "that each child will enjoy school," and then set out to accomplish that goal by any means available to them. They engage in these and other practices primarily from a belief that by so doing they best promote children's learning, and only secondarily because it increases children's enjoyment of school, although the two are obviously related in some ways.

Children's enjoyment in these schools is more a byproduct—albeit a welcome byproduct—of a whole pedagogical approach: of providing significant options and choice; of permitting children to pose and solve their own problems in their own ways; of encouraging children to collaborate; of trusting children; of minimizing differences in performance; of providing consistent order. This is an approach in which children not only seem to learn, but one in which children seem to enjoy learning.

6. "The children . . . are the living aim"

Although she died in 1948, Susan Isaacs has had a profound influence, direct and indirect, on the development of informal education in England. One of the first women to receive psychoanalytic training, she organized and ran (together with her husband, the late Nathan Isaacs) an experimental school for young children in Cambridge in the early 1920s, The Malting House School, which was a precursor of the postwar informal infant school. The observations she recorded during the short life of the school formed the basis of much of Susan Isaacs' writings on learning and child development. Apart from her books and articles, she influenced a whole generation of teachers, head teachers, inspectors, educationists, and educational researchers as the first chairman of the Child Development Department of the University of London Institute of Education.

_____

. . . I am going to write not so much about schools and teaching as about the children who are in the schools. The children themselves are the living aim and end of our teaching. It is their thought, their knowledge, their character and development which make the purpose of our existence as schools and teachers. And it is the modes of their learning and understanding, their physical growth and social needs, which in the end determine the success or failure of our methods of teaching.

From Susan Isaacs, *The Children We Teach* Second Edition (London: University of London Press, 1967), pp. 11, 16, 65–67, 68, 69–70. Reprinted by permission of Schocken Books Inc. and the University of London Press Ltd.

It can be fully admitted that the most far-reaching book knowledge of psychology will not of itself ensure practical success in the classroom. No theory of how things should be done can take the place of the intuitive perception and direct response to children which come from native gifts and long experience. Nevertheless, even a first-rate practical teacher can gain something from a study of children's minds for their own sake, and from looking at the general facts of children's thinking and feeling and doing, as these have been gathered together by the psychologist.

. . . Our standards of work for the children, and our practical ideals in the school, have been changed in many directions by our sounder knowledge of what does really help them to grow in skill and knowledge and understanding and health.

One change which is going on at this moment is a further example, viz. language teaching in the lower forms. We are beginning to realize that it is quite useless to expect clear and fluent expression in *writing*, no matter how good our lessons in composition may be, if at the same time we shut out all chance of the child's learning to express himself in *speech*. The silent classroom is the worst possible training for written expression. But children who are encouraged to talk freely in class about things that interest them, to tell stories, to describe and discuss, soon come to *write* with greater ease and aptness and style, as well as to *think* more clearly and accurately. And enterprising schools are beginning to accept this fundamental truth, and to find ways of encouraging speech and using it constructively . . .

. . . In my discussion of the children we teach, I have so far spoken mainly of the differences between one child and another of the same age. Now I want to go on to their common characteristics, and to the *general* modes of behaviour which can be seen among children as they move through the age groups of the Primary School. When all allowances for the particular ways of particular children have been made, there still remain characteristic modes of thinking and feeling and doing of children in these years. And schools have of course to be planned in the large upon the needs of the general run of their pupils.

Now these general characteristics of the Primary School period will not be shown fully by any one child. No real living child is "typical" or "average." These notions are just useful tools to help us fix in our minds what there is in common between the actual children we observe. Some writers on psychology are fond of talking about *The Child,* almost as if there was a fixed real type that could in some mysterious way be distilled out from the actual children we know. And this leads to all sorts of rigid laws being laid down, and hard and fast notions of development being applied, which leave the practical person high and dry when he comes to deal with the living children in his class. For these reasons, I always try to anchor my own thought to the plural form, to talk of *children* rather than "the child," so as to remind myself constantly of the infinite variety of ways in which this, that, and the other child may depart from the general law.

Having here, however, already considered at length the fact of individual differences, I can now go on to draw the general outline of growth in these years, without misleading my readers.

The first general characteristic of Primary School children to be noted is their need for active movement. Left to themselves and given any chance at all, children of these years are well-nigh tireless in physical activity—running and jumping and climbing, skipping and playing with balls, using their hands to make and to explore, shouting and singing. I happen to live near one of the pleasantest open spaces of London, and in all out-of-school hours and holidays I hear the voices of children who have come to the green grass from the side streets round about, and I can look up to watch them swinging and leaping, playing cricket and football, chasing each other, making tents with a few rags and sticks, arguing and teasing. And I still hear them cheerfully shouting as their unwilling feet take them home at the latest hour of the evening.

And how they rush and run about the playground the moment they are released from the various pressures by which we keep them sitting quiet in the schoolroom! Always their natural impulses drive them *to be doing,* with hands and feet and tongue. This is their spontaneous way of taking the world, and their natural means of growth.

. . . Bodily activity is not with children as with grownups a mere matter of taking enough exercise to keep healthy, nor of mere personal delight. It is these; but it is also a necessity of their education. Without it, they cannot attain full development of skill and power and sensitivity. Nor . . . can they enjoy the freest exercise of their understanding and reason.

The first great duty of the educator is thus to create such conditions as will allow the freest possible and most ample bodily *movement.* When we ask children *not* to move, we should have excellent reasons for doing so. It is stillness we have to justify, not movement. There should be something real to be gained by it, some definite constructive end. Sitting still is a virtue only if it is a means to some purpose beyond itself. The end of education in these years is that the children should grow and develop, and to this, activity of one sort or another is the only key . . .

In general then, our attitude to children's movement in the primary school years should be to *use* it, not to inhibit it . . .

We already make a good deal of wise provision for the direct training of bodily activity, in drill and games and rhythmic movement, as well as in the brief intervals of free play. It is doubtful whether we go far enough in this, however. The health and happiness of children (and their teachers!) would probably be much improved if the actual time given to physical exercise in the open air were increased . . .

But the problem is not just one of sandwiching periods of physical activity in between periods of immobile "headwork." The headwork itself is most fruitful when it is also handwork and bodywork. In these years, the child's intelligence is essentially practical. He thinks as much with his hands as with his tongue; and even with his tongue he can think better aloud than "in his head."

The whole of his education needs to be conceived in terms of his own activity. His desire for movement is part of his desire for expression and for understanding. His delight in rhythm and pattern, in music and dancing, in miming and making things, no less than his love of running and jumping and playing games, show how urgent and how educative his impulse to movement is. We must meet this need by giving him ample experience in the arts and crafts as well as in games and drill.

Even this, however, does not exhaust our practical opportunities for making use of the child's desire for activity. The whole physical setting of the school and classroom should be based upon the creative value of the child's own movements. The furniture and equipment will help or hinder just as readily as our explicit methods of teaching. There is no real place in the Primary School, any more than in the Infants' School, for heavy fixed desks and inaccessible store cupboards. Light movable tables and chairs, individual material arranged so that the children can get it themselves and be individually responsible for keeping it in order, a discipline and a classroom organization built upon the active sharing of work and play, all make for social control as well as for bodily poise.

7. The Educational Implications
of Piaget's Work

After having been virtually ignored in this country for decades, Jean Piaget has come to be recognized as the most important child psychologist of our age. In contrast to the situation in the United States, however, English teachers and teacher educators have recognized the importance of his work for some time. (The late Nathan Isaacs played a major role in that recognition, popularizing Piaget's writings for English teachers and reconciling Piaget's theories with those of Susan Isaacs.)

Since Piaget writes in a difficult and frequently obscure style, the three selections that follow come not from Piaget's own work but from the writings of two of his students who have helped popularize his thinking in the United States. David Elkind, author of the first two selections, is professor of psychology at the University of Rochester. Eleanor Duck-worth, a Canadian teacher, writer, and educational reformer, has served as Piaget's translator when Piaget has lectured in the United States.

In February, 1967, Jean Piaget, the Swiss psychologist, arrived at Clark University in Worcester, Mass., to deliver the Heinz Werner Memorial Lectures. The lectures were to be given in the evening, and before the first one a small dinner party was arranged in honor of Piaget and was attended by colleagues, former students and friends. I was invited because of my long advocacy of Piaget's work and because I had spent a year (1964–65) at his Institute for Educational Science in Geneva. Piaget had changed very little since I had last seen him, but he did appear tired and mildly apprehensive.

Although Piaget has lectured all over the world, this particular occasion had special significance. Almost 60 years before, in 1909, another famous European, Sigmund Freud, also lectured at Clark University. Piaget was certainly aware of the historical parallel. He was, moreover, going to speak to a huge American audience in French and, despite the offices of his remarkable translator, Eleanor Duckworth, he must have had some reservations about how it would go.

Piaget's apprehension was apparent during the dinner. For one who is usually a lively and charming dinner companion, he was surprisingly quiet and unresponsive. About half way through the meal there was a small disturbance. The room in which the dinner was held was at a garden level and two boys suddenly appeared at the windows and began tapping at them. The inclination of most of us, I think, was to shoo them away. Before we had a chance to do that, however, Piaget had turned to face the children. He smiled up at the lads, hunched his shoulders and gave them a slight wave with his hand. They hunched their shoulders and smiled in return, gave a slight wave and disappeared. After a moment, Piaget turned back to the table and began telling stories and entering into animated conversation.

Although I am sure his lecture would have been a success in any case and that the standing ovation he received would have occurred without the little incident, I nonetheless like to think that the encounter with the boys did much to restore his vigor and good humor.

It is Piaget's empathy with children, together with true intellectual genius, that has made him the outstanding child psychologist in the world today and one destined to stand beside Freud with respect to his contributions to psychology, education and related disciplines. Just as Freud's discoveries of unconscious motivation, infantile sexuality and the stages of psychosexual growth changed our ways of thinking about human personality, so Piaget's discoveries of children's implicit philosophies, the construction of reality by the infant and the stages of mental development have altered our ways of thinking about human intelligence.

The man behind these discoveries is an arresting figure. He is tall and somewhat portly, and his stooped walk, bulky suits and crown of long white hair give him the appearance of a thrice-magnified Einstein. (When he was at the Institute for Advanced Study at Princeton in 1953, a friend of his wife rushed to a window one day and exclaimed, "Look, Einstein!" Madame Piaget looked and replied, "No, just my Piaget.") Piaget's personal tradmarks are his meerschaum pipes (now burned deep amber), his navy blue beret and his bicycle.

Meeting Piaget is a memorable experience. Although Piaget has an abundance of Old-World charm and graciousness, he seems to emanate an aura of intellectual presence not unlike the aura of personality presence conveyed by a great actor. While as a psychologist I am unable to explain how this sense of presence is communicated, I am nevertheless convinced that everyone who meets Piaget experiences it. While talking to me, for example, he was able to divine in my remarks and questions a significance and depth of which I was entirely unaware and certainly hadn't intended. Evidently one characteristic of genius is to search for relevance in the apparently commonplace and frivolous.

Piaget's is a superbly disciplined life. He arises early each morning, sometimes as early as 4 A.M., and writes four or more publishable pages on square sheets of white paper in an even, small hand. Later in the morning he may teach classes and attend meetings. His afternoons include long walks during which he thinks about the problems he is currently confronting. He says, "I always like to think on a problem before reading about it." In the evenings, he reads and retires early. Even on his international trips, Piaget keeps to this schedule.

Each summer, as soon as classes are over, Piaget gathers up the research findings that have been collected by his assistants during the year and departs for the Alps, where he takes up solitary residence in a room in an abandoned farmhouse. The whereabouts of this retreat is as closely guarded as the names of depositors in numbered Swiss bank accounts; only Piaget's family, his longtime colleague Bärbel Inhelder and a trusted secretary know where he is. During the summer Piaget takes walks, meditates, writes *and* writes. Then, when the leaves begin to turn, he descends from the mountains with the several books and articles he has written on his "vacation."

Although Piaget, now in his 72d year, has been carrying his works down from the mountains for almost 50 summers (he has published more than 30 books and hundreds of articles), it is only within the past decade that his writings have come to be fully appreciated in America. This was due, in part, to the fact that until fairly recently only a few of his books had been translated into English. In addition, American psychology and education were simply not ready for Piaget until the fifties. Now the ideas that Piaget has been advocating for more than 30 years are regarded as exceedingly innovative and even as avant-garde.

His work falls into three more or less distinct periods within each of which he covered an enormous amount of psychological territory and developed a multitude of insights. (Like most creative men, Piaget is hard put to it to say when a particular idea came to him. If he ever came suddenly upon an idea which sent him shouting through the halls, he has never admitted to it.)

During the first period (roughly 1922–29), Piaget explored the extent and depth of children's spontaneous ideas about the physical world and about their own mental processes. He happened upon this line of inquiry while working in Alfred Binet's laboratory school in Paris where he arrived, still seeking a direction for his talents, a year after receiving his doctorate in biological science at the University of Lausanne. It was in the course of some routine intelligence testing that Piaget became interested in what lay behind children's correct, and particularly their incorrect, answers. To clarify the origins of these answers he began to interview the children in the open-ended manner he had learned while serving a brief internship at Bleuler's psychiatric clinic in Zurich. This semiclinical interview procedure, aimed at revealing the processes by which a child arrives at a particular reply to a test question, has become a trademark of Piagetian research investigation.

What Piaget found with this method of inquiry was that children not only reasoned differently from adults but also that they had quite different world-views, literally different philosophies. This led Piaget to attend to those childish remarks and questions which most adults find amusing or nonsensical. Just as Freud used seemingly accidental slips of the tongue and pen as evidence for unconscious motivations, so Piaget has employed the "cute" sayings of children to demonstrate the existence of ideas quite foreign to the adult mind.

Piaget had read in the recollections of a deaf mute (recorded by William James) that as a child he had regarded the sun and moon as gods and believed they followed him about. Piaget sought to verify this recollection by interviewing children on the subject, and he found that many youngsters do believe that the sun and moon follow them when they are out for a walk. Similar remarks Piaget either overheard or was told about led to a large number of investigations which revealed, among many similar findings, that young children believe that anything which moves is alive, that the names of objects reside in the objects themselves and that dreams come in through the window at night.

Such beliefs, Piaget pointed out in an early article entitled "Children's Philosophies," are not unrelated to but rather derive from an implicit animism and artificialism with many parallels to primitive and Greek philosophies. In the child's view, objects like stones and clouds are imbued with motives, intentions and feelings, while mental events such as dreams and thoughts are endowed with corporality and force. Children also believe that everything has a purpose and that everything in the world is made by and for man. (My 5-year-old son asked me why we have snow and answered his own question by saying, "It is for children to play in.")

The child's animism and artificialism help to explain his famous and often unanswerable "why" questions. It is because children believe that everything has a purpose that they ask, "Why is grass green?" and "Why do the stars shine?" The parent who attempts to answer such questions with a physical explanation has missed the point.

In addition to disclosing the existence of children's philosophies during this first period, Piaget also found the clue to the egocentrism of childhood. In observing young children at play at the *Maison des Petits,* the modified Montessori school associated with the Institute of Educational Science in Geneva, Piaget noted a peculiar lack of social orientation which was also present in their conversation and in their approaches to certain intellectual tasks. A child would make up a new word ("stocks" for socks and stockings) and just assume that everyone knew what he was talking about as if this were the conventional name for the objects he had in mind. Likewise, Piaget noted that when two nursery school children were at play they often spoke *at* rather than *to* one another and were frequently chattering on about two quite different and unrelated topics. Piaget observed, moreover, that when he stood a child of 5 years opposite him, the child who could tell his own right and left nevertheless insisted that Piaget's right and left hands were directly opposite his own.

In Piaget's view, all of these behaviors can be explained by the young child's inability to put himself in another person's position and to take that person's point of view. Unlike the egocentric adult, who can take another person's point of view but does not, the egocentric child does not take another person's viewpoint because he cannot. This conception of childish egocentrism has produced a fundamental alteration in our evaluation of the preschool child's behavior. We now appreciate that it is intellectual immaturity and not moral perversity which makes, for example, a young child continue to pester his mother after she has told him she has a headache and wishes to be left alone. The preschool child is simply unable to put himself in his mother's position and see things from her point of view.

The second period of Piaget's investigations began when, in 1929, he sought to trace the origins of the child's spontaneous mental growth to the behavior of infants; in this case, his own three children, Jaqueline, Lucienne and Laurent. Piaget kept very detailed records of their behavior and of their performance on a series of ingenious tasks which he invented and presented to them. The books resulting from these investigations, "The Origins of Intelligence in Children," "Play, Dreams and Imitation in Children" and "The Construction of Reality in the Child" are now generally regarded as classics in the field and have been one of the major forces behind the scurry of research activity in the area of infant behavior now current both in America and abroad. The publication of these books in the middle and late nineteen-thirties marked the end of the second phase of Piaget's work.

Some of the most telling observations Piaget made during this period had to do with what he called the *conservation of the object* (using the word conservation to convey the idea of permanence). To the older child and to the adult, the existence of objects and persons who are not immediately present is taken as self-evident. The child at school knows that while he is working at his desk his mother is simultaneously at home and his father is at work. This is not the case for the young infant playing in his crib, for whom out of sight is literally out of mind. Piaget observed that when an infant 4 or 5 months old is playing with a toy which subsequently rolls out of sight (behind another toy) but is still within reach, the infant ceases to look for it. The infant behaves as if the toy had not only disappeared but as if it had gone entirely out of existence.

This helps to explain the pleasure infants take in the game of peek-a-boo. If the infant believed that the object existed when it was not seen, he would not be surprised and delighted at its re-emergence and there would be no point to the game. It is only during the second year of life, when children begin to represent objects mentally, that they seek after toys that have disappeared from view. Only then do they attribute an independent existence to objects which are not present to their senses.

The third and major phase of Piaget's endeavors began about 1940 and continues until the present day. During this period Piaget has studied the development in children and adolescents of those mental abilities which gradually enable the child to construct a world-view which is in conformance with reality as seen by adults. He has, at the same time, been concerned with how children acquire the adult versions of various concepts such as number, quantity and speed. Piaget and his colleagues have amassed, in the last 28 years, an astounding amount of information about the thinking of children and adolescents which is only now beginning to be used by psychologists and educators.

Two discoveries made during this last period are of particular importance both because they were so unexpected and because of their relevance for education. It is perhaps fair to say that education tends to focus upon the static aspects of reality rather than upon its dynamic transformations. The child is taught how and what things are but not the conditions under which they change or remain the same. And yet the child is constantly confronted with change and alteration. His view of the world alters as he grows in height and perceptual acuity. And the world changes. Seasons come and go, trees gain and lose their foliage, snow falls and melts. People change, too. They may change over brief time periods in mood and over long periods in weight and hair coloration or fullness. The child receives a static education while living amidst a world in transition.

Piaget's investigations since 1940 have focused upon how the child copes with change, how he comes to distinguish between the permanent and the transient and between appearance and reality. An incident that probably played a part in initiating this line of investigation occurred during Piaget's short-lived flirtation with the automobile. (When his children were young, Piaget learned to drive and bought a car, but he gave it up for his beloved bicycle after a couple of years.) He took his son for a drive and Laurent asked the name of the mountain they were passing. The mountain was the Salève, the crocodile-shaped mass that dominates the city of Geneva. Laurent was in fact familiar with the mountain and its name because he could see it from his garden, although from a different perspective. Laurent's question brought home to Piaget the fact that a child has difficulty in dealing with the results of transformations whether they are brought about by an alteration in the object itself or by the child's movement with respect to the object.

The methods Piaget used to study how the child comes to deal with transformations are ingenuously simple and can be used by any interested parent or teacher. These methods all have to do with testing the child's abilities to discover that a quantity remains the same across a change in its appearance. In other words, that the quantity is conserved.

To give just one illustration from among hundreds, a child is shown two identical drinking glasses filled equally full with orangeade and he is asked to say whether there is the "same to drink" in the two glasses. After the child says that this is the case, the orangeade from one glass is poured into another which is taller and thinner so that the orangeade now reaches a higher level. Then the child is asked to say whether there is the same amount to drink in the two differently shaped glasses. Before the age of 6 or 7, most children say that the tall, narrow glass has more orangeade. The young child cannot deal with the transformation and bases his judgment on the static features of the orangeade, namely the levels.

How does the older child arrive at the notion that the amounts of orangeade in the two differently shaped glasses is the same? The answer, according to Piaget, is that he discovers the equality with the aid of reason. If the child judges only on the basis of appearances he cannot solve the problem. When he compares the two glasses with respect to width he must conclude that the wide glass has more while if he compares them with respect to the level of the orangeade he must conclude that the tall glass has more. There is then no way, on the basis of appearance, that he can solve the problem. If, on the other hand, the child reasons that there was the same in the two glasses before and that nothing was added or taken away during the pouring, he concludes that both glasses still have the same drink although this does not appear to be true.

On the basis of this and many similar findings, Piaget argues that much of our knowledge about reality comes to us not from without like the wail of a siren but rather from within by the force of our own logic.

It is hard to overemphasize the importance of this fact, because it is so often forgotten, particularly in education. For those who are not philosophically inclined, it appears that our knowledge of things comes about rather directly as if our mind simply copied the forms, colors and textures of things. From this point of view the mind acts as a sort of mirror which is limited to reflecting the reality which is presented to it. As Piaget's research has demonstrated, however, the mind operates not as a passive mirror but rather as an active artist.

The portrait painter does not merely copy what he sees, he interprets his subject. Before even commencing the portrait, the artist learns a great deal about the individual subject and does not limit himself to studying the face alone. Into the portrait goes not only what the artist sees but also what he knows about his subject. A good portrait is larger than life because it carries much more information than could ever be conveyed by a mirror image.

In forming his spontaneous conception of the world, therefore, the child does more than reflect what is presented to his senses. His image of reality is in fact a portrait or reconstruction of the world and not a simple copy of it. It is only by reasoning about the information which the child receives from the external world that he is able to overcome the transient nature of sense experience and arrive at that awareness of permanence within apparent change that is the mark of adult thought. The importance of reason in the child's spontaneous construction of his world is thus one of the major discoveries of Piaget's third period.

The second major discovery of this time has to do with the nature of the elementary school child's reasoning ability. Long before there was anything like a discipline of child psychology, the age of 6 to 7 was recognized as *the age of reason*. It was also assumed, however, that once the child attained the age of reason, there were no longer any substantial differences between his reasoning abilities and those of adolescents and adults. What Piaget discovered is that this is in fact not the case. While the elementary school child is indeed able to reason, his reasoning ability is limited in a very important respect—he can reason about things but not about verbal propositions.

If a child of 8 or 9 is shown a series of three blocks, ABC, which differ in size, then he can tell by looking at them, and without comparing them directly, that if A is greater than B and B greater than C, then A is greater than C. When the same child is given this problem, "Helen is taller than Mary and Mary is taller than Jane, who is the tallest of the three?" the result is quite different. He cannot solve it despite the fact that it repeats in words the problem with the blocks. Adolescents and adults, however, encounter no difficulty with this problem because they can reason about verbal propositions as well as about things.

This discovery that children think differently from adults even after attaining the age of reason has educational implications which are only now beginning to be applied. Robert Karplus, the physicist who heads the Science Curriculum Improvement Study at Berkeley has pointed out that most teachers use verbal propositions in teaching elementary school children. At least some of their instruction is thus destined to go over the heads of their pupils. Karplus and his co-workers are now attempting to train teachers to instruct children at a verbal level which is appropriate to their level of mental ability.

An example of the effects of the failure to take into account the difference between the reasoning abilities of children and adults comes from the New Math experiment. In building materials for the New Math, it was hoped that the construction of a new language would facilitate instruction of set concepts. This new language has been less than successful and the originators of the New Math are currently attempting to devise a physical model to convey the New Math concepts. It is likely that the new language created to teach the set concepts failed because it was geared to the logic of adults rather than to the reasoning of children. Attention to the research on children's thinking carried out during Piaget's third period might have helped to avoid some of the difficulties of the "New Math" program.

In the course of these many years of research into children's thinking, Piaget has elaborated a general theory of intellectual development which, in its scope and comprehensiveness, rivals Freud's theory of personality development. Piaget proposes that intelligence—adaptive thinking and action—develops in a sequence of stages that is related to age. Each stage sees the elaboration of new mental abilities which set the limits and determine the character of what can be learned during that period. (Piaget finds incomprehensible Harvard psychologist Jerome Bruner's famous hypothesis to the effect that "any subject can be taught effectively in some intellectually honest form to any child at any stage of development.") Although Piaget believes that the order in which the stages appear holds true for all children, he also believes that the ages at which the stages evolve will depend upon the native endowment of the child and upon the quality of the physical and social environment in which he is reared. In a very real sense, then, Piaget's is both a nature and a nurture theory.

The first stage in the development of intelligence (usually 0–2 years) Piaget calls the sensory-motor period and it is concerned with the evolution of those abilities necessary to construct and reconstruct objects. To illustrate, Piaget observed that when he held a cigarette case in front of his daughter Jaqueline (who was 8 months old at the time) and then dropped it, she did not follow the trajectory of the case but continued looking at his hand. Even at 8 months (Lucienne and Laurent succeeded in following the object at about 5 months but had been exposed to more experiments than Jaqueline) she was not able to reconstruct the path of the object which she had seen dropped in front of her.

Toward the end of this period, however, Jaqueline was even able to reconstruct the position of objects which had undergone hidden displacement. When she was 19 months old, Piaget placed a coin in his hand and then placed his hand under a coverlet where he dropped the coin before removing his hand. Jaqueline first looked in his hand and then immediately lifted the coverlet and found the coin. This reconstruction was accomplished with the aid of an elementary form of reasoning. The coin was in the hand, the hand was under the coverlet, the coin was not in the hand so the coin is under the coverlet. Such reasoning, it must be said, is accomplished without the aid of language and by means of mental images.

The second stage (usually 2–7 years), which Piaget calls the pre-operational stage, bears witness to the elaboration of the symbolic function, those abilities which have to do with representing things. The presence of these new abilities is shown by the gradual acquisition of language, the first indications of dreams and night terrors, the advent of symbolic play (two sticks at right angles are an airplane) and the first attempts at drawing and graphic representation.

At the beginning of this stage the child tends to identify words and symbols with the objects they are intended to represent. He is upset if someone tramps on a stone which he has designated as a turtle. And he believes that names are as much a part of objects as their color and form. (The child at this point is like the old gentleman who, when asked why noodles are called noodles, replied that "they are white like noodles, soft like noodles and taste like noodles so we call them noodles.")

By the end of this period the child can clearly distinguish between words and symbols and what they represent. He now recognizes that names are arbitrary designations. The child's discovery of the arbitrariness of names is often manifested in the "name calling" so prevalent during the early school years.

At the next stage (usually 7–11 years) the child acquires what Piaget calls concrete operations, internalized actions that permit the child to do "in his head" what before he would have had to accomplish through real actions. Concrete operations enable the child to think about things. To illustrate, in one study Piaget presented 5-, 6- and 7-year-old children with six sticks in a row and asked them to take the same number of sticks from a pile on the table. The young children solved the problem by placing their sticks beneath the sample and matching the sticks one by one. The older children merely picked up the six sticks and held them in their hands. The older children had counted the sticks mentally and hence felt no need to actually match them with the sticks in the row. It should be said that even the youngest children were able to count to six, so that this was not a factor in their performance.

Concrete operations also enable children to deal with the relations among classes of things. In another study Piaget presented 5-, 6- and 7-year-old children with a box containing 20 white and seven brown wooden beads. Each child was first asked if there were more white or more brown beads and all were able to say that there were more white than brown beads. Then Piaget asked, "Are there more white or more wooden beads?" The young children could not fathom the question and replied that "there are more white than brown beads." For such children classes are not regarded as abstractions but are thought of as concrete places. (I once asked a pre-operational child if he could be a Protestant and an American at the same time, to which he replied, "No," and then as an afterthought, "only if you move.")

When a child thought of a bead in the white "place" he could not think of it as being in the wooden "place" since objects cannot be in two places at once. He could only compare the white with the brown "places." The older children, who had attained concrete operations, encountered no difficulty with the task and readily replied that "there are more wooden than white beads because all of the beads are wooden and only some are white." By the end of the concrete operational period, children are remarkably adept at doing thought problems and at combining and dividing class concepts.

During the last stage (usually 12–15 years) there gradually emerge what Piaget calls formal operations and which, in effect, permit adolescents to think about their thoughts, to construct ideals and to reason realistically about the future. Formal operations also enable young people to reason about contrary-to-fact propositions. If, for example, a child is asked to assume that coal is white he is likely to reply, "But coal is black," whereas the adolescent can accept the contrary-to-fact assumption and reason from it.

Formal operational thought also makes possible the understanding of metaphor. It is for this reason that political and other satirical cartoons are not understood until adolescence. The child's inability to understand metaphor helps to explain why books such as "Alice in Wonderland" and "Gulliver's Travels" are enjoyed at different levels during childhood than in adolescence and adulthood, when their social significance can be understood.

No new mental systems emerge after the formal operations, which are the common coin of adult thought. After adolescence, mental growth takes the form—it is hoped—of a gradual increase in wisdom.

This capsule summary of Piaget's theory of intellectual development would not be complete without some words about Piaget's position with respect to language and thought. Piaget regards thought and language as different but closely related systems. Language, to a much greater extent than thought, is determined by particular forms of environmental stimulation. Inner-city Negro children, who tend to be retarded in language development, are much less retarded with respect to the ages at which they attain concrete operations. Indeed, not only inner-city children but children in bush Africa, Hong Kong and Appalachia all attain concrete operations at about the same age as middle-class children in Geneva and Boston.

Likewise, attempts to teach children concrete operations have been almost uniformly unsuccessful. This does not mean that these operations are independent of the environment but only that their development takes time and can be nourished by a much wider variety of environmental nutriments than is true for the growth of language, which is dependent upon much more specific forms of stimulation.

Language is, then, deceptive with respect to thought. Teachers of middle-class children are often misled, by the verbal facility of these youngsters, into believing that they understand more than they actually comprehend. (My 5-year-old asked me what my true identity was and as I tried to recover my composure he explained that Clark Kent was Superman's true identity.) At the other end, the teachers of inner-city children are often fooled by the language handicaps of these children into thinking that they have much lower mental ability than they actually possess. It is appropriate, therefore, that pre-school programs for the disadvantaged should focus upon training these children in language and perception rather than upon trying to teach them concrete operations.

The impact which the foregoing Piagetian discoveries and conceptions is having upon education and child psychology has come as something of a shock to a good many educators and psychological research in America, which relies heavily upon statistics, electronics and computers, Piaget's studies of children's thinking seem hardly a step beyond the prescientific baby biographies kept by such men as Charles Darwin and Bronson Alcott. Indeed, in many of Piaget's research papers he supports his conclusions simply with illustrative examples of how children at different age levels respond to his tasks.

Many of Piaget's critics have focused upon his apparently casual methodology and have argued that while Piaget has arrived at some original ideas about children's thinking, his research lacks scientific rigor. It is likely that few, if any, of Piaget's research reports would have been accepted for publication in American psychological journals.

Other critics have taken somewhat the opposite tack. Jerome Bruner, who has done so much to bring Piaget to the attention of American social scientists, acknowledges the fruitfulness of Piaget's methods, modifications of which he has employed in his own investigations. But he argues against Piaget's theoretical interpretations. Bruner believes that Piaget has "missed the heart" of the problem of change and permanence or conservation in children's thinking. In the case of the orangeade poured into a different-sized container, Bruner argues that it is not reason, or mental operations, but some "internalized verbal formula that shields him [the child] from the overpowering appearance of the visual displays." Bruner seems to believe that the syntactical rules of language rather than logic can account for the child's discovery that a quantity remains unchanged despite alterations in its appearance.

Piaget is willing to answer his critics but only when he feels that the criticism is responsible and informed. With respect to his methods, their casualness is only apparent. Before they set out collecting data, his students are given a year of training in the art of interviewing children. They learn to ask questions without suggesting the answers and to test, by counter-suggestion, the strength of the child's conviction. Many of Piaget's studies have now been repeated with more rigorous procedures by other investigators all over the world and the results have been remarkably consistent with Piaget's findings. Attempts are currently under way to build a new intelligence scale on the basis of the Piaget tests, many of which are already in widespread use as evaluative procedures in education.

When it comes to criticisms of his theoretical views, Piaget is remarkably open and does not claim to be infallible. He frequently invites scholars who are in genuine disagreement with him to come to Geneva for a year so that the differences can be discussed and studied in depth. He has no desire to form a cult and says, in fact, "To the extent that there are Piagetians, to that extent have I failed." Piaget's lack of dogmatism is illustrated in his response to Bruner:

"Bruner does say that I 'missed the heart' of the conservation problem, a problem I have been working on for the last 30 years. He is right,
of course, but that does not mean that he himself has understood it in
a much shorter time . . . Adults, just like children, need time to reach
the right ideas . . . This is the great mystery of development, which
is irreducible to an accumulation of isolated learning acquisitions. Even
psychology cannot be learned or constructed in a short time." (Despite
his disclaimer, Piaget has offered a comprehensive theory of how the
child arrives at conservation and this theory has received much research
support.)

Piaget would probably agree with those who are critical about premature applications of his work to education. He finds particularly disturbing the efforts by some American educators to accelerate children
intellectually. When he was giving his other 1967 lectures, in New York,
he remarked:

"If we accept the fact that there are stages of development, another
question arises which I call 'the American question,' and I am asked it
every time I come here. If there are stages that children reach at given
norms of ages can we accelerate the stages? Do we have to go through
each one of these stages, or can't we speed it up a bit? Well, surely, the
answer is yes . . . but how far can we speed them up? . . . I have a
hypothesis which I am so far incapable of proving: probably the organization of operations has an optimal time . . . For example, we know
that it takes 9 to 12 months before babies develop the notion that an
object is still there even when a screen is placed in front of it. Now
kittens go through the same sub-stages but they do it in three months—
so they're six months ahead of the babies. Is this an advantage or
isn't it?

"We can certainly see our answer in one sense. The kitten is not going
to go much further. The child has taken longer, but he is capable of
going further so it seems to me that the nine months were not for nothing . . . It is probably possible to accelerate, but maximal acceleration
is not desirable. There seems to be an optimal time. What this optimal
time is will surely depend upon each individual and on the subject matter. We still need a great deal of research to know what the optimal
time would be."

Piaget's stance against using his findings as a justification for ac-
celerating children intellectually recalls a remark made by Freud when
he was asked whatever became of those bright, aggressive shoeshine
boys one encounters in city streets. Freud's reply was, "They become
cobblers." In Piaget's terms they get to a certain point earlier but they
don't go as far. And the New York educator Eliot Shapiro has pointed
out that one of the Negro child's problems is that he is forced to grow
up and take responsibility too soon and doesn't have time to be a child.

Despite some premature and erroneous applications of his thinking to education, Piaget has had an over-all effect much more positive than negative. His findings about children's understanding of scientific and mathematical concepts are being used as guidelines for new curricula in these subjects. And his tests are being more and more widely used to evaluate educational outcomes. Perhaps the most significant and widespread positive effect that Piaget has had upon education is in the changed attitudes on the part of teachers who have been exposed to his thinking. After becoming acquainted with Piaget's work, teachers can never again see children in quite the same way as they had before. Once teachers begin to look at children from the Piagetian perspective they can also appreciate his views with regard to the aims of education.

"The principal goal of education," he once said, "is to create men who are capable of doing new things, not simply of repeating what other generations have done—men who are creative, inventive and discoverers. The second goal of education is to form minds which can be critical, can verify, and not accept everything they are offered. The great danger today is of slogans, collective opinions, ready-made trends of thought. We have to be able to resist individually, to criticize, to distinguish between what is proven and what is not. So we need pupils who are active, who learn early to find out by themselves, partly by their own spontaneous activity and partly through materials we set up for them; who learn early to tell what is verifiable and what is simply the first idea to come to them."

At the beginning of his eighth decade, Jean Piaget is as busy as ever. A new book of his on memory will be published soon and another on the mental functions in the preschool child is in preparation. The International Center for Genetic Epistemology, which Piaget founded in 1955 with a grant from the Rockefeller Foundation, continues to draw scholars from around the world who wish to explore with Piaget the origin of scientific concepts. As Professor of Experimental Psychology at the University of Geneva, Piaget also continues to teach courses and conduct seminars.

And his students still continue to collect the data which at the end of the school year Piaget will take with him up to the mountains. The methods employed by his students today are not markedly different from those which were used by their predecessors decades ago. While there are occasional statistics, there are still no electronics or computers. In an age of moon shots and automation, the remarkable discoveries of Jean Piaget are evidence that in the realm of scientific achievement, technological sophistication is still no substitute for creative genius.

* * *

Jean Piaget, the Swiss psychologist, has been studying the development of intelligence (adaptive thinking and action) in children for more than 50 years. It is only in the past decade, however, that his monumental contribution to our knowledge of children's thinking has come to be widely appreciated in America. The process of assimilating Piaget's ideas is, however, a slow one both because there is so much to assimilate and because many of Piaget's ideas are contrary to prevailing modes of thought. The slowness of assimilation is particularly evident in the domain of learning where Piaget's ideas have been in contention with a well established body of research and theory.

Perhaps it is because Piaget's views on learning are so different from the prevailing ones in America that they have been among the least publicized and the least available to teachers. Paradoxically, however, many of the new curricula in math, science and social studies derive in part from the Piagetian orientation to learning. Effective utilization of new curriculum materials based on Piaget, demands—or so it seems to me—that they be accompanied by text material designed to acquaint teachers with Piaget's views on learning. While it is impossible to provide such materials here, it might be helpful to briefly introduce and describe three ideas which are central to the Piagetian approach to learning. These ideas are that a) learning is creating, b) learning is developmental, and c) learning is living and growing.

Learning Is Creating

One of Piaget's most important contributions to psychology and education is his demonstration of the creative nature of children's thinking and learning. In the past there were two dominant theories as to how these mental activities operated to provide the individual with a useful picture of the world in which he lives.

One point of view holds that the mind acts like a motion picture camera which merely records a pre-existing world of persons and things. The other point of view, less prominent today, is that the mind is not so much a camera as it is a projector of its own inborn films. From this point of view, the mind never really learns anything new and running the projector (experiencing the world) merely allows the mind to find out what was stored in its own inborn film library.

In contrast to the camera (nurture) and projector (nature) positions regarding the nature of thinking and learning, Piaget argues that the mind is best thought of not as a mechanical contrivance but rather as a creative artist. The true artist never simply copies reality nor does he merely execute some inner vision. Rather the artist brings his experience of reality and his inner vision together by means of a creative process whose result is a product that is not reducible to its components. A good painting is a new reality which at one and the same time captures the artist's inner vision and his real experience.

The products of the mind, so Piaget has shown, are created in much the same way as the artist creates a painting. Perhaps the simplest demonstration of this fact comes not from Piaget's own research but rather from the responses of different individuals to the inkblot test devised by Herman Rorschach. When presented with these inkblots, different people see different things. In the same card one person will see a butterfly, another will see two men supporting a woman while still another person will see a badge with two eagles on it. What people see on these blots depends both upon the character of the blots and upon their own personal predilections. Accordingly, an individual's response to an inkblot is a creation no less than the artist's painting.

What Piaget has shown is that much of our knowledge about the world is of the same nature as the response to the inkblot, a product of our own predilections and of our experience. A child's ideas about number, space, time and causality are never direct copies of what he has been taught or experienced nor are they ever simple projections of some fixed and innate ideas about these matters. We often catch glimpses of this creative process in children's so-called "errors." The child who asks, "If I eat spaghetti, will I be Italian?" expresses an original idea which is neither entirely learned (nobody taught him that!) nor entirely innate (because the child will give the idea up later and innate ideas don't change).

To make concrete how the child creates his world in the very process of learning about it consider the following example from Piaget's research:

The demonstration involves presenting children with two identical glass beakers filled equally high with orange soda. The child is asked if there is the same amount of orange soda to drink in the two glasses. After the child has agreed that this is indeed the case, the liquid from one of the beakers is poured into a much taller and thinner beaker in which it now reaches a much higher level than it did in the original beaker. The child is now asked to compare the amount of orange drink in the tall, narrow beaker with the amount of drink in the low, wide beaker and to say whether one of the beakers has more to drink than the other or whether the two beakers contain the same amount.

When young children are confronted with this demonstration, their performance is quite predictable. They say that the tall, narrow container contains more liquid than there is in the low, wide container. They persist in this judgment even when they're reminded that when the orange drink was in the other beaker it had the same amount of liquid as the low, wide container with which it is now compared. Young children persist in arguing, however, that there is more to drink in the tall, thin container because the level of orange drink in it is higher than the level of orange drink in the other container. For the child, amount of drink is equal to its level in the container.

If the demonstration is presented to an older child (usually ages 6–7), however, quite a different result is obtained. The older child says immediately that the amount of liquid in the tall, narrow beaker is still the same as the amount in the low, wide beaker because "nothing was added or taken away" or because "what it gained in height, it lost in width," or because "if you pour it back, it will be the same." These children recognized that a change in the appearance of a quantity of liquid did not amount to a change in its quantity. Piaget terms this understanding, that a quantity remains unchanged across transformations in its appearance, *conservation*.

Now although Piaget's "conservation" experiments are well known, one feature of these experiments is seldom mentioned. That feature has to do with the fact that once a child attains conservation, he assumes that the equality exists independently of himself and in the materials. In fact, however, the child arrived at conservation by reasoning. This is true because a simple comparison of two differently sized containers partially filled with liquid in and of itself gives no clues to the equality or inequality of the two amounts. The child must, therefore, reason from his previous experience of having seen the two amounts in identical containers at a prior point in time. It is on the basis of that prior experience that he reasons that the two quantities are the same now. In effect, the child arrives at conservation through reason but assumes that he arrived at it through observation.

It is really hard to overemphasize the importance of this unconscious projection of our own mental constructions onto the external world, which has been called "externalization." It is externalization which prevents us, as adults, from recognizing that children are creating while they are learning. Inasmuch as we have already created and externalized our reality it seems to us that the child's task is merely to copy that reality. That is to say, we erroneously assume that we learned about the world by copying a preexisting reality and just assume that children do likewise. Piaget's greatness thus lies not only in having shown us that children are creating while learning but also why we as adults have so much difficulty in perceiving this fact.

Learning Is Developmental

A second major contribution of Piaget to child psychology and education is his demonstration that learning is *developmental* in nature; that is to say, the learning process is not static but rather evolves in a series of stages that are related to age. Again, this position conflicts with accepted opinion which holds that learning involves a more or less fixed set of principles that hold for children as well as adults and even for other species. For Piaget, in contrast, both the way in which children learn and what they learn is very much determined by their level of mental development.

To make this position concrete it is helpful to describe each of Piaget's major stages of development as being concerned with the mastery of a particular "chunk" of reality. The "chunks" to be mastered at each stage are of course, different from one another and when they have been mastered and put together the young person arrives at the three-dimensional, multi-layered reality familiar to adults. The mastery process itself is really the creative learning process we have already described. Accordingly, we can, without exaggeration, describe each of Piaget's stages by means of the "chunk" of reality that the young person must create or recreate during that period.

During the first stage (usually birth to 2 years) the infant is concerned first and foremost with *the creation of objects*. The young infant does not really have any sense of objects as distinct from himself or any sense of himself as distinct from objects. Thus he does not see the difference between the object which disappears by itself (as occurs when his mother leaves the room) from an object which disappears because of his own action (as occurs when he turns from mother and looks away). To the infant, the appearance and disappearance of objects is thus capricious and he attributes no more permanence to them than we do to the shadows cast on the wall by a fire in the fireplace. That is why the young infant does not cry when the mother leaves the room. To him, out of sight is literally out of mind.

By the end of the first year, and with increasing exactitude during the second year, the infant comes to construct or create a world of objects which have permanence and are here to stay. That is, the infant now behaves as if objects continue to exist even when they are no longer present to his senses. Evidence of the creation of a world of permanent objects comes from such observations as the one-year-old child's distress when the mother leaves the room and his fear of "strangers" who threaten his newly discovered sense of personal permanence.

The creation of permanent objects (including the self as object) is largely attributable to the child's increasing capacity to coordinate his sensory-motor activities. Permanent objects are created as the infant becomes progressively able to coordinate his visual, his motor, his auditory and his gustatory experiences of an object into an integrated whole that at once has form, color, smell, taste and texture. The ability to coordinate sensory-motor experiences is thus the ability that makes possible the creation of objects during the first year of life.

At the second stage (usually ages 3–5) the major task of the child is to *create symbols*. Now that he has acquired a world of permanent objects, the child acquires the ability to represent these objects by images and words which greatly extends the utilization of these objects. The representations that emerge during this period are genuine creations. The child who holds up a potato chip and says, "See mommy, a butterfly," has created a symbol which transcends the experiences and abilities involved in its production. The same holds true for the other representations which appear during this period such as can be observed in dramatic play (children dressing up as adults) and in dreams which are first reported after the age of two.

Language, which is the major representational system that appears during this period, is a very special case but even language learning has its creative components. Recent work stimulated by the writing of Noam Chomsky has shown that young children very early attain grammars which are nonetheless different from the grammars attained by older children and adults.

One early grammar is the so-called "Pivot Grammar." With this grammar the child builds two word sentences of the kind, "Bobby up," "Bobby down," "Bobby go," "Bobby eat" and so on, where one word serves as the "pivot" for many different constructions. In language, as in the domains of play and dreams, therefore, children of preschool age are busily creating symbols thanks to the new representational abilities that emerge around the end of the second year of life.

The third stage (usually ages 6–11) can be thought of as primarily concerned with the *creation of rules*. Preschool-age children do not really play or behave according to rules in the strict sense. They make and break rules pretty much as they see fit (usually in ways that make the adult lose the game) and therefore cannot really participate in rule games such as checkers, chess, Monopoly and so on. Nor can they really behave according to rules, and the parents of preschool children must repeat the same prohibitions and demands over and over again. Beginning at about the age of five or six, however, the child develops the ability to reason in a systematic and logical way, from premise to conclusion, with the result that he is able to create and to follow rules.

The school-age child's newly emerged capacity to create rules is evidenced in the personal, social and school domains. On the personal level children of school age have internalized many rules which they will obey even in the absence of an adult. When children of this age break rules, they are very well aware of that fact. In the social domain, school-age children engage in all sorts of games with rules. These range from sedentary card games and Monopoly to active games such as baseball and football all of which involve specified sets of rules. In the academic domain, children are dealing with creating or re-creating rules whether

they are involved in math, science, literature, art or music. The concern
with rules, therefore dominates the elementary school years. It might be
said that many academic difficulties encountered by young people often
result from a deficiency of rule-forming ability or from the formation of
erroneous or interfering rules. In mathematics many children have difficulty because they learn one rule and assume that it applies to all instances and do not see that there are many rules that have to be applied
in different circumstances. Reading too, from the very outset, involves
rule-learning and formal instruction in reading could well be delayed
until the child has demonstrated that he has the capacity to create and to
follow rules.

The fourth and last Piagetian stage (usually ages 12–15) can be said
to be primarily concerned with the *creation of thought*. Elementary
school children think but they do not think about thinking. Adolescents
do think about thinking. This new capacity to conceptualize thought is
attributable to the emergence at about the age of 12 of what Piaget calls
"formal operations." These formal operations enable young people to
create a second, higher order symbol system, a system of symbols for
symbols or language for language. It is this second order symbol system
that allows adolescents to deal with algebra and symbolic logic on the
one hand and to think about thinking on the other.

The adolescent's ability to create the concept of thought is evidenced
by many characteristic adolescent behaviors. Only in adolescence do
young people really begin to talk about and discuss *ideas*. Only at this
stage do words like "belief" and "value" and "conscious" begin to enter
the young person's vocabulary. The proverbial self-consciousness of the
adolescent also derives from his new ability to think about what other
people think about him. Adolescent idealism and impatience with the
slowness of reform derives from the same types of creation. Second order
symbols, in effect, are abstractions, like liberty and freedom, which ideal-
ize reality. Young people believe that it is as easy to realize complete
freedom say for oppressed people, as it is to conceive the possibility of
such freedom. Only with age and experience do young people learn the
relation between the perfection of ideals and the necessary imperfection
of their realization in practice.

Adolescents, then, are busy creating the world of the mind and of the
intellect which complements the worlds of rules, of symbols and of objects created at previous stages. In addition, however, adolescents are
also beginning to integrate these various worlds into the comprehensive
and multilayered reality which is the world in which adults are immersed.
It should be said, perhaps, that the reality of adults does not remain static
but changes too, in less dramatic but equally significant ways. The adult
is progressively able to refine and appreciate the worlds in which he lives
through experience and reflection.

Learning Is Living and Growing

It is apparent from the foregoing discussions that for Piaget learning is not a circumscribed process but is rather an essential part of living and growing. A child does not learn only when he is sitting quietly at his desk or when he is listening to the teacher. The child is learning all the time and the question is not whether he is learning but rather *what* he is learning.

The fact that children are learning all of the time is really not a very new idea, but it is one that we often forget. The slow child who is doing nothing in the classroom is very quick to learn that he is slow. The child who gives the teacher a hard time in the classroom may not learn much about social studies but he acquires a great deal of knowledge about the teacher and what makes her angry and how she reacts when she is angry. He is learning rules but not those he is supposed to be learning.

Adolescents, too, may be more concerned with ideas of ecology or drugs or sex than they are with the ideas of science. They learn ideas about these matters in any case and we can not really blink at this kind of learning. We need to face the fact that young people are learning all of the time and that we need to concern ourselves not just with what we want them to know but with what they are finding out on their own. Piaget's ideas on learning can be most helpful in that regard.

* * *

Everybody in education realizes that Piaget is saying something that is relevant to the teaching of children. For the most part he is understood to be underestimating the value of teaching. He is understood to be saying something like this: Children go through certain stages of intellectual development from birth through adolescence. These stages materialize, fully constructed, when their time has come, and there is little we can do to advance them. What we must do in education is to realize the limits of children's understanding at certain ages, and plan our teaching so it falls within these limits.

In two recent conferences, one at Cornell, one at Berkeley, Piaget made clear that the implications of his psychology for education are a good deal more fecund than this. In fact, the only one of these statements that he would support is that children go through certain stages of intellectual development. Contrary to the view most often attributed to him, he maintains that good pedagogy *can* have an effect on this development.

I will start with the essentials of Piaget's theory of intellectual develop-

Eleanor Duckworth, "Piaget Rediscovered," *ESS Newsletter,* June 1964, reprinted in *The ESS Reader* (Newton, Mass.: Elementary Science Study of the Education Development Center, 1970). Reprinted by permission of the Elementary Science Study of Education Development Center, Inc.

ment, as presented at these conferences, and then go on to some implications for education.

Development of intellectual capacity goes through a number of stages whose order is constant, but whose time of appearance may vary both with the individual and with the society. Each new level of development is a new coherence, a new structuring of elements which until that time have not been systematically related to each other.

Piaget discussed four factors contributing to this development: nervous maturation, encounters with experience, social transmission, and equilibration or auto-regulation. While the first three do indeed play a role, Piaget finds each of them insufficient in itself. His findings lead him to conclude that an individual's intellectual development is a process of equilibration, where the individual himself is the active motor and coordinator of his own development.

What the first three factors have in common is that the individual is passive. Something is done *to* him; his physiological system matures, or he is presented with physical or linguistic material to absorb. But intellectual development is not this passive. Piaget finds it necessary to call upon the factor of the individual's own activity. An individual learns to see the world as coherent, as structured, to the extent that he acts upon the world, transforms it, and succeeds in coordinating these actions and transformations.

Development proceeds as partial understandings are revised, broadened, and related to one another. Piaget's model for this is one of auto-regulation to attain even broader and more stable equilibrium in the individual's dealing with his world.

As far as education is concerned, the chief outcome of this theory of intellectual development is a plea that children be allowed to do their own learning. Piaget is not saying that intellectual development proceeds at its own pace no matter what you try to do. He is saying that what schools usually try to do is ineffectual. You cannot further understanding in a child simply by talking to him. Good pedagogy must involve presenting the child with situations in which he himself experiments in the broadest sense of that term—trying things out to see what happens, manipulating things, manipulating symbols, posing questions and seeking his own answers, reconciling what he finds at one time with what he finds at another, and comparing his findings with those of other children.

Beyond this general implication, Piaget does not claim to be an educator. During the course of the two conferences he made no single discourse on pedagogy. But he made a number of points which I have gathered together here. Most of them are not new ideas, but it seems to me that it is of importance, somehow, to realize that this is what he is saying.

I shall start with comments on one or two teaching practices often associated with Piaget's name because of some relationships to his research. One is the head-on attack on a specific notion in a precise and limited way. This is the type of attack engaged in by psychological experimenters, in trying to teach four- and five-year-olds, for example, that the amount of liquid stays the same when poured into a glass of a different shape. (In Piaget's own research, when a child asserts that the same amount of liquid is conserved, this is taken as an indication of a certain structure of mental operations. For this reason, performance on this task is an important indicator of intellectual level.)

Piaget sees little sense in intensive specific training on tasks like this one. His feeling is that no learning of significance will take place. Even if the child does manage to learn something about this situation, the learning is not likely to have a general effect on his level of understanding.

But notice that he is *not* thereby saying that a young child's mental structure cannot be touched. He is only saying that this type of specific attack is rather trivial. Modifying a child's effective set of mental operations depends on a much wider, longer-lasting, and fundamental approach which involves all of the child's activity.

Piaget amplified this point about the importance of investigative activity in general in reply to a question on cross-cultural comparisons. Montreal psychologists, using Piaget's material as tests, found children in Martinique to be delayed several years compared to children in Montreal. Similarly, there is a significant delay of children in Iranian villages over children in Iranian cities. Piaget was asked what factors in the adult societies might account for these differences.

In reply, he first pointed out that the schools in Martinique follow the same curriculum as the schools in France, so that scholastic preparation was not likely to account for the difference. Then he quoted the psychologist who had done the research in Martinique, who pointed out that the climate is fine, agriculture flourishes, and living poses few problems. There seems to be little call for questioning and struggling for solutions in general, little call for either physical or intellectual activity. Piaget speculated that this could be the significant factor.

Another pedagogical approach often associated with Piaget's name has to do with teaching the "structure" of a subject matter area. This has been associated with him because of the importance that mental structures play in his psychological theory. The word "structure" is seized upon as the link.

The pedagogical idea is that children should be taught the unifying themes of a subject matter area, after which they will be able to relate individual items to this general structure. (This seems to be what Bruner often means by "teaching the structure" in *The Process of Education*.) Commenting on this procedure, Piaget made the following statement:

The question comes up whether to teach the structure, or to present the child with situations where he is active and creates the structures himself. . . . The goal in education is not to increase the amount of knowledge, but to create the possibilities for a child to invent and discover. When we teach too fast, we keep the child from inventing and discovering himself. . . . Teaching means creating situations where structures can be discovered; it does not mean transmitting structures which may be assimilated at nothing other than a verbal level.

Piaget addressed two remarks to problems of teacher training. The first is that adults, as well as children, can learn better by doing things than by being told about them. He was talking about teachers in training, when he said, "If they read about it, it will be deformed, as is all learning that is not the result of the subject's own activity."

The second is that prospective teachers ought to spend some time questioning children in a one-to-one situation, in order to realize how hard it is to understand what children mean, and even more, how hard it is to make oneself understood by children. Each prospective teacher should work on an original investigation to find out what children think about some problem, and thus be forced to phrase the problem and establish communication with a number of different children. Facing the difficulties of this type of research will have a sobering effect on a teacher who thinks he is talking successfully to a whole class of children at once.

Permit me one other point of psychological theory as context for another of Piaget's remarks. Piaget sees the process of equilibration as a process of balance between assimilation and accommodation in a biological sense. An individual assimilates the world which comes down to saying he sees it in his own way. But sometimes something presents itself in such a way that he cannot assimilate it into his view of things, so he must change his view; he must accommodate if he wants to incorporate this new item.

The question arose in this conference as to whether school situations could lead a child to accommodate wrongly, that is, to change his ideas on the wrong basis. Piaget replied:

This is a very interesting question. This is a big danger of school —false accommodation which satisfies a child because it agrees with a verbal formula he has been given. This is a false equilibrium which satisfies a child by accommodating to words—to authority and not to objects as they present themselves to him. . . . A teacher would do better not to correct a child's schemas, but to provide situations so he will correct them himself.

Here are a few other remarks at random:

Experience is always necessary for intellectual development. . . . But I fear that we may fall into the illusion that being submitted to an experience (a demonstration) is sufficient for a subject to disengage the structure involved. But more than this is required. The subject must be active, must transform things, and find the structure of his own actions on the objects.

When I say "active," I mean it in two senses. One is acting on material things. But the other means doing things in social collaboration, in a group effort. This leads to a critical frame of mind, where children must communicate with each other. This is an essential factor in intellectual development. Cooperation is indeed co-operation.

(The role of social interaction is important in Piaget's theory of development. A characteristic phenomenon in intellectual difficulties of preschool children is that they have difficulty conceiving of any point of view other than their own. Coming to an awareness that another child sees something differently from the way he sees it plays an important role in bringing a child to accommodate, to rebuild his point of view, and to come closer to a coherent operational structure.)

The best idea I have heard from a pedagog at the International Bureau of Education in Geneva was made by a Canadian. He said that in his province they had just decided every class should have two classrooms— one where the teacher is, and one where the teacher isn't.

The teacher must provide the instruments which the children can use to decide things by themselves. Children themselves must verify, experimentally in physics, deductively in mathematics. A ready-made truth is only a half-truth.

One participant asked what Piaget thought of having children of different ages in a class together. He replied that it might be helpful especially for the older ones. They could be given some responsibility of teaching younger ones. "Nobody knows better than a professor that the best way to learn something is to teach it."

Yes, the element of surprise is an essential motor in education and in scientific research in general. What distinguishes a good scientist is that he is amazed by things which seem natural to others. Surprise plays an important role; we might well try to develop an aptitude for surprise.

Words are probably not a short-cut to a better understanding. . . . The level of understanding seems to modify the language that is used, rather than vice versa. . . . Mainly, language serves to translate what is already understood; or else language may even present a danger if it is used to introduce an idea which is not yet accessible.

The principal goal of education is to create men who are capable of doing new things, not simply repeating what other generations have done —men who are creators, inventors, and discoverers. The second goal of education is to form minds which can be critical, can verify, and do not accept everything they are offered. The great danger today is from slogans, collective opinions, ready-made trends of thought. We have to be able to resist individually, to criticize, to distinguish between what is proven and what is not. So we need pupils who are active, who learn early to find out by themselves, partly by their own spontaneous activity and partly through material we set up for them; who learn early to tell what is verifiable and what is simply the first idea to come to them.

THREE

The Role of the Teacher

More than anything else, what distinguishes the contemporary informal English schools and the American open classrooms from the so-called free schools, which they resemble in a number of superficial ways, or from the child-centered American progressive schools of the 1920s and 1930s, which they also resemble, is the way in which the teacher's role is conceived and carried out. When open educators suggest that learning may be more effective if it grows out of what interests the learner, they are not proposing an abdication of adult authority, only a change in the way it is exercised. "With our foolish and pedantic methods," Jean-Jacques Rousseau wrote, "we are always preventing children from learning what they could learn much better by themselves, while we neglect what we alone can teach them." Teachers in the informal and open classrooms described in this volume try to make this distinction, but they have no doubt about their responsibility to teach. "From the start," the Plowden Committee declares, "there must be teaching as well as learning: children are not 'free' to develop interests or skills of which they have no knowledge. They must have guidance from their teachers." Since what children are interested in is a function of their environment as well as of their native endowment, it is the teacher's responsibility to structure that environment in the best possible way, and to help it change and grow in response to each child's evolving interests and needs.

Indeed, one of the distinguishing characteristics of good open classrooms is the absolute clarity of this understanding, the hardheaded recognition of and indeed insistence on the teacher's central role. It would be impossible for a teacher in a good open classroom to respond as a teacher in New York's Walden School, one of the citadels of American progressivism, did in the 1920s. Asked if he were the teacher, the young man, who was standing with his back to the room, speaking only when children addressed him, replied, "Well, you can call me that; at least I'm here." (The young man's response also sums up the approach of most teachers in contemporary free schools.)

In the open classroom, the teacher is more than simply "here"; he or she is very much in charge. "It's easy to be a sweet nothing and just say, 'Oh, that's nice,'" one London headmistress told me, "but we are here to teach, not just to let children discover." The teacher "must know clearly what she's trying to do and how and why," Nora Goddard, Inspector for Infant Education in London insists. It is not enough to create a rich environment, as teachers of the progressive era too often were content to do. The teacher must know when, and how, to intervene if she is to achieve the main objective—as Miss Goddard defines it, "helping children learn how to think, to form judgments, to discriminate."

With rare exceptions, too, open educators are careful to avoid confusing sentiment *for* children with sentimentality *about* them. "We must avoid being sentimental," Sir Alec Clegg insists. "Happiness has got to derive from achievement and success, not just having a good time." Concern for the needs of each child, writes John Blackie, a former Chief Inspector of Primary Schools in England, "does not mean being sentimental about children ('dear little things') or forcing them into premature and precocious importance, mistakes that many have made in England and elsewhere. It means regarding them as our responsibility." And that responsibility means teaching them: transmitting, creating, and evoking the skills, values, attitudes, and knowledge that will help them grow into mature, creative, and happy adults. In short, the teacher plays a far more active and creative role in the open classroom than in the traditional classroom.

This part, on the role of the teacher, is divided into four chapters. Chapter I provides an overview of the teacher's role. Chapter II, "How to Organize Time and Space," contains selections describing how teachers can utilize the physical space of the classroom and how they can organize each day. Chapter III, "The Use of Concrete Materials," contains selections discussing the importance of concrete materials and explaining how to scrounge for materials, where to buy them, and how to use them. Chapter IV, "How to Begin," contains selections describing various strategies for making the initial change from the traditional formal classroom to more informal, open approaches. In all four chapters, practical "how to" materials are combined with selections analyzing *why* the various techniques are important.

I

An Overview

1. The Teacher's Manifold Roles

The open classroom is as much teacher-centered as it is child-centered. More precisely, it is a person-centered environment, which is open to the teacher's growth as a thinking, feeling, acting human being no less than to the child's. As Charity James has written in Young Lives at Stake, *"Teachers' lives are at stake, too. They should be experiencing the same kinds of support, respect, and optimism about themselves that we ask them to accord to young people."*

The selection that follows provides an exceptionally lucid and sensitive analysis of the nature of the teaching process in an open classroom, and of the wide variety of roles the teacher plays.

A popular dimension in early education research postulates that a classroom can be located somewhere on a scale of "child-centeredness to adult-centeredness." At one extreme is a classroom completely controlled by the teacher and organized around formal curricular requirements; and at the other end, a classroom in which the children are theoretically setting the entire course of learning—with a wide variety of positions in between. One important finding that emerges from examination of the EDC position is the fact that it does not fit comfortably anywhere on such a scale.

From Anne M. Bussis and Edward A. Chittenden, *Analysis of an Approach to Open Education*, pp. 20–49.

It is obvious on one hand that the EDC approach is child-centered, in many ways just discussed in the preceding chapter. In describing aims of this program, Armington places at the top of his list questions about children's responsibilities for their own activities—e.g., "Are they self directing? Do they take responsibility for their own learning?" It is argued that only the individual child can best determine what is meaningful to learn at a given time and what is the best pace and direction for learning. A breadth as well as a height component to learning is stressed. Children mess around with ideas, they elaborate, they do things over again, they do them in different ways. In the more traditional sense, learning is also seen as taking the form of vertical progression, of upward development. The basic image of the child is one of a constructor of reality . . . in a Piagetian sense, an inventor. The child puts together ideas and things in his own way and comes up with new combinations. From a pedagogical standpoint, it is believed that the growth of personal knowledge and the organization of experience can best take place when the child himself is located at the command center of the process.

The role of the teacher in EDC rooms is in many ways a good deal more difficult to delineate than the role of the child. In part, this is due to the fact that most publications, British as well as American, tend to give considerable attention to the children in open settings but are vaguer on how and where the teacher fits into the scheme. Of greater significance, however, is the fact that our usual dichotomous conception of the classroom can be misleading. We anticipate, for example, that the teacher's role in an EDC child-centered classroom will be the role of an understanding supportive adult—a role which has frequently been associated with teachers in child-centered preschool and early education programs. But any essentially passive conception of the EDC teacher is quite incorrect in several important ways. While it has been pointed out that teachers try to understand children, it is certainly not true that the EDC teacher should be some kind of unobtrusive valet who attempts to foresee and attend to every need.

An inescapable conclusion is that EDC appears to represent not only a child-centered position, but also an adult-centered position. The very advocates of this philosophy are themselves educational activitists who in their own teaching would never be content with a purely nurturant role. A major purpose of the advisory is to stimulate a greater degree of activism among teachers: in selecting materials and equipment; making suggestions; diagnosing; questioning; actively expressing their interests; being honest and adult in their appraisal. The classroom should reflect the teacher and other concerned adults just as it should reflect children. Far from expecting uncritical acceptance or passive conformity to anybody else's views, the advisory staff concentrates on fostering an experimental attitude on the part of teachers, encouraging them to "come alive" in ways that go beyond the passive roles of valet or of conveyor of a curriculum. In summary, good EDC classrooms bring active adults together with active children.

This analysis of the EDC position raises an interesting problem for conceptualization of an early education approach. It becomes apparent that child-centeredness and adult-centeredness might be viewed as independent dimensions in the classroom rather than as opposite ends of a single scale. Thus, we propose the two-dimensional space represented in Figure 1 (below) as a more adequate scheme for conceptualizing classroom environments. To locate a classroom in this space, two sets of questions need to be asked concerning persons who influence the nature and direction of learning. The first set of questions deals with the child as learner. To what extent does he affect what happens to him in that room? The second set of questions relates to the teacher's contributions.

FIGURE 1

Double Classification Scheme Based on Extent to Which (1) the Individual Teacher and (2) the Individual Child Is an Active Contributor to Decisions Regarding the Content and Process of Learning.

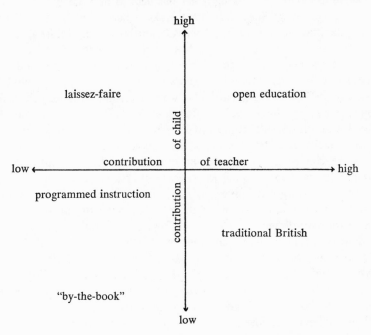

In the upper right-hand quadrant would be located classrooms that have developed considerably along the lines advocated by EDC. In the upper left-hand quadrant are rooms in which the adult plays a very supportive but entirely nondirective role, the children having great freedom which occasionally erupts into chaos. The adult is rated as low in contribution for several reasons, one being her passive acceptance of the curriculum or of some set of "accepted" practices and procedures. While she may seek good relationships with children, such a teacher nevertheless works within set confines. The stereotype of many nursery schools might fall into this quadrant. The preschool teacher here is likely to be a rather bland individual who does not come through very strongly as a person. She may be up to date on child development theory and often tries very hard to understand children and to have a program suitable to their needs. But she is servant more than teacher, the emphasis is on nurturance rather than education. This quadrant would also contain rooms characterized by an extreme "hands-off" or laissez-faire attitude in which the adult generally attempts to avoid expressing personal preference or direct suggestion.

In the lower right-hand quadrant would be classrooms in which the children have little say about what they will do. The teacher may be an active professional woman who examines new curriculum materials with a very critical eye as to their suitability for her classroom. She may be very active in diagnosis, making it her business to find out how the children are progressing. She tends not to take other people's word for it. She may or may not be warm in her relationships with children, but in either case she would come through strongly as an individual adult— the kind of teacher who is often remembered, sometimes with fondness, sometimes with anger. Some high school and college teachers might fit this category. They have a particular way of teaching Shakespeare, for example, that they have evolved themselves. They will throw out the textbook when it doesn't seem to make sense to them. They give a great deal of thought to what goes on in their room and perhaps as to how they are reaching each pupil. On the other hand, they give little credit or chance for decision making to students, preferring to think of themselves in the starring role and occupying "center stage" of the classroom.

The lower left-hand quadrant is the most distant from an open classroom in the two-dimensional space of Figure 1, containing rooms that the advisors would probably consider most dehumanized of all. Unlike the lower right, the teacher here is a passive conveyor of decisions made elsewhere; and unlike the upper left, the children have very little freedom or chance to express themselves. In such a room teachers often teach "by the book" and tend not to question its suitability for them or for their particular children. They accept the words of curriculum experts, of psychologists, of programmed texts, of most anybody, and rarely raise the significant questions themselves. The teachers of this quadrant are given, and depend upon "packages," guides, manuals, and other supportive devices to help them become more effective conveyors of decisions made elsewhere. Advisors argue that these are the rooms where education is seen as a grim business, a preparation for life, rather than life itself.

Somewhere in the middle of this two-dimensional space, at the intersection of the two lines, might be a room taught by an imaginative teacher using creative curriculum materials with emphasis on the discovery method. The children are given quite a bit of room to maneuver, although the external objectives of the lessons are clearly established. The teaching method here has been described as a kind of "sneaky telling." In this central position the emphasis is often on the need for children to understand rather than on the need for them to invent or construct. Similarly, the emphasis might be on the need for the teacher to understand what she is doing and toward what goals she is striving, but not much on her own inventions, constructions, or other forms of departure.

What are the implications of this two-dimensional scheme in which both teacher and children in a classroom are described as being somewhere on a scale from "high" to "low" in terms of their contribution to decisions regarding the content and process of learning? The vignettes presented above have hopefully served to point out at least one important implication—that the scheme has wide applicability. Although derived from a study of EDC, it is not restricted to the classification of EDC classrooms. It is a conceptualization that suggests questions which may be asked of any classroom. It should be stressed in this connection that the classrooms which actually comprise EDC Follow-Through vary greatly—they have indeed come from all four quadrants of the schematic space and they still bear predominant characteristics of all four quadrants. Granting the self-selection feature that is built into Project Follow-Through, it has been our observation that there are extensive differences between localities in the degree to which teachers had an active voice in choosing the EDC program. If this observation holds true for the other Follow-Through programs as well (as we suspect it does), then in reality all Follow-Through sponsors must work in classrooms that reflect a wide variety of teaching styles.

To the extent that the present conceptualization does have generalized applicability, it follows that the objectives of any educational program, when adequately implemented, would result in an "ideal classroom" which could be located somewhere in the space. For example, an educational position which advocates "teacher proof" instructional packages would strive to create a classroom environment that would be located somewhere left of center in the space, with its position along the vertical axis depending upon the degree of choice and freedom extended to students. Thus, it is argued that all Follow-Through sponsors probably work with classrooms located in all parts of the schematic space, but they are attempting to "draw" these classrooms toward some particular point which represents their objectives.

A major implication of this conceptual scheme, then, is its potential usefulness for assessing change in classrooms—more particularly, from our point of view, change toward an open classroom environment. Preliminary attempts to apply this scheme in studying EDC classrooms suggests that there may be rather important differences between teachers who are basically engaged in experimenting with a new image of themselves and teachers who are primarily engaged in experimenting with a new image of children. This distinction between horizontal and vertical movement seems important, because it implies that the influence of the EDC advisory may be less evident in classrooms where the attitudes and ideas of the teacher about her own role are changing and more obvious in classrooms where things are happening with the children. Occasionally, we felt that advisors had had significant influence on a particular teacher, in the sense that she was beginning to question her role in important ways, but these results were not yet clearly visible in what the children were doing. In such circumstances, the advisors tended to feel that they had not accomplished much. Conversely, in a few rooms where things had opened up considerably for the children, we tended to think that the teacher still held an essentially passive image of herself, was doing what she thought the program "expected" of her, and was too dependent on support from the advisors.

The year's study has also suggested the hypothesis that the easiest and most natural change toward an open classroom occurs in a vertical direction—in changing ideas about the capabilities of children and the freedom they can manage. The idea of centering on the child, however that philosophy has been formulated, is not new to a large segment of the American public (at least as set forth in education texts and child care manuals). Teachers recognize, or think they recognize in EDC's position, a view of the child which is not totally unfamiliar. By comparison, change in the horizontal direction seems to be considerably more difficult for many teachers. It requires abandoning the passive role of enacting a program in favor of taking part in creating an instructional approach. For many American elementary school teachers this can require a shift from subprofessional status and self-image to a more professional view of her role. (It is interesting to speculate that British teachers, with a stronger professional tradition, find less discomfort with the active image; possibly, for them, the infant school movement has meant discovering the child—or moving from the lower right to the upper right quadrant.) In any case, such observations and hypotheses are questions which could be submitted to further research. They are raised again in the chapter on "Implications."

In field notes on visits to some EDC classrooms that struck us as being particularly successful, the comment is made that "one has the impression of an open classroom but a tight ship." Although children as individuals had a great deal of influence and control over what went on in these rooms, there was a sense of overall direction and purpose which seemed to stem not only from the purposefulness of the children's activities, but from a sense of community and from the efforts of the teacher. While it is impossible to give any very satisfactory definition of the term "structure" as it is used in the context of open education, it would appear that this sense of classroom direction is what is referred to when educators claim that an "open" approach is not an "unstructured" approach. Because we found it difficult to define the teacher's part in an open setting—to explain how a classroom contains both an active, influential adult and active, influential children—considerable time was spent in trying to examine the teacher's role and come to grips with the more general notion of classroom structure.

As a starting point for analysis, it was helpful to employ Jackson's distinction between activities engaged in by the teacher when children are in the room and those performed when children are not in the room. Generally speaking, research on teacher behavior utilizing classroom observation procedures has tended to focus on the first set of activities. This is the teacher in the role we are most accustomed to visualizing— in a classroom filled with students, performing many maneuvers and functions which are intended to bear on the students' learning. Jackson describes this activity as characterized by "immediacy," both from his own observations and from teachers' self-reports of their classroom behavior. Since unpredicted and unpredictable events will occur during even the most carefully preplanned lesson, there is an immediate "on-the-spot" quality to much of this behavior; and the great bulk of such "on-the-spot" activity has frequently been categorized under the general heading of "Classroom Management." Curiously enough, the notion of classroom management was rarely mentioned by any of the EDC advisors in interviews, and it certainly did not occur as a major theme. What they did stress about the teacher's interaction with children is perhaps best summarized under five general headings: (a) the diagnosis of learning events; (b) the guidance and extension of learning; (c) honesty of encounters; (d) respect for persons; and (e) warmth.

In reading various publications on open classrooms and in listening to the advisors' taped interviews, it also became evident that much of what is stressed about the teacher actually involves behavior occurring *outside* the context of interaction with children. There appear to be three major themes running through these comments which might be summarized as follows: (f) provisioning for learning; (g) reflective evaluation of diagnostic information; and (h) seeking activity to promote continuing personal growth. Considerable emphasis is also placed on characteristics not commonly regarded as "behavior" at all—that is, knowledge, beliefs and attitudes constituting a frame of reference which the teacher brings to the teaching task. For purposes of analysis it seems useful to divide these internal resources of the teacher into two sub-categories: (i) ideas related to children and the process of learning; and (j) ideas related to the perception of self.

Thus, there are ten recurrent themes which we tentatively propose as a way of conceptualizing the role of the teacher who is operating somewhere in the upper righthand quadrant of the two-dimensional space presented in Figure 1. These themes are schematically represented in Figure 2.

FIGURE 2

Analysis of Behaviors Tentatively Proposed as Defining
Characteristics of the "Open Teacher"

Teacher's Internal Frame of Reference	*Activities When Children Are NOT Present*	*Interactive Behaviors with Children*
Ideas Related to Children and to the Process of Learning including: a. Knowledge, beliefs, attitudes b. Trust in ideas c. Valuing processes	Provisioning for * Learning	Diagnosis of * Learning Events
	Reflective Evaluation* of Diagnostic Information	The Guidance and * Extension of Learning
	Seeking Activity to * Promote Personal Growth	Honesty of Encounters
Ideas Related to the Perception of Self including: a. A "beyond the classroom" self b. Responsibility c. Decision-maker d. Continual learner		Respect for Persons
		Warmth

* Components of behavior which are hypothesized to define the horizontal dimension of Figure 1. See text for further explanation.

When this particular picture of the teacher is considered in relation to the two-dimensional space, it becomes evident that not all of the listed behaviors pertain directly to the horizontal "active-teacher" dimension of Figure 1. An overall conceptualization of the teacher's role in open education must be further organized into: (1) those components which are more directly related to the horizontal axis of the schema and would theoretically place a teacher somewhere near the far right of the hypothesized space; and (2) those components which determine the teacher's vertical placement and would serve to locate her position in the upper right, as opposed to the lower right, quadrant. In order to highlight this division, asterisks have been placed in Figure 2 beside those particular components of behavior which are hypothesized to characterize the horizontal axis only.

Considering this set of five (asterisked) behaviors first, it is apparent that they are interrelated in complex ways and that some may even occur simultaneously. While they appear neatly divided in Figure 2, these behaviors are not so readily separated or easily distinguished as such in the on-going life of the teacher. For present purposes, however, the separation into categories does facilitate examination of the active-teacher role in greater depth.

Provisioning for learning. Near the passive end of the dimension in this activity is the teacher who doesn't give much thought to what is in the classroom on any given day. The basal readers and math workbooks are stored somewhere for the children, and their accompanying teacher manuals are filed in a convenient spot. The classroom furniture is standard equipment, arranged in more or less standard fashion. Before the school year began, this teacher may have been allowed to choose between two or three recommended materials in the curriculum catalog or required to decide upon a daily schedule of activities—the latter presumably to be followed the entire year. At the opposite end of the continuum is the teacher image described by Brown and Precious:

> The teacher is in charge of the classroom and it is her responsibility to make the environment (well supplied with suitable apparatus and materials) attractive and thought provoking and one in which there is the widest opportunity for the development of the children's creativity and intellectual ability. . . . Her resources for books, equipment and materials may not always be great, but her imagination and initiative help to make up for deficiencies.

Perhaps the foremost requirement for responsible provisioning is an understanding of the potential value of materials. As several advisors put it during their interview, EDC Follow Through is not simply "having materials"; it is rather an attempt to foster sensitivity to the nature of materials. Even with highly structured materials there is the need for heightened sensitivity. All too often, for example, the teacher's only knowledge of something (be it puzzle, logic blocks, or a Language Master) comes from a manual which states how children are supposed to use the material in question and what they are supposed to "learn" from it. Children, on the other hand, may use any structured material in quite unprecedented ways, gaining unanticipated value from it. Like the child, the active teacher always regards structured material as potentially "fair game" for new and imaginative uses which transform its learning value. Unlike the child, however, she is responsible for understanding in what ways the material lends itself to legitimate educational ends—whether used in an orthodox or unorthodox manner.

It is within the realm of natural and environmental materials, however, that American teachers probably experience greatest uncertainty. On an intuitive level, many think that the gathering of rocks and leaves, the care of live animals, or play with sand and water are all worthwhile learning activities. But it is in justifying precisely such activity, particularly for the upper elementary grades, that teachers are least articulate and most vulnerable to attack. It would appear that part of the trouble stems from the fact that many teachers do lack firm knowledge and genuine appreciation of the learning value of these experiences. Their communication is impoverished because their understanding is hazy. In other instances, a teacher's inarticulateness about the virtue of raw materials may not stem from faulty understanding or limited experience with such material herself; it may instead reflect the complexity of the topic.

After all generalities have been uttered, what specifically can be said about the value of natural and environmental materials? When pushed on this question, one EDC advisor responded with some detailed explanation of the possibilities offered by sand and water. Sand not only lends itself to all kinds of measurement operations (sifting, pouring, weighing) but provides a rich variety of tactile, aesthetic and conceptual experience as well. Wet sand feels and acts differently than dry sand. Dry sand is good for making pictures and designs; wet sand affords the added possibility of three-dimensional construction. Tunnels, bridges, and towers can be made out of wet sand—but not soggy sand. A child can experiment endlessly with the precise consistency required for building different structures. Whole towns and road systems can be constructed, and these in turn may become the subject of mapping exercises as children learn to represent their three-dimensional sand town on a two-dimensional plane. Different symbols are then drawn on the map to identify such things as houses, gas stations, trees, stop signs, etc. In short, the potential for developing quantitative operations and concepts; artistic ability; notions of city planning; rudimentary principles of architecture, engineering, drafting and mapping; and symbolic representational skills—are all inherent in sand and water. Similar examples of the learning potential of raw materials—ranging from plastic bottles for liquid detergent; to food coloring and water; to nuts, bolts, and pegboard—may be found in the accounts of Brown and Precious and Hawkins. In the long run, of course, it is the teacher's own experience with such material in her work with children which provides the essential understanding of its value.

To say that teachers must be sensitive to the learning potential of common environmental material is not to imply that they should plan exactly how children are to use it. To the contrary, any planning of this nature would be quite antithetical to the EDC position. The reasons for *not* planning in such a fashion are well illustrated throughout Hawkins' book, and they are succinctly stated in a quotation which she cites:

> Children, when they construct things in play, normally play after the eolithic fashion: a pointed board suggests the making of a boat, and if the toy, in process of construction, begins to look less and less like a boat, it can conveniently be turned into an airplane. Select the child who appears most ingenious in the making of this class of toys, present him with adequate tools and lumber, give him a simple plan which must, however, be adhered to until completion, and usually his ingenuity gives way to a disheartening dullness. . . .

Other responsibilities for provisioning are more in the nature of practical considerations and "craft." On a purely practical level, as pointed out by one advisor, the teacher should have materials *ready* for use, not just have them "there." Clay, for example, might as well not be in a room if it sits dry and hardened in some pot. On a similar common sense level, activity areas should be arranged so as to facilitate a smooth flow of traffic; and materials and equipment should be placed so as to encourage children to take responsibility. If coat hooks, construction paper, or facilities for displaying the children's work are out of reach, then a child must obviously rely on the teacher or aide for help in performing some act he normally could manage quite well by himself.

Activity areas should also be "attractive" and "appealing" for use by children. It is difficult to define such terms in any precise way, but they certainly do not imply simple artistic arrangement. What they do seem to mean refers more to what might be called "utility" and "balance." If all books in a classroom are centrally stored, for example, this arrangement does not serve a very utilitarian function. A comfortable reading corner well supplied with children's literature is certainly to be desired, but books about the care and feeding of gerbils might better be placed next to the gerbil cage. The term "balance" implies a similar notion. If an activity area is to invite a wide range of interests, then the materials within that area should provide for a range of demands and difficulty levels. If it is assumed that there are diverse ways of "messing about" with a balance beam, then materials near the beam should reflect that diversity of exploratory possibilities. On the other hand, balance beams also lend themselves to more systematic manipulation with problems of increasing difficulty. Therefore, materials such as a set of graduated weights would also be present to reflect and suggest this type of manipulation.

Finally, it is clear that the term "balance" also refers to the totality of a classroom. There should be balance among the activity areas—raw materials, structured materials, reading materials, materials for dramatic play, etc. In addition, the room should reflect some combination of both teacher and child interests, but with the greater weight given to what is relevant for children. This reflection of interests is perhaps most clearly evident in the written and pictorial communications around a classroom. In surveying a room, one might ask the question whether or not these communications are really those of the people who usually live in that room—e.g., do they communicate something meaningful to the children (children's stories or pictures); to the teacher (a favorite poem, a routine reminder about fire regulations); or are they addressed to no interest in particular (a sign: "Spring is Here")? While it may be impossible to determine the relevancy of any one specific communication, the advisors would claim that it is possible to make judgments about the preponderance of communicative material around a classroom.

The topic of provisioning has been treated extensively in this discussion, primarily because it is so central to an educational philosophy that stresses the importance of choice for children and because it is an aspect of the teacher's role which affords many concrete examples. In reality, it is also an area on which the advisors tend to concentrate when they are working with teachers. Other aspects of the teacher's role outlined in Figure 2 will be discussed more briefly.

The diagnosis of learning events. One major goal of provisioning is to provide opportunity for choice—to engage children in activity which they value and find of interest. Only to the extent that children are engaged in such a manner can the teacher gain very much in the way of meaningful information about them. David Hawkins expands on this point:

> What seems very clear to me . . . is that if you operate a school, as we in America almost entirely do, in such a style that the children are rather passively sitting in neat rows and columns . . . then you won't get very much information about them, you won't be a very

good diagnostician of what they need. Not being a good diagnostician, you will be a poor teacher. The child's overt involvement in a rather self-directed way, using the big muscles and not just the small ones, is most important to the teacher in providing an input of information wide in range and variety. . . . I think this is fairly obvious. It doesn't say that you *will* but that you *can* get more significant diagnostic information about children, can refine your behavior as a teacher far beyond the point of what's possible if every child is being made to perform a rather uniform pattern.

Several of the advisors dwelt at some length during interviews on the importance of diagnostic information. One advisor, in particular, voiced concern over the fact that many teachers regard various activities only as providing the child with opportunities for growth. They fail to see this activity as providing *them* with information as well. In her view, the opportunity for children to learn and teachers to assess what is being learned blend inextricably in classroom activity—but many teachers are attuned only to the instructional aspect of that blend.

If there is any key notion at the heart of *how* to obtain diagnostic information, it is the notion of involvement. This was stressed by virtually every advisor, and it is a theme that continually appears in many published works. If significant information is to be gained, you do not observe or relate to children in a vacuum. The active teacher observes children with an involved interest in what they are doing, and she relates to them in the context of involvement in an activity. The very title of Hawkins' paper quoted above—"I, Thou, It"—suggests the nature of this kind of relationship with a child which centers on something of common interest. Such interest cannot be feigned, however, or at least it cannot be feigned for long. A child quickly catches on to the teacher who is really going about the classroom as an informal "tester" (asking questions here and there, making brief observations) and who is more concerned with whether he has learned something than with what he has learned. To become involved and interested in what children are learning does not mean to become a childish adult. Rather, it means setting aside some sophisticated but pre-emptive adult views of the world and learning to appreciate it in new ways. The hard part is the setting aside; but once this is accomplished it is argued that most adults will become better capable of noticing what the child's eyes see and better able to interpret his words and actions.

A final point relating to diagnostic information is that the good teacher knows when to refrain from obtaining it. Frequently, for example, a trip to the zoo or to a museum is followed up immediately by the teacher's request for drawings, written reports, or oral reports expressing what the children "got out" of the venture. It is only natural for a teacher

to want immediate feedback about an unusual experience she has provided for pupils, but to require such feedback can often kill the very
learning one had hoped would occur. To put this principle in a more
familiar context, many adults have experienced the futility of trying to
tell someone "all about" a provocative book they have just finished reading. It is an impossible thing to do. The meaning that is derived from
valuable experience (by adult or child) takes time in evolving; and a
likely result of premature demands for evidence of learning is to interfere with this process and cause the event to be dismissed as "over."
Teachers should certainly look for signs that learning has occurred, but
the impact of a given experience may not reveal itself in the child's behavior until days or even weeks later.

The guidance and extension of learning. What has been said about
diagnostic activity relates closely to the teacher's behavior in guiding
and instructing children. There are few categorical statements that can
be made about when and how a teacher should actively intervene to
divert or redirect the course of some activity or to extend it in a meaningful way. Although teachers feel a great need for guidelines in this
area, it is undoubtedly the most "iffy" and "it depends" topic of all. In
any given instance, it is not likely that even the most experienced teachers
would find themselves in total agreement about what should be done.
The general tenor of their thoughts on the matter might be the same, but
almost certainly they would differ as to specifics. About the only thing
that can be said with any assurance, therefore, is that the teacher is
viewed primarily as a resource person whose job it is to encourage and
influence (in whatever way—asking questions, supplying another material, giving information) the direction and growth of learning activity.

On the negative side of the ledger it does seem possible to offer at
least a few general principles—the "don'ts" rather than the "do's" of
guiding children's learning. In general, for example, the teacher would
be advised not to intervene in any way until she feels fairly certain
what the child is getting from his present activity. In other words, she
would be cautioned to become involved with a child diagnostically before
suggesting any change, extension, or redirection of activity. Secondly,
most of the advisors agree that it is not a good general practice to impose sharp distinctions between fact and fantasy, between what is real
and what is not real. This would be particularly true in the area of reading, for example, where it can be deadly for the child to be told or
reminded continually of such facts as "animals don't really talk." Even
here, however, there are exceptions to the general rule; and the advisors
might not agree that it was any kind of "rule" at all unless the words
"impose" and "sharp" were underscored in the preceding sentence.

At a slightly higher level of certainty is the general principle of not
discouraging choice by any number of subtle and not-so-subtle tech-

niques. While the "you don't really want to do that—do you?" technique is fairly blatant, the "contract system" may not be so obvious at first. A "contract system" refers to the practice of giving children the option of free choice later—*if* they will do something else you want them to do now. The most subtle forms of discouragement are often done quite unconsciously by a teacher, as in the display of highly differentiated interest and values placed on activities. One advisor described this process from personal experience. In her beginning years of teaching, she began to notice that the children were demonstrating an excessive interest in reading—excessive, at least, in light of the variety of other activities she had made available to them. She herself valued reading highly and suddenly realized that her involvement with children most frequently centered on activities related to reading. When her interests and behavior assumed greater balance, there was a corresponding broadening of interests in the classroom.

Reflective evaluation of diagnostic information. The importance of reflective evaluation is apparent in the example just given concerning reading. Had careful thought not been given to the observation that children were "excessive" readers, the teacher might easily have jumped to false assumptions and unproductive efforts. For example, when a teacher observes that children seldom go to a particular activity area, the conclusion often reached is that the activity in question simply is not an interesting one. In many instances, such a conclusion can be quite misleading, for it channels the teacher's energy into an endless search for more "intriguing" materials, as she introduces one new thing after another into the classroom.

In the advisors' opinion, the more usual reasons for children shunning an activity are not to be found in the nature of the activity itself—unless, of course, it is patently inappropriate for those particular children. Rather, they are to be found in such things as the nature of the materials provided for an activity, in the way those materials are arranged or introduced, or (as was the case in the illustration above) in the nature of the teacher's attitudes toward the activity. Whatever the cause, it is insufficient to rest with the diagnostic observation that something "is not working" and therefore hastily conclude that it should be removed. The teacher must also ask "why" it is not working and seek to determine the answer.

Seeking activity to promote personal growth. The importance of personal and professional growth is stressed again and again by advisors, by teachers, by various publications. Growth is defined in ways which go well beyond the type of definition (common to some school systems) that equates professional development with the number of credit hours a teacher may accumulate. One activity thought to be of great importance is on-going communication among teachers in sharing ideas and observations about children and learning. It is such interaction which tends to prevent teachers from working in professional isolation and frequently stimulates new ideas and insights. The same thing would be said regarding communication with other adults (parents, aides, administrators, community residents) who have vital interests in the school and the children. It should be noted, however, that the absence of interaction does not necessarily imply the lack of teacher initiative. The building facilities and/or official policies of some schools are such that they discourage any kind of informal adult interaction.

A second kind of activity stressed by advocates of an open approach is the pursuit of information—particularly information regarding the physical and cultural characteristics of the surrounding community. What games are played by the children outside of school? What activities go on in the community? What services are available? What does the environment offer in the way of interesting places and physical features—e.g., a factory, woods, junkyard, unusual architecture? The immediate environment contains many natural starting points for learning, and it is the teacher's job to become aware of these. Also important is the need to be aware of new materials on the market and to consider the opportunities they might provide for learning. It is even more essential, however, that the teacher explore for herself some of the materials and equipment she has already provided for the children. What interesting possibilities does she find in them? While it is certainly not expected that the teacher becomes an "expert" in every field, it is expected that she pursue some topics of interest in greater depth. There are several informative but non-technical sources (some supplied by EDC) from which the teacher can learn more about the subjects included in the curriculum of early education.

Finally, and in some respects most important, is the teacher's involvement and growth in some area of purely personal interest—be it in music, learning how to fly an airplane, or photography. It is assumed that the adult who continues to grow personally is an adult who exemplifies what she hopes to promote in children. Here, as in the classroom, the particular content of learning is less important than the process.

The behavior patterns and characteristics discussed so far seem to constitute essential directions of growth toward active and responsible teaching which EDC and other American and British educators are attempting to promote. As suggested previously, they represent what would be involved in movement along the horizontal dimension of Figure 1. These directions of growth, however, do not deal specifically with the quality of personal relationships in a classroom. Thus, they fail to encompass other aspects of the teacher's behavior which are considered vitally important in the creation of an optimal learning environment. The qualities regarded as necessary in the teacher-child relationship are most frequently described by such words as "honesty," "trust," "respect," "confidence." While these terms are suggestive, their meaning is unclear and their connotations would apply to virtually all interpersonal settings. Since few publications attempt to deal with this problem, we tended to press the advisors rather hard for concrete illustrations. The following discussion, therefore, is based almost entirely on material obtained from the EDC advisors—although there is certainly reason to believe that the views they expressed are shared by many other educators as well.

Respect for Persons. The word "love" is rarely found in either publications or discussions centering on open education, but the phrase "respect for children" appears continually. While it is impossible to define respect in all the various contexts in which it is used, the *process of respecting* seems quite closely related to what Carl Rogers has described as the process of "valuing in a mature adult." Briefly, Rogers described mature valuing as re-establishing an internal locus for evaluation, subsequent to socialization and the necessary acceptance of various external standards and criteria for behavior. In other words, the adult begins once more to look to his own feelings (as all infants do) in determining what is good or bad, what is worthy of attention and what is not. One major result of re-establishing the "self" as a legitimate source for guiding behavior is that the adult starts to place great value on individuality and freedom of choice—for himself and for others. It is this particular kind of valuing process which we suspect underlies a great deal of what is implied by the word respect.

How does one evidence respect? Obviously there are any number of ways, but at least three kinds of evidence seemed particularly important to advisors. First and foremost perhaps is the valuing of involved activity, and of the products of such activity, in their own right—not only (or even necessarily) as steps in an overall pattern of growth. As discussed above, this does not mean that the teacher will always have a personal interest in the activity or place personal value on the product; but she does value the activity or product as a legitimate expression of another person's interest. Secondly, the *ways* in which children operate—their personal and cognitive styles—are also to be respected. If a teacher values the right to work in her own individual way, then she respects that right for children as well. It is thought that one outcome of such respect is greater freedom and willingness to experiment with different ways of doing things (e.g., the usually careful and reflective painter can make an impulsive and bold sweep of the canvas). Finally, the advisors are quite sensitive to the need to respect children's ideas. The problem is how to do this. How do you tell a child (other than by words) that his ideas are worthy of attention? Displaying children's work is one approach, which may or may not get the message across depending upon how it is done. One advisor suggested other possibilities: e.g., do the stories children have written become legitimate reading material for other children; do the games they invent become incorporated into the classroom as a legitimate activity; where feasible, are their suggestions acted upon?

Honesty of encounters. A concern for honesty which appeared in one form or another during many interviews centered on the need to direct a child to another resource if the teacher cannot provide adequate help or understanding. The cause of her inability might be temporary and situational (involvement with another child, not feeling well); it might be lack of knowledge about the subject; or it might be more personal (fear of examining a dead animal). Whatever the reason, if it would severely limit her capacity to help the child, then she should be willing to say so and direct him if possible to a more appropriate resource. Aside from providing for the child's need at the time (assuming availability of another resource), it is argued that such behavior also encourages children to feel that there is nothing wrong about admitting human limitations—that it is "okay" to express lack of understanding, fear, uncertainty. In addition to these ramifications, the honest admission of limitation would seem to negate any "traffic cop" image of the teacher as the *only* person who can direct the flow of learning. This kind of honesty, then, suggests one specific way in which the teacher creates and reinforces a classroom atmosphere of shared responsibility for learning.

A second type of honesty which was stressed involved the teacher's evaluation of children's products. This is a tricky subject and certainly an "it depends" area of behavior, but at least a few things seem relatively clear. First, the repeated use of pat and stock phrases which reflect little individuation ("isn't that nice," "how lovely," "how interesting") generally leads nowhere. Even more damaging, in the opinion of many advisors, is the thoughtless use of global praise without any real examination of the product being considered. Not only does this fail to provide the child with examples of differential criteria which might be internalized, but it may serve to stifle his verbalization as well. If the teacher really doesn't understand the meaning of some product or find it very interesting, a better approach would be not to feign appreciation but simply to ask the child what it means to him. On occasion the teacher might openly express her own preferences in the matter, but in such a way as not to discourage the child's interest or devalue the product.

The more difficult case in evaluation arises when, in the teacher's opinion, the child's product is rather shabby. The advisors approached this topic rather gingerly and from many different directions, but one generalization does seem warranted from their remarks: poor quality, *as such,* is not to be praised. If a child put considerable effort into the product, then that is what the teacher should focus praise on, while perhaps at the same time seeking ways which might help him to improve his work. On the other hand, if a teacher knows the child is capable of much better productions, then her response should in some way suggest the recognition of a discrepancy—perhaps in a very casual manner if she thinks he was merely "horsing around," or in a more probing way if there is reason to believe something might be bothering the child. In summary, honesty in evaluating children's products is thought to be extremely important, but it is definitely a contextual ethic and the teacher's behavior should be tempered by judgments about the particular child and the particular product in question.

A final kind of honesty mentioned by some advisors actually amounts to "being realistic." While the teacher strives to create opportunities for choice and self-expression in an open classroom, there are nonetheless obvious limits and rules. Free choice, for example, is necessarily limited —by the nature of materials in a room, by the number of people who can work at an activity at any one time, by other considerations. Self-expression cannot be interpreted to include the destruction of material or of other children's work. While the necessity of limits and rules is the common sense knowledge of almost every teacher, these matters can inadvertently be played down or remain unexplicit in an enthusiasm to implement free choice and to "open up" the classroom. When this happens, the lack of clear cut guidelines can undermine, from the very start, even the most committed attempt to create a productive atmosphere. It seems important to emphasize this aspect of honesty (or realism), because our field observations suggest that it might be a critical factor underlying the difference between those classrooms where intentions were uniformly good but the results varied considerably.

Warmth. The qualities of respect and honesty discussed above certainly apply to the child's emotional as well as cognitive life. Feelings are as much respected as ideas or products, and they are to be dealt with honestly. In fact, one of the primary objectives of advisors is to communicate in every way possible the integration of feeling and thinking in behavior. They are by no means separate or separable entities; and any attempt to divide the day in "feeling times" and "thinking times" is not only misguided but potentially harmful. Although it is quite possible to stifle emotion and get the child to regard himself as a more or less divided individual, many educators feel that genuine growth takes place *only* to the extent that emotional and intellectual resources are brought into play and merge in behavior.

This emphasis on the importance of emotion and the importance of accepting it as legitimate, poses some rather special problems for the teacher of an open classroom. Since significant growth is expected to be accompanied by a wide range of emotions, it is recognized that at times children will become not only joyful but quite unsettled, doubtful, perhaps anxious. A number of advisors stressed the importance of risktaking, with its associated feelings, as a sign of growth. A critical characteristic of teaching, then, would appear to be the ability to recognize emotions differentially and to act as a stabilizing and reassuring influence when necessary. To do this successfully (to be able to stabilize and encourage emotional expression) requires the warmth necessary in any human relationship where one person (the child) is willing to depend on another (the teacher) for assistance in handling some difficult aspects of his emotional life—aspects that might not find expression in more traditional classrooms.

The chapter began by raising the question of how it is possible to bring an active, influential adult and active, influential children together in the same classroom. The analysis of the teacher's role presented here is intended as a partial answer to that question. The topics of provisioning, diagnosing, seeking professional growth etc. describe some ways in which the teacher is an active contributor; but it is the nature of the human relationships (the qualities of respect, honesty, warmth) which appear to be central in understanding how the adult and child can work together. When a child has learned that the teacher is true to her word, that there is no hidden curriculum, that she respects honest efforts on his part regardless of where they lead—then the relationship between teacher and child is such that any suggestions she may make to him are not taken as commands or veiled threats. If good relationships are established, it means that the activitist teacher can offer suggestions, introduce materials, demonstrate ways of doing things, with the expectation that children will react to the content and merits of such instruction rather than trying to guess the intent of the instructor.

In concentrating on the role of the teacher we may have inadvertently portrayed it as an impossible one—a role attainable only by superteacher. Certainly energy and effort are called for, but it has been our observation that a great many "ordinary" teachers begin to move into such a role rather naturally when they find some support and encouragement for their efforts.

2. The Teacher as Adviser and Supporter

One of the roles that the teacher in an open classroom plays is that of adviser—of someone who is there to provide advice and assistance when children need it. But that role is not enough; the teacher must be prepared to intervene directly when a particular child or group of children needs specific guidance. A large part of the artistry of teaching in an open classroom consists of knowing when to play one role and when to play the other—when to stand back, and when to intervene. Below, an experienced woman teacher in an English infant school describes the way in which she plays these two disparate roles.

The selection is taken from one of the pamphlets in the series produced by the Anglo-American Primary School project. Ann Cook and Herb Mack, who have taught in both English and American informal schools, are co-directors of the Community Resources Institute of the City University of New York, which trains teachers and administrators for open classrooms in the New York City public schools.

———

I think of myself as an adviser to the children—someone who is there when the need arises, when the children need to take the next step—not only in academic things but in the social sphere as well.

I'm learning to fulfil this role more efficiently and effectively as time goes on. I've learned to work in different ways with different kinds of children. Some need considerably more direction than others. Some will come and say: "I wonder how this works." "I've just noticed that," or "I wonder why this is?" I can leave them to it.

With other children, my role must be more supportive. They don't come up with suggestions. They are satisfied with very little. To these children, I would have to say: "What about your working with this, and seeing what you can find out?" Some are very willing to go off and follow the suggestion. We need much more time with such children, to stretch them more. I would say that a child of this kind would learn more here than in a formal environment because there are things to direct him into.

I was very bogged down when I first began working in this way. I was worried if the children weren't all doing some writing and reading. Then, as soon as an interest appeared, I would feel I had to abandon skills and get them going on the interest.

Now I'm finding that once one gets the right kind of routine and organization, once one has a place for everything and is several steps ahead in simple things like mixing paints, and cutting paper and having books and pencils available, one can step back and blend the interests and the skills. Now I'm ready for the children to bring interesting things to school and to follow through. This is the most difficult thing—being available for all their interests.

In the beginning, one gets terribly worried. Although, inside, one knows that this is the way one really thinks children should work, that they shouldn't be ruled by bells, that they should be able to carry on with something that interests them, one feels: "Well, it may be all right for everyone else, but it's no good for me. I just can't cope with so many children wanting so much individual help." But, somehow, one does.

One discovers that one can't follow up every single interest, but that the children are learning and that their attitudes towards one another are good. And one discovers that every part of the child is developing.

As the children acquire the basic skills, this way of working becomes easier. Most of mine can write and read now; they can stretch themselves considerably and can take themselves from one step to the next. They can find out information. This frees me a little.

I'm not so tied up with children saying every minute: "What shall I do now?" or "Can you help me with this?"

I'm also more confident myself and I can stand back and not worry quite so much. I can throw out half a dozen comments and suggestions, almost without knowing I'm doing it.

I know that a certain amount of learning is going on even if I'm not there, because I hear the children discussing things—about why something works in a particular way or how it's put together. I listen in on conversations and sometimes I think: "They could almost go on without me here."

I choose when to intervene. If I hear a discussion that is going nowhere, or is becoming an argument, or is dealing with something they can't solve, I come into it. I have learned to listen to what's going on, even in areas across the room, and I watch what's going on, also. Sometimes, I think that, working this way, one needs eyes and ears in the back of one's head.

I look for involvement. If, for example, they're playing in the home corner, there's a terrific amount of drama in that. There are also things like laying tables, and counting cups, and deciding how many cakes are needed for those people who are coming to tea. I might go along and say: "How many people are you inviting?" "Four," they might say. I would then ask: "How many cups of tea will you need? How many plates?" and so on. There would be a lot of counting. Even those children who were not very verbal would be chattering away in this area.

I would go along to the water-play area, and we would discuss why the water goes through something fast or slowly, or why bubbles are coming out. I try to stretch them to the next point. The next point would depend on the level of the particular child. Very young ones need to feel the water; for older ones, this would be a waste of time because they have already experienced it a lot.

If the room is set up properly, there isn't any area of the room where some learning can't take place.

I believed in this kind of school before I started to teach here, but when one arrives, and is faced with forty children, and has the responsibility of getting them to a reasonable standard by a certain time, one can't help being afraid it won't work.

When someone spends all day painting or several days painting, one finds oneself saying, "That's lovely, but don't you think you should be doing some writing?" I realize now that, if the environment is right in the classroom, and if I'm aware of the children's potential, aware of the rate of development, then concentrated activity for long periods of time is what's right for particular children. I'm not the least concerned— although three years ago, I would have been. I wouldn't have trusted the child or the way of working sufficiently.

One grows to trust this way of working. Now, there may be children who will drift from thing to thing, who will really need keeping on top of. They need direction and, if necessary, particular tasks. I find that if I don't provide in this way for these few children, they are very unhappy and achieve little or nothing.

I think there's a danger that a lot of people, when they are lecturing, will make this way of working sound as if there are no problems, as if every child will learn naturally if provided with a lovely, stimulating, interesting environment—that they will all learn to read, write and so on. The majority will, but a few won't, and one has got to be there, behind those few, to help them.

Recently I was away for a few days, ill, and when I returned all the dressing-up clothes were thrown about. I gathered the children together and said: "Look, I want all those clothes hanging in the right place, and you, you and you, sort it out." I didn't give them any options. One child stood there grinning at me and said: "It's a good thing you're around sometimes, isn't it?" And I said: 'What do you mean?" He said: "To bully us. Otherwise we'd never do anything."

We have to spend a lot of time helping children to learn to work independently and to be able to make choices from a stimulating environment. I myself experienced this problem when I was at college. The teachers tended to throw us right into the most marvellous environment —particularly in art. They had everything imaginable: fabric-printing, tie-dyeing, collage, oil painting, sketching.

I stood back and said to myself: "I can't do any of that." The whole thing was too overwhelming and for ages I didn't do anything. The same thing happened to me in music. When we came to discuss music at college, I cringed. I thought, "This is all right for people who know about music, but not for me." Fortunately, I had an instructor who noticed this and said: "Don't worry, you *can* do this; it's very simple, come and do it." He made an opening for me.

Some children have to be pushed a bit, opened up to new things and encouraged. One can only do this when one knows the children and has had sufficient experience oneself. I can now see possibilities where, before, I couldn't. As one works this way, one gains insight into the individual child.

Some teachers who have never worked in this way will become sceptical because it is all made to sound so easy. When they come to do it, they find it isn't, and they don't succeed. Finally they say: "I'm just making a hash of it; it doesn't work." They'll abandon it, just like the child, and go back to the thing that's safe, that they feel secure with. I find it makes people much more confident when one tells them that one, too, has had all these problems, that one has had failures, and that one worried about the children not writing or reading. These things are often left unsaid.

Keeping track of what the children are doing while at the same time trying to work from their interests, is very difficult. In the maths area, for example, though I'm no expert, I have a feel for the stages of progress and I try to develop an awareness in the children of maths all around, in everything—in the shapes of symbols, in the shapes of leaves, church spires, in movement, in one child's being taller than another. If one can develop this general awarness to the point where children will notice and comment on size and numbers, I think this is ideal. I feel that if I could get in maths the sort of climate I have in music—where they'll tap out interesting words, try instruments, and so on, I would feel it was right. But there is a lot to do in maths that I still have to learn.

Now a lot of schools which would agree that it's important for children to learn concepts rather than sums, would still use things like work cards for the children. The teacher would know, then, whether the children had covered measuring, weighing, money and so on. Cards make it easy, because one assumes that the children are getting experience in this and that thing because they have the task cards. But, these mathematics cards also mean that one is getting away from reaching maths through the child's interests, and one begins to find children who will say: "I've done my maths." They've done the thing one has set them to do, and they don't see maths in anything else.

I find it terribly difficult to keep track of a child's progress in maths; to know whether a child has done enough weighing, enough work with numbers, with shapes, with measurement. It's always hard to remember from one time to the next whether a child has gone through particular stages.

I have finally got round this, to some degree, by giving every child a maths book. The children use these to keep records of what they are doing and I can then glance back and get some idea of where they are. Now that they can write easily, I ask them to date each entry. I glance back and say: "Good heavens, this child has done nothing with numbers for a very long time," or, "He's done lots of weighing."

I might work with a child on groups, and find he knows nothing about groups of two, or grouping in general. I might then direct him to something in that area. The child's book gives me a way of knowing more specifically at what stage he is.

Sometimes you find a child who will spend days and days on one particular thing. Perhaps he needs to stay at that point for a long period, but there comes a time when you feel he is capable of moving on. It's difficult to keep in close touch with every child. I've devised a way to handle this which seems to work well for me.

I concentrate my attention, for a week, on checking up on one area such as maths. To make sure the children are doing and getting enough mathematical experience, I focus on anything that may be happening in that classroom in that particular week; for instance, on one occasion, we did a project on Indians. I drew the children's attention to the size of the Indian wigwams, measuring perimeters, noticing shape and design. In the music corner, I drew attention to the size of the instruments. I gave my attention to mathematics for that particular week in every area of the room. Such a "boost" will give impetus, for a while, to more concentrated interest in a subject.

The next week, I might give my main attention to, perhaps, creative writing, or just writing in general: attention to formation of letters, to using dictionaries, to all that goes with writing; attention to the creative side of it; to construction of stories (I would lay a great stress on this, so that they would all be very excited about writing). Meanwhile, the boost on the mathematics would still be carrying through, and one would find things inter-relating.

Another week, I might give my attention to the music corner. That doesn't mean I would do nothing else, but I would make myself aware of that particular area of learning, and make sure that I'd given enough to it, and that various children were getting enough from it.

For reading, I'd go into the book corner and talk to the children about the books they were looking at, read to them, and listen to them read, help them make up stories, and, generally, stimulate an interest in reading.

I might do the same sort of thing with art—introduce, or re-introduce, some technique like printing, because the children had forgotten all about it. I might bring in a few new ideas, like tie-dyeing, or work a bit more with collage.

In this way, in about six weeks, I would have covered the main areas of learning. Then I might start all over again. If one could do this sort of thing uninterrupted, it could work very well, I am sure, as it would be the easiest way of making certain that no area of learning was completely left out.

As I've said, there are four or five basic areas in any classroom: areas for writing, reading, maths, creative activities, and arts. I would always add a music area. I'm particularly keen on that, and I would like to see such an area in every infant room, even if it's for homemade instruments. Then there are other areas for interests as they crop up. At the moment, I've got an entire area devoted to growing things, and to little creatures from the garden. The children had already become interested in these things, which were spread all over the place until I put the whole lot together and developed an area, with books and so on.

I'll develop this kind of area until the interest dies. Then I'll just replace it, leaving more space for writing and reading, or something else that seems of interest.

I find the main difficulty is always time. Those children who aren't involved in a major project, will get on with other work, though this does need watching. What can happen is that the teacher gets so involved in a big project that the children who, for some reason, are not particularly interested in that project, may drift about and do nothing. I try to keep things going as usual, with some mathematics and some interest in growing things. But, if an interest becomes very strong and is shared by most of the class, then I'll throw the rest to the wind for a few days, and we'll just concentrate utterly on doing the project. . . .

. . . In my room the children sometimes come in before I arrive and start their work. If they want to play, they must stay in the playground. I find that if the children come in slowly, a few at a time, it's much easier to get started. Some teachers want the children to sit around them before the day begins, and discuss what they will do. I used to do this, but often the children would have no idea of what to do. Now if I did this, if I said: "Who would like to paint? Who would like to work with clay? Who would like to do mathematics? Who would like to read?" there might be far too many children wanting to do a particular thing. If, instead, I leave it to them, most will tend spontaneously to move into the things they want to do and work quite steadily. Then you are left with four or five little drifters. I suggest something, and if that doesn't work, I direct them to something.

When the children are all busy and most of the parents have left, I may take a small group who are ready for a skill and work with them. Or I may hear an individual child read. I try not to let such activities drag on so that all I'm doing is hearing reading, because this can easily happen. I attempt to be available to the children when they need me.

Generally, the children are busy without interruption until 10:30. Then we have assembly. On two days a week, we work on the large climbing apparatus and that's another disturbance of the children's time for concentrated work.

After assembly comes playtime when some children like to stay in, to finish things they are doing. When they all return, I may remind them of what they were doing before assembly. Some will drift off to something new without having finished what they were doing or putting their things away. When everyone is working, I may again pull out a small group to do something specific.

I may help a child find a word in his word book, or help him use a proper dictionary. So the morning goes, with 101 things happening. We usually clear up at about 11:50, and sometimes have ten or fifteen minutes of music. I don't do this so much nowadays because I find that, by now, the children have had so much more experience with music that I can see which ones are genuinely interested and get a lot from the music corner.

We may need to get together to discuss the work the children have been doing in the course of the morning, or again, we may discuss a project that is involving a large number of the children. We may come together to hear a poem, or something else I feel is of interest. Or, I may comment on something in the room.

I don't spend the whole lunch break in the classroom, but I find I have to use some of it mixing paints, sharpening pencils, or preparing something I want to have for the afternoon.

Some of the children want to work in the room during all the breaks. And, although we do have set playtimes, I think we could well do without them because for many of the children they are just an interruption of things they are really enjoying getting on with.

The afternoon is much the same as the morning. Children come in and follow their own interests through. I go from group to group. I may set aside some specific time when I want to work with certain children on something in maths or writing, like getting their letters the right way around—anything specific. I may talk with a small group about how to construct a story because they have been writing: "This is a house. This is a flower. Anna is walking down the road," for weeks on end, and I feel they are ready to begin writing stories.

The extent to which I expect a child to follow through on an activity depends on the individual child. If he is writing a long story and I can see that his hand is very tired, I will suggest he stops writing and does more in the afternoon or next day. Sometimes a painting which a child may have worked on for a long time isn't completed but the child seems quite tired. He may want to finish it but, if I feel he is too tired to go on putting the same effort into it, I will say to him: "Rather than spoil it because you're tired, leave it, and come back to it tomorrow or later."

On the other hand, you get the children who start something and, after an interruption, like assembly or playtime, will not return to the activity. They could spend day after day like this, never really achieving anything, and I usually say to them: "Go back and finish it up." Sometimes, if they've forgotten to finish, I'll remind them.

I really do want children to follow through on things they begin. If a child had written a story: "Once upon a time there lived a cat, he went down the road and he met a horse. The end." I might say: "Is it really the end? It seems to me, it's only the beginning." Or if this were actually a lot of writing for that particular child, I might say: "Let's leave it a while and pick it up later," rather than just letting him leave it at that.

If it's playtime and the children want to carry on, I'll rarely say "no," unless I know it's a child who won't really carry on, but just wants to stay in the classroom and muck about. Or I might feel that a child needed to have a good run around in the yard before he'd be able really to settle again.

. . . Of course, out of school, one spends time planning, thinking of ideas, and getting background information on things the children are looking into. Once a week, I take the music club at school, and I also like to plan that.

I do find though, that I don't have to do as much overall planning as I used to, because the environment is now such that it creates its own momentum. I plan according to whatever interests crop up. Last term there was a terrific interest in ships and I found that I had to go off to the museum myself to find exactly where the ships could be seen.

I also use "flow charts" to think through ideas. When we did work on "the sea" last year, I would jot down "seashore," and think of the various things that could emerge from this: natural science, creative writing, art, mathematics, music, movement, stories about the sea. Sometimes the things I thought of wouldn't develop, and usually I wouldn't use half of them, but I find that doing this makes me aware of the possibilities in a subject.

One idea can lead in many directions. Often the children will really forge ahead, and I learn a lot from them. They lead the teacher very often. That's what the head means when she says "the teacher grows." The children's interests can lead one on to something one hasn't ever thought of tackling before.

3. The Teacher as Observer

A teacher has no way of deciding when to intervene and when to stand back unless he or she knows—really knows—each child. The teacher must be aware not only of what each child is doing, but of what each child is capable *of doing. To know the children in this way—to be able to make on-the-spot judgments, not only about* whether *to intervene, but about* how *to intervene—the teacher needs to observe his or her students in ways that are rare in traditional classrooms. In this selection, a teacher in an inner-city English infant school talks about the way observations of his students relate to the other roles he plays.*

I feel it's important to regard all children as individuals, to allow them to see and choose, of their own accord, what to do in the room. The room is theirs to use as they wish. From what the teacher sees the children are doing with the room as it is, with equipment that is in it, he decides what else to provide.

The teacher considers in what ways the room needs rearranging. He decides what the needs of the different children are, in what direction they should be pushed a little, what particular aspect of the room they should be exposed to more often. All these things are constantly on my mind.

I provide things, and encourage the children to prepare something particular, to think about this, to read about it. I attempt to extend their environment, to extend their experience, in a way that has been shown by my observation to be necessary. This is the role of the teacher: the provision of the basic environment, and the extension of it to suit the children as their needs evolve.

It is an 8a.m.–6p.m. day in which the children are present from 9a.m.–3:30p.m., with a break at lunchtime. But I think a class teacher's responsibility begins when he gets up in the morning and ends when he goes to bed at night. This doesn't mean I advocate spending every hour of every day on something connected with the child. But I do feel that, if one is aware of children and if one is responsible for them and their development, it goes far beyond the school hours and the academic concerns.

This is what the integrated day is all about. It is the complete integration of everything to do with the child's development, physical as well as mental, emotional as well as physical.

It's practical work some of the time. If painting or craft is an important area of children's work, as I think it should be, then one has got to provide materials for them to use. One must cut the paper; one must mix the paints. But one has also got to think what sort of paints they want or, if they've done lots of painting, what other materials one can provide for them to do something different with.

One must think in what way one could introduce some new idea, or suggest a new technique. A new technique may require the provision of another type of material which one must go to find or must think about, or must persuade the headmistress to buy. One has to think how to provide needed direction.

The school can't teach academic skills only. It has also to help the children develop as people. We can't sit them down and expect them to do things with mathematics until they've learned to work with materials of all sorts. They've got to go through the developmental stages.

The freedom of our situation here allows and encourages them to talk to each other most of the time. For 95 per cent of the day they have the chance to speak to whom they like about what they like. Most of the time they will be talking about what they are doing. The ability to talk to each other is developing their language, their fluency of speech, their confidence to explain.

Many children haven't got this fluency of speech when they come to school; they aren't ready to learn to write; they aren't ready even to understand. The first stage is talking, being able to describe what they see, so that later they can begin to write, and be able to express themselves in that way.

I think it is absolutely essential that children have freedom of movement. Often a child has a real need to move physically. As a male teacher, I also think it essential that a child should be able to go to a woman teacher, as well, or to the headmistress. If necessary, she can see him on his own; she can talk to him. She can observe the quality of conversation between herself and the child. In this school, the quality of intimate conversation is valued so much more than in any sort of formal class.

My whole approach to teaching is an integrated, undifferentiated one; to provide an environment and equipment which children will use. From this they will get experiences that will help them develop as whole persons. It is the fact that the children have freedom of choice, that they are able to move, able to talk to each other, that enables them to develop.

At this school, we start *where they are,* as individuals, and build from there.

In this school, we're not concerned with age at all. We have vertical or family grouping. We feel that, if one splits children into age groups, one will get some children who will perhaps be able to read at five and others, of the same age, who can't read at all. If they are all five-year-olds, the children at the extremes will be isolated. Perhaps there might only be a single good reader, and a single bad reader.

By mixing the ages, one tends to get more than one child at the extremes, and usually the variations are not so acute. One finds that the more able six-year-old can work with a seven-year-old, just as a particularly immature seven-year-old will be able to work more naturally with a five-year-old. In such situations a child is probably aware that the child he wants to play with, or do something with, is younger or older, but, since they're both in the same class, he doesn't feel difficulties about working at the other child's level.

I find that vertical grouping is also good for the teacher. The fact that we've done away with any sort of streaming, even by age, forces me to think of the children as individuals. I would hope that even if I were in a school where I had a horizontally-grouped class, I would still think of the children individually, but perhaps I wouldn't be able to. The vertical group *forces* me to think of children as individuals, in order to provide equipment and situations in the classroom that will enable any child, whatever his stage, to work at his own level.

Really to see the children, it is important that I observe all the time what they are doing, what they do around the room, what they do with different pieces of equipment. I must observe their balance of work, their choice of activities, which activities they never do, which activities they do the majority of the time.

All this information goes in, and the resulting output takes the form of various decisions on what further directions to provide for the children, what ways to extend pieces of work they've done. Can I help? If so, how?

One can only make such assessments on the basis of watching the children work. If one observes children working in a situation one has provided, one sees all the faults in it immediately. They may just lie in the physical arrangement of the room—that is something one can change easily. Or one may realize that one hasn't provided anything for a particular aspect of work. For instance, I might notice that I have provided no constructional toys. If I consider this important, and there seems to be a need for it, and if I see children starting to construct things with books or chairs, then obviously, I shall realize that there is need for construction equipment. If I haven't got it, I must get it. This is the way of directing.

If there are plenty of books, and an attractive book corner, but the children aren't going there of their own accord, the teacher's role is to encourage them. Perhaps one should try to find a way of explaining something to the children, or to each child in turn, that will make them realize that they want to read. The quality of books is also important. There must be attractive books; and there must be books that appeal to a range of abilities.

With older children, one can be more directional. One might say: "Surely you want to read the paper when you are older." If the child is a boy interested in the World Cup, this might be a start. One might follow up by showing him books on football and talking about the players.

One can almost teach the child to read a particular paragraph in this way, and will also be reminding him about the book corner. He will go away, thinking, "Yes, I must look at the book corner. Jolly good books on football. I'll have to have a look." This will perhaps encourage him to go to books, of his own accord.

I can direct only from my observation of the children, of what stage they are at. In the example mentioned above, I would use perhaps twenty words about football. If the child were only five, I would make no attempt to get him to read more than the two words that form "football." A complete non-reader would have learned two words which he would be able to read just by remembering.

With an older child, I could tackle more words, some of which he would probably know already. This is the way to direct children to the use of the book corner, especially when one is on one's own with thirty or forty children. One cannot "hear" all those children every day—assuming that they are all able to read.

Therefore, if one wants reading or books to be part of the children's integrated scheme of things, their undifferentiated day—and obviously it must be part of their day—then one must find ways of getting them interested on their own. We are indirect about it and we are prepared to be slow, in the hope of being sure.

We try to see that reading and books are part of children's daily routine, or part of the work that they do. It is to be hoped that the older child, who is beginning to read, will do some kind of reading activity every day. Here, we do not mind whether this is before school or after school, during morning school, during afternoon school, or in the lunch hour. We don't mind when it is. We just want reading to happen. This is a long-term aim (and something that we can achieve to some degree by making the book corner an attractive place, and having the right sort of books there).

We also read stories to the children, in such a way that these are enjoyed, show them books that may encourage them to care for books, and help them to choose books that they will like. We talk about the books, about why they like them, and they are able to look at books on their own, quietly, at any time.

With so many children in the class I couldn't read to each one individually each day. It would be impossible. One has got to get the children working on their own as far as they are able. There are many things they can work at, on their own.

I am not saying that we are making children teach themselves (although sometimes this is appropriate and acceptable). I want to encourage them to pursue an activity as well as they can, on their own, in my absence.

To me, for the child to choose, even if I have influenced him indirectly, to go to the book corner (for even ten minutes) to look at and enjoy a book (even if he can't read it), is quite satisfactory. It is developing the love of books, which we mentioned before, and this is very important to me. To put the pleasure back into learning is an important aim, and applies particularly to reading.

Most of the parents of the children here *can* read. They can read their daily paper, but they don't ever read for pleasure beyond that. They don't use the library. They may have a dog or a cat, but they've never read a book about cats or dogs or about the care of them. They haven't got the interest to find a book about unusual dogs, to look at pictures of them, to read about them, hear how people in other parts of the world care for pets. They are not outward-looking about books or about hobbies. This is sad, especially in an age where people have more and more leisure time.

When the children I am teaching now are older, and perhaps working a three- or four-day week, they will have a lot of leisure time. What are they going to do with that leisure time? If these children have an interest in school now, and like it, perhaps they will want to go to evening classes when they are working. Perhaps they will be prepared to do further studies in connexion with their jobs or perhaps, if they are interested in books, they will go to a library to get a novel, or a book about their dog or their cat—using the skill of reading for pleasure and for information.

I think this is where teachers now play a part: teaching the skill of reading and an enjoyment of books. I think the mistake that was made in the past was to teach reading too quickly. We now have children at school for much longer than formerly, and we can afford to take our time a bit, and improve the quality. This is our aim.

Working in an integrated-day framework, and developing children's ability to choose, is part of making school a pleasant experience. It helps them to enjoy work, to enjoy the learning process. If this can continue through their school life, perhaps learning and the pleasure of it won't end on the day they leave school. Perhaps they will continue, when they don't understand something, to have the desire to find out about it.

4. The Teacher as Learner

One of the reasons that ordinary human beings can make the change from formal to informal teaching is that the open classroom removes the superhuman burden of omniscience that teachers in formal class-rooms tend to carry. When children are free to ask their own questions instead of being confined to answering someone else's questions, and when classrooms are organized on a basis of mutual respect and trust, teachers feel free to admit their ignorance. Equally important, when the teacher abandons her role as The Source of All Knowledge, she begins to see herself as a learner. As Celia Houghton puts it in the brief essay below, the teacher becomes "a collaborator in the learning proc-ess." An Englishwoman with many years of teaching experience in Eng-lish infant schools, Mrs. Houghton is Director of the Teachers Center at Greenwich, Greenwich, Connecticut, and Advisor in the Open Cor-ridor Program in the New York Public Schools. Open Education Work-shop, an in-service, teacher-training organization sponsored by and located at the Convent School.

Some conditions under which active learning can take place.

1. *Mutual Respect*

Piaget sums up the right relationship between teacher and child as the relationship of "mutual respect," the respect the teacher has for the child as a person, for his uniqueness and his needs; the teacher must be willing to be personally involved with each child, so that he may best respond to the individual needs of each child.

The child's respect for the teacher is respect for a caring person who has his best interests at heart, and on whose help and fair judgment he can rely.

Children may also be led to recognise and appreciate the individuality and personal dignity of all other children.

2. *Freedom*

In the relationship of mutual respect there can also be freedom; free-dom for the *child* to do his own learning, to create and invent and dis-cover, and especially he must be free to question.

The *teacher* must be free to make his work relate to the changing needs of his class of developing children.

3. *The Role of the Teacher*

The teacher must have an open mind and be ready to go on learning; he should have sound academic knowledge, at least in some fields, but

Celia Houghton, "The Teacher," mimeographed (Greenwich, Conn.: Convent of the Sacred Heart School).

few teachers could have the knowledge to meet all the individual needs of a class of interested and enthusiastic children and when a child wants to explore fields which are unfamiliar to the teacher, the teacher should know the available sources of material and accurate, if elementary, information which will help him. The teacher thus becomes guide, resource person, and a collaborator in the learning process.

The teacher must be able to diffuse his attention, he must be aware of what is going on in all parts of the room, he must be ready to give help and advice when needed, but must also be willing to withhold help and advice when to give it would deprive a child of the joy and value of discovery. The teacher must have knowledge of child development, of how a child grows and how a child learns, if he is to be able to guide subtly rather than teach overtly.

4. *Organisation*

Good powers of organisation are necessary for the smooth running of a large and active class to avoid waste of time and materials.

It is important that children be trained in good working habits, and in housekeeping; the children should learn to manage the environment as well as use it.

5. The Teacher as Senior Partner

What appears to be casual and spontaneous activity in an open classroom in fact is the result of careful planning on the part of the teacher. The appearance of spontaneity is deliberate; as one English headmaster puts it, "the educator's task is to maximize the occasion." But if the teacher is to be able to maximize the occasion, he must make the occasion possible in the first place by the kind of environment he creates and maintains. "In a sense there is no spontaneity at all," says Mary Brown, co-author of a standard English text on open education, "since we select the materials that are available. We are structuring all the time; that is what teaching is."

One of the most difficult problems for teachers who are making the change from traditional to open education is learning how to mesh their planning with the opportunities they provide for individual student choice. The two selections below provide fascinating analyses of the problem and its resolution. The first selection comes from a summary of the discussions and workshops conducted during three teachers' conferences held in England in 1969; the summary was written by Douglas N. Hubbard of the University of Sheffield Institute of Education and

John Salt of Thombridge Hall College of Education. The second selection comes from the transcription of a long interview which Professor Courtney B. Cazden of Harvard Graduate School of Education had with Miss Susan M. Williams, then headmistress of Gordonbrock Infant School in London, the day before the beginning of the 1967 school year. Professor Cazden's questions are italicized; Miss Williams' answers are in ordinary type.

————————

Perhaps the most important question that was raised during the conferences was that of the degree to which children's work should be planned beforehand and positively guided during its accomplishment. At every point profound questions about the real nature of a teacher's work underlay the discussion. Indeed it soon became clear that a proportion of those who attended the conferences had begun to wonder if the accepted role of the teacher was in danger of abrogation.

What exactly do we mean when we say that teaching should be based on the declared interests of the child? If we accept this dictum, does it mean that effective planning and preparation are to a large extent rendered impossible? And does it further mean that the more positive aspects of the teacher's role are threatened with extinction?

An obvious point is, of course, that a teacher must be capable of distinguishing between a relatively deep-rooted interest and a transient whim. Again, on a purely commonsense level, it is up to the teacher to steer children away from danger and from frustrating academic *cul-de-sacs*. Few teachers, for instance, would encourage a class's interest in making quantities of mustard gas! Nor is it unreasonable to expect a teacher—whose knowledge of children, their instincts, capabilities and motivation are her basic stock-in-trade—to be able to *forecast* children's evolving interests with limits which still allow for unpredictable contributions of the imaginative and creative child. In these circumstances the potentialities of planning are by no means limited. It is simply that the plan must be more flexible and more comprehensive than in traditional teaching, and certainly there will always be avenues that limitations of time and problems of sustaining motivation with primary school children will render unexplored.

In any case, what is interest and how is it generated? Increasingly in recent years we have come to realise that many attributes of the individual's personality previously considered to be instinctive were, in fact, socially-determined. To this constantly extending list it would seem

From Douglas N. Hubbard and John Salt, *Integrated Studies in the Primary School: Teachers' Conferences Report* (Sheffield, England: Institute of Education, University of Sheffield, 1970), pp. 8–12, 16–18.

that, with some reservations, interest has already been added. It is, of course, no mere coincidence that the school—and here we are thinking of a specific example—where the children's interest in music is at its most radiant is also the school which has a "musical head" and assistant staff. Many teachers at the conference, in fact, drew attention to the element of "teacher drive" in the promotion of enthusiasm in specific areas of interest such as music and art. Interest is not the chance, wild, capricious thing that many of us might have assumed. Like so many other things it grows from the interaction of personalities, not least of which is the personality of the teacher. What integrated education is really about is the need to make that interaction a more genuine inter-action by making the child a *more considered* partner in the process.

Now note the choice of words. They do not say—and Heaven forbid! —"the master of the process." Nor do they say even "an equal partner." The changes in the teacher's role associated with the spread of integrated learning are subtle and profound, but they do not represent role re-versal. In any process of learning at this level the teacher is, and must be, the senior partner with responsibilities for guidance and creative assistance as deep as they ever were.

In the field of integrated education, as in other fields of educational "revolution," there are, in fact, complex variations in the pattern of change. No system, old or new, is ever completely self-contained or entirely distinctive, and an interesting point is that some of the aims of integrated education must have been attained in more traditional situa-tions when a given relationship was established between sensitive and enthusiastic persons. It was a sobering experience for many of the younger delegates to hear this point put so clearly by their more ex-perienced colleagues. Most of us can remember the occasional teacher whose talents were such that the more stereotyped aspects of his role became of little importance—the teacher who, perhaps unconsciously, made us *want* to ask questions and to make contributions and who had an apparently inborn talent for building on our enthusiasms. Such people, however, can rarely have felt at ease with a rigid timetable, and possibly in their free moments they were the unwitting pioneers of integration as we understand it today.

Perhaps an incident from a fieldwork session during the conferences might help to sum up what we have been trying to say in this admittedly rather difficult section. In the course of this session a group stopped at a telegraph pole and a "teaching situation" was consciously created. Note that the tutor knew that the pole was there and had listed it in the work plan. It was pretty likely that he would engineer a stop at that point!

Now no one in his right mind would suggest that the group had an intrinsic interest in a telegraph pole. The likelihood is that no member of the group would have noticed it or even the metal plaque on it. A good point here—human beings have to be taught *how* to look (as one conference member commented) and teachers need to develop a greater awareness of things and their relationship to each other, an awareness which is not characteristic of the preoccupied adult in the modern world. It is only, in fact, when this awareness has been cultivated that there is possibly the full communion which represents the joy of integrated teaching.

To go back to the telegraph pole, in the absence of intrinsic interest, ought a consideration of the pole to have been excluded from the morning's activities?

"The answer depends on what we mean by interest and what we conceive the essential job of the teacher to be. *Obviously the tutor,* in this case, unless he was grossly insensitive, felt reasonably confident that he could create a situation in which interest could be *created,* that he could bring it about in that process of give and take that is characteristic of a learning situation. There are needs that a child has, and there are needs that a teacher can create. In general the tutor was pretty sure of his plan of campaign, but was willing to concentrate on any specific interest that he might arouse, although as a realist he did not expect an identical degree of interest to be shown by every member of the group at any given point. Here, in fact, was anticipating planning in the sense in which we have used it in this section, and interest deriving from the engineering of a social situation and a conviction that the group needed positive but unobtrusive leadership to extract educational value from it. . . .

. . . Throughout the conferences a fundamental question that was posed was: if children are to have a large degree of freedom, how can we ensure that each receives a balanced "diet" of the essential ingredients (mathematical, artistic, linguistic and so on) that make up education in the wider sense?

Perhaps we should begin by questioning what we mean by "freedom." More than fifty years ago Sidney Webb pointed out that what we mean by freedom is, in the last resort, no more than a choice of alternatives which in themselves tend to be far more limited than we often assume. What is true of the wider social system is also true of the class, which in its own way is a social system in miniature.

The positive responsibility of the teacher for excluding alternatives that are, for instance, dangerous or pointless has already been touched on in this paper. In any case the equitable use of resources is likely to put a limit of the individual or group's endeavour in any particular field: one could not, for instance, accept a situation in which half-a-dozen children monopolised the woodwork bench and tools for three months. In these circumstances what freedom boils down to is the provision of *viable* alternatives, and the engineering of genuine discussion with the child in the matter of responsible choice. One lecturer, in fact, graphically described how he and a child would together prepare an individual work plan.

Clearly there are complex questions of balance and emphasis here, and in many ways it will be seen that integrated learning in its true sense is an attitude of mind rather than a set of techniques to be learned.

On the general question of balance, much depends on the length of time over which integration is visualized as taking place. Perhaps in this respect the much used term "integrated day" is to some extent misleading in that it seems to imply that the educational balance sheet should be totted up, as it were, at the end of each school session. Obviously the circumscription of educational effort by such a rigid time sequence militates against that true flexibility characteristic of integrated learning.

But how long should a child be allowed to concentrate his energies in a particular area of knowledge? And over what period should "balance" be achieved? A lot depends, of course, on the outlook, inclinations and maturity of the individual child. For some children a relatively long process of "catching up" in a less-favoured field might hardly be associated with the enthusiasm and drive characteristic of the best primary school work. Here, in fact, we are thinking of a child with an intense and rather narrow interest in one branch of activity in which he rarely encounters boredom. Other children can be more easily guided into broadening the scope of their work at any given point or happily steered into almost any field.

A lot, too, depends on the wealth of resources for learning provided by the school, on the proportion of group and class activity to individual work, and on the efficiency of the teacher's method of keeping fairly elaborate records of the individual child's work and progress. The child himself is, of course, his own record but there are, in fact, few fields where the evolution of new methods by practicing teaching is of more obvious importance. Tribute ought also to be paid to Local Education Authorities who have consciously recognized this problem, being aware of the changing situations in our primary schools. One record card produced at the conferences seemed to have much to recommend it. . . .

. . . Why did so many teachers wish to attend these conferences? Essentially, we learned, because they wished to find out whether integrated-learning was a mere fad or a real avenue of educational advance. Essentially, too, because they wished to find out what its requirements were in terms of knowledge and techniques, and what precisely the role of the teacher was in the integrated school: in other words, how professional effectiveness was to be gauged (and not least by the teacher himself) in the new situation. In this paper we have sought to pose these questions honestly and to present the conclusions that were reached. In some places, however, it was suggested that a more open mind should be kept, and on these occasions there have been mentioned doubts or additional questions which were thought to merit further attention.

A number of points, however, are worth enumeration.

1) Integrated learning is not simply a superficially attractive fad.

2) It grows logically out of the way in which we view the child, his emotions, needs, attitudes and potentialities.

3) Ultimately it is concerned with the establishment and reinforcement of a unique partnership in the process of education.

4) It is concerned with standards of excellence in the basic skills of numeracy and literacy which are related to all learning processes in our society.

5) This makes the task of the teacher more complex, but it *in no way* undermines the position of the teacher as one who stimulates, guides and, on numerous occasions, consciously initiates learning, albeit with more sensitivity and pragmatism than was characteristic of earlier systems. On the other hand, the integrated approach involves neither the rejection nor the depreciation of aspects of formal learning where their existence is central to attainment of worthwhile ends.

There is no fanaticism here, no rigid structure of "thou shalt not," and where apparently traditional methods offer a commonsense way of tackling a particular problem there should be no fear of undermining a newer system. Nor are the ultimate aims of education in bringing about the all-round development of the child, socially, morally, intellectually, aesthetically and in every other way changed. Ultimately, as we have stressed, integrated education is a philosophy, an attitude of mind: it is revealed in the characteristic life and outlook of the school.

*   *   *

What are some of the major differences between the traditional class-room and what happens at Gordonbrock—not in terms of physical arrangement but in terms of the kinds of things the teachers and the children do?

The difference, of course—the great difference—is that the teacher doesn't go along saying to herself, "This is what I'm going to teach the children today." She goes to school prepared for anything. Because it's going to come from the children. She doesn't say to herself, "I'll go

From Courtney B. Cazden, *Infant School* (Newton, Mass.: Education Development Center, 1969), pp. 2–21. Reprinted by permission of Courtney B. Cazden and Education Development Center, Inc.

today and I will teach the children addition,"—shall we say, just for example. She goes to school, and addition might come out of something which the children are doing. A child might be building with bricks, and he'll say to another child, "I want 12 more bricks to finish this." We seize on any opportunity. And then, once that is begun, we continue with it. You might have the children counting in 2's. Or you might say, "There were two girls here, and two girls over there." But let the children discover it for themselves. "How many girls are here?" "Two." "How many little girls over there?" Adding the twos. Not going along and writing on the blackboard "2 + 2 is ___" and then saying to the children, "Copy that down. Now take out your counters." Do you see? It's not teacher-directed. It is child-directed. It's what happens— it's happening constantly. You can't shut your eyes to it.

A child comes along and says, "Your coat is the same color as mine." Well, then, what a lovely talk you can have about colors. You can—if the child is ready for it—make up a book about colors. You can cut out pictures of ladies dressed in yellow dresses, and that can be the yellow page. And the child will really get it established. And the green page, and the red page, and so on. And you can have "My book of colors," so that when they want to do their creative writing, instead of coming to you and saying, "How do I spell 'yellow'?" they go to the color book, and the child discovers how to spell "yellow." It's part and parcel of living—learning. The child educates himself, really, through his own needs, through what he discovers.

He suddenly discovers, by looking at a book, that the first letter of his name is exactly the same as the first letter of somebody else's name. He says, "Oh, look! You've got that and so have I!" And then if you are there, you say, "Ah, yes, that says 'buh' for Bobby. And that says 'buh' for Betsy. What else can we think of that starts with 'buh'?" You see how different it is? It's coming from the child. Not teacher-directed. I would say child-discovery, and then guided by the teacher. It's a talking together just as you and I are talking. Here we have already learned from one another. You've told me all about what you were doing in Scotland and what you'd found out about the Edinburgh Festival. You see, you have enriched my—not exactly experience—but my—knowledge? I've been educated. And it goes on constantly.

A mother, when she is training her child, doesn't sit down and give the child a talk on how to use the spoon and pusher. She shows the child and knows that when the child is ready, the child begins to take. The mother doesn't sit down and say, "Now, tomorrow we are going to use the spoon and pusher," does she? I know that's taking it to a great length. It really has not much to do with what we were talking about with the school. But it is the same sort of idea. It's got to come naturally. But the teacher has got to be at the ready. That, I think, is the main difference. She's got to be aware—all the time. She can't stand back, and say, "Well, I've written it all up on the blackboard. Now I've talked to them about it. They must all have taken it in because I've told them about it." You know the little sponges are not taking it in. Otherwise they wouldn't be flicking things around the room or pulling somebody else's hair. If they were really interested, they would be with her all the time.

Another difference I would say with this method is that you can see when the child is ready. The method as we used to have it—you took it whether the child was ready or not. But now the children are doing different things in the classroom. They select what they want to do. And they are learning from the material they have selected. From each child, the teacher—the teacher who is aware—can discover something, and she can enrich that child's knowledge. But she's got to be aware. I think that is one of the big differences. You can go to school, as I did when I was a young teacher, with a lesson beautifully thought out. Tell the children a wonderful story; try to get them interested; have something for them to do at the end of the story; and think, "Oh, I've done a wonderful thing because they've all copied it out. The writing from some of them was absolutely beautiful." But ask those children to read about it two or three days later, and I doubt whether more than one in ten would really be able to read all of it. Except fluent readers.

You said the teacher doesn't go to school with a lesson plan of what she's going to teach that day. But what kind of planning does the teacher do?

Now don't misunderstand me. I didn't say that she doesn't have a plan. She must have some idea of what she's going to do. Starting from scratch, when we go back tomorrow,[1] the teacher doesn't really know what's going to evolve, because she's starting off with children who before were—oh dear, you do realize that mine is a family group school, don't you?

Yes.

So when the teachers go back tomorrow, the children who are the oldest in the class are going to be what used to be the middle group— the middle group in age.

They'll be seven?

They will all be seven by the end of next August—the oldest child by about the end of next week. But there's not a child in the school who's seven years old at the moment. Then during the week, the new children will arrive. So that the oldest ones are six-plus, then the five-plus's, and then these others who are coming into school. Some of them are already five-plus, and some of them are rising-fives.

[1] This interview took place on the day before the beginning of the new school year.

The teacher doesn't really know what's going to evolve, but she has got in mind what she will do tomorrow. She'll set about arranging her classroom, of course. And she will introduce the children, perhaps in a new room altogether, because we change around. And she'll just refresh their memories: this is where we keep different things. And then of course, a whole lot of talking about the holidays and what they did. No doubt a holiday book will be begun. The children will each write or paint or do something about what they did in the holiday. They might create something with the sand. We do know that will happen during the day. I expect my teachers have already got their stories prepared— perhaps a story about the seaside or a story about the country. You see, that will definitely be there.

Stories that they will read?

Read or tell. They must have that in mind. Now as the term goes on, and the different ideas evolve, then the teacher can get her work prepared. You can't just leave it to chance.

When people see Lillian's movie[2], what you don't see is the planning that happens behind the scenes so that this wonderful life in the classroom goes on and gets somewhere. People seeing it think that this is just incidental and accidental learning. You can't see how the teacher plans to bring about a real progression in the child's knowledge and understanding and skills.

No, I don't think that does come out in the film. How can I put it? Well, supposing it's getting near November the fifth. Of course, the children will be thrilled about that. It's Guy Fawkes Day, which we celebrate still with fireworks and so on, as you might have on All Hallows—Halloween. Now that is coming along, and the children get awfully keen on this. So, we take the child's interests. You've got to have sticks of a certain length for your rockets. So that requires measuring. If you make banners, you'll need some measuring on that, too, won't you. You'll hear the story of Guy Fawkes. If you're going to have a Guy Fawkes party, that involves making the cakes. So along comes your weighing, directions for cake-making, making the cakes, time the cakes take to cook, the costs of the cake. A certain amount of science will come into it. Why is the top of the oven hotter than the bottom? What happens? I'm saying this very quickly, and this is quite general.

But then, you see, the children are at different stages. Some children will write how they made the cakes; some might be just content to paint a picture—"I made some cakes"—this is according to their own particular level. This has nothing at all to do with the age of the children in the classroom, because we find that fives work quite happily with sixes, and sevens can work quite happily with fives. It all depends on their

[2] A film, *Infants School,* which Lillian Weber made of a day at Gordonbrock.

experience and their readiness. But the children who are most able will write quite lovely little—creative works of art, shall we say: paint pictures of what they've been doing, and then write lovely descriptions of how they made the cakes, and whether any of the cakes got burnt, and what time they put them into the oven, what time they took them out, how long the cake took to rise.

A lot of the knowledge the teacher has given—you could say— "incidentally," but not really incidentally because no teacher does it incidentally. She's got something and she wants to put it over to the children, doesn't she? She's not just throwing out little pearls here and there. She really has got that in her mind that these children want to make cakes right. "Now what can I get from teaching these children to make cakes?" The feel of different things—the fatty feel of the butter, the soft feel of the flour. Even from that you can go on and find out how do we get flour. You can do quite a lot, according to the age of the children, their knowledge, and their desire to know.

Let's say she finds out, because of the work of making the cakes, that a child is having trouble in dealing with fractions that are involved in cooking. How could she plan to work on that in the subsequent days?

Ah! Now that will be going on in quite a number of other ways, because with their water play they have the opportunity to find out how many of these make a whole one. That all comes in their incidental work as well. The whole of it is there in the classroom. You can find out that two half-pints make a pint. We have fraction games that they play where you can find out that two semicircles put together match up with a complete circle. You do quite a lot of talking, too, you see, about halves when they cut the cakes. How many children? How many made the cakes? From that you can go from your halves to your quarters, your fifths, your sixths, your eighths.

Would she ever take the initiative in gathering together one, or two, or more?

Yes! Oh, definitely!

And actually do what you might call a formal lesson . . . ?

Oh, definitely! Oh, yes! You see, you started by asking me how does it differ. The difference is in the approach. But teaching remains teaching throughout. If you find that children are having difficulty with one particular aspect, and you want to make quite sure to establish that, then you gather these children together. And you work away at that until you are sure that they understand. Then you send them back again to their play with this knowledge. Let's take the cake-making again. They've been making the cakes; they've been weighing them. And then the puzzlement about how many ounces make a pound, shall we say? Four ounces make the quarter, and eight ounces make the half—and some couldn't quite grasp that. The teacher gathers the group together, and they have a long—no, not a long, about twenty minutes—but, at any rate they do have her entirely to themselves while they all work out, with the scales, that the four ounces match with the quarter of a pound weight. They weigh different things. They really get that established. And then she sends them back again to make their cakes with that knowledge.

How large might that group be?

It could be anything from four to ten, accordingly.

Does that happen very often?

It happens all the time. This is a way that I can tell you: sometimes I have children myself. I go to a teacher and say, "Have you got any children I can have for a little while who need some special help with numbers?" She says, "Oh, yes." And she takes out a little group—we have a good look first to see that we're not dragging them away from some other special interest. But generally I can gather a little group. If I can't get enough from her, I say to another teacher, "Have you got any?" Then I take the children out—they can come out into the hall with me—and we talk. We count the children who are there; we count somebody's buttons—this is purely counting. We walk up and down my stairs—I've got all the stairs numbered, and they go up and down the stairs. Then we have a lovely time picking out the number symbols. You wouldn't say that at the end of that time every child in that group would know all those number symbols. But I do think that every child in that group would know at least one number symbol. Then I can have them again the next day, and on we go from there. You can do it so many different ways. You don't need a great deal of the apparatus that's on the market. You can manage quite easily with everything that's around you. You want four—well, you can have four boys; you can put two children together, and they've got four legs on a chair. All of that helps to establish in the child's mind the four. And then matching the symbol: "You draw four lines for me." "You draw four people." "Go find four of anything for me and bring it to me." Oh, yes, we definitely take the groups. And we take the whole class, too. We don't talk just to individual children all the time. We take a whole class. Why not? Why not have the whole class and talk about time?

The whole class is a mixed-age group?

A mixed-age group. But you can do it.

That would be how many children?

Forty. Forty children. We find that with the stories, children all enjoy the stories. You'll have your children who roll around on the floor—we get it quite a lot sometimes from some of our little immigrant children who aren't used to sitting and listening to stories. It seems to us—I may be quite wrong—but quite a number of them, we find, do tend to roll around. We let them roll. They don't upset the other children. But if we find that a child really cannot concentrate, then we let him go and play quietly in the house corner. But you'll find very soon those children will creep back to the group and sit down and enjoy the story. We take stories that will be suitable for the very young—you know, the little nursery stories. And we take stories that are suitable for the older children because, naturally, they've got to reach on—they want a little bit more. We find that the younger children will listen to these stories just as well. A story is a story, isn't it? I remember one of my staff told me that when she was a little girl at home ill with measles—this was an experience I never had because radio wasn't even invented when I was a child—she was at home ill and her mother put on a program—I suppose it was something similar to "Woman's Hour"—where a serial was being read. She said she thoroughly enjoyed it. She hadn't got a clue what it was about, but she thoroughly enjoyed it. It was a story, and the children will listen to stories.

Suppose you go around and ask a teacher, "Do you have some children who need help with numbers?" For the teacher to answer you, she has to know her children—what they know and what they don't know, and exactly where they are. Does she keep this in her head? Or do you keep records?

She jots. She jots during the day, and she writes it up at the end of the week. She keeps a very comprehensive record about her children, about their characteristics, when they show that they're beginning to take leadership, when they are apprehensive. With this, you really know your children. Not only are you aware of their needs, intellectually and physically, you also have the opportunity to stand back from the children and observe. It's only in observing children that you really do know your children. If you're sitting there, and you've got all the little ones all doing the same thing at the same time, what opportunity have you really to know your children? But if they can select what they want to do, and you can find out the thoughts that are going on in the child's mind, you really do begin to know your children. Couple that with the fact that you can see the parents—talk to them, find out a little what it's like in the home, whether they're sharing a house or whether they're living in two rooms, whether there's a baby arrived, whether the child is the middle child. Couple all that with your own observations in the classroom and the fact that with this family grouping, you do keep your children the whole time. At the end of the two years, or three years in the case of some children, you really do know them. That has a great deal to do with the way that you are going to teach your children. You know the child who is going to be quick to grasp something. And you know the child who's got to be led along very, very slowly and very gently.

Is writing down part of her job? Is it something she really must do?
Oh, yes.

Are these notes kept about the individual child, or is it a log of the whole group activity?

No, there's a page for each child. It's individual. But side by side with that, she has a quick jotter where she might write down things under headings—shall we say, "Fluent speaking," "Answers in mono-syllables" (these are just certain headings that you could have), "Reading readiness," "On an introductory book," and so on. Then she would put the tick underneath that (that is very quick), or she might put the date. Just so she can look at it quickly and see what is happening. Again, with numbers, she might write down, "Can recognize number symbols to five" or ". . . to ten," "Can count to . . ." whatever it might be. She must keep a record, otherwise she's going to get hopelessly bogged, isn't she? We teach the sounds, too, the phonetics. Well, then you must tick off for those. You must know whether your child knows the sounds or not.

You mentioned that the teacher must be aware of individual children. If she has forty children in her class, it seems such a difficult job for her to be aware, for her to spend time with individual children, capitalizing on and using their experiences as they work at the workbench or whatever, and also do the kind of small group teaching that you've described. How does she get around?

She generally begins her day with a chat with the children. They have different ways of starting. I've got experienced teachers who just take it in their stride. But I'll try to describe it from the point of view of somebody who's coming fresh to it. I've had quite a number of youngsters straight from college. My advice to them, first of all, is: Talk to the children. Find out what they have elected to do straight away, and then insist—you've got to have order, you can't have chaos in your classroom. So, by the time that four children have said, "I want to play in the sand,"—"Right, four children. Not more than four children." You see, you make your rules as well. "Two children may go and play with the water." "Two people have said they want water; that's the end." "So many children may go and play in the house corner."

You have all these different—"activities" I'll call them, for want of another word. They're all round the classroom. A child hasn't got to rack his brains and think, "Now what do I want to do?" It's all there for him to see. Very often the teacher will put exciting material down which will suggest something to the child. She might put some card-board boxes and think, "That will give the children an idea. They might start making a train." Then she must be prepared to find that it's been turned into a robot. She'll put material which will set the children thinking. Now, don't think that the children all work individually, be-

cause they don't. We're most of us gregarious, aren't we? The children
will get into little groups. There's always a leader of a group, and the
children work together. So your group is naturally formed for you.

Don't think of the harassed teacher dashing from one child to hear
her read, to another child to explain some mathematical problem, because that isn't so. That is the impression in the film, but nobody could
live that way. We'd all be dead. We'd be dead in a week. You couldn't
do it. The impression is conveyed in the film because it had to be done
quickly. The camera swung from one thing to another. The children
were getting their materials, and they were starting. Then a long time
goes by while the children are working with those materials and the
teacher, perhaps, is hearing a little group read. Or she's got another
little group who've arranged themselves, and they're doing some creative
writing, and she goes to them. I know, the film gave me that impression.
When I saw it, I thought we couldn't possibly work at that speed. You
know that it couldn't be so, and your common sense would tell you this
is just a case of little points being picked up by the camera, showing
the children, showing what they can do, and then leaving you to think
out, "What did they get from it?"

*Let's say the children are working at different things, and the
teacher sits down with a few children who are doing creative writing.
Will children from other activities come over to interrupt her for help?*

Yes, yes, they do.

Then what does she do?

Very often it's merely a question of saying, "Well, now, go back and
try it that way." And the other children will take that for granted.
Imagine yourself with your family. You're busy showing your eldest
daughter how to cut out a dress. Both of you are really getting involved
with it, and you're both thoroughly enjoying it. This is what is happening with the children who are doing their creative writing. They're
thoroughly enjoying it, because there is their teacher with them. She's
there to help them if they say to her, "I don't know how to write this."
She is there to say, "Go and get the dictionary, and we'll find this word.
Look for it on the page where the words start with "puh." Or start with
"P," according to the progress of the child. Some of them would do it
with sounds, and some would do it with the names of the alphabet. Then
while you're busy helping your daughter with her dress, your husband
comes in, and he says, "Have you any idea where I put that letter from
old So-and-so?" You say, "Just a moment while I help Daddy." You
say to him, "I think we tucked it away with these different papers,"
and he goes ahead and hunts through it to find what he wants. There is
your child coming from another group to interrupt. You then return to
the dressmaking, and your other daughter comes in. She wants to know

something, and so again you spare just a few moments to talk to her and put her right, so that she can go on with what she's doing on her own. You have to use your common sense quite a lot over this. After all, if you are taking a whole class of children, nobody would expect the teacher to talk to each one individually, although you do know that each one of those children has got a problem.

Supposing you tell me how they take a class in America, and then we'll see what the difference is. How do you do it when you're taking a class? Then I can see what the problems are.

I think the major difference—at least, judging from what you're saying and the film—is the intensity of the experience for the teacher. If you're taking a class—first you have a discussion with the children, and then you set them to do some arithmetic examples, or do some writing, or read—and you can relax a bit.

Yes, but what are they writing about? What are they reading about? And what are they doing their arithmetic examples about? What does it come from? That is the basic difference, isn't it? You take them out of the air and you say, "We're going to learn this. I'll give you some examples. Now, dear little children, sit down and just work out the examples. And if you can work out the examples, I will assume that you understand it." But you see, we don't assume that. We want to know that the child really does understand it. You can give as many examples as you like, but it doesn't necessarily follow that when a child has worked out quite a number of examples of "6 plus 2 makes 8," "5 plus 2 makes 7," "9 plus 2 makes 11," that the child really does know what "plus 2" means. But if you get right down to the basic with a child who is just discovering it—that he's got two hands and his friend has got two hands, so they've got four hands, and somebody else has got two hands, so they've got six hands between them—that is a discovery. And then you can give your examples. You could set those three children down quite happily, and they could work from a whole page of examples. My word, they do enjoy writing down their sums, as they call them. But the sum is not the discovery. The sum is not the experience. The sum is merely a fact, isn't it?

When the children choose—four to work in the sandbox, two to work in the water—does the teacher ever try to influence those choices, or say, "The first thing this morning I'd like to work with so-and-so"?

Yes, that must come sometimes, because we have such large classes. If we hadn't got the large classes, it wouldn't be necessary because the child would have more time with the teacher. We are defeated, as you are, with large classes. Sometimes she might say, "I'd like you and you to come with me first thing this morning. I want to go on with something we were doing yesterday. So I'd like you please to stay with me." By the time the children really know their teacher, they know that no more than so many can be working at different things. Of course, as the term goes on, the children have got embroiled, so they know what they want to do, and they automatically go on with that.

When the child has finished with the sandplay and comes to the teacher and says, "Would you like to come and see what we've made," then she'll go to the sandplay, and the child will say, "You see, we've made a castle here, and that's the road, and that is something else." Then the teacher can step in and say, "What sort of castle is it? What do you call this little tower on the corner? Do you know anything about castles as they used to be?" And as she begins to talk about what the children have done with the sandplay, the other children will begin to come around. And before she knows where she is, she's sent one child off to the library to get a book about castles, and then they all talk about castles. There is your opening for your history stories, and all your creative writing is going to be about castles. The children are going to make their own suits of armor. They're going to make their own lances, and so on. What great vistas are opened up, just from sandplay!

With the children who are less experienced, the teacher can say, "That is a very little sandpie, and that is a big sandpie. Which one is the largest?" And the child is learning comparison there. That one's larger than that one; that one's smaller than that one. "How many sandpies have you made?" "I've put four sandpies there, and John has put two sandpies over there." "How many sandpies altogether?" "1,2, 3,4,5,6." "Oh, yes, four shells here and two shells there. How many?" "1,2,3,4,5,6." And so she goes on until the child realizes: four and two. But it won't be, of course, with that lesson. She has to remember that. She makes a little jotting of it, or she has a mental note. But she must remember it. And the next day she gathers those same children together and she goes on with it, just as you do with your ordinary formal lesson, don't you? I mean, if you've taken a formal lesson—shall we say, on "plus 2"—you know very well that all your 40 children haven't taken that in on one day. Some children have. And so you also note down—don't you?—and you say to yourself, "Tomorrow I must take that other little group, and I must do that again with them." The teacher's not doing any more than that. The children are gainfully employed; they are learning from their own experiences all the time.

Castles might come up and they might not. But are there some things that the teacher makes sure that the children do and learn? Such as— well, numbers we've spoken of quite a bit. Does she care if castles get talked about?

Oh, no, because it could be something quite else. It could be monsters. It could be prehistoric monsters, and there you are way back again. You're talking about man, and then you make your things out of clay.

You're creating as primitive man did, and you're making all the things that primitive man would have used.

But does she try and bring in some history, whether it's castles or primitive man? Does she care if history comes in at all?

She can't say to herself, "I am going to take 'early stone age' in this term," because it may not come at all. No, she can't say that. You cannot write down, "I am going to do this, that, and the other." But you have got to be ready with what does come along. Mind you, there's nothing to stop her from twisting it into that if she wants to. You see, you can do such a lot. You can direct indirectly. If you are ready to put something for the children to take and to get ideas from, then there's no end to what you can do.

Let's say the children start building castles. Maybe the teacher doesn't know much about castles.

Well, then she says to the children, "I'm awfully sorry, I don't know much about this. Let's go to the library and get a book, and we'll find out together."

Might she then do some intensive research on her own to see where they might go?

Well, it wouldn't hurt her, would it? You see, we find that the children are teaching us so much. I've learnt far more about space and planets than I ever dreamt that I would know. But I've learnt it from the children. I think you have to face it. They know more about modern times than I shall ever know. They know more than we know because they take everything; they accept it. This is their world. To us, it's still very new, very strange, very awe-inspiring. But the child accepts it.

Is there any specialization among your teachers? For instance, might you have one teacher who is especially interested in mathematics? Might she do more with pulling groups of children together for mathematics? Or another teacher who might be especially experienced in reading? Is there any specialization like that?

No, that doesn't happen. But I have been rather fortunate—just this last term, I've had a new member of the staff who is gifted musically. I have used her quite a lot in order that the children should have singing with an instrument accompanying. All my staff have taken their own singing in the classroom. But not one of them played an instrument until I had this person. But that is the only way that I would specialize. You see, if you take children out of the classroom, they are having an experience that the teacher knows nothing about. And so she can't go on with it. You must have the experience *with* your children when they're so young. When they're older, yes. From seven, shall we say, and so on—then I think you could quite easily have your specialists. They could be called in to give the special work that the children would need. But not when they're so young. I don't think it's necessary, and I feel that an infant teacher could cope with all these demands that are made on her, apart from being able to play a musical instrument. We can't all do that, but we can do so many other things.

Let me ask one more thing about the planning. Let's think about it from the point of view of the child rather than of the teacher. How much of a commitment on the part of the child is there? Let's say the child chooses sandbox. Is there much flitting about—doing a few minutes in the sandbox and then deciding that what somebody else is doing over there looks awfully interesting and wandering over? Or is there a real commitment to stay at the sandbox for a certain period of time?

There is a real commitment to stay there. Although the teacher must know her child. There are some children who are not ready to be committed to anything when they first come to school. Or not even perhaps only then. Supposing something happens in the home. Supposing there's a sudden rift between the parents, and father goes off. Now that child is terribly disturbed. And it may be two or three days before the head teacher hears about it. The mother might be too upset to say. And the child comes to school and is not ready to do anything. The teacher has observed, and she suddenly sees John or Joan standing aloof and not getting on with things as the child is used to doing. That would tell her something, if she sees the child begin to flit from one thing to another.

Then we have the children who come to school who are not ready to settle to anything for long. It might be the result of the home, where they've had perhaps too much attention. Or perhaps where too much has been done for them, and they can't continue with one particular thing, and so they tend to flit from one thing to another. But the teacher again watches that, and she encourages the child to stay longer at whatever he's chosen to do. No, the child is not allowed to say, "Well, I want to play with the sand," and after two minutes drift off to do something else. The teacher would say, "You asked to play with the sand, and somebody else couldn't play with it because you wanted to. Now I want to see what you've made." When the children have used something, the teacher wants to see what the child has made with it— if it's a material that's going to show something at the end. If it's water play, what the child has discovered from the water play. If it's junk— what the child has made from it. Whatever they do, they talk about what they've done—if they're unable to write. That is a must.

Does that mean that when the child has finished something, before he may go and start another activity, he must go to the teacher to account to her for what he has done?

Yes. That's it. And then if it's something which needed tidying away, she'll say, "Now I've seen what you've done. Tidy it up." And the child tidies up whatever it is he's had and puts it away. They can't just leave it any more than they could in a home—so that Mother comes in and falls over the train set. If they've finished playing with the train set, Mother no doubt talks about it—any parent does. Where the train's been going, and how many passengers, and so on. But of course, in school it would be taken perhaps even farther than that. The child must tidy up. And talk about what he's done, or write about what he's done.

Perhaps it would be simpler to take an example from reading. The child comes to school and paints a picture. I'll take it with painting and reading only. The child paints a picture—maybe a child from a home where television has ruled the household, and Mum and Dad have been chasing the almighty shilling, and they haven't much time to talk to the child. So from that child you might get just the "Yes," "No,"—or perhaps even the nod of the head. So the teacher talks to the child about what he's done and gives him the words. That is really quite basic. There's another child who has come from a home where Mother and Father have had time to talk with him, and the teacher says, "What have you painted?" And the child will begin to say what the picture is about. The teacher will supply words and, again, build up the vocabulary. She might say to that child, "Would you like to write what you've painted?" The child might, perhaps, have painted a picture of a lady—"That's Mummy." "Would you like me to write 'Mummy'?" The child might say, "Yes" or he might say, "No." If the child says, "Yes," the teacher writes "Mummy" beside the picture. And the child can then go over on top of the writing or copy it out underneath, according to his skill. The next time that child might paint another picture of "Mummy," or there might be a picture of "Me with Mummy." The teacher says, "Would you like me to write what you've painted: 'Mummy—Me'?" Then, you see, the steps go on, farther and farther. The next time it is, "This is my Mummy. This is me." Or "This is Mummy and me going shopping." We do not correct any grammatical error. We write it just as the child says it.

That's a big controversy with us at the moment.

Don't attempt to put it grammatically correct, because the child is only going to read what he said. If he says, "Me is going to do this"— I don't often hear that—"Me is going shopping," you would write "Me is going shopping." Because the next time the child reads it, he would read, "Me is going shopping," even if you write "I am going shopping." So don't waste your time and his. Write what he says.

Then the next step, after the child has been doing that for some time, we get quite a lot of, "This is a house." Children love to paint houses, so you'll get that over and over again. "This is a house." "This is a boat." "This is Mummy." "This is my toy." "This is—" And it keeps coming and coming. You might put one up on the wall. You could also collect the children's work together and make up a "This is" book. When the children have done that for a certain time, you say to the child that you know would be able to do it, "Could you write 'This is' for me, and I'll put the rest of it?" The child has drawn perhaps a picture of his birthday cake, and he goes and writes "This is" on the side. "Can you find the word 'my' anywhere in the classroom?" Yes, because you've got the pictures all round, and you've been talking about them. You've been reading all the words that other children have asked for, and the child might be able to find "my." If he can't, you write it on his paper. And then you supply "birthday cake." That is just showing how very simply and gradually it builds up.

You'll find painting is one of the things that children really love to do. You'll have more than two or three children doing painting. Some of them do it sitting at tables, some of them on the floor, some of them standing at easels. It's a lovely way of introducing reading. But you can also do it with your sandplay. "This is John's sand castle." Or, "A sand castle." And the child copies that onto his paper. And he can do a picture of his sand castle. When he's found out that two half-pints equal or fill the pint, he could draw a picture of two smaller jugs. He doesn't get them, of course, correct in size—you wouldn't expect it. But he might draw a picture of the two smaller ones and the big one and write "a half" on each and "one" on the big one. Or he might be content to write, "I played with the water." He might not write, "Two half-pints equal one pint," but you're content, because he's had his number experience from what he did. And he is getting his reading and writing experience from his creative writing afterwards. There is your reading, all coming from what the child is doing.

6. The Teacher as Facilitator of Learning

Informal educators tend to reject the traditional view of education as the transmission of a fixed body of knowledge. "The object of teaching," as Sir Alec Clegg puts it, "is not so much to convey knowledge as it is to excite a determination in the child to acquire it for himself, and to teach him how to go about acquiring it." It is also to teach the child to know what is worth knowing—to help children learn to discriminate between the valuable and the meretricious. In the selection that follows, Roland Barth analyzes the ways in which the teacher's manifold roles relate to his or her primary function, that of facilitator of children's learning.

We have seen that open educators believe that "if a child is fully engaged in an activity, learning is taking place." The key role of the teacher as facilitator of learning, then, is to *maximize the likelihood that each child will be fully engaged in an activity* for as much of the day as possible, to encourage the active exploration of his world by the child. For purposes of discussion and clarity, we shall distinguish seven important and interrelated activities of the teacher. Since these functions are simultaneous, the order in which they are presented here is of little significance. The facilitator of learning:

Respects children as individuals
Manages the environment
Provides materials
Consolidates children's experience through language
Provides direct instruction
Encourages children's activity
Encourages children's independence

Although most teachers acknowledge the importance of respecting children as individuals, the transmission-of-knowledge model prevents them from *acting as if* they respected children as individuals. There is an inherent conflict between the authority of the material to be learned and the learner. The teacher is caught in the middle, and much of his efforts go into finding a resolution, usually imperfect, to this conflict. Consequently, few teachers or children feel or have an opportunity to act respectfully. In schools where subject matter is the organizing principle which governs the relationship between teacher and student, the teacher can be assured of its conveyance to the children only by setting similar goals and expectations for the entire class, by lecturing, and by requiring the same activities of each child. Learning experiences are *group* experiences, tied to group norms. Teachers relate to students, and students relate to other students as members of a large group—but seldom as individuals. Respect for children as individuals exists only with difficulty under these conditions.

For a teacher to relate individually to many children each day, even for brief periods of time, demands an extraordinary amount of sensitivity, mobility, and energy. He must constantly scan the room, the corridor, and the space outside the room, observing children who are working with different materials and with other children. In deciding when or when not to intervene, he must constantly ask himself the question "Is there some way I can help further this child's exploration?" He must alternate group surveillance with moments spent offering a child his undivided attention, help, and support. As difficult as this is, it does not seem impossible. Within a half hour, one observer in a British primary school saw the teacher contacting all forty-one children:

> She stepped into the corridor to comment on a little boy's painting, stopping off at the woodworking bench to see how the boat was coming. Inside the room she listened to two little girls read, wrote down words in a little boy's private dictionary for the story he was writing, looked over the shoulders of the shape-manipulators and block-builders, corrected a page of sums for a little boy who had been working on arithmetic. . . .

Perhaps no educational practice more vividly reveals underlying assumptions about children's learning and knowledge than the common practice of ability grouping. Ability grouping is a logical extension of the transmission-of-knowledge model of learning. If one assumes that the child learns from an agent outside himself—teacher, program, film —then, given the need to educate large numbers of students, it follows that the more closely students are matched along certain relevant dimensions (e.g., test scores, age, perhaps sex), the more efficiently knowledge can be transmitted to them. Since there is more knowledge essential for everyone to know than there is time in which to learn it, efficiency is of the utmost importance. Ability grouping would then appear to facilitate the most effective transmission of knowledge.

But the price of this kind of homogeneity and efficiency is the limitation, if not the elimination, of important individual distinctions. It becomes impossible for teachers to respect children as individuals when the more children act like individuals (i.e., differently), the more difficult it becomes to group them and instruct them; when the system, in the name of efficiency, is grouping the important individual differences out of each classroom as fast as they appear. In short, most schools pay lip service to the goal of respect for children as individuals but engage in practices which virtually exclude this kind of respect.

Open educators are universal in their condemnation of ability grouping, or "streaming" as it is called in England. They believe that if a teacher is to respect children as individuals, then he cannot arrange and teach them in homogeneous groups. Objections to ability grouping rest on:

1. Inability at the present time of adults and test instruments to accurately differentiate intellectual qualities in children

2. Doubt that capacity for accumulation of knowledge is the most important quality of a human being
3. Undesirable consequences, usually in terms of children's self-confidence and self-esteem, which are associated with ability grouping
4. Close association of ability grouping with the view of teacher as transmitter and student as recipient of knowledge
5. Evidence from educational research that differences between achievement of children grouped by ability and those not so grouped, although generally favoring the former, are confined to the limited area of *measurable* attainment, and often amount to a difference of only two or three more questions right on a test of forty items

Open educators not only acknowledge but deliberately attempt to foster individual differences among children. They balance the numbers of boys and girls. They disregard apparent ability differences. They often practice "family grouping," that is, placing children of ages 5–7 or 8–11 in the same classroom, in the belief that the younger children will be constantly stimulated and extended by interaction with the older, and the older will extend their knowledge by working with the younger (a practice not unlike the old one-room schoolhouses). In these ways, open educators attempt to maximize diversity, in the belief that a child who spends each day with children who vary in age, sex, ability, interest, and background will have a richer learning experience than one who belongs to an apparently similar (i.e., homogeneous) group.

When children in open classrooms are grouped, it is usually for other purposes:

The only scheduled events that I saw during the week were an assembly period for singing and prayers, held each day; a gym period, recess, and lunch. During the rest of the day from 9 until 3, each individual child was free to follow his own choices and interests.

In the course of exploring materials and posing, solving, and verifying problems for themselves, children often spontaneously form groups on the basis of *common interest:*

No, don't think that the children always work individually, because they don't. We're most of us gregarious, aren't we? The children will get into little groups. There's always a leader of a group, and the children work together. So your group is naturally formed for you.

Like ability groups, these groups are functional; but rather than serving a function for the adult, they serve the child. They stimulate and assist his exploration of the human and the material world.

It is also common in open schools for teachers to select small groups of children who have a particular need and want help in meeting it, such as learning how to make papier-mâché or running an adding machine. But these groups are ad hoc, not year-long compartments as are the familiar three reading groups. They are "formed for a particular purpose, and should disappear when the purpose is achieved." Thus the concept of grouping *per se* is not antithetical to learning, or to individual relationships; it is only when the adult tries to legislate the time, place, constitution, and duration of a group that the concept becomes abused, unnatural, and counterproductive.

In short, the teacher in the open school respects children as individuals by stressing the quality of the relationship between adult and child and among children, rather than the frequency or quantity, in the belief that a highly individual contact between individuals is more important for learning than continual group exposures:

> I can give all of my attention to a child for five minutes and that's worth more to him than being part of a sea of faces all day.

One obvious difference between an open classroom and the traditional classroom is the physical environment in which both child and adult live —the way the classroom *looks*. The spatial organization of the open school reflects beliefs about children's learning and about the nature of knowledge, just as a lecture hall reveals belief in a transmission-of-knowledge model of education. But physical arrangements not only *reflect* what child and adult are thinking and doing; they also *influence* thought and action.

The teacher in the open school organizes his classroom not to promote optimal conditions for transmission of knowledge but to extend the range of possibilities children can explore. Children's desks are often removed from the room, and only chairs and tables are left. In classrooms where desks remain, they may not be assigned to individual children; instead, each child may have a small cubby or drawer along one side of the room for storing sweaters, pencils, and other personal belongings. Space within the classroom is divided, often by movable screens or furniture, into "interest areas," each perhaps ten feet square.

Although subject-matter categories do not direct the organization of the open classroom, most materials seem to have an explicitness which causes the object to be associated with a discipline. A book is literature; an adding machine, mathematics; a telescope, science. Thus, "interest tables" are often devoted to math, science, reading, social studies, art, etc. Typically, a mathematics "corner" might offer Cuisenaire rods, Stern blocks, balances, geoboards, number lines, and math books; a science area, batteries and bulbs, different liquids in plastic containers, a microscope, and some bones; a nature area, gerbils, fish, rabbits, guinea pigs, leaves, twigs, stones; a social studies area, maps, globes, artifacts from various countries, books, and models of explorers' ships; a reading corner, an old stuffed easy chair or a mattress on the floor, inviting children to read from a wide variety of books displayed on shelves; an art area, usually near a source of water, paints, easels, paper, charcoal, linoleum blocks, and carving tools. These interest areas are employed more so that teachers will know where to put things and students will know where to find them, than as attempts to categorize experience and knowledge for children.

When a child is given freedom to explore materials in his own way, he is likely to be oblivious to categories in which adults have placed them. If a child is building a boat for the neighboring stream, neither he nor the teacher distinguishes among his activities when he measures, studies a picture in a book, paints the sails, or notices that the current in the river changes after a rainfall, although a traditional teacher might label them "mathematics," "history," "art," and "science."

While in the traditional classroom the child learns at his desk, in the open school *the locus of learning is where something of particular interest to the child happens to be.* With this confidence, the teacher accepts and respects what each child chooses to do and where he chooses to do it. The boundaries most American children carefully draw between "school" and "home" are blurred. Children, like teachers, take things and ideas of interest home to ponder, just as they bring things and ideas of interest from home to school. The result is a more fully "integrated day" and, as Hull points out, "a sense of belonging to a much larger community than that of the individual class."

> There might even be an occasion when a child says, "Can I go into my friend's class? Miss Jones is going to tell a story about so and so, and I want to hear it." Or a child might say, "My friend is making a bridge, and he wants me to go and help him. Can I go and help him?"

Many of the junior schools take their students for a week's trip to a lodge which the county maintains in Wales, or to other camping sites in areas of archeological interest. . . . A few schools have managed trips to Normandy or Paris, in order to supplement their studies of French language and history.

A teacher cannot directly provide a child the exploratory experiences which lead to learning; he can, however, provide materials which will engage the child's innate curiosity and involve him in the learning process.

Open educators' belief in the power and importance of manipulative materials conflicts with the conviction of many educators, parents, and children that firsthand experiences with materials are neither appropriate nor legitimate, that secondary experiences mediated by symbols—numerals, words, pictures—are the legitimate means for learning.

For the teacher in the open school, the problem is one of selection, for through the selection of materials the teacher influences the direction of the child's exploration, and hence his learning. Rather than offering selections of appropriate materials, we shall suggest six criteria which can guide the teacher's selection and which may help in reaching an optimal match between child and materials.

CRITERION 1: *Whenever possible, encourage and permit children to supply their own materials.*

One way a teacher can be sure that the classroom contains materials capable of eliciting children's interest is to encourage children to bring to school items of their own. Since "given the opportunity, children will choose to engage in activities which will be of high interest to them," materials which children select from their real world are likely to encourage their exploration and learning. Furthermore, by bringing their own materials to school, children identify what they are particularly interested in and offer the teacher important clues for subsequent selection of materials. If a child with reading problems brings in model dinosaur bones to assemble, his teacher might find some easy books about dinosaurs for him to read. A child who brings in seeds might plant them, then measure and perhaps graph the plant's growth.

Children's ingenuity and imagination need not be limited to bringing materials of interest into the classroom. When they need materials or equipment *not* available either in school or at home, they can construct apparatus in the classroom: for instance, devices to measure length, time, weight, or light brightness.

Although many teachers in this country have a "show and tell" period each morning to which a child may bring things of interest, usually the goldfish, photograph, plant, or magnet provides an excuse for the child to stand up and talk before the class or to convey to the teacher and the class an interest the child has *outside school,* as if that were some other world. What the child brings in is seldom something he investigates during school time. In addition, teachers usually limit the range of acceptable materials children may bring in to books, maps, stories, newspaper clippings, etc., and in subtle ways screen out animals, bicycles, tools, comic books, sports equipment, and the like.

CRITERION 2: *Whenever possible, encourage and permit children to explore the real world outside the classroom and outside the school.*

Once the notion of the teacher as the child's only source of knowledge is dismissed, the classroom is no longer sacrosanct. It is often possible, permissible, and profitable for the teacher to release children from rigid adherence to a five-hour-a-day schedule in the classroom, so that they may explore the environment *outside* the classroom. In this way, a whole world of possibilities opens up, and the entire environment becomes the locus of the child's learning. The countryside offers a study of nature, creatures of every kind, plants, and streams; the suburbs offer opportunities to explore various forms of transportation (buses, trains, trucks, boats, cars); cities offer opportunities to view construction of roads, bridges, and skyscrapers. All give access to weather, food, buildings, movement, change, pattern and excitement. Wherever there is a school, there is a community which is rich in potential learning experiences.

People are resources as valuable for children's learning as are objects or natural phenomena. Everyone is a potential "teacher," for all humans through their jobs, personalities, interests, and experiences hold something of interest and importance to a child. Differentiating between adults who teach children as a profession and those who don't is unfortunate—certainly not a distinction that children would make. Many British schools, for instance, view their entire staff as a resource for the children:

> . . . in these schools, and others at both the infant and junior levels, the kitchen staff is not isolated. Often the women will be sought out by children for help with spelling words and other academic problems.

Responsibility for the education of youngsters will probably never completely leave the schools, nor is it likely that children will be able to supply all their own materials; the teacher has major responsibility for providing materials *in the classroom* for children.

CRITERION 3: *The best materials for children are common ones, which are inexpensive, familiar, and easily available.*

Many administrators, teachers, and parents assume that *unless* materials are expensive, flashy, and manufactured, children cannot learn very much from them. This reasoning leads to a conception of educational "innovation" as moving from old buses, books, desks, and buildings to new buses, books, desks, and buildings. The question of whether a new twelve-dollar social studies textbook results in more learning than the old four-dollar copy is unasked and unanswered.

Expensive materials are not necessarily the key to children's learning. They often better serve teachers' and parents' needs than children's. Most manufactured items used *in* schools—microscopes, filmstrips, mathematics blocks, encyclopedias—are to be used by children *only* in school, usually under strict conditions laid down by the teacher, who fears their loss or damage. This has the effect of localizing and separating many of the child's learning activities from his out-of-school life.

Common, less expensive materials, on the other hand, have many advantages. In seeking them out, children and adults learn to be imaginative, inventive, resourceful, and instrumental. They learn to master the raw materials of the world around them. They learn to relate in-school materials and activities—animals, clay, sand, tree roots, water—and out-of-school activities. Children tend to respect and care for these inexpensive common materials with an uncharacteristic zeal, whereas they often abuse more expensive school equipment; freedom and independence surround the child's use of ordinary things, in contrast to the constraint, dependence, and resentment often associated with more "valuable" materials. This freedom makes learning more possible.

It is questionable whether American teachers can develop a sense of resourcefulness and competence in making the most of their world in a profession where their horizon is defined, on the one hand, by budget restrictions and, on the other, by the offerings of the Creative Playthings catalog. Unfortunately, most teachers are hesitant to scrounge, unsure of themselves and unsure that what *they* might select will be seen as valuable and acceptable to parents, children, and administrators. This caution, added to the availability of funds for manufactured materials (which obviates the need for creative scrounging), discourages the selection and use of common, inexpensive materials in the classroom.

In British primary schools, teachers who earn only $2,500 a year, working in schools with corresponding budgets, *must* be resourceful. They have no choice but to make the most of what they have and can dig up. In British open schools, teachers and children alike scrounge for all manner of things: old tires for swings, popsicle sticks for arithmetic, roots of trees from nearby woods for sculpture, animals caught in snares for nature study, books discarded by libraries, and the like.

> You don't need a great deal of the apparatus that's on the market. You can manage quite easily with everything that's 'round you.
>
> In none of our visits to schools did we see lavish provision of equipment, books, mechanical aids, tape recorders or film projectors. . . . On the contrary, we found an attitude of making do with the materials that were to hand.
>
> The most valuable materials are the natural ones, sand, wood, clay, water and then paint, paper, materials for sewing and cooking and cleaning, and then dolls, furniture, animals, etc. . . . Expensive manufactured bricks, beads, puzzles, etc., are not necessary; they have their uses and may be available in small quantities, but their educational value is much more limited.

CRITERION 4: *Ambiguous, multiprogrammed materials which suggest to the child a wide number of possible paths of exploration are preferred.*

There is another important reason for preferring common, inexpensive materials over more expensive, manufactured ones: common materials tend to be more ambiguous and less directive, and thus offer each child a greater place in determining their use.

Many manufactured educational materials have been designed to exclude all but one or two possible paths for the child's exploration and thinking. These materials are not only limited but limiting, for they teach the child to depend upon the structure inherent in the material (and upon the adult who constructs the materials) to pose questions, to help solve problems, and to verify the solution. The child, in short, becomes dependent upon a source outside himself to intiate, sustain, and verify his own learning.

Materials structured and "programmed" by adults, which leave insufficient room for children to invent, improvise, modify, and adapt, are revealed by such phrases as "the child will be led" or "orderly stages" and by elaborate directions concerning the proper use of the materials and suggested ways to get children back on the "right" path, should their imagination cause them to depart from it. The child can assemble a plastic model in only one way; he can use the filmstrip viewer only with those filmstrips available to him. The fact that they can be exciting for the child and are legitimate from the adult's point of view makes these materials no less limiting.

Open educators' emphasis on flexibly structured materials rests on the belief that a child should be instrumental in posing for himself both the problem and the path that he will take in pursuing that problem. Materials are to assist him in these choices, not to direct or restrict him. But one must not condemn all materials which have structure, only those whose structure strictly directs and limits the child's thinking. Many common materials exist which have not been designed by anyone for anyone, for any particular purpose, and yet which have definite structure. A magnet, sand, or a set of wooden blocks has definite structure and the capacity to influence and organize children's thought. But they are ambiguous and multiprogrammed; they do not confine the child but, rather, offer him a major part in determining their use, depending upon the questions they suggest to him. With the magnet he can make a motor, a test to see which materials are attracted to it, or a study of polarity with iron filings. With blocks, he can build a balance board, a house, a fort, a highway for his cars, or a stand for his checker game; and with the sand he can build, measure time, draw, etc.

A game that British children frequently play with "junk" provides an illustration. A child will bring to school something he has found. Regardless of the material, the teacher will encourage him to explore over a period of time all the possible uses to which the material might be put. A given object would suggest many different uses to different children. For instance, with a clothespin one child might hold a painting on an easel, make a bob for a pendulum, construct the body of a doll, make a handle for a printing stamp, project a stylized grasshopper on a screen, or hang clothes on a line. To investigate the use of a material in many contexts seems to encourage both flexibility in thinking and imaginative play.

The principle of selecting multiple-program materials, like the other principles for selection, must be employed with reference to the degree of independence of each child. For the child who is dependent upon direct adult control for his learning, structured materials and activities such as checkers or a filmstrip viewer are probably more appropriate, at least initially. The same child might be at a loss at a sand table. For the child who is more independent and self-reliant, ambiguous materials such as clay, blocks, or water—which offer a variety of entry points and paths for exploration—may be more appropriate.

The task of the teacher, then, is to select materials which will provide multiple structures and then to encourage each child to use the full range of possibilities inherent in the materials and in himself. People, like materials, can be more or less directive, rigid, and prescribing. What a teacher encourages children to do with materials has just as great an influence on the thinking and behavior of children as do the inherent properties of the materials. Hopefully, all children will, in time, develop competence, confidence, and resourcefulness when confronted with an unstructured and ambiguous situation: that is, when confronted with the real world.

CRITERION 5: *Select materials which have a high likelihood of initiating, sustaining, and extending exploration.*

Because learning is a necessary consequence of active exploration in a rich environment, it is important for the adult to select materials which will make active exploration likely. It cannot be assumed that all children will wish to explore a random collection of materials. The teacher must provide materials which will invite questions, study, examination, and activity. Although the teacher selects materials on the basis of what he *suspects* children of this age range, sex, and locality will find interesting, he should not be surprised if children use materials in unanticipated ways:

> Very often the teacher will put exciting materials down which suggest something to the child. She might put some cardboard boxes and think, "That will give the children an idea. They might start making a train." Then she must be prepared to find that it's been turned into a robot.

Fortunately, the necessity of selecting materials without benefit of observation of the children who will use them is short-lived. Yesterday, three children made robots out of cardboard boxes, even though the teacher may not have guessed that they would use these multiple-program materials in this way. Today he can provide paint, tin cans, and buttons for these same children, should they want to embellish their robot. He might also have on hand robot books, robot models, and robot pictures.

After the first days, then, the teacher selects materials which will sustain and extend each child's exploration, although he may continue to introduce new materials on the hunch that children will find use for them. His job gradually becomes less speculative and based more on careful observation of what the children are saying and doing.

The timing of the introduction of materials is as important as the nature of the materials to child and adult. Lesson plans, curriculum guides, and literature on child development are of little relevance in making time discriminations. Only keen, firsthand observation can guide the teacher. Thus, one cannot separate the role of the teacher in selecting and supplying materials from the role of the teacher in observing and diagnosing children's behavior. In order to prescribe and select materials to make available to children tomorrow, we must take advantage of what they are telling us today.

Given personal encouragement from the teacher and an environment rich in manipulative materials, a child is likely to engage in a variety of rewarding activities. He learns from essentially private experiences between himself and objects in his real world. His learning, however, does not end with the experiences themselves; when he has learned something, he will feel a need to make explicit the implicit.

Because learning can be refined and extended through the conversion of experience into language, the teacher can exercise a delicate, yet powerful, function: he can encourage the child to verbalize his discoveries, provide the child with a word for a concept or an idea, and help the child to associate a useful symbol with a concrete experience. In these ways the teacher can help the child to translate his experience, which is private, into language, which is public.

The teacher's intervention in the child's encounters with other children and with materials must be subtle. It is as possible for the teacher to interfere with children's learning by labeling and abstracting as by directing and prescribing. As a child investigates a pendulum, for instance, he will invent and use his own words for what he sees and does: "swing," "round trip," "tick-tock." The teacher can help him to develop, establish, and enrich these concepts by talking with the child in the child's words. After the child has worked with the pendulum, the teacher may even introduce the technical words for the child's experience: "period," "amplitude," etc. In any case, learning is labeled by child and adult alike during the time and after it has taken place, not before. Words come out of experiences, not out of predetermined lesson plans and curriculum guides.

For the teacher to help the child in this way demands careful observation and diagnosis of children's behavior. In one way, observing in a classroom full of materials is easy, because of the abundance of *overt* behavior. But in another way, observing children and making sense out of their behavior is never easy. At best, it is risky to infer what children are thinking—particularly for the beginning teacher. When children are given materials and encouraged to explore, they tend not to behave in adultlike ways, nor do they always talk in adult language or think in adult concepts. But when a child does or says something, he sends off signals, even though he may be unable or unwilling to give an account of what he is thinking in a way which would make sense to the adult. The teacher must be very careful that the words he supplies to the child are related to what the child is thinking. He must try to decipher the child's own language; he must also pay careful attention to the child's nonverbal behavior, which often conveys as much information as does his language. Rather than trying to force the child to convey his ideas in adult terms, as most teachers are inclined to do, the teacher must be ready to adapt to the child's thinking, language, and behavior.

The effect of the teacher's consolidating children's experience with appropriate language is to help relate the thinking of the child to the thinking of the adult; to anticipate a more detailed investigation of the phenomenon; to develop the child's vocabulary; to develop a commonly used abstraction, a shorthand that helps the child better recall what he has done and learned; and to enable the child to communicate with others if he wants to. In the final analysis, however, the important question is not whether the child recognizes, understands, or uses the "right" word for his experiences but whether he has developed a working concept of his own. His personal and idiosyncratic concept is more important than the correct word for it, as convenient and as impressive as that word might be. Vocabulary is more important as an aid in the development and extension of concepts than as a medium for displaying them.

Open educators believe that there *are* times when it is appropriate and essential for the teacher to be directive, times when he might even be a transmitter of knowledge. Rather than reacting emotionally against the directive role, or assuming it with unquestioning comfort, it is important for the teacher to understand when and why didactic behavior is appropriate.

There are two circumstances when the teacher must be didactic: when children are unlikely to discover for themselves skills or information needed to pursue activities which are important to them; and when it is likely that a child's exploration will result in significant danger to himself or others or to the equipment he is using. Take, for instance, use of a simple camera. Most children, although fascinated by cameras, initially have little idea of what the different dials mean or how and when to use them. If they use the camera *without* such knowledge, their photos are unlikely to be successful. This will result in frustration and probably put an end to the activity and to that opportunity for learning.

A child interested in a microscope may be strongly absorbed in studying a frog's egg. But in the process of focusing, he may move the lens down into the glass slide or onto the specimen, thereby damaging the lens and perhaps breaking the slide or the instrument in the process. Similarly, the child without sufficient instruction in the use of the camera can damage it or can waste quantities of film. The child trying to light a 110-volt light bulb with forty flashlight batteries may experience pain or be harmed unless he is instructed in the ideas of insulation, voltage, amperage, etc.

There are cases, like these, when the teacher must explain in careful detail to children how to use equipment and what each part does. To

be sure, sensitive teachers can help children to learn the skill by drawing them out in a discussion with such questions as "What do you
think this is for?" and "How do you think this works?" The teacher may
also make good use of one or two children in the classroom who have
already mastered the skill and can convey it to others. But the teacher's
objective is the same: to make sure that every child arrives at a piece
of information or a skill specified and judged by the teacher to be essential to the child's further exploration.

Usually the teacher is given important clues by the children which
help him to decide when to be directive and didactic: "How do I get
the film in the camera?" is a legitimate question and deserves a legitimate
answer. But the teacher cannot rely entirely upon the child's verbalized
need in determining his action. Even if the child *thinks* he knows what
he's doing, even if the child does not ask if it is all right to cut the
concrete block with a crosscut saw, the teacher has a responsibility for
the safety and success of the child and the safeguarding of the tool.
The fact that the child may discover in time, by trial and error, that
cinder blocks make saws dull is not sufficient justification for the
teacher to withhold instruction at the proper moment. Summerhill's
A. S. Neil found himself locking up all his fine tools in a tight closet
rather than allowing children to abuse them. The third alternative, instruction and perhaps supervision in the use of the tools, did not seem
appropriate.

In summary, conditions which require direct, didactic instruction are
those in which there is likelihood that the child's failure will curtail
exploration and those in which there is danger to self, others, or equipment. As in all adult-child relations, the line between helping the child
by staying out of his way and helping by intervening is difficult to draw.
It is very easy to err on either side, as Hawkins has suggested:

> [A] teacher can kill a subject by his own eagerness—egoness—to
> show himself its master.

In his role as facilitator of learning, the teacher must consciously and
actively *encourage* children's activity and exploration. Given a classroom full of interesting materials, the teacher can establish certain conditions which will make children's exploration of these materials more
likely and fruitful. Two are especially important: developing a mutual,
personal trust between teacher and child; and permitting and encouraging the child to make important choices.

Characteristic of most teachers is a chronic, uneasy sense of distrust: distrust of what the children might do that the teacher doesn't
want them to do, and of what they might not do that the teacher wants

them to do. A good deal of a teacher's daily energy output and be-havior is a response to this pervasive distrust and fear of children: teachers are taught not to turn their back on the class but, instead, to write at the blackboard at an awkward angle which permits them con-stant surveillance of the classroom; children often are not permitted to leave the room, let alone the building, without a special "pass"; they are given tests to see if they have done the required work and are placed at a maximum distance apart so that they will not cheat during the tests. This sense of uneasiness, fear, and distrust is reciprocal. Most children fear and distrust their teachers! They expect a test to be sprung on them without warning; they worry when parents and the teacher con-fer, lest the teacher betray their shortcomings; they come to school armed with multiple excuses to fend off unreasonable or unexpected demands made by the teacher; they recoil on report card day, less because they are unaware of the quality of the work they have done over the term than because they see little connection between the work they have done—which is theirs—and the grades which they will re-ceive—which are the teacher's. Just as much of the teacher's daily en-ergy is expended in response to a distrust of children, so a large part of a student's energy is dissipated in anxiety and anticipation stemming from his distrust of the teacher. Thus the conventional relationship between teacher and child is essentially one of adversaries in a con-stant struggle.

A sense of mutual trust and confidence between child and teacher is essential for the child's learning and the teacher's effectiveness. Where teacher and child are threatened, teaching and learning are difficult at best. Only in a situation of trust will children feel free to explore com-fortably, actively, confidently, openly, and autonomously in situations not dominated by adults. The development of mutual trust is closely associated with changes taking place in many British and American open classrooms. It is becoming clear that a child outside the teacher's immediate control need not be out of all control.

As important as it is for learning, a sense of mutual trust is perhaps the most difficult attribute for teachers and children to develop. Trust is a basic personality characteristic, not something to be adopted like a principle for selecting materials. *Lack* of trust is, of course, a charac-istic of most schools and pervades even many open schools. In one American open school, for instance, parents who had sent their child to a situation where he might make important choices by day tutored him in the three R's every night.

The teacher can begin to develop trust between each child and him-self by attempting to arrange the child's environment so that the per-sonal and physical inhibitions to free exploration—a troublesome peer, poor eyesight, an inability to write—are removed, thereby increasing the likelihood of the child's success. When the teacher has made frequent decisions which help remove obstacles to the children's learning,

> . . . the child learns something about the adult which can be described with words like "confidence," "trust," and "respect." The teacher has done something for the child he could not do for himself and the child knows it. . . . If he thus learns that he has the competence to do something that he didn't know he could do, then the teacher has been a very crucial figure in his life. He has provided that external loop, that external feedback that the child couldn't provide for himself; he then values the one who provides the thing provided.

A measure of mutual trust between teacher and child is a necessary precondition for a second major role of the teacher in encouraging children's activity. The teacher must empower the child with a significant degree of *choice* concerning the materials and the questions with which he will work.

In all schools a central question is *who* decides what the child is going to do. Does a child write a composition, for example, because he wants to or because the adult decides that he must? The question is perhaps raised more poignantly by asking, "What if the child decides *not* to engage in the activity? What if he is given a battery and a bulb, and he decides to watch the fish in the aquarium? What are the consequences?" Not behaving in an expected way reveals very clearly wherein the power and responsibility for making classroom decisions resides.

In most schools, adults are the decisionmakers. On the basis of experience, training, and status in the hierarchy, they are assumed qualified to decide what a child will learn and how he will learn it. To be sure, teachers in traditional schools give children some choice, but the concept of choice is distorted and abused. It is a usual practice to offer a child a finite number of alternatives: "Write a report on one of the explorers, Magellan, Columbus, Cortez, De Soto, etc." While this may give the child some sense of being instrumental, of involvement in the decisionmaking process, this is a situation where a child chooses from among problems *posed by the adult*. Choice is also abused when the teacher permits a child to choose from among stipulated alternatives and then rigidly forces him to adhere to his choice. The child who has chosen to write about Magellan may discover, after a few days, that Cortez is more exciting for him. The teacher's usual reply is, "You chose to write about Magellan, and you must write about Magellan." For open educators, choice implies the individual's posing questions for himself which are important to him and pursuing their solution in his own way. He may choose to write about Magellan, or he may choose not to write about an explorer at all.

When most teachers give children a choice, they relinquish important control. Having relinquished something of value, they take something back which is important to the child—his freedom to move. Thus, when most teachers give children a choice, it is often accompanied by resentment and even hostility. It is as if the teacher permits the child to choose for pragmatic rather than educational reasons, out of expediency rather than for sound pedagogy. But there appear to be sound pedagogical reasons for permitting children to make some choices:

> . . . where [children] felt really free in their choice of activities and problems, there was not only more spontaneous enthusiasm but also more genuine achievement.

Many teachers have found a modified "contract system" a helpful way to introduce student choice and to share decisionmaking. In these classrooms, children (say, each Monday) are given assignments they must complete that week. These are teacher-imposed, non-negotiable tasks. However, when or where a student chooses to work on these assignments—at school or at home—is for him to determine. When he is not engaged in this teacher-assigned work he may use his time to pursue projects of his own choosing. This system, although highlighting the distinction between work and play, between teacher-set tasks and those the child poses for himself, does release a large amount of time for children to make decisions each week.

In more informal classrooms, the teacher makes choices concerning materials and the environment. The child knows the adult is doing this, but it does not seem to diminish the child's feeling that he is engaged in his own exploration and is pursuing it in his own way and toward his own ends.

Within this context children also make choices. For instance, a child in a classroom rich in manipulative materials might see a pendulum, start to swing it, and wonder how to make it swing faster. After trying a variety of methods, he might wonder *if* he had succeeded in making it swing faster. All these decisions, while perhaps not deliberate or conscious, are legitimate choices the child has made. He has selected a piece of apparatus, posed a problem with respect to it, considered various strategies for solving the problem, chosen a likely means of solving it, implemented his idea, and determined, in the face of the evidence available to him, whether his solution answers his original question. He also chooses when to terminate his investigation and with whom, if anyone, he would like to share his findings.

Because of prevalent child-rearing practices and previous school experiences, many children are not initially equipped with either the inclination or the ability to make this kind of choice. One difficulty for the teacher in the open classroom is the child who may be capable of serious exploration but who does not "get on with it." The child sitting before a pendulum aimlessly fiddling with it is quickly labeled a "time waster," particularly in efficiency-minded America. There seems to be a large amount of wasted time in open classrooms—far more than in traditional classrooms. But children of all ages spend a great deal of their time, both in and out of school, daydreaming, engrossed in their private worlds of fantasy, "wasting time." In the conventional classroom this is easy to camouflage by sitting quietly behind a book or by moving a pencil across a paper, whereas in the open classroom daydreaming means *not* being occupied with materials. In the former case, "wasting time" is all but invisible (although the child may not have anything to hand in at the end of the day); in the latter, "wasting time" is quite visible. But this is not to say that wasting time is a more common occurrence in the open classroom than in most classes.

The one important question for the teacher with a child who appears to be wasting time is, "What does it mean?" Is the child avoiding an anxiety-making situation? Is he consolidating an experience? Is he refueling? Is he watching? A second question is what to do about it— whether to intervene and how. Unless a child appears to be wasting time for an extended period, or unless he is disturbing others, it is probably best to wait and see whether he regains interest before coaxing him on. Wasting time in an environment full of interesting materials with which other children are busily engaged is not self-reinforcing for most children. It would probably help the teacher's restraint in this kind of situation to acknowledge that adults, as well as children, occasionally waste time—and that it's just as unreasonable to expect of children, as of adults, that they always work at their maximum level.

Many children have to work at assuming responsibility for their own behavior. They have to develop confidence and competence in making decisions. They learn to make judgments by making judgments. The teacher can help these children by providing intermediate levels of choice. He might, for instance, attach written questions to pieces of equipment throughout the classroom: to a scale, "How much do you weigh?"; to a pendulum, "How fast can you make it swing?"; to a battery, bulb, and wire, "Can you make it light?" The teacher might ask a child, "Can you weigh this book on that balance?" He might have available several sheets of paper with directions, accompanied by pictures, for solving different problems: for example, building a clay boat, making a leaf print, playing a math game. These intermediate aids lead successively toward the time when each child can pose problems for himself and work independently toward their solution.

Thus, the teacher's role varies from child to child. For some children, he must be very directive; for others, he merely supplies materials; for yet others, he provides only the time and space in which children may explore with their own materials. In all cases, the teacher must recognize that if a child's choice is to be genuine the teacher must accept it and must accept the condition that what is important to the child is important, that each individual is the best judge of what interests him.

The teacher as facilitator of learning in the open classroom encourages the child's independence and self-reliance. The capacity of the individual to cope with the new is more important than the ability to know and to display the old. It is more important for the child to learn to rely upon his own powers in the long run than to accept adult direction in the short run. Yet children depend upon adults to give meaning, order, control, and security to their experience. Most are still dependent in significant ways when they come to school.

Unfortunately, many adults depend upon children's depending upon them. More than a few teachers find meaning in their work from being needed and depended upon by children. They need children to ask what to do, permission to move about, the correct answer, and "Is it all right if . . . ?" For these teachers, to diminish children's dependence upon them is to threaten their own raison d'être. The child cannot become independent of the teacher until the teacher becomes less needful of the child's constant obedience and affection, until the adult learns that not being *needed* is different from being *superfluous*. The teacher must phase himself out of the dependent relationship which has dominated the learning of the child since birth. This is a particularly selfless job, for not only must the teacher resist the constant, comfortable, and powerful temptation to impart knowledge, but he must also resist the temptation to have children "do as I say." The latter task is most difficult because it often gives comfort to both adult and child.

When a child asks for help, the teacher can encourage independence by asking *himself* a series of difficult questions: "Is this child really asking for help by what he is doing?" "Does this child really need help?" "What will happen if he doesn't get help from me?" "If he needs help, is it in his best interests for *me* to provide it, or can he get it from some other source?" "What sources other than myself can he make use of?" "How *little* help can I give so that the child can sustain his exploration and yet so that I will not interfere?" If these questions are honestly asked, and if each situation is carefully assessed, the teacher will probably often exclude himself from children's experiences. His withdrawal may well have the effect of helping the child find a solution for himself.

The teacher can also encourage the child's independence by helping him to become aware of his behavior, by helping him to analyze his own experiences and to modify them on the basis of previous consequences. By encouraging the child to pose his own problems, solve them, and verify them, by providing situations in which the child can work independently and experience success, the teacher can help the child to become autonomous. Open education stresses the present, not the future; living, not preparing for life; learning now, not anticipating the future. But in the sense that development of self-reliance and independence on the part of the child will be the best assurance that he will be equipped for whatever may come, open education becomes a preparation for the future.

In a sense, everything a teacher does in school in some way "facilitates children's learning," or should. We have already discussed several direct means. But the teacher in the open school has less direct, managerial functions which also ultimately enhance children's learning. The phrase "managing children" may appear to contradict much of the foregoing. It need not. A certain amount of management of children by adults, a certain amount of imposed order, structure, and control, is a necessary precondition for independent exploration. Reasonable, consistent restrictions on children's behavior ultimately enable them to be more free and productive. We shall discuss two functions of the teacher as manager of children: the teacher as authority, and the teacher as evaluator.

Many Americans have "authority hangups." For them the word "authority" is a loaded and pejorative term. A great number of those drawn to the ideas of open education question the right of anyone to set himself above children or to consider himself different in knowledge, discipline, and power. It is useful to repeat a distinction made by Duberman:

> A crucial distinction must be made between authority and authoritarianism. The former represents accumulated experience, knowledge and insight. The latter represents their counterfeits: age masquerading as maturity, information as understanding, technique as originality. Authoritarianism is forced to demand the respect that authority draws naturally to itself. The former, like all demands, is likely to meet with hostility; the latter, like all authenticity, with emulation. Our universities—our schools on every level—are rife with authoritarianism, all but devoid of authority.

In Duberman's sense, it is both a legitimate and a necessary role of the adult in the open classroom to be an authority for the children—a source of accumulated experience, knowledge, insight, maturity, leadership, arbitration, strength, judgment, and stability. It is vital to the successful functioning of the open classroom that the teacher be an authority, without becoming an authoritarian. Distinction in the classroom between adult and child can be blurred only up to a point. There is no escaping or hiding the fact that the adult is bigger, stronger, older, and perhaps wiser than the child. But he need not be boss; he need not be arbitrary. The teacher is not one among equals but holds a unique place in constructing and maintaining the learning environment.

The teacher as classroom authority faces the temptation of taking advantage of his special place—to establish and enhance an adult-child power relationship—to become an authoritarian. Forces at work in the school climate press for the establishment of such a superordinate-subordinate relationship, and the teacher must consciously resist these forces if he is to maintain his important place as authority in his daily relations with children and help the children learn to control their own lives. If he can restrain himself from dominating and controlling children's behavior, there is some indication, as William Hull and others have observed, that children will come to be authorities themselves and that they will control their own behavior:

> The scene reminded me of an adult audience waiting for the beginning of a concert. When it was time for the assembly to begin, the children, well aware that something was about to happen, stopped talking, though we could not detect the signal to which they were responding . . . perhaps it was merely that everyone had now arrived. I had never before seen a community of young children behaving with such freedom and self-restraint. They demonstrated an awareness about the group and a sensitivity to it, together with an ability to control their own behavior.

A material-centered approach suggests another definition of the "problem child": In most schools the problem child is the one who behaves overtly, who makes noise, gets out of his seat, talks excitedly with other children, and the "good" child is the one who sits docilely and passively in his seat. In the open school, however, the situation may be somewhat the reverse. The "good" child is the one who responds to materials with interest, exploration, talk—the one who behaves openly and overtly. The problem child is the one who, for one reason or another, may not behave openly and overtly. He may be frightened of failure, of ridicule, or of being hurt. In most schools the problem child is "helped" by getting him to contain himself; in the open school this child needs help which will enable him to reveal himself.

What if children behave in ways which are destructive to other children and to equipment; *what if* children, given encouragement and a rich supply of manipulative materials, do not choose to explore? What can the teacher do in this kind of situation, besides shut her eyes and hope they will go away?

There are behavior problems in open classrooms, and the teacher has an important place in handling them. In a dispute between children, for instance, perhaps the most appropriate initial response of the teacher is not to interfere in any way, allowing the children to work out their own form of justice, for in the open classroom, teacher and child share responsibility for general behavior, just as they share in the choice of materials. Children care just as much about disruptions which interfere with their activities as adults do, and they find many ways of handling disturbances. Nevertheless, there are times when the teacher must intervene. When a child is behaving in a severely destructive or disturbing way—say, destroying another student's artwork—the teacher will be very clearly a restraining influence. In other instances, the class may be asked to help clarify a problem, and the teacher may gather the children around and discuss the difficulty. Children are usually willing and able to identify what is bothering them and to suggest ways of coping with it. Usually a meeting of this kind, convened in response to disruptive behavior, establishes the fact that the class recognizes and objects to specific behavior on the part of a child, thereby putting him on notice that he is disturbing others.

Open schools are not laissez-faire places where anything goes. The teacher knows and the child knows that an authority is present and that the teacher, no matter how personal and supportive he may be, is that authority. Teachers believe that although a child may appear to work for disorder, no child enjoys disorder. All recognize that unless *someone* is in charge they will not be able to move freely, explore freely, and choose freely. In many open classes there are only two rules: (1) no destroying equipment; and (2) no destroying or interfering with the work of other children. These rules seem sufficient for establishing and maintaining a climate in which learning can flourish.

The authority, in addition to providing situations for setting rules, has an important place in punishing their infraction. A teacher may take away from a disruptive child the privilege of working with materials and with other children until he comes up with a plan for productive, constructive activity in the classroom. This is often a very effective sanction, one which makes more sense in terms of the goal of teaching children to respect and value learning and human relationships than assigning additional math problems or requiring three compositions as a disciplinary measure.

In short, when children are given guidance by the adult authority, in interpersonal relations as well as in their work with inanimate objects, they can both identify problems and come up with solutions. Children learn that if they persist in disturbing others or in damaging equipment *something will happen* as a consequence. If they do not successfully handle disruptions, by themselves or with the help of the adult, the adult authority *will* intervene. Thus, in the classroom the best interests of a group of individuals are as important as the best interests of an individual.

In the eyes of the deviant child, the adult authority may be seen as an authoritarian and resented as such. Or the deviant child may run to the authority for help in controlling his behavior. But in either case, in the eyes of the children the teacher is the authority whose rules they respect and accept, even if they do not always help to formulate them, for these rules and this authority permit them the freedom to carry on their own activities, unobstructed.

7. The Teacher as Person

The teacher who comes from a traditional educational background has to make two profound changes in attitude or approach: one in the way in which he or she views children, the other in her conception of her own role. The first change, as Anne Bussis and Edward Chittenden suggest, may be somewhat easier for American teachers than the second; despite the authoritarian character of most American schools, we never have fully abandoned the rhetoric of child-centeredness that developed during the Progressive Era.

It is a lot harder for teachers to change their conception of their own role. They have to abandon their traditional passivity, whereby they merely carry out a curriculum someone else has created, in favor of creating, or working with others in a collegial relationship to create, their own materials. When they do so, teachers begin to act as if they were members of a profession rather than a subprofession—a change in their self-image as well as in their status. To change in this way, teachers need the kind of introspection about their work that Anne Fryer, headmistress of a Leicestershire infant school, discusses in the following selection.

Have you ever looked at a photograph of yourself and exclaimed, "It doesn't look a bit like me." Maybe not, but what possibly happens is that it doesn't look much like the self you see in the mirror each day. My photograph always makes me look much fatter than I really am! or is it that I have got used to selecting the information that the mirror

From Anne Fryer, "Self," address given at National Association of Independent Schools Workshop (mimeographed), The Beauvoir School, Washington, D.C., 1970. Reprinted with permission of the National Association of Independent Schools.

image presents and ignore the bits that do not conform to my mental picture? Perhaps this is what we do when making an assessment of ourselves at work.

I heard of an interesting experiment which might make it possible for a teacher to take a more detached look at himself at work in a classroom. Equipment will be set up so that for an unknown half hour period during the day a video-tape recording is made which will then be available for the class teacher only to view—entirely on his own, in his own time—and then to immediately erase.

It can be as hard to change our ideas as it is to alter our appearance, but first there must be an acceptance of our imperfections so that we have sufficient motivation and drive to endure the rather traumatic experience of scrutinizing our attitudes and philosophy. We must try to view ourselves through the camera's objective lens and not adopt subjective defensive attitudes when something less than flattering is revealed. Perhaps a private and confidential dialogue with ourselves will help to give some answers.

"I am" is said to be the most complete short statement ever made; what we are more likely to feel and say is "What am I?" or "Who am I?" or, in deep moments of contemplation "Why am I?"

What led you to the profession you now follow? Was it a set of coincidences, an opportunity that presented itself at the right psychological moment, an arrogant conviction that you are capable of the responsibility that teaching demands; was it a decision that you have since regretted, or have you a genuine passion for working with and guiding young children? Perhaps it was none of these, but in reflecting on our role as a teacher, it might be well to be honest about our motives in having sought this job.

Now that we are qualified, how has our attitude changed from its starting point, and what are the reasons for the change? Are you maybe in a difficult situation and having to work in a way for which you have no conviction, do you feel secure in your present post? What about your relationships with other staff, parents or School Principal—do they admire you, tolerate you, sympathize with you or (in an extreme case) despise you? What attitudes have the children toward you—do you believe they see you as a dragon, a friend, a hard taskmaster, a pushover, a guide to exciting and creative learning, someone who is truthful and just, a boring necessity to be avoided whenever possible? Do they think about you as a real person or do they show no interest in you at all?

How well do you know the children in your class? Have they all got happy and secure homes? What are their parents like? What are their hobbies or special interests, their fears, strengths and weaknesses? If you were asked to write a comprehensive report on the attitude and abilities of any one child I may pick at random from your class register, could you do it immediately and conscientiously with confidence, or would there be some children about whom you know hardly anything at all? Why is this? Have you any difficult children in your class—aggressive, passive but sullen, socially immature, academically disinterested or bored? What is the reason for this? What are you doing in a positive way to help them overcome their problems? Is there anything you do, or do not do, that aggravates or creates difficulties?

Who has determined how you organize your room? Is it just as it was when you took over, or has it undergone a gradual or dramatic change? What equipment have you on your shelves? How much of it has been home-made for individual children or for groups of children? Have you added to it within the past three months? Can you visit other teachers during the working day? What about their organization? Is it the same, better or worse than your own? By what criteria are you judging? Think of the first class you taught. How does the one you have now compare? Are you always on the lookout for new ideas? What about good old ideas? Do you take an interest in journals or publications concerned with educational research? Do you prefer a rigid syllabus and timetable to the responsibility of forming your own program? Were you well taught as a child and teenager? Which teacher do you remember best of all—is it a memory of dislike or affection? How would you like to be remembered by your children?

There is a Chinese saying: "Give a man a fish and you feed him for one day—teach him how to fish and you have fed him for a lifetime." I suspect that in many schools we are guilty of giving children the educational equivalent of a "fish for a day" instead of taking the more demanding role of teaching them "how to fish" which will make them more independent. When we are continually told the facts, the answers, our minds are not exercised on the need to seek the information which might contribute a solution.

Our attitudes are inevitably influenced by the experiences we have had and the quality of the thinking we have brought to our experiences. The quality of our thinking can be improved by the encouragement we receive to develop greater mental flexibility.

How flexible a mind have you developed?

How receptive are you to the ideas of others?

Have you ever done or said anything really original or creative?

Have you felt you are getting stale—that you would give a lot for a year off?

Do you accept the first solution that seems feasible when you meet with a problem, or do you go on searching for a better solution?

Try yourself on this problem which Edward De Bono presents in his book *Uses of Lateral Thinking*.

"Many years ago when a person who owed money could be thrown in jail, a merchant in London had the misfortune to owe a huge sum of money to a money-lender. The money-lender was old and ugly and fancied the merchant's beautiful teenage daughter. He proposed that they let providence settle the debt and told them that he would put a black pebble and a white pebble into a money bag and then let the girl pick out one of the pebbles. If she chose the black pebble she would become his wife and her father's debt would be cancelled. If she chose the white pebble she would stay with her father and the debt would be cancelled. But if she refused to take a pebble her father would be thrown in jail. Reluctantly the merchant agreed.

They were standing on a pebble-strewn path in the merchant's garden as they talked and the money-lender stooped down to pick up the two pebbles. As he picked up the pebbles, the girl, sharp-eyed with fright, noticed that he picked up two black pebbles and put them in a bag.

What did she do? She put her hand in the bag and drew out a pebble. Without looking at it she fumbled and let it fall on the path where it was immediately lost among all the others. "How clumsy of me," she cried, "but, never mind—if you look in the bag you will be able to tell which pebble I took by the color of the one that is left."

Now this is obviously an extreme example of a display of mental agility—I doubt whether one in 5,000 would have come up with the solution as presented, but it does serve to illustrate that there is more than one way of looking at a problematical situation. Nothing is achieved by throwing up our hands in horror—the challenge is to calmly examine the component parts to try and find the ones in which you can capitalize to your advantage.

Translate this to the school situation:

You are in a rough, downtown area, surrounded by shops and factories, located on a busy main road. Your Maths syllabus says you must cover addition, subtraction, money, measurement and time. Your textbooks are uninviting and you have children of a wide range of ability. Your problem is to make Maths a living, meaningful experience for your children. What have you got in your environment that will positively help? Traffic: A group can take a traffic census of the total volume of traffic over a 15 minute period at 9:00 a.m. Within the group some will record American cars, foreign cars, lorries, buses, travelling North/South while others do South/North. Plot these statistics in as many ways as possible as a visual representation—(histograms, cut-outs of cars, etc., model cars). If the traffic flow remained constant during the next ¾ hour, how many buses would have travelled North/South in an hour? etc. Take a census again at 2:00 p.m. and compare results. Which are the most popular cars? Which are the least frequent? Can you find out how much they cost?

How many people does a bus carry? How many, on average, travel by car?

Adjacent environment:

How long is the street in which your school is located? How many different ways can it be measured (yard rule, foot rule, trundle wheel, pacing count, baby steps, string with knots, etc.)? Let groups try out these different ways you have discussed and time the job, discuss the results and find the most efficient. Has everyone got the same stride? Or the same size of feet? Find out and record. Does the height of a person bear any relationship to the size of feet? Measure and record.

How many types of premises in your street? Shops, factory, school, offices? What do the shops sell? Visit and inquire. Select a sample of goods sold by two shops and compare prices. Is there a hairdresser— what do they charge for different services? Make up some problems on this. What is made at the factories. Visit. Do they export? How do their goods get to their customers?

At school:

How many people in your class?—Boys/Girls—record. How many in other classes? How many teachers? What can you find out about your school? On a large scale map, plot the districts where people live. How do you get to school? How much does it cost by bus and how long does it take? How long does it take walking? Do some comparisons of people who live near but reach school in different ways. And so on. . . .

It doesn't matter how arid your environment appears to be, there are always exciting learning opportunities to be found by those who seek them. Do not be inhibited by a forbidding exterior—there are treasures to be uncovered in the rejects of others.

Create an atmosphere where children will talk to you and to each other and listen to what they have to say. Find out what they are interested in and see how you can capitalize on this. Find out what is in the environment, not so that you can answer all the questions, but so that you can know where they will find the answers and also more problems which will create further questions.

Try to look at your classroom through the eyes of a child who is entering it for the first time. What impressions will he get of you from the appearance of your room, the expression on your face, your tone of voice, your regard for the other children, their regard for you.

No one can tell you what to believe, what is right or what should be done. Listen to the evidence, examine the work done by others, make a critical appraisal of yourself and your work, understand the elements and factors which influence your judgment, accept the inevitability of change both in yourself as a teacher and in your role as a teacher, search out informed colleagues who will listen as well as talk, agree as well as disagree, criticize as well as approve the course you have rationally decided to follow.

Don't let it ever be said with reference to you: "Some people's minds are like concrete—thoroughly mixed and permanently set."

II

How to Manage
Time and Space

*To enter an open classroom for the first time is a disorienting experience
for anyone accustomed to traditional formal schooling. As the vignettes
in Part One have indicated, an open classroom does not look like a
classroom. It is, rather, a workshop in which "interest areas" take the
place of the familiar rows of desks and chairs, and in which individualized learning takes the place of what some informal English educators
disparagingly call "the talk and chalk" method, whereby the teacher con-
ducts a lesson for the entire class from the chalk-board in the front of
the room.*

*The reading area in an open classroom, for example, typically is an
inviting place, with a rug or piece of old carpet on which children can
sprawl while they read, a couple of easy chairs or perhaps a cot or old
couch for additional comfort, a table and chairs where children can write,
and a large and tempting display of books at child's height. The arithmetic area (or "maths area," as the English call it) most likely will have
several tables pushed together to form a large working space. On the
tables, in addition to a variety of math texts and workbooks, will be a
box containing rulers, measuring tapes and sticks, string, and the like;
other boxes, containing pebbles, shells, stones, rocks, acorns, bottle tops,
and anything else that can be used for counting; several balance scales,
with boxes of weights as well as more pebbles, stones, rocks, feathers,
and anything else that can be used for weighing. To complete the picture,
and without allowing for the idiosyncratic arrangements that distinguish
one teacher's classroom from another even in the same school, there
typically is an art area, with easels, paints, brushes and paper, and a
science area, with rocks and shells, leaves and other local flora, candles*

*and jars, perhaps some small motors, batteries, bulbs, and wire, and in
all probability, an animal or two or three, be it rabbit, turtle, hamster, or
kitten.*

*In informal English infant schools, and frequently in the lower grades
of an informal junior school, there might be a large table-height sandbox
and a specially constructed table at about the same height, for water play,
both of them located near the maths area. (Both the sandbox and the
water table come "equipped" with an assortment of empty milk cartons
and bottles, plastic detergent bottles, pitchers, and plastic containers, all
with their volume (⅓ pint, ½ pint, quart, gallon, etc.) marked on them,
for practice in measuring.) There may also be an oven: following a recipe
for muffins or cookies provides still another application of simple mathematical notions, along with practice in reading.*

*Somewhere in the room (probably near the art area), there will be a
table, or perhaps several cartons on the floor, containing blocks, Tinkertoys, "junk" (so marked), i.e., empty cereal and soap boxes, egg cartons,
the rollers from used-up rolls of toilet paper and paper towels, pieces of
wood and cardboard, scraps of wallpaper and fabric, oaktag, cigar
boxes—anything children might use for constructing airplanes, trucks,
cars, steamrollers, robots, spaceships, houses, office buildings, bridges,
or for making collages or murals. In one corner, or perhaps in a converted closet, will be a "Wendy House," a child-sized playhouse furnished with dolls, furniture, dishes, kitchenware, and a pile of castoff
adult clothing for children to dress up in. And all this, in England, in
classrooms which as often as not contain as many as forty children!*

*How do they find room? In good measure by replacing the desks and
chairs with a smaller number of tables and chairs. There is no need to
have a seat and desk for each child: when the teacher does instruct the
class as a whole, the children simply gather around her, pulling up chairs
or sitting on the floor. But teachers also create space for the various interest areas and activities by using closets, cloakrooms, indeed every con-
ceivable nook and cranny, and by spilling over into the halls, lobbies,
playground, and other common space.*

*A visitor accustomed only to formal classrooms is likely to be dis-
oriented by the sound and movement of an informal classroom as much
as by its physical arrangements. To photograph a formal classroom in
action, one needs only a still camera with a wide-angle lens; to photograph an open classroom, one needs a motion-picture camera with sound,
for the initial impression is that the children are all in motion.*

*In a typical informal English primary school or a good American open
classroom, at any one moment some children may be hammering and
sawing at a workbench, some may be playing musical instruments or
painting, others may be reading aloud to the teacher or to a friend, still
others may be curled up on a cot or piece of carpet, reading in solitary*

absorption, oblivious to the sounds around them. Elsewhere in the room, there are likely to be children seated at a table or sprawled on the floor, writing a story. Others are in the maths area, counting or weighing acorns, bottle caps, and what have you, or measuring the perimeter of the room, or the teacher's desk, or the length of a visitor's shoes, or one another's height, and writing it all down; others are measuring the ingredients of a cookie recipe, getting them ready for the oven. There are children playing in the sandbox and others at the water table. And always there is the sound of children talking—to themselves, to their friends, to the teacher, or to the visitors. As one becomes acclimated to open classrooms, one learns to assess the nature of the sound: is it just noise and aimless chatter, the sure sign of a badly run classroom; or does it reflect purposeful activity?

Given the radically different look and sound of an open classroom, it is understandable, if unfortunate, that many American teachers, principals, and parents have confused form with substance and so have concluded that the prime ingredient of open education is to replace rows of desks and chairs with interest areas or, worse yet, to break down the walls between several adjoining classrooms to create large, open spaces.

Nothing could be further from the truth! By itself, dividing a classroom into interest areas does not *constitute open education; creating large open spaces does* not *constitute open education; individualizing instruction does* not *constitute open education. Important as technique is, it is less important than serious, systematic, and sustained thought about education. For the open classroom, as we have argued already, is not a model or set of techniques; it is an approach to teaching and learning—a set of shared attitudes and convictions about the nature and purposes of teaching and learning, about the nature of childhood and adolescence, and ultimately, about the nature of man.*

Unless a teacher understands why one room arrangement or one time-table may be superior to another, all the physical changes in the world will have little or no impact on the nature of the learning process within that classroom. In short, to talk about room arrangements should not be merely to talk about whether the furniture should be placed this way or that; it should be to talk about the educational purposes the teacher has in mind and the educational processes by which she hopes to achieve them.

Thus, the artifacts of the open classroom—interest areas, concrete materials, wall displays—are not ends in themselves but rather means to other ends. In general, open classrooms are arranged so as to facilitate individualized learning more than whole-group instruction, but to accommodate the latter when it is appropriate. In addition, open classrooms are organized so as to encourage

* *active learning rather than passive learning;*

- *learning and expression in a variety of media, rather than just pencil and paper and the spoken word;*
- *self-directed, student-initiated learning more than teacher-directed learning;*
- *student initiative and responsibility in caring for materials, books, and equipment.*

1. "It takes more than moving the furniture."

"The flexible use of space and time in informal English primary schools encourages children to feel that the classroom, and indeed the school as a whole, belongs to them," Casey and Liza Murrow argue in the excerpt that follows. More important, they suggest, the room arrangements and the absence of a rigid timetable make it far more likely that children will feel that learning itself belongs to them. Opening space and time can help open a child's mind to the world around him—but only if these first steps are reinforced by an atmosphere of trust and respect.

British primary schools, like their counterparts in America, vary enormously in quality and design. Some are massive Victorian monuments to education, built to last forever; some are tiny village schools that take in expansive views of the countryside; others are modern structures full of sunlight, and a few are examples of inspired design. Whether the school is in a suburban area or a rundown neighborhood with a rapidly shifting population, the visitor can learn a great deal about the quality of life in the school by observing the ways in which teachers and children use the building. The imaginative use of space, in the classroom and throughout the school, is an exciting aspect of primary education in England, as well as an ingredient essential to the achievement of fine work.

The philosophy of a school is often reflected in the degree of mobility granted to the child. In a great number of good schools, he is not confined to a specific desk or classroom throughout the day. His teacher may well expect him to move around the room or the school, attending to work in progress. Some teachers and educators recognize that the working needs of children are no different from those of adults. That is, different modes of work require different working spaces. The child needs a variety of areas in which to pursue painting, writing, drama, woodwork, mathematics, pottery, and so forth. The school which can provide this diversity in its surroundings can greatly enhance the child's learning conditions.

The classroom itself is indicative of the school's response to the children. As we have described earlier, the infant class makes great use of small tables and chairs in groups. In old schools, lacking new equipment, these "tables" may be four old desks pushed together; elsewhere, four or five children often share a round table. As the children sit in groups, engaged in similar projects or different tasks, they are free to talk and discuss the work at hand. In fact, both the grouping of desks and the round tables encourage worthwhile discussion, focusing inward on the small group. Teachers know that children learn from one another, and the arrangement of the schoolroom furniture promotes this interaction.

In both infant and junior classes, the room is often divided into distinct working spaces, or bays, by partitions made of the best available material: sometimes heavy cardboard, a bookcase on wheels, a cabinet, or a screen. In many cases, these partitions are temporary and the teacher can easily change them. In one corner, there may be a table for displays of different sorts. One week the teacher may set up an exhibit of pottery with some pieces from the local museum; another week might find the table covered with a project recently finished by the children.

The display area contrasts with the groups of tables for general work and with other corners set up for specific purposes. The library corner is one such space, an area set apart for quiet reading. It is often the most pleasant and comfortable place in the classroom and includes small, stuffed armchairs, rocking chairs, and a rug (an addition which makes a great difference.) Attractive displays of books line the shelves and tables. The corner is usually divided from the rest of the room, and one or two children often sit there to read quietly to themselves or each other.

In infant classrooms, an enclosed space encourages quiet responses from the children. They know that there are other areas of the room where they can make noise. An open end of the room is used for water and sand play (each in its own plastic trough). Here, the floor is covered with a material which can easily withstand spills, and the children can scoop sand or pour water from one container to another without having to worry about making a mess. If they do spill, equipment is handy for them to clean it up. There may also be large easels nearby where the children can paint, and a big table for other messy work.

Teachers in many infant schools, both old and new, feel that their classrooms are never big enough for the forty children who so often occupy them. Some of these schools have expanded to include the outdoors as part of the classroom space. The architects of new schools often design an outdoor play area for groups of classrooms. Doors open out onto these paved surfaces, and in good weather in the spring, fall, and summer terms, the children move water tubs, easels, and building blocks outside. They work in full view of the teacher, who can glance outside now and then to watch their progress.

Woodwork is also an ideal outdoor activity for both infants and juniors. Out on the paved area or on the grass, the children are free to bang away without disturbing the rest of the class. The tools for the infants are small and simple: tiny saws, hammers, screwdrivers, and vises. These are not toys, but well-made, usable tools. The children know they must be careful, and they are. The child who saws away vigorously at a future airplane gains practice in small motor skills and feels the pleasure of involving his whole body in the work. In this case, the outdoor space is a great asset.

A few infant schools are now lucky enough to have an aide who serves a couple of classrooms. She can work outside with the children, relieving some of the congestion in the classroom. This gives the teacher the chance to continue work indoors with smaller groups of children.

Some old schools, especially those in urban areas which are starved for space, have added enclosed outdoor working areas to the classroom. Here the children work at large, messy activities. Other schools have extended a plastic roof over a portion of the playground adjoining the building. Unless it is bitterly cold, the children can go out and work there (an added advantage for those who have little place to play outside school). In any case, the purpose is usually to expand the existing teaching space. What goes on outside is intrinsically related to what takes place in the classroom.

All of these different spaces imply a recognition, on the part of the school, that the primary child needs to move, to make noise, to talk. He needs room to build things, to take things apart; room to sit quietly, to think, to engage in fantasy play and drama. Spaces for role playing and games are just as important as the areas set aside for writing, math, or quiet reading.

The intelligent use of flexible spaces in the classroom can stimulate the child's interest in different activities. In addition to the ingenious arrangement of furniture, there is the added stimulus of work displayed on the walls of the room. Some schools have done away with the bulletin boards so common to English and American classrooms and have covered their walls with extensive amounts of corkboard or corrugated paper. The entire wall surfaces are open to display paintings, poems, stories, and art work made of three-dimensional materials. These displays are changed constantly throughout the year and are different from one part of the room to the next.

Junior classrooms seem to suffer more from lack of space than do infants'. In part, this is because the children are bigger, and the work that they undertake often requires more room. For example, a group of children in one school made a series of large mobiles depicting the development of space flight from Icarus to Apollo 12. There were a number of boys at work on this project, and they needed a great deal of space to spread out their materials, the books they were reading, and the mathematical calculations they had made. The English teacher who works with thirty-five to forty junior-age children, in a classroom overflowing with students and equipment, faces a predicament that is familiar to many an American teacher. Both wonder how they will be able to provide nearly forty children, some of them approaching adolescence, with sufficient space to pursue a number of different activities.

Some teachers, in England and in the United States, feel that the only way to deal with this issue is to sit the children at their desks and have them work as a group. Others, in both countries, have found that this is not always fair to the children and that there are ways to open up even the smallest room. Many English teachers have rid themselves of the old belief that each child must have a place to sit and a desk in which to store his books, pencils, and notebooks. They realize that, with some children standing in a corner painting, a few down the corridor practicing the recorder, two out on the playground involved in some complicated measurement, a few in the library, there is little need to provide a seat for each child. They cut down on the number of chairs and push existing desks together. This opens up the room and expands the working area.

Many teachers at first react negatively to the removal of furniture. Where, they may ask, do the children sit if the teacher wants to call them all together as a group? And where do the children keep their work, if not in their own desks?

The children sit on the floor or on tables if there is no other place to sit. This is seldom a problem. When the school comes into the hall for an assembly, they naturally use the floor, for chairs would be a hindrance in a room that serves so many purposes. The removal of chairs and desks does not mean that the teacher never calls the children together in the classroom—far from it. Most classes, working in a free manner, come together a number of times during the day, apart from the numerous occasions when the teacher calls a momentary halt in order to point out the work of one group, to throw in new ideas, or simply to ask a question or make an announcement.

The British teacher's answer to the second question would be to affirm the child's need for a place to keep his things. A number of simple arrangements have been made, the most successful being a drawer for each child set into the wall or mounted in a movable cart. These drawers, made of light plastic, are about twelve inches wide, eighteen inches long, and three or four inches high, and are often removable. If a child needs his books or pencils, he can take the drawer out of the wall and carry it with him. Needless to say, the contents of the drawer are his property, just as if he had a desk of his own.

In the late fall, we asked an experienced infant teacher whether the child of five, on his entry to school, needs to claim a chair or a specific place in the room in order to feel secure. She felt, as do many other teachers in England, that this was not necessary. She pointed out that in her classroom, the children were told that the *whole room* belonged to them. Whether it was the math apparatus, the table in the corner, the rocking chair, or the pet guinea pig, each new child soon learned that he shared ownership with the other members of the class, and thus did not feel the need to guard a special corner of the room for himself.

Many children in England find themselves in classrooms which belong to them. This feeling of sharing is enhanced by the school's attitude toward time. In schools where there is no fixed timetable, and where the children often choose the time at which to work on a specific task, there is no need to fight for a place in the home corner or wait around to be next with tie dyeing. The child knows that he can work there later in the day, or the next day if he wants to, and that the teacher will do his best to give each child a fair share of his classroom's activities.

This is certainly very different from the atmosphere that overwhelms many American classrooms. There the child often struggles to be first in line or to leave the class first at the end of the day. He fights for a place near the teacher or competes with his neighbor to reach the head of the class. If classrooms belonged to the children, if each child shared equally in learning, and worked at his own rate, perhaps the intense struggle to be "first" would not be necessary, and children would no longer attempt to get what they want, regardless of others. The sharing of experiences, spaces, and materials in English classrooms leads to attitudes of cooperation and caring.

There is another, more crucial, implication of the English attitude mentioned here. In a classroom where the books, the class pet, the reading and math corners, and so on, are the property of each child in the class—where the school itself is a domain shared by all the students—the child is more likely to feel that learning also belongs to him. This is an issue raised in the American context by George Dennison in his book *The Lives of Children* and by John Holt in a review of that book. Holt was speaking of American students, from the youngest to those of college age, when he wrote:

> . . . their schools and teachers have never told them, never encouraged or even allowed them to think, that high culture, all those poems, novels, Shakespeare plays, etc. belonged or might belong to them, that they might claim it for their own, use it solely for their own purposes, for whatever joys and benefits they might get from it.

Obviously, it takes more than moving the furniture and placing the school at the child's disposal to convince him that the world of learning belongs to him. It is our belief, nonetheless, that many English children have been started in school feeling that they can take part in learning and, furthermore, that learning is an enjoyable, interesting, and compelling experience. Opening the school to the child is a first step in the process of opening the child's mind to the world around him. An important lesson in trust is conveyed to the child when he is allowed to move about the class and the school with few restraints. This must, of course, be reinforced by respect for the child, belief in the interaction between child and teacher, and by the other concerns, mentioned previously, which bring these schools to life. No arrangement of a school, no matter how ingenious, can compensate for poor, unimaginative teaching.

In good schools, freedom of movement extends to the child's use of the entire building. This mobility arises from the school's eagerness to share information and ideas. Children often participate in activities taking place in other classrooms, while many teachers are involved in various forms of cooperative teaching. Both children and teachers profit from the chance to see what others are doing.

We saw a class of juniors experimenting with silk screening. They had never tried it before, and a small group was hard at work with their teacher in an attempt to find the best method of making a clean print. At that moment, the deputy head, who also had a class of junior-age children, walked in to borrow something, and stayed for ten minutes to watch. He was not at all worried about being away from his class. He returned with knowledge about an art form that was new to him and a determination to try it with his own group. This sharing of ideas leads naturally to a sharing of materials among children and teachers and to a feeling of cooperation throughout the school.

Good head teachers and their staffs consciously try to make their buildings conducive to participation and increased mobility. They may create centers in the school which draw children and teachers together. A display of children's work has this effect, as does a central exhibit with a unifying theme. Whether based on metal work, glass, Japanese art and Haiku, or the stages involved in weaving cloth from natural wool, the objects are sure to include a cross section of items, combined with children's writing and art work. It is not uncommon to see a child seated in front of such an exhibit, making an accurate drawing of an old pewter teapot or any other object seen there.

Whatever the age of the building, an effort is made to use every inch of space available. Narrow tables are set up in the corridors of many schools (still leaving ample space for children) and contain everything from a model of an English village to complicated mathematics apparatus. The children use these hallways as part of their working space, not just as passageways from one area to another. In one school, the corridor often resounds with the soft, clear tones of the large xylophone which has its place against the wall. Now and then, a small group of children pass by, listen to a girl who is picking out notes, and go on to their class-room, humming the tune.

2. Providing for Activity and Choice

This discussion of various ways to arrange an open classroom is particularly helpful because of the diagrams showing specific room arrangements, and because the authors explain why they propose one room arrangement or another. Mary Brown and Norman Precious are headmistress and headmaster of primary schools in Leicestershire, England.

. . . ideal conditions [new building, quiet, spacious grounds] are not essential to the successful practice of the integrated day. Old school buildings can be modified and adapted to fit in with newer methods of education. These often have a warm friendly atmosphere which in a new building takes time to develop.

The school is part of the community in which the children live, but when they go to school for the first time, they are starting life in an environment which is different from home and is strange and new to them. However carefully planned this environment may be, it is still, in comparison with home, an artificial situation. Here, as the child meets a wider group of peers and adults than before and as he uses the materials in the school environment, his development and growth is encouraged and continues.

The child is given the freedom to choose the things with which he wants to become involved and this can be achieved more easily where there is no parcelling out of time or directing of groups of children to different activities. The spotlight has, in effect, shifted from the activities or subjects, to the child and his particular interests. Children just entering school will need time to get used to the new situation. If they join an existing group of children, a vertical group for example, they adjust easily and quickly. If however the class is a whole group of reception children, more care must be taken to see that the amount and variety of materials is not so great that the child is overwhelmed by the formidable task of "choosing." Too wide a choice would seem paradoxically to be almost as limiting as too little and many teachers feel the need to withdraw certain things from the classroom and reintroduce them at what seems a more appropriate moment.

As the children arrive at school first thing in the morning, they come straight in and quite naturally start to do things. Many will be continuing an activity from the day before. Some will be attracted by a stimulating piece of equipment in maths or science. Some will become immediately involved with creative expression in various media. Others will go straight to the section for domestic or dramatic play, some to the reading area or any of the other activities available in the room and some will just chat with a friend. This is the start of the day. For this to happen, the materials and apparatus must be readily available and within easy reach. The children need to feel responsible for organizing and using their own materials and clearing up adequately and well. Even the young children are capable of this discipline and it is a very necessary part of a well run classroom.

Children engaged in activity use their initiative and are challenged to work, to think, to communicate and are given time to follow what is important to them in their own way and at their own speed. With all this in mind, division of the day by timetabling is now unnecessary and is an interruption in the child's natural flow of interest.

The teacher watches what is happening as the children explore the materials. She will see evidence of the child's immediate interests and needs, will see him meeting and solving problems and it is round these ideas that she makes her plans. The teacher must not be too obtrusive and yet must be aware of what is happening in the room. The children must be able to feel her support when necessary and the room needs to be so arranged that she can see where and when her help is needed. At times, the child may feel the need to withdraw from the teacher or from other members of the class. Some children often prefer to work in bounded areas and these are things to be taken into account when planning the room. Careful consideration must be given to the physical arrangement of the environment. Each classroom varies considerably in shape and size and in the actual arrangement of furniture lies much of the success or failure of the room. The classroom is divided into areas for various activities. Obvious essentials are that the children should be able to pursue the noisier activities without disturbing the rest of the group, and that painting and water play should be as near as possible to sink facilities. Construction work is safer in a part of the room where the buildings will not be continually knocked down by passers by. The reading and writing area will need plenty of light and the domestic corner access to an outside area if possible.

It is a good idea to draw the room to scale on graph paper. Each piece of furniture can then be drawn to scale and cut out so that it is possible to arrange the activity or subject areas in miniature and easily find what

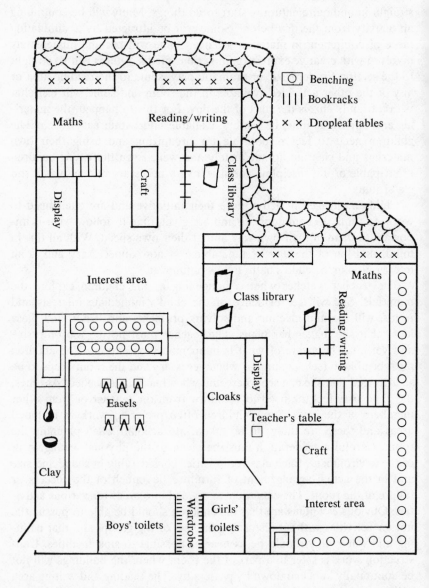

On this and the next page are two arrangements of rooms suitable for infant and junior age children. These are only suggestions and incorporate some of the ideas expressed in the text. It should also be remembered that these arrangements must be flexible and capable of frequent adaptation to the pre-vailing needs of the children.

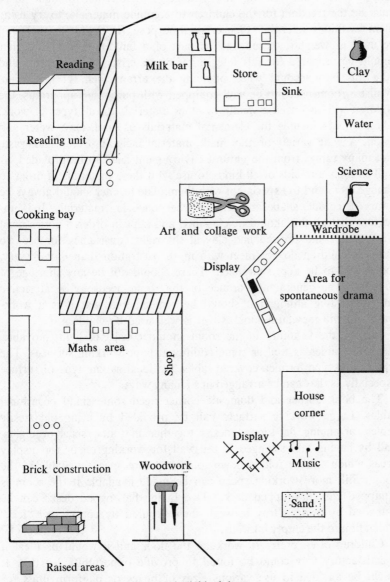

Raised areas

Cupboards or lockers with individual drawers

Beanstalk containing materials

seems to be the most advantageous arrangement. Definite places will need to be devised for the storage of the various types of material and apparatus. It must be remembered however that where the day is a mêlée of activity with no definite dividing line between the various activities, or indeed between the child's range of interest and thought, there must be the freedom for the children to combine materials, to try using them for things other than their original purpose. Blocks for example can be used as weights, or magnets as part of a building and the teacher should be prepared for this integration of materials and apparatus and take this into account when planning the arrangement of her room. Whilst a room needs to be well equipped with purchased apparatus, the children will also need a wealth of other materials for all types of work. These should include the elemental materials of sand, clay, water and wood. A wide variety of man made material including scrap and waste and many things from the natural environment need to be provided, as well as tools and aids of all kinds to use with these materials in order to change them and to experiment with them. The teacher should always be aware of colour, shape and texture when choosing materials. It is important that all this should be classified and kept in order. Fabrics must be kept flat and pressed and clay at the right consistency for use. So that the children do not meet with more frustration than is necessary, tools need to be kept sharpened. There should not be any shortage of supplies. The general appearance of the room needs to be attractive and interesting although it should be remembered that it is a workshop and will inevitably look as if it is well used by children.

Ideally, the furniture in the room should consist of light, movable, stackable tables as well as some additional large working surfaces. The trapezoidal type formica-covered tables are ideal as one type of surface especially as they can be arranged in so many ways.

The book corner and domestic corner need some small occasional tables. Large working surfaces can be provided by using old trestle tables, arranging flat-topped desks together in fours, sixes or eights, and by having tables hinged to the wall for working on or for display areas which can be folded down to make more space available in the room. Still more working space can be made available if the room is equipped with flat-topped desks. Two facing flat-topped desks can be extended by using a tray between them secured by cotton reel "feet" which fit into the empty inkwells.

Children often prefer to work on the floor and it would be ideal if a satisfactory way could be found to provide opportunity for this. It might be an idea to use various sizes of boxes or platform units for children to assemble their own raised areas. A platform about a foot or eighteen inches from the floor is an excellent working area especially if it has an easily cleaned surface. There is no longer the need for a

A variety of arrangements of trapezoidal tables.

place to be available for each child. Seating accommodation may include ordinary chairs, benches, window seats, comfortable armchairs, stools, a rocking chair, rugs, carpets and cushions. Sets of open lockers or locker units on castors about 3 feet high and 4 feet 6 inches long with a pegboard back make excellent room dividers, and if these have a section fitted with individual small drawers, each child can have a place to keep his own books and belongings. The Wendy House is a familiar piece of equipment in infant schools but a plentiful supply of three sided screens made in double pegboard which can be assembled for various uses such as shops and houses or as room dividers and display boards seem more useful and adaptable pieces of equipment.

Pinboard areas on the walls at a suitable height for children to use are essential. There will have to be some provision for storing dressing-up clothes, junk materials and bricks, which could be boxes, wire baskets, a "beanstalk" or low cupboards. A fixed wall blackboard for the children's use, painting easels and trays, baths or tanks to hold clay, wet sand, dry sand, water or other such materials are needed. The polythene tank with a tubular steel stand on castors is ideal for water because of its transparency, but anything can be pressed into service here, from a six-foot tin bath to a rubber dinghy. Book corner standing units, fitments or book trolleys which display books to show the front covers will make them more attractive to children.

Some plans of arrangements have been suggested but each teacher must, by trial and error, plan a room which is suitable to her own particular circumstances. The placing of the large furniture inevitably

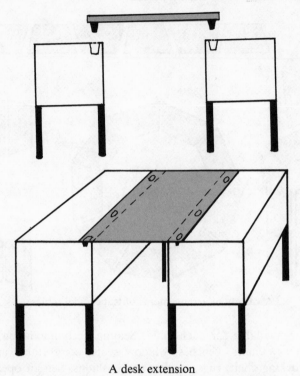

A desk extension

determines the storage of the apparatus and materials. It would be an impossible task to prepare a comprehensive list of materials needed in the primary school and it would not be expected that the list provided as an appendix to this book would be present in its entirety all at the same time or in any one room but it is offered as a suggestion.

3. How to Build and Equip Your Own Classroom

When the Headstart program began in the summer of 1965, Allan Leitman and Edith H. F. Churchill, then staff members of EDC's Elementary Science Study, received a request for help in developing a model Headstart classroom. Working with a group of students from Wheelock College in Boston, they put together a classroom, which they called "Approximation No. 1," in an old warehouse. Their object was not to create the ideal classroom for all time, but rather to see what they could do in a brief period—to find out "just how much it takes in terms of

people, money, and materials to do the job in ten days' time." Many
items were chosen, therefore, not because they were the best or cheapest
way to fulfill a particular function, but because they were available—
which of course is what classroom teachers have to do all the time.

Although new suppliers and new kinds of materials have appeared
and some old suppliers have gone out of business since "Approximation
No. 1" was built, Leitman and Churchill's description remains valuable
for anyone concerned with the primary grades because of the detailed
diagrams, instructions, and lists of equipment and suppliers they provide.

Allan Leitman is now director of the Advisory for Open Education
in Cambridge, Massachusetts; Edith Churchill is a staff member of the
EDC Follow Through Program.

This classroom is our answer to a question which arose when we were
asked to set up a model Headstart classroom, namely, "what can be
assembled in a limited time to provide an adequate learning environment
for young children?" We have placed the classroom in an old warehouse
so that we could familiarize ourselves with the problems of building such
a classroom from the ground up. We have used this opportunity to find
out in reality just how much it takes in terms of people, money and materials to do the job in ten days' time. We have tried to make the room
as attractive and inviting to children as possible, but our emphasis has
been on materials for children's use rather than on furniture. The room
has been organized to include objects which are familiar, and to provide
maximum possibilities for young children to explore materials and to
find and solve problems. . . .

An important part of teaching consists of being able to step back
and watch children's activities. Through their play, children give clues
and signals which thoughtful teachers can use for planning and decision-
making. The room arrangement allows the teacher to be aware of what
is happening, and allows the child to be aware of the teacher's support
without being overwhelmed by her presence. The teacher can move
easily to a child who needs her assistance in using materials or in playing
with other children: a child can move out of the immediate presence
of the teacher when this is what he needs: a child can learn to go to
adults for help, or use their support more indirectly.

The layout of the room makes materials readily available and offers
an organization that may be a first experience with an orderly environment for many children. The arrangement of materials in this classroom

From Allan Leitman and Edith H. F. Churchill, *A Classroom for Young Chil-*
dren: Approximation No. 1 (Newton, Mass.: Education Development Center,
1966). Reprinted by permission of the Elementary Science Study of Education Development Center, Inc.

reflects our conviction that children can *learn* to use these materials responsibly. All the materials are, therefore, located where children can reach them without adult assistance. It may take some time for children coming into this environment to know just what to do with the materials and how to explore and manage them.

We are also well aware that this wide a variety of materials is too overwhelming for the first day of school, so our classroom more nearly represents the situation we hope to achieve after some period of time—perhaps a week or two after school starts, but quite possibly much longer. We visualize building up to this total classroom by introducing materials gradually.

For example, we show the woodworking area with the hammers and saws accessible. Some teachers may prefer not to introduce tools right away. Each teacher will have to make her own decisions on timing and will establish such rules for tool use as her judgment and the temperament of her group of children dictate.

With animals, we anticipate that before the animals appear, children will set up the equipment, prepare the environment and talk about what is needed to care for animals. When the teacher feels that the children are ready to be responsible for the care of animals, she will introduce them in whatever way seems best. The choice of the animals to be used in the classroom must be left to the teacher, whether they are mammals, reptiles, fish, or none.

The work of the class should help children become really involved in their own learning and be successful on their own terms. In this way children achieve a feeling of their power to understand and to change their world.

As the room was developed we consulted Frances Hawkins of Boulder, Colorado; Ilse Mattick of Boston University and Headstart: Leonard Sealey of Leicester, England; Elizabeth Ann Liddle, Henry Haskell, Lynn Gehri, and Alice Kelliher, all of Wheelock College.

In final determinations we have based our decisions upon experiences gathered at our work in Jamaica Plain Day Care Center, Boston; Houghton School, Cambridge; Shady Hill School, Cambridge; Hills and Falls Nursery School, Wellesley; the Red Barn Nursery School, Weston; The South End Settlement House and the Dorchester Settlement House.

We do not believe that this room is finished or that it should be considered as *the* model for Headstart classrooms. It is, at best, a trial set-up that will have to be tested under real conditions in order to be proven. We do not believe that these particular materials are vital for helping children learn, and we are sure that many teachers, with far less than we have assembled here, will be able to build excellent programs. By assembling this room, we hoped that we might be able to provide a starting point for teachers who are setting up their own rooms.

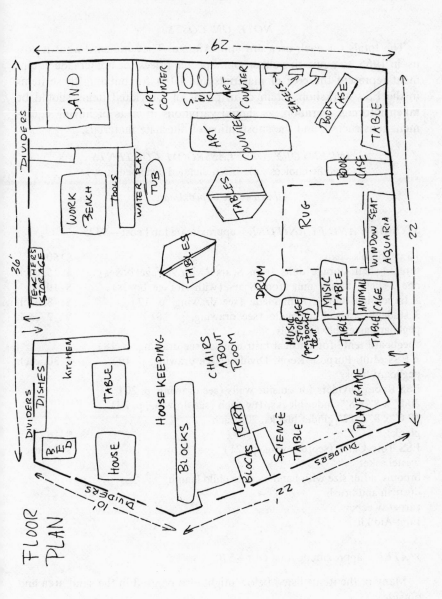

FLOOR PLAN

NOTE ON COSTS

The totals for each area are approximate. They indicate what it cost us, in 1965, to equip this classroom. Specific prices for homemade equipment represent the cost of materials and labor for building these items in the ESS workshop. Changes in prices of individual items should be taken into consideration, as should variations in costs of having equipment constructed, and the substitution of alternate materials.

INVENTORY OF CLASSROOM CONTENTS
(Specific choices were often dictated by expediency)

All prices are approximate.

STORAGE AND FURNITURE   approximate total cost—$375.

16 children's chairs	$150.
three 4-shelf storage units from Sears (with storage boxes)	$ 15. each
one 3-shelf storage unit from Sears (with storage boxes)	$ 10.
8 trapezoidal tables, homemade (see drawing, p. 17)	$ 8. each
3 student easels, homemade (see drawing, p. 18)	$ 2. each
pegboard assembly for tools	
"pegboard tent" for musical instruments (see drawing, p. 18)	
2 ESS Multi-Purpose Room Dividers (see drawing, p. 19)	$ 30. each
pegboard hooks	
ESS Room Dividers for outside walls (see drawing, p. 20)	
20 8" x 8" x 8" cinder blocks, 16¢ each (see drawing, p. 20)	
19 6" x 8" x 12" cinder blocks, 20¢ each	
planks	$ 16.
ESS Tote Carts (see drawing, p. 21)	$ 23. each
wastebasket	
brooms, adult size with handle cut to child length	
dustpan and brush	
carpet sweeper	
First-Aid kit	

WATER   approximate total cost—$70.

Many of the items listed below might also be used in the sand area and outside.

Water sink with high mounted faucet
Til Tub and homemade stand (see drawing, p. 22)
plastic pails:
    two, 11-quart size
    one, gallon size
    one Lug-a-jug (5-gallon, collapsible)
    one collapsible pail

round plastic dish pan
string mop, with handle cut down to child-size

A large collection of plastic bottles, from gallon size to the tiniest, with as many different sizes and shapes as possible, such as liquid detergent bottles, ice cream containers, plastic ketchup dispensers.

funnels
strainers
scoops
measuring cups
plastic beakers
cigar tubes with stoppers
TV-dinner pans
straws
basters
droppers
hand pump
syringes

Vaseline
sponges
Ethafoam (Dow) expanded polyethylene
styrofoam balls
Plasticene
marbles
short pieces of doweling

SAND   approximate total cost—$78.

Many of the items listed below will find use in other areas, particularly outside. Of course sand will also invite adoption of materials from other areas for use here.

39 concrete blocks (8″ x 8″ x 8″ and 30″ x 12″ x 3″)	$ 1.	each
12′ x 16′ tarp (war surplus)	17.	
3 entrenching tools (war surplus) shovels		
garden shovel		
4 rubber mats—at entrance, to wipe feet	.80 each	
600 lbs. of sand		
3 trowels		
2 shrub rakes		

watering can
2 plastic pails
stones (gathered locally)
driftwood

sieves
scoops

wooden and plastic spoons
empty soda bottles and sprinkler tops
empty cans—many different sizes
pie plates
funnels
large assortment of various size and shape containers, such as
    the ones used in water play

An old rug and some pillows were placed between the bookcases and
the animal area to encourage quieter moments for animal-watching,
reading and music.

BOOKS   approximate total cost—$100.

Thirty books were selected to be enjoyed by the children, and included many picture books, favorite stories, and poems to be read to
the children. There were also a number of home-made cloth "feely"
books with buttons, zippers, shoelaces and the like.

In addition, seven music books were provided for the teacher's use.

ANIMALS AND PLANTS   approximate total cost—$75.

ESS gerbil cage (see drawing, p. 23) $50.
2 gerbils—mated pair $ 6.
dirt

15-gallon aquarium
aquarium divider
goldfish bowl
aquarium gravel
refrigerator dishes

fish net
floating thermometer
quart pitcher
measuring spoons
baster

guppies
polliwogs and frog eggs

plants—for decoration of room as well as for aquarium or
    terrarium

Gerbils:

Tumble Brook Farms, Inc.
Brant Lake, New York

$3.00 each

shipped REA Express in cage-like wooden box with food for
    a day or two.

Other equipment in this area included:

rug
pillows
telephones (on loan from NET&T)
Polaroid camera and film
tape recorder

MUSIC   approximate total cost—$125.

Record player and records	$95.
Autoharp	$23.
Raw materials for homemade instruments:	$ 7.

6 cardboard paint buckets with lids @ 15¢ each
nail keg
dowels
white glue
wrapping paper
scrap pieces of wood
bamboo (rug rollers)
string
rope
sandpaper
coconuts
nails
tin cans
salt cartons
scarves
flat elastic or knit cuffs
small bells
inner tube
wire

Some of the homemade instruments were: (see drawing, p. 24)

drums: paint bucket drums, tin can drums, nail keg drum
drumsticks, mallets
rhythm sticks
tambourines
coconut shell clappers
bamboo chimes
bamboo rattles
bongo shakers
stretch cuffs with bells
sand blocks

ART   approximate total cost—$75.

4 packages colored construction paper (100 sheets, assorted
colors)

newsprint paper
Manila paper
bogus art paper
shelf paper
colored tissue paper

large container of crayons
15 small packages of crayons
white and colored chalk
school pencils
felt tip markers (washable)
2 pairs large scissors (for teacher)
small scissors (including some left-handed)

white glue
paste
Scotch tape
masking tape
twine
scraps of yarn
stapler
rubber bands
paper clips
paper punch
compass

powder paint, 1-lb. tins: red, yellow, blue, black, white
frozen juice cans
brushes, 5 each of #134, #AA3, #111
old shirts for smocks

liquid starch (mix with powder paint for finger paint)
soap flakes
liquid detergent

two 5-lb. bags flour
one 5-lb. bag of canning salt
cooking oil

shirt cardboards
tongue depressors
paper plates
art pipe cleaners
straws
clothespins
glitter
seeds (corn, lima beans, kidney beans)
toothpicks
wax paper
paper towels
1-lb. box cotton batting
set of food coloring

macaroni shells
egg cartons
paper tubes

recipe for play-dough: 2 parts flour to 1 part salt. Add a little
   cooking oil and water to desired consistency.

HOUSEKEEPING   approximate total cost—$65.

Many of the items listed below might be used in other areas as well.
The large refrigerator carton might well serve as a store one day or a
den the next. Here, too, cinder blocks and planks serve as storage, and
an old wooden dairy box is an all-purpose chest.

cinder blocks and planks (see drawing, p. 20)
cardboard shelves
play sink (crate holding 2 square plastic dishpans)
play stove (cinder blocks supporting plywood top with real
   stoveknobs attached)
pegboard with hooks to hang scoops, etc.
2 small aprons
broom, floor mop (adult size with handles cut down to child
   size)
scrub brush
dustpan and brush
plastic bucket
sponges
plastic scouring pad
dinner plates
plastic juice pitcher
adult size forks, spoons, knives—4 of each
adult size plastic milk glasses, juice glasses, insulated glasses—
   4 of each
baby bottle
plastic mixing bowls
egg beater
spreaders—2 wooden mixing, 1 icing
sifter
measuring cups, spoons
cookie cutters
rolling pins
metal juice cans
empty egg cartons
empty food containers

wooden milk box to house dress-up clothes
full-length mirror
hand mirror

dress-up clothes: hats, scarves, gloves, pocketbooks, ties, fur
  stole, shirts, blouses, skirts, dresses, material remnants, scraps
  of yarn, old shoes, boots, plastic sun glasses, eyeglass frames,
  shaving brush and blank razor
buttons, material with buttonholes

child's bed—homemade with foam mattress
small pillow
crib blanket
dolls, Negro and white
doll clothes
clothespins and rope
stethoscope
rug
magazine pictures
refrigerator carton—large, used as a playhouse

TOYS   approximate total cost—$50.

Homemade toys:
    wooden toy trucks
    toy train
    wooden airplanes
    toy cars
    animal and people figures

Fisher-Price Creative Blocks
Lego
Blockhead
Slinky
Frame Mosaic
Playskool Parquetry Blocks

dominoes
picture dominoes
Giant Lotto
Colorforms
8 wooden puzzles
ESS Attribute Blocks—2 sets $16. each
ESS Pattern Blocks

curtain rings (to string)
shoelaces, yarn, elastic cord
plastic snap beads

stuffed animals
hand puppets
metal toy trucks

BLOCKS AND SOME OTHER BUILDING MATERIALS
approximate total cost—$230.

Much of the building equipment listed below is used outside as well as inside.

Hollow Blocks—Half School Set from Community Playthings	$110.
Unit Blocks—Half School Set from Community Playthings	$ 98.

set of ESS blocks
ESS Playframe
Tinkertoys—large set
assorted springs
assorted wood turnings
assorted empty cardboard boxes
small pulleys
nuts and bolts
string
rubber bands
wheels
assorted strips of pegboard

SCIENCE-RELATED MATERIALS approximate total
cost—$15.

ESS balance (paper plates)	$ 2.
ESS balance board	$ 2.

lead sinkers
Rubbermaid Lazy Susan plus 3′ square Masonite top

light bulbs #41 (flashlight)
flashlight batteries
copper wire
lamp bases

flashlights
flexible mirrors (small squares backed with fabric)
*assorted colored transparent plastic sheets, 20″ x 24″
assorted hand lenses and prisms
dilutions tray and food colors and medicine droppers
assorted magnets
measuring sticks, assorted lengths

*plastic sheets in colors from:
    Gelatine Products Co.
    459 Adelphi Street
    Brooklyn 38, New York

    55¢ per sheet 20″ x 24″
    minimum order of $15.

A letter to ESS will bring information on sources for unusual
materials.

WOODWORKING   approximate total cost—$50.

The scrap lumber used in this area will be useful in some sand area
projects.

work table	$4.
2 woodwork vises	
back saws	
coping saws	
keyhole saw	
2 hammers	
hand drill and set of bits	
combination pliers	
screwdrivers—small, medium, large	
folding 6′ rule	
assorted nails, tacks, and screws	
coarse and medium-coarse sandpaper	
white glue	
twine	
scrap lumber and hardboard	

OUTDOOR EQUIPMENT   approximate total cost—$260.

Many of the items listed under "Sand" will be used outside as well.

2 8′ all-purpose boards—Childcraft	$12. each
Ladder box—Childcraft	$65.
2 nesting bridges—Childcraft	$28. each
2 high (24″) sawhorses—Childcraft	$12. each
2 low (12″) sawhorses—Childcraft	$10. each
refrigerator shipping box—cardboard	
large wooden reel (from cable or rope)	
½″ rope	
outside balls	
ESS walking board	$14.

Pumping Station (ESS) consists of:

single tub—Sears	$ 7.
jumbo size tub (see *Water* section)	$ 9.
kitchen force pump	$16.
stool to mount pump	$ 5.
50′ hose	$ 3.
assorted hose connectors and nozzles	$ 7.

CHILDREN'S
TABLES

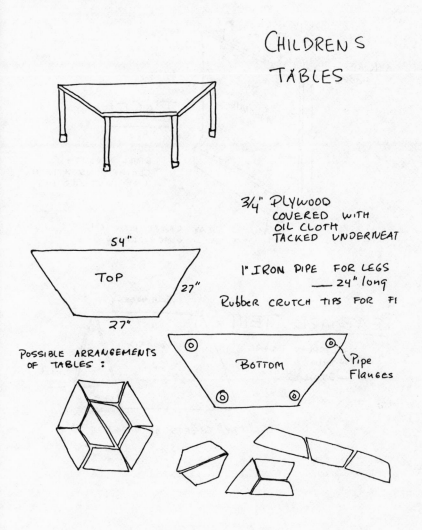

3/4" PLYWOOD
COVERED WITH
OIL CLOTH
TACKED UNDERNEAT

1" IRON PIPE FOR LEGS
       — 24" long
Rubber CRUTCH TIPS FOR FI

54"

TOP

27"

27"

POSSIBLE ARRANGEMENTS
OF TABLES :

BOTTOM

Pipe
Flanges

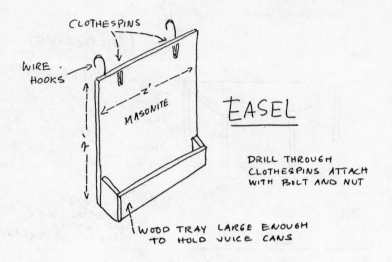

CLOTHESPINS

WIRE HOOKS

2'

MASONITE

EASEL

DRILL THROUGH
CLOTHESPINS ATTACH
WITH BOLT AND NUT

WOOD TRAY LARGE ENOUGH
TO HOLD JUICE CANS

PEGBOARD TENT

— DISPLAY BOARD
— DIVIDER
— STORAGE

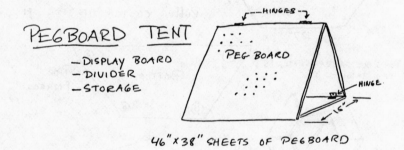

HINGES

PEG BOARD

HINGE

46" X 38" SHEETS OF PEGBOARD

ESS MULTI-PURPOSE ROOM DIVIDER

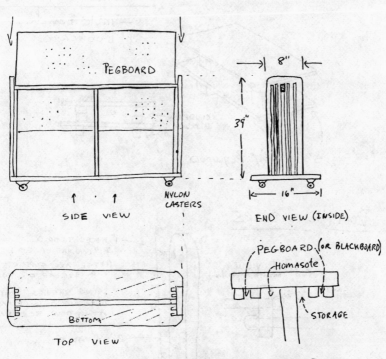

SIDE VIEW

PEGBOARD

NYLON CASTERS

39"

8"

16"

END VIEW (INSIDE)

TOP VIEW

Bottom

PEGBOARD (OR BLACKBOARD)

Homasote

STORAGE

SLOTS ARE SPACED SO
THAT ON ONE SIDE A
PEGBOARD PANEL CAN
BE REMOVED, REVEALING
A HOMASOTE BOARD, AND BE
STORED BEHIND A PEGBOARD
ON THE OTHER SIDE.

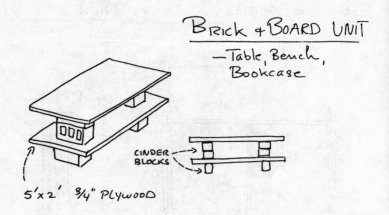

BRICK & BOARD UNIT
—Table, Bench, Bookcase

CINDER BLOCKS

5'x2' 3/4" PLYWOOD

ROOM DIVIDERS

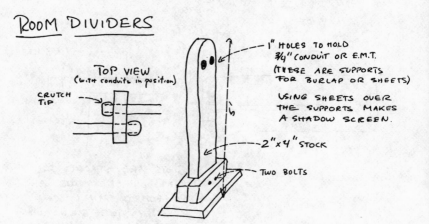

TOP VIEW
(with conduits in position)

CRUTCH TIP

1" HOLES TO HOLD 3/4" CONDUIT OR E.M.T. (THESE ARE SUPPORTS FOR BURLAP OR SHEETS)

USING SHEETS OVER THE SUPPORTS MAKES A SHADOW SCREEN.

2"x4" STOCK

TWO BOLTS

NOTE: THESE DIVIDERS WERE NECESSARY FOR US IN ORDER TO DEFINE THE AREA OF THE WAREHOUSE WE USED AS A CLASSROOM.

ESS TOTE CART

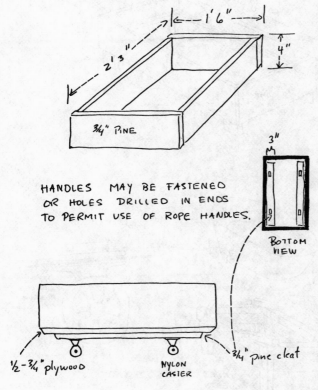

1' 6"

2' 3"

4"

3/4" PINE

HANDLES MAY BE FASTENED
OR HOLES DRILLED IN ENDS
TO PERMIT USE OF ROPE HANDLES.

3"

BOTTOM
VIEW

1/2 - 3/4" plywood

NYLON
CASTER

3/4" pine cleat

CASTERS SET IN FROM EDGE TO PERMIT STACKING

HOUSE CORNER BED

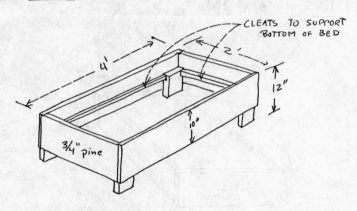

CLEATS TO SUPPORT
BOTTOM OF BED

4'

2'

12"

10"

3/4" pine

'TIL' TUB

AND STAND

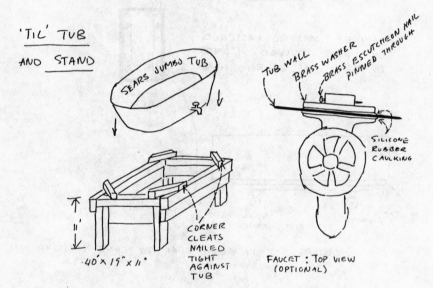

SEARS JUMBO TUB

11"

40" x 19" x 11"

CORNER
CLEATS
NAILED
TIGHT
AGAINST
TUB

TUB WALL

BRASS WASHER

BRASS ESCUTCHEON NAIL
PINNED THROUGH

SILICONE
RUBBER
CAULKING

FAUCET : TOP VIEW
(OPTIONAL)

ESS ANIMAL CAGE

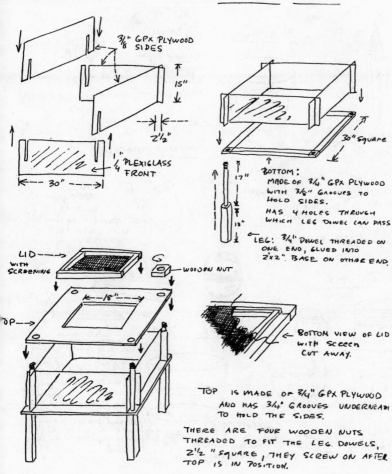

3/8" GPX PLYWOOD SIDES

15"

2½"

¼" PLEXIGLASS FRONT

← 30" →

30" square

17"

13"

BOTTOM:
MADE OF 3/4" GPX PLYWOOD WITH 3/8" GROOVES TO HOLD SIDES.
HAS 4 HOLES THROUGH WHICH LEG DOWEL CAN PASS

LEG: 3/4" DOWEL THREADED ON ONE END, GLUED INTO 2"x2" BASE ON OTHER END.

LID→ WITH SCREENING

←WOODEN NUT

←18"→

TOP→

←BOTTOM VIEW OF LID WITH SCREEN CUT AWAY.

TOP IS MADE OF 3/4" GPX PLYWOOD AND HAS 3/4" GROOVES UNDERNEATH TO HOLD THE SIDES.

THERE ARE FOUR WOODEN NUTS THREADED TO FIT THE LEG DOWELS, 2½" SQUARE, THEY SCREW ON AFTER TOP IS IN POSITION.

MUSICAL INSTRUMENTS

JINGLE CUFFS

PAINT BUCKET (paper) DRUM

brown paper dipped in 1 pt. Elmer's glue to 5 pts. water

String

BELL

STRETCH CUFF

BAMBOO CHIMES

SANDPAPER

WOOD

tacks

SAND BLOCKS

BONGO SHAKER

paper paint buckets glued together with stones INSIDE.

DRUMS

COCONUT SHELL CLAPPER

DRUM MALLETS

elastic

CRUTCH TIP

Dowel

cloth over cotton batting or cloth over wrapped string

inner tube
wire
nail keg

inner tube

#10 juice can

TAMBOURINE

cut off paper paint buckets — one covered with brown paper dipped in glue mixture as above second bucket placed over the first and bottle caps on wire loops added.

BAMBOO RATTLES

CORK

bamboo with stones or seeds inside

ESS PLAYFRAME

MATERIALS :

¼" PEGBOARD ¼" HOLES
¾" x ⅝" PINE STRIP
¾" x 2" PINE STRIP
ASSORTED NAILS, WOODSCREWS,
BOLTS, WINGNUTS, LAGGED STUDS
AND GLUE

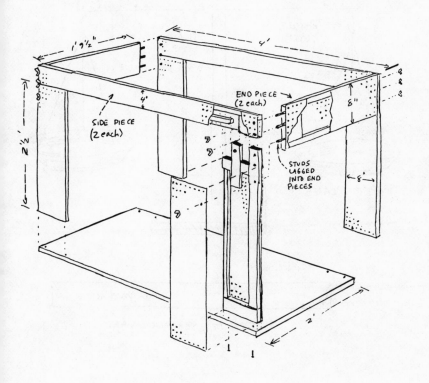

1' 9½"

4'

4"

END PIECE
(2 each)

8"

2'½'

SIDE PIECE
(2 each)

STUDS
LAGGED
INTO END
PIECES

8'

8'

2'

1

1

ESS BALANCE

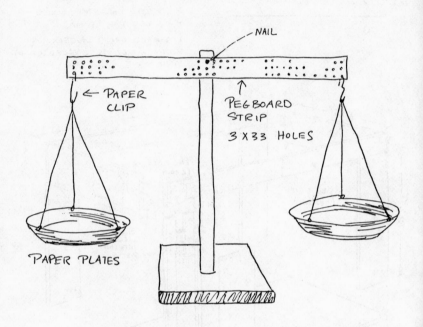

NAIL

← PAPER
CLIP

PEGBOARD
STRIP
3 X 33 HOLES

PAPER PLATES

SOLID MASONITE

ALTERNATE BALANCE ARM

ESS   4-FOOT BALANCE BOARD

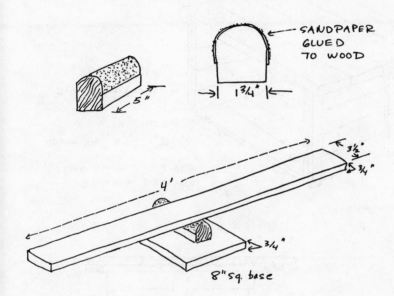

SANDPAPER
GLUED
TO WOOD

1³/4"

5"

4'

3½"

³/4"

³/4"

8" sq. base

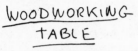

WOODWORKING TABLE

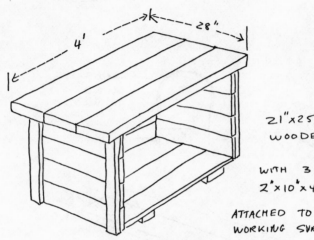

21"x25"x40"
WOODEN CRATE

WITH 3
2"x10"x4' FIR BOARDS

ATTACHED TO PROVIDE
WORKING SURFACE

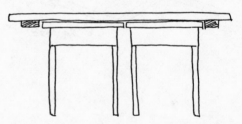

SIMILARLY A TOP CAN BE ADAPTED
TO FIT ACROSS TWO DESKS

ESS WALKING BOARD

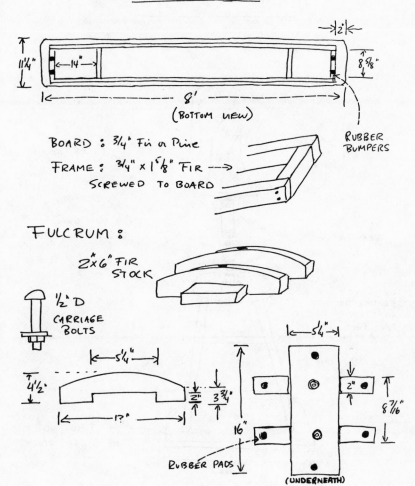

(BOTTOM VIEW)

BOARD : 3/4" Fir or Pine
FRAME : 3/4" x 1⁵/8" FIR ──>
SCREWED TO BOARD

RUBBER BUMPERS

FULCRUM :

2"x 6" FIR STOCK

1/2" D CARRIAGE BOLTS

RUBBER PADS

(UNDERNEATH)

ESS PUMPING STATION

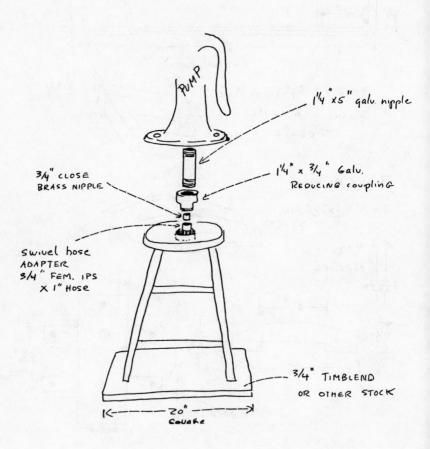

PUMP

1¼" x 5" galv. nipple

1¼" x ¾" Galv. REDUCING coupling

3/4" CLOSE BRASS NIPPLE

SWIVEL HOSE ADAPTER 3/4" FEM. IPS X 1" HOSE

3/4" TIMBLEND OR OTHER STOCK

|← ——— 20" ——— →| SQUARE

4. The Territorial Imperative

The most widespread misunderstanding about open education is the belief that its implementation requires large open spaces. As a result of this confusion of open education with open space, all too many school administrators and architects are breaking down the walls between two or three or even four classrooms, or are putting up expensive new buildings with huge, cavernous spaces designed to hold as many as a hundred and twenty children.

In these notes reporting the impressions he formed during a five-week study of informal English primary schools, Edward A. Chittenden suggests that closed space is as important as open space. While schools of course should be designed to permit and encourage an ebb and flow from one room to another, both teachers and students need some sense of privacy as well. Indeed, the more thoughtful and creative teachers are, the more likely they are to want their own piece of turf, which they can stamp with their own personality and interests as well as those of their students. (This selection is filled with other insights about the nature of the teaching and learning process in the schools that Chittenden visited.)

For five weeks in May and June, 1971, I had the opportunity to visit a number of primary schools in England, and to look in on several research and development projects related to the education of children. The visit, made possible through a travel/study award from the Ford Foundation, was undertaken in the context of our general research efforts on open education, and assessment and evaluation.

In this article I want to pull together some impressions about issues that seem important for an understanding of what is happening in England. It is not my purpose to describe an informal primary school setting, since this has been done in a number of books and articles.

One major conclusion of some of our earlier research on open education was that adequate evaluation and assessment of such an approach requires examination of both the teacher's and the child's roles. Unlike a number of other models in early education, open approaches place as much stress on a creative decision-making role for the teacher as for the child. This sort of educational position is in an opposite corner from that represented by the idea of the "teacher-proof" curriculum. With this in mind in considering schools in England, I was interested in two

From Edward A. Chittenden, "Notes on Visits to Primary Schools in England," *Outlook*, Winter 1971. Mountain View Center for Environmental Education. Based on memorandum written for distribution at Educational Testing Service. Reprinted by permission.

broad groups of questions: 1) What is the teacher's role in creating and implementing more open, informal approaches to instruction? How did she come to adopt such views? What are the sources of leadership and assistance? How much is she pushed? Pulled? Assisted? 2) What is the child's role in the more open settings? How is his learning affected by what the teacher does? How valid are some of our proposed approaches to the assessment of the child's learning and development in school?

The Schools

I visited twelve primary schools and ten research projects associated with either a university or a foundation. Eight of the schools were junior schools, for children ages seven through eleven; two were infant schools, for children ages five through seven; and two were all-through primary schools for children ages five through eleven.

The schools served a variety of communities: a rural village, working class housing projects, new suburbs, and central cities. Areas visited included Hampshire, London, Shropshire, Leicestershire, and Nottingham. While the schools were all exploring ways to broaden their programs for children, they differed widely in the extent to which they had evolved informal, individualized approaches to teaching. In some schools wide differences were evident in styles of teaching; other schools had more homogeneous staffs. While I saw no rows of desks, and little formal lecturing, beyond this there were all sorts of variations. The great majority of teachers appeared to be working with some combination of formal, prescribed methods, and more individualized, more open approaches. I found vertical grouping in some junior schools, but the practice is not as common at the junior as at the infant level. Much has been written of late about the changes taking place in British primary education. I do not know to what extent the schools I visited were representative of a general pattern of change. A number of educators told me that informal practices were widely adopted throughout England at the infant school level—that at that level there is a broadly accepted and reasonably well-defined approach to education. The junior schools present a much more mixed picture, nationally. Some stay with rigid, conventional methods, while at the other extreme, it was claimed, some have gone overboard in uncritical endorsement of informality, with a slight shift back toward more structure evident recently. A great many schools, in any event, are experimenting critically with informal approaches; some are conservative, some more radical. My guess is that the schools I visited covered the range from conservative to more radical experimentation. I should stress that some of these schools have been building their programs for ten or fifteen years. For others, the move away from highly formal programs is much more recent. . . .

Influences on Change in the Junior School

One generalization that I had derived from reading about England before my visit was that changes in the junior school were best thought of as an upward extension of the infant school model. While there is some truth to this, I believe that describing what is going on as an "infant school movement" may impede rather than facilitate an understanding of the course of change in British junior schools.

In every junior school I visited I inquired about the origins of the practices I saw. Rarely was the influence of infant school methods stressed, neither a particular infant school nor a more generalized "model." If the progressive approaches in the schools I visited are the results of creeping "infantschoolism," then this must be very much an underground movement. Other influences were apt to be pointed out: unstreaming, the demise of the eleven-plus examination (although it is still alive in many places), the movement toward comprehensive secondary schools, Piaget, Nuffield mathematics, key H.M.I.'s (Her Majesty's Inspectors), the Froebel Institute, workshops. Finally, quite a few heads and teachers felt that they had been moving in more open directions since their first days of teaching. I did not find much reference to Leicestershire, or to any other single center in the country, as a source of powerful influence. In sum, all kinds of influences were cited, and the infant school and integrated day was one influence among them. Perhaps I was running into a bit of professional rivalry. After all, what junior school head would want to be told, or would want to admit, that his school is really just a version for older children of what is done with infants?

I was also surprised to find that in general the junior schools did not keep close contact with their own local infant schools—the schools that "feed" them. Sometimes the heads did not get along too well; sometimes the local infant school was viewed by the junior school as too much of a play school. Quite often the heads and teachers were "just too busy to get together." Sometimes the junior school was freer than the infant school.

Another oversimplification that I took along to England, based on the reading I had done, was the idea that the changes in primary education had been initiated and sustained by the teachers on the front lines. This is true to some extent (perhaps in some places to a considerable extent) but it is also true that much maneuvering and manipulation has been going on behind the scenes. Good heads have sometimes been placed in key positions, as have good advisors, H.M.I.'s, etc. I did not and could not attempt to unravel the various lines of influence, but it seems that the formula for reform in England has probably been in equal parts teacher enthusiasm and administrative leadership.

Again and again heads would stress the importance of encouraging teachers to develop teaching methods that they could verify against their own experience. Each head had his own tale of what happens when change is too hastily imposed from above. On the other hand, the heads, the primary school advisors, and others in leadership positions do not sit around twiddling their thumbs, simply waiting for teachers to move. Since heads have the power to appoint their teachers when vacancies exist or in new schools, one effective strategy is to build a staff by choosing those teachers with a desire to work in the directions set forth (broadly but explicitly) by the head. Other heads, out of choice or necessity, have had to work with existing staffs, mainly not of their own selection. Here I encountered somewhat more discussion of "change mechanisms" such as team teaching, open plan, environmental studies, workshops, new approaches to mathematics. Any of these, and other avenues as well, may serve the purpose of encouraging teachers to introduce more variety and individualization into their instruction. Again, however, the warning was sounded that these cannot be imposed as a "program."

"Teaming," Open Space, School Size

A variety of issues and concerns were spontaneously brought up in conversation with the heads and teachers, but there were two topics that seemed to have special salience for English teachers: "teaming," and open space. A third topic that came to be important to me but which was taken for granted by the English was school size.

"TEAMING"

In many schools staff members were exploring ways in which they could usefully interact with one another, in an effort to loosen the boundaries of the self-contained classroom. Shared corridor areas and shared trips had been a start in this direction, but teachers were trying other forms of cooperation. In two schools I visited, a teacher without a class took on the role of floating teacher for a year, with the opportunity to develop projects with children and other teachers in great depth; she would return to a class of her own the next year and someone else would take on the floating assignment. Various ways of swapping pupils for different activities were being tried out. Although a great many qualifications were offered and a variety of warnings were sounded, teamwork among teachers was generally considered to be a good thing, something that should be fostered. Two points were frequently made: 1) Cooperative teaching must be built upon the initiative and planning of those who are actually going to be involved in it. Otherwise it becomes a gimmick, with little to recommend it. In some instances, particularly with inexperienced teachers, the heads felt that teaming (they tend to avoid the phrase "team teaching" as having too many extraneous connotations) should not be pushed. Teachers, they argued, need to discover and consolidate their own capabilities. They are better off working in loose confederation. With experienced staffs, however, the opinion was that the encouragement of teaming could pay more immediate dividends. Older teachers, with more established approaches, could perhaps be jostled a bit through the experience of accommodating their ways to those of others. 2) It was also stressed that the purpose of cooperative teaching is as much to stimulate teachers' professional growth as it is to spread the resources of the staff. Thus, it might start out with "I'll-do-math-and-you-do-music," but ideally it should serve to bring mathematics and music together, not to compartmentalize them, just as it should bring the staff together, not promote specialization.

Teaming needs to be viewed as one major way of promoting the competence and creative energies of the staff. (In some areas, regularly scheduled workshops have also had the effect of promoting professional development.) The particular pattern of teamwork was considered much less important than the professional climate in which it was carried out. In some schools more than in others I was struck by the lively interaction between staff members. In these schools, educational matters were taken seriously, and the formulation and expression of opinions were valued; it seemed clear that the adults were learning in such schools. Visits to these schools made me much more conscious of the fact that we so often think of a school only as a setting for children's growth when, in reality, as a place for learning it can profoundly affect teachers' development. For open education this is a key matter if pupil development is seen as a direct function of the teacher's continued involvement. Schools can foster common sense and creative involvement in their teachers or they can nurture mindlessness and convention.

OPEN SPACE

A second topic of considerable interest to English educators had to do with the physical layout of the school building. How do furniture, walls, spaces, affect the interaction of children and teachers? Four of the newer schools I visited had been constructed with such concerns in mind. In some of the other schools internal modifications, such as knocking down some of the walls, had been undertaken. One pattern involved the use of three-walled classrooms, the fourth side of which opened onto a large work area which was shared by several classes. This design was felt to be a have-cake-and-eat-it plan, as it could be adapted to both the self-contained and the sharing styles of teaching. Another plan emphasized flexibility by making use of movable partitions. Still another dispensed with corridors altogether and simply connected one room directly to another—with the disadvantage that some of the rooms served as major thoroughfares.

I have mixed feelings about the success of some of the newer open plan designs. Often, I was quite aware that the staff had to contend with someone's predetermined model of what the ebb and flow of the inhabitants of the building *ought* to be. (Admittedly, old-fashioned buildings can be just as dictatorial.) The most successful arrangement seemed to be the four-walled room with a movable partition in one wall for flexibility, combined with enlarged corridors. This plan combines some sense of territory with the possibility of interaction. Junior school children (more so than infants?) seem to like some sense of territory in a school. More important, I also had the impression that the most creative teachers, the ones who gave considerable thought to their work, were the clearest in their territorial imperatives. It seems obvious that efforts toward teaming and opening up space will need to contend with that fact. For instance, I recall two quite imaginative teachers who shared some common space working alongside each other at times but at other times working within their own room with their own class. Their pattern was one of friendly rivalry and stimulation; they certainly did not constitute interchangeable parts of a team.

In summary, the interest in teaming and open plan in the schools I visited seemed to have evolved naturally out of earlier efforts to develop less formal programs. It may be that when teachers begin to work with children in more open ways they quite naturally start to consider both the physical plant and their colleagues as part of the resources for their own and the children's development. In the United States a different pattern for the evolution of educational practice is sometimes advocated; open space and/or team teaching may be promoted as the forerunner, instead of being seen as an extension, of open education.

SCHOOL SIZE

It is important to consider the size of schools in any examination of the changes going on in primary education in England.

The English fuss a lot less about *class* size than do Americans (35–40 children in a room, while not desired, is not too unusual), but they do give more thought to *school* size. They are appalled at the huge American elementary schools, and they are beginning to have second thoughts about their own recent moves toward large secondary schools. From their point of view, the ideal junior school size is about eight or ten teachers and 300–320 children. (Interestingly, I found these statistics widely agreed upon around the country.) The largest school I visited had thirteen teachers and over 400 children, the smallest, three teachers and about sixty children. Most of the others had 200–350 children.

A number of observations were made in response to my inquiries about size. 1) In a school of no more than 300 children the head and most of the teachers can get to know every child and, by the end of four years, know him quite well. No child gets lost, and this is important for an informal school. Indeed, in visiting classrooms in the company of heads it was clear that they and the children did know each other. 2) The head can work with a staff of ten in ways which involve him primarily in educational matters; only a small proportion of his time needs to be devoted to administrative paperwork. Heads often organize and lead field trips, fill in temporarily for teachers who need to be away for a few hours, and take on special projects with small groups—carpentry, the study of rocks, etc. Staff communication is simple; the lengthy announcements, bulletins, staff meetings, and intercom messages which characterize many American schools are noticeable by their absence in English schools. The head gets out of his office and into the classrooms; he knows what is going on in his school, and he holds himself accountable just as he holds his teachers accountable. In a school of manageable size the head can devote most of his energies to working directly on the most important matters—staff development and the education of the pupils. 3) Geographically the school is a community school; children walk to school and there are no elaborate bus schedules. One head (but only one) mentioned the greater opportunity for parental involvement in modest-sized schools. 4) In some regions, the very small village schools are seen as training grounds for heads and teachers. The head of a small school of fifty pupils is forced to deal with each child as an individual regardless of his educational philosophy. The experience of knowing children individually is considered very valuable in preparing a head for a larger school. As one head told me, he has to operate in a community of children, and he cannot construct barriers between himself and his staff and pupils.

To recapitulate, a school with about 320 children is seen as large enough to permit some breathing space and variety, but is still small enough to be a community rather than an institution.

Teachers and Children

Although the schools I visited were child-centered in many ways they were also, without exception, clearly organized and run by adults. Teachers' expectations about children's performance were often quite exacting, but there was an attempt to tailor these expectations to each individual case. The children's work which was on display seemed to have to show some special quality, such as original thought, special care, or personal significance, in order to merit being displayed. Work was not displayed simply because it had been completed.

As I visited classrooms accompanied by heads I noticed that it was not unusual for the head to be called upon by the teacher or by a child for critical comment on someone's work. Sometimes the comment was simply a compliment; sometimes it might be a correction—for example, one head pointed out inaccuracies in a graph depicting the number of children enrolled in the school. I rarely saw signs of apprehension on the children's part regarding the head's comments. It was clear from their behavior that he was a frequent and welcomed visitor. He knew their names and often seemed to know about the origin and status of various projects in the classroom.

There was an unhurried, unfrantic quality to the school day that I found attractive. There were seldom bells and buzzers. While children typically moved about in schools a great deal, working in corridors and under staircases, there was not the push from one classroom to another that I have seen in elementary schools with departmentalized instruction. Although there were definite schedules for opening assemblies, periods in the gymnasium, playground periods, lunch, these schedules did not appear to cramp the day's activities.

I saw a number of classrooms where I thought that both the teachers and the children were uncertain about the purpose of what they were doing, but I never saw chaos, and rarely did I see a classroom in which the teacher was just barely keeping things going. Several teachers, however, did tell me about chaotic experiences they had had in the past. Others said that they had introduced informal methods quite gradually, in order to build in some organized patterns for the children to learn to follow. They stressed the fact that considerable time is required (at least one year and more often two) to create a productive, open pattern with a group. For this reason some schools make it possible for teachers to stay with the same group of children for two years. It is true, I believe, as others have noted, that the English child is given considerable responsibility. One finds five-year-olds using sharp tools, first-year juniors cooking with flame, children getting about on public busses, and children cleaning up their classrooms and taking care of animals. My impression was that both in the lively classrooms and in the more ordinary ones social systems were working quite adequately. Not much teacher time was spent on scoldings, moralistic lectures or punishments. A well-placed word or two from the teacher or from another child seemed to suffice. Whereas teachers in the United States have to forbid disruptive behavior, these English teachers didn't even expect it. They were firm and consistent to varying degrees; they were willing to listen to children but not to argue with them.

I have the general impression that even in the more open schools, the English child moves in more well-defined paths than his American counterpart. Watching the children relate to each other and to adults I was reminded much more of children I have seen in our rural schools than in our suburban and city schools. This may partly be a function of the size of the schools. I suspect, however, that in rural America as in much of England the patterns of social interaction are more codified, the roles of adult and child more clearly defined. On the positive side this may mean that schools can establish good working relationships more readily; on the negative side, these more defined patterns may mean fewer options for the child.

At the risk of gross generalization, I would say that I was more struck by the responsibility of children in these schools than by their initiative. This should be immediately qualified by saying that they certainly demonstrated plenty of initiative. I felt, nevertheless, that in many of the schools the teachers had more difficulty in stimulating the children to come up with original, unexpected lines of inquiry than they did in encouraging them to follow up a line of interest, once identified, in a responsible way. In a number of open schools in the United States the reverse may be true; there are plenty of good ideas but both teachers and children have difficulty in transforming these ideas into projects which sustain interest and learning. As partial documentation of this impression, my taped interviews with children reveal a pattern of responsibility in answering my questions, but show less initiative in turning the question about or in putting forth new lines of inquiry. Although these interviews occurred in corners of informal rooms, and although the children knew me from a number of previous visits, there were few instances of someone asking such things as "Where did you get that machine?" or "Why are you asking these questions?"

There was another aspect of responsibility that seemed to characterize many of the schools. Children were expected to assume an active role in creating a successful educational setting; they contributed materials and ideas, they made suggestions about better ways of doing things, they were expected to work cooperatively and constructively. In other words, they were producers as well as consumers of what the school had to offer. The open, informal setting is not simply a cafeteria in which the child takes what he wants or finds interesting. Teachers seem to see giving and taking as directly rather than inversely related. In fact, one head went so far as to assert that the informal approaches work best with children from poorer homes who "have more to give because they have more to take."

In view of the demonstrated emphasis on respect for children, and the stress which is placed on building on individual differences, I found it hard to understand why some of the teachers used unnecessarily global labels in describing children, labels such as "backward," "dull," and "lazy." I might be introduced to a pupil with the phrase, "Here's a bright boy," or I might be told, in partially audible tones, that the girl working so hard at her sewing was a "rather dull student." I also found that the teachers were frequently quite aware of the measured ability of the students in their schools, either according to intelligence tests or the eleven-plus examination. And while most of these educators voiced the view that such measures had little value, they might at the same time refer to some students as "a low ability group." Perhaps in one sense this was a realistic view of the children, but it may often lead to serious underestimation of the children's potential for intellectually creative work.

In general, however, I was most impressed with the attitude of teachers and heads toward children. One anecdote seems to me to reveal the tone of much of the instruction in these schools:

> A teacher and her class of ten- and eleven-year-olds were discussing their trip, just completed, to the top of a nearby mountain. Why were there no large trees at the top, only scrubby ones? A number of variables were proposed and explanations offered. The teacher then told the class about the theory of a five-year-old who had been along on the trip. He had said, "There really are big trees, but you see they have a long way to grow up through the mountain and so just their tops are showing." (Later at the bottom of the mountain he had shown the teacher a piece of root as supporting evidence!) The value placed on the process of original thinking was evident in the teacher's telling of the story, and in the response of her class.

Other Notes on Teachers

I was struck by the fact that teachers did not seem at all put off by my visits to their classrooms or teaching areas, often in the company of the head. The welcome seemed genuine. (It is important to note that unlike some schools in England, the ones I saw had generally not been over-visited.) We were usually able to talk informally with some of the children and with the teacher, if he happened to be unengaged, without disrupting the proceedings. Although most of the children had more interesting things to do than to talk with visitors, there were always a few who wanted to communicate something to the head, and sometimes to me.

Some of the young teachers I saw reminded me very much of young American teachers. They had good ideas and nice ways of working with children but they were also struggling to establish priorities in their teaching. How much do they really value the clay? The mathematics? If these teachers shared a common fault it was their impatience with children when the children seemed too childish and wouldn't dig into their work. Yet this was also a virtue in these teachers, since they did want the children to take advantage of all the possibilities. Heads often seemed to allow young teachers plenty of leeway to make their own errors and discoveries. It was also evident that heads can challenge as well as support. A number of teachers with four or five years' experience mentioned to me the important role that a head, or some other teacher, had played in the early development of their teaching ability. They mentioned the encouragement, support, and criticism that heads had given them while they tried some of their own ideas. In fact, certain heads had reputations as trainers of young teachers, and a teacher might be referred to as one of Mr. X's teachers, even though now she was teaching in a different school. Opinions varied about the best situations for teachers to start teaching in. Some educators felt that the average teacher, straight from college, should ideally start with a small group of children, and work in close cooperation with experienced staff members. Others emphasized the important effect upon the staff of a young teacher's enthusiasm and new ideas.

Teachers, of course, differed in many ways. Some of these were: 1) their involvement with the children in learning. At one extreme were teachers who merely monitored what was happening. At the other extreme were teachers who jumped into the activities with the children; 2) the social-political meaning of their work. Some teachers expressed more concern with the total life of the child and what school would or would not mean in his life. Others saw in the informal approach a better method of instruction but not something that would radically alter the lives of the pupils; 3) the ability and/or willingness to analyze what they were doing. Some teachers were quite clear, in words as well as actions, about what their work meant while with others it was much harder to detect a plan.

Men are important in English junior schools. Although I didn't keep a tally, I would estimate that in the average school 30–40 percent of the teachers were men. Unlike American elementary schools, where one finds one or two token male teachers, these schools had a broad masculine representation, with as much variation in teaching style among the men as among the women. Most of the heads were men. With some exceptions, men were most commonly teaching the upper grade levels, the ten- and eleven-year-old children. The older men in classroom teaching were especially interesting to me; I felt they added something important to a school's staff. In the United States such men are rare, having gone into administration or business.

It is worth noting that when the children enter junior school, at about seven, most of them are reading to some extent, and many are well past the beginning reader phase. It seemed to me that this helped free the first- and second-year junior teachers from some of the anxiety about reading that is so prevalent in American primary grades; the English junior school teacher may feel freer to experiment with approaches to the teaching of reading. Books of all sorts were in evidence and very much used, displayed on tables or placed in easily accessible book racks in classrooms and corridors. "Basal readers," so dominant in American schools, were not noticeable. I certainly never saw twenty or thirty copies of the same book in a classroom. Many teachers, however, did use a series of books (color-coded or otherwise marked for level of difficulty) which children read individually and in small groups on occasion. There were often magazines, newspapers, and the children's homemade books in the classrooms.

Teachers generally seemed less confident about what they were doing in mathematics than in other areas. The materials they used ranged from boxes of peas to programmed instruction booklets. Perhaps most evident were work cards, both published and teacher-made. Each card typically posed a problem to be solved or a task to be carried out: flip a coin twenty times and tally the heads and tails; make an equilateral triangle out of a thirteen-inch piece of yarn. Workbooks were also used. Most of the schools had adopted some mathematics scheme around which the teachers would build their program. Such schemes might be fairly comprehensive (for example, the Dienes Multi-base Arithmetic Blocks or Algebraic Experience Materials) or might be a more narrowly defined series of work cards. In a few schools the teachers were developing their own program in its entirety, but in most cases they seemed to lean more or less heavily on some published program. A number of people felt that the teachers simply did not have the background in mathematics to enable them to be as creative as they would want to be.

As other visitors have recorded, the quality of work in the arts and in craft was truly remarkable. I was also intrigued by classes in "movement." This is a kind of cross between physical education and self-expression through use of the body. I know of no counterpart to it in the United States.

Conclusion

There is indeed much to be learned from the British experience. Perhaps they have the least to offer concerning the relationship of school and community, where there seems to be considerably more experimentation and action in the United States. They have a great deal to show us about children's learning in more open and challenging school environments. And perhaps they have the most to teach us about how schools can promote the creative capabilities of their staffs.

5. "There is never a typical day"

Time is a servant, not a master, in a good open classroom. In this selection, an experienced teacher in a large informal infant school located in a racially mixed, low-income neighborhood of an English city talks about the relaxed way in which the day begins, with parents hanging around for a half hour or so, getting to know the teacher and the other children in the class. She discusses the way she gets different children started on different activities and the way she organizes her own time so that she can stay on top of things.

There is never a typical day, but a day might work out along these lines. I would get to school about 8:15. I would go and start work in the classroom—put in clean water, mix new clay, get everything ready for the children.

At about five to nine, the first children appear with mothers, and from then on it's a question of talking to a mother or a group of mothers.

The parents always stay until 9:30 and I like this. They are really *in* the room and you even find parents forming relationships with children other than their own, whom they never see outside.

Jonathan's mother, who is a marvellous person with great personality, has a fine relationship with Donald. She and Donald never meet except during that half hour, but every day she comes in and Donald is waiting for her. When mothers come in like this, they get to know the children, and I get to know them.

They come into the classroom and we sit and chat; the same thing happens at half past three. I find parents rarely ask how their children are getting on because we are talking about these things all the time. They come in and look at the things in the classroom. Some of the children want to show their mothers what they've done, and we talk about that. This is happening all the time.

By about 9:30 we get started, though some children get busy with independent work earlier. We begin by talking informally, sometimes about school, sometimes not, sometimes about things that happened on the previous day.

I may also talk about things that have happened to me. I find they're fascinated by the fact that one has a life as well. They just don't believe things happen to the teacher.

Then we talk about what we are going to start off by doing. The majority of children prefer to tell me what they are going to do. I don't insist on this but I encourage it.

I sometimes try to generate an interest by saying, as though it were something wonderful, "Who's going to do some mathematics?" or "Who's going to do some writing?" so that I will encourage the children whom I want to participate in that particular activity to go and do it.

I find I don't need to do this very often, because things develop from what's going on in the room. If I want to follow up with some form of mathematics, for example, they might get at it through cooking.

Sometimes one finds that something needs developing. Once, when we were talking about families and difference in ages, I felt a small group could benefit. I drew a few children together and we made a book.

I break my day up so that sometimes I am working with a group doing a certain thing, and sometimes I wander from child to child. I try to avoid wandering round all day, because I find I have nothing at the end of it. Though it isn't a set thing, I try to start off each morning in the writing corner. This sometimes takes up a lot of the morning. In the afternoon, I try to concentrate in either the mathematical or the creative area.

It's always changing, though, because I try to respond where I'm most needed. It must be understood that this doesn't always work out; quite often my attention is called to something else. Still I do try to focus my time in particular corners. If I think to myself in the morning, "I am going to try to start in the writing corner," this keeps my own organization going to a certain extent.

It's a most difficult thing, because you find that some other areas, like reading and mathematics are developing also, or that you could spend every day and all day with creative work. In fact sometimes I find I'm spending most of my time in one area for two or three days, because I've found a sudden surge of interest from a group of children who demand my help.

Or I may find that the creative work is suffering, that the children are losing interest because I haven't given any impetus to it, brought in any fresh ideas for a while. Then I will have to go and spend a concentrated amount of time in that area. It is a changing situation all the time.

I usually finish off the morning with a story. This is a good time— either at the end of the morning or at the beginning of the afternoon— for the class teacher to hand the story over to somebody else and to take a group out somewhere. A few of us can run down to the river and have a look at it, or we can get to the park and wander round.

I try to do this with children who need more language development. At other times, I may take out a group needing some specific help with their reading, or writing. If I can find someone to take a story, it frees me to do these special things.

I eat my lunch with the children every day, and I usually follow this by having a chat with the staff who are specially employed to supervise the children at this period. I wander out into the yard to see that everything is going well.

Generally, the staff will all meet in the staff-room after lunch for coffee, and invariably we talk about school. It's like having a staff meeting every lunchtime.

Of course, during the day there are all sorts of other things going on. There will be a group of children who do some reading, and then watch a television broadcast; or a group of children might go to do some music. I might take the children on the PE apparatus. That's more or less how the day goes.

My children are free to wander into the corridors or into any class, but I find, in practice, that most of them don't.

This, too, very much depends on the individual child. Some children are at a disadvantage, wandering round. But this would depend on how long it went on, and on the individual child.

I finish off the afternoon, from about 3 o'clock, with a story. I linger a few minutes, talking to parents. I don't attempt to do anything in the room at this point. I talk to a child or two, and then I leave at 3:50.

I find that things at school needing my attention creep up, so once in a while I spend a whole evening there working until 10 or 11 p.m. I do this about every fourth week, when the whole room needs cleaning up and there are things to be made.

I don't formally plan things out; I think about them a lot in relation to what's happening. I never plan, "I'm going to do this, that and the other." But, lying in bed in the morning or evening, or when I'm driving the car, I will think of the various things that are happening, about ways of developing them, about new things to try. Teaching, for me, is thinking a lot, but not necessarily writing it down.

Even with records, however much you try to keep written records, it's not terribly useful. I can't see the point of it. I don't really see that if you were suddenly removed from the situation, and somebody else had to take over, the written records would be much help.

I have thirty-two children in my class. I couldn't keep a very good record of everybody's progress all the time. I can see what's happening with the children, and I keep a superficial record for each one. A lot of the information about a child I keep in my head.

In addition there are always some children who don't participate voluntarily—children who seem to stand on the periphery of things, whatever one is doing. I keep a record in which I study those particular children in depth. I study their family backgrounds and visit their homes. I keep some of their paintings and I try to make a study of them. I might ask a child to draw a picture of his family, and from it try to get some idea of the family relationship.

I've now taught most of my children for nearly two years and I've talked to all their parents on many occasions, so I do think I know them well.

6. Planning for the Free Day

What appears to be unstructured, and to an unseasoned eye almost chaotic, in fact has a pattern and rhythm of its own, with a mixture of "free" and scheduled activities and of individual and group learning. As Lillian Weber points out in the selection that follows, the scheduled activities that bring all the children together are seen in a positive way. Far from setting limits to the freedom of the open classroom and the open school, they are means of integrating the children into the communal life of the school. Learning, after all, is a group as well as an individual experience.

The plan of the day—the timetable—was a key factor in implementing the concept of informal education that stresses the free flow and wholeness of school living. An infant school timetable could consist of *simultaneous use* with *fixed points* moving toward what has been variously called the *free day,* the *undifferentiated* or *integrated day;* or it could consist of an *activity period* with simultaneous use and a *skills period* with simultaneous varied grouping. The order of activity period and skills period could be reversed and this too had consequences.

Simultaneous use refers to the use of various aspects of the environment—one aspect by one or a few children, another aspect by others, singly or in a group, at the same time.

Simultaneous use was at the least a phenomenon of the activity period, a period of free choice for the children from all the areas of the environment—plastic (sand, water, clay, paint, woodwork), housekeeping, music, acting, sewing, measurement and weighing, books, games, etc. Even when it characterized solely the activity period, simultaneous use meant availability of books and number as well as of other materials. Even in such a division of the day aspects of the environment available during the period of free choice were used for the focused "skills" work, as when sand was used for weighing and water for measuring.

In all schools, the existing situation was of simultaneous varied grouping, no matter what the timetable arrangement. No skills work was taught *entirely* in a block classroom way, with *one* lesson for all. Even where skills were unrelated to "activities"—interpreted narrowly as painting, games, sandbox, house-play, acting—there was *always* a breakdown into several different groupings of children doing different things appropriate to their own point of progression, though all were linked in general sub-

From Lillian Weber, *The English Infant School and Informal Education,* pp. 89–94, 114–118. Copyright © 1971 by Lillian Weber. Reprinted by permission of Prentice Hall, Inc., Englewood Cliffs, New Jersey.

ject. Usually in such a skills period unrelated to activities, one group might be doing reading, another writing, another number work or measuring, or perhaps individual children were engaged in these activities. Thus, the children were not all doing the same thing at the same time. Usually, even if the whole group was doing number, children were doing three or four different activities, on different levels, handling different things. The most structured situation, for example, might be one group weighing, another measuring, another counting with number trays, another "smashing" a number such as eight and turning it into its relevant groupings.

Nevertheless, if the timetable called for the skills period to *precede* the activity period, the result was very little interpenetration of focus and interest and very little sense of the wholeness implied in informal education. This sequence of timetabling resulted in most completely isolating the free activity from the rest of the scheduled day, the least degree of free flow, the least use of the environment. Few schools timetabled in this way.

More likely, some aspect of the activity period interpenetrated the skills and vice versa, and what was done was thus entirely individual. The important thing was the constant use of the concrete in the environment to give meanings to all learning. There was a constant search for what would involve children in what interests them and the intensified learning that stems from this. Therefore, activity stemming from the children's firsthand experiences took precedence over verbalisms, over "take-in" from the teacher. Plowden recommendations as well as publications of the Nuffield research teams support further development of this simultaneous multiple use of the concrete environment. Gardner's view is that activity "in isolation from the rest of the time-table . . . loses some of its potential value as providing a motive and purpose for other work."

In planning for the free day there is no separation of activities or skills and no separate scheduling of any one activity other than the fixed points (Morning Service, P.E., Music and Movement, and lunch) designed for all children in the school. As a result, one might see all aspects of the environment—reading, writing, number, painting, acting, music—in use at all times. A group getting the teacher's special help or stimulus could be found at any time.

At some time of the day a child did number, reading, and writing, adjusted to his stage of progress and depending on his interest and his need of the moment. Gardner, describing this day, says:

> Good teachers have done so much to foster the interests of the children and open up fresh possibilities to them that in some schools there is no need to safeguard particular "subjects" such as reading, writing and arithmetic by reserving special times for them, since the

children can be relied upon to choose them sufficiently and sometimes for longer periods than would have been allocated by a timetable.

Sometimes the schedule was thought out over a period longer than a
day and it was not felt necessary that every child do every thing every
day. In such a school a child who was engrossed in something could
continue exploring the bounds of his work without regard for schedule,
at least for a while.

In Bristol, after some period of use of this undifferentiated day plan,
it was clear that *play time* as a release into movement from an immobile
learning situation was no longer necessary—the children had freedom
and movement all through the day. Of course, some teachers have criticized this because the discard of play time means a loss of these free
moments for the teacher, who remains responsible *all* day. While there
is a loss of *group* free time, teachers continue to take a break for coffee
sometime during the morning.

It should be emphasized that the undifferentiated day was not conceived simply in terms of simultaneity of all different aspects of the environment, nor in terms of a child's use of any one aspect as a separate
use at a single moment in time. The English viewed a child's use of the
environment as cutting across subject areas in pursuit of his interests.
This kind of scheduling not only supported a child's integration of experience but also sustained his involvement.

Not only my observations but the literature also seemed to indicate a
trend towards *more* simultaneous varied grouping and towards the undifferentiated or integrated day. In fact, most of the schools visited had
for the greater part of the day a combination of the activity period related
to skills and simultaneous varied grouping. Schools with activity periods
unrelated to skills were in the minority. For the most part, the schools
that were family-grouped had an undifferentiated day.

Some steps towards a looser timetabling had been made by all the
schools of my sample, but the variety of their arrangements indicates that
the undifferentiated day is the end point of a continuum. The work of
the Froebel Institute focuses on a child's free choice of activity rather
than on the free day, and recognizes that some teachers

> might still think it indispensable to set their children (at any rate
> from 7–8 onward) some definite broad theme. They might perhaps
> also want to start from a prepared talk, and to introduce further
> such talks, or in fact lessons, at intervals. This might then become
> an arguable question of degree. . . . It might well be felt by a
> good many thoughtful teachers that some such carefully limited
> degree of direction would lead to more positive and valuable results,
> anyway from 7 to 8 or 9 onward, than any quite unplanned freedom

of choice. But so far the trend of our evidence rather points the other way. In that connection it seems particularly worth noting that some teachers began along partly pre-planned lines but themselves became more and more critical of these as they went along. They found in fact that the less pattern they imposed, the better appeared to be the results. . . . And it seems important to register that there may well be room for a great variety of different procedures and techniques, determined, at least in part, by what comes naturally and easily to the teacher—provided only that the last word always rests with the child.

The Nuffield Teacher's Guide, dealing expressly with problems of transition to informality in the junior school and recognizing the difficulties of this approach for many teachers, suggested that "it is best to begin in a fairly formal way and to introduce new ways gradually." The teacher then "can meet a limited number of problems at a time instead of being faced with many all at once." For teachers used to a stricter timetable, the Guide suggests small blocks of one hour of time as a starter, though it describes some teachers who seem able to make the change in one step. Earlier accounts of the development of this kind of planning in the infant schools also suggested activity periods of one hour as a starter. These accounts described the necessary changes in room arrangement and the process of overflow to the whole day as activity period and skills were related. Mary Brown, writing after Plowden (and of the integrated day), speaks of the necessity for the teacher to have *evolved* to this.

The undifferentiated day has attracted great attention in the United States as a major, and by implication, necessary and immediate, feature of what I have called informal education. Examination of English writing however, indicates that there was a continuum of many steps in its evolution in the infant school. Furthermore, the English anticipated that such a continuum would characterize the evolution of informal education in the junior school.

The Plowden Report confirms the undifferentiated day as a desirable goal and terms the trend towards this "widespread." It stresses that free use of the rich environment is connected to looser timetabling.

The strongest influence making for the free day has been the conviction of some teachers and other educationalists that it is through play that young children learn. . . . The tendency is spreading in junior schools. Children may plan when to do work assigned to them and also have time in which to follow personal or group interests of their own choice.

Within the undifferentiated or free day, a child's life had a pattern or rhythm even though the day had no specific schedule except for the fixed points listed below.

On arrival he might help with the preparation of the classroom workshop or with the care of the animals; in effect, he entered the school as a responsible participant, knowing that materials were accessible and available to him—to prepare, to use, to restore. He might get to work on something already underway, resuming his investigation almost without pause. After a period of satisfying work, he and all the other children joined in the Morning Service. He then returned with his class to his room and teacher, who perhaps suggested that he work for a short while on a specific skill task appropriate to his own needs. After this work he could return to his own pursuits elsewhere in the classroom, corridor, and hall, or even outside in the playground. He might need to consult with the teacher on a beginning of a new investigation. As the morning wore on a child might join his class for the scheduled Music and Movement or work on the P.E. apparatus. Until then, and while other groups had their scheduled periods, he might continue his own work.

The hall had to be cleared for lunch use. A child knew where he might safely put aside his work, ready to be taken up later. He replaced materials already used, doing his part with all the other children to restore the school to working order for the afternoon. Earlier he might have helped collect dinner money and also, in answer to his own question, computed the amount collected. Now he might be one of a group of children helping set the lunch tables.

After lunch he again met with his classmates and teacher before another period of his own investigation, mixing use of "free" activities and skills. His teacher might join him at his work—the measuring, the reading, the acting, the painting, the weighing—discussing it with him in the terms of his purposes but also posing new possibilities for trial the next day. Or she might suggest trial of a new area altogether.

Nearing the end of the day, as he and other children reached the end of their work or a reasonable point of interruption, they began to tidy their work areas knowing that materials not returned to storage centers would not be available for their use the next day. If he finished earlier than the others, he might read, play a quiet game, hold a guinea pig, talk with a friend, or help with another's tidying.

The day might end with the reading of a story or some poetry and a discussion. Thus, a child's day had a rhythm of sustained involvement in his own work, interposed with periods of coming together with his fellows in class and school.

Whether timetabled for activity period and skills or for the undifferentiated day, the plan of the day also included scheduled activities—Morning Service, P.E., Music and Movement, lunch, and playtime. These activities became the fixed points of the day, though their scheduling (except for lunch) often reflected some flexibility. The Morning Service, for example, the only officially required activity in an English school, was supposed to take place the first thing in the morning, but many heads found that it came more appropriately after some activity, and had quietly made their own adjustment of schedule. The Plowden Report notes this flexibility.

In an attempt to produce greater impact and intimacy, the heads of some schools arranged for a classroom kind of Morning Service a few mornings a week and an all-school service only once or twice a week, but this was not the usual procedure. In a few schools the 5s did not, either as a group or even regularly, join the Morning Service. In a very few instances a number of other departures from the pattern of all-school gathering may be noted.

Obviously the activities that brought together all the children or utilized the big hall limited some of the free-flowing use of the school. But the significance of these activities is not that they set limitations to free flow or to the free day, for more than timetable was involved. These activities were considered to be integrative for the children and for the school. They were expressions of the communal life of the school. . . .

Ideally English educators considered free access to materials an essential element in the support of a child's individual pattern of learning, which is the essence of informal education. They therefore believed that materials and equipment should be placed throughout the school. The amount and variety tended to be full and rich in all schools, far more so than is customary for this age group in American schools. All English teachers aimed for this profusion of materials; they maintained that a high level of supply was needed to sustain stimulation and that having just one or two interesting items was insufficient. The following categories of materials were the minimal standard in the infant schools:

Library	Workbench and Materials
Book Corners	Junk Materials
Esthetic Corners	Blocks (Bricks)
Musical Instruments	Manipulative and Construction Toys
Wendy House	Math, Concrete and Structural: Number,
Dress-up Items	Weighing, Measuring, Exploration of Time
Sewing Materials	and Money
Puppetry	Science: Nature and Interest Tables and Other
Acting Platforms	Materials (Pendulums, Pulleys, Thermome-
Cooking Materials	ters, etc.)
Clay	Water and Equipment
Sand	Animals
Paint	P.E.: Agility Equipment, Balls, Hoops, Ropes,
Art Materials	Tires, Sticks
Printing Materials	

The natural materials—*clay, sand,* and *water*—were to be found in every single room in many schools.

The *agility apparatus,* utilized in P.E., which resembles the climbers that are located outdoors in most nursery schools, is more complex and involves greater skills. The children used it in individual ways—finding different spatial areas to go through and trying out different kinds of balance. A great variety of other material—ropes, balls, tires, sticks, all kinds of balancing boards, and tall boxes for jumping—was also in evidence. Every school had a trolley, like a shopping cart, ready to be used outside or inside, stocked with these extra things. Individual grace and skill and balance, a commando kind of agility, was encouraged. Inventiveness seemed prized. The emphasis in P.E. was obviously individual rather than on a mass kind of conformity, even though P.E. was usually conducted with a class working together.

Painting supplies were often available in the big hall or corridor in addition to the usual very full provision in the classrooms. A child's organizing of his experience in representation and image was considered essential to the development of his understanding, and children were given every opportunity to do this on their own level. In painting, a child integrated his experiences and it was considered that variety and richness of experience in other areas fed the variety and richness of representation and image. Thus poetry, stories, trips, science, even math, could feed the development of image. Most of the schools offered a variety of art materials, including supplies for printing, weaving, and so forth.

The *workbench* was sometimes situated in a classroom, but the hall or corridor or outdoor bay was usually its place, thus making it accessible for several classes. A *stove* for cooking might also be located in the hall for general use.

For the school as a whole there almost always was a *special area*—perhaps a corner in the hall—with easy chairs and books, and on its walls were exhibits of some poems written large, well-mounted children's paintings, or reproductions on loan. This area might also be an esthetically pleasing corner, full of a lovely display of glass, or fabric, or sculpture, or pebbles, shells, and leaves. The arrangement of this display was often worked out by a group of children and often changed. A very attractive room frequently served for a regular *library,* and if the school had more than one corridor, distinct book areas could be found in the corridors all over the school. Book areas also existed in every classroom.

Additional standard equipment included the *large semi-circular hollow blocks.* Several of these blocks put together by children could be turned into an acting platform or an acting area. Costumes and drapes of material suitable for role playing could be found all over and were left to children's ingenuity for use; sometimes a couple of drapes would

PLAN OF CLASSROOM

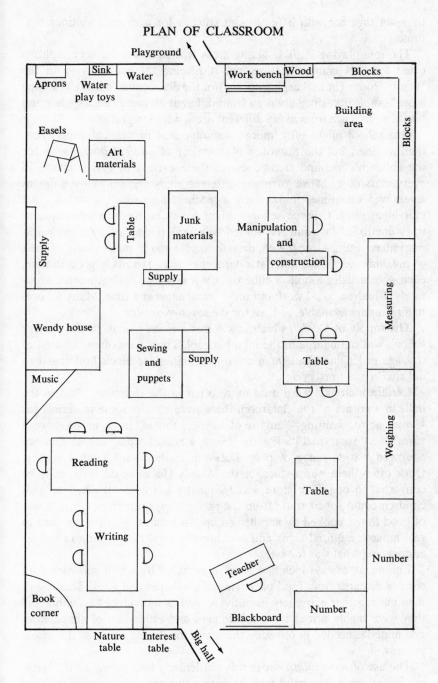

Sketch of classroom plan from a quick on-the-scene drawing.

be sewn together with a few rough stitches for a more ambitious costume.

The role playing in these acting areas was considered a very sophisticated form of communication, not displacing the role playing in the Wendy House (housekeeping corner) of the classrooms, but often adding more complexity, since children from different classes came together and bits of experience from many different areas were integrated.

One school might offer more encouragement of musical experiences than another, but the provision of a variety of *musical instruments* for the children's use and free access to these existed in every school, in every classroom. Music of many different kinds and on many different levels was sometimes initiated by a teacher: sometimes it was a quiet individual pursuit. Some schools might have amazingly interesting and truly fine-toned instruments—tuned bells, xylophones of different kinds, marimbas, drums—for the children to handle and to make music of their own. Chime-bars were fairly standard; they were extremely good in tone, each note usually a hollow tube on a wooden bar, each mounted separately. Children could work out tunes using a few at a time. Many schools had recorders available, at least for the seven-year-olds.

The supply of *blocks,* which was sometimes very small in the nursery school, was quite large in the infant school. Thus, very often children of this age in England had far more opportunities for block building than did children of nursery age.

Certain materials were used more often in the classroom than in the hall. In a corner of the classroom there were usually some materials for sewing or for knitting—lengths of fabrics, thread, large needles, wool yarn. Every room had its *Wendy House,* a housekeeping corner that encouraged a wide range of play. Dress-up clothes were located nearby. Quite often there was a store, or the Wendy House could very easily be converted to one. The store was frequently moved to the hall so that children could solicit trade from a larger group; sometimes the sale was of good things cooked by another group. Such sales, with transactions in real money, required signs and occasionally even the printing of a flyer announcing what was for sale.

Equipment always included "junk materials," by which was meant all sorts of discards from food packaging of all shapes and sizes. These were then put together extremely inventively, and as individual "assemblages" they were highly prized for the judgment and estimation of shape, size, and material needed in covering them and for the ingenuity of the whole process.

The use of *manipulative toys* was particularly interesting. In the nursery school, so-called baby toys, such as color cones, were used with an emphasis on hand manipulation, concentration, the puzzle aspects, and general enjoyment. In the infant school the same manipulative toys were used in the concrete math corner. Thus, the old Russian toy doll (with its seemingly infinite insides), or the color cone, or the nesting boxes were utilized to illuminate the concepts of seriation, order, and larger/ smaller. This idea of using materials encountered earlier in new ways, and of letting a child return to these and discover new uses for them, seemed to be an important one in the provision of material.

III

The Use of
Concrete Materials

There are few aspects of open education in which the change in the teacher's role is as profound as it is with respect to the use of materials. In the conventional classroom, the teacher's choice usually is limited to deciding between two or three recommended texts or between a handful of recommended materials found in standard catalogues. In an open classroom, the teacher generally chooses everything that is in the room— books, textbooks, workbooks, and concrete materials of every sort. Hence learning how to select materials, which means learning how to find and create them, as well as where to buy them—in Bussis and Chittenden's phrase, learning how to "provision" the classroom for learning—is one of the most difficult changes that teachers experience in making the change from traditional to open education.

The reasons for this emphasis on an abundance of concrete materials go to the heart of the rationale for open education. The starting point, in fact, is the conviction, based on the work of John Dewey, Susan and Nathan Isaacs, Jerome Bruner, and Jean Piaget, that the child is the principal agent in his own education and mental development. A child, that is to say, learns by doing—his doing, and no one else's. The child—or, for that matter, the adult—must create understanding for himself. He must actively invent and re-invent what he wants to under-stand. To know something is not merely to hear it or to see it but to act upon it. Hence there must be far less telling on the part of the teacher and far more doing on the part of the student. At least until youngsters are old enough to handle verbal abstractions easily—what Piaget calls the stage of "formal operations," which for most children develops between the twelfth and fifteenth year—the teacher's job is to present the child with situations that encourage him to experiment, to manipulate things and symbols, trying them out to see what results they produce.

Since the child must "do" at his own rate, the teacher must arrange the classroom environment so as to permit children to learn in their own way as well as at their own pace. This means providing young children with an abundance of concrete materials they can explore, manipulate, and handle. It means placing the materials so that children can get at them easily. If children have a rich array of materials to work with and if the materials are easily available and can be used safely, the teacher will be far better able to allow children to work on their own, without her constant supervision.

And yet there is no magic in concrete materials. A classroom can be rich in materials and still be intellectually as well as emotionally sterile. Materials are useful only to the degree to which they are used—used with the mind as well as the hand. Learning occurs when students use materials as an instrument of learning and as a source of imaginative play—two sides of the same coin, since play is an important means of learning. Children and teachers supply the meaning to the materials; by using their minds and their imaginations, they transform what otherwise would be inert materials.

What this means, of course, is that the teacher cannot simply select materials on the basis of someone else's list, although lists can be valuable for the beginning teacher. Rather, the teacher must decide what specific books and materials she wants in each part of the room, and how they are to be initially arranged, on the basis of the kinds of learning activities she wants to foster.

It is not enough, for example, simply to create a math area filled with concrete mathematical materials. The teacher must think through her goals, deciding, at least in general terms, what kinds of mathematical experiences are appropriate—for these particular children at this particular time. This, in turn, means thinking through the kinds of activities that might interest the children, e.g., counting, measuring, weighing; the kinds of materials that are likely to foster these activities; and the way the materials should be arranged. If the math area is to permit a wide range of interests and accommodate a wide range of ability, the materials must provide for different activities and levels of complexity.

Hence the teacher must understand a great deal more about math in the informal classroom than in the conventional classroom where, if need be, she can simply stay one or two lessons ahead of the children. That means a lot more planning, which means a lot more thinking about math—and about children. If, for example, she is going to place Cuisenaire rods in the math area, she has to understand the various ways in which the rods can be used; if she is going to put out "attribute

*blocks," she has to understand how they can be used. But at the same
time, the teacher also has to learn to regard even the most structured
materials as fair game for unexpected and quite unorthodox uses. For
if children are encouraged to explore on their own and to ask their
own questions, they may use conventional materials in quite unconventional ways. And these novel uses may lead to learning even more
directly or effectively than the expected ones.*

1. The Triangular Relationship
of Teacher, Student, and Materials

*The teaching-learning process of the open classroom can be understood
best in terms of a triangular relationship, consisting of the child, the
teacher, and the materials of learning, Professor David Hawkins of the
University of Colorado argues in this widely reprinted and influential
paper. These three points correspond to Martin Buber's "I," "Thou,"
and "it"; as the child (I) becomes involved with the concrete materials
(it), the teacher shares his involvement, so that it becomes "we" confronting "it."*

*The presence of concrete materials—what the English refer to by the
technical term of "stuff"—makes it easier for teacher and child to form
the triangular relationship, Hawkins argues. In part, this is because some
children are better able to develop relationships if they can deal first
with the inanimate world. In good measure, however, it is because
involvement with materials helps teacher and child come alive for each
other, and makes it possible for them to communicate on a new level
and with a new dignity.*

*A philosopher and scientist, David Hawkins became interested in open
education during his tenure as director of the Elementary Science Study.
As he wrote in the Foreword to* The ESS Reader, *"We who have been
involved in this study of science and children have ourselves been
changed in the process—in some way not easy to voice, we have been
liberated." In part, the liberation came from the discovery that it was
impossible to improve the teaching of science in the elementary school
without improving, and radically changing, the nature of the teaching
process itself, a process that has led Hawkins, together with his wife,
Frances Pockman Hawkins, herself a gifted teacher of young children,
to spend several long periods studying, and for a time, teaching in, informal English nursery and primary schools. David Hawkins is now professor of philosophy at the University of Colorado and Director of the
Mountain View Center for Environmental Education, an advisory
center which provides workshops in open education and also works*

with teachers in their classrooms. The paper that follows was originally delivered to a residential workshop attended by teachers from the Leicestershire (England) schools.

I want to talk about children's understanding in the context of a proper education, more specifically of a good school, for the most fruitful way to understand the evolution of children's mental development is from the point of view of a working teacher. My topic therefore is the relation between the teacher and the child and a third thing in the picture that has to be there and that completes the triangle.

This is a relation that's been much talked about, but truncated too often. People have made analogies between the teacher-child relationship and many other sorts of relationships. For example, in olden times people said, "What this child needs is good hard work and discipline," and that sounds rather like a parent-child relationship, doesn't it? Or they said, more recently, "The child needs love." That also sounds rather like a parent-child relationship. I'm sure that neither of these statements is completely false, but it seems to me they're both very unsatisfactory and that the relationship between the teacher and the child is something quite unique that isn't exactly paralleled by any other kind of human relationship. It's interesting to explore a little bit what is involved in this relationship.

I know one rather good teacher who says he doesn't like children. He says this, I'm sure, with a rather special meaning of the word "like." He doesn't like children to be bewildered, at loose ends, not learning, and therefore he tries to get them over this as soon as possible. I mention him because I think the attitude of love, which is the parental attitude, isn't really the appropriate one. Perhaps the word "respect" might be more appropriate. I don't want to deny a very important element of affection for children in the make-up of good teachers, but the essence of the relationship is not that. It is a personal relationship, but it's not that kind of personal relationship. I want to talk about this in the context of the kind of thing we've been investigating in recent years, in the context of a kind of schooling which we are interested in exploring further, marked by the more frequent and more abundant use of concrete materials by children in schools, *and* by their greater freedom of choice within this enriched world. I'd like to talk

From David Hawkins, "I, Thou, It," *Mathematics Teaching,* The Journal of the British Association of Teachers of Mathematics, No. 46, Spring 1969.

about how the third corner of the triangle affects the relations between
the other two corners, how the "It" enters into the pattern of mutual
interest and exchange between the teacher and the child. Being an in-
curable academic philosopher, I'd like to start on a very large scale
and talk about human beings—of which children are presumably a
rather typical example. . . .

Children are members of the same species as adults, really, but
they are also quite a distinct sub-species and we want to be careful
about not exaggerating the differences and not forgetting them, either.
It seems to me clear that there are many complicated, difficult things
they learn, or hope to learn, and such learning occurs in an environment
where there are other human beings who serve, so to speak, as a part
of the learning process. Long before there were such things as schools,
which are rather recent institutions in the history of our kind, there
were teachers. There were adults who lived in the village and who
responded to the signals that children know very well how to emit in
order to get attention from adults. These adults managed quite spontaneously, and without benefit of the theory of instruction, to be
teachers. I really need a kind of electronic analogy here for what goes
on in a child's mind. If you think of circuits that have to be completed,
things go out along one bundle of channels, something happens, and
signals come back along another bundle of channels, and there's some
sort of feedback involved. Children are not always able to sort all of this
feedback for themselves. The adult's function, in the child's learning,
is to provide a kind of external loop, to provide a selective feedback.
The child's involvement gets some response from an adult and this
in turn is made available to the child. The child is learning about himself through his joint effects on the non-human *and* the human world
around him.

The function of the teacher, then, is to respond diagnostically and
helpfully to a child's behavior, to make what he considers to be an
appropriate response, a response which the child needs to complete the
process he's engaged in at a given moment. Now, this function of the
teacher isn't going to go on forever: it's going to terminate at some
time in the future. What we can say, I think, and what we clearly ought
to provide for, is that the child should learn how to internalize the
function which the adult has been providing. So, in a sense you become
educated when you become your own teacher. If being educated meant
no longer needing a teacher—a definition I would recommend—it would
mean that you had been presented with models of teaching, or people
playing this external role, and that you had learned how the role was
played and how to play it for yourself. At that point you would declare
your independence of instruction as such and you would be your own

teacher. What we all hope, of course, is that as the formal, institutional part of education is finished its most conspicuous and valuable product will be seen to be the child's ability to educate himself. If this doesn't happen, it doesn't make sense to say that the processes we try to initiate in school are going to be carried on when people leave school.

The image I want, then, is really the image Shakespeare is working with. You grow as a human being by the incorporation of conjoint information from the natural world and of things which only other human beings are able to provide for in your education. I sometimes think that working in the style we like to work in—which is much farther along in English Primary Schools, I'm sorry to say, than in American schools —we forget the unique importance of the human role. We tend to say "Oh well, if children just have a good, rich, manipulable and responsive environment then everything will take care of itself." When you visit a class which is operating in this way, with a teacher who has a good bag of tricks, you're often impressed that the teacher doesn't seem to be very necessary. You know, he can leave the room and nobody notices it. If *you* don't have that bag of tricks, and know the difficulties, you always rather marvel at what goes into it. After everything is accomplished it all looks as though it's very spontaneous. But of course that's a very dangerous illusion. It's true only in those frequent periods when children don't need the external loop. When they do sometimes need it and there's no one around to contribute the adult resonance, then they're not always able to carry on the process of investigation, of inquiry and exploration, of learning, because they need help over a hump that they can't get over through their own resources. If help isn't available the process will taper off, and that particular episode, at least, will have failed to accomplish what it otherwise might have.

Now, I'm speaking as one very much in favor of richness and diversity in the environment, and of teaching which allows a group of children to diversify their activities and which—far more than we usually think proper—keeps out of their hair. What seems very clear to me—and I think this is a descriptive, factual statement, not praising or blaming— is that if you operate a school—as we in America almost entirely do— in such a style that the children are rather passively sitting in neat rows and columns and manipulating you into believing that they're being attentive because they're not making any trouble, then you won't get very much information about them. Not getting much information about them you won't be a very good diagnostician of what they need. Not being a good diagnostician, you will be a poor teacher. The child's overt involvement in a rather self-directed way, using the big muscles and not just the small ones, is most important to the teacher in providing an input of information wide in range and variety. It is input which potentially has much more heft than what you can possibly get from the merely verbal or written responses of a child to questions put to him or tasks set for him.

I think this is fairly obvious. It doesn't say that you *will* but that you *can* get more significant diagnostic information about children, and can refine your behavior as a teacher far beyond the point of what's possible if every child is being made to perform in a rather uniform pattern. But of course you will not get the information, or will not use it, if you are just sweetly permissive and limp, if you don't provide the external feedback loop when you think it is needed. We know children never do behave uniformly even when they're supposed to. When it appears they are it's just because they've learned the trick of pleasing you—or displeasing you if they're all on strike!—and then you aren't able to make the needed discrimination. But I think the real importance of teacher intervention comes out in situations where a child is not involved by very many things, is not responsive to anything you provide. That child may be a problem, the child who doesn't give you much information, who is tight and constrained, often called "good." But you get little suggestions or inklings of interest and involvement, you get hunches about what might prove absorbing to him. If you have enough of these hunches and enough persistence you find *something* that works and when you do you have laid the basis for a new relationship between yourself and that child, and this is the thing that is really important. The rest is good and important and not too hard to describe: when children are being diverse in what they're doing, selective in what they're doing; when you're giving them genuine alternatives about what they will do, then you are bound to get much more knowledge of them from reading the language of their behavior. Of course, you certainly aren't going to succeed all the time with every child in this diagnostic and planning process. There are going to be several misses for every hit, but you just say "Well, let's keep on missing and the more we miss the more we'll hit." The importance of this in the "I-Thou" relationship between the teacher and the child is that the child learns something about the adult which we can describe with words like "confidence," "trust" and "respect." You have done something for the child which he could not do for himself, and he knows it. He's gotten going on something new which has proved engrossing to him. If he thus learns that he has the competence to do something that he didn't know he had, then you have been a very crucial figure in his life. You have provided that external loop, that external feedback, which he couldn't provide for himself, and he values this.

What is the feeling you have toward a person who does this for you? It needn't be what we call love, but it certainly *is* what we call respect. Another person is valued because he is uniquely useful to you in helping you on with your own life. "Love" is, perhaps, a perfectly good word, too, but it has a great variety of meanings and has been vulgarized, not least by psychological theory.

With different children the relationship which develops will be different just because they are different children. When *you* give a child a range from which to make choices, *he* then gives you the basis for deciding what should be done next, what the provisioning should be for him, and that is *your* decision, it's dependent on *your* goals, it's something *you* are responsible for—not in an authoritarian way but you do have to make a decision and it's your decision, not the child's. If it's a decision to let him alone you are just as responsible for it as if it's a decision to intervene.

The investment in the child's life that is made in this way by the adult, the teacher in this case, is something which adds to and in a way transforms the interest which the child develops spontaneously. If as sometimes happens a child gets particularly interested by a variation on a soap bubble theme which you've already given him, you can just happen to put nearby some other things that might not at first seem related to soap bubbles—some geometrical wire cubes, tetrahedra, helices, and wire with a soldering iron. The resulting soap films are almost bound to catch the fancy of many human beings, including children. What has it got? Well, it's got a certain formal geometrical elegance, it's got color: when you look at the films in the right kind of light you see all those marvellous interference colors. Such a trap is bristling with invitations and questions. Some children will sample it and walk on; but some will be hooked by it, will get very involved with it. Now, this kind of involvement is terribly important, I think. It's aesthetic, or it's mathematical, or it's scientific. It's all of these potentially, and none of them exclusively. The teacher has made possible this relation between "It" and the child or the child and "It," even if this is just by having "It" in the room; and for the child even this brings a third person, the teacher as a person, a Thou, into the picture. For the child this is not merely something which is fun to play with, which is exciting and colorful and has associations with many other sorts of things in his experience: it's also a basis for communication with the teacher on a new level, and with a new dignity.

Until the child is going on his own the teacher can't treat him as a person who is going on his own, cannot let him be mirrored there, where he may see himself as investigator or craftsman. Until he is an autonomous human being who is thinking his own thoughts and making his own unique, individual kinds of self-expression out of them, there isn't anything for the teacher to respect. So the first act in teaching, it seems to me, the first goal, necessary to all others, is to encourage this kind of engrossment. Then the child comes alive for the teacher as well as the teacher for the child. They have a common engrossment for discussion, they are involved together in the world.

I had always been awkward in certain kinds of situations with young children, I'm sorry to say. I didn't know them very well and I'd sort of forgotten that I'd once been one, as we mostly do. I remember being very impressed by the way some people, in an encounter with a young child, would seem automatically to gain acceptance while other people, in apparently very friendly encounters with the same child, would produce real withdrawal and, if they persisted, fear and even terror. Such was the well-meaning adult who wanted to befriend the child, I and Thou, in a vacuum. It's traumatic, and I think we all know what it feels like. I came to realize, I learned with a good teacher, that one of the very important factors in this kind of situation is that there be some third thing which is of interest to the child and to the adult, in which they can join in outward projection. Only this creates a possible stable bond of communication, of shared concern.

My most self-conscious experience of this kind of thing was when a few years ago I found myself with two very small tykes who had gone with me and my wife to the hospital to get their mother, who had just had a third baby. The father was ill and there was already some anxiety. With Frances Hawkins they were fine, indeed it was she who had earlier been *my* teacher in this art. They were perfectly happy with us two but they'd never been with me alone. Suddenly the nurse announced in a firm voice that children could not go beyond this point, so my wife had to go in and I had to stay. It was one of those moments when you could have had a fairly lively scene on your hands. Not being an adept I thought quite consciously of the triangular principle. There had to be some third thing that wasn't "I" and the two children, otherwise we were all going to be laid waste. And there wasn't anything! I looked around and there were bare walls, a bare hospital corridor. But on one wall there was a collection of photographs of some recent banquet that had been given for a donor, so in desperation I just picked them up, rushed over to it, and said "Look!" That's a sort of confession, because I'm sure many of you would know how to handle this kind of situation. For me it was a great triumph and it was a demonstration, if an oddly mechanical one, of a consciously held principle. And it worked.

It seems to me that this kind of episode, which is in itself trivial and superficial, can symbolize a lot that is important in terms of the teacher-child relationship, namely, the common interest, the common involvement in subject-matter. Now of course, you never really deceive children in important matters, so this interest can't long be feigned, as it was in my story. If you don't find something interesting, and try to feign an interest you don't have, the investment won't last. But if there is that common interest it may occur. You need to be capable of noticing what the child's eyes notice and capable of interpreting the words and acts by which he tries to communicate with you; it may not be in adult English, and the reception of it requires experience and close attention.

Here's a long transparent corked plastic tube with two liquids in it. Many years ago I would have thought that this was rather trivial, rather silly, and would have said "What's there to be learned from that?" To tell you the truth, I honestly don't know. We can use a lot of words in physics that have something to do with it: or we can talk about color and motion and other things of some aesthetic importance. By now I've seen enough children involved in this particular curious little thing to be quite convinced that there's a great deal in it—and I don't mean just this particular tube but all sorts of artifacts and things from the natural world. It can serve as an extraordinary kind of bond. The child is in some sense functioning to incorporate the world: he's trying to assimilate his environment. This includes his social environment, of course, but it also includes the inanimate environment, it also includes the resources of the daily world around him, which he's capable of seeing with far fresher eyes than ours, for the most part. The richer is this adult-provided contact, therefore, the more firm is the bond that is established between the human beings who are involved.

Finally, I'd like to mention something which is perhaps of special interest and which takes me into psychological theory. It has to do with how human beings come to attain the sense of objectivity, the sense of reality, with how they come to get a stable, reliable vision of the world around them and how, without losing their capacity for fantasy they are able to make clear discriminations between what they know, what they have learned, what they merely believe, what they imagine, and so on. It has to do with how they are able to get straight the orders and kinds of belief and credibility. This is one of the most important accomplishments of a human being.

It seems to me that for some children and not for others this sense of fitting things together into a coherent whole, into a coherent pattern, comes first mostly in terms of their relations with the human world, while for other children it comes first mostly in their relations with the inanimate world.

The capacity for synthesis, for building a stable framework within which many episodes of experience can be put together coherently, comes with the transition from artistic behavior to exploratory behavior. The first is guided by a schedule which is surely inborn, and is connected with satisfaction of definite infant needs. The second has a different style, and is not purposive in the same way, not aimed at a predetermined end-state. Its satisfaction, its reinforcement as a way of functioning, comes along the way and not at the end; in competence acquired, not in satiation. Both modes of behavior are elaborated through experience, but exploratory behavior is not bound and limited by a schedule of needs which must, to begin with, have the highest priority. A child's first major synthetic achievements in exploratory learning may come in relation to the human world, but they may come equally, and perhaps more readily, in his exploration of the things of his surrounding physical environment, and of their responsiveness to his testing and trying. In either case, or so it seems to me, the exploratory motivation, and its reinforcement, is of a different kind than the libidinous, aimed as the latter is at incorporation and possession. And the child's development will be limited and distorted if it does not, by turns, explore *both* the personal and the non-personal aspects of his environment; but explore them, not exploit them for a known end. Most psychologists, in my reading and my more extensive arguing with them, tend to say that at the root of human motivation lies an interest in human things, in persons. They say that the fundamental dynamics of the child's relation to the rest of the world as he grows up stem from his relation to his mother, his relation to other close figures around him, and that these will be the impelling forces in his life. It is, of course, in such terms that Freud built up his whole systematic theory and although perhaps there aren't many very orthodox Freudians around nowadays this key feature of the theory persists, I think—the feeling that the only important formative things in life are other human beings. And if people pay attention to the non-human world—it may include animals and plants as well as the physical environment, enriched to contain bubble tubes and soap film—one tends to trace this to some desire to exploit the human world: for example, the child does something because he thinks it pleases you or because he thinks it displeases you or because he's escaping you or because he wants wholeheartedly to do what he's doing. In other words, there's been a systematic tendency to devalue children's thing-oriented interests as against their person-oriented interest. All I would like to say is that I think the interest in *things* is a perfectly real, perfectly independent and autonomous interest which is there just as genuinely as the interest in persons is there in young children. And some children are *only* able to develop humanly by first coming to grips in an exploratory and involved way with the inanimate world.

We've certainly seen examples of children who very early have gotten onto the tricks which I suppose in some sense babies are born with but which infants can elaborate as they grow older, tricks for getting what you want from persons by planning how you behave. It's exploiting, and some very young children are very skilful at this. If you know such children as a teacher you'll know they're smarter than you are because they've put a lot more investment into this kind of thing than you have. You have to be very shrewd to cope with them. One thing such a child cannot do is to get wholeheartedly involved in anything else; he has to be watching all the time to see what the adults and the other children think about it. But if you can set enough traps for him, if you can keep exposing him to temptations, if he sees other children involved and not paying any attention to the teacher, he's left out in the cold. So the temptations of bubbles or clay or sand or whatever it is are reinforced by the fact that other children aren't playing his kind of game. If such a child once forgets his game, because he *does* get involved in shaping some inanimate raw material, in something that's just there to be explored, played with, investigated, tried out, then he has had an experience which is liberating, that can free him from the kind of game-playing which he's gotten so expert at. He comes, after all, from a species that is called *homo faber*. If he doesn't get free of manipulating persons somewhere in his life, that life is going to be a sad one. In the extreme case perhaps it will even be a psychotic one. Children of this extreme sort are a special case but, being extreme, in a way they tell you a lot about what is involved in the three-cornered relationship of my title.

One final remark. It seems to me that many of us, whether our background was in science or not, have learned something about ourselves from working with children in this way that we've begun to explore. We've begun to see the things of the physical and biological world through children's eyes rather more than we were able to before, and have discovered and enjoyed a lot that is there that we were not aware of before. We don't any longer feel satisfied with the kind of adult grasp that we had of the very subject matter that we've been teaching; we find it more problematic, more full of surprises, and less and less a matter of the textbook order.

One of the nicest stories of this kind that I know comes from a young physicist who was very learned and very technical. He had just gotten his Ph.D. and, you know, he understood everything. (The Ph.D. is called by a friend of mine "The certificate of omniscience!") My wife was asking him to explain something to her about two coupled pendulums. He said "Well, now you can see that there's a conservation of . . . Well, there's really a conservation of angle here." She looked at him. "Well, you see, in the transfer of energy from one pendulum to the other there is . . ." and so on and so on. And she said "No, I don't mean that. I want you to notice *this* and tell me what's happening." Finally he looked at the pendulums and he saw what she was asking. He looked at *it,* and he looked at *her,* and he grinned and said, "Well, I know the right words but I don't understand it either." This confession, wrung from a potential teacher, I've always valued very much. It proves that we're all in *it* together.

2. The Nature of Choice

A rich supply of materials in a classroom makes it possible for children to exercise their innate capacity for choice, Frances Hawkins argues, and so encourages them to take a large part in the design of their own learning. But the use of materials affects teachers' choices—and learning—too. The teacher has to choose at two levels: in the selection of the materials to be placed in the classroom; and more subtly, at the level of teaching itself, in choosing whether or when or how to intervene. To make the latter kind of choice well, the teacher has to learn about the children by studying the kinds of choices they make.

This selection comes from The Logic of Action, *Frances Hawkins' exquisitely sensitive account of her work with a group of six deaf children in an inner-city slum school. The book is filled with illuminating insights into the nature of teaching, learning, and childhood. Mrs. Hawkins is now a staff member of the Mountain View Center for Environmental Education in Boulder, Colorado.*

There is, then, no difference in kind between verbal logic and the logic inherent in the co-ordination of actions, but the logic of actions lies deeper down and is more primitive; it develops more quickly and overcomes more rapidly the difficulties it meets, but they are the same difficulties of decentration as those that make their appearance later on the verbal plane.—Jean Piaget, *Studies in Education; First Years in School,* published for The Institute of Education, University of London, by Evans Bros. Ltd., London, 1963.

There are six stories recorded in these pages, but they rely on translation from the originals—which were told in the language of action. To the infant of our species this is a universal language. But for these particular four-year-olds it was still their only means of communicating; they are deaf. Through the misfortune of deafness rather than by design, therefore, we have before us for study some matters of learning and communication which involve only the language of action. Of necessity these are heavier with logic and richer than studies assisted and diluted by the speech of children who hear.

From Frances Pockman Hawkins, *The Logic of Action: From a Teacher's Notebook* (Boulder, Colo.: Elementary Science Advisory Center, 1969), pp. 3–5, 13, 21, 26–28.

Among those who hear, beginning in their earliest days, the universal language of action is interwoven with the second language which is spoken. From reliance on the second language most of us have lost our ability to enact or to easily comprehend the first. But not all of us have lost it, and none beyond recovery. Marcel Marceau creates poetry for us with no words. For a physicist friend of mine, watching that mime's enactment of a man climbing up five flights of stairs with his arms full was a short treatise on the physics of human moton: of balance, of muscle action, of momentum transferred and energy spent.

Some of us must keep and add to our understanding of the early action-language for more practical, though not less interesting, reasons. The loss of it is in turn a kind of deafness, an adult disability in work with all children, but an obvious and absolute loss in work with children in preschool or first grade who vary so in their ability to speak. This ability cannot be equated with competence of mind. The two are related but there are some nice exceptions to the fashionable belief that they are the same.

I speak of the language of action in this study for another reason: because it is also, and almost synonymously, the language of choice. We choose as we act, we act as we choose. The account of these six children is one of manifold encounters with a planned but unprogrammed environment, and of their choices within it. The restrictions which circumstances put on us affected planning and the range of materials we could bring and are described in the days reported here. These notes and observations illustrate, and perhaps help to elaborate, an essential principle of learning: that given a rich environment—with open-ended "raw" materials—children can be encouraged and trusted to take a large part in the design of their own learning, and that with this encouragement and trust they can learn well.

From my own years of work with children (from ages three to about nine) I have found that this principle of choice has a far wider and more massive support than the present study provides. Yet I do not underestimate the contribution these six deaf children—in less than two score hours—have made to my understanding and the extension of it. The quality of time cannot be measured by the clock's hands. Who among us—teacher, poet, analyst, lover, physicist, or child damming a stream of water in gutter or gully—does not understand something of time's perversity? The history of these six is very intense in places, then slow and almost becalmed in between. Work with children that reflects their tempo is often this way; but through these mornings the richness of our nonverbal communication had to be the touchstone, and that makes the rhythm more conspicuous.

Others than those who teach are concerned with the way in which learning is coupled to choice, active choice. Philosophers, psychologists, and therapists bring special insights which those of us in schools can use; but it is a teacher who must provide the materials from which choices are to be made in a classroom. Later, when a child is less dependent upon his immediate environment for learning, he can better survive a narrow classroom, though why he should have to is yet another issue. . . .

. . . Just how much and what a teacher should know in advance about the children in her class is a matter of disagreement in the field. I prefer to be told little, to be forced to observe much. Far from implying that I do not value a child's out-of-school life, this preference means that I do not trust the effect of an information filter of the sort created by others' observations and evaluations, on my own early analysis.

What concerns me as a teacher is the child's behavior as it reflects his anxieties and joys; his physical posture, energy, and health; his choices and refusals; his habits and humor. To get so wide a picture of a child outside his home requires a classroom rich in challenge and variety with a climate of probing, trying, weighing. If this cumulative information proves inadequate for me to provide well for a child, *then* I must seek help from a parent, a social worker, or a therapist. In this spirit then, let me provide only brief preliminary information for the readers of this report. . . .

. . . In their programming for young children neophytes commonly see their role as either-or: either completely in control, or completely withdrawn. It takes time and experience to find a more natural way of stepping in and out. That kind of detail cannot be laid out in advance . . .

. . . In planning for this first working, but still essentially diagnostic, morning, therefore, I wanted to increase the input. I asked myself how best to tap the children's *existing* energies and innovative powers for using beginning language, and how to find new concepts for their wider learning, separate from words but readied for verbal expression. That was the general aim. In designing the morning I was especially conscious of two sorts of conditions that are always necessary in competent teaching.

In the Preface I speak of the principle of choice as it contributes to learning when there is richness in the environment and children are using well their innate capacities for choice. The first condition is met by providing materials from which children make choices. And this being school, there is a corollary about teachers' choices and teachers' learning. In order to learn about the children a teacher must choose at two levels: first, in the selection of materials to be provided and then, more subtly, at the level of teaching. A teacher must make choices as to whether, when, and how to intervene in the learning process when it is not going well and when it is going very well indeed. Thus, to meet the second condition a teacher must *plan to learn* about the children through *their* choices and so begin to acquire specific content and definition, from each child, for the variables of *significant* choice and quality of involvement. It is only through such learning, in turn, that a teacher can modify initial goals and materials or intervene successfully to enhance the ongoing process. The ability to expedite learning depends upon how fast and accurately a teacher learns to assess and analyze children's individual patterns, strengths, and needs.

Let me speak first of my own need to know. I had formed some strong impressions about these children and the narrow range of their response to school. But it tempers audacity to enter, as I was doing, a field unfamiliar though closely related to one's own. Accepting gross differences around the fact of deafness, I aimed at the identification of likenesses between these children and their hearing cousins, and then again at the uncovering of differences (over and above individual variations) in their ways of being alike. I needed to test my first conclusions, and refine them. I needed more samplings and soundings from the children themselves, at work, and more thinking about these observations.

Both for these reasons of my own, and because the narrowed channels for receiving would require from me a greater input planned in greater detail than beginnings usually need to be, I selected carefully from materials whose potentialities I had tested pretty well in the past, and extrapolated in certain areas for these children. Local circumstances also affected the choice. We traveled some distance to the school and had to carry our materials each time. Any school innovator will realize that there was also the problem of "keeping school property clean and neat." I did not want to put Miss M. in the position of having to defend our messy junk or store it; so I brought it and took it back, a car trunk full each time. This eliminated much—sand, for example, and growing things.

But now to the children's needs. Careful planning must avoid the trap of narrowness. To program learning often means to hamper it by restricting children to the stereotyped anticipations of the programmer. With four- and five-year-olds of normal hearing our schools tend to do this, to restrict the curriculum or weight it with puzzles that demand the "right" answer, with questions that ask the child to guess what is meant, with activities that fail to invite innovation.

Not long before my Fillmore experience I had observed a nursery school where bells rang, lights flashed, and other forms of strong praise exuded to reinforce the right performance in a context of present goals and predigested content. So I was on guard and cautioned myself not to straighten and confine the offering but to broaden it, to build in an initial multiplicity—and to trip some laughter. The fact that one tries to provide this multiplicity in teaching "normal" children only underlined the proposition that here it would be indispensable.

Such a multiplicity of things to do, things important to children, can have a kind of thematic unity centered around related phenomena. This is one way of planning for the youngest, but it is not lesson planning.

I want to be very clear about this distinction, in view of the loose and conventional use of such words as "structured" and "unstructured," "authoritarian" and "laissez faire." These terms may be useful in specific cases to suggest something measurable on a linear scale, but they only confuse the description of complex settings where learning, not parroting, is the focus for young children. How a child selects and uses material from the initial provisioning depends upon him and upon his unique store of experience. His behavior expresses his present *and developing* resources and concomitantly increases my understanding of how and what to plan with and for him.

This plan is thus a joint and dynamic kind of product, better seen *as a plan in retrospect than in prospect*. But the teacher must assume with care the first responsibility—to select well—in order that the child can accept and exercise his own responsibility. It is in this way, in this web of activity, that the two kinds of conditions for good teaching and learning can both be satisfied. . . .

Most but not all of the children were unable to use these open-ended materials except in a stereotyped or directly imitative way today. I began to judge such behavior compulsive. Ordinarily when material responds to a child's manipulation, evidencing its physical properties, the child responds in turn to these phenomena, and, as I have said, the character of this response is often of critical importance for a teacher. If the response is merely the next link in a chain of behavior already become habitual, then there is little evidence of deep involvement or discrimination. If the response is merely imitative, one judges that attention lies elsewhere than on the material at hand, and again any evidence of discrimination or learning is lacking.

Sometimes the particular thing chosen by a child is not after all his cup of tea, and he seems temporarily to lose the ability to make a search for what will be his. Perhaps he has had troubles at home. In any event something interferes with the coupling between child and material, which we know he has great capacity for. A teacher has here a unique role. It is not the role of mother or therapist or peer, but that of one who values learner and learning professionally and wants to help such a child regain and develop his capacity to probe and test, to summon his sleeping resources of imagery, control, and understanding—in short, to learn, not memorize. In this process home troubles can recede because learning is sustaining in its own way. And here there is at least one tangible, sure-fire aid: if the adult in the situation is himself simultaneously and genuinely exploring the material (and not just observing how the child uses it) then a bridge may be started to the child's reinvolvement. This is as valid a reason as any I know for having in a classroom enough materials with challenging possibilities. Is it utopian to propose that our teachers be permitted and expected to learn, too? I have known teachers who first developed interests in science, at their own level, because of their perception of children's needs. . . .

It is clear that in introducing a totally new activity a decision is made by the teacher about how much and what kind of structure will accompany it. Let me use as an example my thinking about introducing food color for these children. The cluster of materials here, while including water as something known and recently enjoyed, is still inherently new to most children and esthetically vivid. The road to chaos can be short. It has been my experience that there is more enjoyment and exploration if the introduction of food color is "structured." On this particular morning, when I decided to turn to the back table where the food color and related materials were waiting, I made another judgement. A time for quieter activity with teacher involved was needed. Had the early part of the morning followed another kind of pattern, I might have cancelled these plans. On a Monday morning, for example, after a cold and confining weekend, I have found children so deeply in need of self-direction in familiar paths, with adults far in the background, that I have put away "structured" plans. Guidance at such times courts trouble, competes with needs of higher priority, and solidifies a reaction of wandering attention.

3. Communications With, and Through, Materials

In thinking about the subtleties of when to intervene, Anthony Kallet suggests, teachers may find it helpful to conceive of the interaction between a child and some material as a kind of conversation or dialogue. Just as a sensitive person would not think of barging into a conversation between two other people without first listening to what is being discussed, reconstructing something of what has gone before, and considering how to make his own remarks useful, so a teacher needs to size up the "dialogue" a child has been having with his materials before intervening. The teacher also needs to know what it feels like to work with materials, which means undergoing the actual experience himself. "A person who is not used to handling materials in a free way," Dr. Kallet writes, "who is not used to listening to them, is not likely to be sensitive to the two-way communication between the child and the materials. He may readily enough see what the child is doing with the materials, but he is less likely to consider what the materials are suggesting to the child and what it feels like to engage in this kind of interaction."

Anthony Kallet is an American psychologist and teacher who spent several years in England as a member of the Advisory Centre for the Leicestershire schools. He is now a member of the staff of the Mountain View Center for Environmental Education.

While visiting an infant classroom recently, I spent a few minutes watching and working with six-year-old Karl. He was building a pyramid out of colored X blocks, which as their name suggests, are X-shaped blocks that interlock with one another in interesting ways. Karl's pyramid grew to be about seven or eight blocks wide at the base and perhaps six blocks high with the apex placed symmetrically at the top. When he had finished, there were still several blocks left, and, after some hesitation, he started another column up one side of the pyramid. This left the apex asymmetrically placed. After further thought Karl rearranged things so that symmetry was restored. He was obviously pleased with his construction.

After we had both admired it for a while, I asked Karl whether he had ever tried making the same structure and then taking a few blocks out to leave some X-shaped holes. He didn't understand my question, so I asked him to help me remove one of the blocks. The result left him wide-eyed with excitement, and he ran off to bring over the teacher to see the hole. I then helped him to remove five more blocks, and after each removal, he called over the teacher to view the result. My role was largely one of steadying the structure as Karl eased the blocks out. I could see him hesitate before each removal, and once or twice he apparently changed his mind as he contemplated the way the structure was put together. After one near-disaster, his intuition became excellent, and he was able to remove blocks that did not serve a vital structural function. When the pyramid finally fell, it was less because too many holes had been punched in it than because it was handled too roughly during a removal.

Watching and working with Karl and later talking with people about what I had seen, have led to a number of thoughts about the relationships between materials and their users, and between materials, their users, and an onlooker who may want to participate in what is happening. I want to present some of these thoughts, not as fully developed conclusions but as starting points for further exploration.

From Anthony Kallet, "Some Thoughts on Children and Materials," *Mathematics Teaching,* The Journal of the British Association of Teachers of Mathematics, No. 40, Autumn 1967. Reprinted in *Outlook* No. 6, Autumn 1972, Mountain View Center for Environmental Education.

It may be useful to think of a dialogue between a child and materials, accompanied by a second dialogue, or monologue, which the child carries on in his mind. No words need be uttered, although, especially with younger children, materials may provoke spoken commentary. At times no words may be involved at all, much of the "dialogue" being an interplay of images or unverbalized thoughts. But there surely is some sense in which materials "speak" to a user before, during, and after they are used. In some instances the user's actions prompt a response: if Karl placed a block insecurely, the structure wobbled or fell—a rather forthright kind of "No" or "Watch out." Sometimes materials seem to initiate the dialogue: the shape of the pyramid and the pile of unused blocks suggested to Karl a further addition to the structure. There was evidence of internal dialogue too. At times I felt quite certain, in the context, what possibilities Karl was considering, and I could then see which he tried. One can obviously never know for certain what another person is thinking, but where thought leads to choice and action, some fairly shrewd inferences can be made.

Thinking in terms of child-material and child-self conversations suggests a style of approach that might be useful to the onlooker who is interested in what is happening and wants to participate in it. Imagine that you are approaching two people talking about something that interests you and you want to join the conversation. If you are hopelessly obtuse, you will simply barge in, all elbows, and will often be confronted by thoroughly raised hackles. If you have some sensitivity, you will generally listen for a few minutes to find out what is being discussed, to reconstruct some of what has probably been said, and to consider how to make your own contribution relevant. You will try to judge in advance its effect on each speaker; you will try to put yourself in the position of each speaker and to anticipate his reactions. All of this sizing-up is normally done quickly and without much conscious thought. Seldom will it be carried out sequentially as I have outlined it here, but some such process of evaluating the existing situation and one's probable impact on it often does take place.

It seems to me possibly useful to make a fairly direct translation of this process to the child-materials situation in which an onlooker wants to participate. Looking at what is happening, one can often infer what has led to it. I could, for example, tell from the height of the pyramid when I first noticed it that Karl must have had a considerable number of "Yeses" from correctly placed blocks, and it was reasonable to assume, although I didn't put it in these terms at the time, that he was having a successful conversation with the blocks. I was thus prompted to suggest an extension that might prove challenging. I introduced an entirely new element, but at a time and in a way that seemed natural, because Karl's conversation with the blocks seemed to have reached a pause.

If I had felt that this was a pause following a series of failures, I might have suggested a different task or I might have refrained from intervening at all.

In order to join a conversation, you must obviously know what a conversation is about—not just the specific conversation at hand but conversation in general. You must know what it feels like to take part in a discussion. My analogy suggests that to join a child-material dialogue, one must know what it feels like to work with materials. It will also help, of course, if one remembers what is feels like to be a child. If you are used to confronting new materials, this shouldn't be too hard! A person who is not used to listening to them is not likely to be sensitive to the two-way communication between the child and the materials. He may readily enough see what the child is doing with the materials, but he is less likely to consider what the materials are suggesting to the child and what it feels like to engage in this kind of interaction.

Just as conversation with other people is an active process, so communication with materials involves a user reaching out and taking meanings. It is not a passive waiting for something to happen but a probing for possibilities, and it depends to a considerable extent on what the user brings to the situation. A good teacher will have had a lot of experience with materials in general and perhaps with the specific ones the child is using, but he will rely on his own experience as a general guide to some possibilities, not as a limitation on what can be done. He should be aware that children approach materials with differing expectancies and competences and may receive from them quite different meanings and proceed in many different directions. Sometimes, because of his general or specific experience, the teacher will see connections between uses the child sees as separate, and his contribution to the dialogue may be to point out some of the connections. This is, of course, often what a third party contributes to a conversation—a fresh view of the possible fitting together of old elements.

It may be useful to think of materials as having two different kinds of meanings, following the semanticists' approach to words. To use the awkward but well-established usage, words have both extensional and intensional meanings. Extensional meanings are those that can be agreed on, the dictionary definitions so to speak. Intensional meanings are the personal associations words come to have for individuals—and they differ from one person to another. Semanticists point out the danger of using words in a discussion and assuming that only extensional meanings are involved or that we understand fully other people's intensional meanings or that they are the same as ours.

In thinking of materials, the extensional meaning might correspond to the obvious use, the use originally intended for the materials, the use most people agree it has—blocks are to build with, paper is to paint on. In a classroom a wider range of agreed-upon uses may develop over a period of time as a result of what children and adults do, and these become new extensional meanings—blocks are also weights for balances, and paper can be rolled into logs and built with.

No matter how many uses are agreed upon, however, it is important to remember that a child at work with materials will probably have his own set of intensional meanings for them. Just as in conversation it is often important to bring into the open differing intensional meanings of words, so it may be an important part of a teacher's job to discover and to encourage the development and sharing of as many intensional meanings of materials as possible. In doing this the conversations of all may be enriched, and a silent dialogue between a child and materials may, in good time, lead to a pooling of what has been discovered.

Some materials seem richer than others in providing opportunities for a variety of intensional meanings to develop. Some objects have such a dominant built-in use that it is difficult to see what other uses or meanings might develop. Materials may differ in what can be called their transparency, the ease with which they can be seen into by someone approaching them for the first time. Some extremely rich materials may be quite opaque. To take music as an example, a piano seems more transparent than a violin because the keyboard invites the absolute beginner to take action and provides some satisfying results, whereas the strings of a violin require such specialized treatment that the beginner is not likely to achieve much satisfaction. There are often things a teacher can do to increase the initial transparency of materials and thus make it more likely that children will become involved with them.

Things are not people, and although I find the social analogy useful, it must not be allowed to obscure some of the differences between things and people. One important difference may be that things are more often seen as neutral, not as adversaries. That is, one's general approach to materials does not assume that they are trying to hide a meaning or a use, although there may be an infinite number of meanings and uses there to be discovered. In dealing with people, even with friendly people, such an assumption is not always safe. In human social situations one quickly learns to be alert to motives and to the possibility that things may not be intended as they are apparently offered. One may say to a person, "Why didn't you tell me that earlier?" With materials the reaction is more likely to be, "Why didn't I think of that before?" Perhaps another way of putting this is to say that whereas we *discover* the meanings of people, we *invent* the meanings of materials—although I'm sure that the distinction between discovery and invention is not always a clear one.

Finally, it is interesting to contrast the ways in which materials and people disagree or contradict. Materials disagree by failing to respond as one predicts or wishes. Instead of staying up, the improperly placed block falls down and thus communicates in no uncertain terms that something went wrong, that one didn't correctly understand its meaning in that situation. Whereas material may communicate "Something went wrong," people are much more likely to communicate the idea, "You are wrong." One might say that materials pass judgment only on a specific act or situation, while in many human relationships, there is at least an overtone of judgment of the doer of the deed, not just of the deed. It may be for this reason that children are often able to accept with equanimity the sudden collapse of a building they have been working on for twenty minutes, whereas the slightest social provocation may, on occasion, release torrents of tears. This is really a restatement of the fact that generally (and with many exceptions) materials—"nature"— are not seen as being "out to get you", whereas so often even friendly people play the game of oneupmanship. Another reason why teachers must themselves deal extensively with materials in the same spirit as will the children in their classes is that the perception of the neutrality of materials may be important as one observes and helps children who are using materials.

4. How to Equip a Classroom: The EDC Guidelines

While life undoubtedly is a good deal easier for teachers who have at their disposal the kind of budget that the U.S. Office of Education has made available to classrooms in the EDC Follow Through Program, large amounts of money are not necessary for open education. On the contrary, teachers can operate open classrooms successfully without any commercial materials at all.

Indeed, natural materials, homemade materials, and "junk" should form the bulk of any classroom environment, since they have a number of advantages apart from cost. For one thing, using everyday materials in the classroom helps break down the false dichotomy between school and the rest of life and substitutes a sense of continuity between them. For another, natural and homemade materials tend more often to permit multiple uses than commercial materials, which may inhibit both the teacher's and the children's imaginations. When the teacher, the students, and parents cooperate to supply and create natural and homemade materials, moreover, the classroom is more likely to reflect their interests and their ingenuity—and the students are more likely to feel that it is their room. And an abundance of noncommercial materials makes it easier for teacher and students to change the physical environment of the classroom from time to time to reflect their changing interests and activities.

The guidelines EDC has developed for schools participating in its Follow Through Program are useful for teachers anywhere, regardless of their budget, since most of what is included in the list of general equipment for the classroom can be acquired free or at relatively little cost. (The EDC equipment lists for specific curriculum areas will be shown in the relevant sections of Part Four, on curriculum.)

Some First Principles

Instructional aids and materials have no inherent power. A classroom can offer a rich material environment yet be sterile and lifeless. Materials —"stuff" in the broad sense—acquire value only as they are acted upon by children's and teachers' minds. Even such highly structured apparatus as Cuisenaire rods are, of themselves, powerless. They do not and cannot teach. Learning arises when children use such materials as aids to intellectual activity and as stimulants to feeling and imagination. Children and adults *invest* the materials with meaning; they literally *invent* multiple meanings, uses, and interpretations. By using their powers of mind and imagination children and teachers work transformations on inert materials and give them life.

Open classrooms *can* be successfully operated without *any* commercial materials. The natural materials, homemade materials, "junk" materials mentioned in the list have by far the widest application (you will find them repeated over and over again in almost every section) and are by far the most basic and essential part of the material environment.

Another priority is an abundance of really good books—for reference, for enjoyment, for stimulation, both at teacher and student levels.

The large list of commercial materials presented here is intended as a view of what is available; very few are absolutely necessary but we believe that teachers should have a choice so as to provide for the unique interests of their children in a way in which the teachers are comfortable. Please read carefully any introduction to a section so as to make the wisest use of the list.

Practical Implications

These philosophical realities have practical implications for the provisioning of the classroom environment and the use of this materials list.

From *Instructional Aids, Materials, and Supplies—Guidelines,* rev. 1972 (Newton, Mass.; Education Development Center, Follow Through Program. April, 1971). Reprinted by permission of Education Development Center, Inc.

1. Things which the children and their teacher bring to the environment, as an expression of their interest, are often more important than what the school provides. The enclosed list is no substitute for such natural and spontaneous enriching.
2. The physical environment of each classroom should be constantly changing to reflect the interests and activity of the children. No two classrooms will be alike.
3. There is no standard materials list for every classroom, but a wide variety of materials should be available to teachers so that they can quickly respond to the unfolding needs and interests of their children.
4. The attached list is neither complete nor final. Teachers will want to add to it, and so will we. From time to time revisions and supplements will be issued.

Specific Suggestions to Follow Through Directors*

1. Since it is impossible to anticipate the *special* needs of next year's classes it is important that each teacher reserve one third of the allotted amount of the materials and supplies budget for major purchases during the school year.
2. From that same materials and supplies budget approximately $100 per classroom should be kept in reserve for teachers to use as petty cash for smaller classroom needs during the school year.
3. The materials and supplies budget recommendation is as follows:

$1200 per classroom new to the program
600 per classroom already in the program

The breakdown for the materials and supplies budget might look like this:

---

* The figures recommended here were specifically developed for a federally funded program which provided resources above regular school budgets. They represent generous amounts, nice to have, but not necessary to start an open classroom program. In fact, the availability of ample supply budgets can result in overstocked rooms with many underused commercial items and few contributions from the teacher and children.

We do recommend strongly for any open education program:

1. Allocating a sum of $100 per classroom as a reserve petty cash fund for the teacher to spend during the year.
2. Reserving up to ⅓ of the money for purchase later in the year *if* that is possible. In most school systems all orders must be in early to assure any delivery.
3. Gradual introduction of materials into the room during the year.

We still believe that accessible material and supply centers and teacher participation in the process of ordering materials and supplies are vital.

(These are guidelines only and should be tempered to the individual needs of school and classroom and to the special needs of particular teachers.)

a) For a classroom new to the program
1) Materials and Supplies (including books) purchased in advance of school year $700
2) Materials and Supplies (including books) purchased during school year 400
3) Petty cash for use during the school year 100

Total $1200

b) For a classroom already in the program
1) Materials and Supplies (including books) purchased in advance of school year $300
2) Materials and Supplies (including books) purchased during school year 200
3) Petty cash for use during school year 100

Total $600

4. It is important that a readily accessible materials and supplies center be established so that teachers may conveniently examine and obtain materials for their classrooms. Such a center should facilitate the sharing of equipment and instructional aids.
5. It is essential that teachers be involved in the total process of selecting and ordering materials and supplies.

ADDRESSES OF SUPPLIERS

Alexander Steel Equipment Corp.
101 River Street
Waltham, Massachusetts 02154

Bell & Howell Company
Audio-Visual Products Division
7100 McCormick Road
Chicago, Illinois 60645

Brault-Bouthillier Ltd.
205 Laurier East
Montreal 14, Quebec
Canada

Cambosco Scientific Co.
342 Western Avenue
Boston, Massachusetts 02135

Childcraft Equipment Co., Inc.
155 East 23rd Street
New York, New York 10010

Community Playthings
Rifton
New York

Constructive Playthings
1040 East 85
Kansas City, Missouri 64131

Creative Playthings, Inc.
Princeton
New Jersey 08540

Cuisenaire Co. of America, Inc.
12 Church Street
New Rochelle, New York 10805

Economy 5 & 10
1730 Massachusetts Avenue
Cambridge, Massachusetts

Edmund Scientific Company
100 Edscorp Building
Barrington, New Jersey 08007

ETA Division
A. Daigger & Co.
159 West Kinzie
Chicago, Illinois 60610

Flex Products Corp.
445 Industrial Road
Carlstadt, New Jersey 07072

Funtastic, Inc.
Mail Order Division
5902 Farrington Ave.
Alexandria, Virginia 22304

James Galt & Son Ltd.
Export Division
Brookfield Road
Cheadle, Cheshire
England

J. L. Hammett Company
Hammett Place (195 Pearl Street)
Braintree, Massachusetts 02184

Herder & Herder
232 Madison Avenue
New York, New York 10016

LaPine Scientific Company
375 Chestnut Street
Norwood, New Jersey 07648

Liberty House
Box 3468
Jackson, Mississippi 39207

W. C. Long Co.
P.O. Box 311
Chatsworth, Georgia

Magnamusic—Baton
6394 Delmar Boulevard
St. Louis, Missouri 63130

McGraw-Hill Book Company
Webster Division
Manchester Road
Manchester, Missouri 63011

M-I Sales Company, Inc.
200 Fifth Avenue
New York, New York

Milton Bradley Company
P.O. Box 1581
Springfield, Mass. 01101

National Audubon Society
1130 Fifth Avenue
New York, New York 10028

National Products, Inc.
c/o Paul B. Segal
33 Bartlett Road
Randolph, Mass.

Parallel Mfg. Company
32 East 10th Street
New York, New York 10003

Peripole, Inc.
51-17 Rockaway Beach Blvd.
Far Rockaway, New York 11691

Philip & Tacey, Ltd.
69–79 Fulham High Street
London S.W. 6
England

A. E. Piggott Ltd.
All Saints Road, Bath Lane
Leicester LE3 5AB
England

Ranger Rick's Nature Club Services
381 West Center Street
Marion, Ohio 43302

Responsive Environments Corp.
(REC)
Learning Materials Division
200 Sylvan Avenue
Englewood Cliffs, New Jersey
07632

F. A. O. Schwarz
745 Fifth Avenue
New York, New York 10022

Scott Scientific Co.
Sigma Division
600 Fort Collins Industrial Park
P.O. Box 2121
Fort Collins, Colorado 80521

Selective Educational Equipment
(SEE), Inc.
3 Bridge Street
Newton, Massachusetts 02195

Shindana Toys
Div. of Operation Bootstrap, Inc.
6107 South Central Avenue
Los Angeles, California 90001

Taskmaster Ltd.
165–167 Clarendon Park Road
Leicester, England

Transparent Products Corporation
1727 West Pico Blvd.
Los Angeles, California 90015

Tri-State Plastic Molding Company
Box 337
Henderson, Kentucky

Tri-Wall Containers, Inc.
Educational Materials & Services
Division
One DuPont Street
Plainview, New York 11803

Ward's Natural Science Establishment
P.O. Box 1712
Rochester, New York 14603

Welch Scientific Company
7300 North Linder Avenue
Skokie, Illinois 60076

Western Printing Company
Racine
Wisconsin

Wollensak 3M Company
3M Center
St. Paul, Minnesota 55101

Workshop for Learning Things
5 Bridge St.
Watertown, Mass. 02172

Order British Books From:

British Book Centre
Fairview Park
Elmsford, New York 10523

GENERAL CLASSROOM EQUIPMENT

Elmer's glue
Rubber bands
Masonite scrap
Knives
Muffin tins
Pens
Magic markers
Grease pencils
Bowls
Buckets
C-clamp
Chicken wire
Erasers
Containers:
   plastic
   glass jars
   cans
   cartons
   bottles
   jello molds
Toothpicks

Wallpaper paste
Rubber cement
Paper
Pencils
Scrap:
   wood
   fabric
   metal
   plastic
Crayons
Paint
Plasticine
Plaster of Paris
String
Yarn
Wire
Rope
Ribbon
Thread
Straws
Cardboard

Bottle caps
Cups:
  flat
  conical
Seashells
Stones
Spools
Peas, beans, seeds
Macaroni
Nuts & bolts
Nails, Screws, washers
Hooks
Pipes
Tubes:
  plastic
  wood
  metal
  cardboard
Popsicle sticks
Tongue depressors
Pipe cleaners
Dowels
Canes
Broom handles
Sugar cubes
Plastic bags
Pegboard
Food:
  salt
  vinegar
  sugar
  flour
  cornstarch
Baking soda
Glycerin
Food coloring
Soap flakes
Rulers, tapemeasures, yardsticks
Measuring cups & spoons
Quarts
Egg timer
* Stop watch

Minute minder
Clock
Fabric:
  felt
  burlap
  cotton
An old bedspread
Lamp, tensor light
Candles
Dust pan & brush
* Oven—if possible
Knives
Hammers
Scissors
Screw drivers
Drill
Brace & bit
Matt knives
Wrenches
Sponges
Tape:
  scotch
  masking
  duct
Tri-wall
Fasteners:
  paper clips
  thumb tacks
  metal rings
  brass fasteners
  stapler, staples
Rubber bands
Sand paper
Unit blocks
Wax paper
Aluminum foil
* Hot plate
Workbench & vise
Paper cutter—one paper cutter per
      200 children is ample
* Long arm stapler

* Items to be shared by several classrooms.

SPECIAL EQUIPMENT

Note: Items may be shared by several classrooms.

ITEM	CATALOG REFERENCE	SUPPLIER	COST
Wollensak Tape Recorder	1520	Wollensak 3M Company	$184.95
Wollensak Listening Center	for 8 headphones	" " "	14.00
Wollensak Headphones		" " "	51.80
Language Master Unit		Bell & Howell	250.00
Headphones	#36407	" "	28.00 per set
Dual Headphone Adapter	#40720	" "	3.75
Blank Card Set 4″ x 14″	072481	" "	9.50 per set of 100 cards
Blank Card Set 3½″ x 9″	072475	" "	6.00 per set of 100 cards
Small electric stove for cooking			
Small kiln for pottery			
Transparent Plastic Storage Boxes			
6¹³⁄₁₆ x 3¹³⁄₁₆ x 1⅝	82	Tri-State Plastic	30.00/100
7⅜ x 5⁵⁄₁₆ x 3⁵⁄₁₆	C69	" "	42.75/100
10⅜ x 7⁹⁄₁₆ x 3¾	195F	" "	100.00/100
Cardboard Storage Trays (order in lots of 100)			
2″ x 12″		Alexander Steel Equip.	12.00/100
4″ x 12″		" " "	14.00/100
6″ x 12″		" " "	16.00/100
8″ x 12″		" " "	20.00/100
12″ x 12″		" " "	22.00/100
Tri-Wall Cardboard			
42″ x 54″		Tri-Wall Containers	2.41/sheet*
(minimum order 20)			1.34/sheet for 100 or more
4′ x 5′		" "	1.69/sheet
(minimum order 100)			
4′ x 6′		" "	2.06/sheet
(minimum order 100)			
4′ x 8′		" "	2.86/sheet
(minimum order 100)			
		(subject to a plus or minus 10% production run)	
		(prices subject to change without notice)	
Hot Plate	27–92	Cambosco	5.25
Portable Cassette Tape Recorder		Sony's is the best, sells for 99.50; there are many cheaper models.	
Polaroid camera			
Playframe	XSEEPF	SEE	78.00
Printing Press:		Brault-Bouthillier Ltd.	
Presse a volet 13, 5 x 21 materiel complementaire A ½ police script, type 18 no. 1			117.15†
extra ½ police of type			12.80*
Styrofoam storage & display trays (12 compartments)	P-80, 090	Edmund	4.98/6
Record Player		buy locally to suit classroom's or school's needs	

* Price includes freight on 42″ x 54″ size in lots of 20 only.
† Canadian money.

5. How to Use Community Resources in the Classroom

There is an abundance of resources for an open classroom available for the asking in most communities. In this selection, Peter C. Madden of the University of North Dakota's Center for Teaching and Learning explains where and how teachers can acquire concrete materials of all sorts without cost. He also discusses ways of using two other important resources, people and places, explaining ways of taking children out of the classroom into the community, along with a number of ideas for bringing the adults of the community into the classroom. Teachers may also find his bibliography of value. (The Center for Teaching and Learning came into being in September 1972, through a merger of The New School for Behavioral Studies in Education, the entity that pioneered the creation of open classrooms in North Dakota, and the older, more traditional School of Education.)

Regardless of educational philosophy, teachers who attempt to lessen their dependence on stultifying pencil-and-paper student tasks face a common problem: finding alternative classroom materials to replace the traditional avalanche of paper. Teachers seeking alternative sources of materials can move in one of two directions. You may be able to purchase the high-priced, sleekly packaged educational materials that are constantly being developed and offered to schools which can afford such luxuries.

If, however, you cannot make large investments in supplemental materials, you do not have to forego the development of exciting, multi-dimensional classrooms. Instead, I suggest that you merely have to look more closely at the wealth of materials available free or quite inexpensively in your own community. Not only will the cost of locally obtained materials be far lower than items purchased on the educational market, but the usefulness of this material, in terms of the needs and interests of your particular group of students, may actually be much higher than you expected.

The ideas in this paper came from a variety of sources. Most important among these are the teachers of North Dakota who shared their experiences with me during the past year. In addition, a number of other writers have begun to offer suggestions on the educational use

Peter C. Madden, "Exploring and Exploiting Your Community." Reprinted by special permission from *Learning*, Magazine for Creative Teaching, May, 1973. Copyright © 1973 by Education Today Company, Inc.

of locally obtained materials. Those publications which seem particularly useful are listed in the annotated bibliography found at the close of the paper.

One logical way to consider the use of community resources in the classroom is to divide the discussion into three parts: things, or materials, people and places. Since *integration* of learning activities is a primary goal in modern classrooms, there is bound to be some overlap between these divisions. However, each will be treated more-or-less separately in the beginning.

Things

The sources of useful classroom materials are legion. The first and easiest place to look is within the homes of your own students. Broken or castoff equipment of all kinds tend to collect in cupboards, closets and garages until the annual "spring cleaning." Given periodic encouragement and reminders, your children can bring this invaluable material into the classroom instead of watching it be thrown away.

Among the items we collected last year were lawn mower engines, television sets, clocks, watches, tape recorders, phonographs, can openers, mixers, rugs, chairs and lamps.

A related source, but one which involves a small amount of money, is the ever-popular garage and rummage sale or auction. For one dollar or less, I have obtained a variety of operating toys and games, an easy chair, a working gasoline engine, a rug, a lamp, several yards of printed cloth, and many similar items. Other garage sale and auction fans I know have stocked their classrooms with operable autoharps, pianos, clay kilns, lumber, motors, animal cages, typewriters, office business machines and furniture—all at prices which were fractions of their original cost.

Local businessmen will also contribute a number of useful items to your classroom supply. With businessmen there is one key rule to remember: don't become a pest or parasite. I make it a rule never to take anything from a business which is not true "junk." If the material has any value at all, I ask the donor to reconsider. As long as no financial consideration is involved, businessmen will generally be happy to keep you stocked continually with new junk as it appears. I ask each cooperating businessman to keep a box on hand with my name and telephone number. Then I go around every few weeks to collect whatever has turned up.

Naturally, this procedure is most effective with businesses where I am a regular customer. However, I have been able to collect two van loads of classroom junk in a few hours from businessmen in towns where I was a total stranger. You can simplify the process of spreading the news about your junk collecting to local businesses by working through the local Chamber of Commerce. Most Chambers have a monthly newsletter in which you can ask for discarded materials and give a telephone where you might be reached.

The newsletter offers you an attractive vehicle to repay your benefactors as well. It is often quite reinforcing to businessmen to provide them with some private and public appreciation of their contribution to your classroom. A note of thanks sent directly to the contributor from time to time is always helpful. Public recognition in the form of a short article in the local Chamber newsletter or town newspaper will not only reward your business friends for the contribution but will enhance the status of such alternative activities in your classroom with a significant sector of the community.

One of the most interesting sources of material is the federal government. Voluminous printed material is available free or at nominal cost through the Government Printing Office in Washington, D.C. 20402. By contacting the Superintendent of Documents at that address you can obtain a current catalog of government publications and be placed on a mailing list for all future catalogs.

The biggest problem with federal publications is just finding out what is available from the vast output in virtually every department and agency in the government. Examples of what can be found range from the annual yearbook of the Department of Agriculture, which is generally a magnificently illustrated scientific document related to land and ecology, to a handy programmed text on basic computers put out by the Army's Quartermaster Corps. The Weather Bureau, now known as the National Oceanic and Atmospheric Administration, will provide you with national weather maps, books of satellite photographs and maps, and some interpretive materials on the use of scientific tools for weather forecasting.

MILITARY SURPLUS

Physical material is also available from a number of government sources. Military bases offer a staggering variety of surplus supplies. Schools have obtained trucks and cars, parachutes, electronic equipment, desks, files, living room furniture, bottles of rare gases, laboratory and shop equipment . . . the list of what local military bases can offer is virtually endless.

As usual with the government, getting your hands on surplus material involves some fairly complex paperwork and procedures—at least the first time around. The government requires that schools obtain a certificate of eligibility which is usually issued by the state. Then surplus material can be "screened" (meaning looked at), tagged if desired and picked up after a period of time if nobody else wants it. There are certain priorities governing who gets what material, but public and tax-exempt schools rank fairly high on the list.

In North Dakota, as in all other states, the state government has simplified the procedure considerably by drawing federal material on its own and storing it in a state warehouse for schools. The claiming procedure is much easier and does not generally require teachers to wait for the material they have selected. (In North Dakota, information can be obtained from the Director of Surplus Property, Department of Public Instruction, State Capitol, Bismarck, N.D. 58201.)

AT THE COUNTY LEVEL

At the local level, several state, county and federal agencies provide integrated facilities to offer conservation and agricultural services. Most of these agencies operate through the county government system. The county agricultural agent and home demonstration agent offer a wide variety of publications and audio-visual aids. Some of these documents are too specialized or technical for general classroom use, but the rest, especially those dealing with ecology, wildlife, plants and personal finance, are quite appropriate for students at the elementary level.

Of unique interest in making community studies are the topographic maps produced by the Geological Survey of the U.S. Department of the Interior. These extremely detailed maps cover nearly all areas of a state in very small sections of about 60 square miles—roughly one average school district per map. Each map costs 50 cents and may be obtained from Washington, D.C., after finding the proper title from the Geological Survey's *Index to Topographical Maps* for each state. This index may be obtained free from Washington or viewed in a good local library.

In a similar vein, aerial photographs of a number of local agricultural areas of the United States may be procured from the local office of the Agricultural Stabilization and Conservation Service (ASCS) which is also associated with the county government. A related agency, the Soil Conservation Service, will supply you with a number of useful pamphlets and can also offer you trees and shrubs at no cost in the spring of the year.

Several schools have become involved in landscaping projects on school property or nearby publicly owned areas. In each case this activity resulted in development of intense feelings of pride and satisfaction—not only in the students who did the planning and work, but in the rest of the community which benefited from the results. Landscaping projects are excellent ways of introducing to children the concept that protection and enhancement of the environment must become personal tasks for each person if the ecology of an area is to be improved.

There are also a number of community sources of reading and other academic materials for your classroom. Some rough-and-ready intermediate boys who seem to have little time for much of the reading material the classroom supplies will spend hours studying advertising pamphlets produced by snowmobile, motorcycle and automobile companies. Large quantities of such materials are available every time new models come out.

Menus and catalogs are prime sources for mathematics activities. A few hours spent creating job cards with problems in Menu Math or Catalog Math will provide many hours of useful classroom activities. Problems can range over several years of ability levels, as the following examples show:

PROBLEM: Which costs more, a ham sandwich or a turkey sandwich?

PROBLEM: Mr. Smith takes his family to dinner. He and his wife each get the deluxe steak dinner. Patty orders veal cutlets. Jerry orders a tuna sandwich, and Jeff, who is angry that night, doesn't eat anything at all. Figure out how much the total bill will be, including a four percent sales tax and a fifteen percent tip for the waiter.

Catalogs are never hard to obtain, especially after they go out of date. Similarly, in this time of constantly rising prices, most restaurants find themselves replacing menus once or twice a year. They will always give you as many of the outdated menus as you want. Look for bright, durable, colorful menus with large print and a variety of items. By picking up menus from several different restaurants, you can also begin to introduce concepts of comparative shopping and relative value into your classroom.

FILMS AVAILABLE

Major business concerns provide numerous aids for classroom use through their public information offices. Films are probably the most common example of efforts to reach students made by large corporations. While there is a little propaganda in most of the films, it is generally innocuous and seldom distracts from the value of the film. The most comprehensive index to commercially produced films is *The Educators' Guide to Free Films,* part of a valuable series which is updated annually.

The simplest way to order large varieties and quantities of free films, however, is to use the Modern Talking Picture Service, which has several regional outlets around the country. The only cost to you will be return postage, which is quite low for films.

For some reason, many teachers feel guilty whenever they show films, as if they aren't really teaching when the lights go out. While anything can be overdone, many children would profit from greater use of filmed material. This is especially true for children who find themselves culturally or geographically isolated in such places as Indian reservations, small farming communities, or ghettos. In addition, improved screens, self-threading projectors and flexible room arrangements make it feasible today for teachers to allow small groups of students to show themselves films at their own convenience, without interfering with the rest of the class. Under these conditions, ordering several films per week in one classroom is an entirely justifiable and useful activity.

PRINTED MATERIAL

Besides films, companies will provide educational booklets (General Motors has a fine series on various types of engines, for example), games such as *The Ecology Game* now being offered through local Coca-Cola dealers, speakers who deal with many topics and even entertaining shows of professional quality, such as the touring company sent around the country each year by Chrysler Corporation. Virtually every major corporation will supply some kind of material for your classroom upon request to their public relations office. Addresses of large companies are listed in *Poor's Register of Corporations,* which is available in most reference libraries.

The ultimate community resource for academic learning is the newspaper. Only in recent years have large numbers of teachers begun to exploit the learning potential available in a local newspaper. The best compendium of teaching ideas involving newspapers I have seen is *Newspaper in the Classroom* by Jerry Abbott, principal of West Elementary School in Grand Forks, N.D. Working with the *Grand Forks Herald,* this dynamic young educator assembled over 500 ways in which students can creatively learn from newspaper activities. Projects involving social studies, current events, language arts, mathematics and physical education may be easily centered around daily use of a newspaper. The newspaper industry has belatedly realized that its future depends upon educating a new generation of readers to use its services. For that reason, many newspapers will subsidize all or part of the cost of using their material in your classroom.

CONSTRUCTION MATERIALS

Finally, construction materials can provide the physical backbone upon which most of your other classroom activities can hang. Small strips of wood can easily be gathered behind the rip saw of your local lumber yard or can be purchased at minimal expense. Large heavy-duty cardboard sheets are available free at any store which sells major appliances or furniture. If your budget allows it, an especially thick, strong form of cardboard called *Tri-wall* can be extremely useful in building classroom furniture and work areas. Costing about two dollars per 4' by 6' sheet, *Tri-wall* will support weight as well as plywood but can be shaped much more easily than lumber.

An interesting source of ideas for classroom construction projects is *The Farallones Scrapbook,* which is published by a free-wheeling education co-op in California. Like *Big Rock Candy Mountain,* a similar publication, the Scrapbook also contains numerous ideas for using ordinary materials and people in unconventional ways within schools.

Construction activities allow teachers to integrate a number of learning areas into one project. Re-creation of a Norwegian home at Christmas, an Indian village, a pioneer cabin or sod hut, or a factory provides welcome relief from the steady academic diet offered children in most classrooms. Some of the skills sharpened in such an exercise are planning, organization, cooperation, art, social studies, history, reading, fine and gross motor functioning and mathematics.

Child labor and scrap materials can also be used to construct learning centers, cubby areas for private reading sessions, puppet theaters, a film and filmstrip corner and partitions between desks which not only reduce distraction when children are working at their seats but provide every child with a personal bulletin board as well.

In summary, once you get started collecting material in your classroom, your major problem will not be getting things you need, but finding space in your room for all your new "treasures." You may even decide that too much room is being taken up by such static space consumers as teacher and student desks. A number of teachers have removed traditional classroom furniture little by little to make room for new material they have gathered, resulting in a more exciting classroom environment than they would ever have been able to plan in advance.

Places

Teachers have traditionally used the places in their community in only a minimal way, by arranging for one or two field trips each year to the local water purification plant or some local point of interest. While these few trips were undoubtedly useful and interesting to the children, they barely scratch the surface of the resources available in most communities.

Actually, field trips are an art in themselves and deserve a little more discussion than they usually receive. Typically, a teacher arranges a field trip over the telephone, takes the entire class to the site on a school bus, leads the children through the site with an employee explaining things along the way to those students who are in a position to see and hear, then follows up the activity with a few questions or an essay the next day.

There are better ways to visit the same place. First, the teacher should, as often as possible, visit the site before the class arrives and take the employee-led tour herself. Then when the class goes through the site, the teacher can do the explaining with the employee acting as escort and resource person in case questions come up. In general, employee-guides know too much about machinery and too little about your children to make effective explanations. They often bore children with needless detail and overlook the whimsical kind of curiosity children display when confronted with a fascinating new situation.

On that first solo trip you might want to take along your camera to make some slides of especially interesting or complicated subjects. In that way you can "prep" your children in advance, whet their curiosity and make some initial explanations which can be reinforced by the actual visit they will make later. Teachers sometimes think this process robs the field trip of spontaneity and interest but the reverse seems to be true. It's often more interesting to see something in actuality after you have seen it in photographs, as any tourist can verify.

The slides will also be useful for follow-up discussions after the trip. By keying discussion or writing to some of the specifics of the trip as recalled by your pictures, you can often generate a much more meaningful evaluation. It is also helpful to "prep" a few of your children with questions to ask, just in case none come up spontaneously. The most painful part of any field trip is the pregnant pause that so often occurs when the guide confronts the class with, "Well, now that you've seen everything, are there any questions?"

Actually, there is no particular reason for the entire class to go along on every trip at the same time, unless great distances or special arrangements are involved. For local visits, a cooperative parent with four or five kids can provide a very effective field trip if the teacher has adequately prepared the children with some of the methods discussed above. Such trips, by the way, are an excellent initial step toward getting parents more involved in your classroom. You might even want to arm your children with a camera and let each small group tell the rest of the class what they learned on the trip.

PICK A RELEVANT SITE

Probably the key factor for successful field trips is picking a site which is relevant to the needs and interests of your children. Most of us as adults tend to overestimate the sophistication of our students—at least in the beginning. If a child can't relate the process or place being visited to his own life, he probably will have little interest in it.

One year I made a special effort to provide a large number of out-of-school experiences for my junior high school students. The least popular trip of the year was a visit to a large metropolitan airport, which included going through the control tower and a large jet plane. Despite the fact that none of the class had ever seen these things before, the trip dissolved in boredom and acting-out behavior. In marked contrast, the high point of the year was a visit to a small hot dog factory located six blocks from the school. The reason: no one in that class could relate airports or jet planes to any real part of his life. But every student ate a lot of hot dogs and had passed that factory hundreds of times before. There was immediate relevance to their present and future lives.

Increasing numbers of teachers are exploring the possibilities of modifying field trips to provide a longer experience for fewer children outside of school—in other words, sending one child, or a very small group of students, to a local office, business or agency to spend one or more full days. Businessmen have some initial resistance to this plan, but as it becomes more widely known through business channels there should be more receptiveness.

Cornell University psychologist Urie Bronfenbrenner has promoted this plan with a number of large corporations after he saw how effectively it worked in Russia. One of his experiments, involving a group of 6th graders who spent three days at a big city newspaper is described in a beautiful film called, *A Place To Meet—A Way To Understand.* The results indicate that children return from these visits with much higher motivation for doing classroom work, apparently because they learned that someday they will actually be expected to do some of the tasks teachers were stressing so abstractly in class. It seems to come as quite a surprise to some children to find that learning can actually be useful upon occasion.

Many other out-of-class activities are possible throughout the year. The growing interest in ecology, for example, will take on little significance in a classroom unless the children can actually get out into the environment to see how it works. With little more than a small investment in a Durham, or fermentation tube, the class can test water samples from various community sources for signs of bacterial pollution. If there is a river in the community, comparison of up-stream and down-stream water samples should be quite instructive for children examining the ecological practices of their own hometown.

All of the public services of the community provide children with fine opportunities to learn science, especially if you can prepare slides to elaborate on visits to water and sewer plants, the electric company, the local airport, and the telephone company. Different trips might be made to the same sites to look from a different point of view. At the water company, for example, you might want to stress bacteriology and lab work on one trip, business and accounting practices on another, chemical content of liquids on another, and pressure relationships on the last.

Another useful ecological venture is monitoring the effect of the seasons upon the environment. Bird counts, for example, can be made several times during the year. Specific trees of several different species can be observed over several months, with conditions and changes noted and recorded at each observation. Weather, usually taught quite abstractly as a "unit" in a science book, is much better dealt with on a ten-minute-a-day basis every day of the year. Students can easily build equipment to measure and record wind speed, precipitation, wind direction, high and low temperature, and air pressure variations over any period of time. The UNESCO *Source Book for Science Teaching* and similar science source books will provide you with hundreds of ideas for using the places and things in your own community to teach science and related subjects.

People

It is even easier to get adults into your classroom than it is to get students out of it. If you can deal with one critical issue, you can get a high level of adult participation in your classroom. The issue is the natural reluctance of people to get involved with situations that provoke anxiety. Adults have one over-riding fear in classrooms: looking foolish or inadequate in front of the children, especially their own children.

Therefore, you must provide some initial structure so that the adults know exactly what is expected of them and are prepared to carry that task out correctly. It is essential that they feel successful in their early ventures into classrooms. The easiest way to handle this problem is to prepare job cards for parents unless they are coming into the classroom to do some very specific task, such as show slides of a trip they took. Even in that case it would be wise to get the adult into your classroom ahead of time if possible and go over the session with him.

Parents in the classroom can tutor individual children (preferably not their own), work with small groups in reading or other academic areas, lead art or music activities with either large or small groups, engage in their own special interests or hobbies with children, show slides, work with motors and tools or any one of a hundred activities which you'll think of when you get to know them.

One of the most valuable things adults can do with children is discuss their own occupations. A recently published booklet called *The Yellow Pages of Learning* provides a number of ideas for using businessmen, craftsmen, professional workers and their respective places of employment to teach children.

Another ingenious idea dreamed up by a primary teacher was inviting adults into the classroom simply to "do their thing" for a period of time. The adults were not expected to make any kind of presentation to the class. Instead, they simply set up shop and modeled their work. As children became interested, they drifted up from time to time, watching the adult at work and asking whatever questions they wished. Some children even began to imitate the adult at work, entirely on their own.

The first such experience involved an artist who spent four days producing an oil painting from scratch. Then a carpenter built a small project in one corner of the classroom. Any number of professional and business people could simply bring the tools of their trade to school for a few hours and work in the classroom for all who are interested to watch.

Local special interest groups will also make a contribution to your classroom if you invite them. Flower and gardening clubs, country dancing groups, local historical associations and professional societies have all volunteered in the past year to work in classrooms I know.

SENIOR CITIZENS

One largely untapped resource consists of senior citizens, who often have a strong craving for involvement and lots of time to give. In this particular part of the country they constitute a unique potential, as there are still many elderly people alive who actually broke virgin sod and settled the land. Most of them came from foreign lands to settle here and have fascinating stories to tell about their pioneering ventures.

The danger in this kind of activity lies in trying to involve an entire class with the visitor. It would be much better to let this person work with a small group of children, who might even have been asked to "interview" the visitor and prepare a report for others in the class. Just as few classroom activities are going to be equally interesting to your entire class, so will few visitors hold the same fascination for every child.

One of the activities these senior citizens might contribute to is an integrated study of your community. Their recollections and souvenirs could provide the basis for construction activities which would reproduce an earlier culture in your community, including housing, art, clothing, speech, political and social interests and any other areas you can uncover. Old books and photographs might appear from several homes. Some children could investigate the local newspaper files to see what people wrote and thought about in an earlier time. Others might find some facinating trivia in nearby cemeteries.

Similar studies might be made about the community as it presently exists. Ethnic groups, politics, geography, architecture, education, historical precedents, art and music, commerce, government and religious institutions are among the topics that might be investigated. One interesting variation on this community study theme might be sharing the information with classes in other parts of the country. In that way, children would learn not only about their own home but someone else's as well. The classes might want to work together to plan their studies and share papers, photographs, maps, etc., at frequent intervals as they progressed.*

In conclusion, I have tried to summarize a few of the ways teachers can introduce reality into their classrooms. At the moment, far too much classroom time is being spent in an artificial world constructed largely of paper. The real world is exciting, challenging and highly involving—the paper world is flat, repetitive and largely boring. The materials of reality are all around you no matter where you teach. Why not reach out, pick them up and use them?

BIBLIOGRAPHY

COMPILED BY PETER C. MADDEN

Farallones Scrapbook, ($4.25). Farallones Designs, Star Route, Point Reyes Station, CA 94956. 144 pages.

This free-flowing book combines classroom arrangement, teaching ideas, construction activities, poetry, domes and a compendium of rapping and opinion in a very pleasant and useful package.

Big Rock Candy Mountain, ($4.00). Portola Institute, 1115 Merrill St., Menlo Park, CA 94025. Published quarterly.

Has a "counterculture" ring to it, like its parent publication, *The Whole Earth Catalog.* Many useful teaching ideas and sources of classroom material are presented in a highly palatable form. Also opinions about education, mostly of the free school persuasion.

Beautiful Junk, (free), by Diane Warner and Jeanne Quill. Project Head Start, Office of Economic Opportunity, Washington, D.C.

A concise presentation of ideas of using common community and home materials for arts, crafts and construction in classrooms. Usefulness definitely extends beyond pre-school years.

Trash to Treasure, ($1.00), by Sue McCord. Project Change, State University of New York at Cortland, Cortland, N.Y.

More nice ideas for using castoff materials in the classroom. Stresses art projects. Well illustrated.

* I will be happy to serve as "middleman" for classes which want to share community studies (or anything else) with each other. At the moment, I can direct requests to classrooms in North Dakota, Alaska, New York, New Jersey, Illinois and New Mexico. I'm sure others will develop if the interest exists.

A Starter Catalog of Free Materials, (free). The Resource Center for Man-Made Environment Education, Department of Architecture, North Dakota State University, Fargo, N.D. 58102.

Paul Groth and Rick Engebretson have done a fine job of indexing the resources available to classroom teachers for relating architectural and engineering concepts to more traditional "subjects." Catalog also includes some features of the social environment that teachers might draw upon.

Yellow Pages of Learning, ($1.95). Edited by Richard S. Wurman. The MIT Press, MIT, Cambridge, Mass. 02142.

Very clever discussions of techniques for helping children from the occupations, institutions and objects to be found in any community. Ranges from airport to cemetery to tree stump to zoo. A first-rate and invaluable product.

Sourcebook for Science Teaching, ($5.25). UNESCO, United Nations, New York, N.Y.

First produced as an aid for schools in devastated nations following World War II, this book continues to provide several hundred ideas for making science equipment from the junk lying about the average bombed out city or African village. Will eliminate forever the excuse, "I can't teach science because our school has no equipment."

Film catalogs for classroom use:

(1) Modern Talking Picture Service
     9129 Lyndale Ave. South
     Minneapolis, Minn. 55420

     Many, many good films for your classroom for the price of return postage only.

(2) *State Film Catalog,* from
     North Dakota Film Library
     State University Station
     Fargo, N.D. 59102

     Nearly every state has at least one major film library, which contains purely educational films as well as the commercial varieties available above.

(3) Educators Guide to Free Films ($11.00 approx.) Educators Progress Service, Inc. Randolph, Wisc.

     This book, updated annually, is the ultimate reference for classroom films which are available free. The same company produces similar volumes covering *Social Studies Materials; Tapes, Scripts and Transcriptions; Filmstrips; Science Materials; Teaching Aids,* and *Media and Methods.*

A Place to Meet—A Way to Understand, (free film). National Audio-Visual Center, General Services Administration, Washington, D.C.

A beautiful film about children learning about the world of work through an extended visit to the offices and plant of a major newspaper. Reports on the experiments being conducted by Urie Bronfenbrenner on the merging of school and community.

A-V Instruction Media and Materials, by James Brown, Richard Lewis and Fred Harcleroad. McGraw-Hill Book Co., 1969.

Chapter six, titled "Inexpensive supplementary materials," presents a good summary of easily obtained materials, with special stress on government publications and materials.

Monthly Catalog of U.S. Government Printing Office Publications, ($4.50 per year). Available from Superintendent of Documents, Government Printing Office, Washington, D.C. 20402.

Lists government publications subject and title.

Landscaping for Living, U.S. Department of Agriculture, 1972. Available from the office of a federal legislator.

The current USDA yearbook. Back issues of previous yearbooks also can be obtained from the same source.

Distribution Center, U.S. Geological Survey, Federal Center, Denver, Colo. 80225.

Source of *Index of Topographical Maps* and various local maps ordered from the *Index.*

Soil Conservation Service, a federal office located in virtually every county seat.

Will provide a wide variety of printed material related to conservation, wild life, water resources and plants. Will also (if requested no later than the previous autumn) provide free planting material for shelter-belts and "outdoor classrooms" on school property.

Newspaper in the Classroom, ($3.00), by Jerry Abbott. *Grand Forks Herald,* Grand Forks, N.D. 58201. 1970.

An extremely comprehensive guide for using newspapers at school. The ideas cover most subject areas and range from kindergarten to 12th grades.

A Useful List of Classroom Items That Can Be Scrounged or Purchased. Early Childhood Education Study, Inc., EDC, 55 Chapel St., Newton, Mass. 02160

This handy list is one of the few which breaks down resources by subject areas (math, language arts, etc.). In addition to free materials, this booklet covers a variety of low cost games, toys, puzzles and science aids.

Poor's Register of Corporations, published annually by Standard and Poor's Corp., New York, N.Y.

A more concise and easily obtainable list of major corporations is the annual list of "The Five Hundred Largest Corporations in America" published each spring by *Fortune* magazine. However, only Poor's directory will provide actual mailing addresses.

Tri-Wall Container Corp., Butler, Ind.

The source of Tri-wall, the invaluable classroom construction material. 4' by 6' sheets of Tri-wall are currently selling for $2.09 per sheet— unfortunately, in lots of 100 sheets. Smaller sheets are also available in smaller lots and at lower costs.

6. How to Scrounge for Materials

SCROUNGE LIST

This list contains some suggestions for materials available free from local merchants to use in classrooms. They represent only a sample of the many resources you will find in your area. Many of these materials are normally discarded; if you contact local businesses, shops or factories, and make your intentions known, they are quite often willing to save them for you.

Contractors and Building Supply Companies

lumber, pipes and wire, wallpaper, linoleum, tiles, molding wood, sawdust, wood curls.

You can make arrangements to go to a construction site when they are finishing a job; they will let you collect the scrap building materials.

Plastics Company

trimmings, cuttings, tubing, scrap plastic and plexiglass

Electronics Manufacturers

styrofoam packing, printed circuit boards, discarded components

Lumber Supply Companies and Furniture Factories

scrap wood, damaged bricks, concrete blocks, doweling, sawdust, wood curls, wood scraps for carving

Hardware Stores

sample hardware books, sample tile charts, linoleum samples

Rug Companies

sample swatches, end pieces from rugs

Supermarkets and Outdoor Markets

cartons, packing materials, fruit crates, large cardboards and materials from displays, discarded cardboard display racks, styrofoam fruit trays

Department Stores

fabric swatches (drapery and upholstery samples), rug swatches, corrugated packing cardboard, sample food cans and boxes, packing boxes from appliances such as washing machines, refrigerators, etc.

From *A Useful List of Classroom Items That Can Be Scrounged or Purchased,* mimeographed (Newton, Mass.: Education Development Center). Early Childhood Education Study. Reprinted by permission of Education Development Center, Inc.

Phone Company (call their Public Relations Department)
  excess colored wires; telephones (on loan)

Electric Power Company (call their Public Relations Department)
  telephone poles, wooden cross arms, steel ground rods, wire, large spools that can be used for tables, assorted packing materials

Garment Factories and Button Manufacturers
  a great source for accumulating a wide variety of materials—yarn, buttons, scraps, decorative tape

Camera Manufacturers
  cameras (on loan)

Leather Manufacturers and Leather Craft Companies
Pocketbook, Belt and Shoe Manufacturers
  scrap pieces of leather and lacings

Billboard Companies
  pieces of billboard to use as posters, wall coverings

Ice-Cream Stores
  3-gallon ice-cream containers

Airlines
  plastic cups

Container Companies
  large cardboard sheets

Architectural Firms, Upholsterers, Textile Companies, Floor Covering Firms, Kitchen Counter and Cabinet Makers, Wallpaper and Paint Stores
  color samples; wood, linoleum and tile samples, formica squares, wallpaper books and scraps of all sizes

Bottling Firms
  bottle caps, large cardboard tubes

Window, Storm Door and Siding Companies; Soft Drink Manufacturers
  aluminum scraps

Cleaners and Tailors
  buttons, hangers, scrap material

Restaurant
  ice-cream containers, corks, boxes and cartons

Large Food, Candy and Soap Manufacturers
  sample cans and boxes

Plumbers and Plumbing Supply Companies
  wires, pipes, tile scraps, linoleum

Tile and Ceramics Companies
  scraps of ceramic and mosaic tile; tile by the pound (inexpensive)

Paper Companies
  unusual kinds of paper are often available free in the form of samples, end cuts, or damaged sheets. Paper is delivered to paper companies in

large cardboard tubes which are usually discarded. These make good chairs, tables, cubbies, etc. (See *Building with Tubes,* a publication of the Early Childhood Education Study.)

Metal Spinning Companies

shavings and scrap pieces

Junk Yard and Scrap Metal Yards

unlimited possibilities! Wheels of all shapes and sizes, all kinds of gears and moving parts from clocks, radios, fans, cars, irons, toasters, etc. Handles from doors, cars; knobs; broomsticks; hinges and fittings.

Note: Be on the lookout for packing materials wherever you go. Depending on the nature of the factory or business, they come in an infinite variety of materials, shapes and sizes.

FREE AND INEXPENSIVE MATERIALS

Construction, Sewing, and Woodworking

1. Boxes of all kinds—egg cartons, milk cartons, cookie trays, vegetable cartons and trays, match boxes
2. Plastic bottles, boxes and jugs—bleach bottles, ice cream cartons, detergent bottles, cheese containers, margarine containers
3. Cardboard tubing from toilet paper, paper towels, wrapping paper
4. Broom handles, spools, bottle caps, lids, pipe cleaners, elastic bands
5. Elmer's glue, paste, Scotch tape, masking tape, paper clips, staples, string, rope, wire, brass paper fasteners
6. Wallpaper, swatches of rug and drapery material, tiles, linoleum
7. Scrap metal and pipe, wheels
8. Gears from clocks, radios, fans, cars, irons, toasters; handles, knobs, hinges and fittings of all kinds
9. Scrap wood, fruit crates, large cartons, barrels
10. Nuts, bolts, nails, washers, screws
11. Cloth—various textures and colors: silk, lace, organdy, net, nylon, wool, corduroy, wool, velvet, burlap, felt, cotton, taffeta
12. Yarn, ribbon, rick-rack, fringing, decorative tape, lace edging, thread, embroidery floss
13. Buttons, beads, sequins, buckles, snaps, zippers
14. Needles, pins, knitting needles

Playgrounds

1. Large cartons, fruit crates, barrels
2. Concrete blocks, bricks, large stones
3. Large spools from telephone wire—check phone company
4. Ladders, sewage pipes, ropes
5. Bicycle tires, automobile tires, saw horses, tree trunks, planks
6. Targets painted on boards or on the concrete
7. Wooden structure for a clubhouse

House Corner, Dramatic Play, Shops

1. Old dresses, pants, shirts, blouses
2. Hats: men's, women's, cowboy, baseball, baker, bride's veil, crowns, helmets
3. Shoes: ladies' heels, boots, slippers, men's shoes and sandals, etc.
4. Shawls, coats, capes, scarves
5. Beads, earrings, bracelets, pins, belts
6. Material to use as saris, turbans, trains, capes
7. Fans, glasses, gloves, handbags, wallets, aprons
8. White coats for doctors, nurses, bakers, etc.
9. Hand mirror, compacts, long mirror, clothes rack, coat hangers
10. Old televisions, radios, record players, irons, toasters
11. Old dolls, doll's clothes and furniture, stuffed toys
12. Telephone—perhaps from phone company
13. Brooms, dust pans, brushes
14. Tub for washing clothes, soap powder
15. Fruit and vegetable crates, saw horses, baskets, grocery carts, shopping bags
16. Play money or units for exchanging—pegs, golf tees, popsicle sticks, etc.

Sand and Water

1. Plastic jugs, bottles, cups, etc.—all in varying sizes
2. Old teapots, coffee pots, watering cans, garden hoses
3. Bottles, jars with lids, tin cans
4. Wood, cork, stones, shells, sponges, styrofoam, marbles
5. Rubber balls, balloons, bubble pipes
6. Hand towels, mops, aprons
7. Food coloring, soap, flour, string, wire, rubber bands

Wet Sand

8. Wood, stones, bricks, planks, twigs
9. Shovels, spoons, pails, scoops, rakes
10. Molds, muffin tins, cake tins, paper cups, shells, tin cans, plastic boxes, jars, jugs

Dry Sand

11. Dust pans, brushes, brooms
12. Sugar, salt, coffee, tea, spices, seeds
13. Bags—paper and plastic
14. Straws
15. Cone-shaped paper cups
16. String
17. Net material
18. Cornstarch
   (Materials may be interchanged in 3 categories above)

Balancing

1. Plastic containers for storage—labeled
2. Spoons, scoops, funnels, sieves

3. String, wire, paper plates, paper cups, paper paint buckets, paper clips, plasticine, nails, cup hooks
4. Milk cartons, baby food jars, juice cans, plastic bags, paper bags
5. Materials for weighing and balancing:—
   spools, bottle caps, clothes, pins, stones, shells, buttons, styrofoam; sponge rubber, corks, blocks, washers, nuts and bolts, rubber balls; rice, flour, sugar, noodles, coffee, tea, bran, kidney beans, dried peas, nuts, chestnuts, pine cones, sawdust; soap flakes, small cans of food, rolls of Lifesavers, sugar cubes (for making weights), packages made up to exact weights

Math

1. Materials for counting, sorting, grouping, ordering, and pattern making:
   —shells, stones, golf tees, marbles, toothpicks, straws, washers, bottle caps, buttons, beads and lacing, spools, pipe cleaners, lengths of ribbon, colored sticks, popsicle sticks, cancelled stamps; string, rope, hoops for enclosures
2. Playing cards, dominoes, checkers, dice
3. Old clocks, egg timers, stop watches, wrist watches, metronome, cash register, scales, adding machines
4. Curtain rod with hooks
5. Calendars, train, bus and plane schedules, maps
6. Tape measure, yard sticks, rulers, canes, doweling, unmarked wood, lengths of ribbon and string, straws, paper streamers

Free and Inexpensive—Art Materials

Collage Tray

1. Yarn, thread, ribbon, lace, stones, shells, bottle caps, broom straws, straws, toothpicks, pipe cleaners, twigs
2. Materials—all varieties
3. Scrap paper—all varieties
4. Wood chips, feathers, sawdust, sand, macaroni, rice, excelsior, packing paper, beads, sequins, buttons, foam rubber, cork, scrap rubber
5. Seaweed, leaves, pine needles, seed, wax, chalk, wire, string

Painting

6. Muffin tins, empty plastic squeeze bottles, jars with lids, tin cans
7. Sheets of plastic, newspaper, apron
8. Sponges, string, rope, clothesline and pins for hanging papers
9. Straws, sticks, twigs, toothpicks to be used as brushes, paper towels

Graphics

10. Tin cans, cardboard tubing, rolling pins, pencils, hair curlers, candles to be used as rollers in printing
11. Paper towels—folded to make print pads
12. Objects for printing:—
    forks, spoons, potato mashers, buttons, corks, jar lids, blocks, clay, corrugated board, vegetables, rubber bands, paper clips, string, and material

Clay Work

13. Plastic bags and covered tins for storage
14. Plastic material
15. Tools for modeling—pencils, feathers, twigs, forks, knives, spoons, rolling pins, pebbles, shells, leaves, toothpicks

Sculpture

16. Scrap wood and cardboard
17. String, wire, nails
18. Toothpicks, pipe cleaners, straws
19. Sticks
20. Cardboard, tin foil
21. Assorted paper
22. Elmer's glue

SUPPLIES TO BE PURCHASED

All prices shown below are 1969 prices and may have already changed. Orders for the following school year should be placed by April 15, and you should be sure to emphasize your requirements for delivery by June 15.

ITEM	CATALOG REFERENCE	SUPPLIER	COST
Special Equipment (Note: Items may be shared by several classrooms)			
1. Newcomb monophonic portable phonograph	EDT-20	Newcomb Audio Products	$ 79.95
2. Wollensak Tape Recorder	1520	Wollensak 3M Company	184.95
3. Wollensak Listening Center	for 8 head- phones	" " "	14.00
4. Wollensak Headphones		" " "	51.80
5. Language Master Unit		Bell & Howell	250.00
6. Headphones	#36407	" "	28.00/set
7. Dual Headphone Adaptor	#40720	" "	3.75
8. Blank Card Set 4" x 14"	072481	" "	9.50/100
9. Blank Card Set 3½" x 9"	072475	" "	6.00/100
10. Small electric stove for cooking			
11. Small kiln for pottery			

Tri-Wall Cardboard

Available from Tri-Wall Corporation directly; price does not include freight

42" x 54" (20–99 boards)	$ 2.41 ea
42" x 54" (100 and over)	1.34 ea
4' x 5' (100 and over)	1.69 ea
4' x 6' (100 and over)	2.06 ea
4' x 8' (100 and over)	2.86 ea

In the Greater Boston/New England area, you may pick up small quantities of Tri-Wall at the Workshop for Learning Things, EDC, 55 Chapel Street, Newton. No delivery. Maximum order 30 boards.

42" x 54"	$ 2.10 ea
4' x 6'	2.95 ea
4' x 8'	4.10 ea

Tri-Wall prices listed above are as of November 1, 1970

ART MATERIALS

A wide variety of *papers* of all sorts and sizes is essential.
A wide variety of sizes in *brushes* is essential. Especially important are *large* brushes for painting.

ITEM	CATALOG REFERENCE	SUPPLIER	COST
Papers			
1. White Drawing Paper Vellum 18 x 24		Hammett	$ 7.80
2. Easel Newsprint 18 x 24		"	4.40
3. Black Manila Drawing Paper 18 x 24		"	10.00/ream
4. Bogus Drawing Paper 18 x 24		"	4.00
5. Easy Glide Finger Paint Paper		"	1.70
6. Ruffmeal Drawing Paper 18 x 24		"	4.00
7. Crystal Craft Tissue 29 colors 15 x 20		"	1.00
8. Construction Paper 9 x 12, 18 x 24, 24 x 36 packages of assorted colors			
9. Project Roll Dispenser 36"	#10203	Hammett	8.00
10. Project Roll	6200	"	1.75
Paint and Brushes			
11. Dry Powder Paint		Hammett	1.00/lb can
Basic colors: red, black, yellow, white, blue. Others added as budget allows			
OR			
Dry Powder Paint in primary colors		Hammett	
Brushes			
12. Long Handled Easel Brushes		Hammett	
13. Flat and Round Brushes—½", ¾", 1"			
Chalks and Markers			
14. Binney & Smith Colored Chalk		Hammett	3.96/144 sticks
Small sticks—assorted colors	91212	"	
15. Sanford Deluxe Magic Markers Set of 8 colors	23206	"	5.38
Sharpie Fine Line Marker Pen		Hammett	.49
16. Red	23101		
17. Blue	23102		
18. Green	23103		
19. Yellow	23104		
20. Orange	23105		
21. Brown	23106		
22. Purple	23107		
23. Black	23100		
Clays			
24. Plasticine—10 assorted colors	#76500	Hammett	
Any low-firing natural clay available locally (must have a kiln available)			

ART MATERIALS (Continued)

ITEM	CATALOG REFERENCE	SUPPLIER	COST
Miscellaneous			
25. Scissors—5″ clip point	#21101	Hammett	.47
26. Elmer's Glue—gallon	21911	"	6.00
27. 1″ Masking Tape	24423	"	.76
28. 2″ Masking Tape	24424	"	1.54
29. Scotch Magic Mending Tape ¾″	24425	"	1.21
30. Swingline Stapler	20903	"	6.95
31. #24 bare copper wire (1 lb)	65-835	Cambosco	2.50
32. Craft-stix (popsicle sticks)		Constructive Play.	1.20/1000

Plaster of paris—20 lbs—buy locally
Matt knives
Water based printing inks in assorted colors
Scrap linoleum and scrap pine for block printing
Assortment of gouges and knives for carving blocks—Hammett
Brayers
Glass or masonite to roll ink on

MUSIC

Order all instruments from Magnamusic—Baton, 6394 Delmar Boulevard, St. Louis, Missouri

Note: The following represent a complete ensemble of tuned and untuned percussion which could be shared by several classes. If each classroom bought one item of tuned percussion and one or two of untuned, these could be amalgamated. If only one or two items of tuned percussion are purchased, the starred items would be most useful, as they fall into the range of the child's voice. If three or more are purchased, one from each section would be useful, but of a different timbre; i.e., do not select all metallophones or all xylophones, etc.

ITEM	CATALOG REFERENCE	SUPPLIER	COST
Tuned Percussion—all with suitable beaters			
1. Bass metallophone	BMd	Carl Orff	$172.00
2. Bass xylophone	BXd	" "	156.00
3. Alto metallophone	AMd	" "	57.60
4. Alto xylophone**	AXd	" "	53.60
5. Alto glockenspiel**	ACd	" "	20.80
6. Soprano metallophone	SMd	" "	42.40
7. Soprano xylophone	SXd/a	" "	46.80
8. Soprano glockenspiel	SGd/D	" "	24.60
Other Percussion Instruments (as many as possible to be purchased)			
Standing drums with soft beaters			
9. 12″	P30		29.60
10. 14″	P35		34.40
11. 16″	P40		39.20
12. 2 Tambourines 10″	RST25		11.90 ea.
13. 2 Tambours 12″	RST30		13.60 ea.

MUSIC (Continued)

ITEM	CATALOG REFERENCE	SUPPLIER	COST
14. 2 Pairs Cymbals 10″	C25		15.20 ea.
15. 1 Snare Drum and Sticks	KT30K		38.00
16. 4 Triangles (largest size)	T30		5.80 ea.
17. 4 Pairs Castanets *with handles*	KS1		4.70 ea.

Wind Instruments

18. 6 Plastic Soprano Recorders			3.25 ea.

WOODWORKING

ITEM	CATALOG REFERENCE	SUPPLIER	COST
1. Woodwork Bench	H306DC	Hammett	$46.50

Real Tools, Not Toys—purchase from local supplier
2. 4 small Claw Hammers
3. 1 Crosscut Saw
4. 2 Keyhole Saws
5. 2 Small Screw Drivers
6. Screw Driver Electrical
7. 2 Pliers
8. 2 Coping Saws
9. Wire
10. Wire Cutter
11. Sand Paper
12. Doweling—varying widths
    (wooden squares and circles for nuts) (threading kit)
13. Paint
14. Turpentine
15. Shellac
16. Brushes
17. Wood
18. Pegboard
19. Springs
20. Hinges, knobs, nails, screws, nuts, bolts
21. Large metal pulleys, various sizes
22. Rope, nylon cording

MATHEMATICS

ITEM	CATALOG REFERENCE	SUPPLIER	COST
Construction			
1. Skribble stix	11600	Milton Bradley	$ 5.00
2. X blocks	ESA 7363/001	SEE	25.00**
3. H blocks	ESA 7362/005	"	21.60**
4. Lock-a-blocks	Galt N-1305	"	2.50**
5. Cu-bricks	8M-115	Childcraft	3.95
6. Prism blocks	8M-325	"	8.00
7. System One	8M-327	"	10.00
8. Flexagons	DQ116	Creative Playthings	5.95
9. Geo. strips	INV 141	SEE	8.00

** These items are from British suppliers and the prices are estimated.

MATHEMATICS (Continued)

ITEM	CATALOG REFERENCE	SUPPLIER	COST
Mosaics			
10. Pattern blocks	PBCK01	SEE	9.00
11. Geometric Rubber Mosaic Tiles	DJ115	Creative Playthings	5.00
12. Basic shape sets	INV 140	SEE	5.00
13. Polymosaic	77067	Hammett	2.59
14. Plastic Mosaic Shapes	ESA007	SEE	7.75
15. Mosaic Shapes 9" set	ESA7557/027	"	1.50**
16. Scope		Economy 5 & 10	5.00
17. Halsam Play Tiles		Hammett	2.50
18. Ornabo	ESA008	SEE	15.00
19. Playskool Color Cubes	302	Constructive Playthings	2.00
Structured Materials			
20. Poleidoblocks Set G	ESA021	SEE	20.00
21. Geo-blocks	17523	McGraw-Hill	29.50
22. Grouping set	T110	Taskmaster	15.00**
23. Unifix cubes	TN42-23	Constructive Playthings	2.45 Box of 50
24. Unifix 100 track	TN42-31	" "	4.50
25. Unifix 100 trays	TN42-30	" "	1.50
26. " " "	TN42-16	" "	2.15
27. Unifix plastic markers	TN42-6	" "	2.95
28. Cuisenaire rods	CG-1E	Cuisenaire Company	6.95
29. Cubical counting cubes	8039	Hammett	4.00/100
30. Attribute blocks	AGCKOO	SEE	8.60
31. Mirror cards	18418	McGraw-Hill	10.80
32. Dienes Logical blocks	Z80007	Herder & Herder	19.50
33. Rubber Pegboards	DN113	Creative Playthings	.65
34. Pegs	DN115	" "	.80/100
35. Rubber bands	BAND01	SEE	.30
36. Multi-mat Square sum		"	7.25
37. Multi-mat All squares		"	7.25
38. Shapes Board	T107/3	Taskmaster	3.00**
39. Circle Board	T105/2	"	2.40**
Counting, Sorting, Matching, Ordering, Grouping, Sharing, etc.			
40. Miniature toys by lb.	DB-103	Creative Playthings	$5.95
41. Miniature cars		Buy locally	
42. Miniature animals		Buy locally	
43. Golf tees		Buy locally	
44. Beads	470	Milton Bardley	1.75
45. Bead Laces	471	" "	.70 doz.
46. Counting sticks	64041	Hammett	1.30
47. Colored Plastic Washers	PRM006	SEE	20.00
			6 gross in 6 colors
			3.50 gross in 1 color
48. Counting Chips	PRM008		1.75/200 in 8 colors
49. Assorted Porcelain Tiles	77122	Hammett	1.50

** These items are from British suppliers and the prices are estimated.

MATHEMATICS (Continued)

ITEM	CATALOG REFERENCE	SUPPLIER	COST

Puzzles and games locally available, chess, checkers, etc.

ITEM	CATALOG REFERENCE	SUPPLIER	COST
50. Tangrams Pieces (ESS)	17446	McGraw-Hill	2.40
51. Tangrams Cards (ESS)	17445	" "	4.20
52. Set of 12 Tangrams (fit ESS cards)	SEE004	SEE	4.00
53. Set of 12 Tangrams (different pieces)	ESA024	"	4.00

CONSTRUCTION

Note: We suggest
(a) that some items be ordered from each of the groups.
(b) that any central store set up should carry examples of all items listed.

ITEM	CATALOG REFERENCE	SUPPLIER	COST
Junior Engineer	ESA 7453/029	SEE	$18.00**
Giant Engineer Construction Kit	ESA 9884/408	"	38.00**
Mechanical Building Set		EDC Workshop Store	97.93
Fischer Technik 200	DT751	Creative Playthings	14.95
Play panels	8M383	Childcraft	4.95
Clink-a-Links	8M324	"	4.00
Playplax rings and squares		Economy 5 & 10	9.95
Octons	GALT L540	SEE	4.50**
Hex-upon		Economy 5 & 10	7.95
Rising Towers	DR255	Creative Playthings	3.00
Ji-gan-tiks	8M310	Childcraft	2.98
Top towers	8M399	"	3.00
Join-Ems	8M116	"	3.95
Snapsticks	8M284	"	4.95
Connector	8M118	"	12.00
Big Boy Tinkertoy	84465	Hammett	5.50
Rig-a-Jig	DT662	Creative Playthings	4.00
Constructo-straws	60563	Hammett	2.00
Geo-D-stix	8M332	Childcraft	4.95
Lego #74	DT666	Creative Playthings	10.95
Minibrix	GALT N-1060	SEE	7.60**

** These items are from British suppliers and the prices are estimated.

SCIENCE

ITEM	CATALOG REFERENCE	SUPPLIER	COST
Electricity			
Pkg. of 48 Batteries	BATT48	SEE	$ 8.60
			17.00/2
100' #20 bare copper wire	BBCK01	"	1.25
GE #48 bulbs	BBCK08	"	4.50/25
			14.50/100
Bulb holders	BBCK10	"	2.25/10
			13.00/60

SCIENCE (Continued)

ITEM	CATALOG REFERENCE	SUPPLIER	COST
Large rubber bands (battery holders)	BBCK14	"	.65/40
Wire Cutters	BBCK16	"	1.25
			1.10 ea/7 or more
Pkg. of 8 spools assorted wires	BB0807	"	11.75
Electrostatics materials	64-208	Cambosco	3.75

Magnetism (* indicates a particularly powerful magnet)

Magnastiks	8M289	Childcraft	7.95
Magnastiks	KR613	Creative Playthings	7.95
Magnetic Needle	Z-4100	LaPine	1.90
Magnetic Compass	59-229	Cambosco	.53
Iron Filings	59-178	"	.63/lb
Encased Iron Filings	DS-741	Creative Playthings	.79
Small Steel Balls	59-173	Cambosco	.38/100
Magnetic Balls	60,508	Edmund	1.00
Flexible Magnetic Strip	60,092	"	1.25
Flexible Magnetic Cord	40,875	"	2.50/10'
Rubberized rect. magnets w/center hole	BBCK18	SEE	.10 ea
			7.00/100
Assorted Rubber Magnets	1804	Welch	2.50
Ceramic ring magnets (12)	8P307	Childcraft	1.95
*1½ lb. Horseshoe magnet	60,215	Edmund	5.75
*Ring magnet (5' dia.)	60,578	"	5.00
Lodestone	Z-3950	LaPine	.35
Alnico bar magnet	Z-4260	"	1.80
Alnico horseshoe magnet ¾' across poles	219-11A	"	1.00
Alnico horseshoe magnet 1¾₁₆" across poles	219-11B	"	1.50
*Alnico hoseshoe magnet 1⅝" across poles	219-11C	"	2.40
*Cylindrical magnets 6 x 50 mm.	Z-4200	"	1.40/pr
Cylindrical magnets 10 x 127 mm.	60,131	Edmund	3.00/pr
Cylindrical magnets 21 x 16 mm.	60,577	"	2.00/10
*Disc magnets (polarized along dia.)	40,419	"	2.00/pr
Disc magnets (polarized along dia.) (with center hole)	60,433	"	1.00/pr
Small ceramic disc magnets (½" dia.)	40,820	"	1.00/25
Ceramic rect. magnets w/center hole	40,637	"	1.00/10
Ceramic ring magnets	40,869	"	1.00/4

SCIENCE (Continued)

ITEM	CATALOG REFERENCE	SUPPLIER	COST
*Ring gap magnets	40,964	"	2.35/4
*U magnets (1¹¹⁄₁₆″ across poles)	40,951	"	2.15/4
*U magnets (1¹⁄₁₆″ across poles)	40,909	"	2.00/10
*Alnico U Magnet (1⅝″ across poles)	59-63	Cambosco	$ 3.45
*Rectangular magnets (1⅛ x ¾ x ¼ ″)	40,906	Edmund	2.10/8
*Ceramic rect. magnets (1⅞ x ⅞ x ⅜″)	40,818	Edmund	1.40/pr

Optics

ITEM	CATALOG REFERENCE	SUPPLIER	COST
Polarizing sheets 6″ x 6″	60,637	Edmund	2.50/4
Mounted Polarizing Filters 4″ x 4″	40,991	"	4.00
Lenticular screens kit	60,589	"	2.00
Moire Patterns Color Kit —Series A	60,530	"	12.50
Color Filters 5″ x 8″ (44 diff. colrs)	60,403	"	8.00
Colored cellophane rolls	(see under Art Materials; p. 412, item 10)		
Telescope & Mount	60,735	Edmund	13.75
Color Paddles (red, blue, yellow)	INV353	SEE	1.00
Magic Reflector (kaleidoscope)	DJ010	Creative Playthings	5.95
Hand Stroboscope	3742	Welch	2.25
Big i Little i	DS050	Creative Playthings	5.95
Small Stand Magnifier	DS170	" "	3.50
Giant Magnifier on Stand	DS374	" "	9.95
Small Cylindrical Magnifier	79-35C	Cambosco	1.95
Reading glass	40,027	Edmund	2.25
" " plastic lens	60,635	"	1.00
1″ Hand Lenses	MGBK03	SEE	1.00/10
Microscope	SEESCO	"	3.25
" (same) with illuminator	SEES01	"	4.25
Micro Bio Chamber Microscope	73-301	Cambosco	8.75
Mirror Cloth	(specify #1 Clear Mirror; also size of mirrors & size of cloth desired)		
½″ x ½″ mirrors		National Products	2.30/sq ft
½″ x 1″ mirrors		" "	2.00/sq ft
1″ x 1″ mirrors		" "	2.00/sq ft
Plastic Mirror (specify ⅛″ thick and desired dimensions)		Parallel Mfg. Corp.	4.00/sq ft
Metal Mirror 4″ x 6″			

SCIENCE (Continued)

ITEM	CATALOG REFERENCE	SUPPLIER	COST
Plastic Mirrors 2½ x 3½	MIRROR	" " "	1.25/3
			.40 ea/10 or more
Round Flexible Mirror	DJ319	Creative Playthings	3.75
Paddle Mirrors and Standing Mirror	DS053	" "	11.50
One-way glass mirror 5 x 15 cm.	57-226	Cambosco	1.20
Concave-Convex metal mirror (75 mm dia.)	Z-4550	LaPine	1.40
Concave-Convex Cylindrical metal mirror (2" x 4")	Z-4555	"	1.55
Concave-Convex Cylindrical metal mirror (1" x 6")	57-244-1	Cambosco	1.00
Perspex (plastic) Prisms (set of 7)	INV680	SEE	17.75
Refraction plate	Z-3100	LaPine	1.25
Flat equilateral prism	Z-5060	"	1.40
Flat right angle prism	Z-5070	"	2.00
Right angle prism (75 x 25 mm)	Z-5080	"	2.25
Equilateral prism (75 x 25 mm)	Z-5050	"	1.75
Equilateral prism (153 x 30 mm)	DS764	Creative Playthings	2.00
Refraction cube	57-315	Cambosco	3.85
Amici Roof Prism	3002	Edmund	1.50
Penta Prism	40,622	"	6.50
Metal Mirror 4" x 6"	PBCK02	SEE	.80
			1.50 pr; .70 ea/10 or more
Magnifier 4X	MAG04X	SEE	3.25
Magnifier 8X	MAG08X	"	3.25

Mechanics/Dynamics

ITEM	CATALOG REFERENCE	SUPPLIER	COST
Swinger (5 suspended steel balls)	SEE003	SEE	8.00
Assorted springs	(local hardware store)		
Spiral Wave Motion Spring	55-116	Cambosco	4.95
Gyroscope	GYR001	SEE	.75
Turntable bearing mount	40,602	Edmund	1.50
Single Pulley	Z-5200	LaPine	.90
Double "	Z-5210	"	1.20
Triple "	Z-5220	"	1.55
Quadruple Pulley	Z-5230	"	1.85
Double Tandem Pulley	Z-5240	"	2.10
Triple " "	Z-5250	"	2.70
Linen Pulley Cord	43-472	Cambosco	.85/25 yds
Styrofoam Balls ¾" dia.	39-110-1	Cambosco	1.80/12 doz

SCIENCE (Continued)

ITEM	CATALOG REFERENCE	SUPPLIER	COST
1″ "	39-110-2	"	2.88/12 doz
2″ "	39-110-4	"	2.76/4 doz
3″ "	39-110-6	"	4.50/3 doz

Sand and Water Play

ITEM	CATALOG REFERENCE	SUPPLIER	COST
Sand and Water Play Table	A64	Community Playthings	49.50
Aluminum Liquid Measures Set	DJ070	Creative Playthings	9.50
Medicine Droppers	KPST12	SEE	.50 doz
Plastic Measuring Cups 1 & 2 cup	Buy locally		
Food Coloring	" "		
Polyethylene Sheeting (6′ wide)		Roy Edwards, Inc.	10/80/100′ roll
Syringe 20 cc	GAST11	SEE	.35
Syringe 30 cc	GAST10	"	.40
Syringe 50 cc	GAST00	"	.60
Aluminum Sifters and Cans	DP233	Creative Playthings	4.75
Paddle Boat	DR035	" "	3.00
Sand Machine	DB632	" "	8.00
Plastic funnel 35 mm	25-465-1	Cambosco	.31
Plastic Funnel 55 mm	25-465-2	Cambosco	$ .36
" " 75 mm	25-465-4	"	.58
" " 100 mm	25-465-6	"	.91
" " 160 mm	25-465-7	"	1.90
Plastic Filtering Flask 500 ml	25-280	"	1.95
Plastic Erlenmeyer Flask 500 ml	25-270-2	"	2.00
Plastic tubes (6′ long x 1⅛″ dia.)	GAST03	SEE	.35 .30 ea/10 or more
Caps for above (min. order 10)	GAST03	"	.03 ea/25 or more
Plastic tubes (6′ long x ⅝″ dia.)	GAST05	"	.25 .20 ea/10 or more
Caps for above (min. order 10)	GAST06	"	.04 ea .03 ea/25 or more
Clear Plastic Tubing (specify ¼″ I.D.)	2080	Greene Rubber Co.	.14 ft (min. order 50 ft)
Plastic bottle w/hole in bottom	KPS007	SEE	.35
Set of 5 caps with different size holes for above	KPS008	"	.50/set
Assorted taper corks	23-15-3	Cambosco	5.00/100

SCIENCE (Continued)

ITEM	CATALOG REFERENCE	SUPPLIER	COST
Miscellaneous			
Thermometer	SEET00	SEE	.60
Fulham Balance	DA383	Creative Playthings	12.50
Equal Arm Balance (from ESS Kitchen Physics)	KPO604	SEE	1.85

DRAMATIC PLAY

Good suggestions for classrooms—probably not necessary for teachers' workshop. Collect wooden boxes and crates out of which to make housekeeping corner furniture.

ITEM	CATALOG REFERENCE	SUPPLIER	COST
A set of dishes			
1. Buy locally: cups & saucers—set of 6; plates—set of 6; silverware—6 knives, forks, spoons, pots and pans			
2. Puppets—Felt Animal Puppets—set of 6	F.P. 600	Constructive Playthings	$ 7.50
3. Rubber Hand Puppets—family 5 (white)	7D145	Child Craft	14.50
4. " " " " 5 (black)	7D146	" "	14.50
5. Wooden Figures—set of 13 farm animals	2001	Constructive Play	2.00
6. " " set of farm family	2002	" "	2.00
7. Dress-up Clothes (see list of free and inexpensive materials)			
8. Bendable rubber family dolls (white)	DB292	Creative Playthings	8.95
9. " " " " (black)	DB492	" "	8.95

LIST OF SUPPLIERS

Alexander Steel Equipment Corp.
101 River Street
Waltham, Massachusetts 01254

Bell & Howell Company
Audio-Visual Products Division
7100 McCormick Road
Chicago, Illinois 60645

Cambosco Scientific Co.
342 Western Avenue
Boston, Mass. 02135

Childcraft Equipment Co., Inc.
40 Forest Street
Lexington, Mass. 02173
    or
155 East 23rd St.
New York, New York 10010

Community Playthings
Rifton, New York

Constructive Playthings
1040 East 85 St.
Kansas City, Mo. 64131

Creative Playthings, Inc.
Princeton, New Jersey 08540

Cuisenaire Company
    of America, Inc.
12 Church St.
New Rochelle, New York 10805

Economy 5 & 10
1730 Massachusetts Avenue
Cambridge, Mass. 02138

EDC Workshop Store
55 Chapel Street
Newton, Mass. 02160

Edmund Scientific Co.
100 Edscorp Building
Barrington, New Jersey 08007

Roy S. Edwards Inc.
29 Crafts St.
Newton, Mass. 02158

E.S.R., Inc.
34 Label St.
Montclair, New Jersey 07042

Greene Rubber Co., Inc.
160 Second St.
Cambridge, Mass. 02142

J. L. Hammett Co.
Hammett Place, 195 Pearl St.
Boston, Mass. 02184
    or
2393 Vauxhall Road
Union, New Jersey 07083

Herder & Herder
232 Madison Ave.
New York, New York 10016

LaPine Scientific Co.
375 Chestnut St.
Norwood, New Jersey 07648

W. C. Long Co.
P.O. Box 311
Chatsworth, Georgia

Magnamusic—Baton
6394 Delmar Boulevard
St. Louis, Mo. 63130

McGraw-Hill Book Co.
Webster Division
Manchester Road
Manchester, Missouri 63011

Milton Bradley Co.
P.O. Box 1581
Springfield, Mass. 01101

Nasco Scientific Co.
Fort Atkinson, Wisconsin 53538

National Products Inc.
c/o Paul B. Segal
33 Bartlett Road
Randolph, Mass.

Newcomb Audio Products Co.
12881 Bradley Ave.
Sylmar, California 91342

Parallel Manufacturing Co.
32 East 10 St.
New York, New York 10003

Parker Brothers
190 Bridge St.
Salem, Mass.

SEE (Selective Educational
    Equipment Inc.)
3 Bridge Street
Newton, Mass. 02195

Taskmaster Ltd.
165–167 Clarendon Park Road
Leicester, England

Tri-State Plastic Molding Co.
Box 337
Henderson, Kentucky

Tri-Wall Containers, Inc.
Educational Materials & Services
One duPont Street
Plainview, New York 11803

Welch Scientific Co.
7300 North Linder Avenue
Skokie, Illinois 60076

Wollensak 3M Company
3M Center
St. Paul, Minnesota 55101

7. Cardboard Carpentry, or How to Build Your Own Classroom Equipment

With the help of some new materials on the marketplace, e.g., Tri-Wall, a three-layer thick laminated cardboard, and the imaginative use of old materials such as cardboard and paste, teachers who are not skilled carpenters can now make tables, chairs, bookcases, room dividers, display cases, slides, climbing apparatus, and other large pieces of classroom equipment at a relatively small cost. Since the new cardboard materials are much easier to use, as well as much cheaper, than plywood or other kinds of wood, building classroom equipment can be a joint effort of teacher and students. The following suggestions are drawn from a catalog published by the Workshop for Learning Things, Inc., an EDC offshoot that set itself up as an independent organization in 1971.

WHAT WE DO

The Workshop Offers These Services:

Advice on purchasing and sources of supply for schools and classrooms

Commercial and general photography and photo-processing

Courses for teachers and others

Custom manufacture of school equipment and materials

Design services

Graphics for schools and for books about school

Illustrative photography, especially in and around classrooms

Publishing, especially books by children

Workshops for teachers and others, here or wherever you are

The Workshop Sells Things Like:

Cameras, film and supplies

Cardboard and the tools for working it

Things to build with, carve with, print with

Furniture things—easels, workbenches, playground equipment, sand tables, etc.

Storage things—cubbies and cubbyboxes

Books—to help you get started and to learn what others have done; several of these are by children

From Workshop for Learning Things, Inc., *Our Catalog*, Fall 1971. (Watertown, Mass.: Workshop for Learning Things, Inc.) pp. 4–7, 13–17.

The Workshop for Learning Things opened more than three years ago to develop and supply innovative materials to teachers who are interested in building informal classrooms and in pushing learning into unaccustomed places. By and large, the materials and books we have developed have been the sort which offer children and teachers experiences not usually found in school—things once described as inappropriate for classrooms, until we began to suspect that classrooms (and kids, and teachers) were tougher than we knew.

One of the pleasures of our first three years has been to watch the unusual become familiar—to see such things as cardboard furniture and classroom photography finding a comfortable place in classrooms throughout the country. . . .

The Workshop for Learning Things began several years ago at Education Development Center in Newton, Mass. as a group of teachers, photographers, writers, designers, and curriculum developers who found themselves drawn together by a common interest in physical changes in the classroom environment . . . in helping to reshape the room where school is. As we became able to involve other teachers in the development of ideas and materials, the Workshop took shape and grew almost without deliberate effort—giving both teachers and ourselves the advantage of this new way of working. . . .

Several years ago, the Workshop first came across triple-thick corrugated cardboard. We began to design and build with it, wondering how many conventional building materials—lumber, plywood, masonite—it might replace. Since then, we've used thousands of sheets of it, much of it in workshops working with people using it for the first time. It has made it possible for anyone to take direct part in shaping learning environments.

This laminated cardboard is three layers thick and comes in very large sheets. It is inexpensive compared to plywood, yet it is satisfyingly strong. Used with a good eye for its advantages and shortcomings, it can be as durable in a classroom as the more expensive materials. Best of all, it can be worked with simple tools and requires few or no woodworking skills. The inventory of things made by teachers in recent workshops is endless . . . chairs, carts, tables, easels, play-see-saws, sandboxes. . . . This combination of cardboard, tools, techniques and people we call Cardboard Carpentry.

Booklets About Cardboard Carpentry

CARDBOARD CARPENTRY WORKSHOP:

A photo essay about a cardboard carpentry workshop one summer, with a nice sense of how people began to learn and the range of things they made.

FURTHER ADVENTURES OF CARDBOARD CARPENTRY:

A cookbook . . . Full of sketches and plans of things other people have made with heavy cardboard. About special structural problems and good ways of using tools to do what you want.

Some Facts About Triple-Thick Cardboard

It's 9/16 in. thick and comes in sheets as large as 4 × 8 ft.

The cardboard is made of tough brown paper and is designed in triple-burger fashion with three layers of fluted corrugations sandwiched between four flat sheets. The fluting gives the board a "grain" similar to that of wood and offers design advantages when you are building for maximum strength.

Triple-thick cardboard is about ⅓ the weight of comparably thick plywood and about ½ the price.

It's easy to work with simple tools even if you aren't accustomed to carpentry. In fact, it's a very "forgiving" material.

It takes paint nicely, can be covered with burlap, makes a great surface to stick pins in . . . paint murals on. . . . One coat of chalkboard paint and it's a chalkboard.

This cardboard is very useful for making "rough drafts" of hard-to-design things. A few good ideas tried out quickly in cardboard can save a lot of hours and money.

As a general rule, it doesn't do to get cardboard wet. Even though we've made a thoroughly seaworthy sailboat and a good canoe out of the stuff, we don't recommend soaking it with water unless you tape the edges and varnish the surface.

Buying Cardboard

The heavy, triple-thick cardboard which serves as the lumber for Cardboard Carpentry is available at the Workshop on a cash and carry basis. We stock three sizes: 3½ × 4½ ft., 4 × 6 ft., and 4 × 8 ft. We try to keep a good supply on hand at all times, but a phone call ahead is a good idea. The Workshop is open from 8:30 to 5:30, Monday through Friday, and our telephone number is (617) 926-3491.

For those living in the greater Boston area, we can arrange to have cardboard delivered to you. For delivery, a 20 sheet minimum order is required. Give us a call and we'll give you the details.

Shipment of cardboard in 100 sheet lots can be arranged direct from the factory. Factory direct prices are substantially cheaper and this method is your best bet if you need large quantities of cardboard. We have a piece of paper which explains all the details, and we'll be happy to send it on request.

You can get started in Cardboard Carpentry with very simple tools.

Your kitchen and the basement will probably yield a handsaw, a paring knife, a yardstick. That's all it takes for a start. The tools we offer are designed to improve the cardboard's versatility and to make it possible to build easily some pretty fancy things. We've chosen the tools in our kits with an eye to having them last a long time in classroom workshop use. They've been in hundreds of classrooms by now and are standing up well, and that gives us conviction about our choices, even when we see that Cheap & Dirty, Inc. has similar tools on sale for less than our price.

PLAYGROUND THINGS

The slide and ladder house are for playing on—they are equally useful inside or out, although the cardboard items shouldn't be left long in the rain. They are for climbing, sliding and spinning; they are exciting for children and, like many adventures, a little scarey, too.

These items are large and hard for us to store, so we aren't able to keep them in stock. Consequently, please allow 90 days for them to reach you.

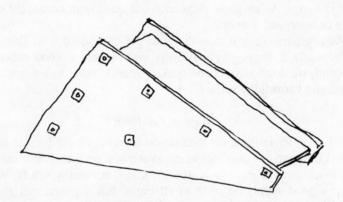

SLIDE: What do we say about a slide? Not much to explain about ours, except that it's also cardboard, about three feet high, fastened with birch dowels, and nuts, is light enough for children to lug around—and works just fine.

LADDER HOUSE: Flat on the floor, it's a "crawl-through"; standing upright, it is a climbing tower, or a hideout. It's made of heavy, folded cardboard and long, stout, threaded birch dowels fastened with wooden nuts.

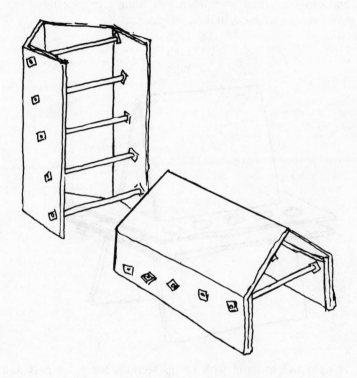

WORKING FURNITURE

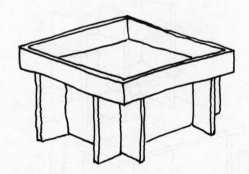

SAND TRAY TABLE: There are so many things a sand table is for! Kids measure and sift; there is dramatic play of many kinds; they make streets and villages; work out roadways for little trucks and cars; invent map making; explore the physical properties of sand. Recreate the world of the dinosaurs! Other science and social studies exploration. A 30″ square sand tray of lacquered wood can be plastic lined for wet sand or growing plants, and can be turned over when you want a regular table top. It comes with a cardboard base, in three heights:

18" high
24" high
30" high

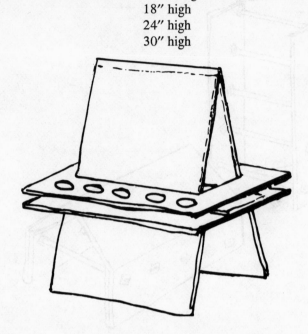

EASEL: A light weight easel with no-tip sections for paint pots and a good sized surface for painting. Triple-thick cardboard.

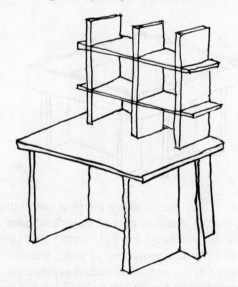

DESK AND SHELVES: Wooden desk with shelves, 47½" high, and 23½" wide.

8. The City as Classroom

The physical openness of an open classroom is designed to symbolize openness in other ways: to other teachers and students in the same school; to parents; and to the community itself. If children are to become self-directed learners outside school as well as inside it, they need to learn how to draw intellectual sustenance from the complex world around them, which means learning how to see and how to listen. And if children are to learn from experience, there are few better sources than a disciplined exploration of the world we all tend to take for granted. The book from which this selection is taken contains detailed suggestions on ways to use some sixty-seven different community re-sources as learning environments. Supported by the Educational Facilities Laboratories, Yellow Pages of Learning Resources *was conceived in response to "The Invisible City" International Design Conference in Aspen, Colorado; Richard Saul Wurman is a partner in the Philadelphia architecture and planning firm of Murphy Levy Wurman.*

Introduction

Why a *Yellow Pages of Learning Resources?*

The city is education—and the architecture of education rarely has much to do with the building of schools. The city is a schoolhouse, and its ground floor is both bulletin board and library. The graffiti of the city are its window displays announcing events; they should reveal its people to themselves, tell about what they're doing and why and where they're doing it. Everything we do—if described, made clear, and made ob-servable—is education: the "Show and Tell," the city itself.

This book is concerned with the potential of the city as a place for learning.

Education has been thought of as taking place mainly within the confines of the classroom, and school buildings have been regarded as the citadels of knowledge. However, the most extensive facility imagina-ble for learning is our urban environment. It is a classroom without walls, an open university for people of all ages offering a boundless curriculum with unlimited expertise. If we can make our urban environ-ment comprehensible and observable, we will have created classrooms with endless windows on the world.

From Richard Saul Wurman, ed., *Yellow Pages of Learning Resources* (Cambridge, Mass.: M.I.T. Press, 1972), pp. 1–3, 85–87. Copyright © 1972 by GEE!

What is the *Yellow Pages of Learning Resources*?

This book is an invitation to discover the city as a learning resource.

The purpose of the *Yellow Pages* is to turn people on to learning in the city and to assist them in taking advantage of the wealth of available learning opportunities. There are three basic parts to this invitation. First, the *Yellow Pages* provides a selection of typical firsthand learning resources that can be found in almost any city. These examples and the others they suggest serve to make vivid the richness of learning potential readily at our disposal. The examples of typical learning resources included in the *Yellow Pages* are intended to indicate the depth and breadth of available learning possibilities. There are thousands of others that might have been considered had there been time and room enough. You will find those that most interest you. The key is to start realizing the learning potential in the people, places, and processes we encounter every day.

Second, the *Yellow Pages* outlines the avenues to follow in order to make these resources accessible. This is the "where" and "how" of converting people, places, and processes into sources of learning. The aim of this book is to encourage readers, through the examples provided, to extend their own entrepreneurial abilities to locate and utilize additional resources for learning. The extent of accessible learning resources is limited only by the reader's imagination and sensitivity to his environment.

We believe that schools are the places for education, and most of the time we know when we are being taught. As a result, most of us are apathetic when it comes to self-learning. We have television, light shows, teaching machines, cinerama, and a whole host of simulation techniques —a vast technology for making the artificial seem real. But in the glamor of our sophisticated informational and educational technologies we often fail to appreciate the reality in our everyday lives; we no longer place a premium on experiential learning. Reality is frequently too obvious, and we are rapidly becoming jaded. Too often we no longer look carefully, listen intently, or yield to our innate sense of wonder.

Yet the city is everywhere around us, and it is rife with invaluable learning resources. Even more than classrooms and teachers, the most valuable learning resources in the city are the people, places, and processes that we encounter every day. But in order to realize the vast learning potential of these resources, we must learn to learn from them.

We should learn to differentiate between products and performance. We must learn to use the city, to explore. We must learn not to overlook the obvious. We must learn to hear when we listen, to see when we look, to ask questions, and to realize that good questions are better than brilliant answers. We must learn to demand from our city that it fulfill its potential as a learning resource. Each of us should recognize his role as the developer of an invitation to learning.

We should be concerned about real experiences and encourage the development of new learning situations that are independent of traditional books and learning products, which focus on student experiences in classrooms and school buildings. We should be interested in the identification and the subsequent communication of the elements that make up the man-made environment. We should understand the need to develop the skills and abilities to communicate information about the environment, both verbally and nonverbally. We should create in a student the confidence that will enable him to develop the criteria that might be used in the evaluation or creation of his own environments. And we should remember that we are all students. We should encourage a sense of ownership of the city and define the extent of the public environment. We should see the "environment issue," not simply as the causes and effects of air and water pollution, but in broader terms: the understanding of the total physical environment, both public and private.

This book is full of questions. These are provided in order to suggest how rich the learning resources can be and to cultivate the learning process by planting the seeds of inquiry. Questions, rather than answers, are the beginning of learning, but too often we find it difficult to pose good questions.

LEARNING FROM PEOPLE

In a very real sense the city is its people. Everybody can be a teacher. From a bank president to the guy next door—including the mailman, Uncle Charlie, a carpenter, a shopkeeper, and everyone else—everybody knows things, has been places, and has answers. The city is full of people to learn from—all we have to do is start asking questions and demonstrate enough interest to deserve the answers.

Then, too, each of us can be both learner and teacher. Once we have unleashed our own curiosity, we can easily appreciate other people's quest to know and understand. We need, therefore, to be open and willing to share our knowledge and understanding with each other. To other people, we are the other people.

LEARNING AT PLACES

Classrooms are not the only places for learning. There are many other spaces that could be used for people to get together and learn in. While we search around for spaces in which to meet, learn, play, rest, or think, thousands of spaces are going unused in every city. Our cities are very inefficient because we do not use effectively the spaces we have. Ironically, we are wasting valuable space by using it for only small parts of the day; at the same time we complain of the need for more classrooms. Office conference rooms, public auditoriums, waiting rooms, movie theaters, churches, building lobbies—just to name a few—are always there, even when they are not being used. How could we begin to take advantage of the city's underutilized spaces?

As well as being spaces for meeting and learning in, many places are themselves learning resources. Very often things can best be learned by experiencing them firsthand. Why read about how a port operates when there is one a short bus ride away? Why read a book about how steel is made if there is a steel plant nearby? Does it make sense to study about crime and police protection services without ever visiting a real police station?

Any place where special things happen or that possesses unique characteristics (and all places do when you think seriously about them) can be a rich learning resource. That it is not fancy or designed for learning makes it especially valuable. Street corners, hospitals (in which one can learn about bookkeeping and food preparation, as well as about medicine), stores, gas stations, airports, electricity generating plants, banks, and insurance companies are all good places for learning, and experiential learning is the most interesting and the most fun.

LEARNING ABOUT PROCESSES

We usually tend to think of things only as products instead of considering the roles they play in larger processes. Telephones are small parts of the process of communication, automobiles are parts of transportation, and doctors are parts of health care. When we enlarge our thinking to seek an understanding of whole processes, we consider cause-and-effect relationships, change over time, interrelationships among parts, and total concepts. Just think of all the processes required daily to make a city possible!

Good questions lead us eventually to want to know how a process works from beginning to end. When we mail a letter, how does it find its way to its destination? By what means do our cities grow and change? Where does the food we eat come from, and what happens to it along the way? The daily processes affecting each of our lives are constant invitations to learning, once we cease taking them for granted.

Who can use the *Yellow Pages of Learning Resources*?

Just about everyone—children, high-school students, parents, and teachers. This book is written so that children can understand it and use it themselves. However, several of the learning resources outlined here are especially suited to group learning experiences—guided tours, field trips, and demonstrations of particular skills. It is hoped that

	Philadelphia, Pennsylvania	Baltimore, Maryland	Cincinnati, Ohio	Albuquerque, New Mexico	Columbus, Ohio	Altoona, Pennsylvania	Wausau, Wisconsin	Tulare, California	Aspen, Colorado
Population	1,948,609	905,759	452,524	243,751	154,168	62,900	32,806	13,824	2,404
Advertising agencies (indoor and outdoor)	330	195	134	38	9	8	8	1	5
Architects	445	175	166	84	15	9	6	n.a.	15
Auto registrations	613,902	269,193	150,841	142,869	100,427	33,000	19,138	9,164	n.a.
Banks	22 main 339 branches	sav. 5 comm. 7 sav. and loan 295	comm. and sav. 116 sav. and loan 246	comm. 6 branches 29 sav. and loan 7	sav. 9 sav. and loan 5	comm. 2 sav. and loan 5	comm. 6 sav. and loan 2	4	3
Department stores	95 main 140 branches	59	53	23	28	15	10	6	3
Doctors (M.D.s only)	4,000	2,193	1,130	347	139	101	65	19	12
Electric meters	539,204	584,308	427,722	98,669	57,621	20,888	28,657	n.a.	n.a.
Gas meters	539,261	421,669	312,059	81,826	48,645	20,580	12,303	n.a.	n.a.
Hospitals (general)	40	29	28 (in area)	8	3	3	4	4	1
Junk yards and dealers	85	52	21	7	6	5	2	n.a.	n.a.

	Philadelphia, Pennsylvania	Baltimore, Maryland	Cincinnati, Ohio	Albuquerque, New Mexico	Columbus, Ohio	Altoona, Pennsylvania	Wausau, Wisconsin	Tulare, California	Aspen, Colorado
Lawyers	5,420	2,458	1,470	432	146	50	53	10	19
Libraries (all kinds)	183 (plus branches)	66 (24 br. free lib.)	66 (35 br. of pub. lib.)	13 (6 br. of pub. lib.)	4	4	5	1	1
Newspapers (daily)	3	2	2	2	2	1	1	1	1
Newspapers, magazines, and trade publications	285	99	69	17	6	5	1	1	3
Photographic processing plants	350	205	170	100	33	17	6	6	7
Printing (printers and establishments)	545	356	241	62	31	19	17	1	2
Schools (K-12)	276	217	109	111	67	27	18 Wasau 6 Joint District	12	3
Schools (elementary)	193	168	74	78	51	22	14	8	1
Schools (junior high and middle)	36	31	17	22	9 (7 and 8)	3	2 (middle)	2 (junior high)	1

	26	18	8	9	7 (9-12)	1 senior / 1 tech/voc	2 high	2	1
Schools (high and vocational)	26	18	8	9	7 (9-12)	1 senior / 1 tech/voc	2 high	2	1
Students (elementary)	175,101	112,484	45,929	K: 1,407 / 40,579	22,502 (K-6)	7,287	4,312	4,200 (K-8)	498
Students (junior high and middle)	50,034	77,084	17,916	20,888	16,700	3,297	2,132	946	393
Students (high school and vocational)	59,232 (including 6,209 vocational)	n.a.	15,454	21,664	15,254	3,280	3,467	2,900 (9-12)	367
Number of students in K-12 system	284,367	193,150	79,299	84,538	41,000 (approx.)	13,800	9,911	7,333	1,258
Number of teachers	12,236	n.a.	2,799	3,030 (not including K)	1,884	615	498	128 (9-12)	67
Ratio of students to teachers	23/1	n.a.	28/1	28/1	28/1	n.a.	20/1	30/1	22/1
Number of classrooms	9,500	6,126 (plus 700 shops and labs)	4,471	3,342	n.a.	n.a.	450	n.a.	57

n.a.—figures not available.

parents and teachers, as well as children, will read this book and find in it suggestions for learning experiences that they can both utilize themselves and share with the younger learners who look to them for guidance.

The *Yellow Pages of Learning Resources* can also be used by people in every city and town. No matter how small your town is, it is rich in learning resources to be tapped. The following chart provides a sample list of resources in many different areas—from a large city of almost two million people right down to a small town of just over two thousand!

How to Use This Book

LEARNING FROM AN ANONYMOUS BUILDING

Now that you have read how different people, places, and processes—those that are part of your everyday experience—can open new areas of interest and investigation, how do you go about finding these resources?

One place to start is a large office building in your town. Most buildings will have a directory in the lobby, which will list the names of the occupants. Sometimes they will also list a director or superintendent's name. To learn more about an individual company, you can ask an elevator operator for the name of the company's director, talk to the building manager, or walk directly into the superintendent's office.

Whichever office you enter, carry a pencil and paper and be prepared with a basic framework of questions and a concise explanation of whom you want to talk to and why you are there. There will generally be a receptionist as you enter. Ask for the director or manager. If these are inappropriate titles for this company, the receptionist will say so. Then give your name and explain your purpose. The receptionist will give you the name of the proper person; if he or she is not available, make an appointment.

In order to give an example of the breadth of possibilities in one building, a survey of an eleven-story downtown office building in an Eastern city was taken and produced the following list of occupants:

Three finance companies	Shoe store
Real estate broker	Tap room
Psychologist	Pizza parlor
Optometrist	Architectural engineers
Four private lawyers	Bondsmen
Public defenders	Two dentists
Four local trade union	Jewelry shop
headquarters	Two community organizations
Beauty shop	Small magazine headquarters

Food concession stand
Collection agency
Wholesale kitchen equipment
   company
Court reporters
Security guard agency
Two city agencies
Political group
Medical laboratory

Building manager,
   superintendent, building
   agent, and other staff
Four insurance agents
Educational organization
Public relations agency
Two accountants
Employment agency

Even if you were to investigate only one-quarter of a list like this, learning all about the company, its personnel, its business, and all of the other kinds of companies and people involved with it, you would learn a great deal about the interlocking of resources and problems in your community.

GUIDELINES FOR GROUP LEARNING

As you have learned, the education and enjoyment potential of the community is great. But reading about the resources is often quite different from actual investigation. Where do you begin? Must you start with a subject area or can you just start with a city block or a building? There are a few general guidelines that may be helpful to you before you embark on your project.

What is the size of the group? Will this be for your entire group, a portion of it (like five people), or, perhaps, is it for only one individual?

Where will the activity take place? Will you go to the place or the person (to the journalist, airport, street corner, etc.), or will the resource come to you (pharmacist or clergyman come to speak before your community group, class, etc.)?

How long will the relationship between you and the resource last? Will it be a one-day visit to a factory or a two-part tour of a hospital by the whole group followed by once-a-week visits by one or two of the group to spend concentrated time with the financial vice-president and a file clerk at the registration desk, or a two-week all-day involvement with a lawyer?

What is the purpose of the investigation? Do you want to get a general overview of a block in your neighborhood? Do you want to know the relationship of city agencies to your street? Are you interested in vocational opportunities? Do you want to know the relationship of one individual to a whole organization (for example, a marketing executive in a cosmetic firm)?

After you are able to answer the preceding questions, also keep the following guidelines in mind.

The planning of the activity should involve the prospective participants. If you are a teacher or a group leader, your students or group members should help define the project's goals and then define the method of reaching these goals—the searching out of the resources, planning and organizing the resources, participants, and schedule.

All projects should allow for discussion and shared-learning periods. This is particularly true of an extended project. But even if it is a one-time visit and you are taking your child or a brother or sister, you should incorporate a let's-talk-it-over session to reinforce new learning or plan for a follow-up session to clear up uncertainties. The discussion should also include an evaluation of the activity, which will help you to plan better for further projects and to be more sensitive to learning opportunities in both everyday and specially planned activities.

As you plan a project, it is advantageous to start with familiar resources before introducing totally unfamiliar ones. When learning about building and zoning codes, for instance, start with your own home and neighborhood (or that of the group). When you are learning about a hospital, start with a doctor or a nurse, before an accountant or a physical therapist.

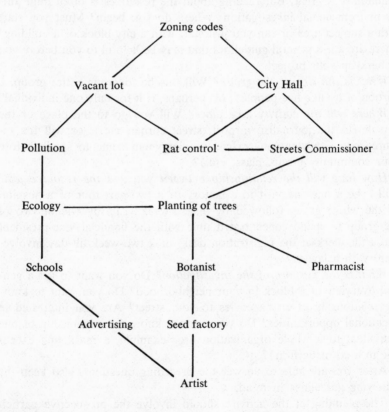

An investigation will tend to be more successful if it involves action, not only study. If you are learning about air pollution, learn who the polluters are. It is far more satisfying to plan an action that might involve reporting an offender, publicizing business or government agencies that break pollution laws, or planning and implementing a publicity campaign for your neighborhood, instructing the residents on how to combat pollution.

Because everything in the community is interdisciplinary and interlocked, it is natural to assume that one well-planned project will lead to many more. For example, start anywhere on this diagram and you will see that everything has some relationship to everything else.

EXPERIMENTING IN ELEMENTARY SCHOOL

When one thinks of actively learning about the community, one usually thinks of an adult or a teen-ager but rarely sees the elementary-age child as an active participant.

One elementary school decided to experiment. There are thirty-two students between ten and eleven years old in this fifth grade class with one teacher. The teacher made all of the initial arrangements; but as these are proving to be successful, other organizations and people are contacting the school directly.

The students are involved for approximately two to four hours a week. The kinds of activities are varied, giving students a broad range of experiences. Each activity involves approximately two to eight students, depending upon the nature of the activity, where it takes place, and the student selection process. The students are generally walked over to their activity by the teacher or by volunteer college students.

Here is a list of some people, places, and processes these students are investigating:

City Hall. The students go to court hearings and sit in the jury box. The judges will often speak to them directly from the bench to be sure that the students understand what is going on. The students also do a variety of clerical activities under the supervision of someone in the office of the City Council. Everything they do is explained—explained both for skill learning (for example, how to file) and for the reason behind it (for example, these are records of housing complaints). They answer phones, type, file, stamp the city seal, address envelopes, use the Xerox machine and adding machines.

YMCA. The students work in the day care center with one- to three-year-old children. They play games and help care for them.

Political Headquarters. The students do the same kinds of things all political volunteers do. They answer phones, address envelopes, file, and interview the candidates on a regular basis. They also attend many of the local political rallies.

Photography. A photographer volunteers his time several hours a week to work with the students. The students have learned how to use still and moving cameras, how to develop their own film, and how to use film to investigate a subject area, for example, city planning.

Board of Education. The students work with the social studies department. They do many different kinds of clerical duties, many of which take them all around the building. As a result, they have become very familiar with the different departments and people involved in the education of the public school students. They also interview many of these people, including the superintendent and his associates. While they are working there, they are also given lessons in African history, since the supervisor in charge of the students is an African scholar.

Science Museum. Because the school is located near the city's Science Museum, several students are attached to the education supervisor. Every morning the students set up the apparatus for the day's experiment. The experiments remain the same for a week; by the end of the week, the students know and can explain the entire experiment. One day a week, the students remain for the presentation to visiting groups and act as aids to the demonstrator.

Food Co-op. The students run the register, pack the bags, stamp incoming products, set up displays, and shelve. As an added incentive to a new way of learning mathematics and organization, the students get a free lunch!

Anthropological Museum. Three anthropology students and their professor from a local university have taken a special interest in these students and each week are teaching them about different cultures through the exhibits. The students have also been involved in taking polls in the area to determine why the attendance at this free museum is not higher and are making and distributing posters to encourage more people to visit.

Stock Exchange and Computer Center. Besides the usual tour and clerical duties associated with many of their other activities, the students also learn to work with computers. They learn to read the stock page, select a company to follow, help write a program for the computer, and then try to predict the stock activity of the company. They also learn how to run a small computer.

Once a week the students spend a good part of the day making presentations to the rest of the class about the week's activities. Not only do they talk about their activities, but they also read extra books on their subject area, show their work (for example, one student at the Anthropological Museum is an excellent artist and displays his drawings of the artifacts while explaining what he has learned), and actually teach the rest of the group. While the students are learning, so is the teacher. It is now unnecessary for her to avoid those subject areas she knows nothing or little about. She has the students work with an expert and learn for themselves.

The success of this program has been largely due to excellent organization and planning and an attempt to match a student's interest to a particular activity. Through this program, the students have become more independent, self-reliant, and outgoing. For many students who were having difficulty with basic skills like reading and mathematics, these kinds of experiences have shown them the practical needs for these skills, offered a more exciting way of learning them, and, more importantly, provided the motivation to learn more.

A NEW APPROACH TO ADULT EDUCATION

An adult discussion group meets biweekly. They have decided to spend a month or two on urban problems. Previously they had speakers come to their meeting place, but this time they decided to do things differently. This time they wanted to actually go out into the community and learn more directly about the problems and the people involved. They also decided that they would establish some ongoing action-oriented program.

The group established the following procedure: The twelve members split into groups of three, with each group specializing in one of the following areas:

1. Housing
2. Employment
3. Mental health (including drugs and alcohol)
4. Education

The group members attempted to meet people involved in these four areas by making appointments with individuals in various agencies or by doing volunteer work. Where this was not possible, group members did individual research on their particular subjects.

One of the two meetings each month is now devoted to discussion and sharing of learning experiences, while the second continues to involve a speaker, in the field that the previous meeting concentrated on. However, the group members feel that with the background provided by the people who have either worked in or researched a particular area, they can appreciate better the monthly lecture. Many of the group members have also found their work in the community personally rewarding, as well as instructive.

IV

How to Make
the Change

How do I begin? is a question teachers who have been persuaded of the advantages of open education inevitably (and quite properly) ask. The first answer is—SLOWLY! The most common mistake that teachers make, in fact, is to try to do too much too soon. Informal teaching is difficult, and it takes time for a teacher to internalize so radically different a role. Indeed, the first weeks and months—for some, the first year or two—can be unsettling and even frightening; the teacher who tries to move too quickly may feel overwhelmed. Children, too, need time to learn to make choices and to assume responsibility for their own learning and their own behavior. Hence the teacher who begins slowly is likely to travel a lot farther than the one who tries to do everything at once.

The second answer to the question, How do I begin? is—in whatever way you find comfortable. Some teachers begin by "opening up" in one subject area, the area in which the teacher is most comfortable, continuing to teach the other subjects in the traditional manner. Others begin by opening up for an hour a day, or one day a week, continuing to use the traditional approach the rest of the time. Others feel more comfortable starting on a larger scale. The point is that there is no single "right way" to begin; how a teacher makes the transition should be a function of his or her interests, knowledge, personality, fears, teaching style, relationships with the students, relationships with other teachers and administrators, and so on.

1. Changing the Teacher's Approach Toward Children and Learning

"There is no one way to begin," Vincent Rogers argues in this selection in which he poses and then answers the questions teachers ask most often about open education. There is only one prerequisite: that the teacher begin to see, and to think about, children and learning in a different way.

Vincent Rogers was first exposed to the informal British primary schools in 1966, when he began a study of British education as a Fulbright Scholar. "I have not been quite the same since," he wrote in 1970 in the preface to Teaching in the British Primary Schools, *a collection of papers by English educators which he assembled and edited. "Seventy-two schools later I still find myself wondering if what I saw was real, if such schools and teachers do exist. Four cartons of notes taken on 3-x-5 cards give material support to the fact that these schools do indeed exist and that they are becoming increasingly influential, not only in Britain but in the wider world as well." ***

Professor Rogers' own writing and lecturing have helped make those schools increasingly influential, as have the innovations in teacher education that he instituted during his tenure as chairman of the elementary education at the University of Connecticut. Professor Rogers is now professor of education at the University of Connecticut and director of the University's Center for Open Education.

This past summer, hundreds of American teachers flocked to England to visit open or informal classrooms, schools here with reputations for "openness" are generally inundated with visitors, and open education has become a fairly common topic of conversation in teachers' rooms across the country.

Let's start, then, with the assumption that you've already read and talked about open education. On these pages I'll attempt to answer specific questions that I'm asked most often about informal classrooms.

Can I start an open classroom in my room alone, or does the whole school have to take the step?

Actually, there are very few schools that have made sudden or in-

From Vincent R. Rogers, "Open Education—Answering Teachers' Questions," *Instructor,* August–September 1971.

* Vincent R. Rogers, editor, *Teaching in the British Primary School,* (New York: Macmillan, 1970).

stant changeovers. In fact, when we find a school that is operating this way from top to bottom, we can usually assume that the change began with one or two teachers who dared to be different. There are some exceptions of course. Some "free" schools, and private schools like Summerhill, may have begun with this philosophy in mind. For any educational innovation to take hold in a serious way, working models are essential. Beginning the change process in a given school by having one or two teachers start is good strategy, and is more likely to bring about successful longterm results than an attempt to convert an entire school at once.

Can I begin gradually, perhaps using some traditional and some open methods, and eventually make the total change?

A few teachers I know have come to open education in the way that some people come to religion. They experience a rather sudden insight or revelation and from that moment on they are converted. But most of us go through a more gradual process, in which we examine and re-examine old ideas, and little by little come to look at teaching children with a new perspective. A typical change pattern might consist of identifying one area, such as language arts, and then setting up a "center" in the classroom, which might include an old typewriter, a variety of other tools to write with, blank paper in various shapes and sizes, handmade books, books only partially completed that invite children to finish them, and so on. Necessary rules for working in the center would be set up, such as "Only one person may use the typewriter at a time," "Only six people may work in the center at one time." As a result, small groups of children spend some of their working in language arts in freer ways.

Some teachers begin by taking one or two time blocks during the week, perhaps Tuesday morning and Friday afternoon, to use for freer activities. One teacher I know began by building with the children a color display in the corridor outside her room that included everything they could lay their hands on that was red. Another started by introducing animals and other living things into his classroom. *There is no one way to begin.* What is essential is that the teacher begin to change his attitude towards children and learning, to become more an observer and listener, to become more responsive to children's interests and needs. It is equally important that teachers be aware of the inconsistencies of their work at this stage. They must realize that one is not an open teacher merely because of opening a reading-writing center or making a color display.

How much should the teacher facilitate and direct?

He facilitates and directs a great deal, although not always in an obvious way. If he sets up a math center and includes certain apparatus in it, he is clearly directing children towards working with that apparatus. The materials that teachers bring to their classrooms, and the learning environment that they create, help determine the responses of children. An empty environment will bring about few responses.

The teacher in an open classroom is still very much in charge. He is a dynamic participant in each day's activities. He is, as John Coe says, "alongside the child" in his work in the classroom. He constantly suggests, prods, challenges, stimulates, and demands—but only in terms of what is "do-able" by each child. *The teacher does not abrogate authority.* He is not a passive observer, nor does he hesitate to set up and enforce necessary rules. And he does not constantly conceal feelings of annoyance, concern, or even anger—for most of all, he is a human being interacting with other human beings.

Are there no standards in open classrooms? Do children never fail?

Many people who have never visited a good informal classroom seem to equate open education with some kind of permissiveness or softness. Nothing could be farther from the truth. In schools such as the Tower Hill School in Oxfordshire, England, the quality of work produced by the children is tremendously impressive. This includes work in all areas: art, music, math, reading, creative writing, and so on. I have often heard the word "craftsmanship" emphasized in such schools, and I think we can translate that into "demand for excellence." Excellence, however, is determined not by comparisons with arbitrary standards but rather in terms of what a given child can do. Teachers, then, must know children well and make appropriate, challenging, yet achievable demands on them. A teacher should not hesitate to return a piece of work and ask that it be improved, or to ask for more, if in his judgment the child can really be expected to do a better job. Such a request does not indicate failure on the child's part, however. It is simply a matter of a teacher's reacting constructively to a child's work, showing him where it is good, where it is not so good, and how it might be better. *Children are not compared with other children. The concept of failure has no part in open education.*

How do you evaluate children in open classrooms? What do you do about marks and grades?

Children are constantly evaluated in open classrooms, and record keeping becomes an important part of a teacher's work. However, the evaluation covers a wide range of talents, skills, abilities, and interests. Teachers keep informal simple records of what books a child has read, what sorts of difficulties he has in reading, what he is able to do in counting, measuring, sorting and so on. In addition, teachers keep folders of children's work, including examples of their drawings and paintings, poetry, stories, and other projects. Items are added periodically so that a look at the folder can show the development of a child's work in a given area over a period of time. Teachers occasionally make notes on index cards concerning such things as the way a child interacts with others, handles animals, or reacts toward adults and younger children. What a child is and what he does are both evaluated. Teachers place great value on the work the child produces, and less value on outside tests of any kind. Marks and grades have little place in an informal classroom. However, thorough and complete communication with parents and other teachers about the child and his work is very much a part of open education.

How do I set up limits and boundaries for student activities and behavior? For example, can I let a child work at one interest center for four days if he wants to?

The open teacher must, above all, become a skilled listener and observer. He must know his children in the most complete sense of the term. Teaching consists of making series of decisions concerning what activities are or are not appropriate, how an activity may be extended, and when it should be stopped. No one suggests that informal teachers dodge or ignore this responsibility. However, when a teacher intervenes, he must do so on the basis of the best knowledge available to him concerning the skills, interests, and abilities of a given child. It may be entirely appropriate for a child who is deeply interested in a project to carry it on over a long period of time. This is one of the greatest assets of the open classroom—there are no periods, bells, or schedules, and a child has the opportunity to become completely involved with an activity. Another child, however, perhaps because he has chosen poorly or because of his own limitations, will need to be encouraged to work somewhere else. Only the teacher can make that decision, and he must carry it out in the most straightforward way possible. There's no need to play games with children, to trick them or charm them into changing activities. The teacher simply says, "You've been at that long enough now. I'd like you to come over here and work with me on your writing book for a while."

Most informal classrooms have a minimum number of rules, but there ARE rules and they must be adhered to. "Only five children may work in the math center at one time," "Animals may not be taken out of their cages unless I give permission," "No children may go beyond the fence when we go outdoors," and so on. An open classroom is not something magical that makes for instant cooperation from all children. What a teacher must try to do, however, is set up a learning situation that is geared to the needs and interests of children, and provide experiences that are challenging, stimulating, and yet nonthreatening. Most children will respond favorably to such efforts. The discipline problems that cause so much concern in traditional classrooms tend to diminish, although they may not completely disappear.

Is open education really unstructured, or merely not structured in the traditional sense?

The best answer to this question is to look inside a hypothetical open classroom. What do we see? Among other things, sand and water tables, Cuisenaire rods, attribute blocks, bottle caps, popsicle sticks, two or three boxes of oddly shaped macaroni for counting and sorting, typewriters, material for printing, "Task" or assignment cards of various kinds, books of recipes, an orange (or blue or yellow or red) table with an invitation to add objects of the same color, animals that are observed, written about, weighed, measured, and loved, and an infinite number of other things. Each is there because the teacher decided there were obvious learning possibilities inherent in these materials. Therefore he structured the classroom environment by utilizing them. This is a different sort of structure from that usually found in a traditional classroom, but it is neither random nor unplanned.

However, no matter how structured the learning environment, remember that the teacher in the open classroom is an astute observer of children. How a child responds to an activity, problem, or a piece of apparatus cannot always be predicted. Therefore, the follow-up may well be something that the teacher has not anticipated. He must be willing, nevertheless, to adjust to its going off in a new direction, or going backwards, or leaping far ahead if the situation calls for it. He notes how individual children react and then builds or structures future activities on the basis of this knowledge. He does not push ahead with an inappropriate program, or a unit or work which is obviously falling flat or producing different responses from those he planned for.

I hasten to add, incidentally, that open teachers use many materials that are found in traditional classrooms, including workbooks, textbooks, programmed materials of various sorts, and so on. However, such materials rarely become the curriculum. They are used with individual children if the material meets a specific need. The difference lies in how such material is used.

What kinds of problems am I likely to run into if I change to open education?

Some teachers make the transition fairly smoothly, while others have the rockiest sort of going. This is partly due to individual differences among teachers. Some are simply more skilled than others. However, it also has a great deal to do with the amount of preparation and serious thought given to such a move by both the teacher and the principal. If, for example, parents have been involved from the beginning and they have had the opportunity to choose among alternatives, you can expect fewer problems from that source. If the teacher has had time to gather and purchase appropriate materials, take part in seminars, visit schools, and talk to teachers already involved in open education, many problems will have been forestalled.

In any case, you can certainly expect a variety of difficulties. It is very hard for a teacher (and her children) to break out of the school culture to which they have become accustomed. Quietness, orderliness, right answers, straight lines, standardized tests, and letter grades are all familiar and comfortable and aren't discarded easily. There will be constant periods of agonizing reappraisal, as you begin substituting a new set of educational values for the old. And don't have any illusions —there will be more mess (although it can and should be cleaned up by those who make it), more activity, more confusion, and more noise and more movement. There will be headshaking, clucking teachers who look into your room at a bad moment and condemn both you and the new ways. But you can cope with these things if you anticipate them.

Initially, you may find it difficult to achieve a balance among the children's activities, as they are drawn to the many opportunities often denied them in traditional classrooms. This problem will diminish when you come to think these activities are as important as pencil and paper work, and when the children themselves, realizing that the new opportunities are not going to be suddenly taken away, begin to choose more broadly.

Record keeping may be a problem too, since so much hinges on knowing a good deal about each child and being able to communicate that knowledge effectively to parents and other teachers. Developing a simple system that works for you will take time and patience.

You will perhaps have some children who are unreachable. Remember that informal education is no cure-all, no panacea. *You will not be able to accomplish what you want with every child, or solve everyone's problems.* There will be children who cannot cope with freedom, who must have their choices limited, and who depend much more upon you than will others. And finally you will have to learn to be comfortable with some ambiguity and uncertainty. You will have to admit you don't always know the answers. Also, children's responses to certain situations may be almost impossible to foresee.

What happens when kids go from an open classroom to a more traditional classroom?

In one way, I think we worry about this question more than we should. Children are really quite adaptable. They may be unhappy at first in a situation that requires them to sit still most of the day, or that greatly limits the amount of material they may work with. Soon, however, they learn the rules of the new game, and serious problems are not likely to occur.

On the other hand, there may be some difficult problems. Suppose the new traditional teacher makes academic demands on a child that he may not be able to cope with. If a child is immature and you have adjusted the pace of his learning accordingly, it may be difficult for him if the next teacher demands third-grade work from everyone. All you can do is to discuss your children with their new teachers and try to help them understand each child's level and the kinds of problems he is likely to have. You cannot, in good conscience, push children in your class to do things that you know are wrong for them. You can only provide the best sort of education possible while they are with you, and try to communicate with the teacher who follows you. And in so doing, you will bring about a kind of education that, to paraphrase Robert Frost, begins with delight and ends with wisdom.

How can I get training in this kind of teaching?

There are an ever increasing number of excellent books that can help you become familiar both with the techniques and the feeling of open education.

Many teachers have found Sylvia Ashton-Warner's *Teacher* (Simon & Schuster) very inspiring. John Holt's book, *What Do I Do Monday?* (E. P. Dutton) will help you develop workable classroom attitudes. My book, *Teaching in the British Primary Schools* (Macmillan) includes essays written by British educators, who give suggestions for managing experience-based programs. *The Integrated Day in the Primary School* (Agathon) by Mary Brown and Norman Precious also gives practical help. Two books of special interest to teachers working in urban schools are Gloria Channon's *Homework* (Outerbridge & Dienstfrey) and George Dennison's *The Lives of Children* (Random House).

If you don't have time to read several books, try *Radical School Reform* (Simon & Schuster) edited by Ronald and Beatrice Gross. It's a very readable volume of excerpts from contemporary works by people who are rethinking American education.

There are also films that are well worth viewing and available at minimal rental fees. *Movement in Time and Space,* produced by British Broadcasting Company, and several others dealing with virtually every aspect of the British primary school, are available from Time-Life Films, New York.

Primary Education in England can be ordered from I/D/E/A, P.O. Box 628, Far Hills Branch, Dayton, Ohio 55419.

They Can Do It and *I'm Here Today* are American-produced films available from Education Development Center, 55 Chapel Street, Newton, Massachusetts 02160.

The best way to get the feel of open education is to visit classrooms operated this way. Talk with the teachers, observe the kids, and ask them questions. Put your observations and ideas together and then take the big step—into your own open classroom.

2. Don't Abandon the Virtues of Formal Teaching

One of the mistakes teachers sometimes make is to assume that an open classroom is one in which children work only by themselves or in small groups. Not so, Elwyn S. Richardson argues in this selection. It is a mistake for teachers to throw away any style of teaching just because he or she is working in an open classroom. There are many times when whole-class instruction is appropriate and desirable. Elwin Richardson is a staff member of the Mountain View Center for Environmental Education at the University of Colorado and author of In the Early World *(New York: Pantheon, 1964), an account of a small country school in New Zealand where he taught for twelve years. (Joseph Featherstone has said that* In the Early World *"may be the best book about teaching ever written.")*

The stories teachers tell of chaotic beginnings in open education are far more common than are stories of less distress and the gradual discovery of something that works well for both teacher and children. *Festine lente,* hurry slowly, might well be the motto for any venture into the unknown; but the *apparent* simplicity of a good open-education classroom seems to lead many teachers to make a greater commitment more quickly than is wise. Often this leads to discomfort and even despair as teachers move too hurriedly after a brief observation of open education. The learner-teacher may quickly absorb some superficial aspects of openness as she sees children working at centers of interest around tables in the room, but she may not take the time to understand the origins of the work, the underlying broad planning, and the variables in organization and in styles of learning and expression which open education involves. Teachers may come away from a short visit to an open classroom inspired but misinformed and race to equip themselves for open education; it is no wonder that poor classrooms proliferate. As a result, what is otherwise a potentially excellent approach to education becomes discredited.

From Elwyn S. Richardson, "Some Problems in Developing an 'Open Education' Classroom," *Outlook* No. 5, Spring 1972. Mountain View Center for Environmental Education.

I want to discuss some of the problems the beginner, and even the experienced teacher, may encounter. I include the experienced teacher because she may feel that she is already functioning satisfactorily when, in fact, there are many aspects of freedom and informality which she does not understand. I cannot discuss more than a few of the problems of open education in a short article, nor is it my intention to suggest that there is *a* methodology; indeed, teachers who teach in freer ways are usually more themselves, more different from one another, than are the traditionally-minded. I want to talk mainly about the roles of the teacher and the child in the open-education classroom.

Some people have the misconception that open-education teaching is easy. It isn't. The teacher has to work extremely hard, and at no time can she relax and feel that she has established a self-propelling classroom. Open education demands a great deal of time and energy, and the good work which can result will stem not only from the teacher's suggestions and guidance but from the ideas of the teacher and the children working together.

I saw how difficult the teacher's job is when I visited a small country school in the south of England recently, along with some other teachers. We went into a classroom of some thirty to thirty-five ten-year-olds, who were actively engaged in a variety of tasks at tables and in corners around the room. One small group was examining rocks on the geology table, and I learned that they had been out collecting flints in a nearby chalk pit. They were writing about their discoveries in their own books, and were referring both to published books on geology and to home-made books from past years which were in the small classroom library. One young fellow had written:

> Rock I. This is a chalk flint. The rock is hard and will not scratch with my knife so I think it is quartz. It has a split on its side like a bottle and it is called a conchoidal split.

The children were using the reference books well, and were also helping each other to put together relevant information—the idea of the conchoidal fracture, for example, was offered by a child who had seen volcanic glass, or obsidian, in a reference book. He suggested to the group that the chalk flint showed the same kind of splitting.

Another group of children was preparing a play based on a local historical story. I didn't find out the details, but I gathered it involved the way a village punished a wicked steward in the Middle Ages. The teacher told us that the group had read the story and had then asked to produce a small play about it, with costumes. One boy had made a fine horse's costume, based on a design used by English mummers of the period, which he had seen in a book the teacher had found, illustrating the dress of those times. I think the sewing machine belonged to the teacher.

One or two of the children were writing stories; another was rewriting some of the words for her part in the play. Still others were engaged in mathematical activities, solving problems set out on cards. They were using concrete materials such as counters and number rods to do what the teacher called "their minimum number work," part of the balanced program she believed in preserving.

Everyone in the classroom seemed gainfully employed. One young girl spent some time talking to us, but I found out later that she was writing us up for their wall newspaper. The teacher's manner brooked no nonsense—all the children seemed to know that if she spoke there was to be no argument: back to work it was! There were no threats, no raising of the voice; they all seemed to have a well-established idea of what was expected of each other. This mutual respect was quite refreshing, but not at all easily arrived at; the teacher had spent more than a year getting to know the children well, and many years before that learning how to work with children in this freer way.

Another visitor who was with me was impressed by the quality of the work, by the way the children went about what they were doing, and by their general activity and interest in the various school tasks. She asked the teacher a number of questions about how to get this kind of education started. One question was whether this was hard work, and hard to keep going. The teacher modestly said, "Oh no, it doesn't require very much hard work at all." In fact, she worked extremely hard to extend the children's interests, to bring into the classroom curriculum ideas that would be worthwhile and productive, and to open up new directions based on ideas expressed by the children. She went daily to the village library, searching out reference books, and was in contact with the science advisor about the class's stream observation project. She was also preparing stories to tell and to be read by the children. And this was only part of her job. It is a serious misconception that open education is easier for the teacher than is conventional teaching.

In discussion with a number of teachers in many places I have found that they usually derive their impressions of open classrooms and their style from observations of classrooms they have visited. Often they assume, incorrectly, that the open classroom is one in which children always work either individually or in small groups. This may be true in some open classrooms, but it is not always true, and the matter needs some discussion so that teachers do not feel obliged to operate exclusively in what may be a rather confining way. The extreme position, held by some teachers, is that one should not talk to the whole class; to do so is thought of as "lecturing" and is believed to have no place in a good classroom. I consider it quite wrong to throw out *any* style of teaching just because we are trying to work in freer ways. In fact, every outstanding teacher I have ever met is rather directive at times. These are the times when it is right to teach the whole class because the teacher has something to say which she feels is important to the whole class. There will be times when the teacher will lecture; such occasions may occur every day or perhaps several times a week. Informal teaching does not imply that all formal teaching techniques are always wrong, and should never be used, even if the teacher sees them as appropriate. One needs to talk often with the whole class, especially to develop those particular personal associations and judgments that the class will have.

The benefit of small groups as we see them in good open classrooms is that children learn from each other. They are also motivated by interests which relate to their everyday life, extending from the classroom out and back into the classroom. They are likely to learn skills such as reading, spelling and writing more easily and more thoroughly than they do when taught formally; this has been borne out by studies in England. I do believe, however, that these skills are not learned in isolation. The qualities of expression in the children's writing will be limited unless the class has a chance to consider such things as the motives behind a child's writing, and its facility. This means, of course, discussion by the class.

Children working in a freer way, exploring their own curriculum rather than the teacher's or the local school board's, will usually learn more than they otherwise would, and will demand to know more than would normally be demanded of them by a set curriculum. The time will come, though, when a child is so involved in his studies that he will be prepared to listen to everything he can hear about his interest. This makes informal teaching very demanding, and advocates of this form of teaching are often not prepared to provide the information that children need. The teacher will have to become informed about her environment in a depth which few of us acquire. For example, it is hardly possible for her to be a good teacher of geology unless she also reads about and studies rocks with the children.

I remember that once a small group of children in my school in the north of New Zealand found a centipede, presumably female, curled about some small, whitish young. It seemed to the children and to me unusual that it was obviously caring for its young. However, there was no question about this; our observations continued day after day, and we were able to prove beyond doubt that the creature was the protector of those young. We weren't able to prove that she found food for them— we surmised that the young probably fed with her. The children were involved in this study for perhaps half an hour a day for a week; other children became involved for shorter periods of time. They did drawings, made diary reports, and attempted a number of feeding experiments, some of which seemed to work. All this led eventually to a high degree of interest in centipedes and millipedes. I found it necessary to get hold of a fairly advanced text, and to obtain other nature books in order to assist this group to extend its knowledge.

Eventually the children asked me to tell them all I knew about centipedes. In addition to what I had found out from my reading, I also brought in a good deal of personal experience. At this point I was talking to the whole group, in what might be called a rather formal "lesson." I might have been accused of lecturing, at least by the cultist open-classroom teacher.

Good open education helps the child to help himself. For example, the teacher may find the relevant books and assist the child to get into the reading, or she may lead the child into collecting materials and information, testing, and assessing what is happening. And, finally, the teacher must provide information in depth.* Informal teachers are told that they should no longer be the authority at the front of the room. Just because the room may no longer have a front, however, the teacher should not resign her position as one who can find out extra information and direct certain kinds of research when she has the ability and the information to do so. The teacher must be sufficiently forceful (but at the same time not *too* directive), must keep in mind the total pattern of what has been accomplished, and must be imaginative about the possible outcomes of the work.

The manner in which the child learns to find information for himself and makes increasing use of his skills will be directly related to his satisfaction and his ability to be a learner. If his research ability is slight and is not growing, if his skill development is minimal, he is not likely to become involved in his own learning. The teacher is responsible for seeing that the various areas of the curriculum are absorbing, for providing a structure within which the children can work—helping them to discover this structure for themselves when possible—and for providing assistance with resource materials. All too often, teachers don't do enough to help children make their research more satisfyingly organized, for example by making charts, using diary reports, making clear statements of fact and opinion, and abstracting general principles. This is vital to the learning process.

A teacher whose pupils were Socrates, Jesus Christ, and Rousseau

---

* Here is one example of the kind of information in depth I am talking about. The phenomenon of caring for the young is uncommon among primitive and lowly creatures, but becomes increasingly prevalent in higher animal forms. Other good examples of caring for young occur in the Cypraea, or money shell family; the Conidae, or cone shells—a branch of which has the most poisonous sting known to man; and in almost every gastropod which has a free-swimming veliger, or proto-shell. The phenomenon is more common in the Arachnida, Crustacea (spiders and crabs), and in fishes and reptiles.

might not need to provide books, information and a structure for them—
they would find their own way and be innovative as they did so. (This is,
of course, what most children do for themselves before they come to
school.) For many older students, however, we do need more structure,
and in moving from formal to informal methods the teacher must have
in mind a wide range of possible ways for integrating subjects. She must
make sure that children will explore materials, will write about their
work, will have the chance for experience in the arts, will have the opportunity for discussion, and will be able to find new ways to employ the
skills they are learning.

The teacher has an important role as "knower." Her teaching will always be better, and there will be a greater chance of children becoming
able to educate themselves, if they see the teacher as a person of knowledge and wide interests. The worst school I have ever seen was a so-
called open education school in which all the teachers refused this role,
refused to accept responsibility for providing engrossing topics for research, refused to provide information of the kind I have suggested.
These folk were not teachers; they had resigned that role. They expected
good things to happen without any effort on their part, without any input.
In fact, the children ran riot and learned very little.

A teacher embarking upon a more open approach to learning should
not abandon *any* technique which seems appropriate in the new situation. She should not abandon the role of teacher of the whole class if
this is at times the most useful way to help children learn. Many social
experiences must sometimes involve the entire class. For example, singing, music, discussion about organization and government of the class
may all most profitably take place when the class meets as a whole. The
class may also profitably come together for discussing the creative products of its members. It is not enough to leave judgments about values to
small groups all the time; the whole class should feel involved in the
esthetic values their room and their work embody. It is, of course, wrong
and of little value to the children if the teacher is the sole judge of such
matters, even if she is a good judge. If she is a poor judge it becomes
doubly important that she learn from the children.

When language becomes a major concern, when its values need testing
and discussion, once again the whole class will need to meet regularly.
And, of course, the teacher may want to share a poem or a story, and
she must feel that she has the right to bring the whole class together for
this if she wishes.

One of the many ways in which informal education departs from conventional teaching is that the open classroom teacher does not necessarily
believe that there is a common body of knowledge, a curriculum that is
suited to the needs of all the children at any one stage of development.
There is a difficulty here, however. In practice, the curriculum is largely

derived from children's needs and their interest in their own environment. But to say that the curriculum is, therefore, totally child-centered is misleading. For example, the child may draw upon his environment for most of his experiences in science, and his day-to-day experiences will provide the wellspring for his expression in writing and in the arts. The teacher, however, should not be without a curriculum "in her pocket," because the time will come when new material needs to be introduced or old material needs revitalizing. The new material can usually be brought in through its relation to an existing interest, and this is the best procedure when possible. But this does not mean that there is never a time for introducing something completely new. I think there is some merit in having an established curriculum for each grade, provided that this is far more suited to children's needs than it usually is, and far more flexible. If there is no curriculum as such, there must at least be some well-thought-out ideas about the subject matter children are involved with.

I want to argue strongly for the need to make a gradual transition from an established way of teaching to a new one. Immense adjustments are required of the teacher making such a change; her orientation toward children will be different, and she, as much as they, will have to find her role in a learning process in which the children are led to discover things which in the old method might simply have been set before them. It is usually best to begin the transition to more open education subject by subject. For example, setting up a freer mathematics table might be all that a teacher could manage at first. There must be time for her to see that what she does is working—there must be time for her to see that the mathematics table becomes the center for the class's work in mathematics, not just "the mathematics table."

If a beginning teacher wishes to introduce informal methods, there is a valuable advisory strategy which can be employed, based on the teacher's request for help in a particular area, or on the offer of specified help by an advisor. This consists of helping to set up an activity in one part of the room. For example, there could be a section of the room devoted to *time*. This would be maintained as a center of interest for the class and each child or group would make a specified commitment of effort. I have worked with many classes in this way. In some cases the classroom remains fairly formal for most of the week, except that on one afternoon the children may write and paint and do crafts as part of a rather freer language-arts program. Whatever is done should be valuable for the teacher and the children. It must "work" and must be actively fostered so that the work progresses not only factually but also from the point of view of the esthetic and cultural values involved in it. Most importantly, the approach must improve human understandings and feelings about the study. The study will then infuse other, more formal work that goes on during the week.

I find it interesting that a teacher who has a firm control of her class and the kind of work that goes on can, nevertheless, embark upon a special activity with a group of children. For instance, several children may have made interesting but as yet inconclusive beginnings in paintings. The teacher might spend some time with this group discussing their initial successes, and stimulating them to go about a new and more satisfying completion of the idea. Her confidence in the progress of this group might encourage her to set up a new corner of interest, for example, a geology or astronomy corner. This might be all the teacher had the energy and ability to do. It is, however, valuable that she do it—and, of course, she may go much further. This kind of commitment, at whatever level of competence she is capable of, is all that I, or anyone, should ask of the teacher.

3. Helping Children Make the Change

Children whose prior schooling has been formal need help in adjusting to open education no less than teachers. In this selection, an experienced teacher in an informal English junior school talks about the way she helps children make the transition.

It's very hard, this way of working. One really has to know a class and get the children working independently before one can step back and think about where to go next.

With children who have had a formal education, seeing results is a slow process. Such children have difficulty in following through on something; they aren't confident in themselves. They need a tremendous amount of approval and support. But one does, after a while, begin to see breakthroughs. It just takes a lot of time, and confidence in oneself, and trust in the children.

Essentially I see discussion as the way to help children develop. Often a child won't know what to do. If you ask him questions or tell him to look for information in a book, he often won't be able to say exactly what he is going to do. Yet the teacher shouldn't have to say: 'Right, now you must go and do such and such.' Rather, she should try to lead the child to the materials, try to put him in a position to discover for himself where to go. It's very difficult to do. Sometimes when one is harassed, it's much easier to say specifically, 'How about doing this?' or, 'Do this!'

When one starts with a new group of children, they are constantly clamouring for attention. It's so easy to say: 'Well, how about finding out about X,' and they will. But it may not be what they really want to find out about. It may be that they don't know what they want to do, and they'll take your advice so easily. This is something I keep working at—being able to give thinking questions to every child and to get every child to find out for himself where he's going.

You've got to push things into the child's way, without being overbearing. You've got to make sure that, if one child begins to do something you brought in for somebody else, there are things available for the other child; you've got to make sure that there are the right sort of books to lead children on; that material is there that can be worked with.

I could never just walk into a class and say to the children, "You can choose what you like and do what you like,' because I know that some of them wouldn't know what to do, or would feel negatively about certain things. They might hesitate to paint, for example, because they hadn't had enough experiences with material.

You must start by giving children lots and lots of experiences and lots of techniques, so that there can be meaningful choice. In other words, you can have painting available in the room, but that in itself doesn't provide choice. In this situation the only choice may be in deciding what to paint.

The teacher must take a wide variety of materials into her class, or be prepared to support activity in a wide variety of topics. First she needs to help the children learn to make choices, and then she must provide an environment in which choice is real and meaningful.

I don't structure topics. I make cards, covering a wide range of information, available, and the children select what information to work with. If they say, 'I want to do some more about this; I know there is something in this book,' that's great. But it's a slow process.

Some teachers worry about how children will balance their interests; about whether children will learn when they're involved in three activities at the same time; about how to get children to make connexions between things. I think a teacher has to start where she feels confident and then move forward slowly. By the time the children are ready to go on, she'll be more confident and ready to move ahead.

I grew with the children. I didn't come here knowing exactly where I was going. I knew what I wanted in a vague sort of way; I knew I wasn't happy teaching traditionally, and I knew I wanted something else, but I didn't know how to go about it. I saw other classrooms functioning in a more open way and I didn't know how they had started or how they had arrived at their current situation.

The head said, 'You must start where you feel confident and not go faster than you feel able to.' One's got to take things slowly, otherwise the whole thing could just become chaotic and then one would say, 'All right, I'll never try again.'

In helping teachers at my new school, I'm stressing this all the time.

'Go slowly, or else you'll be stuck with formal teaching for ever, because you'll get soured. You'll never go back to trying a new way.' One can't expect teachers to read a book about this way of working and then to walk into the classroom and say, 'Today we'll begin to work in this way,' and achieve success. People do approach things in this way and are unsuccessful, and then say, 'I've tried it and it didn't work, and that's that!'

I didn't have the confidence to go in and try to do it that way. At the beginning, I was very unsure of myself, and was fairly formal. Although I had had a reasonably good first year of teaching, and a comfortable second year, by the time I got to my third year, I knew I was teaching in a way I didn't want to, but I didn't really know how to start changing.

I was beginning to be disillusioned about myself, and I thought, 'If I can't feel better than I do or can't do better than this, then what's the point of teaching? I love the children but I am so frightened about where I am going and what kind of teacher I am, that I'm useless.' Also the head we had at that time wasn't keen on new ideas. He was actually against them so that there was no support. It was a new head who gave me the confidence to try to change, to go slowly and to build confidence in myself.

This way of working requires a lot of careful thought. I find myself thinking about how the children learn. I like to see them have a real go at something, really get involved and spend time on it. I'm not happy with children who come up and say, 'I'd like to do something on cars,' and five minutes later are back saying something else. If children are bored with something, there is no point in going on with it. I worry about the children who never settle down to anything. I try to get them to make up their minds.

Another thing I watch for is the child who doesn't want to do anything, who never becomes interested in anything. There must have been something very wrong with the way that child has been approached, because almost every child I have known can become interested in something if one spends time finding out what, and listening to him. I have found that most children want to finish what they've started, unless they forget about it. And they may start something, leave it for a week, and come back to it.

One thing I've noticed, in teaching in this way, is the problem of the person who is more in love with teaching than with children. This is the one who gets things running smoothly, whose classroom is really quite perfect. In such a person's class, I think you find teacher-dominated work.

For example, children who know nothing about art, but get a teacher who is very keen on drawing, will suddenly produce 'perfect' work. You can see it with crayon, for example, where it is a tedious process to get a smooth gloss.

Where you see superb work from first-year children (eight-year-olds), you know that some kind of pressure is occurring, because most first-years don't want to outline their work in black, nor will they naturally choose colour combinations which adults find harmonious. One has to watch that the teacher isn't doing the children's work, or being overbearing in providing direction. I feel that artwork should be an expression of the children's experience, not the teacher's. Wall displays of children's work are often a give-away of how much the teacher has directed the activity.

I don't think one should interfere too much with children's work. I think one finds teachers interfering because the children don't know where to start. Older children who are new to this way of working will say, 'Can you just draw me the size?' or 'Can you start me off?'

I feel very guilty if I do this, though one is tempted to give a starting point when they ask. But in general I think it's a very bad thing, and the longer I teach the worse I feel about it. This is why I like working with young children, or children who have been educated in an open way, because usually the damage hasn't been done. The children haven't been convinced they can't do things.

I like to see some sort of progression in subject areas over a period of time. I don't expect children to do a specific thing every day, but I do want them to have a certain number of experiences, because I don't feel confident enough to let them choose exactly what they want to do all the time. But I want them to experience new things *some of the time,* to work with new materials. This can mean my suggesting that they try out something they are unfamiliar with, tackle a new kind of problem or a new sort of equipment.

I find that children will progress through the materials, so I don't worry too much about balance, except in an occasional special case. Although a child will develop a passionate interest in something, and want to pursue it, he will also explore other inviting ideas. For example, I like to paint. I go home after school and paint. But I also watch TV, read the paper, go to visit friends. Most people do achieve a balance.

Relationships with the parents are very important to me. When parents come in, I try to interest them in what's going on in the class. I invite them to come in at any time. If I see them in the school or in the yard, I make a point of talking to them, because I feel that if they know me, they're more likely to be interested in what's going on in the class. This is very important, getting parents on one's side, because most of them were taught formally and are unfamiliar with this kind of work. I want them to understand what I'm doing so that they will support the children. It's really a case of putting over my point of view very clearly and stressing how much I believe in it. I look for cooperation and I find that the more I get, the easier my job is and the more I can get done.

My first experience with parents was very important in developing my attitudes. It all started with a trip to the zoo. When the children came back to the class, I suggested that we make some of the animals. They wanted to build a giraffe, elephant, rhino, and lots of other animals. We started with lots of art materials and the results were smashing. All the animals were made out of wire which was to be covered with papier mâché. But when we got the papier mâché on the wire, it all collapsed. The room was in an awful mess. The head said, 'Why don't you get some parents in to help you?' But I was reluctant. I didn't like asking them. I said I would manage and stayed behind to clean up.

Meanwhile, the head had seen one of the parents. He told her what a mess I was in, and asked if she would like to help. In she came, and she got so carried away that she brought friends in to help.

I was frightened by this parent, Bess, at first, because she was a bit overwhelming; quite a large woman who just rolled up her sleeves, got down on the floor and worked. I had been hesitant even to talk with her, because her son was having some difficulty in my class, and she was not happy with what we were trying to do. It wasn't until she came in and started working, that she really understood. In the end, she stayed, and was absolutely marvellous. The animal project ended up with the whole room turned into an art studio. For the children to work productively in it, the room had to be tidy so that things could be found easily. Bess brought her mop and kept the place looking neat. She worked with the children. She brought in so many people to see the results and talked about how *we* had all done the project. Her attitudes changed and so did mine.

Although I didn't think that Bess would stay after the animal project, she began to come more often. First she came in the afternoon. Then she said, 'Look, I'll give you a hand in the morning, to help you start'; then, 'I'll come over later in the afternoon, too.' And finally she began staying all day.

I had been frightened about having parents in because I thought 'What can I give them?'; 'How can I talk to them?'; 'Will they be judging me?'; 'Will they understand what I am trying to do?' It was pretty frightening at first. And then one realizes how silly one has been, and how much one has missed.

Other mothers started coming in, and it was terrific. We had tried, before Bess came in, to have tea parties for the parents, but many of them didn't come. Bess didn't. It wasn't her sort of thing. She came because of the head saying 'How about giving this teacher a hand?' Bess is the sort of person who hates to refuse to help someone, and so she came.

Children are much more imaginative than I would once have thought they could be. They can do so much more than one expects. The animals I mentioned were made almost entirely by the children, although this involved using heavy wire. My expectations were quite low at first, but the children were very fussy. They had great arguments about how the animals really looked, about how many horns the rhino should have, about whether it was an Indian or an African one. Without being told to, they searched for information.

This sort of thing happens a lot when children are used to working in this way, when they have the freedom, the materials and the environment. The group that made the animals didn't know what it was to fail in art. They could be critical; they would say when they didn't like something they'd done. But they also knew their successes. They weren't frightened; they would never shy away from experimenting. Often they could see possibilities I didn't think of. Children see things we, as adults, don't see, because the doors aren't shut.

4. The Three Stages of Opening a Classroom

Teachers can make the change from formal to informal education only if they decide voluntarily that this is what they want to do. Equally important, Jenny Andreae argues forcefully in this selection, teachers need "the courage to make mistakes, the willingness to hear criticism, the strength to continue when things (they) were certain would work end in chaos"; they must "be able to cope with having more questions than answers and be able to deal with the inevitable frustration and depression that sets in" when things go badly. On the basis of six years' experience helping American teachers make the change, Mrs. Andreae, a young English adviser, describes three stages that teachers go through as they open their classrooms, and themselves.

A former head teacher at The Prospect School, North Bennington, Vermont and director of open classrooms for the New Rochelle, New York public schools, Jenny Andreae is now Director of Advisory Service at The Teachers' Center at Greenwich, Greenwich, Connecticut.

Have you heard about the new British Infant School, the open classroom, the integrated day, the Plowden method? Well, there is a special three-day package deal with fifteen credits where you visit actual schools where *it* is working and where you meet real teachers who tell you how to do *it*. It sounds great! And, my principal said if I go on this tour I can do *it* when I return.

From Jenny Andreae, "How to Make Open Education Really Work," The Teachers' Center at Greenwich, Greenwich, Conn. Reprinted by permission.

Rushing across the Atlantic for a quickie package tour to a few besieged primary schools often in a similar stage of development with one or two discussions with the key people is not a very productive way towards openness. Indeed, it can be disillusioning. We can use a great deal of the thinking and work that has and is being done in many schools in England. But, the idea that something that has evolved slowly over many years within a particular culture can be transplanted and thrive in the same way in a totally different culture is nothing short of absurd!

We are not dealing with an SRA or an IPI program, but with an evolutionary process which involves administrators, teachers, parents, and children who think, interact, communicate, and grow together. Labels attached to an innovation can be very misleading and imply a similarity and standardization. Open education often implies a lack of structure or boundaries, or an uncontrolled freedom where the teacher represses his common sense and anxiety so that the creative development of the children can change. The teacher is assured learning will somehow happen. Unfortunately, this is not the case.

If you look up the word "opening" in the dictionary, two of the definitions are: "a planned series of moves," or "acts as instances of becoming open." For me, opening education or opening a classroom is more accurate than open education or open classroom. Open implies something that is complete or finalized whereas opening implies growth.

We have in this country the beginnings of viable structures within which children can grow. The extent and depth to which this growth develops is dependent on our willingness and ability to implement our understanding. This understanding is based on the following premises:

1. That children learn best when they have rich first-hand experience with concrete objects and situations.
2. That the processes of thinking are action based. Piaget maintains that "thought is internalized action," not verbal repetition.
3. That when experiences and materials match the level of thinking of the child, and there is a link or relationship to a previous experience, the child will learn easily and with interest.
4. That if we concentrate on what the child can do and build on that, we are likely to have his cooperation, confidence, and active involvement in his own learning.
5. That if we provide a rich, stimulating environment the child will discover, manipulate, plan, question, and practice those things that are important for him to pay attention to. This is a natural process.
6. That it is essential for a child to have opportunities for social and emotional growth along with his cognitive development.

Being able to talk, work, and share with other children; having opportunities to relate to the teacher as an individual, to the group, or to another child, on a continuing basis are all part of his growth.

This is the philosophy or basis of our work. It is essential to assess how you personally feel. What are your own interests, feelings, values, and views of life? This will help clarify and determine the extent of your commitment. Only if you decide voluntarily that this is what you want to do, will it have a chance of success. It does not stand much hope if you do it because your principal asked you to, because you think it will be easier to have children all busy with materials and centers, because you heard discipline problems are lessened, or because nothing works for you at present.

If you have a voluntary commitment, faith in the principle, the courage to make mistakes, the willingness to hear criticism, the strength to continue when things you were certain would work end in chaos, you will likely be successful. But you must be able to cope with having many more questions than answers and be able to deal with the inevitable frustration and depression that sets in.

One of the facts that becomes uncomfortably and increasingly clear is that it is you, the teacher, that determines the success or failure of working this way, not the amount of material and equipment, not the size of the room, or the facilities available. It is your ability to use them to your advantage.

Let us look at some of the things the teacher needs to be able to do: (1) ability to form new and more flexible organizations within the classroom, (2) ability to judge when and how to intervene and question students, (3) ability to care and think through problems, (4) ability to structure experiences, (5) ability to understand the potential in materials and the development of the child's growth so that you can make appropriate links between the two (the child and the material), and (6) the ability to be aware and observe children, individually and collectively—their potential problems and present needs. Intuition must be interwoven with all of these skills—based in part on a knowledge and experience with children. The legitimacy of intuition has been dropped in the present rush to identify segmented sequential steps and precise prescriptions. However, I believe intuition is an essential and vital part of being a teacher. Without it, all the resources and techniques will fail.

The task of succeeding this way is an awesome and challenging task and one that can never be mastered overnight or vicariously. In the early seventeenth century, Comenius wrote, "Let the first foundations of all things be thoroughly laid unless you wish the whole superstructure to totter." As with children, so with teachers. There is a definite learning process on the part of a teacher in opening his classroom.

Stage One—When you start doing "it" (actually you began several years ago but did not realize it), you often plunge in too deeply too fast, and then you are surprised you cannot cope with it. Teachers in a summer school set up lovely centers, but soon realize this is not enough. If you have an ounce of common sense, you retrench, take stock of the situation, attack what you believe was the cause and try again—this time more cautiously and carefully. At this stage you need to develop the skills of coping with the overall situation—(1) providing things for children to use, (2) a place in which to use them, (3) how to help children select, (4) a way of keeping track of where children go, (5) how to accomplish clean-up.

Usually the children are excited and much noisier, there are more materials and mess. You find you have to be able to think and do a hundred and one things at once as suddenly the children are dependent upon you for every single move they make (insecurity on their part and a lag in the development of their independence). At this stage, clear overall organization of the class, plus patience, calmness, and perseverance are essential.

Stage Two—You reach the next stage when you establish a regular period of time in which the children are able to function independently using a variety of materials. You have found a place in the room for everything, and trained the children to replace materials in their proper place. But several things begin to disturb you. The children produce interesting things, but always gravitate to certain areas such as the art area, workbook, blocks, etc. No one goes near the book area after you ban jumping on the couch and throwing pillows. No one wants to write and no one is interested in the mathematics area after filling the scale pans dozens of times. You have a problem sharing something everyone has made that day. When do you find time to display their work? What do you do with all the things they have made? The room feels suddenly very cluttered and things disappear at the most crucial moment. As one teacher put it, "I feel as though the walls are going to move in on me at any moment." Gradually you realize your organization must change, so you go through a period of constant furniture rearrangement. You begin putting away materials that are misused or unused and keep only a selected few out (the room at this stage is usually so crammed that children cannot focus or select). You begin to prepare the children more by telling them what is available, by giving them suggestions and directions, telling them how long it is to clean-up time. You explain to them that you will look at a few interesting pieces of work together because you believe they can be of value for the group.

Stage Three—So you come to another stage where you feel more on top of the situation. But you become aware that you have been accepting work from children that is sloppy and of poor quality. You justify this because you wanted to build up their confidence. The children are also repeating an idea over and over and becoming bored. You are getting increasingly concerned that the academic skills are not coming into the children's activities. You are cramming your reading groups, phonetic drill, and mathematics worksheets into one-half the day. Other classes on the same grade level are on page 200 and you are still only on page nineteen. Somehow you keep getting sidetracked. There is not enough time to do everything. Your record-keeping has become a mammoth operation. This is perhaps the stage when the biggest challenges come face to face with you. You are beginning to realize that you are trying to juggle and succeed in two different directions, and that neither, therefore, is being successful. The children are very aware of the differences and define one as play (which they mean when enjoyment, interest, satisfaction, and involvement take place), and the other as work (when they are more difficult to deal with as a class). They find it harder to pretend to listen, and do meaningless and irrelevant exercises. It is this stage where you must think through what you have been doing. You have consciously developed their skill of active participation, enlisted their cooperation and interest, found ways of making their experiences relevant and encouraged their ideas and solutions to problems. You have been a resource, listener, and facilitator during this time. But now this is reversed in order to accomplish basic skills. You are in fact saying to the children that the academic work-time is more important because this is when you become more authoritarian and pressured. Taking this next step requires a lot of courage. You decide that real learning *can* take place if you can provide appropriate situations and tasks. You realize that you need to strive for a balance for each child so he can develop the necessary skills in all areas of growth, *and that you need to provide structures to support that growth.*

All of us have moments of doubt and panic that children are not learning in an "opening" situation. This is partly because it appears more difficult to detect, or rather I should say, we do not trust what we see. Our observations become limited so we revert to judging growth only in previously accepted academic terms—thus seeing only the top of the iceberg. No longer can you reassure yourself on a daily basis that children are getting the information you want them to have, which the workbooks, dittoes and quick tests told us so conveniently. Instead, we have to look harder for instances that tell us more clearly that growth is taking place in different ways. We must remind ourselves that no growth is made on a continuing curve. It goes in spurts with plateaus of consolidation. That it is not confined to one curriculum area but relates to the underlying basis of understanding more about the world. Experiences and learning are inter-related. You, as the teacher, have to make certain you have material from which the children can learn, remembering that children can only explore what is made available to them. You, as the teacher, select it for them. Teachers, like children, learn by doing, by first-hand experience. Each stage is an outgrowth of a previous stage, is essential and cannot be skipped over, and has a consolidation period that is successful for a period at that level. Suggestions and assistance are only utilized if they are relevant to the needs of that stage.

Teachers need to develop the ability to anticipate, select, and focus so that their actions will lead to the development and extension of ideas, materials, and learning. For continuing growth on the part of everyone involved, there must be commitment and support from the administration and parents. This involves reflecting, refining, and relevancy.

5. Dealing with Reality: The Open Corridor Approach

Voluntarism lies at the heart of Lillian Weber's "open corridor" program in the New York City public schools. The term originated as a literal description of what Professor Weber was attempting (see Part One): the program began in the corridor outside five classrooms forming an L at the end of one floor of a Harlem school. "I worked near classes organized in a traditional format," Professor Weber writes in this selection, her own account of how the program has evolved, "and I was anxious to establish the possibility of individual teacher growth without forced intrusion on past patterns." The approach continues to make it possible for Professor Weber and her adviser-colleagues to begin with teachers who would like to change but who are at very different points in terms of their understanding and ability.

The Weber approach stands in stark contrast with the self-indulgent utopianism of the so-called free school movement. "I simply began to utilize the openings that were present and to explore others," Professor Weber writes, "without waiting to convince a whole school, and without waiting to attain perfect understanding myself." Some of the things that were done on purely pragmatic grounds, however, have turned out to have value in themselves. Working with a small group of four or five classrooms sharing common corridor space turns out to be an invaluable means of establishing a community—and developing a community that respects the contribution of each member turns out to be an invaluable source of growth for teachers no less than for children.

Since 1968 a great deal of change in school organization, variously called "open" or "free," has occurred in all parts of our country. It is for the most part of two kinds: One is the creation of completely new, usually small, parent-teacher managed school units—free schools—in place of the old; the other is changing parts of schools, instituting open corridors within schools that remain unchanged in their total organization and that are all within the compulsory school system.

The free schools, organized external to the school system, may have to conform to minimal building and health codes but usually are able to use their space according to their own plans and to bypass the requirements of compulsory education for syllabus, testing, grade level standard, tenure, and staff regulations. The parents and teachers who organize free schools, rejecting what has been the teaching framework of compulsory education, attempt as close an approximation as possible to what they think is ideal. Their frequent references to the English infant school are to the integrated day—the breakdown of subject barriers around experiences developed from interests. They despair over anything short of this ideal. They pay very little attention to the continuum of arrangements within the English informal context or its history. Having bypassed the old setting and working with completely new units, they feel no need to study history for cues to organizational change.

Actually, very little of the impetus for the free schools is drawn from the compulsory English infant schools. Some of them relate more closely to the Summerhill community, which made relatively few changes in teaching rationale. But most of the free school developments result from young teachers' interests in possibilities for their own individual self-determination and autonomous experience in a world where the pressures of automation and computer control are felt strongly. The young parents who support these teachers feel similar pressures and want to avoid them for their children. Freedom and humanization, zest and spontaneity are the words stressed and prized. Workshops stress the teachers' own experiencing.

However, the change from the rejected compulsory school structure to its ideal opposite has in some instances been more rapid than the development of supports for the dynamic of the new setting. Those concerned with this phenomenon have asked if change has been applied too widely and too quickly and if the poor performance of some of the new schools might be a deterrent to applying change elsewhere. Would it have been better not to start? What is appropriate preparation? What support system is needed? All of these questions have been aired in the discussion papers that circulate among those engaged in open education. They are

Lillian Weber, "Development in Open Corridor Organization: Intent and Reality," *The National Elementary Principal,* Vol. LII, No. 3, November 1972, pp. 58–67. Copyright © 1972 by National Association of Elementary School Principals. All rights reserved.

serious questions, and they apply to implementation of open education in both free and compulsory schools.

But the discussion of these questions in the free schools is always of an "it." Organized for small, often congenial groupings and in this sense selective, they ask "Is it right for all teachers? Is it right for all children?" They discuss methodology, relationships, and organization that they assume have already been formulated. It is in this abstract context of a conceptualization of an ideal, of what *ought* to be, that one hears such questions as "Is it open?" "Is this one more open than that?", and so forth.

In contrast, in our case the term "open corridor" was in its inception a literal description—classes opening to the corridor—and its use as a title was accidental. Certainly no metaphysical state was being described in that early period.

It was as a conception of a total environment that the open corridor was first established as an organizational unit. I worked near classes organized in a traditional format, and I was anxious to establish the possibility of individual teacher growth without forced intrusion on past patterns.

This reasoning for the open corridor still has force. It makes it possible to accept each volunteering teacher at the point of her own development, respecting her need for a home base and her own rate of change, yet offering immediate tangential attractions toward common effort, toward interaction and communication, and toward changed patterns. Because the first teachers involved with the open corridor were not used to taking the role of facilitator of the children's direct experience with materials, they were asked to keep their doors open while I worked near them in the corridor with children and student teachers. Teachers told the children that I would be offering experiences for them in the corridor, and when the children left me to return to their still formal rooms, they asked, "Will you come back tomorrow, Mrs. Corridor?"

But much has happened since that time, and I have been asked to discuss the changes we have made within the compulsory system. My interest has consistently been the search for ways to change compulsory education in the United States, impelled by the changes I observed in the compulsory education system in England. The widespread commentary on new developments in open education loosely links both kinds of change—that external to the system and that within the system. But while the intent for children and the change in classrooms may and do have many similarities, the circumstances are very different, and what has occurred may also be very different.

No ideal conception of open education or integrated day is operative for us. Our goal is to better support children's learning than has been the case in compulsory education in the past and to produce a better match between school structure and what we know of how a child learns. Our efforts are toward development of teachers' understandings and how they are implemented in the relationships teachers seek to develop and in their new organizational settings. We bend our sights toward such changes but we know that our success is partial, that the descriptive word for our efforts is "toward." We start with teachers who want changes but whose understandings, focuses, competencies, and training are all at different points, and with parents who similarly want change and who similarly have different starting points. Moreover, we start our changes within a structure that has not changed. What we ask of that structure initially is minimal; indeed, what the structure allows is minimal.

The words of the free school—freedom and humanization, zest and spontaneity—are important words to our teachers. They, too, feel the pressure of the hierarchical organization, the dehumanization of the large school. They, too, are anxious to create situations in which they can respond to the child specifically and appropriately and with zest— even when his interests are outside the prescribed syllabus. And they are anxious for the kind of support and experience that will further their own development so that their response becomes increasingly spontaneous. But the words insufficiently define the direction and intent of our organizational changes.

There has been a vast surge of interest from parents, teachers, principals, and administrators who have visited the open corridors. They have seen changes in school life and relationships, and what they have seen has shown them, at least in part, that change is possible. Indeed there is no difficulty in seeing changes—they are highly visible. And there is no difficulty in reading dramatic accounts of teacher energy, of changed classrooms, arrangements, and teacher-child relations. These changes, developed incompletely and differently in each classroom by each teacher with his own interests and understandings, are sometimes viewed by visitors as terminal and ideal. In fact, whole schools or even systems often attempt to replicate visible changes without understanding their dynamics or direction. Our demonstration of what is possible has evoked from a whole host of people the hope and the energy to aim for change, so it is important that we spell out and underline the realities of our experience, that we dispel the abstractions and mythology that center around the word "open."

The teacher's whole-class control and the self-contained classroom seemed to us a poor match of school structure and learning. These factors were compounded by the prescribed limitations on the time involvement of teachers, and the delimited planning for delimited periods in which a subject was presented and later tested according to a prescribed standard of achievement to be accomplished within a prescribed time period. Supervisory evaluation of teachers determined tenure; testing and evaluation of children determined placement and selection; and recording was limited to these very circumscribed requirements. These limitations, each one with its own necessary testing, measurement, and evaluation, were handed down as a prescription from level to level in a hierarchical and autocratic scheme.

What we all saw was a fixed institution, permanent and impermeable to influence, where a malleable child was "trained" as a dog or horse is trained. That continuity with the child's prior-to-school ways of learning was not the functional purpose of this institution was evident in such "folkloric" phrases as, "The child must adjust"; "He has got to get used to it"; and, in the worst instances, "You've got to break him to it."

These phrases recognized that major adjustment was involved, that a poor match existed. American educators acknowledged that learners were in fact individuals, different in style and pace, and that what each learned was a result over a period of time of selection from different experiences, not necessarily sequential; a result of each learner's different focus and different interests. They recognized that the process for any one learner was uneven but continual. They even knew that the teacher's expectations of whole-class response contradicted this diversity in learner style, pace, and synthesis: The giving out, giving back relationship of teacher and child assumed a passive, nonselective learner and ignored individual focus and interest. Furthermore, the sharp separation of grade levels contradicted the uneven nature of much of human learning.

Educators knew that concrete and firsthand experiences were an essential basis for further understanding, but very little firsthand experience was provided. They knew that children's experience was hard to classify as this subject or that subject, as cognitive or affective; they knew that cognitive synthesis was often given impetus from affect and interest. Nevertheless, planning and scheduling made sharp subject demarcations. Educators knew that a child confirms and extends what he knows as he talks with another child, with the people in his world, and as they talk with him. Yet such communication was completely devalued in classrooms, and each child was adjured to keep to himself. The individual, actively selective, uneven, continuous, and socially interactive patterns of children's learning prior to school entrance, though known to every parent, were bypassed because the school was conceived of as an institution developed for the economical and efficient handling of the masses; it had to be as it was, and educators supposed that it operated well.

Questions about these contradictions were increasingly frequent all through the 1950's and 60's. Even then, compensatory education projects did not question the basic organizational relationships of the school and did not pose the question of better match. They focused on efficiency and proposed tightening the bolts of the old teacher-child relationships. It was the changes already underway in many schools in England that led us to reconsider our own school organization, not with the intent of duplicating what had been found possible in England, but with a view to finding what was possible given our own history.

I stress that our process of change proceeded from the analysis of poor match and from analysis of the possibilities for organizational change, because this approach both evaluates the past and gives us clues to what is desired in the present. This is fundamental for the choice made by new teacher volunteers. What we have presently organized can be analyzed for how far along we are toward better match and for clues to further change.

To be able to define compulsory schooling in terms of its functional support for the continuity of children's growth is our goal. Such an educational philosophy, it would seem, could guide *all* teachers—whether or not they are part of the open corridor communities—to expand their teaching; it would allow for the response that is needed for each child. Within this definition all relationships are possible—individual, group, or even whole-class—depending on the needs of the children and teachers involved and on the particular situation.

The story of *actual* organizational changes is a story of beginnings. First, I simply began to utilize the openings that were present and to explore others, without waiting to convince a whole school, and without waiting to attain perfect understanding myself.

The openings used to begin changes within the existent system resulted from the poor performance of the schools. I could evoke from parents, teachers, and administrators a shared recognition of poor match. They were permissive administrators (though administrators were slower to share my view of poor match), volunteer teachers, and consenting or volunteer parents.

We proposed a minimum of changes, taking hints from the scale and intimacy of relationships in English schools. We did not ask to change class size or the adult-class ratio, although the college interest in the open corridor has produced, in some instances, a surfeit of student teachers, disturbing to the adult/class ratio. In every instance the unit of change was a piece of the school, usually four or five classrooms—the smallest piece capable of setting in motion a process of actual changes in school organization. Although individual teachers had indeed attempted to create better match in their own classrooms, it had been clear to me that, from the base of their self-contained classrooms and behind their closed doors, they had never appreciably influenced others or changed the structure and relationships in the school. One teacher's proposals for change could be ignored. The teacher might even be persecuted and reduced to frustrated conformity or to hidden rebellion (described by Herbert Kohl), pulling the plan book out of the drawer in spurious conformity, for supervisory inspection. A group of teachers and parents, however, could hope for permission to try an alternative.

Changes in organization were requested in order to create new possibilities for support of better match. Thus varied grade levels placed near each other would support the continuity and uneven nature of learning. Teachers encouraged to relate to individuals or small groups in a richer setting might allow for the diversity of children's interests, might allow for children's individual and actively selective patterns of learning. Social interaction might be fostered through the contiguous placement of the classes, the sharing of different interests, and the working together of small groupings. Teachers isolated from each other and stultified in their development by the self-contained classrooms might similarly share and gain from the supportive exchange of a community. Heterogeneous grouping, we believed, was an essential and minimum condition. Thus we asked the administration to allow volunteer teachers and parents of children of different grade levels and of heterogeneous backgrounds to be placed near each other with the aim of building a community, a total environment that would support children's active and individual growth. In addition, support of children's active and individual growth needs a rich environment that recognizes choice, selection, and diversity of interests, and we saw that the environment of learning, which in the almost totally verbal modality of the whole-class teaching of the self-contained classroom had needed very little more than desks, chairs, blackboards, workbooks, and books, would have to be enriched.

In this beginning period my role, external to the job control of the system, was to define minimal initial conditions for change and, with the teachers, to analyze our work for possible further developments, and for cues to further organizational changes. And so, the role of advisor was born, and as the number of schools engaged in change increased, advisory training developed. An advisor was necessary to the support of possibilities for change in the new setting and to the continuing development of the teachers' understanding and resources.

The initial use of the corridor laid to rest the fear of poor discipline there. Children were not working in the empty space of what had been a passageway but in a prepared environment, which joined classes into a total environment by linking them with activities and a pipeline of communication. Use of the corridor raised serious questions about the use of the school, about relationships with custodians and about vandalism and fire hazards. The use of the walls of the school is now established —as a pipeline of communication and as a serious adjunct to reading. The use of the environment (floor and wall tiles, and so forth) for learning purposes is also established. Schools with interior hallways and with single toilet facilities located in the corridor do use corridors for passage, and so building codes have to be carefully examined. Moreover, with the help of custodians and of building and fire departments, we are planning furniture placement that will allow for some shared corridor activities in the total environment. Vandalism as a threat vanished with the appearance of good and interesting displays that aroused the sustained curiosity of older children, who began to offer help to the younger children. The use of the corridor as part of the total environment established immediate accessibility that ensured growth: The work could be seen; it was a public statement to the children of other grade levels not in the corridor community and to the teachers of other classes. Of course the basic accessibility was to the teachers of the corridor itself, to the community, and to the parents.

Our present stress is on the educational reasons for our groupings, on valuing the community interaction of diverse individuals as support for further development. Our prime necessity now is to develop a community that respects the contribution of each individual. Thus the union of four or five classrooms into a community has had significance on many levels.

During those first six months of beginnings, almost every issue was raised that needed accommodation from the school organizational structure and for which in most instances solutions have subsequently been found. Teachers enriching their classrooms with additional materials had problems with housekeeping, with storage of supplies, and with school furniture. The individual desks that provided storage for a child's notebook and basal reader were joined together to provide work areas for groupings of four to eight children, and storage for children's much increased production was provided in various improvised ways. Similarly, when they discarded their desks and positions at the front of the room to move among the children as facilitators and reactors, many teachers found they needed storage files. Dividers to provide for privacy within the class and for quiet corners for concentration have been improvised. Coziness has been achieved for book corners with rugs and curtains.

We criticized our first improvised efforts as inadequate, and one improvisation yielded to another and another. Suggestions and help have come from custodians, parents, other teachers, and children. Teachers have given a great deal of concentrated thought to the design of better storage facilities and have sought advice and support from custodians. The ingenuity and energy employed by many of the teachers have been boundless. Workshops on classroom organization have centered on the classroom as the setting for work and for social interaction. Workshops in which teachers themselves use materials have helped them see how proper organization influences their ability to share and sustain their work, to make decisions, to select, and to be responsible participants in the construction of their own learning environment.

Obviously principals and supervisors have also grown as a result of the serious adjustments they have made to new functions and roles. It is a long time since a supervisor, joining me in a classroom where some children are working in a math area, some molding papier-maché, a few others reading, and a group of six working with the teacher on some phonics, has turned to me and asked in a whisper when I thought the teacher would begin her lesson. Surprising flexibility has been found in supposedly inflexible structures. Supervisors are now accepting plans projecting the new learning environment and adaptations of plans based on observations of children's use.

But during this period an external agent, the advisor, was needed and continues to be needed for change to occur in the midst of the unchanged. The visible changes offering choice were made, but the advisor was needed to draw the teacher to further understanding of the implications for changed planning, recording, reporting, and evaluation that follow inevitably from choice and the break with whole-class teaching.

We are working out ways of recording that reflect what the teacher sees the child doing in the classroom, and the teacher is coming to value both the planning and the recording as helpful to her in sustaining and extending children's work. More and more supervisors and principals are joining teachers in workshops that explore these questions.

Changes in classroom organization, in planning, and in recording are needed to support the children's work. And for some people the work itself is a mystery. "Is there a curriculum?" I am asked. The question reflects the confusion that exists about the distinction between curriculum and syllabus. Children's relationships and knowledge do not grow in an empty set. They grow around content that provides experiences that can be reflected on, discussed, and connected by children. From these experiences children synthesize understandings about the world, other people, and themselves. The experiences provided are selected for their appropriateness to the developmental level of the child and for their relevance and appropriateness to the culture the child lives in. They must relate to what the child has already experienced, to his interests, and to the questions he is asking. They are experiences of the mathematical nature of the world, of the connectedness of the world, and of the human institutions that relate people to each other. They allow him to symbolically represent and express his feelings and understandings—representation and expression that also help him in further synthesis.

Although we are still using prescribed syllabi to some extent in reading and math, we are at the beginning of developing curriculum that really supports extension of a child's understandings at the point of his own focus and grapplings with synthesis. We have made additions to the curriculum that allow for enrichment from often isolated, unrelated experiences, and offer the child a choice. But as teachers we ourselves are only beginning to have experiences that provide sufficiently for expanding our own thinking about broad bands of enquiry and about the different levels of complexities of firsthand experience. Only such experiences will ensure that the teacher responds with empathy to each individual child's experience in a way that supports the complex learning possible for him in terms of his development, his focus, and his interests. And we are only at the beginning of comprehending how diversely understandings of these broad bands of enquiry are reached and how diversely synthesized.

The beginnings I have described are only partial implementations that we are trying out with the expectation that, as a result of teachers sharing these experiences, even more varied and smoother implementations will take place. It is these partial implementations that visitors see and examine and sometimes imitate without the test of reference back to their functional status regarding better match. But it is clear by now that the implementations create only the *possibility* for support of individual and actively selective patterns of learning, only the *possibility* for support of interest and an interaction of points of view.

Teachers who are rooted in past ways of working and still pressured by the demands of the past move slowly and unevenly, dependent on their own backgrounds and focus, to a real understanding that learning is individual and active. We find that initial problems of classroom organization tend to occupy the teacher for the first four or five months and that her changes during that period may be very uncertain or only in one area. We find that teachers need bulwarking from the advisor's confident and long-term view of what is possible over at least a two-year period. We find that all teachers, having become learners, seek to continue their development.

At present, working within the existing demands of the old institutional frame, most teachers still use material from the prescribed syllabus. They continue to use basal readers; they "flog" reading since they are judged by the achievement of reading levels and are even held accountable for at least parts of the prescribed syllabus. But they do *enrich* around the old base; they offer the children some choice and selection in a richer setting, some degree of interaction with each other. Thus there is some easing of the pressure of passive input on the child, and he can retain some space for his active mental functioning around his own search for what he is trying to understand.

These offerings are a first and necessary step for further development of both child and teacher. Some enrichment and diversification, some differentiation of children's experience, was necessary to even set the stage for understanding.

Teachers had to observe children as different before their understanding of this difference could grow. The child and his individual way of learning, his use of what is provided, the focus of his attention, is now visible. He has become accessible to observation by the teacher, just as the classroom and its functioning are now accessible to the community and to the parents. Thus the new classroom creates organizationally a new *possibility* for the teacher's further development, for the child's encounters with his environment.

This is the reality behind the confusion evident in attempts to characterize what is "open." It is the confusion of "open" used as a developed and perfected organizational form, existing in itself, with "open" as a new floor of possibility for further development of better match. It is in this context that I reexamine the question of change. It has been urged that teachers be prepared for change, trained for change, that they delay change until they have understood the underlying assumptions. And it is certainly valid to urge teachers to prepare and study. Certainly they should examine their present context of work and analyze its match to what they know of children's learning. No reason for change exists if poor match is not found. But it is equally true that if poor match is believed to exist, then change and spread of change is necessary. For the beginning teacher understanding does not come suddenly. Understanding is in part a function of the setting in which the implications of change can be seen and understanding can grow and be internalized. One change produces a platform for other changes; the process is developmental.

A beginning is made toward change when teachers perceive both the existence of a poor match and the organizational possibility for a better one. Teachers are not schizophrenic; the effort to accommodate occurs, and they begin changes as an inevitability. Only this conviction of the *necessity* for change can give them the energy and courage to sustain the anxiety of public change, to risk actualizations that are inevitably inadequate and fumbling and that can only be evaluated directionally—that is, how far along they are toward better match. Thus, as their analysis of an existing but heretofore unrecognized poor match becomes conscious and clear, teachers *will* begin to change if the possibility of organizational change exists. Their attempts to change will be partial and will be adapted as they are reflected on. But they will not return to the old. That will be precluded by their analysis that, even when efficient and smoothly implemented, the prescribed syllabus and achievement standard of the teacher controlled, whole-class organization of learning is a denial of the diversity and potential of the learner. It is too narrow to be considered a proper match.

The uncertainties, the fumbling, and the slowness of teacher change can be reduced through support systems. The corridor community supports the participating teachers, and the advisor assists in the growth of this community and in its gradual assumption of autonomous direction. Experiences are shared and reflected on with others. No support system, however, can eliminate all the uncertainties and ensure even and smooth development. In addition to the time necessary for growth of understanding in a setting that allows reflection and further accommodation, specific adjustments of implementations to circumstances must always be made.

Change is slow also because it is still very much rooted in the past pressures of the institutional frame. These pressures are now somewhat eased, and there is, in planning and recording practices, a further development of the possibility for implementing children's active and individual learning patterns. But let us be clear: Teachers are making fantastic changes, but they are still hardpressed by what remains of prescribed curriculum, by definitely prescribed standard achievement tests, and by grade level standards that deny the whole sense of the prolonged experience offered by the corridor and enforce grade repetition requirements.

Initially, administrators gave permission to make changes with very little understanding of what was meant by children's active and individual learning or what was meant by diversity of interest. Even volunteering teachers were inevitably limited in their initial understanding of what we were trying to accomplish. But because the implementations the teacher attempts, as her understanding grows, are facilitated or restricted by the institutional frame, it is equally obvious that the growth of the teacher must be accompanied by *continued* easing of this institutional frame.

The minimal conditions for beginning change provided a platform where what was needed for further implementation could be seen. But if nothing more develops, if a static plateau is accepted, the result will be inadequate match. If the diversified environment is used only manipulatively as "motivation" and the same questions of prescribed standards and essential intake are asked of the new diversified environment as of the old, then change may be too slight. If in the anxiety for exact bookkeeping the diversification is really a machine prescribed and controlled diversification toward a controlled end, there will be very little support for the child's own synthesis of understandings, in his own style and as a result of his own focus and interests. We must evaluate the administrative frame, as we evaluate all implementations, in terms of how far along it is in developing a better match, and in developing functional support for the continuity of the child's development.

At this time, we are beginning to see implications from our growth that involve not only teachers and administrators but the whole community of participants. Our first break with the past has had concentric rings of change implicit in its structure. We wrestle with the implications unevenly as we cope, as a group, with specific situations; in the process, solutions are generalized.

An example of such an issue is voluntarism. Voluntary participation by teachers was and continues to be a precondition, but growth poses problems for voluntarism. Teachers were allowed to make initial explorations, very often as an encapsulated and limited experiment. In many schools a "trial" was allowed of one class on each grade level. But we assumed that other teachers in the school, not included in the trial group, might also be interested. These teachers began to try out their own accommodations of organizations toward better match. We took such beginning changes as evidence that the volunteer applying to join our expansion into another corridor within the school was discontented with the past and had the energy for change. The right of teachers to begin changes is inherent in the right of any human being to modify his actions in accordance with his intelligence. Thus we expected spread, and in each case the open corridor organization has spread within schools, as well as to other schools—as permitted by the administration and as requested by volunteer teachers and volunteer or consenting parents. The initial permission should assume the possibility of such development; an initial condition of encapsulation is unacceptable. However, as change produces a ripple effect, sometimes through a whole school, the option offered teachers must remain real. They must be protected from the pressure of overzealous administrators and parents; their actions must be truly voluntary. It may be that the base for option, a single school, has to be broadened. The option offered parents or that parents demand can also become unreal, especially if it is interpreted as an option of opposites that do not exist.

As such situations become the focus of our advisory discussions, we rethink our first understandings and extend them. Even under the pressure of the first problems of organization, we were clear about the importance of our structure: an open total environment in a piece of a school, not only for the teachers of the corridor but for its accessibility to the rest of the school, the administration, the community, and the parents. This structure created a platform for communication of our educational analysis, making possible an intelligent spread of the open corridor. But pressure of immediate organizational problems resulted in insufficient and inadequate utilization of the possibilities of this open structure. It is this we are now analyzing. It was insufficient to be "open" to visitors. Parents and teachers from the rest of the school must be regularly invited, made welcome, and their questions answered. This is now planned in some schools as a monthly all-school open house. The weekly lunch hour or after school workshop discussions for open corridor teachers have long been open to all interested teachers.

Moreover, though the work of the classrooms was open and accessible to parents (and many wishing to be active participants were accepted as adjunct personnel), parents of the corridor community have sometimes been insufficiently involved in the actual solution of the problems of growth. Teachers struggling with initial problems felt a need for private soul-searching rather than the goldfish bowl of shared consideration of obviously inadequate implementations. Understandable—and perhaps necessary—as this is in groundbreaking for the community, for teachers unused to shared reflection, it results in too small a definition of community. In every case it is necessary that *all* participants—parents, custodians, administrators, teachers, and children—be participants in development, in problem definition, and in evaluation. Otherwise they will assume an external stance of evaluation toward *other* rather than *self*— toward the teacher, toward a situation. What is needed is the stance of a participant, responsible for a constantly assessed development. Only such a community of participants can discuss together the basic accountability of open work, assessed together and adapted for better and better implementation of desired match. Only in such a community will the prolonged experience without grade retention in the multilevel grades of the corridor community be valued as providing better for the uneven and erratic nature of children's learning. Only in such a community will heterogeneity be valued as basic to the very definition that is being explored, emphasizing the commitment to support of each individual. And only such a community will determine whether it is yet possible to redefine the meaning and purpose of compulsory education in terms of its commitment to and support of the further development of each individually different child.

FOUR

The Curriculum

Few aspects of open education involve as much confusion (and as much disagreement among open educators themselves) as the nature of the curriculum. In good measure, as David Hawkins argues in the first selection in Chapter I of this part, the confusion stems from the fact that both advocates and opponents of open education are limited by the terminology usually used in education. Our vocabulary makes it appear that our choices are limited to polar opposites: authority versus permissiveness; subject matter or content versus process; teacher-centeredness versus child-centeredness; and so on.

As the selections in Chapter I demonstrate, and as we have seen in Part Three, these familiar dichotomies misrepresent the complex reality of open education. In a good open classroom, there *is* a curriculum; to assume that there is not is to mistake the syllabus and lesson plan of conventional schooling for the curriculum. Open classroom curriculum is an outgrowth of two sets of choices and action: those of the children, and those of the teacher (and of the principal, superintendent, and so on). There is respect for children and their interests—but there is also respect for the authority of knowledge and of culture. There is a concern for process, for *how* children learn—but there is also a concern for subject, for *what* children learn.

Chapter I of this part presents a number of examples of how informal educators think (and have thought) about curriculum in general. Subsequent sections present theoretical and nuts-and-bolts practical examples of how contemporary open educators deal with the major curriculum areas: reading, writing, and language arts (Chapter II); mathematics (Chapter III); science (Chapter IV); and the arts (Chapter V). (Because of a paucity of useful materials, there is no section on the teaching of history and social studies.)

I

How to Think About
the Curriculum as a Whole

Given the depth and breadth of human knowledge, the rate at which knowledge grows, and the diversity of students' interests and abilities, it seems almost self-evident that there is no single curriculum suitable for all time, or for all students at any given time. "The evocation of curiosity, of judgment, of the power of mastering a tangled set of circumstances, the use of theory in giving foresight in special cases," Alfred North Whitehead wrote—"all these powers are not to be imparted by a set rule embodied in one set of examination subjects." To insist that there is only one curriculum is to confuse the means of education with the end.

This is in no way to suggest that one piece of knowledge is as good as another, however, or that students should learn only what interests them. Knowing one thing is not the same as knowing another, and some things are more worth knowing than others. Hence the content of the curriculum should not be left simply to chance; education is a process that cannot be separated from what it is that one learns. The transcendent objective, to be sure, is not mastery of a body of knowledge; it is, in Jerome Bruner's formulation, "to create a better or happier or more courageous or more sensitive or more honest" human being. But other institutions, especially the family and the church, also have that goal. The raison d'être of the school—society's ultimate justification for creating a separate educational institution, and for making prolonged exposure to it compulsory—is the belief that, as Bruner also puts it, "[t]he conduct of life is not independent of what it is that one knows" nor "of how it is that one has learned what one knows."

To create a classroom in which children have freedom to explore their own interests, therefore, is to recognize that what children are interested in is profoundly affected by the kinds of learning materials the teacher puts in the classroom and the way he arranges them. A child, after all, cannot be interested in something he has never experienced, or heard about, or imagined. The way in which an open classroom is organized and equipped reflects the teacher's idea of what the curriculum is, and should be.

The paradox of the open classroom is that it combines clear notions of curriculum, hence careful advance planning, with a great deal of day-to-day and even week-to-week flexibility and spontaneity. A teacher must have clear goals and plans of his own, but he must leave room in those plans for the children's goals, and he must be ready to modify his own plans on the basis of the children's activities and responses. While the goals are clear and laid down in advance, the path to those goals is completely unpredictable.

1. How to Plan for Spontaneity

It is impossible to predict what is going to happen in a good classroom, David Hawkins argues in this essay, precisely because the teacher is in control. By being in control, Professor Hawkins means that the teacher "is basing his decisions on observations of the actual children in their actual situation, their actual problems, their actual interests, and the accidental things that happen along the way that nobody can anticipate." Every good teacher (and every good learner) knows that the best classroom experiences tend to be the result of "some little accident that happened to direct attention in a new way, to revitalize an old interest which has died out, or to create a new interest that you hadn't had any notion about how to introduce. Suddenly, there it is. The bird flies in the window and that's the miracle you needed."

But the bird in the window is analagous to the great accidental discoveries in science: they come only to those who deserve them, to those who have prepared for them. "If the bird coming in the window is just a nuisance," Hawkins points out, "you don't deserve it and in fact that never happens." But if you do deserve it—if you do prepare for it—or you do think about your goals sufficiently to be able to take advantage of whatever opportunity comes along—the bird will fly in the window figuratively if not literally. In Hawkins' words, "There will be some romance around the corner which will be there to be captured."

This essay, originally given to a residential teacher workshop in Leicestershire, is perhaps the best contemporary analysis of the nature of curriculum in open education.

The reason we made our way to England this year is because we had come, over a period of time, to believe that in England we could find more schools of the sort we wanted to look at, and more people to talk to who were involved in these schools, than anywhere else in the world. I think that is probably true. Since we've been here, since the autumn of 1968, we have, of course, had a chance to get over any romantic illusions we had about the trouble-free schools of your country, but on the whole, as far as we are concerned, the romance holds up pretty well.

I want to talk about a topic that I know is vexing many people nowadays. It vexes you because you have probably got the matter coming up soon and it vexes us because we are trying to start some battles in the United States. I think you will find yourself in a more defensive position, because you have done some things in primary schools which we've been trying, rather unsuccessfully, to get started in the United States. We're more on the offensive because so far we haven't made much of a dent, in terms of changing some of the rudimentary patterns of traditional school life, patterns which you are very familiar with from your own past. It's an interesting historical business. There has been some interchange over a long period between the United States and England particularly with respect to primary education. I think there was a time about three or four decades ago when the slogans of progressive education were probably more resonant in the United States than in England, although in England there have been for a long time the traditions of progressive education, going back to the early influence of Froebel and others. Of course, we have had the same influences. We've produced some fraction of the materials, some of the components of infant school work of the kind that would be familiar to those of you who are infant teachers. And you have produced some fraction of them, and some fractions have come from other sources. There's been a kind of international pooling of workaday ideas about the organisation and the equipment of infant classes.

When we first walked into an infant class in Leicestershire my wife, who has been a kindergarten teacher for many years, sniffed the air, and said, "This is familiar, but I haven't seen it in the United States for a long time." What has tended to happen more and more is that the tradition of a majority of your infant schools was the tradition in the United States of only one year of school, called kindergarten, which was as you probably know the year that was put in under the first grade of our schools, starting at age six. This five- to six-year-old group

From David Hawkins, "The Bird in the Window," transcription of a talk given at the Easter Residential Teachers Course, Loughborough, England, April 1969. (A shorter version of the talk was published in *Outlook,* Spring 1971, Mountain View Center for Environmental Education.)

was not introduced universally in the United States but did come about in many states as a result of this same progressive education movement which managed to get in under the establishment, so to speak. It created a new year of school which had a pattern quite radically different from the pattern which we call primary, a term which in the United States means the years six to seven, seven to eight, and eight to nine. The kindergarten was almost without influence on the later years of school. In a typical American school of the thirties you would see a kindergarten which you infant teachers would recognise as very familiar in style. Then you would go into a first grade which was very formal and almost completely lacking in concrete equipment of any kind, which was dominated by primers and pencil and paper, and which had the children sitting in neat rows and columns. The most extensive influence I know of from the kindergarten in the United States was that there was a great burst of progressivism which resulted in the unbolting of the desks from the floor. But that didn't mean they were ever moved! It was a symbolic achievement. Children were free to move but in fact they didn't.

One of the things which we contributed to this movement was a rather good philosopher, John Dewey. Nobody *reads* Dewey very much but everybody knows how to say some things about him. I think actually John Dewey is very well worth reading, but not unless you're prepared to dig in and not unless you're prepared to argue with him, to try to recover the context in which he was talking, and to talk with your friends about it. Dewey is responsible for some good and very careful thinking which is almost totally unknown in most educational circles. When I was an undergraduate, students in education were usually required to read a book by Dewey called *How We Think,* which is a neat little thing he did for pedagogical purposes at some point. It classifies thinking into stages and talks about the transition from one stage to another. It's a thoroughly dull and unphilosophical work and the important ideas in the book are developed elsewhere much better, with much more sense of qualification and realism and with much more vitality. But there was at least a period in which Dewey was widely known in the United States and in which many people in colleges of education were devoted to him, at least in theory. But these people had very little influence on the schools. So neither the influence of the kindergarten nor the influence of the colleges of education was enough to make any real dent in the American public school system. This system isn't overtly authoritarian: it doesn't keep you out the way that schools in some continental countries might tend to do; it's just very resistant, it has lots of built-in feedback mechanisms for avoiding change. You can get in and you can do something and things will sail along very nicely but two years later you won't find much residue of effect.

Dewey was not only a very good, very thoughtful, very deep philosopher in many ways, but he was also a man who had some personal acquaintance with children and with schools. As you probably know, he was for a time involved in the operation of a school which was called "The Experimental School" at the University of Chicago. The record of that school is quite an interesting one. The pattern of what was generally identified as progressive education was dominant throughout the primary or elementary years. Dewey was a theorist, however, who didn't savour the practical details. He knew them, he learned: there's a quality in much of his writing which couldn't be there unless he was familiar with teachers and schools. But he loved to take off into vast realms of theory and polemic. He hardly ever illustrates what he is saying with any of the concrete stuff that would make a teacher say, "Ah, yes, I really know what he's talking about." So, he is a difficult person in this way. Well, because of the battle we may have to fight—or the battle we would like to fight—I think that this level of concern and of theory, of getting our ideas straight and getting them into a form which we can verbalise clearly and which will hold up against neutral or even hostile criticism if necessary, this is an important thing.

I for one have found that since I've become practically involved in work connected with the early years I've acquired a great distaste for theorising in the old style. I don't like to talk about general questions having to do with learning and teaching in the abstract, because I am so aware that when you do this you talk past people all the time. If they don't already know what you're talking about, if they're not already tuned to your wave-length, you can say things and then when they say them back to you you don't recognise what's happened. This is a very real difficulty, and it isn't a difficulty that has to do with the degree of academic training people have had: I think it's a difficulty in principle. Another way of putting this is to say that I think teachers, not all teachers but those who have a genuinely professional feeling about their work and who have learned and grown in their profession over a long period of time, do know more about things than is codified in any book. I think they know more about the psychology of learning than is written in the books. The psychologists, unfortunately—and I might be forced to name a few exceptions but I don't think there would be many— are unacquainted with this level of operation. They don't know children. They don't observe children. They don't know teachers except as people they teach. They don't regard teachers as their instructors in psychology. To do so would turn upside down some sort of social pecking order and that would be almost unthinkable. But it may need to be done. More is known and understood on the practical level by people who work effectively and successfully with children than is codified in any of the books. And it's doubtful whether the codification which is in the books is for the most part particularly relevant to this level of knowledge and understanding. When you try to formulate ideas about learning and about education you have to get into the psychologists' league and play that kind of game one way or another. You have to try to make explicit, to find ways of verbalising, things which you'd much rather just know in your bones and in your practice. Teachers are craftsmen, artisans, artists, whatever you want to call them, not theoreticians. And just as the good craftsmen of the Renaissance expressed themselves through the work they did and not through writing books about it (or research monographs) so teachers express themselves through the work that they do, through the human beings who have been their pupils, and not by writing little papers.

On the other hand, in the academic world the thing is geared the other way and the end-all and be-all of existence is that you write a little paper. Those of us who are in the academic world are very much torn. If we get involved in school work at a practical level we come to realise how empty a lot of the theoretical discussion is compared to the practice. We either struggle to express it—some of us are foolish enough to keep on trying to do this—or we acquire a distaste for our own academic ways of functioning. And I know that I myself am very much torn as the result of this. I want on the one hand to do battle with the psychologists and a good many of the American educationists, but that requires that I get into their league and read their papers and books and so on. But then I'm very dissatisfied because they're not talking about things I think are important, and I don't myself quite know how to talk about those things that seem to me to be important. So I'm in trouble. Everybody in this business is in one kind or another of trouble. Other people who haven't been in the academic world feel, often incorrectly, I think, that they don't have the means to express themselves, to develop theoretical ideas. In fact, I think they more nearly have the means than do the rest of us, because they have the raw experience, or, rather, the experience they have culled and analysed over and over again to guide their practical work. What we want to do is somehow to get those ideas not only into practice but into the marketplace where they can be argued.

I want to try, with just one or two ideas that seem to me to be crucial, to talk about learning and teaching. It is said, and I think sometimes with justice, that the traditionalists in education have a more cogent rationale for the things they believe in than do the progressives, with whom I would identify myself. We are people who talk in vague generalities and don't really have any consistent theory at all. When we are called on to discuss something we tend to point to particular concrete examples rather than to develop tight, consistent logical positions. I think this is often true. But it has also been true in the past in other places, and the places I know best are in the history of science. I think it's always true in principle that when new ideas are in the process of development those who are devoted to them and who are trying to bring them to definition have a very hard time expressing themselves, whereas those who represent some established order have a very easy time because the language patterns which have been worked out fit their ideas, against which the innovators are reaching. And the language the innovators have to use is, therefore, the language of their opponents, so to speak. You can find many examples of this in the history of science. For example, consider the very slow acceptance of something like the germ theory of disease. People who advocated this point of view were simply laughed out of court because the way they had to talk was in a framework of ideas which made the notion of little, invisible micro-organisms something that just had no reality at all. There weren't yet words for the things which are now part of the established pattern in, say, medical education. You had to coin words, and you had to use words in a new meaning, words that meant something else to other people.

This, I think, is very much our situation now. So, for example, I have said on various occasions that it seems to me a fundamental aim of education to organise schools, classrooms and our own performance as teachers in order to help children acquire the capacity for significant choice, and that learning is really a process of choice. If children are deprived of significant choice in their daily activities in school, if all their choices are made for them, then the most important thing that education is concerned with is simply being bypassed. Children have to be encouraged, supported in self-directed activity. And that means that you give children certain kinds of freedom. But now you're talking a language which has a lot of emotional loading. So, if you believe in giving children a lot of freedom this means, in terms of the emotional loading, that you are withdrawing discipline. To say the child is free is to say you are not coercing him and if you think of discipline as coercive then you are not imposing a discipline on the life of the child in school and that means you are turning him loose to do whatever he wants to, and now we're on the merry-go-round of the old, familiar argument. It's very clear, isn't it, that in traditional ways of thinking the opposition between freedom and discipline is of this kind. Discipline is an externally imposed mode of acting under the influence of something called "authority" and authority is something externally imposed and coercive. Look the word up in the Oxford English Dictionary if you don't believe me. There is no other primary meaning of "authority" except that of constituted authority, legally constituted authority or the authority of a person who has power because he has status or because he has special knowledge or something of the sort. Now, if that's what authority means and if discipline is something which is imposed by authority, then freedom in the usual sense is simply the negative of those, and that means you're getting rid of it. So the stereotype of progressive education is, "Turn the children loose and let them do whatever they want to." If you don't do that then it means you are imposing structure, order, discipline and so you have this dichotomy between two things which are inalterably opposed: that's the way our common, everyday market-place language works. Whenever you get into a futile, frustrating argument with somebody about education, you recognise that this is the pattern you have allowed yourself to fall into. The interesting thing is that you get annoyed at the other person for pulling this trick on you, but you also get annoyed at yourself because you've let yourself get trapped in it. You don't want to say something, but he's made you say it, and you've had to assent because that's the way the ordinary language works. I won't name him but I could refer to at least one well known contemporary English philosopher of education who does precisely this all the time. He just rings the changes on the ordinary stereotypes of English speech and forces you into a corner. He doesn't force you very hard and you may not be much impressed but he thinks he's forcing you. If you take his meanings of the words then everything is pretty clear and cut and dried and people who talk the language of progressivism are mushy and unaware of the logic of their own language.

So I think we are in a difficult position because we're trying to say something that's rather genuinely new, and I don't think that our ordinary modes of expression allow us to do this without falling into traps. We have to think very carefully about what we're saying, how we're saying it, and what kinds of illustrations we use to pin down our meanings. It's a difficult task to argue and to reason cogently at a level which corresponds to the understanding of many practising teachers. "Authority" is a particularly interesting case. If you look at the practice of the best primary schools (I'll reserve to myself the privilege of saying which ones they are but I think you'd probably agree with me) one of the important roles of the teacher in those schools is something that could be described by the word "authority." I think it is a different meaning of the word, and one which isn't in the Oxford English Dictionary or, if it is, it's buried in some special context. Authority is a way in which human beings are related to each other and it is connected with the word "respect." If someone plays a role as an authority in your life this means that you respect him. His activities or contribution to your existence you value because it has proved itself to *be* valuable. If you respect and trust someone you may follow his suggestions or his style, knowing that you are getting something that you will come to value even though you don't yet know enough to develop it for yourself.

In other words, authority is one of the primary sources of learning. To be an authority in this sense, to be a teacher whom children honestly respect because you give them something which helps them on the way and which they know they couldn't get for themselves, is to be a teacher. If you are not that kind of authority, you are not a good teacher, you're not functioning properly as a teacher. Therefore the word "authority" is very important, but if we let it get captured by that kind of opposition which is arguing against the primary importance of encouraging children's autonomous, self-directed learning, then we don't have any way to talk about this important part of teaching.

There's another way you can look at this which is very familiar. The polarity that is in the ordinary language reasserts itself between two stereotypes of the classroom, and I think many of us are guilty of these stereotypes ourselves. There's the old, authoritarian classroom—notice the word "authority" again in the same sense: an authoritarian is one who advocates or who imposes, who believes in the propriety of imposing discipline by authority, and that means by coercion. The word has a disparaging tone. So there's the authoritarian classroom and in opposition to it there is the permissive, *laissez-faire* classroom. Get a lot of good, stimulating environment for children and turn them loose in it and seven years later they'll come up with the requisite education. Or at least they will have been expressing themselves, they will have been creative—and all the other "sloppy" words that the philosophers object to. So, again, we're in this trap. How do you devise ways of calling to people's attention that there *is* such a trap? You can say to an opponent in an argument, "Look, I don't want to accept this dichotomy, this is not what I'm talking about." But then you have to have some general ways of describing what you are doing. You can give illustrations, but your opponent will say, "Yes, that's very nice, but you can't build a whole school on that basis." Or he'll say, "Yes, but that's an unusually good teacher and after all we must be prepared for the ordinary sort of teacher who can't do that." These arguments are all so stale, so repeated, so rehearsed that you can hardly mention them in any audience without getting a lot of people smiling because it's in the experience of all of us. Well, let's try.

One scheme that I've tried is to say, here is the authoritarian classroom, the stereotype: children are doing things in unison, they're told to open the spelling book at page 23 and do the following and when they're busy doing that the teacher goes and gives some similar busiwork to other children or perhaps has *all* the children doing the same thing at the same time. I won't develop that, we all know what it is, it's a conventional stereotype of a classroom. Many classrooms have approximated it and still do. Then there is the permissive classroom in which children are running wild and running out of steam, which they will inevitably do if they're given a good environment and then not given any kind of reinforcement and help: they'll try all the things that are tryable by them at that stage, they'll exhaust the possibilities and then the possibilities will get narrower and narrower. Finally they won't have any choices left and they'll get into the same kinds of troubles that children get into who live in the authoritarian classroom because both of them are now bored. Children who are bored exhibit similar symptoms no matter what the cause of the boredom is. You have behaviour problems and discipline problems and all that sort of thing.

So, how can you break out of this contrast? Well, one way of doing it is to think of a triangle, a very mechanical little thing. The authoritarian classroom is at one corner, the permissive classroom is at another and at the third is a classroom which isn't either of them. It's as far off that axis as you can be. Because you have that contrast of teacher direction versus child freedom sometimes you look at this classroom from one point of view and it will look authoritarian and other times you will look at it from the other point of view and it will look permissive. In fact it isn't either of them and it's a distortion of the classroom to describe it in this language at all. So, how will you describe this third alternative? Well, one thing I certainly don't want to do is invent a label for it. God help us, I think we ought to get along without labels for things that are really important. Maybe that's a mistake, maybe you have to have a label but I, at any rate, don't intend to invent one. It's a classroom in which there are two kinds of choices being made, one kind by children, the other kind by the teacher. So it isn't either the teacher making all the choices or the children making all the choices. It's a more complex situation, and we all know that it is. We're trying consciously to break out of the stereotype. Sometimes children are making decisions because the classroom, the atmosphere of the school, the behaviour of the teacher are such that they're encouraged to make choices and they have alternatives before them which are meaningful to them: you can properly say they are making choices. The teacher is observing what they are doing, following what they are doing and interpreting what they are doing, diagnosing their state, their level, their special problems and thinking of ways of making provision for them in that situation. This is now the choice, the freedom, of the teacher. What a teacher does in this way is just as genuinely a matter of choice as anything the children do. So it's absurd to say that this is a classroom which is permissive. A teacher may in such a classroom make a choice, sometimes quite properly, which involves a very firm use of the adult role. "Why do you make me do this?" "Because I'm bigger than you are and let's not argue about it." If that was the only kind of choice the teacher was making it would be pretty bad but it's quite another thing to say that no good teacher ever makes choices of that sort, because this is patently false. There are times when coercion in particular is a very salutary thing. There are times when it's the only *educational* thing that you can do. I know a young man who told me in great detail that the first time in his life he thought he might be a normal human being was when a teacher whom he had struck caused him to be arrested and put in jail. This was a vital component of his education. To say that you could have had the same effect with sweet reasonableness is just plain false. He'd had sweet reasonableness all his life and that in fact was the chief malady he was suffering from. On the other hand, a teacher may at other stages be consciously withdrawing, consciously be non-interventionist, may give the child complete freedom with a perhaps anxious calculation that the only way in which that child is going to get over a particular hump is to be entirely on his own in confronting it. These are opposite kinds of decisions made by the same teacher under different circumstances for different children. So the whole range of choices is there. Some are very like the authoritarian model and some are very like the permissive model, but they are quite different in character because this is now a teacher operating, dealing with human beings and using observation, interpretation, wit, strategy, to play the role in reinforcing the self-directed learning of children. It can't be put more simply than that because it isn't any simpler. It seems to me that such a description has to be made and it has to become familiar. I probably don't do it right. I'm only making a rough cut at it, there are lots of qualifications, lots of filling in of detail, lots of discussion about how you know when to do this and that and the other thing. It's a very complex matter. But these are questions that can be solved in practice to some good approximation, otherwise we wouldn't have good teachers. There may not be any elegant theoretical formulation about it but it's still possible to decribe the range of considerations that are involved in a teacher's making intelligent choices.

Once you are committed to the belief in the primacy, the priority of children's choice-making capacities as the main thing that education is after, then there are many things that follow which likewise run afoul of the traditional stereotypes. Once you accept this basic aim of education you discover some other things that come along with it that are vital to the process. For example, if a teacher has children doing things or ostensibly doing things that are pretty much according to a pattern which he has laid down, then the opportunity for observing significantly the child's behaviour is very much diminished. If you tell a child to do a set task and there are many ways of failing and one way of succeeding, solving a particular kind of set problem which has a unique right

answer, for example, then essentially the only thing you can observe is
the success or failure of the child in doing that particular task. This
will divide children into categories, but no more: there may be some
incidental observations you make along the way—some children groan
when set the task, others try to act cheerful about it and so on. But you
don't really learn much from the success or the failure of the children
in a situation where you are requiring uniformity of behaviour from
every child. Whereas, if you encourage diversity, which you're bound
to do if you encourage choice, then you will observe that much-too-large
number of human beings doing different things. The range of choices
they make is very wide and therefore the amount of information you
get about them is much greater. It is just common observation that if
you watch a child working with a particular kind of material quite
successfully and avoiding everything else, you're learning something
about that child which is a much more important guide to your behaviour as a teacher than his success or failure in particular set tasks. If
you give a child a choice, for example, and he does nothing but work
with paints and acquires a certain status in the class because he does
have something of a flair in painting that other children don't have, but
he's a total failure in everything else, he simply avoids everything else,
he doesn't read, he doesn't write and so on, then you know a great deal
about the child that is relevant to you as a teacher. What strategies you
will use now will be very much determined by your knowledge of the
way this child has homed in on one activity and avoided a lot of others.

I have still very limited personal experience in teaching primary
school children, so I only speak as an amateur. My experience has been
with college students and I do believe they're not really so different
under the skin but there are some differences. Mainly, college students
have learned very well how to avoid giving you important kinds of
diagnostic information. They know how to look bright, alert and to
pretend they've turned you on when in fact they've turned you off
fifteen minutes before. Nine-year-olds don't know how to do this or at
least don't care to do it, in my experience. So I learned much more about
myself as a teacher as soon as I went to that age. And even more when
I first, with fear and trembling, got involved with four- and five-year-olds.
One of the things that became very clear to me was that when children
were engaged in a considerable diversity of activities, I had no trouble
at all remembering what they were doing and no trouble recalling information about their behaviour and what it probably signified. Whereas,
when they were all doing the same set piece I'd have to go around and
make records all the time in order to keep up with them. In fact, I
think the familiar phenomenon called "The Test" is largely a crutch
to replace the good means of evaluation we have when we don't suppress children's capacity for choice. Children simply distinguish them-

selves individually when they're working at different tasks in different ways. You get so much more information you don't have trouble remembering.

Many teachers in the United States who've become involved with us and are somewhat interested in the things we are doing, and think maybe they will try some of them, bring up this question: "Yes, but how will we test them, because they'll all be doing different things?" And again, that's part of that stereotyped pattern. How can you test? If people are not doing the same thing you can't compare them. And you say, "Yes, that's true, isn't it." But that's terribly unsatisfactory, because there's that hole left there, that demand for evaluation. Of course you're evaluating much more effectively, in another meaning of the word, but again, you've got to say what that meaning is because it isn't the business of putting people on a linear scale. It's a much richer scale you're putting them on, with many dimensions to it. You're saying, "This child is best at telling stories, this child is best at numbers and—I'm remembering a story—this child is best at catching frogs!" These are three dimensions and each of them gives a different permutation of the children. That's the way human beings really are. It is not the way the traditional demands of education have seen them and therefore we have real problems in meeting the traditional demands, that is, in meeting the people who make the traditional demands with the kind of information we want to give them. So, there is a very close and important relation between children's actual level of choice-making in the classroom, or in the field if they're in the field, and our own ability to interpret and diagnose, but it's not the kind of thing that will yield information on a paper and pencil test of any kind that anybody I know has ever devised. And I doubt in principle whether it can be devised because the paper and pencil test imposes a set of criteria which are preconceived by the tester and this reduces not necessarily just to one but to not very many dimensions of comparison. The teacher who is skilful at this kind of observation can tell you a great deal that's quite important about a child but will not give you numbers on scales because the nature of the thing being measured is not a lot of little points along a line; it's a lot of points that are in different directions defined by completely different qualities and attributes. Many of these are not in any catalogue. They are too numerous to catalogue.

The demand for testing is bound to be one we have to confront, to think through. I'm not making any recommendations for how to cope with this on the practical level. I'm just saying that I don't think the demand for this sort of thing on the practical level should confuse us about our basic thinking, as I'm afraid it sometimes does. We say, "I would like to think that way but it isn't practical." Nonsense! In thinking, the only important question is whether it's true or not, not whether it's practical. When you're making decisions about how you're going to behave, you may have to make compromises but for heaven's sake, let's not start shading our beliefs to make it more comfortable to live in an uncomfortable situation, because it doesn't really make it more comfortable.

Another thing that comes up here has to do with the business of curriculum. There was a time, I think, when the word "curriculum" didn't mean what it means now. I'm not sure what it means in England. In the United States a curriculum is apt to mean the whole works, curriculum, syllabus, timetable, because in the United States many groups of people who have been involved in curriculum development have in fact spelled everything out at a level of detail that's almost giving daily instructions to the teacher about what to do next. This means that the choices are not available to the children: the choices are not even available to the teacher unless the teacher is bold enough to disregard the curriculum guide. The choices are made "up there" by somebody. The word "curriculum" used to mean a general outline of subject matter and areas of competence that children were supposed to be systematically exposed to. You wanted them to understand arithmetic, for example. You didn't list twenty-five number facts for the first three months. That wasn't curriculum. That was something that some teacher might do, but it was no concern of the adult community, because the curriculum was primarily a set of decisions by the adult community about what children ought to be learning and how the general aims of education could be made more specific in terms of areas of competence and skill, subject matter and so on.

Dewey, for example, is very strong in asserting that the Experimental School, which he ran for a time, had a definite curriculum and there was no freedom to depart from this curriculum. This was imposed: it was a pattern which could be argued about, it wasn't sacrosanct, but at any given time there was a curriculum and everybody understood what it was. Within this, teachers were *enormously* free to pursue these general subject-matter situations in any way they wanted to and it was quite clear also, to many of them at least, that an important group involved in making those decisions was the children themselves. I don't know how romanticised they are, it's hard to tell at this distance in time, but if you read some of the accounts of what some teachers and some children in that school did you can see that they were having a great good time making their way through some aspect of the curriculum but diverging all over the place. They were diverging into other areas which were also on the curriculum and nobody regarded it as a waste of time, therefore if in the process of studying some primitive society they got heavily involved in the craft of pottery, because that also was part of the curriculum. So, there was great freedom within a general framework that was rather clearly spelled out. I think today we would find this framework to be a bit special and a bit narrow and would perhaps accuse Dewey of being a bit of a traditionalist about some of it. But it was very interesting for me to discover that Dewey in no sense subscribed to the *laissez-faire* belief that the curriculum was up to the children, so to speak. These were decisions made in the patterning, the organisation of the school itself, and in the provisioning of the school. Well, we all make such provisions, don't we? We can't dodge the responsibility for the things we put in classrooms. These are not put there at the request of children—they may be added to at the request of children, they may be subtracted from because children don't use some of them, but that represents our learning and not the direct decision of the children.

The other problem that we face, however, is that as soon as we talk about self-directed learning this implies, correctly, I think, that we cannot lay out in advance a track that children are going to follow, because we don't yet know the things we will learn by observing them which will cause us to make decisions which we haven't yet thought of. Therefore, there is an essential lack of predictability about what's going to happen in a good classroom, not because there is no control, but precisely because there is control, of the right kind; precisely because the teacher is basing his decisions on observation of the actual children in their actual situation, their actual problems, their actual interests and the accidental things that happen along the way that nobody can anticipate. A power-shovel moves in next door to the school: this throws all your plans for studying batteries and bulbs into a cocked hat—or should! But you say, there are many aspects to science and this is also part of the curriculum. You can't anticipate those things. Everyone knows that the best times in teaching have always been the consequences of some little accident that happened to direct attention in some new way, to revitalize an old interest which has died out or to create a brand new interest that you hadn't had any notion about how to introduce. Suddenly, there it is. The bird flies in the window and that's the miracle you needed. Somebody once said about great discoveries in science, "Accidents happen to those that deserve them." If the bird coming in the window is just a nuisance you don't deserve it and in fact that never happens. If you deserve it, the bird *will* fly in the window or there'll be a door that opens into the jungle. There will be some romance around the corner which will be there to be captured. This is again something very different from the stereotype of the permissive classroom because what's involved all along is a teacher who is making educational capital out of the interests and choices of children and out of the accidents that happen along the way, as well as out of his own cleverly designed scheme for getting something new into focus. He fails part of the time but sometimes he succeeds. When the school year is over, you say—or at least I used to say in my college teaching—the best times were the times when we got off onto something that had no relation whatever to the timetable, something that wasn't envisioned but that turned out to have a lot of relevance to what the course was really about. I just had never had the wit before to see this: it came up accidentally or it came up because of some question or some argument with a student and we got off on a new track and that's when things really came to life. We all know that this is true; we all know that we can't succeed at it all the time or sometimes even very often, but we all also know, I think, that when it does happen it's worth a great deal because in fact far more is learned under those conditions than under conditions of routine presentation of subject matter.

One of the other things one has to fight against is the belief that because the central priority is self-directed learning there is no such thing as instruction or didactic teaching. That's where the word "discipline" comes in again, because people say, "Yes, that's all very well but what about the discipline of the organised body of knowledge?" Have you come across this one? That's a real question. I'm dealing with the opposition with a light touch but I don't want to say that everything they bring up is just foolish, because I don't think *we* know the answers to some very important questions and I think it's foolish to pretend that other people who think they have answers are just completely wrong. It seems to me, and I hope many of you would back me up in this, that there are times—perhaps they have to be defined opportunistically, you can't tell in advance just when they are going to be—there are times when a group of children is very ready to be instructed about something, or is very ready to engage in a set task which might even be rote learning under certain circumstances. Their readiness to do this means that it has become for them a significant choice and therefore it is by no means violating the principle of choice to say there is room, and sometimes a significant amount of room, for quite formal instruction. I think the people who advocate this enormously exaggerate its relative importance in terms of the learning of subject matter. For example, in mathematics as far as I can see the set pattern of the text, whether it be old mathematics or new mathematics, makes very little difference. Some people really believe that the set pattern of the text is *the* way mathematics is to be learned. Or they might grudgingly admit that there are three or four alternatives, but all of them would be carefully sequenced, outlined series of steps. They say, "But you can't *possibly* understand multiplication before you understand addition." Well, I haven't thought too much about that but I'm sure it's false. I know one thing that's very, very common, just to take a little example: there's a widespread belief for some reason that you can't understand subtraction until you understand addition. How can you subtract if you can't add? Well, subtraction, I would suspect, is the more primitive of the two operations. It's easier to think of taking something away from a collection than it is to think of putting two collections together, which is a rather artificial activity that we don't often engage in, whereas we've very often taken candy out of a box, we're depleting a collection by taking things away. I would begin my textbook, if I wrote one, which I'm not going to do, with subtraction and division and then I would introduce multiplication and addition as subsequent and derivative things. The logic is perfectly symmetrical, there is no reason for preferring one to the other from the point of view of the logical organisation. Moreover, we all know that learning doesn't have any very close or intimate connection with logical organisation. The order in which children come to understand a logical pattern is not by following the logical pattern from the beginning. They don't have it yet so they can't follow it. You can lead them by the nose, but that also means they can't follow it. We all agree there is some body of connective ideas and propositions that vaguely we can call mathematics. Nobody has ever written it all down but it's there; all the logical connections that exist among all the ideas in the area which we agree to call mathematics. There isn't any linear order among them. They're connected in a very complex sort of network and you can make your way through them along thousands of different paths, depending on your momentary readiness, your understanding, your fund of analogies and your interests. You can get into it in many different ways. The obvious thing from the point of view of teaching is to say, well, we want to find that way which is optimal for a particular child at a particular time. This will be in terms of all of the things which characterise him as an individual. We don't know how to do this, we're not omniscient, but one of the very practical ways of getting on with it is to give the child himself some free choice. This doesn't mean that he will always, unerringly, choose the way that is best for him but it means that you will get evidence from his choices that will help you to define a pattern for him that will probably be much more effective than a standard pattern that is distilled out of mass instruction of the past.

Just as a personal comment about mathematics, I feel very strongly that there are two things the word refers to. One is mathematics and the other is the pedagogical tradition, and they don't necessarily have a very close relation to each other. Mathematics is what mathematicians do and it's what people do when they're being like mathematicians, solving problems of various kinds, bringing certain kinds of understanding to bear on these problems. . . . I don't want to try to define mathematics. But the pedagogical tradition is something not very closely related to that, because the pedagogical tradition is one particular slice, one particular pathway through this network of ideas, or through part of it. "Through it" is the wrong phrase to use because you never get through it, you get into it. You don't cover it. You get into it by many paths, and some of these have been standardised because they have a certain average level of effectiveness, I suppose, and because they happen to appeal to the taste of people who have been engaged in the teaching process under certain kinds of conditions. But I think many people in education think that mathematics *is* what is in that syllabus. Therefore they talk about going through it because you get to the last page in the syllabus and you're through it. But this isn't the nature of mathematics. Mathematics is infinite and it has this kind of structure and complexity which means you can't reduce it to the linear order of words in a book. There are just too many cross references. You can't put it on a computer, which can cross-index a lot more than a book can, the organisation is too rich for that. People are forever discovering new paths in very old mathematics. Only four or five years ago there was a brand new method found for proving that there are infinitely many prime numbers, by a very able mathematician who just went back and looked at this old problem from a fresh point of view. That's not very important, but it is the nature of mathematics that it should be this way. The thing that is really important is the capacity to function as a human being in this domain. You acquire this capacity for functioning by functioning. Along the way there are many disciplinary elements which you may decide to accept or which you may have imposed on you and completely reject—and of course we know that most children, in terms of the habits of the disciplinary pattern, have in fact rejected. Or they have very cleverly invented a way of accepting it only as far as necessary to get through something called an examination, being careful to protect their minds from contamination in the process.

So, the disciplinary argument is really a very weak one. It implies that we progressives are just cutting loose, not giving children the strict order and discipline that is really necessary if you're going to become competent in mathematics, when in fact, the practices of the past have created almost universal failure. It isn't very hard to beat the past record. We shouldn't pat ourselves on the back very much just because children are doing a little better on the eleven-plus as a result of some new mathematics programme. That's a cheerful thing, but it's almost unimaginable that they would do worse, not given three months, but given five or six or seven years of work in the style I think we could recognise as that of present-day progressive tendencies and which we can certainly vastly improve on. But given the opportunity to get children repeatedly exposed to the development of mathematical interests and given lots of material which does in fact embody a lot of the things which we regard as basic to mathematical understanding, they won't do worse. It's almost unimaginable. If you set children to memorizing the multiplication table on day one, then on day thirty they will do better on a test than will children who have not been memorizing the multiplication table, that's perfectly obvious, if the test is a test on multiplication tables. But we're not interested in one-month results, we're interested in, let's say, seven years. And here—and partly I'm safe in saying this because the seven-year test hasn't been made yet—it does seem to me almost unimaginable that people could point and say, "See? It's a disastrous failure, they don't know mathematics the way they used to." All I can say is, Hurrah! Because I have for years had freshmen coming into American colleges with two or three years of secondary school mathematics who are totally non-functional in any interesting use of mathematics applied either to science or applied to itself. Using mathematics to learn more mathematics is something that has never entered at all. This isn't their fault, it isn't the fault of their teachers. I suppose in some historical sense it isn't anybody's fault; it's the way things have evolved. But it certainly is a fault which we ought to correct. It seems to me that by making some propositions, and maybe my formulations aren't the right ones, of the general sort that I've tried to make, putting a few important things in the centre and saying that these have top priority and now let's look at other things and see where their priorities come, we can begin to develop a way of talking about the things we believe in which makes sense to us, which perhaps helps us in our own planning and thinking and which provides some sort of cogent bulwark against the kind of opposition which is based on traditional stereotypes. I've only tried to illustrate this with two or three sample topics that come up and to suggest the need to try to formulate ideas in this field, simply not giving in, not surrendering to the pattern of the prevailing language of the market-place. I think we really do have the problem. As in the history of science there have been times when you've had to forge genuinely new ideas and build them into some theoretical structure which will seem strange and odd and which people will continue to misunderstand for a while. This is the way new ideas come. It's not a painless process. I believe that it is much more important to demonstrate the practical working of progressive methods in schools than it is to simply talk about them but I think it is of great importance also to learn to talk about them, partly because we need this for our own thinking and partly because we operate in a world where we have to be able to do battle in public debate with people who do not share our intuitions and our refined understanding of things. We've got to become explicit and this is just my small effort.

2. The Need for Flexibility and Balance

In this excerpt, the Plowden Committee describes some of the ways in which English teachers integrate the various parts of the curriculum.

Learning is a continuous process from birth. The teacher's task is to provide an environment and opportunities which are sufficiently challenging for children and yet not so difficult as to be outside their reach. There has to be the right mixture of the familiar and the novel, the right match to the stage of learning the child has reached. If the material is too familiar or the learning skills too easy, children will become inattentive and bored. If too great maturity is demanded of them, they fall back on half remembered formulae and become concerned only to give the reply the teacher wants. Children can think and form concepts, so long as they work at their own level, and are not made to feel that they are failures.

Teachers must rely both on their general knowledge of child development and on detailed observation of individual children for matching their demands to children's stages of development. This concept of "readiness" was first applied to reading. It has sometimes been thought of in too negative a way. Children can be led to want to read, provided that they are sufficiently mature. Learning can be undertaken too late as well as too early. Piaget's work can help teachers in diagnosing children's readiness in mathematics, and gives some pointers as to how it can be encouraged.

At every stage of learning children need rich and varied materials and situations, though the pace at which they should be introduced may vary according to the children. If children are limited in materials, they tend to solve problems in isolation and fail to see their relevance to other similar situations. This stands out particularly clearly in young children's learning of mathematics. Similarly, children need to accumulate much experience of human behaviour before they can develop moral concepts. If teachers or parents are inconsistent in their attitudes or contradict by their behaviour what they preach, it becomes difficult for children to develop stable and mature concepts. Verbal explanation, in advance of understanding based on experience, may be an obstacle to learning, and children's knowledge of the right words may conceal from teachers their lack of understanding. Yet it is inevitable that chil-

From *Children and Their Primary Schools* (*The Plowden Report*), Vol. 1, para. 533–550, 739. Reprinted by permission of the Controller of Her Britannic Majesty's Stationery Office.

dren will pick up words which outstrip their understanding. Discussion with other children and with adults is one of the principal ways in which children check their concepts against those of others and build up an objective view of reality. There is every justification for the conversation which is a characteristic feature of the contemporary primary school. One of the most important responsibilities of teachers is to help children to see order and pattern in experience, and to extend their ideas by analogies and by the provision of suitable vocabulary. Rigid division of the curriculum into subjects tends to interrupt children's trains of thought and of interest and to hinder them from realising the common elements in problem solving. These are among the many reasons why some work, at least, should cut across subject divisions at all stages in the primary school.

These beliefs about how children learn have practical implications for the time table and the curriculum. One idea now widespread is embodied in the expression "free day" and another, associated with it, is the "integrated curriculum." The strongest influence making for the free day has been the conviction of some teachers and other educationalists that it is through play that young children learn. Nursery schools began by devoting half an hour to free play. This is still done by many kindergartens which we visited abroad. Now the whole day is spent on various forms of play, though groups of children may break away to enjoy stories or music with an adult. Infant schools usually give at least an hour a day to play, though it may be called by many different names. If teachers encourage overlap between what is done in periods of self chosen activity and in the times allocated, for example, to reading and to writing, a good learning situation will probably result. Children who are not yet ready to read can go on playing and building up vocabulary while other children are reading. Play can lead naturally to reading and writing associated with it. Children do not flit from activity to activity in their anxiety to make use of materials not available at other times of the day. Some infant schools are now confident enough in the value of self chosen activity to give the whole day to it, except for times which are used for stories, poetry, movement, and music—and even these may be voluntary, particularly for the younger children. The tendency is spreading in junior schools. Children may plan when to do work assigned to them and also have time in which to follow personal or group interests of their own choice. In a few infant and junior schools the day is still divided into a succession of short periods. In the great majority, we are glad to say, there are longer periods and these can be adjusted at the teacher's discretion.

These changes represent a revolution from the type of time-table implied by the forms completed by schools for local education authorities until quite recently. Heads were expected to show exactly what each class was doing during every minute of the week and to provide a summary showing the total number of minutes to be spent on each subject. In extreme cases, the curriculum was divided into spelling, dictation, grammar, exercises, composition, recitation, reading, handwriting, tables and mental arithmetic. It is obvious that this arrangement was not suited to what was known of the nature of children, of the classification of subject matter, or of the art of teaching. Children's interest varies in length according to personality, age and circumstances, and it is folly either to interrupt it when it is intense, or to flog it when it has declined. The teacher can best judge when to make a change and the moment of change may not be the same for each child in the class. In many schools, as we have said, children plan much of their work. Yet the teacher must constantly ensure a balance within the day or week both for the class and for individuals. He must see that time is profitably spent and give guidance on its use. In the last resort, the teacher's relationship with his pupils, his openness to their suggestions and their trust in him are far more important than the nominal degree of freedom in the time table.

The extent to which subject matter ought to be classified and the headings under which the classification is made will vary with the age of the children, with the demands made by the structure of the subject matter which is being studied, and with the circumstances of the school. Any practice which predetermines the pattern and imposes it upon all is to be condemned. Some teachers find it helpful in maintaining a balance in individual and class work to think in terms of broad areas of the curriculum such as language, science and mathematics, environmental study and the expressive arts. No pattern can be perfect since many subjects fall into one category or another according to the aspect which is being studied. For young children, the broadest of divisions is suitable. For children from 9 to 12, more subject divisions can be expected, though experience in secondary schools has shown that teaching of rigidly defined subjects, often by specialist teachers, is far from suitable for the oldest children, who will be in the middle schools. This is one of our reasons for suggesting a change in the age of transfer to secondary education.

There is little place for the type of scheme which sets down exactly what ground should be covered and what skill should be acquired by each class in the school. Yet to put nothing in its place may be to leave some teachers prisoners of tradition and to make difficulties for newcomers to a staff who are left to pick up, little by little, the ethos of a school. The best solution seems to be to provide brief schemes for the school as a whole: outlines of aims in various areas of the curriculum, the sequence of development which can be expected in children and the methods through which work can be soundly based and progress accelerated. It is also useful to have a record of experiences, topics, books, poems and music which have been found to succeed with children of different ages, and for attention to be drawn to notable experimental work. In good schools, schemes are often subject to a process of accretion which may make them so long that few teachers have time to read them. It is better for them to be sifted and revised, for matter to be dropped as well as added. Individual members of staff, with such help as the head and others can give, will need to plan in more detail the work of their particular classes. Often it will develop in an unexpected direction. A brief report on the topics, literature and so forth which have absorbed children during the course of the year will be necessary for teachers who take them later in their school career.

The idea of flexibility has found expression in a number of practices, all of them designed to make good use of the interest and curiosity of children, to minimise the notion of subject matter being rigidly compartmental, and to allow the teacher to adopt a consultative, guiding, stimulating role rather than a purely didactic one. The oldest of these methods is the "project." Some topic, such as "transport" is chosen, ideally by the children, but frequently by the teacher. The topic cuts across the boundaries of subjects and is treated as its nature requires without reference to subjects as such. At its best the method leads to the use of books of reference, to individual work and to active participation in learning. Unfortunately it is no guarantee of this and the appearance of text books of projects, which achieved at one time considerable popularity, is proof of how completely a good idea can be misunderstood.

A variation on the project, originally associated with the infant school but often better suited to older children is "the centre of interest." It begins with a topic which is of such inherent interest and variety as to make it possible and reasonable to make much of the work of the class revolve round it for a period of a week, a month or a term or even longer. Experience has shown that it is artificial to try to link most of the work of a class to one centre of interest. It has become more common to have several interests—topic is now the usual word—going at once. Much of the work may be individual, falling under broad subject headings. One topic for the time being can involve both group and class interest, and may splinter off into all kinds of individual work.

When a class of seven year olds notice the birds that come to the bird table outside the classroom window, they may decide, after discussion with their teacher, to make their own aviary. They will set to with a will, and paint the birds in flight, make models of them in clay or papier maché, write stories and poems about them and look up reference books to find out more about their habits. Children are not assimilating inert ideas but are wholly involved in thinking, feeling and doing. The slow and the bright share a common experience and each takes from it what he can at his own level. There is no attempt to put reading and writing into separate compartments; both serve a wider purpose, and artificial barriers do not fragment the learning experience. A top junior class became interested in the problem of measuring the area of an awkwardly shaped field at the back of the school. The problem stimulated much learning about surveying and triangles. From surveying, interest passed to navigation; for the more difficult aspects of the work, co-operation between members of staff as well as pupils was needed. For one boy, the work on navigation took the form of a story of encounters of pirate ships and men-of-war, and involved a great deal of calculation, history, geography and English. Integration is not only a question of allowing time for interests which do not fit under subject headings; it is as much a matter of seeing the different dimensions of subject work and of using the forms of observation and communication which are most suitable to a given sequence of learning.

Another effective way of integrating the curriculum is to relate it through the use of the environment to the boundless curiosity which children have about the world about them. When teachers talk about "first-hand experience" what they often have in mind is the exploration of the physical environment of the school, though the expression of course includes other kinds of experiences as well. Whereas once the teacher brought autumn leaves into the classroom and talked about the seasons and their characteristics, now he will take the children out to see for themselves. Rural schools can be overwhelmed by the variety of material on their doorsteps. Crops and pastures, wild flowers and weeds, farm animals, wild creatures of every kind, roads and footpaths, verges, hedges, ditches, streams, woods, the weather, the season, the stars, all provide starting points for curiosity, discussion, observation, recording and enquiry, at every level from that of the five year old to that of the 12 year old and beyond. Much of this material is also available to the newer urban schools though their sites are often laid out too formally to be suitable for children's play or for interesting studies. The most difficult problem of all is not so much that of the older urban school, despite its often restricted site, as that of the school on the large housing estate. But the weather and the stars are available to all; so are the occupations of fathers which offer a way of enlisting co-operation and interest in their children's education as well as an approach to local industry.

Teachers in town schools can make use of railways and other transport systems, and the local shops and factories, all of which can provide suitable material. Building sites are almost ubiquitous and can provide an approach to geography, mathematics and science. We have heard of children doing "traffic counts," discovering from shop keepers the source of their goods and even, in one case, exploring unofficially the sewage system of their area. Museums, geared to children's interests, may also be within reach and are becoming ready to let children handle as well as look, and to lend to schools some of the surplus stock which is otherwise often stored away in basements. It may be well to look a little at this approach as it can work out in a favourable environment. A group of H.M.I.s. working in a division in which some particularly good work is to be found, write as follows:—

> The newer methods start with the direct impact of the environment on the child and the child's individual response to it. The results are unpredictable, but extremely worth while. The teacher has to be prepared to follow up the personal interests of the children who, either singly, or in groups, follow divergent paths of discovery. Books of reference, maps, enquiries of local officials, museums, archives, elderly residents in the area are all called upon to give the information needed to complete the picture that the child is seeking to construct. When this enthusiasm is unleashed in a class, the time table may even be dispensed with, as the resulting occupations may easily cover mathematics, geology, astronomy, history, navigation, religious instruction, literature, art and craft. The teacher needs perception to appreciate the value that can be gained from this method of working, and he needs also energy to keep up with the children's demands.

Another possibility is to take children out of their own environment into a contrasting one, either for the day or for a longer period. This of course applies as much to rural children visiting towns as to urban children visiting the countryside. Such visits, carefully prepared for and not just sight-seeing, are generally used as the culmination of an interest or interests. They would often serve better as starting points. For day visits, when the school situation makes it possible, those places are best which are near enough for children to visit and to revisit, individually, in groups or as a class when new questions arise. There is then a strong incentive for them to look closely at the objects which have made a further visit necessary.

In one northern city a school, well situated in a park on the outskirts of the city, is being used for a fortnight at a time by children from the central slum areas. The school has a small resident staff and is well equipped. Since the visiting children's own teachers accompany them, they can be taught in small groups of 15. During the summer months the school day is extended into the evening so that the children, who are conveyed by buses, can gain the maximum from their experiences.

Authorities can help schools, as some indeed do, by providing hutted camps and other residential centres which do much for children socially as well as educationally. Useful experiments have also been tried in linking country and urban schools and arranging for exchange visits. Expeditions too far afield are to be avoided, as they are generally speaking pure sight-seeing tours. We have considerable doubts about overseas expeditions for primary school children.

A third possibility, which is open to all schools, is to make the school environment itself as rich as possible. Nearly all children are interested in living forms, whether they be animal or plants. Some acquaintance with them is an essential part of being educated. To care for living creatures offers an emotional outlet to some children and demands discipline from all. However rich the locality, emphasis must always be put on the school itself, which is an environment contrived for children's learning.

A word which has fairly recently come into use in educational circles is "discovery." It includes many of the ideas so far discussed and is a useful shorthand description. It has the disadvantage of comprehensiveness that it can be loosely interpreted and misunderstood. We have more to say about the value of discovery in the section on science. The sense of personal discovery influences the intensity of a child's experience, the vividness of his memory and the probability of effective transfer of learning. At the same time it is true that trivial ideas and inefficient methods may be "discovered." Furthermore, time does not allow children to find their way by discovery to all that they have to learn. In this matter, as in all education, the teacher is responsible for encouraging children in enquiries which lead to discovery and for asking leading questions.

Free and sometimes indiscriminate use of words such as discovery has led some critics to the view that English primary education needs to be more firmly based on closely argued educational theory. Nevertheless great advances appear to have been made without such theory, and research has still a long way to go before it can make a marked contribution. At many points even so fruitful an approach as that of Piaget needs further verification. What is immediately needed is that teachers should bring to bear on their day to day problems astringent intellectual scrutiny. Yet all good teachers must work intuitively and be sensitive to the emotive and imaginative needs of their children. Teaching is an art and, as long as that with all its implications is firmly grasped, it will not be harmed by intellectual stiffening.

It is clear that to change a school run on traditional lines to one run on free lines requires faith and courage. The fact that a substantial number of schools have made the change is evidence that these qualities have not been wanting. They are certainly the first requirements in a reforming head, but they are not the only ones. It is not a question of saying "freedom is in, discipline is out," an attitude which could lead to instant disaster. The change involves the total life of the school, and the staff, or a substantial proportion of it, must at least be ready for change and must understand something of the philosophy underlying it. A small country school which had been run on traditional lines was able to make the change quickly because the staff of two retired simultaneously, and were replaced by a man and his wife who knew what they wanted to do and were able to set about it without delay. The children responded and, in less than a year, the school closely resembled that described at the beginning of this chapter. On one occasion the headmaster was obliged to be absent for two days and was unable to obtain a substitute. The children in his class were then left to their own devices, with only such supervision as the infants' teacher in another room was able to give them. "There was no trouble" said the headmaster, "and they had done two good days' work when I got back." A ten year old boy at this school observed to a visiting H.M.I.: "The trouble with this place is that we haven't enough time to do all we want. We are trying to get Mr. . . . to start a night school for us, so we can get on with our work in the evening." There will be many readers including teachers, who will find this story almost incredible, remembering, as they will, the instantaneous, disorderly relaxation which used to characterise a class when the teacher went out of the room. The change is a major one which is beginning to revolutionise the primary schools of England, but it needs teachers of great personal qualities, strong character and a deep understanding of children, and it also needs first rate organisation. If, for example, children are allowed choice in what they do the choice must be genuine and the alternatives interesting and worth doing. Boredom is a deadly enemy. Time wasting occupations and exercises "to keep the children quiet while the teacher is busy, or marking the Registers" are fatal to good discipline and to good learning and there is no place for them, or need for them, in the kind of school we are discussing. Furthermore, although in such a school rewards and punishments in the ordinary sense may seem to have little or no place, there is in fact a substitute in the form of approval and disapproval. The more sympathetic a teacher is, the more successfully he or she establishes with the children a relationship of affection and respect, the more clearly will approval be a reward, and withdrawal in some sense a punishment. Such a system is preferable to arbitrary authoritarianism, but it involves the abrogation of one kind of power, it bestows another and must be used with understanding and scrupulousness. Children like to know where they stand and what to expect. They must depend upon adults for their moral standards and for guidance on what behaviour is tolerable in society; an adult who withholds such guidance is in fact making a decision which involves as heavy a claim for his own judgment as is made by the martinet. There may be occasions, as the children grow older, when such guidance ought to be withheld so that children can think out problems for themselves, but this only underlines the fact that the teacher has a crucial role to play at every point in the "free" school.

3. How to Think About the Curriculum

The English take their Royal Commissions and Parliamentary Committees far more seriously than we take the reports of our presidential or congressional commissions. A series of reports in the early 1930s by the so-called Hadow Commission, a group much like the Plowden Committee, has had a profound effect on the thinking of English teachers, heads, and inspectors. One measure of its continuing influence is the fact that Her Majesty's Stationery Office felt compelled to reprint the 1931 report on primary schools just ten years ago.

In the selection reprinted below, the Hadow Commission addressed itself to the role of the academic disciplines in primary education. While it is important to emphasize the traditional subjects at a later stage of the educational process, the Commission argues, such an emphasis is not the best way to meet the needs of young children. As the Commission put it in a widely quoted phrase, "primary education would gain greatly in realism and power of inspiration if an attempt were more generally made to think of the curriculum less in terms of departments of knowledge to be taught, and more in terms of activities to be fostered and interests to be broadened." The starting point of the curriculum should be "the experience, the curiosity, and the awakening powers and interests of the children themselves."

. . . The essential point is that any curriculum, if it is not to be purely arbitrary and artificial, must make use of certain elements of experience, because they are part of the common life of mankind. The aim of the school is to introduce its pupils to such experiences in an orderly and intelligent manner, so as to develop their innate powers and to awaken them to the basic interests of civilised existence. If the school succeeds in achieving that aim, knowledge will be acquired in the process, not, indeed, without effort, but by an effort whose value will be enhanced by

From *Report of the Consultative Committee on the Primary School* (The "Hadow Commission" Report), London: Her Majesty's Stationery Office, 1931, reprinted 1962.

the fact that its purpose and significance can be appreciated, at least in part, by the children themselves.

Thus conceived, the curriculum of a school acquires a higher degree of unity than is possible so long as it is regarded as a series of separate, if related, subjects. It is unified by the common relevance of the growth of children of the different elements composing it. Growth is, from one point of view, and a point of view which is peculiarly vital for young children, a physiological process, and the foundation of a school's activities must clearly be care for the physical well-being of its pupils. . . . But the child is not only an organism with biological needs; he is also a member of the human family. His environment is a civilisation created by man. Just as, if he is to survive, he must adapt himself to the requirements of the physical world, so, if he is to be at home in that civilisation, as one free of the house, he must acquire some familiarity with the elementary processes which civilisation employs and catch a glimpse of the foundations on which it reposes. Language, as the expression of thought and the instrument of human intercourse, constructive work which at once stimulates the intelligence and gives an insight into the significance of the great historic crafts, the appreciation of beauty and the creation of beauty in simple forms, the enlargement of the individual's horizon by contact with other minds through literature and the discovery that life has a past and future as well as a present, some knowledge of the simpler facts of the material world—these things, it will be agreed, lie at the basis of an intelligent participation on the life of society, and are to be regarded, therefore, as fixing the general character and direction of the school curriculum. What is important is not that a high standard of attainment should be reached in any one of them, but that interest should be quickened, habits of thoroughness and honesty in work established, and the foundations on which knowledge may later be built securely laid. The production of juvenile authors, mathematicians and scientists is neither to be anticipated nor to be desired. It is reasonable, however, to expect that in the primary school children should learn, within the limits of their experience, to use the noble instrument of their native language with clearness and dignity, a matter in which English education has hitherto been noticeably inferior to that of France; that they should acquire simple kinds of manual skill and take pleasure in using them; that they should admire what is admirable in form and design; that they should read some good books with zest and enjoyment; and that they should learn that the behaviour of the physical universe is not arbitrary or capricious, but governed by principles, some at least of which it is possible for them to grasp.

Such a curriculum includes several different elements. Each of these elements, language and speech, manual work, art, history and geography, mathematics, science and the study of nature, obviously opens unlimited vistas. Each is the sphere of a different specialism and each is often described as a separate subject. For certain purposes, and in certain connections, the description is just. The technique of learning or of teaching one of them is different from that which is required for another. But divergent streams spring from a common source in human experience, and methods appropriate to children of an age when they can follow specialised interests along the lines of logical development are not necessarily best suited to a stage when curiosity is strong but the capacity for logical analysis and consecutive reasoning is still relatively weak. Subjects are not independent entities, but divisions within the general field of knowledge, whose boundaries move, and should move, backwards and forwards. They are artificial, in the sense that the classification which they represent is not an end in itself, but the means by which some measure of order and system is introduced into the complex world of intellectual interests. At one stage of education it is important to emphasise the characteristics peculiar to each as a separate discipline, at another the common experience which underlies them all. Both these aspects of the truth are vital, and neither must be sacrificed; but they are not equally relevant at all periods of life. In the secondary school, which is designed for children over eleven, that which may more properly be emphasised is the first, not the second. In dealing with children of the age when they attend the primary school, the more important aspect is the second, not the first.

We agree, therefore, with the large number of witnesses—the majority, indeed, of those coming before us—who pleaded that the pursuit of primary school studies in the form of distinct and separate "subjects" was not the method best calculated to meet the needs of young children. We think that the time has now come to consider these conventional categories with a view to relating the curriculum more closely to the natural movement of the children's minds. In making this statement, we wish to guard, at the outset, against possible misapprehensions. We are far from desiring to remove the backbone of intellectual discipline from the work of the school, or to imply that, even within the primary school, the same method of presentation is equally suitable for pupils of different ages, or to lend countenance to the suggestion that teachers should follow any stereotyped system or rely on any single device, however attractive. There are obviously certain parts of the curriculum—for example, reading, writing and arithmetic—which are the tools of education, and a reasonable proficiency in which requires regular practice. As children advance in years, they approach more nearly to the stage when different branches of knowledge become the subject of special study. Teachers must be guided by their own insight and experience, and must use the methods which they are conscious they can use best. With these qualifications, however, we are with the majority of our witnesses strongly of the opinion that primary education would gain greatly in realism and power of inspiration if an attempt were more generally made to think of the curriculum less in terms of departments of knowledge to be taught, and more in terms of activities to be fostered and interests to be broadened. Hitherto the general tendency has been to take for granted the existence of certain traditional "subjects" and to present them to the pupils as lessons to be mastered. There is, as we have said, a place for that method, but it is neither the only method, nor the method most likely to be fruitful between the ages of seven and eleven. What is required, at least, so far as much of the curriculum is concerned, is to substitute for it methods which take as the starting-point of the work of the primary school the experience, the curiosity, and the awakening powers and interests of the children themselves.

Whether such an approach to the problem is to be described by some special name, such as the "project" method, is of minor importance. The essential point is that the curriculum should not be loaded with inert ideas and crude blocks of fact, which are devoid of significance till related to some interest in the minds of the pupils. It must be vivid, realistic, a stream in motion, not a stagnant pool. Nor are we concerned to elaborate in detail the precise procedure to be deduced from these premises. If the point of view for which we plead is generally accepted, teachers will find little difficulty in translating it into practice. The fundamental idea of starting from a centre of interest and exploring in turn the different avenues which diverge from it is involved, after all, in all intellectual activity which is not merely formal or imitative, and if its educational significance is sometimes overlooked, the reason is not that it is novel, but that it is too familiar. What is needed in education, as elsewhere, is a little cold realism, or in other words, the art that overcomes art. A boy is interested in steam engines; let him start from his interests, make a rough model of an engine, discover something about the historical process of its invention and improvement, read a little about the changes in the life of society which have been produced by it, make a map of the transport system of his own town and country, learn something about the lives of famous engineers, and study in outline the part which steam plays in linking together different parts of the world. A girl has heard her parents discuss the price of food: let her learn something about the countries from which it comes, the processes by which it is conveyed, the crafts concerned in its production and preparation, what agriculture is and the changes through which it has passed and is passing, the life of the rural population in her own country and elsewhere. Children visit a place of historical interest, a church, a castle, the site of a British or Roman camp; let their work before and after the visit be planned round it, and the pupils be told of its place in history, paint such features of it as they can, make a map of the surrounding region, and act where possible some of the famous scenes associated with it, making the dresses and scenery for themselves.

Such methods of giving concreteness and reality to the work of the school are already often practised and need no lengthy explanation. They will naturally vary from place to place, and from town to country. In the latter, indeed, they should be specially easy and profitable. We do not share the view sometimes advanced that a special curriculum should be devised for rural schools; it is even less desirable that the education of the country should be urbanised. The business of the school is to make good human beings, not countrymen or townsmen; nor is it irrelevant to point out that a large number of country children will later live and work in towns. What is necessary is that the curriculum of the school should make every use of the environment of the pupils. It will use one sort of material in a colliery or textile district, and another in an agricultural village, where nature supplies living specimens for children to observe, where plants, birds and animals, the configuration of the country and its geological characteristics, can be studied at first hand, where the weather is not merely an unavoidable inconvenience but a significant phenomenon, and where gardening and the keeping of animals can be carried on without difficulty. What is important in each case is that, while the indispensable foundations are thoroughly mastered, the work of the school should be related to the experience and interest of the children. Education must be regarded not as a routine designed to facilitate the assimilation of dead matter, but as a group of activities by which powers are exercised, and curiosity aroused, satisfied, and again aroused.

4. Changing the Center of Gravity of the School

More often maligned than read, John Dewey unquestionably is the greatest philosopher of education the United States has produced. One reason for his greatness is that he disdained the philosopher's usual aloofness from the grimy affairs of men. His basic ideas on education, for example, were tested and developed experimentally at the Laboratory School of the University of Chicago, which he founded in 1896 and directed for eight years. The School and Society, from which this excerpt is taken, is the most widely read of Dewey's writings on education. The book originated as a series of three lectures which Dewey delivered in 1899, in part to refute charges that the Laboratory School was subversive, in part to help raise funds for the school's support.

Dewey's practical knowledge of schooling is reflected in the opening anecdote, in which he describes the difficulty he encountered in trying to buy furniture appropriate for the kind of classrooms he was creating. As one thoughtful supplier explained the problem to him, "You want

*something at which the children may work; these are all for listening."
To which Dewey adds, "That tells the story of the traditional education."
He goes on to elaborate on the passivity and uniformity that grows out
of this emphasis on listening rather than working; in the traditional
school, the center of gravity is in the teacher or the textbook. What is
needed, Dewey argues, is to shift the center of gravity to the child, who
should be the center around which the educational process is organized.*

Some few years ago I was looking about the school supply stores in the
city, trying to find desks and chairs which seemed thoroughly suitable
from all points of view—artistic, hygienic, and educational—to the
needs of the children. We had a great deal of difficulty in finding what
we needed, and finally one dealer, more intelligent than the rest, made
this remark: "I am afraid we have not what you want. You want something at which the children may work; these are all for listening." That
tells the story of the traditional education. Just as the biologist can take
a bone or two and reconstruct the whole animal, so, if we put before the
mind's eye the ordinary schoolroom, with its rows of ugly desks placed in
geometrical order, crowded together so that there shall be as little moving room as possible, desks almost all of the same size, with just space
enough to hold books, pencils, and paper, and add a table, some chairs,
the bare walls, and possibly a few pictures, we can reconstruct the only
educational activity that can possibly go on in such a place. It is all made
"for listening"—because simply studying lessons out of a book is only
another kind of listening; it marks the dependency of one mind upon
another. The attitude of listening means, comparatively speaking, passivity, absorption; that there are certain ready-made materials which are
there, which have been prepared by the school superintendent, the
board, the teacher, and of which the child is to take in as much as possible in the least possible time.

There is very little place in the traditional schoolroom for the child
to work. The workshop, the laboratory, the materials, the tools with
which the child may construct, create, and actively inquire, and even the
requisite space, have been for the most part lacking. The things that
have to do with these processes have not even a definitely recognized
place in education. They are what the educational authorities who write
editorials in the daily papers generally term "fads" and "frills." A lady
told me yesterday that she had been visiting different schools trying to
find one where activity on the part of the children preceded the giving of
information on the part of the teacher, or where the children had some
motive for demanding the information. She visited, she said, twenty-four

From John Dewey, *The School and Society* (Chicago, Illinois: University of
Chicago Press, Phoenix Books, 1956), pp. 31–38. Originally published 1899.

different schools before she found her first instance. I may add that that was not in this city.

Another thing that is suggested by these schoolrooms, with their set desks, is that everything is arranged for handling as large numbers of children as possible; for dealing with children *en masse,* as an aggregate of units; involving, again, that they be treated passively. The moment children act they individualize themselves; they cease to be a mass and become the intensely distinctive beings that we are acquainted with out of school, in the home, the family, on the playground, and in the neighborhood.

On the same basis is explicable the uniformity of method and curriculum. If everything is on a "listening" basis, you can have uniformity of material and method. The ear, and the book which reflects the ear, constitute the medium which is alike for all. There is next to no opportunity for adjustment to varying capacities and demands. There is a certain amount—a fixed quantity—of ready-made results and accomplishments to be acquired by all children alike in a given time. It is in response to this demand that the curriculum has been developed from the elementary school up through the college. There is just so much desirable knowledge, and there are just so many needed technical accomplishments in the world. Then comes the mathematical problem of dividing this by the six, twelve, or sixteen years of school life. Now give the children every year just the proportionate fraction of the total, and by the time they have finished they will have mastered the whole. By covering so much ground during this hour or day or week or year, everything comes out with perfect evenness at the end—provided the children have not forgotten what they have previously learned. The outcome of all this is Matthew Arnold's report of the statement, proudly made to him by an educational authority in France, that so many thousands of children were studying at a given hour, say eleven o'clock, just such a lesson in geography; and in one of our own western cities this proud boast used to be repeated to successive visitors by its superintendent.

I may have exaggerated somewhat in order to make plain the typical points of the old education: its passivity of attitude, its mechanical massing of children, its uniformity of curriculum and method. It may be summed up by stating that the center of gravity is outside the child. It is in the teacher, the textbook, anywhere and everywhere you please except in the immediate instincts and activities of the child himself. On that basis there is not much to be said about the *life* of the child. A good deal might be said about the studying of the child, but the school is not the place where the child *lives.* Now the change which is coming into our education is the shifting of the center of gravity. It is a change, a revolution, not unlike that introduced by Copernicus when the astronomical center shifted from the earth to the sun. In this case the child becomes the sun about which the appliances of education revolve; he is the center about which they are organized.

If we take an example from an ideal home, where the parent is intelligent enough to recognize what is best for the child, and is able to supply what is needed, we find the child learning through the social converse and constitution of the family. There are certain points of interest and value to him in the conversation carried on: statements are made, inquiries arise, topics are discussed, and the child continually learns. He states his experiences, his misconceptions are corrected. Again the child participates in the household occupations, and thereby gets habits of industry, order, and regard for the rights and ideas of others, and the fundamental habit of subordinating his activities to the general interest of the household. Participation in these household tasks becomes an opportunity for gaining knowledge. The ideal home would naturally have a workshop where the child could work out his constructive instincts. It would have a miniature laboratory in which his inquiries could be directed. The life of the child would extend out of doors to the garden, surrounding fields, and forests. He would have his excursions, his walks and talks, in which the larger world out of doors would open to him.

Now, if we organize and generalize all of this, we have the ideal school. There is no mystery about it, no wonderful discovery of pedagogy or educational theory. It is simply a question of doing systematically and in a large, intelligent, and competent way what for various reasons can be done in most households only in a comparatively meager and haphazard manner. In the first place, the ideal home has to be enlarged. The child must be brought into contact with more grown people and with more children in order that there may be the freest and richest social life. Moreover, the occupations and relationships of the home environment are not specially selected for the growth of the child; the main object is something else, and what the child can get out of them is incidental. Hence the need of a school. In this school the life of the child becomes the all-controlling aim. All the media necessary to further the growth of the child center there. Learning? certainly, but living primarily, and learning through and in relation to this living. When we take the life of the child centered and organized in this way, we do not find that he is first of all a listening being; quite the contrary.

The statement so frequently made that education means "drawing out" is excellent, if we mean simply to contrast it with the process of pouring in. But, after all, it is difficult to connect the idea of drawing out with the ordinary doings of the child of three, four, seven, or eight years of age. He is already running over, spilling over, with activities of all kinds. He is not a purely latent being whom the adult has to approach with great caution and skill in order gradually to draw out some hidden germ of activity. The child is already intensely active, and the question of education is the question of taking hold of his activities, of giving them direction. Through direction, through organized use, they tend toward valuable results, instead of scattering or being left to merely impulsive expression.

If we keep this before us, the difficulty I find uppermost in the minds of many people regarding what is termed the new education is not so much solved as dissolved; it disappears. A question often asked is: If you begin with the child's ideas, impulses, and interests, all so crude, so random and scattering, so little refined or spiritualized, how is he going to get the necessary discipline, culture, and information? If there were no way open to us except to excite and indulge these impulses of the child, the question might well be asked. We should either have to ignore and repress the activities or else to humor them. But if we have organization of equipment and of materials, there is another path open to us. We can direct the child's activities, giving them exercise along certain lines, and can thus lead up to the goal which logically stands at the end of the paths followed.

"If wishes were horses, beggars would ride." Since they are not, since really to satisfy an impulse or interest means to work it out, and working it out involves running up against obstacles, becoming acquainted with materials, exercising ingenuity, patience, persistence, alertness, it of necessity involves discipline—ordering of power—and supplies knowledge. Take the example of the little child who wants to make a box. If he stops short with the imagination or wish, he certainly will not get discipline. But when he attempts to realize his impulse, it is a question of making his idea definite, making it into a plan, of taking the right kind of wood, measuring the parts needed, giving them the necessary proportions, etc. There is involved the preparation of materials, the sawing, planing, the sandpapering, making all the edges and corners to fit. Knowledge of tools and processes is inevitable. If the child realizes his instinct and makes the box, there is plenty of opportunity to gain discipline and perseverance, to exercise effort in overcoming obstacles, and to attain as well a great deal of information.

5. Education Must Be Both Child-Centered and Subject-Centered

Both the advocates of Progressive Education and the traditionalists make a fundamental error, Dewey argued as early as 1902, in posing an opposition between child-centeredness and subject-centeredness. There is no difference in kind between the child's experience and the subjects that make up the usual curriculum. The academic disciplines are themselves experience—the cumulative experience of mankind, experience that has been organized in a systematic way. If traditional education tended to ignore the educational value and dynamism of the child's own experience, Dewey warned, the reformers ran the risk of ignoring the heuristic value of the various intellectual disciplines and thus of inhibiting children's potential growth. "Nothing can be developed from nothing; nothing but the crude can be developed out of the crude—and this is what surely happens when we throw the child back upon his achieved self as a finality, and invite him to spin new truths of nature or of conduct out of that."

The fundamental factors in the educative process are an immature, undeveloped being; and certain social aims, meanings, values incarnate in the matured experience of the adult. The educative process is the due interaction of these forces. Such a conception of each in relation to the other as facilitates completest and freest interaction is the essence of educational theory.

But here comes the effort of thought. It is easier to see the conditions in their separateness, to insist upon one at the expense of the other, to make antagonists of them, than to discover a reality to which each belongs. The easy thing is to seize upon something in the nature of the child, or upon something in the developed consciousness of the adult, and insist upon *that* as the key to the whole problem. When this happens a really serious practical problem—that of interaction—is transformed into an unreal, and hence insoluble, theoretic problem. Instead of seeing the educative steadily and as a whole, we see conflicting terms. We get the case of the child *vs.* the curriculum; of the individual nature *vs.* social culture. Below all other divisions in pedagogic opinion lies this opposition.

The child lives in a somewhat narrow world of personal contacts. Things hardly come within his experience unless they touch, intimately and obviously, his own well-being, or that of his family and friends. His world is a world of persons with their personal interests, rather than a realm of facts and laws. Not truth, in the sense of conformity to external fact, but affection and sympathy, is its keynote. As against this, the course of study met in the school presents material stretching back indefinitely in time, and extending outward indefinitely into space. The child is taken out of his familiar physical environment, hardly more than a square mile or so in area, into the wide world—yes, and even to the bounds of the solar system. His little span of personal memory and tradition is overlaid with the long centuries of the history of all peoples.

Again, the child's life is an integral, a total one. He passes quickly and

From John Dewey, *The Child and the Curriculum* (Chicago: University of Chicago Press, Phoenix Books, 1956), pp. 4–7, 9, 11–12, 17–18. Originally published 1902.

readily from one topic to another, as from one spot to another, but is not conscious of transition or break. There is no conscious isolation, hardly conscious distinction. The things that occupy him are held together by the unity of the personal and social interests which his life carries along. Whatever is uppermost in his mind constitutes to him, for the time being, the whole universe. That universe is fluid and fluent; its contents dissolve and re-form with amazing rapidity. But, after all, it is the child's own world. It has the unity and completeness of his own life. He goes to school, and various studies divide and fractionize the world for him. Geography selects, it abstracts and analyzes one set of facts, and from one particular point of view. Arithmetic is another division, grammar another department, and so on indefinitely.

Again, in school each of these subjects is classified. Facts are torn away from their original place in experience and rearranged with reference to some general principle. Classification is not a matter of child experience; things do not come to the individual pigeonholed. The vital ties of affection, the connecting bonds of activity, hold together the variety of his personal experiences. The adult mind is so familiar with the notion of logically ordered facts that it does not recognize—it cannot realize— the amount of separating and reformulating which the facts of direct experience have to undergo before they can appear as a "study," or branch of learning. A principle, for the intellect, has had to be distinguished and defined; facts have had to be interpreted in relation to this principle, not as they are in themselves. They have had to be regathered about a new center which is wholly abstract and ideal. All this means a development of a special intellectual interest. It means ability to view facts impartially and objectively; that is, without reference to their place and meaning in one's own experience. It means capacity to analyze and to synthesize. It means highly matured intellectual habits and the command of a definite technique and apparatus of scientific inquiry. The studies as classified are the product, in a word, of the science of the ages, not of the experience of the child.

These apparent deviations and differences between child and curriculum might be almost indefinitely widened. But we have here sufficiently fundamental divergences: first, the narrow but personal world of the child against the impersonal but infinitely extended world of space and time; second, the unity, the single wholeheartedness of the child's life, and the specializations and divisions of the curriculum; third, an abstract principle of logical classification and arrangement, and the practical and emotional bonds of child life.

From these elements of conflict grow up different educational sects. One school fixes its attention upon the importance of the subject-matter of the curriculum as compared with the contents of the child's own experience. . . .

Not so, says the other sect. The child is the starting-point, the center, and the end. His development, his growth, is the ideal. It alone furnishes the standard. To the growth of the child all studies are subservient; they are instruments valued as they serve the needs of growth. Personality, character, is more than subject-matter. Not knowledge or information, but self-realization, is the goal. . . .

What, then, is the problem? It is just to get rid of the prejudicial notion that there is some gap in kind (as distinct from degree) between the child's experience and the various forms of subject-matter that make up the course of study. From the side of the child, it is a question of seeing how his experience already contains within itself elements—facts and truths—of just the same sort as those entering into the formulated study; and, what is of more importance, of how it contains within itself the attitudes, the motives, and the interests which have operated in developing and organizing the subject-matter to the plane which it now occupies. From the side of the studies, it is a question of interpreting them as outgrowths of forces operating in the child's life, and of discovering the steps that intervene between the child's present experience and their richer maturity.

Abandon the notion of subject-matter as something fixed and ready-made in itself, outside the child's experience; cease thinking of the child's experience as also something hard and fast; see it as something fluent, embryonic, vital; and we realize that the child and the curriculum are simply two limits which define a single process. Just as two points define a straight line, so the present standpoint of the child and the facts and truths of studies define instruction. It is continuous reconstruction, moving from the child's present experience out into that represented by the organized bodies of truth that we call studies.

On the face of it, the various studies, arithmetic, geography, language, botany, etc., are themselves experience—they are that of the race. They embody the cumulative outcome of the efforts, the strivings, and the successes of the human race generation after generation. They present this, not as a mere accumulation, not as a miscellaneous heap of separate bits of experience, but in some organized and systematized way—that is, as reflectively formulated.

Hence, the facts and truths that enter into the child's present experience, and those contained in the subject-matter of studies, are the initial and final terms of one reality. To oppose one to the other is to oppose the infancy and maturity of the same growing life; it is to set the moving tendency and the final result of the same process over against each other; it is to hold that the nature and the destiny of the child war with each other. . . .

If, once more, the "old education" tended to ignore the dynamic quality, the developing force inherent in the child's present experience, and therefore to assume that direction and control were just matters of arbitrarily putting the child in a given path and compelling him to walk there, the "new education" is in danger of taking the idea of development in altogether too formal and empty a way. The child is expected to "develop" this or that fact or truth out of his own mind. He is told to think things out, or work things out for himself, without being supplied any of the environing conditions which are requisite to start and guide thought. Nothing can be developed from nothing; nothing but the crude can be developed out of the crude—and this is what surely happens when we throw the child back upon his achieved self as a finality, and invite him to spin new truths of nature or of conduct out of that. It is certainly as futile to expect a child to evolve a universe out of his own mere mind as it is for a philosopher to attempt that task. Development does not mean just getting something out of the mind. It is a development of experience and into experience that is really wanted.

6. The Progressive Organization of Subject Matter

The danger of which Dewey warned in 1902 became more and more of a reality in the 1920s and 1930s, as Progressive Education took on an increasingly romantic, and at times almost anti-intellectual, cast. As a result, Dewey became Progressive Education's most telling critic as well as its principal philosopher and prophet. In this selection, which applies equally well to the contemporary scene, Dewey elaborates on his earlier analysis of the role of subject matter in a progressive school. Using the child's own experience as the basis for teaching and learning is important, he argues, but it provides no more than the starting point. The teacher must go on to help the child develop and organize what he has already experienced in ways that will lead to further learning. "No experience is educative," he insists, "that does not tend both to knowledge of more facts and entertaining of more ideas and to a better, a more orderly arrangement of them."

———

Allusion has been made in passing a number of times to objective conditions involved in experience and to their function in promoting or failing to promote the enriched growth of further experience. By implication, these objective conditions, whether those of observation, of memory, of

From John Dewey, *Experience and Education*, reprinted in Reginald D. Archambault, ed., *John Dewey on Education* (New York: Random House, Modern Library, 1964), pp. 373–386.

information procured from others, or of imagination, have been identified with the subject-matter of study and learning; or, speaking more generally, with the stuff of the course of study. Nothing, however, has been said explicitly so far about subject-matter as such. That topic will now be discussed. One consideration stands out clearly when education is conceived in terms of experience. Anything which can be called a study, whether arithmetic, history, geography, or one of the natural sciences, must be derived from materials which at the outset fall within the scope of ordinary life-experience. In this respect the newer education contrasts sharply with procedures which start with facts and truths that are outside the range of the experience of those taught, and which, therefore, have the problem of discovering ways and means of bringing them within experience. Undoubtedly one chief cause for the great success of newer methods in early elementary education has been its observance of the contrary principle.

But finding the material for learning within experience is only the first step. The next step is the progressive development of what is already experienced into a fuller and richer and also more organized form, a form that gradually approximates that in which subject-matter is presented to the skilled, mature person. That this change is possible without departing from the organic connection of education with experience is shown by the fact that this change takes place outside of the school and apart from formal education. The infant, for example, begins with an environment of objects that is very restricted in space and time. That environment steadily expands by the momentum inherent in experience itself without aid from scholastic instruction. As the infant learns to reach, creep, walk, and talk, the intrinsic subject-matter of its experience widens and deepens. It comes into connection with new objects and events which call out new powers, while the exercise of these powers refines and enlarges the content of its experience. Life-space and life-durations are expanded. The environment, the world of experience, constantly grows larger and, so to speak, thicker. The educator who receives the child at the end of this period has to find ways for doing consciously and deliberately what "nature" accomplishes in the earlier years.

It is hardly necessary to insist upon the first of the two conditions which have been specified. It is a cardinal precept of the newer school of education that the beginning of instruction shall be made with the experience learners already have; that this experience and the capacities that have been developed during its course provide the starting point for all further learning. I am not so sure that the other condition, that of orderly development toward expansion and organization of subject-matter through growth of experience, receives as much attention. Yet the principle of continuity of educative experience requires that equal thought and attention be given to solution of this aspect of the educational problem. Undoubtedly this phase of the problem is more difficult than the other. Those who deal with the pre-school child, with the kindergarten child, and with the boy and girl of the early primary years do not have much difficulty in determining the range of past experience or in finding activities that connect in vital ways with it. With older children both factors of the problem offer increased difficulties to the educator. It is harder to find out the background of the experience of individuals and harder to find out just how the subject-matters already contained in that experience shall be directed so as to lead out to larger and better organized fields.

It is a mistake to suppose that the principle of the leading on of experience to something different is adequately satisfied simply by giving pupils some new experiences any more than it is by seeing to it that they have greater skill and ease in dealing with things with which they are already familiar. It is also essential that the new objects and events be related intellectually to those of earlier experiences, and this means that there be some advance made in conscious articulation of facts and ideas. It thus becomes the office of the educator to select those things within the range of existing experience that have the promise and potentiality of presenting new problems which by stimulating new ways of observation and judgment will expand the area of further experience. He must constantly regard what is already won not as a fixed possession but as an agency and instrumentality for opening new fields which make new demands upon existing powers of observation and of intelligent use of memory. Connectedness in growth must be his constant watchword.

The educator more than the member of any other profession is concerned to have a long look ahead. The physician may feel his job done when he has restored a patient to health. He has undoubtedly the obligation of advising him how to live so as to avoid similar troubles in the future. But, after all, the conduct of his life is his own affair, not the physician's; and what is more important for the present point is that as far as the physician does occupy himself with instruction and advice as to the future of his patient he takes upon himself the function of an educator. The lawyer is occupied with winning a suit for his client or getting the latter out of some complication into which he has got himself. If it goes beyond the case presented to him he too becomes an educator. The educator by the very nature of his work is obliged to see his present work in terms of what it accomplishes, or fails to accomplish, for a future whose objects are linked with those of the present.

Here, again, the problem for the progressive educator is more difficult than for the teacher in the traditional school. The latter had indeed to look ahead. But unless his personality and enthusiasm took him beyond the limits that hedged in the traditional school, he could content himself with thinking of the next examination period or the promotion to the next class. He could envisage the future in terms of factors that lay within the requirements of the school system as that conventionally existed. There is incumbent upon the teacher who links education and actual experience together a more serious and a harder business. He must be aware of the potentialities for leading students into new fields which belong to experiences already had, and must use this knowledge as his criterion for selection and arrangement of the conditions that influence their present experience.

Because the studies of the traditional school consisted of subject-matter that was selected and arranged on the basis of the judgment of adults as to what would be useful for the young sometime in the future, the material to be learned was settled upon outside the present life-experience of the learner. In consequnce, it had to do with the past; it was such as had proved useful to men in past ages. By reaction to an opposite extreme, as unfortunate as it was probably natural under the circumstances, the sound idea that education should derive its materials from present experience and should enable the learner to cope with the problems of the present and future has often been converted into the idea that progressive schools can to a very large extent ignore the past. If the present could be cut off from the past, this conclusion would be sound. But the achievements of the past provide the only means at command for understanding the present. Just as the individual has to draw in memory upon his own past to understand the conditions in which he individually finds himself, so the issues and problems of present *social* life are in such intimate and direct connection with the past that students cannot be prepared to understand either these problems or the best way of dealing with them without delving into their roots in the past. In other words, the sound principle that the objectives of learning are in the future and its immediate materials are in present experience can be carried into effect only in the degree that present experience is stretched, as it were, backward. It can expand into the future only as it is also enlarged to take in the past.

If time permitted, discussion of the political and economic issues which the present generation will be compelled to face in the future would render this general statement definite and concrete. The nature of the issues cannot be understood save as we know how they came about. The institutions and customs that exist in the present and that give rise to present social ills and dislocations did not arise overnight. They have a long history behind them. Attempt to deal with them simply on the basis of what is obvious in the present is bound to result in adoption of superficial measures which in the end will only render existing problems more acute and more difficult to solve. Policies framed simply upon the ground of knowledge of the present cut off from the past is the counterpart of heedless carelessness in individual conduct. The way out of scholastic systems that made the past an end in itself is to make acquaintance with the past a *means* of understanding the present. Until this problem is worked out, the present clash of educational ideas and practices will continue. On the one hand, there will be reactionaries that claim that the main, if not the sole, business of education is transmission of the cultural heritage. On the other hand, there will be those who hold that we should ignore the past and deal only with the present and future.

That up to the present time the weakest point in progressive schools is in the matter of selection and organization of intellectual subject-matter is, I think, inevitable under the circumstances. It is as inevitable as it is right and proper that they should break loose from the cut and dried material which formed the staple of the old education. In addition, the field of experience is very wide and it varies in its contents from place to place and from time to time. A single course of studies for all progressive schools is out of the question; it would mean abandoning the fundamental principle of connection with life-experiences. Moreover, progressive schools are new. They have had hardly more than a generation in which to develop. A certain amount of uncertainty and of laxity in choice and organization of subject-matter is, therefore, what was to be expected. It is no ground for fundamental criticism or complaint.

It is a ground for legitimate criticism, however, when the ongoing movement of progressive education fails to recognize that the problem of selection and organization of subject-matter for study and learning is fundamental. Improvisation that takes advantage of special occasions prevents teaching and learning from being stereotyped and dead. But the basic material of study cannot be picked up in a cursory manner. Occasions which are not and cannot be foreseen are bound to arise wherever there is intellectual freedom. They should be utilized. But there is a decided difference between using them in the development of a continuing line of activity and trusting to them to provide the chief material of learning.

Unless a given experience leads out into a field previously unfamiliar no problems arise, while problems are the stimulus to thinking. That the conditions found in present experience should be used as sources of problems is a characteristic which differentiates education based upon experience from traditional education. For in the latter, problems were set from outside. Nonetheless, growth depends upon the presence of difficulty to be overcome by the exercise of intelligence. Once more, it is part of the educator's responsibility to see equally to two things: First, that the problem grows out of the conditions of the experience being had in the present, and that it is within the range of the capacity of students; and, secondly, that it is such that it arouses in the learner an active quest for information and for production of new ideas. The new facts and new ideas thus obtained become the ground for further experiences in which new problems are presented. The process is a continuous spiral. The inescapable linkage of the present with the past is a principle whose application is not restricted to a study of history. Take natural science, for example. Contemporary social life is what it is in very large measure because of the results of application of physical science. The experience of every child and youth, in the country and the city, is what it is in its present actuality because of appliances which utilize electricity, heat, and chemical processes. A child does not eat a meal that does not involve in its preparation and assimilation chemical and physiological principles. He does not read by artificial light or take a ride in a motor car or on a train without coming into contact with operations and processes which science has engendered.

It is a sound educational principle that students should be introduced to scientific subject-matter and be initiated into its facts and laws through acquaintance with everyday social applications. Adherence to this method is not only the most direct avenue to understanding of science itself but as the pupils grow more mature it is also the surest road to the understanding of the economic and industrial problems of present society. For they are the products to a very large extent of the application of science in production and distribution of commodities and services, while the latter processes are the most important factor in determining the present relations of human beings and social groups to one another. It is absurd, then, to argue that processes similar to those studied in laboratories and institutes of research are not a part of the daily life-experience of the young and hence do not come within the scope of education based upon experience. That the immature cannot study scientific facts and principles in the way in which mature experts study them goes without saying. But this fact, instead of exempting the educator from responsibility for using present experiences so that learners may gradually be led, through extraction of facts and laws, to experience of a scientific order, sets one of his main problems.

For if it is true that existing experience in detail and also on a wide scale is what it is because of the application of science, first, to processes of production and distribution of goods and services, and then to the relations which human beings sustain socially to one another, it is impossible to obtain an understanding of present social forces (without which they cannot be mastered and directed) apart from an education which leads learners into knowledge of the very same facts and principles which in their final organization constitute the sciences. Nor does the importance of the principle that learners should be led to acquaintance with scientific subject-matter cease with the insight thereby given into present social issues. The methods of science also point the way to the measures and policies by means of which a better social order can be brought into existence. The applications of science which have produced in large measure the social conditions which now exist do not exhaust the possible field of their application. For so far science has been applied more or less casually and under the influence of ends, such as private advantage and power, which are a heritage from the institutions of a prescientific age.

We are told almost daily and from many sources that it is impossible for human beings to direct their common life intelligently. We are told, on one hand, that the complexity of human relations, domestic and international, and on the other hand, the fact that human beings are so largely creatures of emotion and habit, make impossible large-scale social planning and direction by intelligence. This view would be more credible if any systematic effort, beginning with early education and carried on through the continuous study and learning of the young, had ever been undertaken with a view to making the method of intelligence, exemplified in science, supreme in education. There is nothing in the inherent nature of habit that prevents intelligent method from becoming itself habitual; and there is nothing in the nature of emotion to prevent the development of intense emotional allegiance to the method.

The case of science is here employed as an illustration of progressive selection of subject-matter resident in present experience towards organization: an organization which is free, not externally imposed, because it is in accord with the growth of experience itself. The utilization of subject-matter found in the present life-experience of the learner towards science is perhaps the best illustration that can be found of the basic principle of using existing experience as the means of carrying learners on to a wider, more refined, and better organized environing world, physical and human, than is found in the experiences from which educative growth sets out. Hogben's recent work, *Mathematics for the Million,* shows how mathematics, if it is treated as a mirror of civilization and as a main agency in its progress, can contribute to the desired goal as surely as can the physical sciences. The underlying ideal in any case is that of progressive organization of knowledge. It is with reference to organization of knowledge that we are likely to find *Either-Or* philosophies most acutely active. In practice, if not in so many words, it is often held that since traditional education rested upon a conception of organization of knowledge that was almost completely contemptuous of living present experience, therefore education based upon living experience should be contemptuous of the organization of facts and ideas.

When a moment ago I called this organization an *ideal,* I meant, on the negative side, that the educator cannot start with knowledge already organized and proceed to ladle it out in doses. But as an ideal the active process of organizing facts and ideas is an ever-present educational process. No experience is educative that does not tend both to knowledge of more facts and entertaining of more ideas and to a better, a more orderly, arrangement of them. It is not true that organization is a principle foreign to experience. Otherwise experience would be so dispersive as to be chaotic. The experience of young children centers about persons and the home. Disturbance of the normal order of relationships in the family is now known by psychiatrists to be a fertile source of later mental and emotional troubles—a fact which testifies to the reality of this kind of organization. One of the great advances in early school education, in the kindergarten and early grades, is that it preserves the social and human center of the organization of experience, instead of the older violent shift of the center of gravity. But one of the outstanding problems of education, as of music, is modulation. In the case of education, modulation means movement from a social and human center toward a more objective intellectual scheme of organization, always bearing in mind, however, that intellectual organization is not an end in itself but is the means by which social relations, distinctively human ties and bonds, may be understood and more intelligently ordered.

When education is based in theory and practice upon experience, it goes without saying that the organized subject-matter of the adult and the specialist cannot provide the starting point. Nevertheless, it represents the goal toward which education should continuously move. It is hardly necessary to say that one of the most fundamental principles of the scientific organization of knowledge is the principle of cause-and-effect. The way in which this principle is grasped and formulated by the scientific specialist is certainly very different from the way in which it can be approached in the experience of the young. But neither the relation nor grasp of its meaning is foreign to the experience of even the young child. When a child two or three years of age learns not to approach a flame too closely and yet to draw near enough a stove to get its warmth he is grasping and using the causal relation. There is no intelligent activity that does not conform to the requirements of the relation, and it is intelligent in the degree in which it is not only conformed to but consciously borne in mind.

In the earlier forms of experience the causal relation does not offer itself in the abstract but in the form of the relation of means employed to ends attained; of the relation of means and consequences. Growth in judgment and understanding is essentially growth in ability to form purposes and to select and arrange means for their realization. The most elementary experiences of the young are filled with cases of the means-consequence relation. There is not a meal cooked nor a source of illumination employed that does not exemplify this relation. The trouble with education is not the absence of situations in which the causal relation is exemplified in the relation of means and consequences. Failure to utilize the situations so as to lead the learner on to grasp the relation in the given cases of experience is, however, only too common. The logician gives the names "analysis and synthesis" to the operations by which means are selected and organized in relation to a purpose.

This principle determines the ultimate foundation for the utilization of *activities* in school. Nothing can be more absurd educationally than to make a plea for a variety of active occupations in the school while decrying the need for progressive organization of information and ideas. Intelligent activity is distinguished from aimless activity by the fact that it involves selection of means—analysis—out of the variety of conditions that are present, and their arrangement—synthesis—to reach an intended aim or purpose. That the more immature the learner is, the simpler must be the ends held in view and the more rudimentary the means employed, is obvious. But the principle of organization of activity in terms of some perception of the relation of consequences to means applies even with the very young. Otherwise an activity ceases to be educative because it is blind. With increased maturity, the problem of interrelation of means becomes more urgent. In the degree in which intelligent observation is transferred from the relation of means to ends to the more complex question of the relation of means to one another, the idea of cause and effect becomes prominent and explicit. The final justification of shops, kitchens, and so on in the school is not just that they afford opportunity for activity, but that they provide opportunity for the *kind* of activity or for the acquisition of mechanical skills which leads students to attend to the relation of means and ends, and then to consideration of the way things interact with one another to produce definite effects. It is the same in principle as the ground for laboratories in scientific research.

Unless the problem of intellectual organization can be worked out on the ground of experience, reaction is sure to occur toward externally imposed methods of organization. There are signs of this reaction already in evidence. We are told that our schools, old and new, are failing in the main task. They do not develop, it is said, the capacity for critical discrimination and the ability to reason. The ability to think is smothered, we are told, by accumulation of miscellaneous ill-digested information, and by the attempt to acquire forms of skill which will be immediately useful in the business and commercial world. We are told that these evils spring from the influence of science and from the magnification of present requirements at the expense of the tested cultural heritage from the past. It is argued that science and its method must be subordinated; that we must return to the logic of ultimate first principles expressed in the logic of Aristotle and St. Thomas, in order that the young may have sure anchorage in their intellectual and moral life, and not be at the mercy of every passing breeze that blows.

If the method of science had ever been consistently and continuously applied throughout the day-by-day work of the school in all subjects, I should be more impressed by this emotional appeal than I am. I see at bottom but two alternatives between which education must choose if it is not to drift aimlessly. One of them is expressed by the attempt to induce educators to return to the intellectual methods and ideals that arose centuries before scientific method was developed. The appeal may be temporarily successful in a period when general insecurity, emotional and intellectual as well as economic, is rife. For under these conditions the desire to lean on fixed authority is active. Nevertheless, it is so out of touch with all the conditions of modern life that I believe it is folly to seek salvation in this direction. The other alternative is systematic utilization of scientific method as the pattern and ideal of intelligent exploration and exploitation of the potentialities inherent in experience.

The problem involved comes home with peculiar force to progressive schools. Failure to give constant attention to development of the intellectual content of experiences and to obtain ever-increasing organization of facts and ideas may in the end merely strengthen the tendency toward a reactionary return to intellectual and moral authoritarianism. The present is not the time nor place for a disquisition upon scientific method. But certain features of it are so closely connected with any educational scheme based upon experience that they should be noted.

In the first place, the experimental method of science attaches more importance, not less, to ideas as ideas than do other methods. There is no such thing as experiment in the scientific sense unless action is directed by some leading idea. The fact that the ideas employed are hypotheses, not final truths, is the reason why ideas are more jealously guarded and tested in science than anywhere else. The moment they are taken to be first truths in themselves there ceases to be any reason for scrupulous examination of them. As fixed truths they must be accepted and that is the end of the matter. But as hypotheses, they must be continuously tested and revised, a requirement that demands they be accurately formulated.

In the second place, ideas or hypotheses are tested by the consequences which they produce when they are acted upon. This fact means that the consequences of action must be carefully and discriminatingly observed. Activity that is not checked by observation of what follows from it may be temporarily enjoyed. But intellectually it leads nowhere. It does not provide knowledge about the situations in which action occurs nor does it lead to clarification and expansion of ideas.

In the third place, the method of intelligence manifested in the experimental method demands keeping track of ideas, activities, and observed consequences. Keeping track is a matter of reflective review and summarizing, in which there is both discrimination and record of the significant features of a developing experience. To reflect is to look back over what has been done so as to extract the net meanings which are the capital stock for intelligent dealing with further experiences. It is the heart of intellectual organization and of the disciplined mind.

I have been forced to speak in general and often abstract language. But what has been said is organically connected with the requirement that experiences in order to be educative must lead out into an expanding world of subject-matter, a subject-matter of facts or information and of ideas. This condition is satisfied only as the educator views teaching and learning as a continuous process of reconstruction of experience. This condition in turn can be satisfied only as the educator has a long look ahead, and views every present experience as a moving force in influencing what future experiences will be. I am aware that the emphasis I have placed upon scientific method may be misleading, for it may result only in calling up the special technique of laboratory research as that is conducted by specialists. But the meaning of the emphasis placed upon scientific method has little to do with specialized techniques. It means that scientific method is the only authentic means at our command for getting at the significance of our everyday experiences of the world in which we live. It means that scientific method provides a working pattern of the way in which and the conditions under which experiences are used to lead ever onward and outward. Adaptation of the method to individuals of various degrees of maturity is a problem for the educator, and the constant factors in the problem are the formation of ideas, acting upon ideas, observation of the conditions which result, and organization of facts and ideas for future use. Neither the ideas, nor the activities, nor the observations, nor the organization are the same for a person six years old as they are for one twelve or eighteen years old, to say nothing of the adult scientist. But at every level there is an expanding development of experience if experience is educative in effect. Consequently, whatever the level of experience, we have no choice but either to operate in accord with the pattern it provides or else to neglect the place of intelligence in the development and control of a living and moving experience.

II

Reading, Writing, and Language Development

As with every other aspect of the curriculum and of classroom organization, a discussion of the role of reading and writing in the open classroom should begin with the question of purpose: why *do we teach reading and* writing? *The answer is not self-evident; to look at most traditional classrooms, one might think that teachers had but a single objective—to teach children* how *to read and write. This impression is strengthened considerably if one also considers the standardized reading tests that are a fixture of almost every American public school, for the tests are concerned only with children's technical facility in reading.*

Teachers in open classrooms have other objectives as well. They are concerned with giving their students proficiency in the technical skills and mechanics of reading, to be sure. But they are equally interested in what the children use their proficiency for and in the pleasure they derive from it. "Reading for what?" the head of a London infant school asked me. "If my children get perfect reading scores and then grow up to read only the tabloids and movie magazines," she said by way of answer, "I shall have failed. My job is to develop attitudes and values as well as skills—to make music, art, poetry, beauty experiences they will enjoy throughout their lives. I don't want to develop a generation of readers who lack humane values."

It is not enough, therefore, to ask whether children know how to read. Of course they must learn how; without the technical capacity to read, education is virtually impossible. But if we are to develop lifelong, self-directed learners, we have to ask other questions as well:

- *Do children* enjoy *reading?*
- *Do* they in fact read?

- What *do they read? Are they developing some sense of discrimination, some esthetic criteria by which to judge the quality of what they read? Does their reading show breadth as well as depth?*

- *What do they learn from what they read? Are they able to use literature as a means of clarifying, understanding, and extending experience?*

The same kinds of questions have to be asked about writing. Children have to learn how to write, of course. They must learn how to form letters and how to assemble the letters into words with enough clarity so that they and others can read what they have written. But mastery of the technical skills of writing is a means to other ends, not an end in itself. Children (and teachers) need to understand that writing is a means of ordering and clarifying their ideas and feelings in their own minds as well as a means of communicating those ideas and feelings to others.

Besides asking whether children know how to write, therefore, we must also ask whether they enjoy writing, and whether they in fact write —whether they write with ease and facility. We need to ask, too, whether they write with imagination. And we need to ask whether they write with precision. Do the students, in short, have ideas, experiences, and feelings they want to communicate, and do they have the capacity to communicate them?

Clearly, then, a teacher in an open classroom takes a radically different view of the role of reading and writing than a teacher in a conventional classroom. Reading is not a "subject" studied in isolation; nor is writing. They permeate the entire life of the classroom.

1. Reading As an Extension of Experience

The starting point in thinking about the teaching of reading is to understand that reading is an extension of language development. Language, which is rooted in personal experience, makes it possible for the human being to organize that experience and clarify and extend his understanding of it. Reading vastly expands the individual's capacity to do that by making available to him the wisdom and thought of others. It is not too much to say that the ability to read puts the cumulative experience of mankind at the disposal of each person.

The teacher of young children must understand this relationship between the personal and the universal, according to Molly Brearley, former Principal of the Froebel Institute College of Education and member of the Plowden Committee. (The book from which this selection comes was edited by Miss Brearley and six of her colleagues at the Froebel

Institute.) A child is more like to read easily and fluently if he sees reading as a means of illuminating and extending his own experience.

It would be a mistake, however, for teachers to focus only on the personal; schools must facilitate the shift away from the egocentricity that characterizes children of nursery-school age and encourage children to put themselves in the position of others. Literature in general, and telling stories aloud to the class as a whole in particular, can play an important role in this process of emotional and intellectual growth.

It would be true to say of many, if not most, teachers that their first encounter with a group of children involved the telling of a story. This is because the opportunity to listen to a story produces an immediate response from children and is one of the surest ways of establishing a rapport between them and an adult. It is not easy to know how this happens. While the power of great literature to gain and hold attention can be appreciated, with children the same result can be achieved with a comparatively trivial story, and many teachers have been puzzled by the rapt attention given by a whole class of young children to one of their number telling a long and sometimes incoherent story. It is clear that story-telling can evoke an intellectual and emotional response from children which is deeply satisfying. Adults gain this communal satisfaction at the theatre or cinema, and for children the physical presence of the teller is important. This is recognized in such wireless programmes as "Listen With Mother": when these programmes are used in school, the teacher's presence still seems to be necessary as a representative of the unseen story-teller.

Part of the emotional satisfaction may arise from the personal relationship which is set up between the individual listeners and the story-teller. Although the story is told to a group of perhaps forty children, each child hears his own personal story and pays attention to the features which are relevant to *him*. In this way, the semblance of an intimate and highly personal relationship between him and the teller is established.

This personal relevance in a child's response to a story draws attention to an important aspect of any art form. A person looking at a picture or listening to a story responds to this in so far as he recognizes in it something of his own feelings, behaviour or experience. This order may be concerned with ideas or emotions.

Since very young children are still in the egocentric position of not being able to put themselves into the position of an imagined boy or girl

From Molly Brearley, ed., *The Teaching of Young Children* (New York: Schocken Books, 1970), pp. 52–57, 60–62, 67–68. Reprinted by permission of Schocken Books Inc. Copyright © 1969 by Basil Blackwell Publisher.

they respond best to stories in which they are the main characters, or in which the plot or content resembles closely their own actions or experiences. This need for personal reference is still observable in nursery children and in young infants, when a story about a particular child or about a model which has been made will produce intense interest. As the shift away from egocentricity takes place children are able to put themselves into the position of imagined persons and situations (provided these bear adequate relation to themselves) and therefore begin to appreciate stories of increasing complexity. Stories, indeed, can make an important contribution to the decentering process by encouraging children to put themselves into the position of other persons, thereby elaborating their "views" of people and experiences. Further, one story can give the differing impressions of a number of characters, thus encouraging a child to look at a situation from different points of view. *Big Sister and Little Sister* by Charlott Zolotow, for example, looks at the relationship from the point of view of both sisters, an illustration of the structuring function literature can perform. This story can serve as an illustration of the play aspect of literature referred to earlier as it provides an abstraction of experience which "plays" with ideas, among others, of caring, loss, sadness and happiness.

The combination of these aspects of play and abstraction which a story incorporates encourages the move from play to thought. This is particularly important in relation to social and ethical understanding, for while scientific knowledge can be tested and confirmed or negated by reference to concrete situations, it is not possible for all social and ethical knowledge to be tested in this way. Stories therefore can provide opportunities of reflecting on these situations both in setting out possibilities for consideration, and in allowing children to test out ideas in their own stories.

Whilst the discussion so far has been concerned mainly with the match between stories and the intellectual understanding of children, reference has also been made to the relationship with emotional response. Intellectual and emotional response are recognized as interdependent. A child's emotional response is towards *what* or *whom* the story or poem is about, though how he is feeling at the moment will influence what he pays attention to in the story. As was suggested earlier, literature is in the unique position of being able to "represent" any of life's countless experiences because verbal expression can be more precise and explicit, perhaps, than any other art form. What is more, these "re-presentations" are likely to be in differently arranged relationships, and may therefore arouse either previously experienced or different emotions. In this way children's emotional response can be helped to develop in complexity and subtlety. Further, it is possible for a child to identify himself with any of the characters and therefore to experience something of the conflicting emotions which the same situation may arouse in each. The manner in which a story is told, and the emphasis made by the teller will certainly affect the listener's response. In this way, an adult, through the medium of literature, can influence the development of emotions in children—and also of attitudes and values. . . .

So far literature has been considered in its oral form, i.e., as being read or told to children, but during the first school period, of course, most children learn to read and their opportunity for literary experience is thus greatly extended. This is not true for all children. At the end of this period some will only just be beginning to make a formalized approach to learning to read, while others will be fluent readers, finding great satisfaction in books. It is not proposed, here, to consider techniques in learning to read, but to draw attention to principles which should underlie children's reading, whatever method of teaching is being used.

Reading is an extension of language development. Language is grounded in and develops out of personal experience, enabling an individual to codify, clarify and extend his understanding of objects, situations and relationships. Reading performs the same function, but provides much greater opportunities, by making available to one person the cumulative thought of others.

It has been said that knowledge is universal but learning is personal, and this needs to be emphasized in relation to reading. A child must himself see the purpose in reading and find that his personal experience is illuminated or extended thereby. What he reads must have a meaning to him: the mere reading of "words" lacks any purpose, as it can be a mechanical skill having no effect on his intellectual and emotional life.

In the first place, therefore, he must perceive that visual verbal signs are representations of oral verbal signs and thus of experience, and in the second place he must discover that these signs not only represent, but also extend experience. No one can teach a child these facts, but it is one of the most important functions of the first school to put children in the way of learning them. Learning to read can add a new dimension to the life of a child and the major responsibility for making it possible for this to take place rests on the teachers of young children. Most are fully aware of this responsibility, but this can lead to over-anxiety and pressure to achieve results. However, much anxiety is allayed when it is recognized that the most satisfactory learning situations exist in schools where books are an essential and integral part of the environment, where teachers naturally and frequently refer to books themselves and share them with the children, and where there is a basic expectation that most of the children will be able to read at seven years of age. In such schools only the children with particular intellectual or emotional difficulties fail to respond. It must be remembered that the adult's ability to read brings great pleasure and satisfaction to a child, and, as with other admired skills, is one which he will be anxious to achieve.

Children who come to school linguistically deprived have their own special problems, and for these one of the important functions of a school will be the development of oral language: written language may have to wait. However, the recognition of the problem is likely to lead to satisfactory attempts to solve it, especially if, in such instances, the junior schools accept the responsibility for introducing these children to reading.

Whatever degree of reading skill is achieved in the first school, the spoken story or poem is still important. Reading is essentially a private experience encouraging personal reflection, while the spoken word is a communal activity often producing a deeper emotional response. Both aspects are important. The shared experience of a story contributes both to the individual child and to the total life of a classroom. When visiting a theatre with friends most people are aware that personal appreciation and enjoyment is heightened when it is shared. This is true also of an individual child who can discover similar social satisfaction when listening to a story or poem, and as a result be helped in his social development. Such a shared experience can also provide a starting-point for discussion among children, which may develop interest in other areas of the classroom. For example, the story of "The Little Red Engine" told to a class of five-year-olds led to a series of paintings, models, music and counting of coaches and engines in which the whole group was interested because of the original communal stimulus.

Opportunities must be provided for hearing and reading a wide variety of stories, poetry and books if we are to satisfy the literary needs of a whole class. This variety must allow for a wide range of content and complexity which will match the mental and emotional levels of the children. Book corners and libraries can be equipped with a changing supply which will sustain and develop individual and group interests. Many schools recognize the importance of making book corners attractive areas of the classroom where the provision of rugs, comfortable chairs and flowers adds to the enjoyment of the books.

At this stage, written verbal expression becomes established as a satisfying medium for children to order, clarify and communicate their ideas and feelings. It is one among many which will be used, but language controls and organizes experience and expression with a precision not possible in other media. It must be emphasized that this expression is concerned with ideas and feelings arising from a child's total interaction with his environment. . . . Children must have something to talk and to write about if they are not to become inarticulate or illiterate, or to be forced back into fantasy experiences. One of the functions of school is to provide situations which will interest children and therefore provoke thought and emotional involvement.

2. The Classroom Community and the Need to Communicate

The key to the teaching of reading and writing in the open corridor program, Lillian Weber argues in this unpublished paper, transcribed from a talk she gave to teachers in the program, is the creation of a community in which children feel the need as well as the desire to communicate with a variety of individuals and groups, both adult and peer. That, in turn, means providing an environment in which children can be involved in a variety of different activities, an environment in which they can see different possibilities in the same activity or material, and an environment in which children are encouraged to express their understandings of their own experiences in different ways and at different levels. "These two things are built in," she writes, "people to communicate with, and things to communicate about."

The role of community is crucial, Professor Weber suggests, but often misunderstood and underestimated, which leads to an overemphasis on individualized learning. Contrary to a widespread impression, she writes, a classroom in an informal English infant school does not have "thirty individuals wandering around in space. What it has are children able to be individuals, experiencing things in somewhat different ways, acknowledged to be different, but in a community setting that is a very conscious community setting and where most of the time children are working in groups because they have similar interests."

I am not of course an expert on language, nor am I planning to tell you *what,* in specifically different terms, characterizes language work in open classrooms. Rather I will try to trace with you how our concern for communication influences what we do organizationally. Our concern was for language development, for the development of conceptualization. The concern of the '50s for "Johnny can't read," the concern of the '60s for the language or non-language of the disadvantaged, the concern for the evidence of downward spiraling of conceptualization at fourth grade level, was also our concern. In our concern we *also* focused on the schools and we evaluated the school organization, its whole-class, teacher-

From Lillian Weber, "The Open Corridor and Communication."

controlled, prescribed input-output, as a mismatch with what we knew of how the child, individually different and active, synthesizes his understandings in interaction with things and people, unevenly but in a continuum within himself. We evaluated the traditional school organization as providing a mismatch for what we knew of how the child naturally develops language and thinking.

My observation in England and my analysis of the rationale underlying informal education centered on the English thinking about language development, about the relevance of experiences to language development, and about the implications for the role of the adult. Out of such analysis reaffirming what was already known to us of the child's development and out of such observation of organizational possibility, came clues for the organizational changes we strive to affect.

This focus on language development and on the process of conceptualization dominates our advisory development sessions. We assess the effect of our organizational changes and search constantly for further understanding of the factors that affect the child's language development and for ways we can support the teacher's further understanding of these factors. We try, as we work with teachers, to have our understandings clearly expressed in our actions as well as in our mind so that what we react to will give clear indication to the teachers of our considerations. We think we are creating in our open corridors an environment that fosters communication, and that makes possible a more supportive frame or context for children's language development . . .

The Open Corridor community of several heterogenously grouped classrooms of different grade levels is a natural setting for children to help each other. With whole-class teaching ended, and difference in interest as well as pace provided for and supported, one group of children has something to share with and tell another group. With children working together, perhaps without the teacher, on various aspects of a common theme, the interaction and various viewpoints expand the possibilities and understandings. With the teacher expanding and adapting from whatever is the child's starting point, the effort to communicate and to interact with this mind and with that mind and to "step into" the viewpoint of the other is prized. Communication with one group or one teacher is not enough—there are always others who are interested and would like to know and so explication and consolidation are or can be natural concomitants of the organizational frame in a community of many adults and many children of diverse interests and diverse starting points.

The community presupposes that interaction of the various participants—children and teachers and parents and administration—sharing experience is a positive good, supporting with interchange of viewpoints and the introduction of new possibilities the reframing process that is integral to new learning, supporting the continuity of the development of teacher and child. The respect for the potentiality of each participant and for his contribution in interchange is inherent in this structure.

It is these possibilities that have been observed of language development by the linguists who have worked with our advisory group as positive aspects of the Open Corridor organization supportive of language development. One of the linguists, discussing with our group of advisors the child's need to have his thoughts and language understood and affirmed pointed also to the somewhat different need that the child *explain* and make explicit his thought in language. The Open Corridor, with its community of different teachers, offers a natural support for the child's need to explain. In this environment in which different children may do different things and see different possibilities in similar material—and in which the end result is not completely prescribed or controlled—what the child explains to the teacher or to other children may actually need explaining. He may offer a new view of great interest and stimulation to others, and may be so received. One of the linguists has discussed with us the negative effect of the pressure to produce and the positive effect of the chance for rehearsal. In the Open Corridor communities the pressure of whole-class standard is reduced and the chance for rehearsal in children's talk to each other, to animals, to puppets and in dramatization is maximized.

The evidence seems to be that for the learning of a second language it is best to allow a long intake period, just like a baby has of seven or eight months, with no demand on production but a context of experiencing and interaction with the adult in the experiencing. The demand for production seems to inhibit intake and narrow synthesizing of the forms of a new language. The Open Corridor organization offers the possibility for support of these conclusions of international bilingual research.

I've often heard a young child or a child with difficult speech speaking to a rabbit or at a rabbit with another child nearby. Of course we still live with the demand for production, the teaching of a narrow patter that in fact is not the English language at all. "Say it in a sentence." "What kind of a day is it today?" "Hot." "Say it in a sentence." I hear kids tortured by "Today is Monday the fifth day of the tenth month." And I say to the teacher afterwards, "How about it? You going out today?" And she says, "Nah. It's hot." Or she says nothing, or she says "Yeah." She doesn't say it in a sentence. If she would ask the child another question, interestingly enough, it would come out right. It might be a limited sentence, but it would be a sentence. As the conversation progresses, one notices that the pattern of English sentences, or whatever language it is, comes out.

*

Professor Weber goes on to state that there is linguistic evidence that the child who has had a chance to hear many words and to synthesize them as he develops, learns the pattern of language, even the pattern of a second language. And she illustrates one of the ways that this kind of language development occurs when a mother and a young child converse.

*

The child says, "Mommy's shoes?" and the mother says, "Yes, would you please get them for me?" just assuming that the whole thing has been said. And out of that the child develops language. This has enormous importance for bilingual programs where the tendency is still to emphasize in class after class "Say after me . . ." The evidence is that young children in that 5–7 period still can learn a second language as the two-year-old did, only we're terribly uncomfortable with a seven-year-old coming at us with those two words like the two-year-old did. We were perfectly comfortable with a two-year-old doing that and we filled it out, but we don't with that seven-year-old. We demand production which then makes the child stand back, get self-conscious about the language learning and we duplicate the problem of adult language learning rather than utilize what could be.

The Open Corridor arrangement affords possibilities for the child to express his understandings in many ways and on many levels and to use many avenues of experience in his synthesizing of his understandings. It is a context that allows the connection of affect and interest to effort—and presumes that effort, attention, sustainment, concentration increase as this connection is strong. It is a connected context in which there is the possibility for experiencing across subject barriers . . .

The evidence is that language learning is rich in a context of meaning and experience and interchange—especially where free conversation *around* experience is encouraged. But in addition to language this context encourages thinking and the possibility for thinking, for symbolic expression and development in all kinds of ways is of enormous importance and is related to language. Voyat points to the importance of dramatizing and representation in symbolic development and in the support of language development. I think it is enormously significant that the Carinis who studied language development in the Prospect School in Bennington, Vermont, look at a classroom for the quality of the drawing when they are estimating it as a reading classroom. In our open classrooms, we've created a floor of new possibilities and so the child can draw and paint. At least there's a chance, and that is significantly better than before, but we are almost completely ignorant about the real value of that painting. We don't look at painting as symbolic development essential in the child's synthesizing of his understanding, and as giving us clues to this understanding. We don't look at the spatial transformations. We undervalue the painting. We really in our heads think of painting and all the expressive activities as soft goods. We are often so busy with the skills of language we can't take time for these expressive activities—painting or drama or poetry—that support the synthesizing of understandings of experience and the rich context of symbolic development. Thus we value the exercise of language rather than the richness of language, rather than what language is all about.

The chapter in *The Teaching of Young Children* by the Froebel Institute on the meaning of literature is one of the most significant chapters. I recommend it to everyone. It reminds us that education is about development from an egocentric stance to a wider stance and reminds us of the function of literature in this, in the building of empathy for things that cannot be experienced. In this question of language and experience, not everything can be experienced. The child experiences. He can correct his inadequate first frame—that pre-verbal logic, pre-verbal thinking that he develops in his first frame of experiencing—by re-experiencing. But he corrects also because he interacts on his experience with others who have experienced that same thing differently or in a slightly enlarged frame with additional components. He is confronted with some discrepancies and corrects his first frame. And the role of the adult as reality-corrector and someone who has walked that path before and knows of additional possibilities that can be presented to the child linguistically and in actual experiences is enormous. So you have built in all the time these components—experience, re-experiencing expressively, linguistic clarification of experience and addition to experience in literature and in human relationships with peers and with adults.

I would never be the one to minimize the importance of language. Nor could I be the one to match language development with meaning in a mechanistic way. I was surrounded by language—poetry from my mother, explanations from my father, talk and talk and talk from brothers and sisters. Perhaps I was too much surrounded. My reluctant speech before bursting forth in a still unceasing flow resulted in the name tag "dumb doll." But from that surround, whether used or not, I have in my head a thousand bits of rhyme and song that my mother must have thrown at me and around me when I was very small and that had and have absolutely no meaning to me except of pattern and wonderful sound and feeling. Thus, when I talk of meaning I am not demanding that the child understand everything he hears. I remember parents who told me "he doesn't understand yet" when I said, "Well, don't you talk to him?" And I thought "My God, how's he ever going to understand if you don't talk to him." Certainly it never occurred to me to ask my children if they understood me when I recited bits to them, because they and I loved the sounds.

The youngest child takes in the sound, the pattern, the intonation of words. He learns language by hearing it. He is surrounded by the assumption that he is part of the language context and is surrounded by people willing to respond to his attempts to join the context. The absorption period, described by linguists as necessary for the synthesizing of the forms and logic of the language, allows for enrichment from an emotion-filled surround that can convey these forms and logic. This usually happens in the home but should be continued in the surround of the classroom—in what is read to children, in the poetry and song. Parents do not plan for this surround. They place no demand that the child produce a prescribed pattern. They just talk around if not to the child. They understand or half understand the child, and, answering as though his expression was complete, they extend this expression.

From the context of my own language learning—as child and parent and teacher—long before I went to England, I had become fascinated with the miracle of development and I was interested in language. I brought to my look at the schools what I already knew about children and this led me to discard linkage of "little language and therefore little thought." I had to discard the prescription of prescribed and controlled input as too limiting, as contradictory to what I knew of language development. Nevertheless I could not push off this question of language and perhaps of limited vocabulary.

I think about the many children of three I have known with inadequate speech. But from three on, the middle-class child, if he has limited speech, will be centered on by the concerned adult. The adult will feel that he must try with all his ingenuity to help the child do what he wants to do in ways that create a need for language. He will try to break through. He will try to meet with understanding any response the child makes. He will try to make opportunities for use of language and, as he talks with the child, he will try to forge connections to meanings. On the other hand, it may be that many children live in circumstances where after they are three they are less nurtured by adults. Because of their premature independence, the children begin to rely for response more from their peers than from the adults. So perhaps, as one factor, the nurturing process has been inadequate and needs enrichment. I was reminded of this, reading in the newspapers a few weeks ago the latest research of Herbert Birch and others telling about middle-class children with minimal brain damage coming out all right, poor children with minimal brain damage not coming out all right.

But most "disadvantaged" children *have* language and it is Bernstein who has added to the story of mismatch, of non-acceptance in school of children's different language, of non-understanding and so discontinuity with the child's prior-to-school language development. All these analyses of language development reinforce the direction I already knew. The genetic stereotype, the prescription of pattern for a whole group, was one found unacceptable. The necessary surround was a language surround of accepting the language of the child, understanding it, expecting that it would develop further in a context that encouraged use, and interchange around interesting experiences.

All the controversies, all the questions on language, were with me while I was in England and before I went to England. Everything I looked at in England was constantly with reference to the question of language, to the question of experience in relation to language. This linkage of experience and language development was prime in the English discussion. Those who study child development are necessarily concerned with the child's experiences in the objective world, with other people, and with his own understandings of these things. It is in this setting of the outer world and human relationships that the child learns—unevenly, actively, and individually.

Now, the question of language—which comes first, the chicken or the egg? the language or the experience?—is never resolved in the English discussion nor do I think it can be. That the child develops language in interaction with people but he understands these words that he is hearing and uses them functionally as he experiences and attaches experience and language together I think is one statement. It isn't a question of the mimicking of the sounds that are possible for the human being. The trying-out of sounds—like my 7-month-old grandchild trying out his new complex of sounds and looking at me for a smile—is an overture which is miraculous and which only the human being can do. It sorts itself out for the particular language of that culture and for the meanings that the child attaches to it, as the child is guided by the responses he gets to his overtures. That language grows and is used in a meaningful context is what I would stand with and what the English are operating with. When I've discussed with them the training for pattern for words, the pattern "this is my pen," they laugh because they say, as I think we should say, that that's been tried a long time and that describes a limited aspect of the growth of language. They say that the growth of language occurs in the richer context of use and of interaction. They do not under-rate specific language learnings, but they stick with something I think we have under-rated—the importance of social interaction.

I've heard the English infant school described as though the children were unrelated individuals experiencing in space. Newspaper articles describe everybody doing what they want to, everybody following their interests—30 different interests. Naturally our teachers are totally confounded: how could they do it if kids have a different interest every moment? But of course it isn't that way. The English infant school doesn't have 30 individuals wandering around in space. What it has are children able to be individuals, experiencing things in somewhat different ways, acknowledged to be different, but in a community setting that is a very conscious community setting and where most of the time the children are working in groups because they have similar interests. They may be experiencing and sharing these things in somewhat different ways, but they are not separate individuals. Susan Isaacs spoke about the child learning speech with the mother, about the child learning speech in a context where someone was very interested in what the child was experiencing and interactive with it, and also the child in free conversation with other children who share his experiences. In addition to the joy of just the sounding, in addition to the joy of patter and the music that comes from poetry and song, there is the *growth* of language richly in a context of us and meaning and interaction.

Summing up: Our view on this, deeply concerned by the controversy on language in this country and in England, was that the changes could be considered as changes for the maximization of communication . . . In open corridors, consciously built in, is the aspect of interaction of several adults. There is a minimum of four teachers because we are working with a group. We feel that this makes possible the interaction of the teachers on their experience, reflection on their experience, which therefore assists the continuity of development of the teachers. In addition, the child experiences and tells the teacher what he has experienced, and there is another teacher who can be referred to as an interested party who doesn't know about it. There is no interruption involved. Miss So-and-So would like to know about it. And the kindergarten children would like to know about it. And the children who haven't tried this would like to know about it. And so, not in a rote way but in a natural way, there is a lot of repetition and consolidation of what the experiencing has been. From the very beginning I send children to tell principals, who I claimed to be anxiously waiting to hear, about this thing that they had done. I must say that some of the time, some of the principals greet the children with "Huh, what's that?" and that was that. However, most of them are men of good will and they were indeed interested and said, "Well, tell me about it," and it's been salutory for them. What we did opened the door to the classroom again to some principals who had been too overburdened by administration to participate actively with the educational program and know what the children were doing.

Discarding the whole-class teaching format and providing for the individually disparate nature of children's learning and interest, was basic to what we did. Of course we're all rooted in the past and most of our classes do have some whole-class conformation and some whole-class conformation can be a strengthening of the sense of community. But at least some of the time there is a recognition of diversity. By providing for this diversity we have, in my opinion, created another thing that some linguists talk about: the *need* to communicate. Providing for this need was very conscious in my mind. I remember my mother visiting, my turning to my children and saying "Tell Grandma about that," and they looked at me as if I was absolutely daft and they said, "You were there. You tell her." This is analogous to the situation in a traditional classroom. There is no communication; there's question and prescribed answer. Question and answer, not communication based on the desire and need to share an interesting thing with an interested person. Now when people are doing different things there is the reality that not everybody has experienced this thing and possibly there is the reality that people are interested, adults are interested and other children are interested in what is happening. These two things are built in: people to communicate with and things to communicate about, because not everybody has had the same initial experience. And this recognition of different experiences rather than a pattern of *one* thing, we think is of absolutely enormous importance.

Let us get past the accident of the use of the word "open" or all the adjectives now associated with this use—"happy" for instance. I read all these adjectives, and I wonder what they're talking about. Now a person does feel happier when he's not pulled apart by the mismatch I've described. That's true. So that if a person, a child, is helped to function in a way that is in the direction he is already headed, I would be sure he will be happier. And if a teacher doesn't have to constantly deny the theoretical formulation of her own understanding of children's development and can conform her action with her thinking, I think the teacher will be happier. I think both these things are true. But happiness is not the central issue. It is development and development does have disequilibriums as well as coherence. The child's frame of reference is being challenged all the time. The teacher, now in the position of a coherent continuity of her own development, does have challenges to her past frame of reference —and this is painful, not just a matter of happiness. Better than the word "open," we are talking about, more appropriately, developmental, responsive, interactive education, but we are organizationally in the compulsory sector. Thus we are inevitably questioning whether the aims and organization of compulsory schooling can be reformulated, whether the structures can be bent so that indeed schooling becomes a support system for the continuity of development of the child and the teacher—the two things go together. Our applications have bent the old structures. We are discovering some possibility for reformulation but we are really at the very beginning and have a long way to go to create true support for the child's development. This development of the child, his synthesizing of understanding, will have to include the curriculum that includes the information on the questions he asks of the world. It will include skills.

It will include language but it will really center on communication because language isolated from experience and social interaction is for far too many a limited or unsuccessful learning.

And so we encourage oral development, language of children in a meaningful setting, in a setting of emotional affect. If, as we encourage, we attach, from the very beginning where it applies, the written words, the spoken word, and the printed word altogether, and if the material is enlarging and is used frequently—not in a 20-minute period but all through the day where it applies—then we have at least a beginning and basic frame of techniques.

All our teachers—and this is no apology—are still using basal readers. The pressures of the institution—of prescribed standard, of testing, of curriculum—still exist and we are at a beginning, working in a *direction* of maximization of communication. We meet the teachers where they are, just as we want the teachers to meet the children where they are, provided they want to go further, provided they want to look at this picture of language acquisition, language development, and the development of the child. If they say they're comfortable with their reading group, etc., fine. But we expand so that the songs the children know will also become reading material. We break up dictionaries that are far too difficult for children and we put the words that make a sentence around that experience, three or four around each experience, at the point where the child can begin to write his own stories. So that he can find the words he is seeking or ask another child for them. In all these ways we attempt as hard as we can to pin language and experience together with the growth of the child. And we ask for an immersion of everybody in what language acquisition is about and that they report what they learn of the developing process of language acquisition in the child. The organizational structure we have set up allows this study. We can learn more. We do not have last words yet and try not to bypass the problem by saying "Piagetian!" The last word will be found from continuous observation of the young child. So there will be another last word and another last word and another last word. And more and more and more. The learning more, it seems to me, is the task—for us and for language teachers—not the compiling of new tests or the correction of old ones.

3. How to Teach Children to Read

The emphasis on creating an environment in which children have people to talk to and experiences to talk to them about does not mean that having created such an environment, the teacher can then sit back and assume that children will learn to read automatically. "The child has no natural impulse to learn to read," Nora L. Goddard, Inspector of Infants Education for the London schools, argues in the following selection, taken from the third edition of her standard text on the teaching of reading in the infant school. "Reading is a skill that the human race developed late." Hence making sure that every child does learn to read "cannot be a haphazard operation." This selection provides a systematic analysis of the ways in which the teacher who believes that play is the principal means of learning in early childhood can make sure that children learn to read.

We need to have two aims when we teach children to read. First, we should try to discover the best way of teaching the individual child *how* to read. At the same time, we should not be so taken up with technique and method that we forget our second aim, which is to guide the child in his choice of *what* to read. If we give our children only the tool of reading, they may, as adults, progress no farther than to read those daily newspapers that demand the least thought. If, in addition, we try to pass on to them a love of books, their later reading may be of the kind that will give them real and lasting pleasure. Both method and material are important. . . .

To teach a child to read, as all practising teachers know, is an exacting task, demanding skill, patience and ingenuity. It is a worth while task, but one that is not complete if we have not also awakened in him a love of books and of reading. Such an attitude to reading will arise partly from the satisfaction and sense of achievement that come as the skill is successfully mastered. It is also something that our children will, as it were, "catch" from us. It is our whole attitude that the children will imitate and to which they will respond.

If enthusiasm for reading arises in some measure from the sense of achievement, our methods must be such that right from the beginning the child has a feeling not of frustration and failure, but of achievement and success. An older child can see a distasteful task as a means of achieving a remote, but desirable, goal. For the younger child, however, the task needs to be of immediate interest. If he is successful in the early stages his success will be an incentive to further effort. This sense of achievement and success will be most likely to arise if we can base our methods of teaching upon known facts about how the child naturally learns and develops. . . .

An outstanding characteristic of the child when he enters the Infants' school is the attraction his immediate environment holds for him. He is

From Nora L. Goddard, *Reading in the Modern Infants' School*, 3rd ed. (London: University of London Press, 1969), pp. 8, 9, 11, 12, 20–27, 30–66. Reprinted by permission.

interested both in the things that happen to him and in those that take place around him. He is eager to talk about the things he does with his mother and father, and to tell us about his baby, his birthday party, or his new clothes. He is delighted with his increasing manipulative skill, and anxious for our approval of his painting, or the tall tower he has made with his bricks.

When he first comes into school, the child should have the opportunity to talk freely about all these things that engage his attention, for the ability to use words in speech must come before learning to read and write them. Our task is to observe the child's natural interests and to give him freedom to talk to us, and to other children about them, since they give rise directly to the early work in reading, writing and number.

In approaching reading through interest the natural sequence is: first, that the child has something he wants to say, second, that we write it down for him, and last, that he reads it, and *wants* to read it because it tells of something that is of real interest to him.

In the reception class three boys joined in making a rough and ready train from "junk" materials. They were greatly excited about what they were doing, and when the teacher made some wall sheets about it saying:

> *"John made an engine*
> *"Terry helped him*
> *"They used boxes*
> *"They used tins"*

they greeted everyone who came into the room with the words, "We've made an engine *and* we can read about it." Such an approach to reading is more likely to meet with success than the method of presenting a sentence of "the cat sat on the mat" variety.

Interest can be a driving power, and we try to get the child's absorption in what he sees and does to overflow into reading and writing about those things. In this way the driving force of his interest will help him through the first steps of reading. To help him to acquire the skill of reading is the first of our aims. If his first reading material is alive and interesting, so that he is successful with it, there will be an association in his mind between reading and pleasure. By providing material of this sort we shall be more likely to achieve the second of our aims, and our children will grow towards a lasting and increasing delight in reading. . . .

The need for the widening of experience that the preparatory period provides will vary according to the home background of the individual child. Some of our children who come from privileged homes will, by the time they come to school, have had many experiences such as we perhaps can remember from our own childhood. Such a child will have played with water; made mudpies in his garden or sandcastles on the beach; experimented with plastic materials, such as plasticine or pastry or dough; made his first attempt at writing and drawing; cut out things, and stuck things, and built things with his bricks. Books will have been part of his environment and he will have been read to. Most important of all, he will have been able to talk freely to his mother or his father, or some other sympathetic adult, about his play.

It is this talking about what he is doing that is so necessary as a preparation for learning to read. The child will not be successful in learning to read words that describe things that are outside his experience. For this reason we seek to extend and supplement the experience of the child from the less fortunate home. We leave him free to experiment in a carefully prepared and planned environment, and we let him talk to us and to the children round him about what he is doing. In this way the number of words that he can use with understanding will be increased. He will also become more skilled in expressing his thoughts and ideas in words.

All young children need the opportunity to experiment, to create, and to play with other children; such play is essential if their personalities are to grow and mature. Those for whom it is a new experience are the ones for whom such playing and talking is an essential part of the preparation for learning to read.

Before we plan our classroom environment we need to think carefully of the activities that a five-year-old naturally enjoys, and to consider how far his home environment has given him opportunities for them. We have to decide how we can add to and widen the experience of the child from the unprivileged home, while at the same time developing those of the child whose home life has been rich in experiences of the right sort. Some of the activities that can be used in this way are described below.

1. PLAY WITH WATER

Playing with water is an occupation which most young children enjoy, and there are few who do not find the opportunity for doing so, either with or without the approval of an adult. Even the child from the home where Mother has no time to approve such play or to organize it will play in puddles, in gutters, or in the pond in the park. For some children there will be all the joy of playing in the bath, or helping Mother on washing day, of blowing bubbles and perhaps even having a pond in their own garden. Through these varied activities they will satisfy their need to play with water, and they will begin to learn about its properties from first-hand experience.

When he comes to school at the age of five, the child will find that he is free to play with water if he wishes. There will be a zinc tray or bath full of clean water, and close by it a collection of exciting water toys. There will be boats and corks and rubber toys that float, and heavy articles that sink. There will be small containers and large ones so that he can pour water from one to the other. There will be tins with holes pierced in the bottom so that the water comes through in a spray.

At first he will play freely with the water, experimenting with it, and will be expected to conform only to those rules that are part of his training in consideration for others. The play need not be confined to the water-trolley. It may be possible occasionally to have a doll's washing day, or the Wendy House may need to be spring-cleaned. From play of this sort, the child will get all the joy that he experiences in imitating an adult, as well as the pleasure of playing with water.

The teacher will talk to small groups of children as they play. Gradually such words as "sink," "float," "heavy," "light," "spray," "full," and "empty" will be added to those that they can use with real understanding.

2. PLAY WITH SAND

One has only to watch young children at play on a sandy beach to realize how deep is their satisfaction in what they are doing. They will be engrossed for long stretches of time in their play. They will make sandcastles with spades or with their hands, patting them into shape, tunnelling out passages, and decorating them with shapes turned out of buckets or shells. Sometimes older members of the family will be drawn into the game, and when this happens there will often be a discussion about what is going on. In this way the younger children will learn a whole group of new words.

Some of the children who come into our schools will have been fortunate enough to have had such experiences in the secure and happy atmosphere of a family holiday. Some may have had the joy of playing in a sandpit in their own garden. For many it is unfortunately true that school provides the first opportunity for play of this kind.

In the classroom, the sand can best be used in a fairly deep zinc tray, and it should be kept damp if the children are to enjoy building and modelling with it. Dry sand may also be used, for the experiences that it provides are the different ones of pouring and sifting rather than of modelling and moulding.

Near the sand tray or trolley should be kept a tray or box of sand toys. Here, there should be small spades or other implements for digging, and a selection of moulds or shapes for making pies or turrets or sandcastles. A variety of everyday objects can be used for this purpose, such as jelly moulds or plastic eggcups and containers of all sorts. From time to time, new and interesting toys can be added. In one of our classes there was on the tray of sand toys a collection of gaily-coloured paper flags stored in a jar. The children were delighted with these and used them a great deal in their play.

When they first come into school the children will play quite freely and imaginatively with sand. Sand play is always a popular activity with young children, but equally important from the point of view of the teaching of reading is the fact that they will be talking to each other, and to us, while they are playing, thus helping to build up their vocabulary. They will learn such new words as "dig," "pour," "castle," "shape," "tunnel," "sieve," "mould" and so on.

3. PLAY WITH CLAY AND OTHER MALLEABLE MATERIALS

Children enjoy playing with materials that are soft and pliable, and that can easily be moulded into different shapes. The school provides a variety of materials of this sort of which clay is probably the most satisfactory. It is a medium that is delightful to use and most children will enjoy modelling with it. From time to time the child will also have the chance of using flour and salt paste, papier-mâché, plasticine and dough.

Play with materials of this kind gives him the joy of making something; it widens his experience; and it provides an outlet for his imagination. As in all the other activities of the preparatory period, the child will talk as he plays and so he will become increasingly ready to learn to read.

4. CREATING WITH JUNK MATERIALS

As a preparation for learning to read, the function of play with junk materials is similar to that of the other creative activities, in that vocabulary is enriched both by the addition of words that describe the actual processes and by the child's attempts to tell us about what he has made.

Part of our classroom equipment will be a large box painted or decorated attractively, and in it will be a collection of suitable and interesting waste materials. Cardboard containers of all kinds, wheels from old toys, cotton reels, things that will make chimneys, coloured paper, silver paper, odd bits of material, tape, string and corrugated paper are all materials that the children can adapt to their own purposes. In addition to these they will need paint and brushes, satisfactory adhesives and scissors. Interest in the junk box may fluctuate, but in most classrooms there are times when the children are vitally stimulated and challenged as they play with it.

5. BUILDING WITH BRICKS

Many children older than those in the entrants' classes enjoy playing with bricks. Such play seems to have a very wide appeal. It provides an opportunity for imaginative play, and many so-called difficult children will be completely engrossed in it.

We should provide as many kinds and shapes of bricks as possible, and it is often a good idea to have a box of small toys for use with them. There can be cars, animals and small figures, and many children will enjoy incorporating these in their imaginative play.

Part of the joy in playing with bricks for the youngest children may be in knocking down again the models they have made. But many children's play will be really imaginative. It is interesting to watch them using the models they have made. They will unload ships in the dock; drive cars into the garage; make boats and then sail them under the bridge, and so on. It is helpful if the children can play where there is as much floor space as possible. If a hall is available this is a most suitable place, as here the children can spread their models over a wide area without being in anybody's way, and without the danger of having their bricks knocked over.

6. PAINTING

Painting is often one of the child's first attempts to express himself on paper. Before he comes to school he may scribble on a piece of paper with a crayon, with a pencil or with a paint brush, and tell us that "That is a spider." In the early stages we should accept what the child does. We should not attempt to criticize or show him what to do. When he first comes to school, we should try to give him the sort of atmosphere in which he is free to paint what he likes, and not what he thinks will please us. If the atmosphere in our classroom is right, then the child's first paintings will be vivid and alive.

We should give the young child a wide variety of materials and because his manipulative skill is not yet fully developed, all the materials should be large. We should give him large sheets of kitchen paper, of sugar paper and even of newspaper, and we should try to avoid it always being of the same shape. We should give him large brushes and powder colour, both wet powder colour mixed in jars and dry powder colour in patty tins, with a plate or saucer on which to mix the colours.

In the beginning the child will paint straight away with a brush. We should try to provide conditions where there is plenty of room for arm movement. When they have finished painting, or indeed while they are actually painting, children will often want to talk about what they have painted. Our role is to listen and to appreciate. It is never to compare or to criticize.

As well as giving our children experience in painting, we try also to let them use non-smearing crayons, chalk with large boards, and occasionally charcoal. There seems to be for them a great joy in making strong black marks. Painting is one of the child's first methods of expression. By painting he begins to externalize his thoughts. It is the forerunner of creative writing and, being another way of expressing thoughts and ideas on paper, it is closely allied to reading.

7. DOMESTIC PLAY

Most children seem to enjoy playing at mothers and fathers. Even children with little opportunity for play of this sort at home can play in this way in streets, squares, playgrounds and parks. In school we can give them such materials that they will get real joy from their play.

Children like the feeling of being able to go inside somewhere. So in our classroom we can provide either a Wendy house or a home corner made from a clothes horse covered with material or paper.

The Home Corner should be furnished with a table, chairs, a dresser, a gas stove, a doll's bed and bed clothes, a pram, one or more dolls that can be dressed and undressed, a tea service and a cooking set. The dressing-up box may well be used in connection with play of this sort. The children as they play in the home corner will identify themselves with their parents or other adults. They will play out the sort of things they see happening at home.

Domestic play can be a valuable preparation for learning to read. If the early reading books tell, as it is so suitable that they should, of the everyday life of children in a family, then home play will be giving the children the same kind of experiences that they will read about there. Through these experiences the children will be adding to their vocabularies the words that they will meet in their reading books. Experience, speech, and reading will be centred upon the same theme.

8. LEARNING ABOUT LIVING AND GROWING THINGS

Most young children are naturally interested in things that are alive and in things that grow. If their home is of the sort in which there is enough time and understanding to give them the right kind of experiences, by the time they come to school they will already have had the opportunity of watching and caring for living and growing things. Perhaps they will have had a pet that they have helped to look after. Almost certainly they will have helped in the garden, and they may have had their own patch of garden where they could plant seeds and watch them grow.

It is this kind of experience that we try to give our children when they come to school. The nature table is accepted as part of the environment that we provide. Those of us who teach in town schools find that it may tend to become rather a dusty and dreary affair.

If it is covered with plain-coloured American cloth, it is easy to keep the Nature Table fresh and to deal with spilt water. Ours is a town school in the midst of large blocks of flats. Few of our children have gardens of their own, and for some of them the school provides almost their only experience of growing plants. Therefore the nature table should have on it, not only the familiar little jars of neatly labelled flowers, but also things that the children really can watch as they grow. In this way we shall be achieving through interest in nature what we set out to do in the preparatory period. We shall be widening and extending the children's experiences.

It is not always a simple matter to keep pets in school. In our school, where many of the children have little opportunity for keeping pets at home, we have found that their obvious delight in having an animal in the classroom has made the venture well worth while. The children themselves feed the animals and keep them clean. They form the habit of doing this regularly and thoroughly, and they learn to be gentle with creatures that are weaker than themselves.

9. LOOKING AT BOOKS

The children we teach will vary very much in the extent to which they are familiar with books. Part of our task in preparing the children to learn to read is to introduce them to books as things to be valued and from which come pleasurable experiences.

In order to do this, we provide a book corner or book table as an essential part of the classroom environment. This is an attractively set-up and carefully kept table on which are a collection of suitable books. The teacher sits at the table and reads to a small group of children, just as Mother or Father would do at home. Books will begin to be a familiar part of the children's background. They will like being read to and they will enjoy looking at the pictures.

There are other activities that will go on in the classroom from time to time. Examples of such activities are: woodwork, playing with puppets, and playing with puzzles and games. There will also be very lively current interests continually cropping up. For instance, there may be a visit of the circus to the neighbourhood; or a Harvest Festival service in school; and all the activities of Christmas will always arouse a spontaneous interest that we can use as a basis for reading. Physical education and music, too, are pleasurable experiences that will add many new words to the child's vocabulary. By providing the right sort of environment, we are giving the child the opportunity to mature as a person, as well as fulfilling our narrower purpose of bringing him nearer to the threshold of reading.

The child has no natural impulse to learn to read. Reading is a skill that the human race developed late, and if we are to help the child to acquire it, we shall need to be aware of the innate impulses that each child possesses in varying degrees, since these can be the driving force as he begins to acquire the skills of reading, writing and number. He has a natural impulse to imitate adults. He is self-assertive, and he is by nature curious. His desire to imitate will make him want to learn to read and write as he sees his parents, his teacher, and his brothers and sisters doing. The impulse of self-assertion will want to make him succeed, and his innate curiosity will give him an attitude of wonder and interest towards much that he sees going on around him.

In the initial stages of reading, we try to follow the emerging interests of the child. We need to be sensitive so that we follow his real interests, and not what we imagine that these interests should be. Here, our knowledge and experience will provide us with some guiding principles that apply to many children.

We know, for instance, that most children are interested in events in their own lives, in their homes and families, in things that they themselves make, in living and growing things, in listening to stories, and in new experiences that come to them within the secure environment of the home or classroom. It may not be easy to discover the interests of the shy, slow or difficult child, but play in the kind of environment we discussed earlier in the chapter will help him to reveal his interests to us.

Subject only to the well-being of the classroom community, the child will for a considerable part of each day be allowed free activity within this carefully planned environment. His tasks will be self-chosen. By watching him at his play and seeing which activities really hold his interest, we shall be guided to provide him with the right reading material.

It is a good plan to provide some sort of reading material as soon as the children come to school. So many of them come in a mood of keen expectation. They think that they are going to learn to read and write and do sums, and it can be a real disappointment to them if they are made to engage in what they call "play" all day. So, for those children who want it, and perhaps are ready for it, let us provide some simple reading material. This could be in the form of a simple sentence written in large script on a big sheet of paper saying,

"We have started school this week"

The children can then "read" this sentence. This reading will at first only be repeating the sentence with the teacher, but if they can do this the keen children will not feel disappointed. These children should also be introduced to the Book Table and given access to paper and pencil so that they can "write" if they wish.

The following are some ways of approaching reading through interest.

1. FREE DRAWING OR PAINTING LEADING TO THE WRITING
   OF INDIVIDUAL OR CLASS NEWS

It is often by painting or drawing that the child first tries to put his thoughts into visible form. Most children by the age of five years, if given access to suitable material, will want to draw or to paint. Usually, when we have gained their confidence, they will want to talk about their drawings, their paintings, or about the model they are making. It is upon such lively interests as these that we shall base much of our earliest reading material.

When the children have settled into school and have got used to handling brushes and paints and crayons, we give them each a news book. Not all of them will be ready for this book at the same time; and those who are not ready, or whose manipulative skill is poor, will go on painting and drawing on large sheets of paper or blackboards. These children may meet their first reading material through the class news sheet, or we may put a big label on their painting saying,

"David painted this ship"

They will not in any way be given a feeling of failure if they are not quickly able to use a news book.

The news books should be large in size. A page that is twelve inches long and ten inches wide is a satisfactory size to begin with. These books can be made from kitchen paper if they are not included on the requisition list. Books of the exercise book size are not big enough for this purpose, as children of this age will not have acquired the fine muscular control that is necessary to use them satisfactorily. The drawing and writing may be done either with thick greasy crayons or with beginners' pencils.

At first the children will draw in the books, being told to use only one page at a time. While they are doing this the teacher will go from child to child, listening to what they have to say about their drawings. When the children have got used to drawing in this way, the teacher suggests that she should write under the picture, telling what it is about. This writing should be as nearly as possible in the child's own words, as these are the ones that he will remember. So at first he may ask us to write:

"My baby"
or *"Me and my mummy"*

As his confidence and his command of language increases he will make sentences:

"This is my baby"
"I am going shopping with my mummy"

For a while the child may do no more than accept what we have written under his picture and remember the sense of it when he looks at the page again next day. He will have taken the important step of associating written symbols with meaning, and it does not matter at this stage if he does not remember exactly what has been written. After this, we may suggest to him that he write with a different coloured crayon over what we have written, and in doing this he should be encouraged to write the words from left to right. When he can do this with some skill he can take the further step of copying the sentence underneath rather than over the original letters.

When they are writing news the children need considerable help from the teacher. The teacher can most successfully give the children the help they need by not having the whole class writing news at the same time. A group of twelve or fifteen children can be drawing in their news book while the rest of the class is engaged in occupations of the quieter type. The task of the teacher is to let each child talk freely about what he is drawing and then to write for him the sentence that he wants to describe the picture.

Writing in this way can provide the opportunity for some incidental teaching about the technique of writing. For instance, the sentence being written may be:

"My new baby is called Michael"

The teacher will say the words as she writes them, and when she comes to the word *"Michael"* she may very well say, "Michael, and we begin it with a capital M because it is the baby's name." She may in a similar way comment on the formation of individual letters. This teaching should be incidental. It should not be laboured so that it becomes a burden to the child. If the situation is sensitively handled by the teacher the child can begin to acquire good writing habits from the work he does with his news book.

Working with only a group in this way will give the teacher the opportunity to do some useful work with each child. As well as writing on the new page she should turn back to previous pages and help the child to remember what he has written there. Writing news in a group rather than as a whole class means that each child will add only one or two pages to his book every week and in this way he will be more likely to remember what is written on the previous pages. He will of course be free to draw or paint what interests him on the days on which he is not using his news book.

When he has been copying sentences for some time, or towards the end of the preparatory period, the child will begin to try to write his own news. This is the stage at which he will need a great deal of help and encouragement. To write in this way he will need to be able to recognize words away from their original context. In writing his sentence he will copy some words from reading material that is available in the classroom, and the rest he will either guess or ask his teacher to write on a slip of paper for him.

For instance, a child may want to write:

"I went to play in the park with my sister"

He will know the word *"I"* because it begins so many of the sentences in his news books. He will know the word *"play"* because it comes in the sentence, *"We play with sand here"* which is written over the sand trolley. He may know the word *"park"* because in the class news there is a sentence that says *"We all went for a walk in the park."* The word *"sister"* is to be found in the reading cards that he has learned in preparation for his first reading book. These words, interesting because they mean something to him, he will have learnt to read in other contexts, and he will be able to find and copy them when he is writing his news. He will need help with the less familiar words, and with those that have no distinctive shape by which he can recognize them, and this help we can give him when we sit by him and hear about his picture.

It is worth while spending a considerable amount of time with the children who have reached this stage of news writing. It usually begins when the child is ending the preparatory period and beginning formal reading, and it is a stage at which he can easily be discouraged. If we do discourage him, then what he writes will be stilted and lifeless, and he will not progress towards vivid and lively descriptive writing.

While he is at this stage of transition between copying and writing for himself, we should be readily available when help is needed. We should also show the child how to use all the reading material that is at his disposal. Above all, we should be patient and encouraging, and to this end it is worth while sacrificing, for a short period, time that would normally be given to other aspects of work in the skills. When he is through this difficult period, during which he needs so much help, the child will begin to write stories and descriptions that are clear, spontaneous and interesting.

The class news book also has a place in the work of the preparatory period. It can be used most successfully to record news that is of interest to the whole class. Generally speaking, news that relates to one child only is best put into that child's own book. The class news book should tell of interesting things that happen in the school, such as the Harvest Festival, or the Christmas party. It may include information about class pets, or about a model that is being made. The sentences should be short, for the class news is for the whole class and should not be so difficult that many of the children find it impossible to remember it.

Most teachers find it satisfactory to have the news written on large sheets of paper and joined in some way at the top. The writing should be done by the teacher and should be in clear well-formed script. When one achieves some skill with a ball-pointed lettering pen, this writing can be done quickly and satisfactorily. Alternatively, if a crayon is used the news can be written at once instead of being added later as it must be if a pen is used. There will usually be many volunteers among the children to illustrate the news.

It is impossible to say precisely how many sheets a week should be added to the class news book, as this will depend partly upon the situations that arise needing to be recorded in this way. There may be some weeks when nothing at all is added. Our school is in an area in which many of the children have not good reading backgrounds, so that for us it is a mistake to add to our news sheets too quickly. To do so is to have a news book whose contents the majority of the children cannot begin to remember. Usually not more than one or two sheets will be added to the book each week.

As in the case of the individual news books, the class news should be written as nearly as possible in the words of the children themselves. This may not be possible when the grammatical errors are too glaring, but the children will remember sentences in the form in which they, themselves, make them rather than as we may carefully change and word them. The class news sheet should be used as a tool for the direct teaching of reading. Its contents should be repeated and remembered. This need not be in any sense a form of drudgery that will destroy the children's interest in reading. Rather it can be a game in which each child has the opportunity to satisfy his impulse for self-assertion by successfully remembering sentences or words that are within his range of ability.

The children who are mentally not ready to read with a book, or who are slow even with the work of the preparatory stage, can work as a group with the class news book, using the book itself and flash cards based on it. This, too, should be approached as a game, and the children will begin to remember the words and sentences that describe happenings that are of real interest to them. Individual apparatus based on the sentences in the news book can be used as another means of ensuring that the children really become familiar with the words. News writing, using as it does the day to day living interest can be one of the most satisfying ways of approaching reading.

2. THE WALL STORY

In the preparatory period the wall story may often be similar in content to the class news sheet. As he reads it the child approaches reading through sentences that are full of meaning for him. In this way it is very different from the material that we used in the early days of the sentence method. This was often in the form of verses which not only did not spring from the living interests of the child, but in many cases were not even understood by him. The wall story as we use it today is the continuous record of a story, or of classroom happenings in which the children are interested. Its continuity distinguishes it from the isolated sentences of the news sheet.

A wall story may be introduced after the children have been in school for some weeks and after they have had some experience in repeating the sentences of the class news sheet. It should not be a story that the teacher plans carefully, thinking that it should interest her class. She should be sensitive to their real interests, and these should be the basis of the wall material. Their interest in what is being said will help the children to remember the sentences. It will make them want to remember, and this remembering with interest is the first step along the road to reading.

In one of our entrants' classes the children wanted to play at mothers and fathers. They had no Wendy House in their room, and so they set about making one from a clothes horse. With the help of their teacher they painted bricks on strong paper which they nailed on to the clothes horse to make the walls. They left a space for the window at which they put curtains. In the Wendy House they put the table, chairs, doll's bed and dresser that they already had in the room. These, if they had not been part of the classroom equipment, could very well have been made. They made a rug with strips of material on a box-loom, and having put the doll's tea service and kitchen set and their dolls into the house they were ready for imitative play.

This was obviously an interest that could provide material for a wall story. The story was written in short sentences.

> *"We are making a house"*
> *"It has red brick walls"*
> *"It has a window"*
> *"It has curtains at the window"*
> *"Inside there is a table"*
> *"There are some chairs"*
> *"There is a bed"* and so on.

These sentences were written by the teacher in large bold script on sheets of kitchen paper. The children took it in turns to make the illustrations. These illustrations may either be drawn straight on to the sheet, or several children may make a picture illustrating the sentence and then the class can choose which one is to go on the wall. There will be interest and excitement in watching the story grow.

The story of the house is an example of a story that lasted over a fairly long period, but the skilful teacher can seize upon and use much more transitory interests. One morning, one of our classes went for a walk in the nearby park and the park-keeper took them into one of the greenhouses and gave them two potted plants to take home. The children were thrilled and excited about this. During the dinner hour the teacher wrote the first sentence about their outing:

"We have been for a walk in the park"

and the children drew a picture of the whole class walking in the park. The next two sentences followed quickly. They were:

"The keeper gave us two plants"
"Here they are"

In this case interest in the adventure of going out of school with their teacher was a powerful factor in aiding memory.

A well-loved and well-known story can sometimes be used to make a wall story. When this is the case, it is often possible for the story to be told verbally in such a way that some of the familiar phrases can be incorporated into the written story. *The Tale of the Turnip* (by Elizabeth Clark) could be used in this way:

"Once upon a time
"There was
"A little old man
"A little old woman
"A little girl
"A little black and white cat
"And a little tiny mouse"

Repetition of words and phrases helps the child's memory. So when he meets the words *"A little"* in one sentence after another he will begin to recognize and remember them.

When, at a latter stage, the sentences are long enough to require several lines of lettering, the child will begin to develop rhythmic eye movements as he reads. When this time comes the lines should be of even length and not broken up by pictures, so that the eye can move steadily along one line and then make the backward sweep to the beginning of the next. In the early wall stories the child is not reading in this way. He is remembering sentences, phrases, and words because of their interest for him, because of their shape, and with the help of the picture. We do not, therefore, need to be so much concerned about the even length of the lines, and sentences can very well be broken according to the sense and phrasing rather than when the end of a line is reached.

It is not sufficient to provide the children with a wall story, well-lettered and well-phrased, illustrated in a lively way, and based on real interest. That is only the first step. The wall story must be intelligently used by the teacher as a basis for some direct and definite teaching. To provide the right material is to take the first step, but that material must also be used skilfully. How then shall we use our wall story? Each teacher will work out in detail her own way of doing this according to the needs of the particular group of children she is teaching. The following is a possible way.

When the first sheet is to be shown the children are gathered in a group round the teacher and they may talk freely about whatever interest the wall story is going to describe. As she talks to the children, the teacher will use the words that are on the first sheet. She can then say to the children, in the case of the story about the house, "Shall we write a story about the house? Here is the first part. It says, *We are making a house.*" The children then repeat these words once or twice with the teacher, and the first sheet is pinned on the wall. By the next day the picture will have been made to go with the sentence, and this can be stuck on while the whole class watches and then reads the sentence again. Another sentence is next decided upon by the children and written by the teacher on the blackboard. On the following day the wall sheet with this sentence written on it will be shown to the children, and the next picture will be made. In this way the sheets will be introduced at the rate of about two a week, so that there is not more new material than the children can remember.

Each day the class will read the sheets in a short lesson of five minutes or so, so that the sentences are memorized. Sometimes the children themselves are so anxious to get on with the story that the reading sheets have to be produced more quickly. The wall story should all the time be within the scope of the child of average or slightly below average ability. The child who is obviously going to be a natural reader can be given more difficult material in other ways.

The first wall story should be short, and the children may not progress beyond the stage of remembering each sentence as a whole. This story should not be discarded, but may be kept and re-read. Very soon the phrases within the sentence will be recognized and this process may be helped by the use of flash cards. These can be made so that the lettering is of the same size as that on the sheets. The cards should at first be exact copies of whole sentences. These can be shown to the children and matched by them with the corresponding sentence of the wall story. When this can be done accurately flash cards of phrases can be made and matched with the phrases in the original sentence. The last stage is the matching of the words within the sentence, concentrating at first on the significant words that have a distinctive shape.

When some children are nearing the end of the period of preparation for formal reading, we can introduce into the wall story some of the vocabulary from the introductory reading book. It is not always possible to do this, as the current interest may provide a vocabulary that is quite different from that of the book. The story of the house, in the class in which it was used, helped the children to learn many of the words from the introductory book of *The Happy Way to Reading*. Other stories can be used in a similar way, so that when the child begins his first reading book much of the vocabulary is familiar. Of course the wall story is not the only available means of becoming familiar with the vocabulary of the first book. Many reading series provide preparatory sheets and cards for this purpose. The wall story may, however, often be used to supplement this published preparatory material.

When the wall story is ended it should be made into a book and hung near the book corner where the children can still read it. Some teachers find too that the children enjoy small copies of the wall story, which can be made of manilla card and put on the book table. Individual word matching and sentence matching apparatus can be made from the words and sentences in the wall stories. So the wall story may be used in three ways: it may be read by the whole class; it may be made into a book and used by a group; it can also be used as a basis for individual apparatus which will profitably employ the children during the practice period in the skills of reading, writing and number.

Reading the wall story will continue after work with the first reading book has begun. It can very well continue in every class in the infants' school. When many children are reading the first books of the series, those who are not mentally ready to take this step can use the wall story as their chief reading material. Short class lessons in reading the sheets will still be taken, but, in addition to these, the children who are slowest in beginning to read can work in a group with their teacher, practising and repeating sentences from the story. These lessons will be taken rather as a game than as a drill, and the smallest successes should be praised.

In one class in our school the teacher sits for this group lesson on a small chair with a blackboard resting on the floor and propped up beside her. One or two sheets of the wall story are taken from the wall and pinned to the blackboard. The children sit on a rug in a loose group facing the board. One has only to watch these children during what they call their reading lesson, to know that they are enjoying it. Sentence matching, phrase matching, and word matching go on just as they do in the short class lesson, but the pace is slower and each child in the group has a chance to take part, and to feel that he is succeeding. Sometimes this group will develop a separate interest and when this happens their reading material will be based on it. The teacher tries, without too obviously dictating the sentences, to ensure that this group which is slow to develop meets the words of the first reading book in as many contexts as possible.

3. READING AT THE BOOK TABLE

There are three reasons for regarding the book table as an essential part of the classroom environment.

(*a*) The home experience of the child is supplemented by the book corner. In it he can experience the fascination of books and stories and the world of make-believe.

(*b*) Throughout his school life the child can find books on the book table that he wants to read, and that it is within his power to read. The carefully made selection will always include books that are suited both to his mental age and to his interests.

(*c*) In the book corner the child will begin to develop the right attitude of mind towards books. In the preparatory period the child's attitude of mind towards reading is all-important. As we gather a small group of children around us in the book corner and read a simple story to them, the situation approximates to that of the family group in which stories are a joy, and books treasured possessions. We should read our children stories, and we should tell them stories that are carefully chosen and well-prepared. They will catch our enthusiasm, and be influenced by our choice of words.

(i) THE ARRANGEMENT OF THE BOOK TABLE

The amount of space that is available will be a controlling factor as we decide how to set up our book corner or book table. The term "book corner" may be discouraging to teachers who have small classrooms, large classes, and furniture that is difficult to move. But, however difficult our situation, we can usually contrive something in which the right atmosphere can be created.

It is possible to keep the books in a number of ways. When there is a real shortage of space we can use hanging bookshelves. These are quite simply made and can be painted in an attractive colour. Alternatively, pockets can be made to hang on the sloping surfaces of a painting easel; when not in use the easel can be folded and left to stand against a wall where it will take up very little room. Pockets made of strong material can be made to hang on the wall. These are all improvised storing places.

For rooms in which there is more space, furniture can be bought for this purpose. A wooden book-screen is a satisfactory place for housing a small number of books. A wooden book trolley has the advantage of being easily moved to any part of the room. On it we can keep books satisfactorily and display them attractively. For the preparatory stage, when the books are relatively few and often changed, some teachers prefer to use a spare small table.

In whatever way we may decide to keep or store our books, the place in which the children sit to read them must be as attractive as we can make it. The use that the children make of the book table will partly depend upon how attractive it looks. There will be no irresistible attraction in a neglected-looking orange box filled with dirty, old and tattered books. The book table needs constant attention if it is always to look fresh and inviting. This need not be an additional daily task for the teacher. The children can take their share in caring for it.

However crowded our classroom may be, it is well worth while trying to create a feeling of quiet and privacy for the children who are reading in the book corner. A clothes horse, covered with cotton material that can easily be removed and washed, makes a most satisfactory screen for this purpose. Placed between the children who are reading and the rest of the class, it will shut them off from the many attractions and distractions of the other part of the room, and it will help to suggest quiet. When not in use it can be folded and put out of the way.

Inside our book corner we shall put a few children's chairs. If there are no spare chairs the children can bring their own when they come to read. Generally speaking, about six is the maximum number of children who can use the reading corner satisfactorily at one time. If the classroom is furnished with desks, two of these can be pushed together so that their tops join to make a flat surface. This surface should be covered with a clean and attractive cloth made, if possible, from similar material to that on the clothes horse screen. If a table is used instead of desks, it too should have a table cloth and a vase of flowers that is kept always fresh, and is of such a shape that it cannot easily be overturned. We shall all find our own way of planning our reading corner so that it looks attractive, and so that it fits into the pattern of our whole classroom.

(ii) THE CHOICE OF BOOKS

Our choice of books for the book table will be guided by the age, the interests and the mental abilities of our children. In every class there will be a considerable range of mental ability, and a great diversity of constantly changing interests. This is true of a class in which the chronological ages of the children are roughly similar. These differences and diversities are, of course, much greater in classes where there is a difference of one or two or even three years between the youngest and the oldest child.

In considering the books that we shall provide, it is always the reading age of our children rather than their age in years that must guide our choice. Thus, in the entrants' class at the end of one or two terms in school, there will be some children who are only ready to look at picture books, to talk about them with us, and to listen to simple stories that we read. There will be in the same class some children who are able to make a fair attempt at reading by themselves a very simple book of the type that has one sentence on each page. A few children may be capable of more than this. The book table must supply books that are of the right degree of difficulty for each stage.

An intelligent three-year-old may sit on his mother's knee and revel in the words and the rhythm of *Bad Sir Brian Botany* or he may be fascinated by *Winnie the Pooh,* and even begin to remember whole stretches of the familiar and much-loved dialogue. This is the beginning of the right feeling for books, and the child who has an experience like this is fortunate. If the books are worn and have been used by his brothers and sisters before him, if they are kept in a special place and taken down and read as a great treat, he begins to know that they must be treasured and treated with care.

Unfortunately, many children are given by their parents unsuitable books of the "annual" type, or others that are of poor quality in every way. The print is small and not clear, much of the subject matter is remote from their real interests, and the pictures are badly drawn and crudely coloured. Small print and difficult subject matter may sometimes be acceptable in the books that are read to children as distinct from the ones that we provide at school for them to read for themselves.

It matters very much what sort of books the school provides. The teacher will have some that she keeps carefully in her cupboard. These she will read to the children, showing them the pictures and building up an attitude towards books similar to that fostered in a good home. As well as these, there will be the ones in the book corner.

These need not be elaborate or expensive. Until recently the number of suitable published books has been small. There is happily an increasing number of such books, and a list of some of them will be found at the end of this book. They should be attractive to look at, the pictures should be clear and in good colour, and the print should be of fair size. They should either be strong, and be able to stand up to much handling by little children, or if they are less durably made the worn copies should be frequently replaced.

Some of the books, especially during the first term, should be of pictures only. Coloured photographs or well-produced pictures of known objects and familiar happenings provide the opportunity for talking that some of our children need. They should be encouraged to talk to us about these pictures, so that they become increasingly able to express themselves in coherent sentences.

Other books should contain pictures each with a simple sentence underneath. This sentence should be closely related to the illustration so that the child who is used to looking at the picture, and talking about it, takes the next step of accepting and remembering the printed words that describe it. New books can be introduced in story time. The pictures are discussed and the simple story read aloud, sometimes more than once, so that the children begin to remember the words. We can then put the book on the book table, and read it sometimes to small groups of children there.

(iii) BOOKS THAT CAN BE MADE

During the preparatory period we shall almost certainly find it helpful to make some of the books ourselves. In this way we can follow up any

A book made by the teacher for the children in the preparatory stage.

activity that interests either a group of children or the whole class. If any child is absorbed in an interest or phantasy of his own we can make a book that is primarily for him. Often there will not be a published book that is suitable.

The children will enjoy helping to make these books. They will bring pictures and will be able to help with cutting them out and sticking them in. They can suggest the wording that goes under the pictures, and, because they have joined together in expending time and effort to make the books, they will all be the more likely to care for them and respect them.

We can make these books in a number of different ways. The material used should be durable or the pages will quickly tear, and the children will be disappointed because their effort has been wasted. We can punch holes in thick cardboard and join the pages together with coloured card or elastic. Manilla card can be used in a similar way, or we may choose sheets of strong thick paper. A paper book will last longer if the cover is made of rather thicker material. The cardboard, manilla or paper should be attractive in colour, and several different colours can be used for one book.

Home-made books need not be of a unifom shape. For a book about houses, all the pages could, for instance, be cut in the shape of a house. Similarly, books about trains or ships could be made in the appropriate shapes. Some books can be square, some rectangular or some made to open like a concertina. Some will necessarily be large, for they will be made by joining together the sheets of a wall story.

The material inside the books will be as varied as their shape and form. In some there will be one picture on each page with a descriptive sentence underneath. Some pages will contain a collection of pictures of one kind, such as a page of birds, and a page of animals or flowers. If we are making the books ourselves, we should give some thought to the lay-out of the page, the placing of the pictures, and the spacing of the writing. We shall greatly increase the attractiveness of our page if we leave margins at the top and bottom and on each side. Any well-printed book will illustrate the pleasing effect that results from the right use of margins.

For the lettering a ball-pointed lettering nib is easy to use, and it produces clear script of an even thickness. We can use any waterproof ink or paint that does not smudge, provided that the colour contrasts sufficiently with that of the paper to show up clearly. The following are some suggestions of books that the teacher can make. Many more will arise from the special interests of each individual class:

Things I can do, A book about boys, A book about girls, Hymns we know, Poems we like, Things that help me to grow, A book about the Zoo, My book of animals, Things we do in school, Games we play, My family, A Thank You book, A Christmas book, A book about holidays, A book of shops.

(iv) READING ARISING FROM THE CENTRE OF INTEREST

In the preparatory period the centre of interest is of a less permanent nature than it is at a later stage. There is seldom one for the whole class. Rather, there tend to be many activities in which the children are engaged. Some of these will hold the interest of a group of children for several weeks. Others may absorb their attention for only a few days. Sometimes the introduction into the classroom of a new pet or a new toy will interest the whole class.

There will be interests that come and go, but that of playing at homes and at mothers and fathers is common to most children. The appeal of this sort of play will be stronger for some children than for others, but most of them possess the impulse to imitate the behaviour of loved adults.

This impulse may lead to other kinds of imaginative play, but for many children it finds its outlet in domestic play.

This means that there should be in the entrants' classroom some sort of home corner. Here, for the first weeks in school the children will play freely, cooking meals, laying tables, making beds, taking the baby out, going shopping to imaginary shops and doing all the other jobs that they have seen their mothers and fathers do. At first they will play alone, or in small groups, but gradually they will begin to play together in larger groups. One child will be "Mother," one will be "Father," and there will be the baby and various other members of the family.

When the play reaches this stage, some reading material can be introduced. If the introductory book of our reading series tells of the activities of a family, the material arising from the home interest will be an invaluable preparation for it. In our school we use *The Happy Way to Reading* so our home corner becomes *"Tom Bell's house."* The children, as they begin their play, hang labels round their necks saying either *"I am Mother"* and *"I am Father,"* or *"I am Mrs. Bell," "I am Mr. Bell," "I am Joan Bell."* Thus the vocabulary of the first reading book gradually becomes familiar by being used in play situations.

Playing at homes leads quite naturally to playing at shops. The shopping play may in the beginning be entirely imaginary. The child will go to a certain place in the room and pretend that he is shopping, and he will not feel the need for any external aids to his imagination. When play of this kind persists, the teacher can suggest that a shop is introduced into the room. At first it is likely that this will be a general store. It can be very simply set up and given a name. Articles to sell in the shop can be made in the creative period, and a list of things that are for sale can be made.

In addition there will be a notice saying:

"Come and buy at our shop"

and there will be notices saying when it is "open" or "closed." Sometimes the interest in shopping grows and the children want not one shop but several of different kinds. When this happens the scope of the reading material is naturally widened. Each shop will have its own name and its own price list. This is the sort of development that does not come in the first term in school, but rather at the end of the first year, or at the beginning of the second. Shopping play and home play can each provide the material for a wall story.

The domestic interest is the most common and the most lasting one, but there are others that arise from time to time and that can be used with advantage as a basis for reading. Some of these last only for a short while. An interest of this kind may be seen when the school is preparing for a harvest thanksgiving service. A sheet can be prepared saying:

"Next week
"we shall have
"a harvest service"

This can be followed by another which says:

"We shall bring
"these things"

Then will come sheets on which the teacher writes the names of all the fruits and vegetables that are brought, and on which the children draw them. The gifts as they are brought can be gathered together and labelled, either with their name, or with a sentence saying who brought them. During this week it is often convenient and suitable that the nature table should become the harvest festival table. Words that will frequently be met in reading, and sooner or later needed in writing news can be learnt in this way.

In one class a group of boys was particularly absorbed in floor play with bricks. This interest developed when the class took its creative activities into the hall. Here, there was plenty of space and play with a train set could be incorporated into the imaginative play with bricks. Soon the children were building roads, stations, bridges, tunnels, houses and fields. The farmyard animals and trees were introduced into the play, and model cars were brought to put on the roads.

This play persisted over a period, and the teacher wisely devised some reading material around this interest. There was a short wall story about a train which the group learnt to read, but the most valuable material was that which the children used in their play. This consisted of labels that could be used with the model as it was made. There were names of stations and labels for houses and bridges, and these of course were put in different places as the model was differently built each day.

It is possible for an absorbing activity and a wall story to be used as valuable aids to reading independently of each other. Although in practice it very often happens that the activity provides the opportunity for the making of a wall story, with young children it does not always do so, but can, nevertheless, provide a valuable basis for reading. The children will use labels and notices in their house or shop or model, and in their news books they will begin to try to write about their play.

(V) READING ARISING FROM NATURE INTERESTS

The nature table should in the widest sense be a focal point in every classroom where there are young children. Children will not only be interested, but they will experience a sense of wonder as they care for things that live and as they watch things that grow. Even at the preparatory stage much reading will arise from these interests.

The most common form of reading material is the label that identifies the flower or leaf or twig. These labels can all too easily stay on the nature table for so long that they cease to be noticed. If they are really to be of use they need to be collected regularly and put out again in their right places. This can be done as a game, sometimes by the whole class and sometimes by a group. Collecting the labels also means that it is easier to keep the table fresh and well cared for, as the opportunity can be taken to dust it and throw away dead flowers.

In one class the labels were so made that the children could replace them correctly without the help of the teacher. Made of thick manilla, they bore on the front the name of the flower, and on the back an actual specimen, pressed, and secured behind cellophane. The making of these labels took time, but no one going into that particular class would have doubted that these children were interested in their nature table.

It is also a good idea to label specimens that the children themselves bring, with a sentence:

> *"John brought these shiny conkers"*
> *"Diana found these bluebells in the woods"*

Here again, the labels should not just be put on the table and left there, but the children, especially the ones who brought the specimens, should be encouraged to read them.

There can be other, more general, labels introduced in connection with the nature table at the preparatory stage. The children will be particularly interested in watching the progress of things that grow. If they have planted beans there can be a series of labels appearing at the appropriate times:

> *"Watch our beans grow"*
> *"There is a white root"*
> *"The leaves are beginning to grow"*

Similar reading material can arise from planting grass, or mustard and cress, or anything that will not take too long to germinate.

Young children like to see things happening, and their interest is most easily aroused by plants that will grow quickly. This does not mean that they will not enjoy things like bulbs, but that their lively interest in watching something sprouting in a very short time can be used in helping them to learn to read about what they are seeing.

Five-year-olds will delight in caring for the nature table and a chart may be made showing them who is to do this job each day:

> *"Please tidy the nature table today"*
> *"Peter"*
> *"Susan"*

The sentence can be written on a sheet of manilla card and the names inserted into slots underneath. In this way the children will not only learn to read the sentence telling of this job to be done, but they will have a real incentive to begin to recognize their own names. Charts may also be made, telling who is to care for any pets that there may be in the room.

"Please feed the goldfish today"
or
"Please look after the guinea-pig"

Notices may also be made listing the food that the various pets like to eat.

"Our guinea-pig likes to eat these things,
carrots,
apples,
lettuce"

Occasionally the nature table may be used to show all the things that a particular pet eats. In one of our classrooms where there is a guinea-pig there was a label over the nature table saying:

"Brownie likes to eat these things"

and on the table with their appropriate labels were a lettuce, some apples, some carrots, and a saucer of milk.

In another class of five-year-olds, Sally, the guinea-pig, became at one time the centre of interest. Wall sheets with illustrations were made saying:

"We have a guinea-pig"
"Her name is Sally"
"She lives in a box"
"She makes her bed of hay" and so on.

The children, in their first term in school, were really interested in reading the story of Sally.

Reading arising from nature interests can be of four types. There can be word or sentence labels; there can be duty charts; there can be records of growing or living things; and there can be a wall story, arising from a nature activity that interests the whole class.

6. READING ARISING FROM THE WEATHER CHART

Another activity that is closely linked with interest in nature, and which the children enjoy is the keeping of a weather chart. In the pre-reading period this can be very simple. A most satisfactory chart can be made from a piece of wood or very thick card roughly two feet six inches in size. Hooks are screwed into the chart, and on these are hung cards giving the day, the date, the month, the weather, and a picture of the day's weather. These cards are changed every day, and the children will often watch the weather and change the card which says "It is raining," or, "It is sunny," once or twice during the day.

An interesting weather chart.

There are many interesting variants of this kind of chart. One teacher hinged together two empty picture frames of the same size so that they would stand quite steadily on a table or window sill. One of these was backed with plywood and into it were hooks on which to hang labels as in the case of the chart described above. In the other empty frame was suspended a swing. Jennifer, a doll made from balsa wood, sat in the swing. In a box were Jennifer's clothes, a mackintosh for wet weather, a woolly jersey and skirt for cold weather, a cotton frock for sunny weather. So as well as recording the day, the date, and the month, this weather chart had cards saying:

> *"It is wet*
> *"Jennifer wears her mackintosh"*
>
> or
>
> *"It is sunny*
> *"Jennifer wears her summer frock"*

This quickly captured the interest of the children and they had little difficulty in remembering the sentences.

7. SOME OTHER WAYS IN WHICH READING MAY BE APPROACHED
   THROUGH INTEREST IN THE PREPARATORY PERIOD

It is impossible to give a comprehensive account of reading of this sort, for it will vary from class to class and from term to term. Unlike the news book, the wall story and the book table, such material is not an essential part of the preparation for reading. It arises from time to time, either spontaneously or when the teacher decides that a particular class is ready for a particular piece of reading material. The following are some examples.

(*a*)   *Action cards.*   These are short sentences, written by the teacher on manilla or thicker card, giving certain instructions:

> *"Stand up"*
> *"Sit on your chair"*
> *"Clap your hands"*

The children read the cards, and obey the instruction. These cards can be used as a game either with a group of children or with the whole class. The children will learn to read the cards because they want to be first to do the action that is required. It is possible, of course, to ask individual children to read the cards and to perform the action while the rest of the group watches, eager to see if it is done correctly, and ready to do it themselves if it is not.

Another type of card is the one that the teacher holds up, or gets a child to hold up, when there is to be a change of activity in the classroom.

> *"Five minutes more"*
> *"Begin to put your work away"*
> *"Please stand by the door"*

It is a good plan not only to hold these cards up and to ask the children to do as they say, but quite frequently to ask them to read them aloud.

(*b*)   *Classroom labels.*   There was a time when it was the custom to fix a label to every window, door, cupboard and piece of furniture in the Infants' classroom. These labels were left in position for whole terms at a time, and after they had been fixed for a week or two the children ceased to notice them.

There is a value in having such labels in the classroom from time to time. Words like *"window," "cupboard," "door," "table,"* and *"chair"* are ones that the child needs to know. He will want to use them in his news, and he will find them sooner or later in his reading book. Like the labels on the nature table, these, too, need to be collected frequently and then put back again, as a game in which the teacher holds up a label and asks the children to show her or tell her where it goes. In this way they can be used to some purpose and they will soon be recognized and read.

Labels of a slightly different kind also have a place. These can show, first of all, where in the classroom the varying activities will take place. Examples of labels of this kind are:

> *"Play with sand here"*
> *"The reading corner"*
> *"This is Tom Bell's house"*
> *"The nature table"*

Like the labels on furniture and parts of the room, these should be frequently read.

It may not be practicable to collect them and put them in place again, but they can be read, and words from them can be found in other parts of the room. For example, when the game is being played of putting the classroom labels back in their right places the teacher, when she comes to the word *"table,"* can ask the children where in another place they can find the same word. They will find it in the label *"The nature table,"* and so they will begin to recognize words out of their original context.

Children's work may also be labelled. The label may be a general one, as, for example, one over a row of mounted paintings saying:

> *"Here are some of our paintings"*
> or *"We like to paint"*

Individual children's paintings may also be mounted and labelled:

> *"This is Mary's house"*
> or *"Tom painted this motor car"*

Models that the children make in clay or Plasticine or waste material may be treated in the same way. There can either be a collective label saying:

> *"We have made these things"*

or there can be small ones for individual models.

Most teachers will, in practice, alternate between the two ways of labelling. Generally speaking, the collective label will be of greater interest to the whole class than the individual one. There will be times, though, when one child's model or painting captures everybody's interest, and that is the occasion for the individual label or caption.

In one of our classrooms was a piece of apparatus that was not strictly either a duty chart or a label. The children used it with obvious enjoyment over a period of several terms. In a place that was easily reached

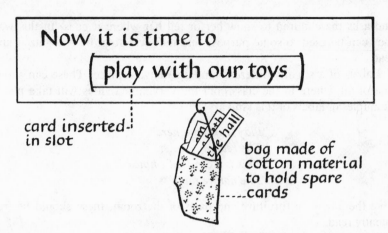

card inserted
in slot

bag made of
cotton material
to hold spare
cards

by the children, was fixed a long strip of card, with the beginning of a
sentence written on it. The words were:

"Now it is time to"

and there was a slot at the end into which cards could be slipped. Underneath hung a bag, in which were many possible endings to the sentence.

"play with toys"
"have our milk"
"say our prayers"
"go into the hall"

At first the teacher made a point of asking children to change the
cards every time they were going to do something new, and she made
sure that they did it correctly. Later, whenever there was a change of
occupation someone quietly went and changed the card. When a piece
of apparatus of this kind is first introduced it is often quick children
who use it. When it has become thoroughly familiar, it ceases to be a
challenge to the more able children, and the slower children, having
gained confidence through seeing it day after day, begin to use it successfully.

(c) Charts of classroom duties. These charts will tell the children
about the duties that are performed regularly in the classroom. They will,
of course, vary in the course of the year, but some typical ones are:

"Please give out the milk today"
"John"
"Mary"
"Please look after the flowers"
"Tom"
"Joan"

During the several short periods that the teacher gives every day to reading the wall material with the children, and helping them to remember it, the sentences on these charts will be read, and words from them compared and matched with words in other parts of the room.

(*d*) *Reading arising from games.* Some valuable reading material can be introduced arising from well liked games and activities. The following is an example: during the creative period the children play quite freely on the floor with bricks. Later in the day, when the activities are more specifically concerned with learning or preparing to learn the basic skills, there is play with bricks again. This time a pile of cards is put with the bricks, and on each card is a different instruction:

> *"Build a tall tower"*
> *"Build a house"*
> *"Build a big bridge"*

To help the children, a drawing of what is to be built is put by the sentence.

Very soon, they are able to read the instruction on the card as soon as they pick it up, without reference to the picture. The teacher can word the sentences in games of this kind to include much of the vocabulary that is already being presented to the child in other reading material in the room, or which will be found in the first reading books. This use of the same words in several contexts proves to be a valuable aid in building up a reading vocabulary.

These are only some of the ways in which, during the preparatory period, reading can arise from the natural interests of the children. The ways of approaching reading that are of the most constant value are the writing of news, the wall story and other reading material based on the centre of interest, and the book table. In the first two of these the reading material can meet the needs both of the able and of the less able children. It can unobtrusively be guided by the teacher, who can ensure that each child not only progresses, but progresses at the right speed. It can most truly be said to arise from the children's own interests. The third main approach to reading is the book table, for it is here that, even in his first year in school, the child's desire to learn to read is fostered.

In any class there will be a wide range of mental ability. No teacher can discover immediately what is the intellectual capacity of each child in her class. Nor can she know at once whether the home environment and the developing character traits of each child are of a kind that will help him to make full use of his innate abilities. For the child, the preparatory period is one of adjustment and level finding as well as a time of widening experience and interest. For the teacher, it is a time for observing and assessing, as well as for providing the right environment and guiding the children in their use of it.

In a town school a group of forty or so children may begin school on the same day. The first five years of their lives will have been spent in widely differing home conditions. As well as this, some will be the only child in the family and others will have watched or joined in the occupations of older brothers and sisters. Some will have advanced mentally beyond the average, and others will have been slow to develop.

The classroom environment will provide for the differing needs of all these children. It will widen the experience of children from unprivileged homes. "Only" children will be able to play with others. All children will play with their contemporaries, which is a different experience from play within the family group. There will also be the opportunity for each child to work to the level of his own ability. In the first weeks, the reading material will be for the whole class.

Before long the teacher will find that some children are much quicker than others at remembering this material. She must see that these children do not monopolize the short class reading lessons and she will praise the slower children for much smaller successes. In short, the teacher will soon discover within her class a group of children who are ready to go ahead quite quickly with reading.

The preparatory period provides the opportunity for this group of children to progress as quickly as they are able. They will work as a group with the teacher. They will proceed from remembering the sentence to flash card work in recognizing sentence, phrase and word. They can work with individual apparatus that gives them practice in this phrase and word recognition. They will soon want to try to write their own news and they may be encouraged to look at and to read, first with the teacher, and then alone, the very simple books on the book table. Before long they will be led by the teacher to reading the first books of the graded series. In this way, the children of superior mental ability will progress at their own rate, and will not need to wait until more of the class is ready.

The whole class will continue with all the approaches to reading through interest. They will all continue to read the news sheet or the wall story, to put labels on the nature table and to work with action cards, and so on. At these times the teacher will make certain that everybody has a chance to feel successful. In addition, the children who are progressing more quickly will work as a group with the teacher at a separate time.

The first group may be ready for a reading book while the next group has only reached the stage of recognizing phrases and words, and the rest of the class is still recognizing whole sentences. So it will go on until a small group of children is left who cannot handle the preparatory work with sufficient confidence to be ready for the first reading book.

The group of children who, by the end of their first year in school, have not begun to read with a book, will not have developed that attitude of resistance and disinterest towards reading that is characteristic of the older backward reader. They will not have struggled day after day with the same dirty, dog-eared page of the first reading book. They will have been introduced to books in an attractive way. Even if they have not been successful, they will have realized that written and printed symbols tell us about things that are interesting to know.

ASSESSING READING READINESS

It is necessary to find a way of judging a child's readiness to read the first book of the graded series. Some authorities say that when a child reaches a mental age of six years he is ready to begin formal reading. This is probably true, but it is possible to find a simpler way of judging a child's reading readiness than by finding his mental age.

We can give the children a variety of informal reading material. We can let them become thoroughly familiar with the idea that written symbols convey meaning, and then observe carefully each child's reaction to the reading material with which he finds himself surrounded. We let the children who show obvious ability work more intensively as a group for a short time each day, and then we introduce them to the printed material that is preparatory to the first reading book. At this point we begin to keep a careful written record of their achievement, and when they are really confident with the preparatory cards and can recognize about 15 or 20 words away from the original context, we judge them ready to read the first book with a good chance of being successful.

After a few weeks there may be another group who are ready to do the work that is directly preparatory to the printed book. With these children we shall work rather more slowly. Again we shall keep detailed records of the words and phrases that they know.

There may very well be in the class a large group of average ability which after a while will divide quite naturally into two or three smaller groups. These children, both when they are working with preparatory material and when they begin a book, will need to tackle smaller amounts of reading, and to prepare much more slowly and carefully. As with other groups, we shall consider them to be ready for the first book when they can recognize 15 or 20 words out of their original context.

We shall be left with a small group of perhaps 6 or 8 children who, at the end of a year in school, or having reached a chronological age of six, show little sign of being ready to begin to read a book. Some of them, if left to develop at their own rate and not made to feel that they have failed, will quite suddenly be ready to read and be successful in doing so. In a few, progress may still be very slow throughout the second year.

When the first group of children is ready to begin to read the first book of the graded reading series, we need to find ways of organizing the teaching of reading so that we can keep the right balance between the more formal and systematic side of the work and the approach through interest which is so important throughout the child's life in the Infants' school. The work of the second year, when all except the very slowest children begin to read the graded series needs to be considered and planned very carefully. At this stage most children need a lot of help from the teacher, and the work of the day must be planned so that she is available to give this help, for it is vital that at this point the children should not fail and be discouraged.

There are many series of reading books available, and our choice will be guided partly by the needs of our particular school, and partly by our own views and preferences. It may vary according to the home background of our children. If many of them come from privileged homes where they are helped and encouraged to read, our main reading series can be one that progresses quite quickly. If, on the other hand, the home environment for the majority of the children is poor and lacking in any interest in reading, we shall choose a series in which the first books at least do not present difficulties that are likely to be discouraging.

We shall, if it is possible, have more than one series available. Whatever our circumstances, whether ours is a country school or a town one, whether our children are fortunate in their environment or whether they come from homes that are less privileged, there are certain qualities for which we should look as we choose our reading series.

1. SUBJECT MATTER

In the first place, the subject matter should be suitable and of interest to the children who are to read it. This means that the first books of the series should tell of people and events that are familiar, for young children are interested in people who are close to them, and in happenings that are within their own experience. For most children the familiar environment is that of home and school, the people in whom they are interested are those whom they meet from day to day, and the happenings that concern them are those that form part of their own life.

So the first books of the reading series should tell the story of the ordinary life of children in an ordinary family. They should describe the things that happen at home, the games that the children play, the people that they meet, how they go to school and what they do there. This is familiar, secure ground and its appeal will be general.

This does not mean that in choosing reading material we ignore the children's imaginative play, and the phantasy life that is often so real to them. A child may go through a phase when, for the time being, he literally is a ship, or a Red Indian, or a Cowboy. He may have an imaginary companion who is sometimes just as real to him as any of his family. These interests, which are often individual, find expression in the child's painting and in his creative writing. Sometimes they are shared by several children, and if this is so the group will have a "centre of interest" in the true sense of the words. Certainly we shall base reading on interests such as these. They are however, peculiar to individual children, or to groups of children, and therefore they do not provide such suitable material for a series of reading books as do the people and situations that are within the experience of most children.

If the subject matter of the reading book is of this familiar kind, there is a natural link with the play interest of the preparatory period. The spontaneous playing at mothers and fathers can lead to playing at being the family in the reading book, so that there is the link which we try to make on every possible occasion between reading and the child's natural interests.

The choice of a reading series may be guided in some measure by whether the children live in the country or the town. Town children may be ready to read about farms and the country by the time they reach the third or fourth book of the series, but material of this sort is not the most suitable for the first books. The converse, of course, is true of country children. Between the ages of six and seven, as they progress through the reading series, the children's interests and experiences are widening all the time. This should be reflected in the subject matter of their reading books. As their interests develop so the range of suitable reading material extends. The last books of the series should contain some well-known fairy stories told in simple language. If this is the case, reading with his reading book will gradually become for the child the same thing as reading stories for pleasure. If the stories are worth while and the language carefully chosen, the first step will have been taken towards developing the child's literary taste.

2. RANGE OF VOCABULARY

Thinking of the language that is used leads quite naturally to the second point that we should consider in choosing our reading series. We should try to find one in which the vocabulary is carefully chosen and controlled. The choice of words will of course depend very much upon whether the book makes a predominantly sentence or phonic approach.

If the majority of the words used in the first and second reading books are ones that can be "built" phonically, the resulting reading material is likely to be stilted, unnatural and lacking in interest. If, on the other hand, we are going to ask the child to read short sentences about familiar events, and well-known characters, we must be certain that we are not expecting him to remember more words than he is ready for. The vocabulary of the first books needs to be systematically planned. There should not be too many new words on each page. For the first few pages one sentence on a page is enough, and there should be repetition of words and repetition of phrases from page to page.

It is a help to the teacher if new words are listed beside their page number at the back of the book. This enables her to see at a glance which are the new words on any page, and thus time is saved in preparing new work. These lists of words are not necessarily to be read painstakingly by each child before he passes on to a new book. Children vary in their ability to recognize words out of their original context, and it is the experience of the teacher, rather than the exact number of words read, that will help her to judge when the time for a new book has come.

The first two books, then, need only a few new words on each page, these should be often repeated. The good series provides sufficient repetition without being dull. A small amount of reading material on each page means that the child will get the feeling of achievement that comes from sucessfully reading a page and turning over to a new one. This experience can be taken one step further if the first books of the series are short, so that there is also the achievement of finishing one book and going on to the next.

The feeling of pleasure that comes with success as he begins to read is important especially for the average and below average reader. If he likes reading he will be ready to co-operate with us as we try to help him through the more difficult phases. The child will be the more likely to like reading and to gain confidence if his reading vocabulary increases at the right pace and in a planned way.

3. ILLUSTRATIONS

It is a natural progression to pass from thinking about vocabulary to considering the pictures with which the book is illustrated. They need to be considered both artistically, and from the point of view of helping the child to read the text. Not all the pictures with which our reading books are illustrated are equally successful in helping the child to read. But it is possible for the picture on each page to illustrate the text so closely that the child, with a minimum of help from the teacher, reads the correct words. This close co-operation between the artist and the writer is particularly desirable in a series that uses the sentence method.

The child at first relies on remembering the sentence, and a picture that helps to recall the exact sentence is invaluable. To achieve this result the illustration must be clear and bold, avoiding distracting and fussy detail. The books we give children to read in school will be helping to mould their taste, not only from the point of view of their subject matter and literary value, but also through the artistic merit of the pictures with which they are illustrated.

Many of our children see in their homes, books that are a part of the great mass of badly presented and artistically poor material that is produced for children. Unconsciously, children will accept the standards with which we present them at school in this connection. One of the things we should look for in a reading series is that the pictures should be good both in line and colour.

Not only should the pictures be good, but the whole book should be attractive and well-bound. Children cannot satisfactorily be led to care for books that are so poorly bound that they fall to pieces with only normal wear and use. Children like books that look attractive and whose covers show the different books in the series quite clearly either by colour or pattern.

The print should be of the right size for the children to read comfortably. Broadly speaking, young children need larger print than older children. Their eyes have not yet developed the fine control that is necessary for reading small print easily. So the first books of the reading series should have clear and well-spaced print. The books that are to be read by older children may have smaller print, but the pages should not be broken up by pictures interspersed in the text, as these interfere with the rhythmic eye movements that are necessary for fluent, easy reading. The pictures should be either at the top or at the bottom of the page, or on a page by themselves.

4. APPARATUS

Individual and group apparatus can be used with the reading series, and in choosing a series we should look for one that has suitable published material of this sort. Types of apparatus that are most generally useful are flash cards, word and picture matching, and reading and doing cards of all kinds. Modern methods demand thought and hard work from the teacher. Much of the material that she provides for her class is suitable for that class only and could not be found in any printed or published form.

4. The Fatal Defects of Reading Tests

Standardized reading tests do a grave disservice to both children and teachers because they subject both to a system of evaluation based on standards and goals that ignore, and in many instances do violence to, the ways in which young children learn. This indictment of the Metro-

politan Achievement Test, one of the most widely used tests of reading, is valuable for its author's point of view about reading and its insights into the ways in which children think. Deborah Meier is a staff member of the City College Advisory Service to Open Corridors.

The reading test mystique is, despite the number and respectability of its opponents, decidedly more widespread and powerful than ever before. Faced with a growing demand for "accountability," school administrators increasingly tend to exploit testing as a cheap and easy way of defining goals as well as of measuring success.

As a result, every parent and citizen is alerted to and armed with very precise test statistics. A child is no longer "a good reader," "a poor reader," or even "a non-reader." Now Johnny is a 2.7 or a 4.1 reader. Schools, too, are consistently classified by reading test scores—above grade level or below, and almost all "performance contracting" is based upon payment according to such test score results.

The Social Context

It is not only the poor minority parent, with a history of legitimate suspicion about the good intentions of the school system, who is the "true believer" in the reading tests. It is not only 3R-conscious "middle America." The faith embraces also highly educated parents, including many advocates of open classrooms, "relevant curriculum," and free schools. At meeting after meeting, many such parents—while demanding the introduction of freer and more relevant schooling—will inquire about the comparative test scores of open vs. formal schools and use past test scores to prove the evils of traditional education. Well-educated and well-off parents have told me how they "had to" change schools or hire tutors because their 9-year-old *scored* low, or anyway insufficiently high! ("But does he read well?" I ask in vain.) Others praise John Holt and A. S. Neil as their educational gods and then tell me proudly that they have just learned that their fifth grade son is an 11.3 reader. In short, almost all parents "believe in" these tests. They "believe in" them even when the scores defy their own observations about their own child's reading ability, and despite a nearly total ignorance of test contents, scoring methods, or, certainly, their own child's actual performance on the test.

Test scores are hard to resist, given their widespread use by school systems, their utilization in reputable studies on education, their quo-

From Deborah Meier, "What's Wrong with Reading Tests?" (New York: Notes from City College Advisory Service to Open Corridors, March 1972), pp. 3–17.

tation in the most scholarly journals, their yearly publicity in the *New York Times,* and the passing references made to them by the best intentioned educators when boasting of their own favorite programs. (Furthermore, the statistical exactitude of the testing lingo adds to an aura of scientific accuracy.) If this is the case with parents who know their own children, and school people who presumably know their own classrooms, it is certainly understandable that the public whose taxes support the schools should accept test scores as hard data regarding the success or failure of school programs.

Yet an examination of the tests themselves, their scoring methods, and, most important, the manner in which children handle them, demonstrates that they do a grave disservice. They subject the young child to an evaluation system based on standards which neither child, parent, teacher, nor school may agree on or even be consciously aware of, and thus, often unwittingly, drive schools and teachers into adopting pressure-cooker programs to meet the needs of the tests, not children.

This combination of circumstances may account for what has become an open scandal in New York City schools: the widespread cheating done with regard to reading tests, not merely by students but by the educational establishment itself—including traditionalists, reformers, and radicals.

While teachers and administrators congratulate themselves on the fresh wind of humanism that is blowing across the nation's schools (albeit amidst an inhumane poverty of funds), they have paid too little attention to the entrenchment of a system of measurement that could serve as the excuse for the death of any reforms.

"Why such passion? What are you afraid of? Aren't such tests 'merely' a tool to measure a child's ability to read, which you also are eager to improve?" say well-intentioned colleagues. But what is reading? How do such tests measure it? And if they do not measure reading development, what is it they do? And how dangerous is their effect?

It is a cliché to note that education does not take place solely within the four walls of a school. In fact, *between* the ages of 6 and 16, children spend only about a fifth of their waking hours inside schools. But what is apparently less obvious is that it is therefore not possible to devise a standardized group test that measures only the data printed upon the mind by the school teacher.

Or, put another way, no standardized group test by its very nature can be without bias. Nor should it. It has to have a particular content of some sort. Furthermore, it has to have a style and a "jargon." It has to have a "format"—a way of getting to what it is after. And finally, it must be built in such a way that it can be "objectively" scored for right and wrong responses.

The Trouble with the Tests

Two major "biases" exist in the reading tests given to young children. One that has been well publicized is the class and cultural bias regarding choice of content. As testing critics have noted, tests reward not only "the ability to read" but also knowledge of particular words, ideas, places, and experiences, commonly linked more with one socioeconomic group than another.

While one can *understand* the argument that a high school diploma (or a college degree) should indicate knowledge of a certain "common curricula territory," it is not the tester of reading who should be deciding on the territory. Furthermore, to aim for this from the primary school is absurd. Worse, it is dangerous. For the task of the teacher of the young is the very opposite one. Early childhood education seeks to emphasize words, concepts, and reading material that will help a child sort out the here and now, that will provide continuity between his pre-school learning and his school learning, between the different parts of his own life and environment. It stretches out beyond the world of intimacy only slowly, as experience, interests, and needs widen.

A test that ignores the nature of childhood separates—with a tool of apparent scientific neutrality—children of one kind of background from those of another. An examination of the way children deal with the test documents this fact in a startling fashion. As one listens to bright, articulate black children from our inner city schools attempt to make sense of the bewildering array of test questions, the bias involved is painful and shocking.

The second bias, less apparent and probably more insidious because of its subtlety, is the extent to which standardized tests are rigged against the nature of the thinking of all young children. What appears to many teachers, in their effort to coach their students to success, as "immaturity" (if not stupidity) in dealing with test questions, is simply the normal developmental style of thought of any 7- or 8-year-old. Middle-class children, because of their familiarity with certain key phrases and styles (conditioned responses), short-cut the process and succeed in producing "right" answers even though they do not carry out the logical thought implied by the question. They get it "right" for the "wrong" reason. The bright lower-class child, who cannot fall back upon a lifetime of familiarity with certain language, picture or word-association patterns, is dependent upon real mental ingenuity to make the necessary "logical" connections. As a result, even if he has equal reading skill and utilizes greater intelligence in his effort to think through the particular question on the test, he is bound to answer wrong more frequently. A 7-year-old child, still engaged in "pre-operational" thinking, or, at most, in what Jean Piaget has described as "early concrete operational thinking," is simply not in the same world as the adults who fashion such tests. It is for this reason that such a child's ingenuity and good judgment are not only useless to the task, but often even detrimental to it.

In labeling such children "slow," or seeking test-oriented get-rich-quick schemes, irreparable damage is done. Schemes to help such children "score better" (however well meant) invariably seek to substitute conditioned responses for good thinking. They block off the rich vein of associative thinking, imagery, spontaneity, and attendant self-confidence that the world makes sense upon which intellectual growth depends.

In relying on drilled associations to link specific terms or words, they divorce language from conceptual and experiental growth. They fashion their own curriculum demands which focus not on children's interests or their developmental needs but on preknowledge of the nature of the test contents. The tendency for "school thinking" to become disassociated from "sensible thinking" is thus reinforced. In short, in order to "look good" in second grade, we risk a child's potential for later growth.

To make matters worse, the scoring methods currently in vogue lead to their own absurdities. Test scores are reported by grade level norms: a second grader taking the test in April is "average" if he scores 2.7 (second year, seventh month). Towards the two ends of the scale the grade-level equivalents go wild. On one of the tests examined here, 77 out of 84 right scores 3.7, 4 more right jumps it to 5.2, and a mere 3 more catapults a student to 8.4. At the other end, average luck at guessing will place a second grader taking this test at 2.0. A few bad guesses and he zooms down to 1.3. For this reason, a poor reader is best advised to take the most advanced test he can, where, assuming he skips nothing and has average luck, he will score amazingly high in terms of grade level. The test makers admit the scoring system is misleading. They argue that it is hard to find one that will better satisfy the public.

How Children Handle Tests

Following the spring 1971 testing period in New York City, I spent two weeks talking about the tests with second and third grade children with whom I had worked for some years in a central Harlem school. All had just completed one of two tests: Primary II or Elementary I of the Metropolitan Reading Achievement tests. These tests are fairly typical, and the following comments are not intended as criticism of this particular set. For while in certain respects it has improvable qualities, this set is no worse than any others and better than some.

These tests are given to all second through fourth grade children (7- to 9-year-olds) in New York City each spring. I met with about 15 children in small group discussions and individual sessions, taping their comments so that I could review them later with other colleagues. Most of the children had had a limited period of skillful pre-test coaching, were among our best students academically, and had spent at least a year in fairly informal classrooms. These conversations led me to note at least four broad areas of competence that seemed to be involved in an ability to score high. Few of these competencies seemed necessarily connected, however, to "reading," "word knowledge," or "comprehension," the specific aims of the test.

The most startling realization was the extent of confusion in most children's minds about what they were being asked to think about or do. The test directions involved thinking skills that were inappropriate for most 7-year-olds; not only was there a poor choice of wording but also a mismatch between the test tasks and the minds of the children for whom the test was intended. For example, one part of the "word knowledge" subtest consists of simple line drawings followed by a choice of four words. The child is asked to select the one that "tells what the picture is about." Generally children had no difficulty thinking of a name for the object in question. But if that name did not work, the children were not always able to refocus in order to select the possible word association that the testmaker might have had in mind. A child in second grade looking at a drawing of a merry-go-round sought vainly for the word "merry-go-round." "The only word that begins with an 'm' is 'mile,'" she wailed. "It couldn't be right, could it?" she inquired insecurely. A few chose "run," because the horses in the picture, they said, might be running. The correct answer, incidentally, was "turn." Similarly, a few good readers were stumped by the picture of a ball! They went over and over the possible answers. Afterwards some insisted that there had been something wrong with their test! The "right answer," b-a-l-l, must certainly have been somewhere. They were unable to even consider "round" as a possible answer, although, as with "turn," most were quite able to read and use it appropriately.

Another section of the "word knowledge" subtest requires children to note the underlined word in an incomplete sentence, and then choose one of four words which "best completes the sentence." The sentences are of the type: "*Afraid* means . . ." "To *know* is to . . ." or "*Quiet* is the opposite of . . ." What the test seems to be seeking are synonyms and antonyms. But the children invented their own game of word association. A synonym is only one approach to "word definition" and involves a quite abstract notion about the replaceability of one word for another. If pressed for a "meaning," children (and adults) generally give a story example that describes the word or which uses it appropriately. When I asked what "afraid" means, children told me *when* or *why* you might be afraid, e.g., "Afraid means like when you go someplace new and you get afraid." They often selected the right answer, "scared," to complete this sentence because it was natural for them to use it in the context of "afraid." ("I get scared when I am afraid," seemed to make sense.) However, and for precisely the same reason, the children were divided more or less equally between right and wrong answers on the sentence "to *keep* means to . . ." The four choices included "carry" and "hold." The ones who got it right said, "If you want to keep *something* you got to *hold* onto it." The others, who answered it wrong, said with equal logic, "If you want to *keep* it you better *carry* it." In both cases the children were explaining the relationship in life between two words.

For some children of 7 and 8, "opposites" were difficult and were confused in their mind with the concept of "very different." When I tried to explain the notion of opposites, I began to grasp how complex and abstract this "simple" idea was. Familiarity leads most children to the correct answers. But for some children, "tall" and "far" were opposites, just as clearly as "tall" and "short," and no reasoned argument in the world could demonstrate otherwise at this age. Their failure again was not due to an incapacity to read the right answer, but rather an inability to focus on the specific relationship involved. While this kind of data is of interest to a good teacher in assessing a child's mode of thinking and classifying, it tells us very little about his "word knowledge" and his ability to read. There might well be a statistical correlation between children who are "advanced" in such tasks and those who succeed in school and become good readers. However, if we are merely seeking a statistically predictive tool, one that will serve our purposes quite well already exists, one carefully documented in the Coleman Report, which proves that the best predictor of all is the income/educational background of a child's parents. Such statistical correlations are merely indicative of the degree to which schooling is too often made irrelevant—not proof of the extent to which schooling is used effectively. Statistical *correlations* are not always sufficient evidence as to whether or not we are in fact measuring a relevant cognitive skill.

For our purposes, what is vital to know is whether a child answers a question incorrectly because he cannot read, because the vocabulary is unfamiliar or confusing to him, or merely because he has interpreted it in accord with his own common sense, in a manner appropriate to his age and his own experience. Even his "right" answers should be scrutinized with these same kinds of questions.

A similar confusion over the meaning of the test directions plagues many children in handling the "reading comprehension" subtest. Despite persistent efforts during the pretest coaching to help children understand the relationship between the story paragraph above and the incomplete sentence tasks below, some children "refused" to grasp it.

They stubbornly insisted upon inventing answers as though the previous paragraph did not exist, selecting answers instead based on their own personal experiences, intuition, or fantasies. They did so even when I reread the paragraph aloud to them, in order to get them to check their own answers. The very connection upon which the validity of this part of the test is based failed to make sense to them.

The language and subject matter are largely inappropriate for young children. For example, "a fair day is one that is . . ." The answer is "clear." But many children quite capable of reading the four choices offered had never had any reason to connect "fair" with weather. "Fair means," they explained to me, "when a teacher doesn't be unfair," "when you go on rides, that kind of fair." Similarly, few and far between were the children who were able to give me an example of where "point" and "place" were synonyms or went together in *any* way. Other words were often unfair in a test to be used with city children—as inappropriate as landlord, subway, crosstown, apartment, junkie, or project (meaning a big apartment building) would be for rural youngsters or comfortable suburbanites. We are so unconsciously biased in the world of schools in favor of 19th Century America and suburban Westchester county, that we quite forget that some words have dropped out of urban usage. Nor can one see why a *reading* test for 7- and 8-year-olds should presume that any child's verbal, much less written, knowledge should include knowing that a "canoe" is a "kind of boat" rather than a "kind of ship," that "oats" are a "kind of grain," or that "clay" is a "kind of mud." And imagine the adult mentality that asks a 7-year-old child to select just one right answer to "A *giant* is . . ." "huge," "scary," "fierce" or "mean."

It is hardly worth belaboring the absurdity of testing reading by asking 8-year-olds to read and answer questions regarding Amazon ants, the discovery of penicillin in 1928 by an English scientist, Guy Fawkes Day and the Gunpowder Plot against the British government 350 years ago, or the contents and meaning of Egyptian religious art. It would be comparable to testing the average literate adult's reading ability by giving him passages to read from Einstein, Piaget, or an advanced trigonometry text. Thus the test *makers* seek to impose a curriculum on the primary grades—one that covers the terminology appropriate to a study of medical history, the geography of the world, and the history of Western civilization. To imagine such a curriculum actually being covered in an average school day is patently absurd; to attempt it would be educationally criminal. All good early childhood education begins with the language of the child, values his own life and experiences and emphasizes reading and writing as natural extensions of this verbal communication.

Even the narrowest skills of reading—phonetic decoding ability and the possession of a good basic sight vocabulary—are poorly measured.

Every attempt is made to "trick" readers into betraying phonetic lapses and sight-word confusions. For example, among the four choices offered alongside a drawing of a human mouth are both "mouth" and "month." A majority of our good readers selected "month" because it came first. The u-n reversal is, we know, common up until fourth grade even among many fluent readers. Reading experts almost universally urge a casual approach to such reversals unless they are also associated with other reading problems. Yet the test had a number of such pitfalls which, to be avoided, would require a cautiousness toward reading (a word-for-word vocalization) that would indicate poor reading habits. *Month* and *mouth* and *log* and *leg,* for example, are hardly likely to be confused in a real reading situation.

Despite good sight word knowledge, strong decoding skill and a substantial verbal sophistication, some children still get into serious trouble over their interpretations of pictures or stories. For example, when shown a picture of a little boy at the beach with his hand on a girl's shoulder, almost everyone interviewed selected "push" as the best answer. While many did not understand the word "wade" (which was the "right" answer), they did not change their minds even when I explained what it meant. The word "push" seemed good enough and closer to their own experience with such a situation. Similarly, every second grader and all but one of the third graders misinterpreted a picture showing birds flying above and below some trees. Those birds, they insisted, were "flying many ways." Only one boy chose the correct answer, "flying in a flock." While this indicates that many of these 7- and 8-year-olds were unfamiliar with the word "flock," it also means that most of them had an interpretation of the phrase "flying in many ways" that was different from the test maker's.

In another drawing, a boy is waving toward three boys talking together in the distance. Most children incorrectly and empathetically thought the boy by himself in the foreground was "lonely because he does not have any friends." While I found the children's answer sensible, I had spontaneously answered it "correctly" by selecting "John and some boys belong to a club." Apparently I had unconsciously responded to a small suburban-type clubhouse in the background, because afterward I had a hard time defending my answer to the children or to myself! In still another drawing, bright and imaginative Karen worked out a very skillful interpretation of a picture that stumped many children. The picture showed a man in the foreground painting a wall, and some other men in firemen's uniforms in the background carrying some small objects. "The man up front is painting," Karen explained proudly to our group. "But the answer isn't this one about painting, because how would we know he was a fireman! He hasn't a fireman hat on. So they must be talking about those men back there who are carrying things, especially see this man in the fireman's hat and that must be stuff for putting out fires." So she selected, "The fireman has the tools for putting out a fire." She convinced most of the children, including those who had correctly answered, "The fireman is doing some painting," and others who had said, "A fireman works by himself." Her mistake was not recognizing a fireman's uniform minus the hat and/or being too suspicious of the test. The children who were right generally had not bothered to read all the answers, but had simply noticed the word "painting" in the first answer given, and on that basis alone picked the right answer. Two children engaged in a charming verbal battle over a drawing of a lady shopping. "The man weighs the fruit before Mother buys it" just didn't seem right to one girl. "Where will Mother put the fruit he's weighing, since she's already carrying one bag that is too full?" "Well," said her classmate, "she could carry two bags." Her own mother does that sometimes, and she demonstrated how it could be done. The first little girl remained dubious.

Another picture puzzled many children, who could not see the logical connection between any of the sentences and the picture. The right answer was dependent on first noticing the detail of rain streaks outside the window, connecting these streaks to the idea of a rainstorm, then linking a rainstorm to a power failure and finally, all of this to the candle on the table! In still another scene, we see a smiling well-dressed girl in raincoat and rain hat. Surely she was not going to let her books get wet, was the general consensus. She must have covered them, although it was hard to tell from the picture. Most children selected one of two wrong answers: "The rain will not hurt the books" or "Mary is taking good care of the books." I arrived at the right answer by following deviously deductive logic: if Mary had been conscientious and covered her books there would be two equally correct answers. This cannot happen on a standardized test. Therefore, "Mary's books will get wet in the rain" must be the preferred answer. Yet all three answers were equally easy to read and equally defensible as descriptions of the picture.

So convincing did I find the children's arguments in support of many of their wrong answers, that I often had to seek verification and counterarguments from other adults. One might claim that some of their explanations were too labored, too imaginative, or relied on a very limited personal experience. But in only a few of the cases would greater reading skill, no matter how we defined it, have helped this group of children avoid their mistakes.

For all these reasons it should not be surprising that the second graders scored best on the last and most obtuse reading comprehension paragraph. The topic was sound vibrations and a technical description of how they are made. I "dishonestly" told the children not to bother to read it for "understanding." Instead, I suggested they start with the incomplete sentence tasks and go back then to find phrases that coincided with the possible answers. Almost every child, using this backward strategy, managed to get two out of four right, and many answered all four correctly. In the easier paragraphs, in other words, they were penalized precisely for having sought to comprehend what was written. As a result, for example, some children thought Bill was "handsome," rather than "kind," to teach his brother to ride a bike. (Ugly was equated with meanness, and handsome with generosity.) Several insisted Mike must have had "wise parents" rather than "courage" to learn to ride a bike. And virtually all the children capable of reading the story about the architect thought his most important tools were his "paper and pencil" rather than his "ideas."

For most 7-year-olds, who have just begun the reading process, reading is still a laborious word-for-word activity in which so much energy goes into decoding and recalling that precious little is left over for genuine comprehension of any sort. This situation is intensified when the subject and vocabulary are unfamiliar and require dealing with new ideas. For most children there are simply too many intellectual tasks to perform at one time, and the test is thus merely a huge miserable confidence-shattering experience. Yet they often did no worse, if we were able to hold them together long enough to answer every question, than those described here who have mastered the first stages of real reading and who were therefore in a position to bring their "living" intelligence into the test situation.

Conclusion

Schools can make a difference. But neither educational equality nor educational quality can be demonstrated or measured through standardized group tests for young children. The mistaken set of assumptions that underlie these tests are not merely absurd. They lead to disappointment, misplaced bitterness, understandable paranoia, frantic parents, educators, and public rushing from one educational panacea to another, and finally, despair about the utility of school reform altogether.

Learning is a complex process and much remains to be understood about it. But an evaluation system must, at the very least, take into account what has been painstakingly learned from years of careful research and observation about a child's mode of thinking, growing, and learning. To use a tool to measure a child's growth that ignores the personal, individual, and often idiosyncratic nature of a young child's language cannot help us evaluate either his language or his reading skill. Finally, and perhaps most important of all, it is essential that we demand that testing devices become the tool—and not the shaper—of our educational objectives.

Suggested Readings

Carini, Patricia, "Productive Thinking and Achievement," Material presented at Follow-Through workshop, Lebanon, New Hampshire, January 1968.

Carini, P., Blake, J., Carini, L., *A Methodology for Evaluating Innovative Programs,* from the Prospect School, Title 3, Project 825. Bennington, Vermont: Supervisory Union, June 1969.

Chittenden, E., and Bussis, A., *Research and Assessment Strategies,* NAEYC, Minneapolis, Minnesota, November 6, 1971.

Chittenden, Edward A., "What is Learned and What is Taught," *Young Children,* Vol. 25, No. 1, October 1969.

Cole, Michael, and Bruner, Jerome, "Cultural Differences and Inferences about Psychological Processes," *American Teacher,* October 1971.

Feldman, Shirley, and Weiner, Max, "The Use of a Standardized Reading Achievement Test with Two Levels of Socioeconomic Status Pupils," *Journal of Experimental Education,* Vol. 32, No. 3, Spring 1964.

Natchez, Gladys, and Roswell, Florence, *Reading Disability,* Basic Books, 1971.

Voyat, Gilbert, "Minimizing the Problems of Functional Illiteracy," *The Teacher's College Record,* December 1970.

Wasserman, Miriam, "Testing Reading in New York City: A Critique," *The Urban Review,* January 1969.

5. Learning to Find Pleasure and Excitement in Language

"Perhaps the most dramatic of all the revolutions in English teaching is in the amount and quality of children's writing," the Plowden Committee observed. "In the thirties, independent writing in the infant school and lower junior school rarely extended beyond a sentence or two and the answering of questions, and for the older children it was usually a weekly or fortnightly composition on prescribed topics . . ." Now, anything and everything a child does may provide the occasion for an essay, story, or poem. Writing is no longer a "subject" to be studied for thirty minutes a day; it is a form of communication that pervades the entire curriculum.

One of the ways in which teachers can encourage children to write, Celia Houghton writes in the first selection, is to encourage a conscious interest in words and their distinctions by communicating the excitement and pleasure that can be derived from language. She suggests a number of ways in which teachers can do this.

In the second selection, Tony Kallet describes a number of word and sentence games that children seem to enjoy and that teach them some of the structural properties of the English language.

---

1. Children do two kinds of writing in school, and both are important in the educational process. About 90% of the child's writing is RE-CORDING; writing about social studies, science, mathematics and so on; many of the words and phrases used will be taken from books, or from notes he has taken down, rather than from his own store of words. PERSONAL writing is the child's writing about his personal experiences, impressions or imaginings. Expressive prose, and poetry is personal writing, the child using his own store of words for it.

Growth is not truly individual, is it? A child grows in relation to others, and he learns by shared experience. His interest and involvement in an experience brings a need to communicate this interest and involvement. As language is an instrument for exploring our world, the more competent a child is in use of language, the clearer is his understanding of his experiences. So it could be said that writing builds the writer, and to the degree that a child does not have language competency, something of an experience must surely be lost to him.

It is interesting to discuss how much of education should be a "putting in" (and of what?), and how much a "drawing out." A child feels—intensely—and needs help to express his feelings; personal writing is one way, expressive movement, painting, clay work, music-making are others. Each of these helps the other; the child's ability to express himself well in creative dance, for instance, will help him express himself in clay work, or creative (personal) writing. If a child cannot express his feelings with words, they do come out in other ways. Unfortunately, if he has no "legitimate" way of expressing his feelings, they will often come out in anti-social, aggressive ways.

We have all seen how a young child, in dramatic play, plays many roles, and will often act out his fears and painful experiences, so that familiarity makes them more bearable; the writing child will also play many roles, some necessary for him to come to terms with a hurt, to accept it and so make it less painful.

In building a child's competency in personal writing, we are looking for opportunities to give him direct sensory experiences; first-hand experiences in which he can become interested and involved, which he will feel a *need* to communicate; and we make these experiences rich for him, through making him *aware,* making his involvement intense. This

From Celia Houghton, "Curriculum Papers," The Teacher's Center at Greenwich, Greenwich, Connecticut. mimeographed.

is what is important. Then, of course, he has to be helped to find words for the experience, and his understanding of it, his impressions, his feelings. He has to have the words and he has to make words his own through his involvement in what they express.

And all this in a climate of trust, support and encouragement. In expressing one's feelings in words, spoken or written, or in fact in expressing one's feelings through dance, or any other medium, so that these feelings are communicated to others, one (child or adult) feels vulnerable. The importance of a trusting, supportive climate cannot be over-stressed, and part of this is the teacher's understanding that the privacy of a child's expressed feelings must be protected; before a piece of writing goes on the bulletin board, or in the school newspaper the teacher needs to make sure that the writer is quite happy to have his work on show.

An important part of the teacher's job in helping the child express himself through the sensitive use of language, is to communicate to him the excitement and pleasure of words, making him competent in describing the experiences his senses give him. "Close your eyes, what, exactly, do you hear? What does the wind sound like?" Getting details, helping the youngster explain, describe, with precision and detail. "What sound does a bubble make, exactly, when it bursts?" The child *listening* to bubbles, searching for words, trying new ones, arriving at satisfying ones.

It helps a lot to take the children out. Let them *feel* the sun and the wind and the rain, and let them get down low onto the dewy grass, to smell and touch and hear the early morning; the small things, the spider's web, the blade of grass, the busy ant—and give them time—"What is this life if, full of care, we have no time to stand and stare?" How can one *find* a sense of wonder, much less preserve it, without the time to be still? And how can one foster sensitivity "on the run"? How pleasing this phrase is: "the sunny slow lulling afternoon . . ."

I'm afraid we seldom give children time to grow well, we get behind them and push—we push them through first grade, through fractions, through tests, through school, as fast as we can, it seems; we really don't give them a chance to live fully at each stage. Only the baby can take his time, there isn't much one can do to push him through learning to talk, to walk, to be toilet-trained; but then we start on him, pushing him through his childhood as fast as we can. What a pity!

Sometimes it seems very difficult to get first-class, first-hand experiences for children. The weather, people, places, animals are good to talk about and write about, and one can blow bubbles in class, light a piece of paper and watch it twist into crisp, grotesque black shapes; take off on a flight of fantasy over an old rusty key, and so on; but of course we also want to read often to children, stories, and poems and any pieces of writing we find where words are used imaginatively, interestingly; where they are precisely relevant. D. H. Lawrence's "Fish" is an example of a really interesting use of words, I think.

> I have waited with a long rod
> And suddenly pulled a gold and greenish, lucent fish from below.
> And had him fly like a halo round my head
> Lunging in the air on the line.
>
> Unhooked his gorping, water-horny mouth, and seen his horror-
>   tilted eye,
> His red-gold, water-precious, mirror flat bright tye
> And felt him beat in my hand, with his mucous, leaping life-throb.

And who doesn't enjoy these phrases,—"when the world is mud-luscious . . ." "when the world is puddle-wonderful . . ." that e e cummings uses in "in-just."

Many poems have a use of words which appeals strongly to young children; first graders love this kind of thing. (by Spike Milligan)

> On the Ning Nang Nong
> Where the cows go Bong!
> And the monkeys all say Boo!
> There's a Nong Nang Ning
> Where the trees go Ping!
> And the teapots jibber jabber joo . . .

Haven't we all wondered about "the land where the bong tree grows," and been intrigued by "a runcible spoon"? A wholly delightful sequence in the B.B.C. (Time-Life) film "Movement in Time and Space" shows, in the children's interpretation, how much they enjoyed "jabberwocky."

Older children will see and enjoy the relevance of the words in Southey's poem, "The Cataract of Lodore":

> Dividing and gliding and sliding,
> And falling and brawling and sprawling,
> And driving and riving and striving,
> And sprinkling and twinkling and wrinkling,
> And sounding and bounding and rounding,
> And bubbling and troubling and doubling etc.

and may like to use the same way to write on themes to do with some games and sports, in fact any action theme.

Let us give children lots of opportunities to play with words, to make lists of "warm" words and "cold" words, rough and smooth words, etc. Children soon appreciate that "lively" words have a different personality from "sleepy" words. We should encourage them to collect words they like for any reason.

Sometimes, in reading stories to children you can take them "inside" the story. Reading the description of the ride on the lion's back in C. S. Lewis' "The Lion, the Witch and the Wardrobe" you feel yourself really taken into the situation, instead of being outside looking in.

Some music is very good to use as a stimulus to writing; it is best not to give the name of the piece of music because if you give the title of "In the Hall of the Mountain King," the children will all write about Mountain Kings! Likewise, if you use pictures it can be inhibiting or confusing to give the children the titles. Some pictures by Umberto Boccioni, Kandinsky, Escher, Miro, Monet, Max Ernst are good to use; you can get prints from the public library, or slides from UNESCO or art museums.

Some public libraries have a record lending department. Some records that have inspired children to write are:

Peer Gynt Suite, Grieg
Night on Bare Mountain
Pictures at an Exhibition, Moussorgsky
Grand Canyon Suite, Ferde Grofé
The Leminkinan Legend, Sibelius
La Mer, Debussy
The Firebird Suite, Stravinsky
The Planets Suite, Holst

Apart from records of music, sound effects are useful; if you cannot find records of the sound effects you want, try experimenting with a tape recorder, using various recording and playing-back speeds.

I feel that we should encourage children to write poetry; it is a very appropriate and natural way for a young child to write before he has the facility and language to write prose; in a sense, the young child, writing poetry, expresses more than he knows he knows; he vaguely understands a wide field of experiences, but only gradually does he learn to see things sharply, analytically, to focus narrowly on something and dissociate it from its surroundings. Sharp clarity is a quality of good prose and this writing comes at a later stage of the child's development, when he learns to understand his environment in this way. In writing poetry the young child writes in a way that corresponds to his experience, and expresses it without its being logical or analytical.

Reading children poems written by children of about their own age, from Richard Lewis' "Miracles" for example, will encourage them to write poetry.

Should the child's personal writing be corrected? Yes, but only at each child's level of competency, individually: teacher and child working together. For the most part the skills of handwriting, spelling and punctuation can be left to the bulk of the writing a child does in school, the "recording." In personal writing we are concerned with drawing out from a child what is in him, helping him communicate this, enriching his world. If we criticise his spelling, he will write about "cats on mats" instead of exploring other possibilities.

But when personal writing has become a regular part of the work in the school, the children take a great interest in improving their work, and they will re-write their poems and prose, carefully and correctly, decorating their books with pictures and designs, if encouraged to do so.

* * *

Many games can be played with words and sentences which, apart from being fun, may illustrate some of the structural properties of the English language. Of the suggestions which follow some are mine, some are borrowed. The substitution and transformation games were first brought to my attention by David Armington.

1. *Sentence expansions and contractions.* If you start with any sentence—for example, "The dog ran quickly"—you can make substitutions according to a rule which will expand or contract the sentence. Let's consider expansions first. Suppose that the rule is that two words will be inserted for any one word in the original sentence. "The dog ran quickly" could become "The pink tiger ran quickly," which, in turn, following the same rule, might become "The pink tiger ate pancakes quickly" and then "The pink tiger ate pancakes with ketchup," and so on. There is, of course, no limit to how far the expansion can be carried. A group of ten-year-olds started with a four-word sentence and ended up with a thirty-odd word monster.

One point which emerges from an activity like this (and from many of the games suggested below) is that *sense* and *sentenceness* are not the same thing. A sentence may be grammatically and syntactically impeccable and yet be absolute nonsense. I think this is an important, as well as enjoyable, point to make about language.

The converse of the expansion game, contractions, works best if a long sentence is used to start with. I prefer humor in my starting sentences and one which I recall is, "The bowl of ripe fruit balanced dan-

Tony Kallet, "Fun and Games with the English Language," *Outlook* #2, Spring 1971. Mountain View Center for Environmental Education, University of Colorado, Boulder, Colorado. This is a revised version of an article which first appeared in the *Primary School Broadsheet*, Leicestershire, England.

gerously on the end of the diving board while a sheepish banana screwed up its courage for a backwards somersault." Again, a two-word rule can be used; any two consecutive words in the sentence can be removed and replaced by a single word which does not violate *sentenceness*. With practice it seems possible to reduce most simple sentences to a single word using this rule. When this becomes routine, try substituting a single word for three consecutive words.

It is often more fun, in both the expansion and contraction games, if each new sentence is written out in full. This way the progress (if that is the right word) of the expansion or contraction can be clearly seen. To illustrate the contraction game, let me start with a sentence somewhat shorter than the one above.

> Six sad sheep sat silently mourning the midnight moon.
> Slippery sheep sat silently mourning the midnight moon.
> Slippery sheep sat silently mourning the dawn.
> Rupert sat silently mourning the dawn.
> Rupert is mourning the dawn.
> Stop mourning the dawn.
> Behold the dawn!
> Behold Jello!
> Oops!

2. *Substitutions*. For any word in a sentence almost endless substitutions can be made so long as only the *sentenceness* must be kept inviolate, not the sense. For example, consider the sentence "All boys chop wood cheerfully." The sentence is still correct if "cows" or "teaspoons" are substituted for "boys." It is still a sentence if "muffins" is substituted for "wood," or if "My" replaces "All." In every case, the word to be substituted is tested in the original sentence.

The game might be organized on paper or a blackboard as follows:

All	boys	chop	wood	cheerfully
Some	girls	sing	dirges	dully
Do	cows	invent	poems	gaily
Can	teaspoons	mutilate	muffins	often
Seven	rockets	destroy	crocuses	everywhere
My	teachers	spread	people	dynamically.
(One)	(man)	(pushes)	(rug)	

In parentheses I have indicated some "illegal" substitutions. Looking just at the legal ones, and moving freely through the rows and columns, the possibility for humorous invention is considerable: "Some rockets destroy poems everywhere"; "My teachers invent people often"; "Can cows mutilate crocuses dynamically?" And so it goes.

It is worth noting that nonsense words can be substituted for real words. The sentence "All doples glip fibbets dabically" sounds very much like an English sentence such as "All boys chop wood cheerfully." It may be interesting to discuss with children why this should be so, and to have them invent other nonsense sentences which correspond to "real" sentences. Another interesting point for discussion can be the difference between the nonsense of "All doples glip fibbets dabically" and the nonsense of "Boys wood cheerfully chop all."

3. *Inventing sentences using random words.* With a bit of imagination and a carefree attitude it is possible to use any words at all in a sentence, adding the necessary connecting words and "filler." For example, suppose the words are "can," "sky," "filibuster," "pickle," "truck," and "violate." One possibility is: "Can you look at the sky during a filibuster designed to prevent passage of a law saying that any pickle truck can violate all traffic laws?"

A good start for this game can be to have a number of people write down several words each. Collect a word from each person up to a total of, say, three, and ask if anyone can use all three words in a sentence. For example, consider the words "water," "measles" and "naturally." Forgetting about order, one might say that "Water naturally causes measles." If the rules made it necessary to retain the order of the words, the sentence might be "Water should not be drunk if you have contracted measles naturally."

One enjoyable way to obtain large numbers of words, which can be used in this game and others, is to have everyone write down as many words as they can think of in five minutes. (When asked "can you write down twenty words?" many children, in my experience, react with a horrified, "Oh, no." But once they start they often go on and on and on. It helps to make it clear that correct spelling is not important.) I've found that the long rolls of paper tape used in adding machines are ideal to write such lists on, and they have other uses, as well, some of which I suggest below. When someone has made a long list, have him close his eyes and put a finger down anywhere on the list. Then ask him if he can use the word nearest his finger and the one following it in a sentence. Then try the two following words, then three, etc. I was recently playing this game with some ten- and eleven-year-old children. When we had compiled a list of twenty words I asked if anyone could use them all. No one volunteered, so I demonstrated how it could be done, whereupon one of the boys rattled off a sentence using all the words in reverse order; his story was just as fluently told as mine had been, and even more amusing.

4. *The long story.* Children and adults alike have had great fun writing long stories—literally long, since they are written lengthwise on adding machine tape, which is cheap and comes in several widths as required.

A perfectly ordinary story can become more fun when written out this way, and the length of the tape often encourages the writer to keep going. The resulting tape can be fastened to the wall (perhaps in the corridor) to be read by all. One might suggest writing the longest possible sentence, or a sentence long enough to go all the way around the room.

And then there is what I call the Möbius sentence. If you join with Scotch tape the ends of a three or four foot length of paper tape to which you have given a half turn, you have constructed a Möbius strip. Topologically this is a strip with only one side, as you can easily demonstrate by placing a pencil on it and making a continuous line down the middle. Eventually you will discover that without having ever encountered an edge, you have come back to your starting point—and when you look at the tape what appear to be both sides have been covered, thus proving that "both sides" are in fact only one side. (I don't pretend to understand this but it does work!) Now, the point of all this, as far as writing goes, is that it is possible to invent sentences which come back on themselves, end to beginning, and with care these can be written on a Möbius strip, so that once you start reading you go on and on. Here is one such sentence: "When you stop cantering and dismount, the horse will smile, bow, thank you, and ask politely for a lump of sugar, because he has learned that. . . ." It is also possible to write stories in which the end leads back to the beginning, much in the fashion of the old song, "There's a hole in your bucket, dear Liza."

5. *Arranging words in sentences.* This game seems especially useful in suggesting some of the features of words which determine their position in sentences. Write down a fairly straightforward sentence (without capitalizing the first letter): "the car sped down the street" might do. Cut up the sentence into individual words, tell the person playing the game that there are six words, and then give him one word. Ask him to decide what your sentence might be, based on the one word he has, and to write down his hypothesis. Give him a second word and ask him to place it where he thinks it goes in relation to the first word. Again he should write down what he thinks your sentence is. Continue giving him one word at a time until he has all the words. It may be, of course, that the sentence he finally arrives at is technically correct but does not make sense: "The street sped down the car." Or he may have a correct sentence that differs from yours: "Down the street sped the car." Are any other variations of a correct sentence possible?

It is clear that the word that one receives first makes a difference in how quickly one's sentences begin to look like the "correct" one. If the first word one gets is "car" one knows more than if the first word is "the." A discussion of this point may help reveal the function of various kinds of words.

6. *Inventing words.* Why are "bat," "cat," "fat," "hat," "mat," "pat," "rat," "sat," and "vat" all real English words, whereas "dat," for example, is admitted only now and then and "lat," "nat," and "wat" are never allowed? Surely there are thousands of words just waiting to be invented, not just mechanically, as I have done here, but creatively. Why not "crackerfluff" or "tingletalk"? What about "slapish" or "timble"? (A book called *Ounce, Dice, Trice,* by Alastair Reid, illustrated by Ben Shawn, is devoted largely to the invention of just such words.)

Define "bilp" and draw a "patchpawg."

7. *Words as they happen.* Sentences, phrases, words, near-words and interesting letter combinations can be found in many places. As part of a general effort to help children enjoy the sounds and shapes of language, they might be encouraged to be on the lookout for oddities. For example, car license plates in England and in some American states consist of three letters and three numerals. Some of the letter combinations are intriguing. I have recently encountered "NUT 355," which leads me to wonder where the other 354 nuts are driving, and "RUT 847" which suggests that the car and driver are well set in their ways.

Signs, often quite baffling to adults, may be even more incomprehensible to children. Ogden Nash has immortalized the familiar "Cross CHILDREN Walk" in a verse the next line of which is "Cheerful CHILDREN Ride." Traveling across the Atlantic on the *S.S. United States* many years ago I came across a sign bearing the legend, "All dogs must be fully released before opening the hatch." I eventually discovered the true meaning of the message, but meanwhile some delightful images sprang to mind. It may simply be the personal quirk of a perennial punster, but I find it fun to take literally such signs, statements, and the like. Across from my hotel in Cleveland I once noticed "Avenue Cleaners" and was sorry I hadn't any avenues to be cleaned. And in Leicester, England, there is a chain of shops each of which has its name over the front door: "The Three Sisters. Hosiery, Drapery, Linen." I often felt the urge to go in and ask for Miss Drapery.

8. *The music of words.* Carl Orff's method of helping children make music as well as listen to it employs extensively the sounds and rhythms of words and names. (Of course, many other people, before and after Orff, have also used the cadences of language musically.) The line between "just words" and poetry and music can become blurred and meaningless at times. For example, list a few of the common objects in a kitchen, such as teaspoon, coffeepot, can opener, sink. One can use these words to explore a number of interesting rhythmic effects:

> teaspoon
> coffeepot
> can opener
> sink

Translated into musical values, these words might be represented by two quarter notes (teaspoon), two eighths and a quarter (coffeepot), a quarter and triplet eighths (can opener), and an emphatic eighth or sixteenth (sink). Try rearranging the order:

> coffeepot
> sink
> can opener
> teaspoon

If you distort "coffeepot" so that the accent comes on the "fee" you are into syncopation. And so on. Any words can be used. Orff gets good results with flower names, trees, and, above all, the names of people. A good start can be made by asking children to produce (on tone bars or a xylophone or a piano) two notes, then sing their own names, distributing the syllables over the two notes in the most natural way. The next step might be to combine two or more names spoken or sung at once.

Two years ago, after I had introduced some of these ideas to a group of teachers, one of the teachers said that on a fine summer's day she and her children had been shelling beans out on the lawn. One of the children had suddenly started chanting, "Green beans, August tenth, 1963," and the others had picked it up until all were in hysterics! There are few sentences that can't be sung.

9. *Non-stop speaking and writing.* Many people never seem to stop talking, but have you ever set yourself, or children, the task of speaking for a solid minute without pause? The ground rules might be that it doesn't matter what you say; you needn't even make sentences; but you must keep talking. At first people may be reduced to reciting the alphabet or listing the objects in the room. Fine. With some practice, and a willingness to be "silly" if need be, children and adults alike may find that they can become quite fluent. From here it is not too far to writing without stopping for a minute or perhaps even three or five minutes. Again, the ground rules may be that anything goes, and that if nothing comes to mind, letters or numerals may be written down. The semanticist, S. I. Hayakawa, writes that, working with adults, if this exercise is done regularly, many people who have at first had the greatest difficulty become quite fluent in getting something down on paper and, as with speaking, the results gradually become more coherent. (One ten-year-old to whom I proposed this task spent five minutes describing in minute detail everything I did while she was writing!) As with all these games, of course, it is important that this not become a chore, and that there be a certain lightness of touch and spirit, and that the effort be abandoned when it becomes tiresome.

10. *Convergence in Webster's.* This is a delightful and challenging

game invented by Professor Hassler Whitney of the Institute for Advanced Study at Princeton. It is a two-player game in which player A writes down a short sentence (perhaps four words) and player B tries to discover what it is by constructing test sentences. The game can best be explained by giving an example.

Player A writes down his sentence, making sure that player B cannot see it. Suppose the sentence is:

How fragrant are halibut.

Knowing nothing of player A's sentence except its length, player B writes down his first test sentence:

Monday mornings never pass.

He hands this to player A who compares each of the four test words with the corresponding word in his sentence. If a test word comes before the corresponding word, alphabetically, he writes under it the letter "B." If it comes afterwards, he writes "A." When he hands back the first test sentence it will look like this:

Monday mornings never pass
a   a   a   a

All four of the test words came later in the alphabet than the corresponding words in player A's sentence. Player B, thus, knows something about player A's words. With this knowledge, he constructs a second test sentence:

Good grief, he groaned.

Player A looks at this sentence and puts the letters "b," "a," "a," and "b" under the four words. Player B, in this example, has adopted a useful strategy, which I won't reveal! The game proceeds. Within five or six test sentences it is likely that player B's words will all begin with the correct letters; alphabetizing continues with second letters, then third, etc. When player B eventually hands a sentence to player A which contains a correct word, player A writes an "=" sign under it. The game continues until all words are correct.

I have found that the game is somewhat less frustrating if, when player B correctly identifies a word but presents it in the wrong tense, player A "gives" him the word and corrects the part of tense. When players become more skilled, this may not be necessary. I also find that it is a good idea, at least at first, to rule out proper nouns: the game is difficult enough with fairly simple words until one has had considerable practice. Toward the end of the game, it may be hard to set test sentences which make sense. My advice is not to worry about this in the slightest. Much of the fun of the game, for me at least, comes in trying to make ridiculous test sentences which, nevertheless, serve my purpose.

Prof. Whitney says that on average it takes about fourteen test sentences to identify correctly player A's entire sentence. Interestingly, the number of test sentences needed does not depend on the length of player A's sentence since, in each test, all the words are being tested. After one or two words have been correctly identified, of course, grammar and syntax will help with the remaining words.

11. *Place names.* A study, light-hearted or serious, of place names can be most rewarding. George R. Stewart has recently written a book, "American Place Names," which gives the origins and some of the lore about thousands of names. I have enjoyed simply making lists of place names which appeal to me. A good source of names is a booklet called "National Zip Codes", which is widely available both in bookstores and at the larger magazine stands, and is published by Larron, Inc., Berrien Springs, Michigan 49103, at one dollar. I don't want to rob anyone of the pleasure of browsing through this booklet, but I can't resist ending this article with a few of my favorite place names: Allgood, Alabama; Bumble Bee, Arizona; Dowdy, Arkansas; Needles, California; Hygiene, Colorado; Howey in the Hills, Florida; Enigma, Georgia; Goodwine, Illinois; Bippus, Indiana; Agenda, Kansas; Head of Grassy, Kentucky; Pippa Passes, Kentucky; Plain Dealing, Louisiana; Meddybumps, Maine; Chance, Maryland; Prides Crossing, Massachusetts; Brutus, Michigan; Tea Garden, Mississippi; Knob Noster, Missouri; Plentywood, Montana; McCool Junction, Nebraska; Parsippany, New Jersey; Horseheads, New York; Crisp, North Carolina; Pepper Pike, Ohio; Boring, Oregon; Hop Bottom, Pennsylvania; Crazy Horse, South Dakota; Finger, Tennessee; Scroggins, Texas; Dutch John, Utah; Creenbackville, Virginia; La Push, Washington; Droop, West Virginia; Embarrass, Wisconsin; and Thumb, Wyoming. Oh, by the way, there's an Agnew in California and several Nixons are dotted around the country from New Jersey and Pennsylvania to Texas.

6. Teaching Children to Write Creatively

"Teaching children to write creatively," according to Vernon Hale, headmaster of an Oxfordshire junior school, involves "understanding how they live and how they grow; and ultimately valuing the integrity of each personality searching for fulfillment." Children are more likely to write creatively in a classroom which nurtures the imagination and provides a variety of sensory experiences: "listening to the plop of bricks in the water tray, touching the roughness of bark, or tasting the

saltiness of a shell." In such a classroom, Hale writes, children "feel the rhythms of life around them and become aware that their own bodies can respond sympathetically. Using words to communicate these rhythms becomes an inherent need, and where a skilled teacher creates an environment delicious to the senses, a child's speech and writing patterns can change radically."

————

I was watching an infant boy of six taking part in a movement lesson. He was sitting so still that I almost forgot the other children around him; they were sliding and undulating and making a cacaphony of sounds impossible to isolate from the situation. He stayed like this for two or three minutes until he lifted himself up and balanced on one leg with a total control over his body. It seemed to me that the boy was floating. Quite soon he sat down and waited for his colleagues to finish; he was content with two simple movements and was unconcerned that the others were still active.

The next day I happened to go into the boy's classroom and he came straight to me to show me a swan he had made from a fallen twig, on which he had glued two feathers of a dove. He told me that he could "blow it along the water like the wind does." I asked him whether it would float, and although he did not answer the question directly he was interested in what else could be done with the feathers other than using them in the simple artifact. However, I was impressed so much by our dialogue that it seemed relevant to relate the two incidents that I had observed.

In the English primary school the children begin their explorations with simple experiences that involve the senses: listening to the plop of bricks in the water tray, touching the roughness of bark, or tasting the saltiness of a shell. They feel the rhythms of life around them and become aware that their own bodies can respond sympathetically. Using words to communicate these rhythms becomes an inherent need, and where a skilled teacher creates an environment delicious to the senses a child's speech and writing patterns can change radically. This becomes especially true when the philosophy of the school is based on integrated learning.

The content of school experience changes for the growing child, but imaginative potential is constantly being nurtured whether the activity is movement, music, mathematics, or science. Language therefore grows organically as I will try to illustrate by bringing to life a group of older juniors I had the pleasure of observing.

From Vernon Hale, "Teaching Children to Write Creatively," in Vincent R. Rogers, editor, *Teaching in the British Primary School* (New York: The Macmillan Company, 1970), pp. 130–153. Copyright © 1970 by Vincent R. Rogers. Reprinted by permission of Macmillan Publishing Co., Inc.

These children were enacting the feeling in their fingers of the sharpness of thorns; they were stretching their arms like a tree growing and shaping their bodies in a tangle. Groups of three and four came together to make the thickness of an old hawthorn and moved with the heaviness of leaf; they made the light scratch of birds with their nails and swayed to the wind turning across the fields.

We had been listening to Stravinsky's *The Rite of Spring* (*Le sacre du printemps*) and through a series of movement sequences we were trying to understand the rhythms and undercurrents of music that vibrated and celebrated the mystery of life. There was so much of spring in the wild patch outside the classroom: the busy rooks high in the elms; the alders shivering with leaf—ginger-colored in the sun; spawn slobbering on the edge of the pond; the scrabbling of shrews through grass tunnels. The children were free to wander in this environment collecting and identifying specimens or simply waiting and watching for a revelation. There was much to observe and record, yet the children were ready to experience what D. H. Lawrence called "plant consciousness, insect consciousness, fish consciousness, animal consciousness . . . The natural religious sense." They were ready to make imaginative use of their bodies to explore the sources of growth, of order, of burgeoning in nature. They felt a need, too, to reinterpret their discoveries with painting, printing, and drawing—but particularly through imaginative language.

Two girls who had responded especially well to the Stravinsky music wrote for about one quarter of an hour, standing on the step of the classroom and watching the change of light and color under swiftly moving clouds. They wrote:

> Sun shining on ginger alders,
> Water lifeless lies.
> Then wind whips,
> Howling
> Whirling whistles.
> Water shedding its skin,
> Snake skin of ripples.
> Reeds in beige light,
> Calm, to be disturbed
> By the scampering rat wind
> Which stops to gnaw.
> Gull inland
> Shines silver,
> Flashes.
> Is gone.

Tangled growth withered
As clouds hide the sun.
    Jayne and Terry (10+)

The first impression of the wild fields, humpy as far as the school fence, is one of complex, maze-like growth. In winter the dominating colors are brown and dun except for the black tracery of branches. Underfoot it is so wet that a darkness spreads over the grasses and sedges. This setting is a source of eerie wonder in the children, and frequently it has been a starting point for talking about strange landscapes and distant places. Often, we have sat quietly in the classroom at the end of a January afternoon and watched the sky empty of all but the cold dampness and the pools of water hardening into ice-moons. These occasions have been opportunities to read poetry and listen to music, thus extending the area of imagination and enriching the vocabulary of the children. The worlds created have been quite alien to the actual area. One boy wrote:

The sounds echo on the walls and bounce off in all directions. The wind twirls into a cone of music and plays round the old ruin. It makes its way across the distant desert and creates a blinding terrifying sandstorm. A camel train goes slow. Then the wind blows over the sea and lashes the water to a white foaming top and the ships dip between mountains. Finally the wind finds a deep valley and destroys all things that are weak and defenseless. People go low as the wind surges harder and harder, until it blows itself out.
    Andrew (10+)

It was interesting that when this piece of writing was read aloud, it stimulated the rest of the class: two girls made a monochrome of curling abstract shapes like a wind of barbed wire; a boy made a brown-and-white collage from sample pieces of wallpaper, creating a picture of ice that seemed to be drawn by the moon along furrows of waves where birds floated like thrown sticks. Others sketched the grass tangles in a series of charcoal studies, which in turn gave rise to talking and writing about strange plant forms such as the giant hogweed, the exploding seed pods of impatiens roylei, or their own "death flowers." One child was inspired by this discussion and wrote a poem:

She turned back into the soil
And curled over the roots and buried things.
She felt her large brown leaves

And her stem which went deeper.
Her petals bore a crystal of snow.

Katherine (9+)

The dialogue was enhanced by bringing objects and pictures to the classroom and displaying them in a context of color, shape, and texture. I gathered together fabrics in browns, greys, and blacks and arranged dried grasses, roots, and branches as well as stone from local quarries, animal skulls, and bones. In the center of the display I placed a painting by Giuseppe Arcimboldi called *Winter,* which portrays a face made as a dead tree stump, with hair of entangled ivy and two grey fungi for lips. I allowed the display to grow and change as I was able to introduce the childrens' poems, their descriptions, their art. The experience became one in which the children were exercising all their senses and demanding a wide range of related media for communication.

In spring, summer, and autumn it was possible to be closer to the environment and to study it in detail. Many more particular references to fauna and flora were contained in the childrens' writing:

The willow is hollow. The bark is ridged and bumpy. Thin moss clings to the trunk. Underneath there is ripe brown wood. Down at the bottom are insects crawling in holes. The tree trunk makes winding and twisting shapes with spinning leaves hanging. The sun glitters through zigging twigs. Ledges step up in the hollows in which lie small pieces of broken wood, twigs, left leaves and wood dust. Black wood spirals around in the holes.

Diane (9+)

A blooded breast;
Eggs of rust and white
In a den of thorns,
Watched by a black bird.
Moss-padded walls,
Grass of bronze makes the nest.
Eyes looking for food.

Nigel (10+)

A weasel flashes by after a rabbit.
A flurry of fur and bone,
Bones of weak ivory.
Weasel and rabbit are gripped,
A clutching of throat
A squeezing.
The rabbit's jaw is separated from face,

Eyes torn, once looking like diamonds,
Now broken glass.
The weasel eats.
Again the survival of the fittest,
The weasel the fittest.

David (10+)

This quality of thought arises in an integrated situation where the children are involved in activities essentially interrelated and continuous. They need a flexible classroom structure where they are free to respond in many ways to stimuli offered by a spirited teacher. It would be limiting if a teacher merely encouraged the exploration of the environment with a set of reference books and a microscope and failed to understand that children have a natural inclination to be totally involved through the senses. At the same time, the imagination must be enriched by perception of detail and evaluation, which we can call "the scientific attitude." For example, the poetry of John Clare is full of precise observation that may be found in the notebooks of a meticulous naturalist. It reveals a patient waiting; he is the scientist in the field, yet with words Clare penetrates a mystery unrevealed by mere facts. So many children are artists in this sense and assimilate the complexities around them and make order.

It is interesting to see how children respond in an idiosyncratic way to the things they find around them. The teacher may intend the classroom display to be thematic, but pupils have a way of isolating an object, or plant, or flower arrangement and studying it for its own sake. Such an object frequently begins a train of thought that preoccupies a child for as long as a week. Perhaps it is dissected and examined under a microscope, or sketched in ink, or used as a lino-cut or woodcut design, or becomes the subject of a poem or prose piece. One arrangement of bulrushes, for example, elicited all these activities and after the velvety texture had been felt and the seeds magnified, and the designs had been cut Terry wrote:

Proudly the bulrushes hold their prizes which have burst from within them. They droop upon us, admit all their secrets. The leaves of the bulrushes twist and curl, just to remind us that they are part of the miracle as well. Seeds fly everywhere as though drawn towards the earth. Some escape through the open window and disappear into the sky.

The classroom displays are often supplemented by exhibits on loan from the local museum school service, including textiles, pottery, sculpture, embroidery, and stuffed animals and birds. For Jill, a William Morris design of golden flowers became "The Chrysanthemum Forest":

Fighting harder and harder,
Stalks tangling around each other,
Not letting my body through.
Heads towering above,
Swaying in the wind that makes it harder.
Touching them and getting a shower of petals.
Birds cheeping,
Bees buzzing down to the nectar.
Quiet,
Then the disturbing wind whistles.
Ants, slugs, snails creeping up the endless stalks.
All the Jack the Giant Killers.
Thicker, thicker, then thin,
Then fades away.
I look back at the chrysanthemum forest.

For Alan, the heron displayed in tall sedges comes alive:

The high judge of the river
Stands like a statue,
Its slender neck folds bent.
Its beak holds still,
The eyes move slowly across the water
Scanning its territory.
Its legs are like burnt branches;
Grey back and snow white,
Elegant in its own way.
Then it darts spearing the poor fish.
The meal is quickly devoured
And across the river in marshland
The female sits on the blue eggs.
Beyond, the curlew calls.

During the year the class creative writing folder was filled with work written about foxes, Victorian ginger jars, sprigs of traveler's joy, a policeman's truncheon, a railwayman's cap, a waterboatman, a copper kettle, a ceramic cross, a fan, a piece of iron railing, and a giant pumpkin.

Primary children have the capacity to explore more fundamental themes, as well as responding to everyday experience. Many teachers still underestimate their pupils, but it is clear from traditional stories and nursery rhymes that from infancy the world is seen to be a serious place.

> Barney Bodkin broke his nose,
> Without feet we can't have toes:
> Crazy folks are always mad.
> Want of money makes you sad.

This rhyme might be about any number of things: the intolerable frailty of the body, the inconsistency of adults, the pressure of day-to-day family life. Young children do work out such problems as they mature, and it has been my experience in helping them to develop their language skills that their most profound achievements are made when they recognize personal anxieties and aspirations. In the later primary stages, the children show a considerable perception in dealing with things that will be with them for life: loneliness, sorrow and mutability, personal fulfillment and happiness, cruelty and compassion, violence and war, class and discrimination, and the ultimate meaning of life. If the relationship between the children and their teachers is a sincere one then frequently the creative writing is of deep personal significance.

Perhaps the most important new factor in English primary education is that children and adults have more common ground because discovery takes place at many levels, and although communication varies in sophistication, the intensity of experience is shared. In the classroom it is now generally felt that the teacher will be personally affected by the creative process that he sets in motion and will be extended by the insights and imagination of his children. The teacher has the resources —the "producible vocabulary"—to structure the environment; but like the artist, he releases a magic that works on everyone in the situation. In attempting creative work at his own level, the teacher inevitably reveals standards, beliefs, and inadequacies. His sympathies grow for the frustrations and joys that children feel in taking the devious routes to understanding. Teaching involves the faculty for appreciation, for discrimination which grows with our own pain and fulfillment in the creative process. I believe that we should expect a great deal from our teachers. Wordsworth might have been speaking of them when he said of the poet, "a man endured with more lively sensibility, more enthusiasm and tenderness, who has a greater knowledge of human nature and a more comprehensive soul. . . . a man pleased with his own passions and volitions, and who rejoices more than other men in the spirit of life that is within him; delighting to contemplate similar volitions and passions in the goings-on of the Universe. . . ." For children to live and work with such adults can do nothing but good during years when children are searching for life standards.

The interrelationship can best be illustrated by describing one of my first contacts with a class of ten-year-olds, after a long period of working with adolescents. We began by remembering the incidents of our earlier years, and I read the children a poem of my own about a legendary character, Wayland the Smith, who once lived for me on the distant chalk hill beyond my home. I described how I imagined the texture of his skin, the long hard nails, his groping in the hole under the ground, the ringing of his anvil across the downland, the frightened horses left in the dark. I told my class how the myth had receded as two years passed, during which time I bought a bicycle and cycled to the place where previously only my thoughts had flown. The children were beginning to understand the concept of passing time and how it can suddenly change awareness. I showed them how the Cornish poet, Charles Causley deals with this theme in his "Nursery Rhyme of Innocence and Experience" in which he describes three years in the life of a child who longs for the sailor to bring her toys from across the sea. Three summers later the sailor returns with the plum-colored fez and a drum once desired, but the child asks, "Why have you brought me children's toys?" I read this poem and it immediately evoked graphic reminiscences. One boy described his new birthday penknife and how he found himself whittling into the wood of a loved doll. Another told us about his waiting on the wall looking at the base of a horse chestnut tree and seeing a thrush fly down. He described how he took a catapult from his pocket and shot a stone, which thudded into the bird's speckled breast. My pupil said, "A drop of blood came from its beak and I cried. I hid my catapult in my dad's garage." For these children the dialogue was a profound oral release and therefore complete. Others wanted to write about it, but it would have been artificial to ask all the class to do so. If we accept that our work must be child centered, then they must have the freedom to assimilate ideas in their own way and if necessary reject them. Creative writing is a natural means of communication for many children but the primary way is speech. Therefore to suggest that written work could always follow experience would result in frustration and superficiality. This view is substantiated by the compositions of children being educated in formal subject situations where style is cultivated and overgrown. Then it becomes difficult for the teacher to deal with the basic skills that ought to be acquired in a context of need. Here are a few pieces, the economy of which resulted from ordering real responses, which were deeply felt and unimpaired by teacher-centered discipline:

> My old bear had no legs and I had to tie up his back with a stick. He didn't say much from his mouth that used to be a line of stitches. I hung him up from my bed on a piece of string and every

night I kissed him and twisted him around to make him twirl. One morning he had fallen on the floor and I forgot to pick him up before going down to breakfast. The dog tore him to shreds but I didn't seem to care.

John (10+)

A pair of eyes came out of the dark at me. It was an owl sitting in the fir tree at the end of the garden. One day I drew a picture of an owl on a big piece of paper and the yellow eye I put in made me tremble from head to toe. So I fetched a pair of scissors and cut it up and scratched the piece of paper right across. Then I found a piece of wood to make an owl but my knife wasn't sharp enough and the wood was hard. I went on to something else.

Susan (10+)

John stood by the clump of trees where some cows had left turds and he looked into the water. He thought of all the fish that Henry had described on their trips to the Oxford canal. He remembered the spiny-finned perch with the stripes you could see under the water, especially when it was sunny. That upset Henry when it struggled on the end of his own hook.

[J:] Bigger than what?

[H:] On your tackle he might be quieter.

[J:] He's on yours.

[H:] He wouldn't have torn and bled.

[J:] You are always ripping them. If you throw him back now the bacteria won't eat him away.

Martin (10+)

When the children's themes begin to take shape and truths emerge, there are many opportunities to introduce literature which can enrich their learning and take the children on other journeys of discovery. Unquestionably the teacher must use prose and poetry that he has enjoyed and evaluated as an adult. Sometimes, it is superficial to search for appropriate "Children's books" and debilitating to search through school anthologies of mediocre verse. There is a wealth of material in the English language—both traditional and modern—and translated from world literature. In recent years, however, the quality of children's literature has improved enormously.

For the winter theme I chose *Elidor* by Alan Garner—a book full of strange and wonderful magic, pervaded by the symbols and myths common to men. It is an exciting contemporary story with some of the qualities of science fiction, yet powerfully affected by English history and landscape. The total impact of the novel is one of continuity and permanency. In it there are the ancient monuments of our civilization, such as standing stones and castles; caves go deep into the earth; morality is polarized, and men stand shining in light or live in darkness; the silver unicorn snorts and thunders and finally lays its head in the lap of a girl. The children in the story find a ruined church in a city redevelopment area and are called by Malabron into Elidor, the Green Isle of the Shadow of the Stars. There, they are entrusted with four treasures that are the symbols of enlightenment. Roland, Helen, Nicholas, and David bring these back into their own world, yet are pursued by the forces of darkness even into the safe world of suburbia. This book was especially significant for the children in my class because we were able to relate the wild uncultivated land around the classroom to the desolation of Elidor. Consider this fragment:

> Roland looked back: but he had nowhere else to go, and at that distance the castle was a tortured crag. He clutched a handful of gravel and rubbed it against his cheek. It hurt. It was real. He was there. He had only himself.
>
> Within the forest the road dwindled to a line of mud that strayed wherever there was ground to take it: fungus glowed in the twilight, and moss trailed like hair from the branches. There was the silence of death over everything: a silence that was more powerful for the noises it contained—the far-off crash of trees, and the voices of cold things hidden in the fog that moved in ribbons where there was no wind. Oaks became black water at a touch.[1]

This kind of writing has an immediate effect upon the children's shaping of experience. It is as though they have been given a key to unlock the store of language patterns and vocabulary that have been accumulating since infancy. The physical actuality of light and shade, of softness and hardness, of growth and decay, of hills, trees, distant towers, they can take within their imaginative grasp and set in order. The words they find, or the materials that are to hand set in motion a questing, which the teacher must encourage with further infusions of ideas, by introducing the other arts, by aiming for "an exquisite sensation of wholeness."

At one point in *Elidor* Roland passes through a door in a mound of earth, into an underground passage. When I read this episode, the children's faces were a mixture of excitement, curiosity, and fear as though they were being drawn under the ground to an experience quite overwhelming. This observation was borne out by their intense interest

---

[1] Alan Garner, *Elidor* (London: Collins, 1965), pp. 28–29.

in the subject of caves and mines; many of them found reference books on physical geography and recorded many facts, but again the research was valuable in helping them to be precise in their speaking and creative writing. Further, this discovery work also formed the basis for a series of movement sequences when we concentrated upon the contrasts of space and confinement; we listened to Bartok's *Music for Strings, Percussion and Celeste,* the third movement of which begins with sounds like the slow drip of water echoing in deep galleries. The children also made their own sound effects on a range of Carl Orff instruments, taping their compositions at one speed and replaying them at a slower one. They pinpointed each sound: the liquid flow of darkness, the tap of picks at the coal face, the sudden rush of sea against cave walls, the creak of pit props, the abrasion of sand and shells.

Drip, drip, drip. The water drops into the dark pool and ripples run across it. I stand silently watching. The walls are jagged and roughly cut around me. It is frightening, yet wonderful like a new world without light, an underground world. I move on slowly over the rough floor. The cave is damp and water trickles in little streams over the floor and over my wet feet. I carry on walking and wonder what else will come before my thrilled eyes.

Michael (9+)

Rushing water
Beating the rocks
Forming over centuries
A cave now complete.
Calm water goes in and out as it pleases.
Shadows of rock make queer shapes,
The shape of a needle
Formed on the water by a great stalagmite,
Ages to grow, ages.
The sun shines through the entrance
And I see a lizard-like creature.
The jutting rock like whales' teeth,
Rugged rock.

Alan (9+)

The underground is a world of its own. The blackness is at full strength and God is only just with me and my sense of feeling is floating through the tips of my fingers. This low dark tunnel of seeping limestone echoes every move I make. A strange power has overcome me and I seem to be led through row on row of dismal tunnels. This in my mind will go on for ever, for ever, for ever.

Andrew (11+)

I was able to gather this small group of boys together and follow up their work by reading them selections from writers who I felt had explored similar themes both factually and imaginatively, including George Orwell and Franz Kafka, Coleridge and Mark Twain.

Alan Garner's novel finishes with a reinterpretation of the unicorn legend. Findhorn—"silver and dark with wounds"—is being pursued relentlessly by the men of darkness carrying spears. The great animal rests finally in the lap of Helen who is holding one of the treasures. The children know that Findhorn must sing to save Elidor and in a magnificent climax, when the last spear pierces the beast's heart, "a brightness grew on the windows of the terrace and in the brightness was Elidor, and the four golden castles. Behind Gorias a sunburst swept the land with colour. Streams danced and rivers were set free and all the shining air was new. . . ." [2] Some of the children were moved to tears by this ancient story and wanted to know more about the myth. I obtained pictures of the Flemish "Hunt of the Unicorn" tapestries, now in the Metropolitan Museum, New York. These intricately woven pictures are filled with animals and hunters; the unicorn is milk-white against dark greens and blues and is pursued through a maze of leaf and flowers, until he is finally secured to a pomegranate tree. One girl decided to make her own fabric collage of the story and found as many scrap materials, sequins, and buttons as she could and created a beautiful yellow unicorn leaping into the sky, which seemed to be filled with glittering spears and tattered clouds.

For a number of weeks groups of children discovered similar myths from many cultures and made their own miscellanies. One miscellany even contained the Greek legend about the imprisonment of the Minotaur and the flight of Daedalus and Icarus. The children included in their collection Breugel's painting of the fall of Icarus together with W. H. Auden's poem on the same subject. I read a selection from a contemporary treatment of the maze myth by Michael Ayrton, a British artist. We also devised our own version of Demeter's dancing floor and danced through the whirling, serpentine shapes that we drew on the school playground.

It becomes clear that literature should not merely be seen as an initial stimulus for writing; its value is in its centrality. Literature imbues the child with the communicated and eternal perceptions of mankind. Therefore the committed teacher in the English primary school feels a profound responsibility to the children in valuing the word and views with suspicion those educational technologies and methods that undervalue books. A gross example has been the recent production of creative writing kits and film loops which aim to supplement the teacher's own

[2] Garner, op. cit., p. 159.

resources. There are of course no substitutes for the teacher's vision and his capacity to live a full life.

During the summer months many children learn to swim in the school pool. Swimming is a physical achievement comparable with balancing on a bicycle, or climbing a tall tree, or breaking through a seemingly impenetrable wood. It is a personal triumph over an element, a natural hazard hitherto powerful and alien; the attempt to succeed can cause pain and disappointment, yet with success comes a general growth in confidence often favourably affecting a child's social attitudes. Achievements of this kind are so important that children readily draw upon them when writing:

> My toes dangled into the cool water, forming ripples on the surface and making the blue bottom of the pool disappear. Somehow I felt strangely frightened and yet I was excited by the thought that I might succeed in reaching the opposite side. I pulled my bathing cap further over my ears. My head hurt under the pressure of it. My hair was being strangled. I jumped and water whirled around my body taking my breath away for a few seconds. A splash of water surged down my body, making me see my friends around me. . . .

During our discussion of this piece of child's writing, a boy made a comment that crossing a width of the pool was like taking a long journey; he tried to articulate that distance was relative to the state of mind of the traveler and the hazards that beset him. We tried to compare a flight across a large continent such as South America with a trek of a few miles in the same area, on foot and without the aids of civilization. The children understood that to contemplate the unknown gives rise to irrational fears and exaggeration. I told them of the 16th-century Oxfordshire geographer, Peter Heylyn of Burford, who described Australia as "Terra Australis Incognita or the Southern Continent, Utopia, New Atlantis, Fairy Land, the Lands of Chivalry and the New World in the Moon." We looked at old charts of seas full of strange monsters, whirlpools, and fogs and talked of the myths that Homer chronicled of the wandering Odysseus.

However, in the June of the term we were hearing journalists' dispatches from the Arab-Israeli war front, and I read aloud an account of how Egyptian soldiers were retreating across the Sinai desert, caught in sandstorms, without water, and suffering from wounds. The exchange of ideas that resulted was revealing for I had not expected such a divergence of opinion on war. For most children war was conceived in fantasy terms, and the destruction of a town with bombs was no more real than throwing beanbags at bricks. I decided to confront the chil-

dren with the meaning of war as experienced by soldiers, civilians, artists, and writers through the ages. I mounted an exhibition of photographs, comic strips, and souvenirs loaned by parents; there were shells,
helmets, regalia, service pay books, scrapbooks, and letters written from
the front. We spent time looking at Goya's drawings and read from the
Anglo-Saxon epic poem *Battle of Maldon,* parts of Froissart's Chron-
icles, from Ernest Hemingway's Spanish Civil War dispatches, and
Bertolt Brecht's narrative ballad, *Children's Crusade* 1939.

I suggested that the children might like to interpret war pictorially
and gave them chalks and charcoal, limiting colors to black, white,
brown, and grey. Once again we explored the immediate environment
for inspiration and found a hedge blackened by chemical spray and two
trees whitened by lightning burns. We also looked at a partly demolished
building, with splitting beams and sharp masonry. One abstract charcoal
study was of remarkable quality: a grey storm of ash seemed to spiral
into a blackening sky, taking with it jagged slabs of concrete and white
match-like figures with broken triangular limbs.

One photograph of the German occupation of Paris (confiscated
from a prisoner of war) evoked a lengthy discussion on the morality of
this kind of act, on how personal relationships can break down and how
decent people can be debased by organized and socially approved
violence. The children understood this type of breakdown in social mores
when I described the experience of the boys on the island in *Lord of
the Flies.* This is not a book that can be read to young children in its
entirety, but I was able to read them one small part that I felt might be
a clue to some who may have been thinking deeply about behavior:

> They scrambled down a rock slope, dropped among the flowers
> and made their way under the trees. Here they paused and ex-
> amined the bushes around them curiously.
> Simon spoke first. "Like candles, candle bushes, candle buds."
> The bushes were dark evergreen and aromatic and the many buds
> were waxen green and folded up against the light. Jack slashed at
> one with his knife and the scent spilled over them.
> "Candle buds," "You couldn't light them," said Ralph. "They just
> look like candles." "Green candles," said Jack contemptuously,
> "We can't eat candles, come on." [3]

The manner in which the theme was developing needed careful control to avoid pushing the children into an area of experience beyond
their mental maturity. The extract from *Lord of the Flies* was a break-

[3] William Golding, *Lord of the Flies* (New York: Penguin Modern Classics,
1954), p. 30.

ing-off point. It brought us back to talking about ourselves, how we differ from each other, how we experience the same things in personal ways, how our imaginations sometimes work, or fail to respond. Much of the writing that we finally collected into a book called *The Landscape of War* was a vindication of Coleridge's comment that "Children are much less removed from men and women than generally imagined; they have less power to express their meaning than men, but their opinion of justice is nearly the same. This we may prove by referring to our own experience." In the English primary school it has become possible to accept this general observation and at the same time teach the language skills required to articulate meaning. Consider these pieces:

> It is quiet, but I can hear a child crying beside his mother. He is lucky or is he? He has lost his leg. It's like a ruined world. A chain holds man down to war. Why is there no peace? We are all people. What has happened to the world?
>
> *Robert (10+)*

> Listen to the warning
> Find me out
> From death and darkness,
> And flying dragons
> That pierce the sky with smoke.
> Flames fight with the earth,
> Flames that fall from the sky.
> Ruins and shattered glass,
> Ashes smouldering
> And bodies deadened by fire.
> Clouds that sail in the shape of war.
>
> *Lesley (11+)*

> Burning sand and hot dried up mud. The mud is shrinking. There are the ashes of a plane that has crashed. A great war devil crosses the land, taking the people, telling them to come into the desert to have a better land. They go, leaving behind a happy place. But now it is dark ashes and ruins. The land they seek cannot be found, for there is no such place. But the devil draws them on. Their skin shrinks like the burning mud.
>
> *Susan (10+)*

Although primary children have this sense of justice and natural sympathy, often manifesting itself in a chivalrous, romantic commitment, their grasp of abstract moral concepts is often transitory, and may not survive the immediate context. Children of this age are readily

diverted from ideas about the reverence for life or social responsibility
to discovering how the natural world functions. Yet they are engrossed
by origins (first causes), and it has been gratifying to observe them
following the course of a thunderstorm, or finding out how waves begin
their journeys across the ocean, or waiting for young chicks to break
from the eggs warming in the classroom incubator. They show extraordinary patience in tapping away at rock to find fossils and intense
absorption in the lives of primitive people.

This type of concentration was made clear to me during two out-of-
school activities, a weekend camp and a visit to an Oxford Museum and
Art Gallery, which happened to take place during the same time, and
gave rise to one of our most rewarding themes: The Creation of the
Earth and the Evolution of Life. We had pitched our camp on a piece
of common land in the Oxfordshire Cotswolds, close to some old stone
mines where centuries before raw fissile limestone had been brought to
the surface and exposed to hard frost, split with hammers, and used as
building slates for country homes, farm buildings, and Oxford colleges.
Within the stone were treasures; rich evidence of fauna and flora existing millions of years past, such as ammonites, belemnites, sea-urchins,
fenestella, and cycads. Much of the stone still remains in grass-covered
mounds and on chipping banks, and during camp we lifted the turf and
dug into the ground where we found many samples to take back for
identification. The site was also ideal for other researches, particularly
about the Roman world. We were tracking through a wood when suddenly a boy found a large white shell which we were able to identify
as a species of edible snail first introduced into Britain by the Roman
settlers. This discovery led us on a search for other evidence that would
enable us to construct a realistic picture of life in the Roman centuries.
From the hillside we realized that below us a turf-covered road "petered
out" in the water meadow and was shown as Ackerman Street on the
Ordnance Survey map. Across two fields were the excavated ruins of a
Roman villa with a fine example of mosaic and a well-preserved
hypocaust (heating system). Here, the children discovered a mound of
brick and tile left by the archeologists, in which they found many
discarded examples of Roman materials and returned to school with a
valuable collection.

In the neighboring village stood a simple 13th-century church with
one remaining stained-glass panel—a green saint filtering pale light into
the chancel. There were tombstones dating from the 17th and 18th centuries, and on the other side of the church wall was a 17th-century
lockup where in days gone by the village malcontents were held for all
to deride.

The day of our visit was hot, and as we looked down upon the village we saw the cottages behind nets of sunlight; they were like great fish from ancient seas, scaled in stone. The snails under the walls were drying and falling, the shells showing hollow gapes to the light. The brass cock on a tower rippled in the summer air and seemed to wait for slow and distant winds. The whole atmosphere was such that the children felt themselves in touch with the past; everything they had found demonstrated the continuity of things and people, while the village seemed to suggest permanency.

At the Oxford Museum and Art Gallery we saw the painting "A Forest Fire" by the Florentine painter, Piero Cosino. The work represents his vision of the evolution of man and depicts the struggle for survival during the Old Stone Age. It is full of strange beasts fleeing from a fire, yet beyond its narrative content it evokes the primeval distance and the simplicity common to all creatures, including man. I also showed the children the sepia and pen drawings of Samuel Palmer, the 19th-century English mystic, whose work is a vision of paradise, the Garden of Eden.

After we returned to the classroom, I read *The Dream Time* by Henry Treece, a writer of children's historical novels. His book is about a young boy, Twilight, who discovers within himself the power to use natural materials to represent his world. He rejects the uninhibited violence of his own tribe and comes to terms with life through his art. Not only is the book meticulous in recording the stages by which primitive man ordered his environment and developed an early technology, but it also involves the young reader in the life and imagination of a boy whose aspirations they immediately recognize as their own.

We also made use of a drama series broadcast by the BBC School Service, which helped the children to explore through movement and music the evolution of life from single-cellular squirming to upright man and on to the invention of tools and machinery. The latter presented us with opportunities in mathematics, to experiment with pulleys and levers, with weight. With marbling inks that spread on water the children took prints of swirling shapes and gaseous explosions of color. Finally, many of them wrote about evolution:

> Nothing but space, all nothing, endless. Gas whirling around trying to make something out of nothing. Weird shapes and colours arc. All is careening around. Then it cools, hardening, beginning to be something, to take form. Small life-shapes move. Water. Then on land vegetation gets thick. Screams and cries echo across the volcanic islands. Then eruption. Red lava oozes out and pours down the side like a fire-tide. Smoky pieces of rock hurtle through the air. Life-shapes screech and burn to death in distress. Spitting

and spurting the volcano kills. It burns itself out and it is dead. Murky lava bubbles. The last convulsions of the life-shapes in a changed substance.

The eruption of the volcano expands the island, but in the ground are small creatures which can only crawl across it. Vegetation begins to grow again. But sticky bogs are hidden by the undergrowth. Tempted by the green the larger creatures come to feed, but some disappear into the bogs never to be seen. There is another change. New upright forms have come. They kill animals with sharp tools. They bring fear.

Philip (11+)

The children involved in these many experiences were from a variety of backgrounds where it would still be generally true that their parents place less significance on cultural inheritance than on ultimate material success in a competitive society. Because of this attitude there is always a temptation for teachers to prepare children for the next stage in their education and to forget the immediacy of response that is always manifest. So often there is a gulf between the potential of young children and what teachers expect from them. There develops a separation of school from living, as learning becomes a preparation for social status rather than a continuing part of the life process. Then it becomes necessary for children to use language for social conformity instead of for exploration: the clichés overwhelm their imagination. It is true in children's writing (as it is with literature) that the metaphor and image become the creative factors. These forces are conceived emotionally and intellectually and then exist "out there" for the group; they are powerful enough to reveal truths otherwise unattainable; they are subversive and erode superficial modes of thought. Most children are capable of using language in this way, given that the sources of experience are not confined.

Hitherto, in English education, school has offered pupils fragments of knowledge, only a little wisdom, and strictures about passing examinations. Under this system succeeding generations of the young have withered and become joyless adults, as the teacher and poet, Charles Causley understands in "School at Four-O'Clock":

> Though men may blow this building up with powder,
> Drag its stone guts to knacker's yard, or tip,
> Smash its huge heart to dust, and spread the shingle
> By the strong sea, or sink it like a ship—
> Listen. Through the clear shell of air the voices

Still strike like water from the mountain bed;
The cry of those who to a certain valley
Hungry and innocent came. And were not fed.[4]

Teaching children to write creatively is therefore understanding how they live and how they grow; and ultimately valuing the integrity of each personality searching for fulfillment. In this there is more love than pedantry.

[4] Charles Causley, "School at Four-O'Clock," *Underneath the Water* (London: Macmillan, 1968), p. 8.

III

Mathematics

Why do we teach mathematics in the primary school?

Edith Biggs, who has played a major role in reforming the teaching of math in England in her capacity as Staff Inspector for Mathematics in the Department of Education and Science, suggests three general objectives for primary school teachers. Two of them are familiar enough: to encourage children to think for themselves, and to give them skills in computation. The third goal, as Miss Biggs puts it, "is to give children a knowledge and appreciation of mathematics as a creative subject; of its order and pattern (in number as well as in geometrical form); of its vital presence in everyday life and in the environment, not only in man-made things but in natural forms as well. Children who learn to appreciate mathematics in this way," she suggests, "as a subject in which they make their own exciting discoveries and which holds fun and fascination for them, will have full confidence in their own abilities."

Mathematics is important, in short, because it is one of the most powerful ways by which man has learned to order and organize the world in which he lives. As the mathematician Z. P. Dienes has written, "Mathematics is based on experience; it is the crystallization of relationships into a beautifully regular structure, distilled from our actual contacts with the real world."

1. Why We Teach Mathematics

In this influential monograph published by The Schools Council, Edith Biggs elaborates on the reasons math is taught in primary schools. She suggests three general objectives—encouraging children to think for themselves, enabling them to appreciate math as "a vital presence" in their lives, and giving them skills in computation—and then goes on to translate these general aims into the specific concepts, processes, and facts that children ought to have mastered by age seven or thereabouts.

With discovery methods in mind and encouraged by Piaget's experiments, let us create a dynamic definition for the learning of mathematics. To be brief we might content ourselves with: 'Mathematics is a discovery of relationship.' But if we (or the children we teach) have discovered such a relationship for ourselves we want to communicate the exciting discovery to others. We may first describe the discovery in words to a friend or teacher. Subsequently we may find a more effective way of expressing the relationship; for example, in numbers (as in arithmetic), in letters (as in algebra), by a diagram (as in geometry) or by a graph. Therefore a more comprehensive definition would be, 'Mathematics is a discovery of relationships and the expression of the relationship in symbolic (or abstract) form.' This is no static definition but implies action on the part of the learner, of whatever age and whatever ability. It is the fact that mathematical relationships can be discovered and communicated in such a variety of ways that puts mathematics within reach of children and adults of all abilities. In the following chapters we shall show how young children can learn mathematics by their own efforts and how we can plan the learning situations which will effect this. For this purpose we may summarise the conclusions derived from the research to which reference has been made in this chapter as follows:

(1) Children learn mathematical concepts more slowly than we realised. They learn by their own activities.

(2) Although children think and reason in different ways they all pass through certain stages depending on their chronological and mental ages and their experience.

(3) We can accelerate their learning by providing suitable experiences, particularly if we introduce the appropriate language simultaneously.

(4) Practice is necessary to fix a concept once it has been understood, therefore practice should follow, and not precede, discovery.

From *Mathematics in Primary Schools,* The Schools Council Curriculum Bulletin No. 1 (London: Her Majesty's Stationery Office, 1965), pp. 9–13. Reprinted by permission of the Controller of Her Britannic Majesty's Stationery Office.

No one nowadays will question the desirability of including mathematics in the primary school curriculum. Any doubts should be dispelled by the following excerpt from *Primary Education*.

> Mathematical thought is part, and a great part, of the heritage of the race. . . . By its aid man has measured the distances to the stars, forecast eclipses, navigated the seas and the air, made maps of the earth, built cathedrals and bridges, split atoms and designed machines from the simple lever to the most complicated space satellite or electronic computer; all the elaborate business transactions between men, between groups of men, and between nations are founded on a knowledge of mathematics. And the subject is growing; the need to know more about the structure of the atom led to the development of new algebras and geometries. . . . The elegance, the order, the pattern and the generality which are inherent in even the most elementary work can be appreciated by all children. Clearly the teacher must be aware of these qualities himself and appreciate them.

In this, and in subsequent chapters, we shall be concerned with the content of mathematics courses for primary school children. We shall examine the structure of the mathematical ideas children can learn between the ages of five and eleven years. Bearing in mind the changing trends in education to which reference has already been made, we shall discuss ways of planning the work so that children are enabled to make their own discoveries. Dr. Z. P. Dienes described the classroom situation we want to create when he wrote, 'It is suggested that we shift the emphasis from teaching to learning mathematics, from our experiences to the children's, in fact from our world to their world. We shall then be already well on the way to a solution of our difficulties.' Dr. J. Biggs is no less definite when he writes; 'There are two major aspects to mathematical ability: an ability to rote-learn facts and connections and an ability to deal with the structure; these abilities correspond to arithmetical techniques and concepts respectively.'

Perhaps the classroom situation we want to create will be further clarified by a statement of our aims in the teaching of mathematics. We shall limit these to three. The first is to make children think for themselves. The second is to give children a knowledge and appreciation of mathematics as a creative subject; of its order and pattern (in number as well as in geometrical form); of its vital presence in everyday life and in the environment, not only in man-made things but in natural forms as well. Children who learn to appreciate mathematics in this way, as a subject in which they make their own exciting discoveries and which holds fun and fascination for them, have full confidence in their own abilities. The third aim is to give children a facility with number and quantity relationships or, more briefly, to give them skill in computation.

Sir T. P. Nunn, in *The Teaching of Algebra,* wrote, of mathematics: 'Mathematical truths always have two sides or aspects. With the one they face and have contact with the world of outer realities lying in time and space. With the other they face and have relationships with one another.' To gain an appreciation of mathematics, children must have experience and knowledge of both these aspects of the subject. We shall draw on the first, mathematics in the environment, as a basis for the discoveries of the abstract mathematical relationships implied by the second.

Children come to school at five years old with very varied mathematical backgrounds based on situations which have arisen naturally in their day-to-day experience inside and outside the home. In fact they have already begun accumulating 'that knowledge of number, quantity and space which adults take for granted.' In most infant schools, at least in the first term or so, this experience is continued. Teachers of reception classes make the most of opportunities which arise for introducing mathematical ideas and, more important still, for associating the correct mathematical language with the situations which arise. Thus for example, numbers are not met in isolation from language or experience as the following records show: Alan, aged five years, was very interested in telling the time. He made a clock book and kept adding to it. He learned to recognise the symbols up to 12 by this means. He used the cookery pinger clock and became familiar with five-minute intervals. 'Ten minutes until eleven o'clock. Five minutes more and it is coffee time,' he said. When using the water measures he said: 'I want the biggest one . . . a gallon of water in it for my car.' Alan made such rapid progress as a result of these varied experiences that, when the boy who was counting the number of children requiring milk asked him how to write twenty-three, Alan replied: 'You will find 23 in the calendar Paul.'

In another infant school the children had recorded their answers in writing to the question: 'What can you weigh?' These included:

My shoe weighs 10 ozs.
50 small dog biscuits make ¼ lb.
The largest brick weighs 2 lb.
The middle-sized brick weighs 10 oz.
The smallest brick weighs 4 oz.
1 stone balances 14 lb.
46 lemonade tops to balance ¼ lb.
The lightest thing in our room is a feather.
The heaviest thing in our room is a radiator.

'Our Zoo Number Book' at yet another infant school contained the following passage:

> Uncle Jack took me to the Zoo today. It was 9d. for Uncle Jack and 6d. for me. How much did he pay for the tickets. ⅓d. I had a bag of 12 buns. I threw 5 of them to the bears. How many buns had I left. 7. First we went to see the monkeys. There were 9 big monkeys and 4 baby ones. How many monkeys did we see. 13. It was lovely to see the kangaroos. There were 5. How many legs had they all. 20. Elephant is big and heavy. Mouse is little and light. Tortoise goes very slowly. Giraffe is very tall. We went in at 10 o'clock. We left at 4 o'clock. We stayed 6 hours.

But such mathematical opportunities as arise naturally in the classroom, though excellent in themselves as a continuation or extension of earlier experience, are rarely sufficient and broad enough even at this stage. We, as teachers, shall need to provide the right kind of experience to serve as a basis for more systematic learning. In order to do this we must examine the mathematical concepts which it is possible for most children to learn by the age of seven years. (Some children will, of course, learn considerably more and others far less, according to their abilities.)

Here is a summary of these concepts, processes and facts.

   i. Sorting and classifying objects into sets. Comparing sizes of two sets (the number of objects in each set) by matching or one-to-one correspondence; learning the language, and later the symbols, of inequality; is greater than >, is less than <.

  ii. Counting the number of objects in a set (cardinal number). This, in effect, involves putting each object into one-to-one correspondence with one in the series of number names. Conservation of number. Composition of numbers up to 20 known without counting on or counting back.

 iii. The number line. Numbers in sequence or in order up to 100 (ordinal numbers). 'Nodding acquaintance' with numbers beyond 20 but, except for a few children, no written manipulation of these numbers in isolation from experience. Growing awareness of place-value in the number notation.

 iv. Measurement and money. Conservation of measures. Knowledge of the relationships between one unit and another (the common units of weights and measures which normally come within the experience of young children).

  v. Simple fractions: halves, quarters, three-quarters.

    vi. Varied aspects of the operations of addition, subtraction, multiplication and division as these arise in the real situations of the classroom.

   vii. Shape and size (Proportion).

Before each of these aspects is considered in more detail the part which oral discussion and written recording can play in the work should be assessed. Reference was made in the last chapter to the importance of associating the appropriate language with the experience. This oral discussion, between a teacher and a group of children, or between children, serves many purposes. The suggestion has already been made that the learning of concepts is accelerated by discussion. Children frequently learn by their attempts to put into words what they are doing, and what they have discovered. 'How do I know what I think till I see what I say?' is an adult version of this aspect of learning. By talking to the children teachers can find out the stage the children have reached in learning a concept. A child can work through an assignment card and answer every question correctly and yet still fail to grasp important aspects of the concept. Such a failure is usually revealed only in discussion between teacher and child.

An example of this, which occurs quite frequently, is of children who were given oral practice, as a class, in adding 10 to different numbers less than 10. By the time the teacher had selected a child to answer $10 + 6$, for example, most children had had time to count on from 10 to 16 and had the answer ready. The children were then given a written exercise on this and nearly all of them obtained full marks. But subsequent questioning revealed that one child only, of a group of 24, had discovered the pattern $10 + 3 = 13$ (or $3 + 10 = 13$), $10 + 4 = 14$ etc. and so did not need to count on in ones to find the answers. A few minutes' discussion with small groups of children at less frequent intervals is always far more effective than oral class work of this kind.

It sometimes happens, too, that a child, using structural apparatus, may give the impression that he understands a concept when, in fact, he may be enjoying the visual pattern without appreciating the mathematical significance at all. For example, a six year old, using structural rods, was asked to find all the pairs of rods which together were of the same length as a given (black) rod. The boy soon discovered that when he had found one pair of rods together equal in length to the black rod he could then reverse the order of the rods and so obtain a second pair. With evident pleasure he matched up, in a similar way, all the pairs of rods (and reversed pairs) which were equivalent to the black rod. Although the boy was able to assign numbers to the rods he was quite unaware that he was on the brink of an important mathematical discovery: that in addition the order of adding two numbers does not matter (e.g. $3 + 4 = 4 + 3$, the commutative law). The teacher talked to the boy, focussing his attention on each pair and reversed pair in turn and asked him, as she did so, to name the number pair. After each pair of two rods she asked the boy if he noticed anything interesting. At first, he looked puzzled but, at the third pair, the boy's face lit up and he said: '6 and 1 and 1 and 6 are the same', and then proceeded to name all the other pairs. It was quite clear that if the teacher had not discussed the number patterns with the boy, and questioned him, he would not have made the discovery at all.

Since language has such a fundamental part to play in the learning of mathematics, it follows that children working as suggested are learning English and mathematics simultaneously. (It is important to remember this when the question of time allocation is raised!) If vocabulary is restricted, the experience provided for learning mathematics can also be used as one means of learning to read. One headmistress has stated that the children in her school learn to read at least six months earlier now that reading and recording have such an important place in the learning of mathematics. A five-year-old in his second term was trying to read a card which said, 'Which is heavier, a cup of peas or a cup of rice? Guess first.' The boy found the words 'heavier' and 'lighter' on a pair of scales. He matched the words 'peas' and 'rice' with the labels on the jars containing these objects. He then asked an older boy what the word 'guess' was. He said aloud, 'I guess peas because they are bigger.' He was astonished to find that the cup of rice was heavier. He repeated the experiment three times and was still puzzled. He discussed the result with his brother, an eight-year-old, who, apparently, had done this experiment the day before. This boy's explanation was: 'Rice grains are littler but you get more in t'cup.'

At a later stage, when children are writing their findings entirely in their own words, very good opportunities are provided for written recording. Some children who find other forms of expression difficult excel at this kind of direct recording based on their own experiments.

2. Learning Math Through Exploration and Play

The experiences on which mathematics is based begin with the earliest explorations of infancy, as the child discovers such phenomena as sequence, continuity, and the permanence of objects. (Infants initially assume that when an object is out of sight, it no longer exists.) In the elementary school, the mathematics curriculum should continue this process of exploration and discovery. For this to happen, teachers need to understand the continuity between the kinds of exploration and play in which children engage before they come to school and the activities that are encouraged in an open classroom. They also need to understand the ways in which all kinds of activities, e.g., playing with sand or water, learning nursery rhymes, building things with blocks, can extend children's mathematical thinking. Last but not least, teachers need to understand the basic ideas and concepts that form the beginnings of mathematics.

The two selections below, designed to give teachers these kinds of understandings, suggest the enormous variety of ways in which teachers of young children can integrate mathematical learning with almost any classroom activity. The selections come from two parallel Teachers' Guides published as part of the Nuffield Mathematics Project, the most influential English curriculum reform project in math.

Introduction

This volume is concerned principally with children in their first few years at school and how their experiences of life gradually extend their mathematical thinking. But this guide is a 'beginning' in another way; it is concerned with some of the basic ideas at the beginning of mathematics itself. It is hoped, therefore, that teachers of older children will also read it.

Because of this double 'beginning,' new ideas have been introduced in the classroom context. For example, sets are introduced in terms of animals and flowers rather than abstract symbols {a, b, c . . . } and so on. In this way it is hoped that the teacher will more readily find the guide *applicable*. Suggestions for the classroom are indeed interlaced with the material designed to help the teacher himself to understand the 'new look.'

1 Pre-school experience

The world of mathematics is one of abstractions largely concerned with symbols. These symbols have been and are being invented by man to help him discover, discern and record the structures, patterns and relationships within the universe.

This world seems utterly remote from the small world of the pre-school child, the world of home, garden, family and neighbourhood, the world of things that can be seen, heard, smelt, touched and tasted. Yet if we are to consider the developmental pattern within which a child begins to perceive the patterns and relationships of mathematics we cannot ignore the early years.

Early experiences will be outlined under four headings:

A. Experience with materials—'continuous' and 'discontinuous.'

B. Experience of space, shape and size.

C. Experience of containing, matching and measuring.

D. Experience of number words and symbols.

All these experiences can and should lead to the all-important growth of *language.*

It is impossible to over-emphasise the importance of pre-school experience. Throughout their education children draw upon resources gained through previous experience to enable them to assess a new situation or tackle a new problem. The roots from which language will grow lie in the early home environment and we are beginning to realise more fully the relationship between the language of the early environment and intellectual growth and development. It is impossible to lay down any programme in this field for a child of any given age, but it is vital to realise that we can only develop what is there already and build on what has gone before.

Development of ideas and vocabulary, hand-in-hand.

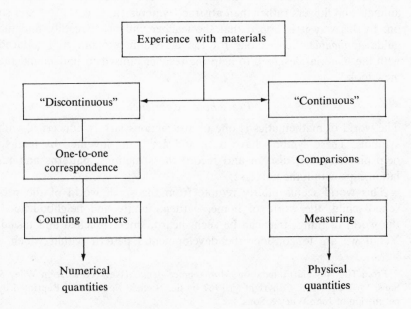

Effective development will depend on:

1. the quality and variety of the experience,

2. the availability of a companion and particularly an understanding adult with whom to talk,

3. the quality of the language used.

A. Experience with materials—'continuous' and 'discontinuous'

A young baby is able to grasp small things, and, largely by trial and error, transfer an object to his mouth. At this stage his mouth is all-important. The object may be his own fist, his mother's finger, part of her necklace that he has managed to grasp, or some toy attached to his pram. The coloured beads on strong elastic thread stretched across a baby's pram offer endless possibilities. They feel hard, unlike most other things in the pram. They move. They can be pushed along, or turned round. And they don't all do it at once. The beads in contact with the baby's hand can be moved about while the others remain in the same position. The string of beads is composed of *separate items* ('discontinuous').

The child of two, three or four years comes in contact with different materials throughout his waking day. He will learn to discriminate between them within different frames of reference, e.g. how the material *feels,* or 'what I can *do* with the material.'

He has a box of bricks. These can be emptied on to the floor, and are then seen as separate items. They can then be built up vertically to form a tower. It soon becomes too tall and rather unsteady, and eventually topples to the ground. The bricks are again seen clearly as separate items.

Alternatively, the bricks can be assembled in a long horizontal line, and pushed along as an imaginary train. The train bumps into another object, perhaps a chair, and disintegrates. Again the separate items are distinguishable.

Outside, in the gutter, is a puddle of water. There seems no connection between this and the water in the bath—yet they both behave in the same way. The child hits the bath water, and it makes a lovely splash. He scuffs a puddle, with the same result.

After the tower of bricks has tumbled, the separate bricks are clearly seen. The child may refer to *a lot of bricks* and in this instance he is manifestly dealing with 'separate items.'

After the splash in the puddle—a puddle of water remains. Although the child may refer to *a lot of water* in this instance the content of the puddle is not separate items but a 'continuous' stream.

B. Experience of space, shape and size

A baby in a pram experiments with all available materials. He sucks, grasps, releases, pushes and pulls things. Later he becomes aware of a world beyond the pram. He grasps something, moves his hand beyond the edge of the pram, and releases the object. It has disappeared from view—hitting the ground with a thud. Here is the first experience of the law of gravity. It is an incredible piece of experience for the baby, who cannot accept it, and will go on experimenting, i.e. dropping things out of the pram, just as long as a co-operative adult will retrieve them.

The key to the awareness of space is movement. As the child becomes more mobile so his world enlarges. The baby who cannot yet crawl will nevertheless try to move if placed on the floor. This early exploratory movement is almost always circular. For movement to be directional, i.e. from A to B, the motivation must be strong. A young child will struggle to move in a specific direction, either crawling or walking, to reach a desired object or person.

Young children have plenty of experience of being enclosed within a confined space, at first a cot, then a pram, then a playpen, a room, a house and a garden.

Covering a board with chalk, or a piece of paper with paint, is an early experience of covering space.

Early experiences of shape arise in a variety of situations. A building block is found to be of very different nature from a ball. Place a building block on the floor and it stays put. Put a ball down and it will probably roll away. You can pile building blocks on top of each other, but you cannot do this with balls. A child allowed to help Mother unpack the shopping basket will see and handle many different shapes, a large number of them cylindrical and rectangular.

Jigsaw puzzles give specific experience of shapes that fit together, but there are many examples of things that fit inside containers. The toothbrush fits into its own slot; the crayons fit into the box (but only if they are put in the right way).

To gain any understanding of what size means to a young child we have to imagine the appearance of, say, a room from the eye-level of a three-year-old. Chairs, cupboards and tables are comparatively enormous. The situation is further complicated by the fact that the child grows. Shoes that were called *too big* soon become described as *too small*.

Fortunately some things remain constant, and he will meet situations that do not vary. He will discover that he can never get that particular toy on that particular shelf, because it is always *too big*.

C. Experience of containing, matching and measuring

Containers serve different purposes, and these purposes are related to the nature of the substance contained. The young child meets problems concerning containers almost every day. If he knocks the box containing a jigsaw puzzle off the table he can easily pick up the pieces and return them to the box. If he upsets a jug of water there are no *pieces* to pick up. You simply wipe it up.

He might have milk and biscuits for his lunch. He can hold the biscuit in his hand, but the milk has to be contained in a mug.

Children who are allowed to help Mother with the cooking will have plenty of experience of materials removed from one container to another, mixed together, and transformed by the process of cooking.

Laying the table for a meal provides much experience of matching. A cup goes on a saucer, a knife with a fork. 'A plate for Mummy—one for Daddy—one for me.'

When Mother takes the child to buy new clothes they are matched against him for size. When she knits him a sweater she might match it against him to see if it is long enough. Wallpaper is matched to the wall, new curtains to the window. All this is valuable pre-measuring experience.

Some fortunate children still see large scales with pans on each side— weights on one side and potatoes on the other. But with the growth of sale by price rather than weight (in this era of pre-packed goods), children may rarely have this experience in the normal course of events.

D. Experience of number words and symbols

a. *Vocabulary*

Long before they go to school children come into contact with numbers as names. They see and may recognise numerals, e.g. number symbols as names. The words five, eight, two, etc. form part of their vocabulary almost as soon as they learn to talk.

On buses they will hear *'Two nines,* please.'

In a shop they will hear 'That will be *sixteen* and *eight.'*

At home they will hear these words occurring frequently in normal conversation.

Sometimes these words are used as names in relation to objects: 'I live at number *eighty-two.'* This, to the child, is the *name* of the house.

'We'll go on a *twenty-seven* bus today.' This is the *name* of the bus.

In some strange way these words seem to identify or describe the objects to which they refer. Similarly they seem to be used to describe the child himself. 'Yes, hasn't he grown, he's *four* now.'

Quite soon children learn to recite these words in a particular order—
'One, two, three, four, five, six'—and so on.

This is a satisfactory activity in that it seems to delight the adults!

b. *Folk tale and nursery rhyme*

As soon as children are old enough to enjoy traditional stories and
nursery rhymes these words appear again, this time involved in fantasy,
embodied in the world of nonsense, wonder and magic.

Some words appear regularly, e.g. *three* and *seven*.

> The three little pigs.
> The three billy goats gruff.
> The three sillies.
>
> The wolf and the seven little kids.
> Snow White and the seven dwarfs.

The sequence of number words appears in rhymes.

> One, two, three, four, five,
> Once I caught a fish alive.
> Six, seven, eight, nine, ten,
> Then I let it go again.
>
> Two, four, six, eight,
> Mary at the cottage gate,
> Eating cherries off a plate,
> Two, four, six, eight.
>
> One, two, buckle my shoe,
> Three, four, knock at the door,
> Five, six, pick up sticks,
> Seven, eight, lay them straight,
> Nine, ten, a big fat hen.

There seems to be very little difficulty concerning this aspect of
vocabulary growth. These number words arise naturally and in a variety
of contexts.

We are, however, a long way from establishing a notion of number,
and thereby making these words meaningful.

c. *Number symbols*

Some children will be able to identify the symbol on the front door
of their home at a very early age. Home is very important to a young
child, and this symbol on the front gate identifies this place as 'mine.'

If the symbol is a simple shape such as a seven the young child may even be able to reproduce it.

7

Obviously the child who lives at number five hundred and sixty-two will have far more difficulty both in remembering the sounds that make up the words and identifying the complex sequence of shapes which form the symbol.

562

Number symbols, or numerals, are all around us and it would be a mistake to suppose that children first meet them in school. It would also be a mistake to suppose that they are as yet meaningful to the child in a mathematical sense. Essentially they are concerned with *naming and belonging*.

Some other examples of situations in which children meet number symbols early on:

> Birthday cards
> Car numbers
> Buses
> Telephones
> Shops—price tickets.

Summary

In this chapter we have been concerned with the variety of experiences a child might encounter before he comes to school. His intellectual growth and development will largely depend upon three factors:

1. The quality and variety of the experience.

2. The availability of an understanding adult with whom to talk.

3. The quality of the language used, for this will influence and even determine the growth of the child's vocabulary, and his ability to use language with ease, flexibility and fluency.

The background of experience of the child determines the starting point when he comes to school. If he has not been fortunate enough to have enjoyed a rich and varied set of activities in these early years— if he has not been able to discuss these with someone who uses language with flexibility and imagination, then these opportunities must be made available in school as a first priority, for on such a foundation does his future development depend.

* * *

1 Pre-school experience

From the age of only a few months babies begin to explore the world about themselves—they splash and play in their bath water, given a chance they play with their food and drink, and taste or bang everything within reach.

From this natural curiosity and desire to explore and discover on the sensory level, the child will gradually gain various experiences of spatial relationships although, until he enters school, these will probably not have been consciously put in his way, or enlarged upon.

Slowly, from everyday life situations, the child will build up a vocabulary to describe these physical experiences. The very common words 'big' and 'little' will be combined with others to give some idea of amount, e.g. big lot of water, little bit of cake. Mother will say 'careful with the cup—it's very full.'

However, when the child uses and imitates words during these early years he does not necessarily understand what he is saying. For example, so many words descriptive of amount, size and place are relative to the adult but to the child this relative use of big, little, wide, long, high, can be confusing. Often the words will be used more in the nature of a *name* —the *tall* cupboard, the *high* chair. . . .

The fact that language is learned by imitation tends to cause confusion in a young child's mind. Returning to the frequently used 'big' and 'little,' the child often describes his environment with these:

> Daddy is big, Mummy is big.
> The house we live in is big.
> The stools in our kitchen are big.
> I am little.

These are straightforward ideas in that the people and objects concerned *are* all big in relation to the child himself, who after all is the central character in his own life during these early years. However, at the same time the child hears:

> You have eaten a big dinner.
> The baby is growing big.
> What a big bruise on your knee!

The eventual arrangement the child makes in his mind about these two sets of statements is going to determine whether he understands that the words 'big' and 'little' are used *relatively* and are not absolutes.

The same idea of the relative use of words will apply to the whole range of language which has been referred to in the past as *'number* vocabulary'—although it has not been, and is not, concerned *only* with number —many, few, most, least, high, low, narrow, wide, deep, shallow, tall, short, etc. When the child comes to school our aim should be to give as many and as varied experiences as possible so that the child realises that all these words describe *relative* size, quantity, proportion and place.

We have to accept that a statement such as 'the puppy is smaller than I am because it is little' is not wrong but is a stage of thinking: the idea of relative size and command and control of language have not yet become aligned. A more advanced stage is this: 'The classroom is wider than me because if I stretch my hands, I cannot reach the walls.' However, it would not usually be reached in the child's development before entry into school, although the experiences given in the home environment and the innate ability of the child will eventually decide where the starting point for the teacher will be.

2 Background to activities

As this guide deals with the beginnings of 'environmental mathematics,' it will of necessity deal with situations found more often at the infant stage than at later stages of the child's school life. However, if a child has had very little experience with a particular material the play and free experiment stage will have to be experienced sooner or later.

At five this may take several months but at the age of eight it may take only days. The activities covered are those most often found in schools, but it is hoped that the teacher will be able to apply the same approach to other situations which are not dealt with in this volume. Many of these activities were provided in the first instance to give very young children a rich and stimulating environment in which they could develop socially, emotionally, physically and intellectually. Because the *primary* motive was not intellectual the attitude still prevails—'as children grow older they do not need to play'—but many teachers have realised through their own experience that *more* learning and indeed more enjoyable learning can be gained by working through the interests of children and many of these interests do, in fact, arise during play.

With many activities during the early stages a complete year, or even two, of free play is desirable with as much variety of equipment as possible within the basic activity. This is necessary because, although a child may be developing well in one direction, in another there may be difficulties—some highly intelligent children are not socially adjusted, other slower children can mix well and find friends but need much more practical experience through which to learn. Through the activities children are gaining physical skills—the ability to use hand and fingers with control and to co-ordinate sight and touch with thought and speech.

They need to be able to pour water without spilling it, to build and balance bricks easily, to fit shapes together.

The seeming misuse of material may be due to physical control but is more often the result of an emotional problem. The child who throws sand, who turns the sand tray into a morass, who squirts water over everyone, who delights in destroying other children's models and buildings, who mixes up shop and home equipment, is often responsible for these activities being denied to other children on the grounds that 'they get nothing from them, they just mess about.' But many children have no need to 'play out' difficulties and, given a challenging environment and situations carefully structured by the teacher, they will begin to experiment and discover on their own initiative. Unfortunately, we often provide basic activities with a set of minimum equipment and then leave them as places where most children will play for weeks and even months with no progression taking place either in the form of the play or in the use of the intellect.

To get the maximum amount of satisfaction and learning out of the classroom, each activity needs its range of stimuli varied and extended regularly.

3 Creative work

a Sand play

Ideally children should have access to trays of sand, both coarse and silver, wet and dray. In practice, however, there is rarely enough room for this.

Each class could, however, have a large tray of coarse sand, sometimes allowed to become completely dry so that some experience will be gained of the properties of the wet and dry material. On the other hand, an old water tray, zinc bath or wooden tray (perhaps 18 in by 24 in) which would fit on a table and which could be shared between classes, could be used for silver sand.

Buckets, tins, plastic cups, mugs, beakers, washing-up liquid containers cut open in various ways,

spades, rakes, ladles, spoons, sieves of all shapes and sizes can be provided. When sand is being used dry, funnels may help the children to pour, as do containers with lips and handles.

Vocabulary and points to bring out of the play

One vocabulary will be concerned with the shape and size of the containers and the various relationships between them; another will be concerned with the sand itself.

i Containers

Wide, narrow, thin, thick, tall, short, deep, shallow, round (later *circular, curved*), *flat, straight, how many, how few, full, empty.* Children will undoubtedly use *big, bigger, biggest, bigger than, small, smaller than, smallest,* but the teacher should encourage them to explain what they mean: for example, on a particular occasion when the child says 'bigger' he may mean 'holds more than,' 'weighs more than' or even possibly 'is longer than.'

The children may be led to notice the differences and similarities between the look of a container and the shape 'inside.' For example, a round tin will make a round sand pie. Young children often make symmetrical patterns with sand pies, and although no observations may come from the children at this stage, it is useful for the teacher to have a knowledge of symmetry when patterns are being made in the sand and a variety of differently shaped containers are being used.

ii The sand

How much, how much more, how much less, all leading to the use of the word 'amount' (volume of sand).

Mathematical and scientific discoveries cannot be separated. Where does the water go when the sand dries out? Why does silver sand run more freely than coarse? Why does dry sand run smoothly while wet sand doesn't? Why won't dry sand make castles and models? Where does sand come from? These and many other questions will arise in talk with young children playing at the sand tray. Investigation of such problems will almost certainly involve some mathematics.

The frequent complaint—'there isn't enough sand'—can lead to discussion about the situation, that is, there could be more sand added, there could be a smaller share for each child, or there could be fewer children playing with the existing quantity.

While the children are playing, the teacher will be able to observe them matching, sorting and counting in many situations. . . . From the very beginnings of play with sand and buckets and tins, children are having the experience of filling three-dimensional space, leading eventually to the concept of volume . . .

A pair of scales will give children extra opportunities for discovery.

A crude balance made by the teacher would be sensitive enough for this purpose; indeed, sand might well damage new and expensive apparatus. Teachers will probably find that taking balances to the sand,

rather than sand to the weighing table, will be a more practical proposition, especially with younger children.

After considerable free play a point to bring out is the comparison
of size between *two* containers—which holds the more sand? Even at
an early stage the children can be asked to guess or *estimate* the answer
before discovering for themselves. Some children seem to find the comparison easier by filling the containers with spoonfuls of sand and comparing the numbers needed rather than pouring from one to the other,
but this may be the result of insufficient experience of matching and
comparison. Results can be recorded as shown on the following pages.

Children who have had much experience of filling containers by various means (cups, spoons, scoops, shovels full) might suggest weighing
the sand in each container as a quicker method of finding which contains the more. This will lead to extra vocabulary: *heavy, light*. A child
of seven was able to transfer his experiences of sand play to a problem
about the size of two tins. He was asked which of the two held more
and replied that he thought the blue: in fact he thought 'it was about
twice as big as the green.' When asked how he could find out if he were
right, he said 'I could fill the tins with sand and then weigh the sand.'

Three or four boxes of various shapes and sizes, a spoon or some
scales, and a tray of silver sand will provide much thought and experiment for children at later stages of sand play.

If the children are able to write with some ease, they can record their
findings in words.

Even at this stage children may discover that two containers of different shapes will hold the same quantity of sand—an important experience leading towards the concept of invariance of volume. If the children are on the way towards establishing the concept, they will be able
to answer the question 'If the two boxes hold the same amount of sand,
what can you say about the *amount of space* inside each of them?'

If a child does not understand this question, then much more experience of filling and emptying of containers is necessary, not only with
sand but in other ways to be outlined in subsequent sections of this
guide. Also it will be necessary to find time to talk about what the
children are doing as they play, to make sure, for instance, that they
understand what we mean by the *size and shape* of a container, and
what we mean by its capacity: the amount of space inside it.

Of course, the teacher wishing the children to make discoveries will
see to it that there really are some tins in the sand tray which, although
of different shape, do hold just about the same amount; that is, the
situation will be structured in order to enable the children to discover
something. The teacher's observation, insight and skill will play an important part in the children's success, and must continually be used in
conjunction with provision of material.

b Water play

In this activity there are often trays containing a collection of boats or just a set of standard measures. The most valuable equipment is a complete range between these two extremes—various containers of all shapes and sizes, plastic and rubber tubing, sieves, colanders and strainers, jugs, funnels, small corks and sponges, very large stones and small pieces of wood.

It can be seen by the above list of possible equipment (which is by no means exhaustive) that only a selection can be put out at any one time; therefore changes should be made, but not complete replacements.

There will nearly always be at least one child who is needing to play on the sensory or emotional level and has not reached the stage for intellectual discovery. Other children may occasionally regress for some reason and return to more immature stages, so provision must continue to be made for this. Children like variety within an activity; the addition of non-toxic detergent, or alternatively dye or paint in small amounts, to the water will stimulate any flagging interest in the water tray.

The children will be filling containers, as with sand, and from a carefully structured set of equipment will be gaining experiences of volume and capacity. More can be *seen* if some of the items are made of transparent material—for very young children glass is not always advisable (although the skill of manipulating wet and slippery surfaces has to be learned through experience). Water is often regarded as the 'messiest' basic activity with children's clothing becoming soaked and the floor flooded. Care therefore must be taken in:

i protecting and covering the children as much as possible and rolling up sleeves;

ii limiting the number of children playing at a tray—if a zinc bath is used there is even more chance of getting wet; baths and high sinks usually limit the number of young children to two,

iii ensuring that equipment is suitable for a particular group of children, e.g. most 7-year-olds find difficulty in lifting and pouring a gallon of water; young children find a short length of tubing easier to cope with than a long piece; too large a sieve or colander can cause accidents if given too soon.

Teachers will find that the *gradual* introduction of equipment needing a greater degree of physical skill will be most satisfactory.

As with all children's play there will be many opportunities at the water tray to count, match and sort. It is useful sometimes to suggest a change of equipment from water to sand tray, and vice-versa, so that children can find out for themselves why certain items (funnels, tubing, scoops, sieves) are used with one material and not with another. This, of course, would be at a later stage, as 5-year-olds will readily try to play with sand and *anything*.

Vocabulary and points to bring out

All the language descriptive of shape and size of container noted in the last section on sand can be applied to play in this activity.

The characteristics of liquids which are within a child's own experience may be discussed: how a liquid has to be contained in *something*, what happens when a liquid is spilled, poured, heated, frozen, etc., how it takes the shape of the vessel used, how water can be made into a jet, a spray, or a fountain. A 5-year-old said 'If *I* get in my *baby's* bath the water comes over the top.' This was when she was just standing by the water tray. The children's natural observations will often begin a whole train of experiment, discovery and discussion.

Teachers will find that when water is being used, the children will need some help at first to decide on what they really mean by 'full,' and much practice is needed to gain the physical skill by which a young child can obtain the required amount of liquid. Discussion about how milk, squash and lemonade bottles are 'filled' and the amount of space left at the top, will help the children to realise from the very beginning the approximate nature of measurement. Talk about how liquids are measured in everyday situations (e.g. petrol, paraffin, drinks of various kinds, medicines), will provide starting points for play and experiment. The children will be using the language of measurement in their play long before they understand the implications of the words they are using. At 5 and 6 children will refer to *any* quantity of water during their play as being 'a pint' or 'a gallon'; but there is a danger at this stage in attempting to *teach* standard measurement just because children are heard to be using words wrongly.

From the point of view of mathematical concepts water play is important in establishing a basis of experiences which will lead to the eventual and true understanding of volume and capacity. The children will be filling three-dimensional space and discovering relationships between containers.

This is the work of a 6-year-old:

> I pored the water out of the jug into the botall and I fond one that fitted but I could not finde eny mor.

It is interesting to note that this child, *at this stage,* does not draw any conclusions from her discovery. It is an experience, however, which will go towards her later attainment of the concept of invariance of volume.

The next discovery is *reversibility*. If water from a full jug is poured (carefully) into another container, the process is reversible: that is, the water can be poured back again and the jug will again be full. This is a large step towards understanding of the *invariance of mass;* that is, appreciating that no matter how the water (or other incompressible material) is moved about, the amount of it remains constant.

c Picture, pattern and model making

This section refers to painting, drawing, woodwork, the making of collages, the construction of models in all media: paper, clay, plasticine, dough, junk, wire, papier-mâché.

Although many teachers may prefer to keep these activities for purely creative purposes, much incidental mathematical experience may arise from them. The *language* used while engaged on a particular piece of work, and the children's and teacher's observations on various aspects, will help to heighten the awareness of shape, pattern and size in the environment.

These activities fall roughly into two categories:

1 The painting and drawing of pictures and patterns, when children are covering area;

2 Model making, when children are working in three dimensions (for young children, collages are another form of picture making).

Before these activities are engaged upon, tables are frequently protected with plastic cloths or newspaper, and this is also an experience of covering a surface.

i Picture and pattern making

Experiences which may be gained in this activity are those concerned with area, space, length and measurement.

In making pictures and patterns with paint, crayon, charcoal, chalk, gummed paper, pieces of material, etc., children are covering a flat surface, one of the few times when this arises naturally in the young child's school environment.

Young children enjoy 'printing' patterns in various ways: first with their hands, then with small sponges or cut potatoes, and later making their own felt patterns for printing. Their first prints are usually random in character, with no order about them, but occasionally a child will at once produce a highly symmetrical pattern.

When children have had plenty of experience of printing on plain paper, the shape of the paper can be varied; a square or a circle may provide an interesting stimulus. Also the provision of paper with an existing pattern may produce unusual results; checked or striped wallpaper can be used if not of the washable kind.

When children are doing creative work (disregarding all 'laws' of proportion and perspective) it would be ludicrous to intervene on mathematical grounds.

Nevertheless in design work (leading to patterns for textiles, wallpaper, etc.) there is plenty of inherent mathematics which should be exploited. Economy in cutting from a sheet of paper, foil, material, felt, etc., is valuable experience of area and spatial relationships. Young children find difficulty in doing this—they will either cut from one edge or try to cut the shape they require from the centre of a sheet of paper.

Practice in, and experience of, arranging shapes in a limited area is gained when working with gummed paper, felt or material. Length and measurement in their simplest forms, that is, comparison and matching, are used by the children to make their pictures and collages from all these materials.

The symmetrical properties of the children's work may be discussed, as from an early age some children produce stylised and formal patterns quite nautrally which are highly symmetric in character. This is the prelude to much significant mathematics . . .

Counting, comparison and matching often arise in the children's work, and the whole vocabulary descriptive of shape and size is continually being used. One problem of language may be noted here—children *without* experience of balancing and weighing may think that the words 'light' and 'lighter than' refer exclusively to *colour,* so that when discussing shade of colour, opportunity might be taken to discover the extent of the children's understanding of the language they are using.

ii Model making

This activity involves experiences of volume, space, substance, length, and less frequently, area and weight.

While making models children are concerned with the fitting together of pieces of card, wood, junk material, etc. into three-dimensional shapes. Apart from gaining practice in the quite difficult physical skills needed to cut various materials and fix them together, children may also discover facts about shapes. They find that it is easier to stick two rectangular boxes together than it is to stick a rectangular box to the curved surface of a cylinder or sphere. In doing this they are experiencing the nature of flat and curved surfaces. They find that it is difficult to cover the head or face of the doll that they have made, but easier to cover its arms and legs; when fixing wheels to a car or lorry they find that at any rate each pair of wheels must match in size to ensure free running, and that to make the wheel turn properly they need to put the 'axle' (nail or paper fastener) through the centre; they find that a large and heavy box is difficult to stick *on top of* a small, light one, but that the other way round, the task is simpler.

Measuring girth, circumference, length, width, height of cartons or containers by matching lengths of string will make it easier for a young child to cover them with another material, for example, when he wishes to cover the walls of a doll's house or the cylindrical part of a rocket.

With plenty of this type of experience children's powers of estimation will improve. The children will discover relationships between the sizes of boxes, pieces of wood and card, and will find that when another large thing is needed, sometimes two smaller ones will fit instead.

When children are using clay, plasticine and dough mixture (flour, water, salt) they are gaining experience of a 'continuous' solid quantity. If using a limited amount of these materials the children will often 'share out' between themselves. As with sand, they will say that there is not enough, and the possibilities of less clay for one child, more clay being brought to the table, or of fewer children using it, are all mathematical solutions. While using their own individual amount of material the children find that they can make a greater number of small things, a lesser number of larger things or indeed just one really large model. This again is an experience of quantity and also an experience leading to 'conservation of volume' because although clay, dough, and Plasticine are all slightly compressible, the 'amount' that a child is using, without any being added or any being taken away, remains practically the same.

Vocabulary

'Shape and size' vocabulary will be used during these creative activities, but in addition the nature and texture of materials will be observed —whether they are *hard, soft, smooth, rough, spiky, tough* or easy to cut or tear. Other words defining position in space, or of one object in relationship to another are frequently used—*up, down, across, on top of, underneath* (later *over* and *under*), *in front of, behind, next to* (later *left* and *right*). . . .

f Bricks and constructional play

When there is a plentiful supply of bricks and boxes of all shapes and sizes, young children's imaginative play is enriched and much mathematical experience may be gained.

i Very large building

Once imaginative play has begun to develop in a young child there is a desire to play *inside* a house, a boat, an aeroplane, or a car of his own making. If nothing else is available he will use a table or a chair for his make-believe indoors, or a corner of a garden or shed outside. If space is available in a hall, corridor, porch or playground adjacent to a classroom it is most desirable to provide a selection of large constructional apparatus in school.

Tea chests, fruit crates, boxes, barrels, an old table with legs sawn down, planks, boards, tyres, ropes, heavy cardboard rolls, and interesting and stimulating odds and ends such as an old steering wheel, pair of handle-bars, straps, loudspeakers, handles, switches, etc.; all such things will give children an opportunity to build models on a large scale.

ii Building on floor or table

Even if facilities do not allow for construction of models large enough to play *in,* then smaller bricks can be provided, which do not take up so much storage space and which can be used on a fairly small patch of floor (under the teacher's table?) or even on table tops; but where possible these would be in addition to or in conjunction with the materials of (i). The smaller bricks can also be made more interesting by providing smaller boxes, off-cuts of wood, hardboard, chip-board, and polystyrene. They will be used for the building of harbours, airfields, docks, streets, forts, castles, farms, zoos, towns, markets, bus stations, railways, etc.

Road strips which children can lay out to form routes, tracks and circuits are of value as the problems they set are mathematical (fitting together shapes, angles, etc.). This of course also applies to railway tracks and lines.

iii Construction on tables

Construction on a still smaller scale can be carried out by means of the many sets and kits on the market, made of plastic, wood, or metal. These can be stored in a cupboard and easily used on a table. They are, however, expensive in relation to the other means of building and more 'structured' as they suggest, or even presuppose, certain ideas and methods of construction. They are also inclined to include small pieces, which are difficult to manipulate and easy to lose for younger children.

iv Tiles

Tiles of all shapes and sizes may be provided for use, either separately or with bricks, so that the children make floors for their models, or distinguish various parts of their building, e.g. land from sea, one field from another, paths, roads.

Mathematical ideas involved in brick play

Children will have experience of sharing, counting, comparison and matching as they play, and occasionally the teacher may draw attention to this as she talks with them.

They are continually experiencing the putting together of three-dimensional shapes, finding which surfaces fit well together, which bricks make the best walls or seats, which surface balances best; they are frequently *enclosing area* in their play, and this together with discussion of the total area of the floor of the room, corridor or hall may help children to appreciate the adult concept of area. At first perhaps it might be referred to as 'floor space,' as opposed to the 'air space' taken up by an object which is its volume.

A 6-year-old was asked about the submarine he had made. He said it was for one boy inside and one on top. When asked how he could make the inside large enough for the two boys, he immediately suggested extending the length of the model by adding one more box to each side.

The children will also gain experience of length in their constructive play, and this can be linked with other measuring work. Some boys, just 7 years old, estimated correctly that their boat was about three yards long. Further discussion could have taken place about the length in relation to their own height.

The packing away of equipment will afford opportunity of making the best use of a limited space. Many teachers know how often young children fail to pack or stack equipment successfully; they will say that there is not enough room in a certain box or a certain place and with the method they have employed, there is not. But with practice and experience they learn how to use the available space efficiently, and how individual pieces will fit on to, beside, or inside each other.

Vocabulary

This describes space, shape and size. The words *big, bigger than, small,* must be questioned and as soon as possible replaced by more meaningful statements about length, breadth, width, depth, height, space occupied or weight of objects under discussion. If a child is asked in what way a particular brick is bigger than another, he will have to think, to find words to describe his thoughts. If the necessary vocabulary is not within his experience, if meanings are confused or understanding not clear, then a chance is given for the child to learn and the teacher to discover more about the child's ability.

A teacher watched two 5-year-olds trying to decide the bigger of two model cars. The dimensions of each were so similar that eventually they balanced one against the other to discover, by weight, which was the 'larger.'

When describing the shape of bricks, boxes, boards, etc., only the simpler and more common names need be used with young children. However, it is within their power to understand that a solid shape has *faces,* because the word 'face' is already in their vocabulary, and that faces are bounded by *edges;* too often the word 'side' is used colloquially for both face and edge. Bricks with square faces may soon be given the name *cubes,* but others can continue to be referred to as rectangular, triangular or circular throughout the infant school, unless a great interest in shape arises, when the children will force the pace and show their readiness for more knowledge. Before this, the words *surface, flat, straight, round, curved, corner* may be introduced, used and discussed. The symmetry of the various shapes can be discussed, as also can the symmetry of the patterns and models that are made.

3. Teaching Basic Mathematical Concepts

In this selection, a gifted teacher teaching a class of young deaf children explains how she plans her day so as to use her classroom environment to encourage mathematical learning. As Edith Biggs writes in her introduction to the narrative, the teacher "is constantly on the watch for opportunities which will give the children mathematical experiences," and "she follows these up carefully to ensure that the children acquire basic knowledge in number, measurement and shape." The teacher's approach is every bit as relevant to normal as to handicapped children; indeed, were it not for the mention of the children's handicap, the reader would have no way of knowing that the children being described lack any faculty.

The class of four- to five-year-olds with which this work was carried out was an unusually oral and bright group of deaf children. The children came to me with plenty of free-play experience with all kinds of material, including simple sorting for colours, shape, size, etc. They could also count to ten fluently, but they could only *use* numbers up to five or six, as one would expect.

At first, I tried talking to the children in ones or twos as they played, but I found this was not very satisfactory. The children disliked having to stop for a long time in the middle of their play for me to try to get something across to them. I found I was having to repeat myself up to half-a-dozen times as I moved amongst the children. Gathering the class together in an informal group for talks—perhaps on the floor—worked much better. Then, next day, a short comment as the child played, helped the play to be more meaningful and purposeful. In these group talks, I frequently found I had to *tell* them something basic at first, or demonstrate something new and *then* let things develop.

I have grouped the work under specific headings, but of course, it was intermingled throughout the year. Certain topics followed each other in a logical sequence. We began by learning the words 'same' and 'different,' as I felt these would be the most immediately useful. With these we could compare and comment on practically everything around us; and this really pleased the children. Then we tried the words 'a few,' 'a lot,' and 'nothing,' learning them as a group, using all sorts of material. For example, I put my hands into a box of gravel, and scooped up as much as I could. Then I let it fall slowly on to a sheet of paper and said, 'This is a lot.' After they had all looked and repeated, I poured it back into the box and said, 'Now there is nothing.' Then all the children each had a turn. Similarly we tackled the word 'few,' and I found they often 'played out' these group talks next day during free play. We went on to play with other materials—Smarties, other small sweets, sand, acorns, and so on. Then, instead of emptying the material back each time, I said, 'Can you make this few into a lot?' or 'Can you make this lot into a few?' One very young child, under four years old, at first did not know how to reduce a lot into a few, and kept adding more in the hope that the pile would disappear. All the children loved me to ask them to add or to leave nothing. They seemed fascinated by the empty table. Soon, the work became more individual, and we began to use specific numbers of soldiers, rabbits, cars, and other subjects. For example—'Nicola, put out four soldiers . . . Add two more . . . How many altogether? . . . Now take three away . . . How many are left? . . . Well, can you make that into five soldiers? . . . Now, can you leave only one soldier?' (and so on). In time the children became very competent and free with this work.

At the beginning of the morning, we 'marked the register,' using a flannelgraph and felt figures. The blue figures were for the boys, and the red figures for the girls. At first we used a 'one to one' relationship. Picking up a blue one, I would say, 'Peter came to school'—and so on. Then—'But Paul stopped at home'—and so on. Then we counted how many girls and how many boys had come to school and wrote it on the blackboard. I linked the two numbers together. Then we counted how many children there were altogether, and put up the correct felt number on the flannelgraph. At first I used the felt figures myself, and the children sat round and watched. Then they asked to do it themselves, and took over. As time went by, they changed from using names, and, quite rapidly, counted how many boys and how many girls were present, and put up the appropriate numbers of felt figures—boys grouped together, and girls likewise. Then one day I put two of the red figures on one side of the blue ones, and two on the other side, and they were lost! They could only see two girls, and two girls—they could not see four any more! But not for long—the children grew so competent that, knowing there were nine in the class at the time, they knew that there must be three at home if six were in school. This work lasted from about January to May.

We did a lot of number work at milk time—in a group. At first we counted the number of children and the number of bottles, having first checked—'one for Andrew,' 'one for Peter,' etc. We noted that the number was the same. Over the weeks they became aware that these numbers *must* be the same, or there would not be one each. Then I tried taking all the tops off, and hiding them in my hand, asked how many they thought there would be. They had no idea! They were quite intrigued with this relationship between the number of children, bottles, tops and straws—if we were having one each. Then, one day, one of the children separated the bottles of milk on the tray into those for the boys, and those for the girls. This opened the way for more opportunities of addition and subtraction. There was always much amusement if the child giving out the milk held up the last bottle and looked perplexed, wondering whose it was. The children also took turns in putting two straws into each bottle, and it was interesting to see how the quicker ones, if given five or seven straws, could quickly sort them out into two, two, and then an extra one to make up another two. The very slow child always put the straws in one at a time—he did not pick up two of anything until the week before the summer holidays.

At lunch time we all have lunch together in the classroom. Mac, my nursery assistant, and I sit at opposite ends, and the children sit on each side of the table. The length of the dining table depends on how many children are in the class—we simply join enough individual tables together. The children were surprised to find there was a *reason* why I asked them to pass the salt to Mac. It never occurred to them that it was because of the length of the table. They were interested to note how we could pass the salt to each other quite easily if the table was short. As the children were seated down each side, we counted the number of children down one side, and then I counted out the appropriate number of plates, and likewise for the other side. We wrote the two results on the blackboard sometimes, piled the plates together and counted the result; and wrote that on the blackboard. Sometimes—under my very close supervision—I let the children hold the pile of plates to feel how heavy they were. The children were encouraged to ask for specific amounts of food—'a lot,' 'large,' 'small,' even 'very small,' 'medium' and so on. We used numbers of spoonfuls for milk puddings —four or five spoonfuls. Those who loved milk pudding knew only too well that five was more than four, and that six was even greater!

One day I heard that Ruth had been going up a shallow flight of stairs in twos saying 'two, four, six'—so we all went over to the hostel to this shallow flight, with large number cards, one to ten, and laid them on the stairs, one on each stair, with the numbers turned inwards for easy reading and counting. First, we took turns walking up, counting as we went, and then back down again. This was their first introduction to counting from ten down to one. Then we walked up the stairs, two-at-a-time, first using the odd numbers, and then the even numbers. From then on the children really understood about alternate ones out. Back in class we had follow-up games—count-downs for rockets; a sort of 'musical chairs' in which they could only sit on chairs marked with even numbers—or, sometimes, odd numbers—when the drum beat stopped; we also threw numbers on the floor, putting a square around all the odd numbers, and a circle around all the even numbers, to show the pattern of alternation; then we hopped or jumped onto odd or even numbers, saying them as we went.

Before the year ended, I tried a piece of written work on the board. Peter was with me and was quite familiar—from previous work—with the words 'Add one more.' I wrote this on the board and we started, using bricks. Half-way through, Peter suddenly realized what was happening, dropped the bricks, took the chalk out of my hand, and wrote up the rest himself.

Time

We have a large jig-saw clock; one piece holds the central hands, and there are twelve more pieces, one for each number. This was a particularly favourite toy—I think they were fascinated by the idea of the numbers going round—and playing with it taught them the clockwise direction of numbers. Using this, and the school clock, we would talk about 'nearly lunch time—we must wash' and then 'lunch time' and so on. From that they learnt approximate time. This was enough I thought. We also talked about the movement of the days of the week. I made a chart naming each day. Beside each name was a little picture illustrating something special we did on that day, for example, Monday—came to school; Thursday—dancing; Friday—go home; Saturday and Sunday —stop at home. We had a movable pointer which could be moved from Monday downward. Saturday and Sunday were grouped together, and then the pointer moved to the top again. It was a great help to the young boarders to see 'home' day coming nearer and nearer. We could work out—'three more days to going home' then 'two more' . . . and so on.

Weighing

Before we started weighing, I let the children play freely with the balance for a few days. I watched with some amusement as they put something on one side and then wondered why the balance became crooked. They often tried to correct this by straightening the top bar with their hands, and then looked puzzled when they took their hands away and the balance went back to a lopsided position!

Then I gathered the group around me and produced the balance, and a carefully selected number of toys and materials, all of which were either very heavy or very light. First, I picked out half a brick, weighed it in my hand, and said, 'This is heavy.' I passed it round the group for them to feel the weight. Then we put it on one side of the balance to watch the reaction to something heavy. Peter suddenly stood up and imitated the action of the balance. I was delighted! Then we all took turns, so that the children could really understand what was happening when we weighed something, and it was surprising how many children raised the heavy object on high, at first! I drew two circles on the floor and into one we put this heavy object. Thus, into the circles we sorted all the heavy and light objects, after testing. We finished up by counting how many of the things we had weighed were heavy, or light. The children themselves noted and imitated how a pan only moved downward slightly when the toy was light. Then we went on to compare *two* things —perhaps a small piece of metal and a large chunk of polystyrene. At first, I always made sure there was a definite difference. We hand-weighed first—no comment from me—and then I invited *them* to say which they thought was heavy, and which was light. When we had all offered an opinion, we tried weighing them in the balance to check. I found that this young age group did not like a lot of small objects— they preferred a single 'hand-sized' toy or familiar substance. At first, I was able to fool them with a large piece of sponge or polystyrene, but not for long. They became quite intrigued with these substances—so much size, and so little weight. After plenty of experience of differences of weight, I then offered them, one day, two like objects of similar weight. They did not know what to say about them, and looked quite startled when they balanced. Towards the end of the year we went on to small numbers of objects, such as cotton reels. If I put three cotton reels on one side, could they say how many would be needed on the other side to balance them? No, they couldn't! They all looked quite perplexed, and it took some time before they really understood. We only used numbers of reels or bricks up to five. I tried going further— comparing numbers of unlike objects—cotton reels with bricks, or large shells with 'conkers' (horse chestnuts), and entered the results; but only one six-year-old really understood this enough to want to do it on her own during free play. The others enjoyed doing it in the group with my help.

Money

The children bring sixpence for the school fund on Monday. First, we learned the names of the coins, and pointed out the appropriate number on the wall. After some time, I was delighted to note a quibble creeping in—that I should call the small one 6d, and a much larger one only 1d. Then Andrew arrived one day with two 3d pieces—and 'no sixpence!' I tried to show that this was just the same and we wrote it on the blackboard. Only the day before, there had been three boys and three girls in class, and Ruth looked quite startled as the connexion between the money sum and the number sum became apparent. Thereafter, each Monday we put out the money in a row, and noticed all the different ways of making 6d. They had to take my word for it, as their adding was not fluent enough; but they were most impressed and interested— and it did make a start. I also let them write the 6d in my little book each week. Before the year ended we also played a little 'shop' with pennies only, up to 6d, and at least they learned to give me the right number of pennies I asked for, and not just to hand them all over for me to take out what was necessary.

Capacity

At first, I could find no meaningful lead-in, and then a set of standard-sized polythene milk bottles arrived. I realized that in their daily bottle of milk I had a set amount, with which they were all familiar. Just before milk time—so that the milk need not linger in any other container—I brought out the quart, pint, half-pint and one-third-pint bottles. I put them in a row, then produced their bottles of milk. We decided which polythene bottle was the same as their own. I poured a bottle of milk into this one-third-pint bottle, and we all agreed that it was indeed the same. We then looked at the half-pint bottle—I asked where they thought the milk would come up to, and they said, 'the top,' just as it had for the one-third pint. They were all surprised when it did not! Immediately, they wanted me to try the pint and quart bottles—so we poured one bottle of milk into each and they were all most intrigued by the way the level of the milk dropped in each larger bottle. They asked if they could drink out of the new bottles; so I gave them straws, without comment, and we all had quite a bit of fun watching the child who had 'bagged' the quart bottle—his straw would not even reach the milk, and then dropped in! We continued this work until they had a good idea of where the known amount would 'come up to' in other vessels. Then we tried another idea—how many of our one-third pints would fit into the pint bottle, and then into the quart bottle. When we came to try the half-pint bottle, we learned the word 'half,' and I tried to show them how the half-pint bottle held one-and-a-half of their own bottles. Peter argued about this. He thought it ought to be two-and-a-half—he could see a half bottle of milk left, but I had opened two bottles! We learned the words 'full,' 'half,' and 'empty,' and went on to use all sorts of shapes in water play. They particularly enjoyed making

things half full. They wanted to go on to 'quarters' but I thought it
was too soon. When discussing the amount of custard in the jug at lunch
time we used 'a little bit,' 'half,' 'a lot' and 'full.' We also used a wide
variety of containers for free play and experiment with sand.

Length and Shapes

We learned the words 'long' and 'short' first, and discussed how these
were different from 'large' and 'small.' We examined all kinds of things
around the classroom and in the cupboards. We played with lengths of
ribbon, vinolay, string, cardboard, and so on. I would hold up two
pieces, and the children decided which was long and which short. Then,
I might move one piece up or down and ask again which was long and
which short. One or two made mistakes at first, but it did not take long
for them to realize that the length remained the same whichever way
I moved the pieces. Then I tried the same method using strips of the
same length. Funnily enough the 'sameness' of length, regardless of
position, took longer to acquire, but when they were sure that they
were still the same length, I varied the positions of the two strips even
further, and later used three and then four strips, all of the same length,
and in all positions. We would start with them all in a row, so that the
children could see that they *were* the same, and then they all took turns
in moving them around. One day, without comment, I moved the four
'same' strips into a square. They all looked quite interested, and we
learned the word 'square', which I drew and wrote on the blackboard.
Then I held up two long strips and two short strips, and we discussed
how many of each there were. I handed them to a child, and asked her
to make a shape. She immediately made a shape—and then looked
amazed and puzzled. We left her alone for a few minutes, and it did not
take her long to sort it out, and make an oblong. Before I could teach
the word, Peter jumped up, very excited, and said 'Five, no, no, wait a
minute'—and he counted round the oblong. 'One, two' (for the first
long side) 'three' (for the short side) 'four, five', and 'six'. He knew a
square had four sides, and this was his way of describing the new shape.
I was thrilled by the spontaneous effort. I introduced the new shape as
'oblong'—not 'rectangle' as that sounded too much like 'triangle,' which
I wanted to use later. We discussed the fact that it had two long and
two short sides. We examined objects around the room, and picked out
the long and short sides.

Later, we learned the words 'round,' 'triangle'—I simply handed
three strips of paper to a child and asked her to make a shape, and then
introduced the new word—and 'oval'—we used a hoop, slightly squashed
by each child in turn. Then with all these new words, and this new
knowledge, I brought out some boxes. We all examined these, and com-

mented on the various shapes that go to make up a box, for example, a Typhoo tea box has oblong and square sides. To my surprise they described a Vim tin as having two 'rounds' and an 'oblong' shape.

Then I brought out a great pile of boxes and put them in the middle of the floor. I drew a large square on the floor and asked them what it was. Then I drew a large 'round' in another corner; then, as I *started* to draw a triangle they all shouted 'triangle,' I realized that they must have some awareness of angles, for they knew it would not be an oblong. When I had drawn all the shapes, I let them sort the boxes into the various chalked shapes. They loved it. One child asked where a Typhoo tea box ought to go, as it had both square and oblong shapes. I asked her what she thought, and she decided 'oblong,' which it was, predominantly. Another child, with a very flat, squarish cigar tin, looked amazed when it fell open, and 'changed' to an oblong. We let him put it in with the other oblongs. At the end we were left with the large egg carton which had contained all the other boxes. Peter looked around and saw almost nothing in the oval section, so he put the egg carton there. I looked surprised, but Peter pointed out the large egg printed on the side; so we left it there! They loved this kind of sorting, and I was sorry there was not time to sort the same pile of boxes for colour and size.

Afterwards, each child cut up a box and pasted the pieces on a sheet of paper. Then we counted the number of pieces on each child's paper. They were quite surprised to find everyone had six. They also played with large wooden mosaic shapes. They knew that two triangles made a square, and two squares an oblong. They had noticed spaces were left if they used circles, so they were not keen about using these! One day, Ruth thrilled us all by making a square with strips, and then, as she played with some cardboard shapes, a thought suddenly occurred to her, and she tried filling the large square with small square shapes. Then she counted out to us that she had used nine. She was really finding out for herself.

Stories, Art, Dancing, Recipes

I found, as I went along, that the more I knew about the new trends in mathematics, the more I was able to *use* opportunities as they arose. For example, when I told the story of *The Three Bears* everything was drawn on the blackboard, and we discussed who would be likely to use the large bed, and so on, instead of me simply stating who had which. We also had models, and, to my delight, even my very slow child could match each to each correctly. We painted pictures, and all could paint the different sizes beautifully and freely. In free cut-out work all the children could cut out three different-sized bowls to put on the table.

In dancing we found many ways of imitating the three bears. We could crouch low to walk as a baby, medium high for mother, and tall for father. We could take tiny running steps for baby, normal walking steps for mother, and long, slow strides for father. After *Jack and the Beanstalk* I gave them long strips of paper, and we painted a long beanstalk. We painted other long and short things—trousers, socks, and so on; and we cut pictures out of magazines. We made four large wall-charts with the cut-out pictures for 'large,' 'small,' 'long' and 'short.' We made gingerbread from a recipe on the board, just using large or small spoonfuls of things, for example, half a packet of margarine. We rolled the gingerbread and cut out shapes from templates to make a gingerbread house. Peter pleased me by examining one of the templates and showing me how it was made up of a triangle and a square! This work was a little too long, but the children were pleased with the result. The children mostly by themselves, also made orange juice from a recipe on the blackboard, and very competently, too.

4. How to Equip the Math Area

There is no part of the curriculum in which an abundant supply of concrete materials is more important than in math, for in a literal sense, children learn math through their hands. In an open classroom, children typically are engaged in a wide variety of concrete mathematical activities: counting bottle caps, or acorns, or shells, or pieces of elbow macaroni; weighing all kinds of objects on a simple balance scale; telling time; measuring each other's height, or the perimeter of the classroom, or the size of the teacher's desk with the use of measuring sticks or pieces of string; comparing the volume of different-sized containers by pouring water or sand from one to the other; and so on.

As the two lists of equipment below imply, some of the most useful math materials are inexpensive or free, or can be made fairly easily even by a teacher with ten thumbs. As the Introduction to the EDC List points out, and as we have seen in the selections above, a good deal of a child's mathematical experiences will occur outside the math area itself, in the course of his activities with science, art, sand and water play, and so on. Before putting any material into the classroom, teachers need to understand at least some of the uses to which it can be put; as we have seen in Part Three, they need to be prepared, as well, for children's unfailing capacity to devise new uses.

Mathematics—Introduction

This list is a guide for materials which are useful in the area of Mathematics. It is to be used with discretion; if an article is listed as "essential" and you have no idea what it is then look for it in the catalogue; if you still have doubts about its usefulness then ask your advisors about it. Do not order equipment blind!

The first section of the list is a collection of items, both commercial and non-commercial, which we consider to be *essential* for a rich Mathematical environment. We consider these materials *basic* materials as they are open-ended in the ways they can be used and their uses can cover many areas of development.

Although we have labeled this section *essential,* when ordering the commercial materials listed, thought must be given to the allotment of your budget in relation to other areas in the classroom. It may not be possible or indeed necessary to order *all* the commercial articles listed here. We do, however, consider it possible *and* advisable to have most of the non-commercial articles available.

We have included a sample sheet showing how examples of different types of materials from the basic list can be used to cover many areas of development in Mathematics. We hope this will encourage you to look beyond the material to the uses it can be put to.

Much of the child's Math experience will occur outside the recognizable "Math Corner" and will come from activities labeled as "Art," "Science," "Sand & Water Play," etc. For this reason we may refer you to other parts of the materials list for some of the basic materials.

The later parts of this list are collections of most of the available materials which we consider either desirable or interesting (but not necessary) extensions of the basic materials. We suggest that with the construction materials you would be better off to order a large quantity of one type rather than one little set of each.

Omitted from the list are articles which we consider not desirable for this age-group, articles which are too expensive for what they add, and articles we consider poorly made or highly prone to breakages for other reasons.

From Education Development Center Follow Through Program, *Instructional Aids, Materials, and Supplies,* mimeographed (Newton, Mass.: Education Development Center, 1971). Reprinted by permission of Education Development Center, Inc.

	Discrimination Sorting & Ordering	Pattern Relations	Boundaries & Regions (Inside—Outside)	Measurement	Volume	Weight & Balance	Geometric Relations	Logical Relations	Number Work (Computation)	Symbolization (Representation)
1. Attribute Blocks	X	X	X				X	X	X	X
2. Chess & Checkers		X					X	X		
3. Tangrams	X	X	X	X			X			
4. Lego	X	X	X	X	X	X	X	X		X
5. Unifix Cubes	X	X	X	X	X	X		X	X	X
6. Canes, Doweling, Wood Slats	X	X	X	X		X	X		X	X
7. Miniatures—Cars, Animals, etc.	X	X	X	X	X	X		X	X	X
8. Stones, Shells, Spools, Bottle Caps, String, Yarn, etc.	X	X	X	X	X	X	X	X	X	X
9. Sugar Cubes, Beans, Macaroni	X	X	X	X	X	X	X	X	X	X
10. Calendars, Ads, Schedules, Newspapers	X			X					X	X
11. Geo Boards	X	X	X	X			X	X	X	X

Sample applications of some materials to the various areas of mathematical development.

MATHEMATICS—Basic Materials

ITEM	CATALOG REFERENCE	SUPPLIER	COST
Chess & Checkers set	buy locally or		
	163	Milton Bradley	$ 1.30
Unifix Cubes (order at least 3 sets) 10 ea. of 10 colors	102-U-08	REC	4.00
Geo-Squares (geoboards)	G-2	Scott Scientific	8.50/5
Colored Rubber Bands	buy locally or		
pkg. of 200+	BAND01	SEE	.35
10 or more pkgs.			.30 ea.
Beads and Laces	470F	Milton Bradley	6.50
Craft-Stix (popsicle sticks)		Constructive Playthings	1.20/1000
Tongue Depressors	92692	Hammett	2.75/500
Counting Sticks—assorted colors			
2″	64046	"	.60/100
4″	64048	"	.85/100
8″	64051	"	1.30/100
12″	64053	"	1.90/100
Tape Measures	"		
Yard Sticks	"		
Meter Sticks	"		
Canes, Doweling, Wood Slats	"		
Stickers—1″ square	"	(various colors)	
Graph Paper—8½″ x 11″			
1″ squares	12560	Hammett	2.70/ream
½″ squares	12551	"	2.70/ream
¼″ squares	12541	"	2.70/ream
Miniature toys by the bag airplanes, cars, animals, etc.	buy locally (usually available in large 5 & 10 or discount store)		
Straws and Pins	"		
Toothpicks	"		
String, Wire, Shoelaces	"		
Yarn, Ribbon, Cording, Felt, Scrap material	scrap from local companies		
Stones, Shells, Pine cones, Spools, Bottle caps, Buttons, Beads	collect with children's and parents' assistance		
Jars, Cans, Egg cartons, Boxes (all sizes and shapes), Cardboard	collect from parents		
Sugar cubes, beans, macaroni	buy locally		
Calendars, Train, Bus, and Plane schedules	collect locally		
T.V. Guides, Newspapers, Supermarket ads	collect locally		
Large sheets of masonite pegboard	buy locally		
Pegs	NN 115	Creative Playthings	.80/100
Golf tees	buy locally		
Pattern Blocks	PBCK01	SEE	10.75
Teacher's Guide for Pattern Blocks	17560	McGraw-Hill	2.64

MATHEMATICS—Basic Materials

ITEM	CATALOG REFERENCE	SUPPLIER	COST
Geo-Blocks	17523	"	32.50
Teacher's Guide for Geo-Blocks	17524	"	2.46
Attribute Games (ESS)	AGCK00	SEE	8.85
Teacher's Guide for Attribute Games	18479	McGraw-Hill	4.86
Attribute Games with guide	AGCKTG	SEE	12.95
One of these, or one of each type:			
⌐Dienes Logical Blocks (4 × 3 × 2 × 2 = 48 blocks)			
large plastic set	Z 80007	Herder & Herder	19.50
medium wood set	Z 80300	"	6.50
small plastic set	Z 80301	"	3.50
Invicta Attribute Blocks (5 × 3 × 2 × 2 = 60 blocks)			
large plastic set	INVA00	SEE	18.25
⌐ small plastic set	IN1278	"	2.50
Basic Shapes Set	INV140	SEE	4.75
Trundle Wheel	ARN001	"	4.50
Marbles	buy locally or		
10 ea. of 6 colors	MARBLE	SEE	.60
1000 of 1 color	MARBLM	"	8.00
Dice	buy locally or		
½"	DIE102	SEE	.30/pr
	DIE126	"	1.25/6 pr
	DIE172	"	11.50/72 pr
¾"	DIE304	"	.60/pr
	DIE346	"	2.50/6 pr
	DIE372	"	23.00/72 pr
Counting Chips			
25 ea. of 8 colors	PRM008	"	1.75
Multi-Fit master set		Economy 5 & 10	10.00*
⌠Lego #375		"	10.59*
⟨Lego #615		"	16.50*
⌞Lego #004 master builder set		"	22.50*
Playplax Rings & Squares		"	8.50*
One of these:			
⌠Tinkertoy #155		"	5.98*
⌞Connector	OM 118	Childcraft	12.00
Jr. Engineer set 5	ES7453	SEE	17.50
Play money	buy locally		
Cash register	"	(preferably a real one, second-hand, rather than a toy)	
Unit Blocks			
full set (760 pcs.)	OB 357	Childcraft	235.00
half set (380 pcs.)	OB 358	"	119.00
Tangram pieces (4 sets)	17446	McGraw-Hill	2.60**
Tangram pieces (12 sets)	SEEP04	SEE	4.00*
Tangram pattern cards	17445	McGraw-Hill	4.62

*—less 10% discount to schools
**—McGraw-Hill's tangrams are thicker than SEE's; both fit the pattern cards sold by McGraw-Hill.

MATHEMATICS—*Desirable Materials*

ITEM	CATALOG REFERENCE	SUPPLIER	COST
Flexagons	NQ 116	Creative Playthings	$ 5.95
Geo-Strips	INC141	SEE	7.50
Poleidoblocs set G	121-G-10	REC	20.00
Cuisenaire Rods	CG-8	Cuisenaire Co./America	14.95
Mirror Cards	18418	McGraw-Hill	12.95
Teacher's Guide for Mirror Cards	18417	"	3.57
Multimat "Squares of Sums"	GN1356	SEE	7.25
Multimat "All Squares"	GN1357	"	7.25
Wooden Puzzle Assortment	70,205	Edmund Scientific	5.00
Haar Hoolim Perception Games	ALP001	SEE	3.50
Kalah	SG 104	Childcraft	7.00
Psyche Paths	M-8	Cuisenaire Co./America	4.00
Etch-a-Sketch		Economy 5 & 10	3.98*
Multiway Rollway	NR 604	Creative Playthings	6.50
Giant Engineer Construction Kit	ES9884	SEE	58.60
Play Panels	OM 383	Childcraft	4.95
Clink-a-Links	CLK320	SEE	4.50
Hex-Upon		Economy 5 & 10	6.00*
Rising Towers	NR 255	Creative Playthings	3.00
Constructo Straws	60563	Hammett	2.30
Connect	UR 322	Creative Playthings	5.00
Unifix 100 Track (only with Unifix cubes)	118-U-08	REC	4.00
Lego Gear set (only with Lego blocks)		Economy 5 & 10	5.50*
Abacounter	NN 151	Creative Playthings	5.00
Nice Cubes	SJ 360	Childcraft	1.50
Mental Blocks	SJ 363	"	3.00
Linjo	1102	Constructive Playthings	2.00
Intarsio Rounds	OM 320	Childcraft	6.00
Try Circles	UR 323	Creative Playthings	3.50
Geo-Blocks Problem Cards**	17587	McGraw-Hill	11.95
Focus	4808	Western Printing Co.	2.25
Attribute Stickers	18502	McGraw-Hill	3.99
Half-scale Unit Blocks (esp. with Unit Blocks)	NB 647	Creative Playthings	5.95
Set Dominoes	809	ETA	4.95
Giant Grooved Dominoes	NN 146	Creative Playthings	9.95⎤
Tactile Domino Blocks	OG 197	Childcraft	9.95⎦
Trimino	KB 744	Creative Playthings	2.00
Score Four		Funtastic, Inc.	5.00
Top Towers	201	M-I Sales Co.	3.95
Ji-Gan-Tiks		"	3.95
Join-ems	340	"	5.95

* Less 10% discount to schools
** Suggested as teacher resource, *not* as student task cards

MATHEMATICS—Desirable Materials

ITEM	CATALOG REFERENCE	SUPPLIER	COST
⎰ Soma cube puzzle (plastic)	SOMA33	SEE	2.00
⎱ Wood Block Puzzle (soma)	WOOD33	"	1.85
Octons	L 540	Galt	∼1.75
Plastic Meccano Work Box	N 2456	"	∼15.00
Abacus board	INV103	SEE	.70
same with 100 tablets	INC103	"	3.20
Abacus tablets, 160 in 8 colors	INV106	"	4.00
Polyatom	Z 80471	Herder & Herder	6.95
Plastic Spools (white, red, yellow, blue, green—			.84/100
specify colors)		A. E. Piggott Ltd.	8.40/1000
Colored 1″ cubes (wood)	63089	Hammett	4.00/100
Colored 1″ cubes (plastic)	TN 353-1	Philip & Tacey	∼3.00/120
Clear Acrylic cubes	SEE011	SEE	11.00/100
	SEED11	"	52.50/500

MATHEMATICS—Interesting Materials

ITEM	CATALOG REFERENCE	SUPPLIER	COST
Dr. Nim		Economy 5 & 10	$3.50*
Metal Twisting Puzzles	71,164	Edmund Scientific	4.50/20
Knüpferli		Economy 5 & 10	2.98*
Geo-D-Stix	NS 167	Creative Playthings	4.95
Construct-A-Cube	GNO 872	SEE	2.35
Space Panels	OM 141	Childcraft	6.00
Rig-A-Jig	NT 662	Creative Playthings	4.00
Tangled Angles	L-025	F. A. O. Schwarz	5.00
Plastic Mosaic Shapes	INV 143	SEE	7.50
Scope		Economy 5 & 10	4.98*
Design Cubes	OM 380	Childcraft	5.00
Grouping Set	T 110	Taskmaster	13.30
Discovery Blocks	1500	E.T.A.	12.00
Shapes Matching Cubes	GN 1072	SEE	3.00
Fours	444444	SEE	4.00
Think-A-Dot		Economy 5 & 10	1.98*
Scribble Stix	83447	Hammett	5.00
H-Blocks	OM 166	Childcraft	6.95
Avalanche		Economy 5 & 10	4.50*
Pegity		"	
Playsticks	N 550	Galt	∼2.60
Square Domino Game	E-077	F. A. O. Schwarz	2.50
Birds-on-a-Tree Puzzle	NT 650	Creative Playthings	7.95

MATHEMATICS—Materials for Older Children

(7–8 years and up)

Many of the materials in the preceding three sections are suitable for children through all the elementary school years. Those below are probably only useful starting with 2nd or 3rd grade. The Dienes blocks are good building materials for younger children who would not grasp their formal applications; however, they are too expensive to replace other materials in the preceding sections.

ITEM	CATALOG REFERENCE	SUPPLIER	COST
Twixt	MMT110	SEE	$ 7.95
Beeline	BEELIN	"	4.25
Mem	SG 212	Childcraft	6.00
Spirograph		Economy 5 & 10	4.25*
Poleidoblocs set A	120-G-10	REC	16.00
Dienes Multibase Arithmetic Blocks (MAB):			
Complete set (bases 3, 4, 5, 6, 10, with work cards & teacher's manual)	Z 80008	Herder & Herder	118.00
Base 2 set	Z 80016	"	9.50
Dienes Algebraical Experience Materials (AEM): Complete set	Z 80011	Herder & Herder	59.00
Pantograph	55095	Hammett	3.50

MATHEMATICS—Resource Books for Teachers

Nuffield Mathematics Project:

John Wiley & Sons, Inc.
605 Third Ave.
New York, New York 10016

Mathematics Begins	2.25
Pictorial Representation	2.25
Beginnings	2.50
I Do, and I Understand	1.95

Cuisenaire Series:

Cuisenaire Co. of America
12 Church St.
New Rochelle, N.Y. 10805

M. Goutard: Talks for Primary School Teachers	CB-18	1.00
C. Gattegno: Mathematics with Numbers in Color, Book A	CB-A	1.50

Elementary Science Study Teacher's Guides:

McGraw-Hill

Attribute Games & Problems	18479	4.86
Geo Blocks	17524	2.46
Geo Blocks Problem Cards	17587	11.95
Mirror Cards	18417	3.57
Pattern Blocks	17560	2.64
Peas and Particles	17521	3.27
Pendulums	17568	3.12
Primary Balancing (The Balance Book)	17511	5.13
Rocks and Charts	17564	2.46
Tangrams	17444	1.92

Elementary Science Study Working Papers:

Elementary Science Study
55 Chapel St.
Newton, Mass. 02160

Match and Measure	1.00

* * *

Materials for sorting, matching, ordering, grouping, sharing and counting, also for dealing with symbols, number names, making a one-to-one correspondence, and cardinal and ordinal numbers.

Shells, matchboxes, conkers, corks, poppet beads, cotton reels, pipe cleaners, leaves, buttons, washers, marbles, bean-bags, bricks, mosaic shapes, pebbles, plastic rings, bottle tops, spills, straws, coloured sticks, golf tees, miniature cars, animals, and other toys.

Transparent plastic boxes for storage.
Sorting boxes.
String, rope, hoops and coloured card for enclosing groups.
Many things in the environment, e.g., cups and saucers, knives and forks,
　　paint brushes, pencils, balls, bricks, milk bottles etc.
Pegboards and pegs.
100 square.
100 bead chain.
Number lines and strips.
Ladders.
Strip of curtain rod with hooks.
Nesting toys, interlocking cubes, graded stairs.
Abacus.
Plastic numerals or written on cards.
Beads and threaders.
Trays with written numerals in which children can place appropriate number.
Games, e.g., dominoes, skittles, Ludo, Lotto, Snakes and Ladders, Bagatelle.
Dice games, spinning tops, fishing game, etc.
Children can be encouraged to make up their own race games, building tracks with bricks.
Playing cards.
Patience cards.
Sets of cigarette cards with serial numbers.
Cuisenaire rods.
Stern Arithmetic apparatus.
Colour factor, venture etc.

Time and Speed

Real clocks with clear faces placed at children's level.
Toy clocks with gear wheels.
Clock face tracers.
Egg timers.
Ten seconds timer.
Home-made water clock or sand clock.
Candle clock.

From Mimeographed List compiled by Marjorie Kay, Advisor for Infant Schools, Leicestershire, England.

Home-made pendulum.

Pinger.

Photographic clock with stopping device and large second hand.

Stop watch.

Metronome.

Pulsometer.

Balls, toy cars, cylindrical pieces of wood, marbles, etc., to roll down an inclined plank.

Calendars.

Day and date from daily papers to arrange in order.

Radio Times.

Bus and train time-tables.

Highway code.

Area

Mosaic shapes of all types for pattern making, etc.

Assorted shapes which fit together completely and also those which do not.

Plenty of inch squares.

Lino tiles of varying shapes and sizes.

Polystyrene tiles—ceiling tiles.

Templates of squares, triangles, etc.

Transparent squares, rectangles, triangles etc.

Pegboards.

Coloured sticks of different lengths.

Bricks, Stern material, Cuisenaire etc.

Square feet, square yards, cut from packing paper.

Squared paper, gummed squares, pieces of material, corrugated paper, fablon, contact or backing from these.

Money

Orange boxes, tea chests, planks, moveable screens should be available so that shops can easily be set up and arranged by the children, e.g., toys, sweets, grocers, drapers, post office, cafe, milk-bar, bank, etc.

Commodities can often be made by the children.

Coins used should be decided by the teacher to suit the group's ability and experience.

Cash register.

Gummed paper for price tickets.

Price lists.

Capacity and Volume

Containers of assorted shapes and sizes, some unusual shapes if possible.

Rectangular boxes and cartons of all sizes.

Oxo cube box and oxo cubes.

Cylindrical containers, e.g., salt tins, Smartie tubes.

Tins, bottles, beakers, jugs, cups, egg-cups, medicine bottles etc.

Buckets, watering can, basins, funnels, measuring spoons.

Plastic tubes with stoppers 1″ & 1½″ diam. cut to lengths required.

Obtainable from Harrison Jeavons, 5–7 East Bond Street, Leicester.

Standard measures ½ pt., 1 pt., 2 pts.

Milk bottles, ⅓ pt., ½ pt., 1 pt., 2 pts.

Plastic measuring jug.

Flat tins, such as sandwich tins or frying pan, so that children can see 1 pint in a different container.

Sand, marbles, bricks, rice, etc., for filling containers, also water.

Safe colouring matter—McCormicks, 4 colours 2/6d. (obtainable from grocers)

Plasticine.

1 gross of 1″ cubes.

Rubber bands for marking water levels.

Large transparent geometric models with holes in them so that they can be filled E.S.A.

Space Shape Size and Symmetry

Poleidoblocs E.S.A.

Grouping set.

Mosaics.

Jigsaw puzzles.

Hammer pictures.

Graded material commercially produced, e.g., graded shapes and pictures, nesting dolls, (P. & M. Abbott).

Different sized balls, wheels, hoops, tins, tin lids, etc., which can be graded.

Basic shapes set. (Invicta)

Geo. strips.

Large and small cubes, long bricks, flat bricks, cones, arches, planks, etc., for building.

All kinds of boxes and materials for construction.

Collections of round things, square things, etc.

Pegboards.

Geo. boards, elastic bands shirred or rolled elastic.

3D shapes—cuboids, pyramids, prisms, spheres, etc.

Coloured plastic or wooden shapes.

Tins, boxes, bottles of all shapes.

Interesting shapes—pieces of wood, leaves, etc.

Cardboard strips, lino strips, meccano, pipe cleaners, plastic wire.

Templates.

Finding things, e.g., leaves, each part of which would look the same if cut in half or folded.

Kaleidoscope.

Mirrors.

Thin paper for cutting and folding.

Squared paper, coloured paper, pencils, crayons, scissors, etc.

Length and Distance

String, ribbons, braids, wool, ropes, plastic wire, etc.

Laths, canes, dowelling, strips of pegboard.

Meccano strips.

Foot rulers, some unmarked, some marked in inches, halves and quarters, but *"no ends."*

Yard sticks, some unmarked, some marked in feet and some in feet and inches.

Varying lengths from one to eleven inches, some unmarked, some marked in inches.

Plenty of 1 inch tablets. Area tablets (Invicta).

Tape measures.

Steel tapes.

Surveyors' tapes and chain.

Plastic covered rope 22 yards long for home-made chain.

Trundel or click wheels.

Calipers.

Height scale.

Drinking straws, paper streamers, trimmings, obtainable from wall-paper shops, spills, string, paper, gummed coloured paper, etc., for cutting to lengths as needed.

Balance and Weight

Material for weighing; flour, sugar, potatoes, dried peas, beans, conkers, dog biscuits, nails, sand, clay, shells, stones, feathers, corks, cones, foam rubber pieces, etc.

Clear plastic containers.

Scoops and funnels.

Some parcels made up in exact weights, e.g., 6 ozs. 4 ozs.

Scales of all types but *simple balances* are essential.

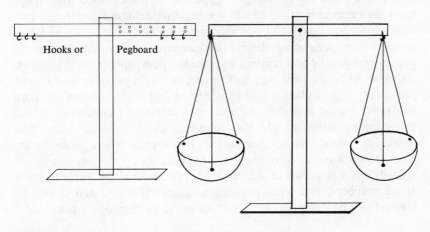

Hooks or   Pegboard

Spring balances.

Letter scales.

Extension type as used for fishing.

Bathroom scales.

Plentiful supply of weights, *at least* 16—1 oz., 8—2 oz., 4—4 oz., 2—8 oz., and weights of 1 lb. and 2 lb. Brass weights are more accurate and should be used for 1 oz., 2 oz., and 4 oz. weights.

5. Mathematics as Adventure

"I was definitely what one would call a 'math cripple,' " Manon Charbonneau writes. "I hated [math], didn't understand it, and quit taking it as fast as my school would allow." But Mrs. Charbonneau is an extraordinarily gifted teacher who discovered some twelve years ago the excitement that mathematics can evoke when, as a beginning second-grade teacher, she was handed a box of Cuisenaire rods. Since then, she has been a member of the staff of the Madison Project, the most useful American curriculum reform project in mathematics for teachers in open classrooms, and has participated in and directed teacher workshops in various parts of the United States; she is presently a member of the faculty of the Colorado Academy. Her description and analysis of how to equip and manage a math laboratory, while primarily concerned with the upper elementary grades, contains valuable insights for teachers of children of any age.

Learning to Think in a Math Lab

A mathematics laboratory is a learning environment more than anything else. It is a place full of "things": games to be played, tools and equipment for experimentation, blocks for building beautiful structures, patterns, concepts; boxes and bottles, shapes of all kinds; scales and balances, rulers, measuring devices in standard and nonstandard units; papers and pencils and crayons and marker pens; spools, little toy cars, trains, dried beans, peas, rice, salt, sugar, coffee, cups, spoons—to name just a few. It is a place where imagination and creative ideas are born and grow, where thoughts and feelings can become certainties, where many young minds decide that mathematics is certainly more than practicing "sums" that teacher assigns. It is a place where problems are created and ways to solve them are thought up by the individuals involved. It is a place where one can learn just about all he wants to know about numbers, and what happens to them "if" . . . and it can be learned slowly, using lots of "stuff" to prove or disprove a point, or it can be found quickly because that eager curiosity moved like lightning that day.

There is so much that can be said for a mathematics laboratory for the use of young children of all ages, really, that it is difficult to be definitive in one's approach to setting one up. In this book I am primarily concerned with the upper elementary grades—the nine-, ten-, and eleven-year-olds. Children vary from school to school, so that one must be acutely aware of and sensitive to the needs of the individual children with whom one will be working when stocking a lab. There are some things I personally could not do without, others that are desirable but not necessary, and then there are the frills—those special tools or games or books or blocks that would be great if only they did not cost so much; but many, many things can be put into a lab which cost little or nothing but the time involved in scrounging them up, or making them in some instances.

I strongly suggest measuring tools of all types: tin measuring cups, measuring spoons, quarts, pints, half pints, half gallons, gallons (milk containers that can easily be gathered and replaced with use), all sizes of boxes, bottles, containers that are cylinders or odd shapes, styrofoam shapes of all sizes, yardsticks, meter sticks, foot rulers, trundle wheels in yards and meters and odd sizes, tongue depressors, sticks of various lengths, floor tiles (9″ by 9″ and 12″ by 12″, etc.), scales of all kinds, gram weights and ounce weights, marbles—which can be used for weighing very effectively. Bottles and jars can come from any kitchen or medicine cabinet. Never throw away odd-length sticks; these can be sanded down and used for measuring with nonstandard units. Tongue depressors are ideal for many things, and doctor fathers are often willing to donate a box or two of them! String of all lengths and weights, yarn, rope—all can be easily collected, and once you start looking, boxes of all assorted shapes and sizes start popping up. These are great for volume and surface area problems. Quart plastic containers with rice, dried cereal, macaroni, dried beans, dried peas, coffee, tea, sugar, salt, flour, sand, popcorn are all great things to weigh and measure and compare. Standard cups, medicine cups (small paper ones), plastic spoons or scoops for getting the stuff out of the containers, or for use in weighing small quantities are just ideal. (I have had children balance one cup of rice against plastic spoons or marbles instead of weights—and often it's fun just to see how much tea will balance one half cup of rice etc.) Children can invent many, many ways themselves to tell you "how much" a thing weighs, and when getting started with this sort of thing, nonstandard units are more interesting and fun than standard ones. And, when you find out for yourself, with the gram weights, just how many grams equal one ounce, it sticks—far longer than going to a table of reference in a book—and it's more fun!

One tremendous motivator in the area of measurement is a beautiful full-color chart I received gratis through the mail from the Ford Company on the history of measurement. It tells, quite simply and graphically, the origin of such things as the foot, the cubit, the rod, the fathom, the hand, and goes right on up to such fantastic measuring units of today as angstroms. One group of ten-year-olds I had became so fascinated with the chart that they made their own "feet," "hands," cubits, yards, fathoms, rods, etc., and proceeded to measure everything in sight with their own units. They even came to the conclusion that standardized units of measure are a very real necessity, or how else can you be sure of what you are getting? All I did was put the chart on the wall—everything else came from them. If I had suggested the study, I doubt that any of the boys would have done more than grunt or snort their disapproval. What they ended up doing took far more work and care than anything I could have thought up for them—and they enjoyed it much more.

As far as blocks go, I am very fortunate. I have in my lab Cuisenaire rods (which I consider indispensable), Dienes algebraic experience materials and multi-base arithmetic blocks, Attribute blocks, pattern blocks, and geometry blocks, all from EDC.[1] I also have a box full of inch cubes and two-inch cubes just cut and sanded from plain lumber.

Games include dominoes, triminoes, fraction dominoes, Vector, Quinto, Twixt, Yahtzee, Tuf, Stocks and Bonds, Milles Bornes, Equations, Hex Hi-Q, and a variety of puzzles that are nameless as far as the market goes. There are lots of three-dimensional wooden puzzles for taking apart and putting back together, Insanity blocks, the Tower of Hanoi, Kalah—a nifty marble game of "count and capture." We even have Scrabble and Spill and Spell—learning doesn't stop with just numerical games!

More things I could not do without are maps of all kinds: railroad systems maps, airlines systems maps, road maps, topographic sheets, world maps, political maps, underwater geographical maps, weather maps, and some Mercator projections of the world, as well as globes—both political and topographic. With the use of string or yarn and a ruler, the children can find distances both "as the crow flies" (airmail) and via roads and railroads and rivers, etc. A favorite game is to bring letters to school from all over the world and find out how far these have traveled to reach the addressees. And half the fun is finding the right map for the job!

Boxes full of compasses (drawing), protractors, simple cutting tools, all kinds of paper and cardboard can lead to scale drawings and then on to scale models, eventually in balsa wood. I have one young lad who

---

[1] Education Development Center, 55 Chapel Street, Newton, Massachusetts 02160.

designs the most beautiful sailing ships to scale, and then proceeds to color and describe them in detail—math, art, and English, all in one lesson. He has even produced some spectacular wooden models—and NOT from a kit, either!

Paper in a math lab is vital—plain typing paper, large sheets of colored paper, rolls of newsprint or large sheets of it, but above all, graph paper; one-inch squares, one half-inch squares, one quarter-inch squares, five squares to the inch, decimal graph paper, centimeter graph paper, large sheets, small sheets—we buy the enormous sheets and cut them down into various sizes. And adding-machine tape by the case—there is a multitude of uses for adding-machine tape. Something I would like to have, but do not, is a supply of very large sheets of centimeter graph paper for recording problems done with Cuisenaire rods. So far, I have found the small 8-½" by 11" size, but nothing larger—and there are times when the big sheets would be very desirable. Cardboard in all weights and thicknesses and sizes is very handy. Mat board is especially useful for scale models—it cuts easily with Exacto knives. Dot paper made for the 25-nail geoboard is also very important.

Geoboards are one of the key materials in the math lab. They could be treated as a subject by themselves! Their value as an exploratory device, as well as for more directed learning, cannot be overemphasized.

Miscellaneous items that come to mind which are very helpful and which the children find interesting to work with: Japanese and Chinese abacuses (the soroban and the swan pan), boards of various lengths (10, 12, 15 feet and 12 to 14 inches wide) for doing rate problems on an inclined plane, all kinds of little cars and trucks (Corgi cars, giant matchbox toys, etc.) and, ideally, an electric train! Problems involving rate, time, and distance mean much more when they can be worked with real "things." And the generalizations can then be more easily transferred to problems found in textbooks. Dice, magic markers, ball point pens, colored pencils, crayons, masking tape, scotch tape, colored tape, stop watches are a few more items that we make tremendous use of during the year.

"Things" come to mind as you work with the children and they work in the lab situation. Lots of things can be scrounged; little cars and trucks, milk cartons, plastic ice cream containers, empty spools, boxes and cartons and bottles. A simple letter to parents asking for cast-offs and throw-outs can bring in loads of materials.

DO NOT FEEL THAT YOU MUST START WITH A LOADED LABORATORY OF MATERIALS! We started with three bookshelves of games and puzzles, and over the course of four years have built up a very extensive mathematics laboratory. I would urge anyone starting in this situation to begin slowly, with a little bit of equipment, for short periods a day, and gradually build up into something which crosses hours, disciplines, and teachers. In making suggestions for stocking a lab, I cannot say strongly enough that you must meet the needs of the children with whom you are working, and as you work with them, ideas for materials and what to do with them constantly keep cropping up. What I have done here is give you a partial list of what is NOW in our lab at Colorado Academy for the elementary school, all of which is used constantly by the various age levels. I guess one criterion I use in deciding if a certain piece of equipment or game is right for our lab is its direct usability by the children. If whatever it is takes a lot of teacher direction or close supervision—in other words, something that the children cannot handle and use by themselves—then it is of very little value to me. I clearly remember Dr. Robert Davis, director of the Madison Project, saying to a child in a lab situation, "Play with it a while and see what it does, then we can talk about other things to do with it." Children as a whole are very creative about the things they work with, and the less you show them, the more they will invent ways to use them or things to do with them. Of course, they can think up destructive ways to use things too. We have two distinct rules in our lab: (1) YOU DO NOT BREAK OR DAMAGE ANYTHING YOU ARE WORKING WITH! and (2) NEVER INTERRUPT ANYONE ELSE WHO IS WORKING! Those two rules will cover almost any disturbing situation that can arise and spoil the lab set-up.

Before going any further with what to do in a lab and how to do it, let me tell you something about myself. I do not want you to think that I have an extensive formal background in mathematics, with degrees to go with it. How I wish I did, or at least had the time to take some more courses in formal mathematics. I was definitely what one would call a "math cripple" . . . I hated it, didn't understand it, and quit taking it as fast as my school would allow, which turned out to be after algebra I and plane geometry in high school. (Since then I have managed a course in college algebra, which was great fun and of tremendous value to me personally.) My initial interest and excitement with numbers came when I was handed a box of Cuisenaire rods the year I started teaching grade two back in 1960. The tremendous gains I made that year with the students, from playing with rods, really opened a whole new world for me. Since then I have been a participant in many interesting and profitable workshops in mathematics and have more recently been a staff member, a position that yields as much learning for me as I hope it provides for my "students"! . . .

I guess what gave me the biggest fright during these years of learning (which I am still going through *constantly* with the children) was saying something or implying something or outright teaching something that wasn't true mathematically, and thereby leading the children astray for future math courses that they might take. A great help in this area is an upper school-level math teacher who is willing to give the time to watch me teach, and/or sit down with me and help me plan not only learning sessions, but worksheets and work cards. I have always found someone in my school most willing to do this. It really is a confidence builder!

The point I am trying to make is that if you are sincerely interested in learning mathematics with the children, there is always some talented mathematician around who is glad to help. Go to him for help, invite him into your classroom—there is so much to be gained on both sides!

Like all adults who have grown up under a traditional system, I have found myself feeling guilty in classroom situations where, perhaps, the children have not done steady practice in the four operations in increasing degrees of difficulty. I have even felt panic-stricken to realize that they must face standardized testing, and "what if they don't know how to do . . ." and I have dutifully assigned practice work, with "so many problems or pages" to be turned in to me daily, with an admonishment to the children of "you must do . . ." What has resulted each time is a situation of teacher fighting student, force against force, and let's see who wins. Yes, I can *make* them do worksheets full of problems, I can keep them in from recess, or after school, or for extra help sessions or study halls, and what results is that I feed my own ego—I have accomplished the work set out, I have made them do the practice I felt necessary, I'm a tough person who demands a lot of work! Yes, I have TAUGHT, but there has not been much LEARNING going on. Time after time, I have seen the same children who fight hardest against deadlines and assignments do twice as much work on their own when told, "Go as far as you like or can; do as many papers as you wish or have time for—come and ask for help if you need to, or ask your buddy for help. Maybe he can help you see where you goofed better than I can." Children like to have some control over their lives instead of constantly being told what, when, why, where, and above all HOW. The little one who constantly lags or does little has very real reasons for behaving in this way—and maybe easing up on quantity, on the degree of difficulty, can make the difference between tuning him out completely and giving him just the kind of help he needed at the right time. Backing off and staying out of the way can be as much help as a personal tutoring session at times—maybe more!

I know what is going through many minds at this time as you read this: What happens when they go on to the next grade, and particularly what happens when they go to junior high school and the grade seven teacher asks, "What happened in sixth grade—didn't that teacher teach anything? Why is this child passed along to seventh grade when he can't do . . . ?" Yes, I've heard it all before, too, but the question that must be answered is do we as teachers do what is best for each child, or do we do what is most expedient for us (teach the class as a group and hope for the best) to meet the next grade-level demands, whether the child is ready or not? How many times have we all heard the statement about children not developing at the same rate, mentally or physically? We all believe it, philosophically, but the minute they get to school we classify and pigeonhole and lock them into step and pass them along, restraining some and dragging along others. WHY? Because it's the easiest way to do it. We even talk of efficiency—teaching or having all the children in one class working on the same thing at the same time. Isn't it more efficient to do it this way? Efficient for whom? For the teacher, yes, but really and truly, how many children are REALLY ready for the same concept at the same time? If they were, would there have to be so much reteaching and going over and "review"? I shall not try to speak for older children, but certainly elementary-age children desperately need to develop at their own pace—some can and should learn long division at grade four, but others can't cope with larger number concepts yet, and waiting until the ripe moment can save hours and days and weeks of agony for young minds and frustrations for teachers. Most teachers do know their pupils very well indeed, sometimes better than parents, even, and it isn't difficult to learn to sense when, just precisely when, this child is ready for, say, three-digit multiplication and two- or three-digit long division, or fractions. As far as passing them along to the next teacher is concerned, it certainly isn't THAT hard to sit down and talk about the children who move, their strengths and weaknesses, their interests and abilities. It isn't hard to pick up each child exactly where he is and take him as far as he can go each year. Some years will show tremendous growth, some years not so much— just as in the classroom, some days or weeks, great leaps are made, others seem to show only a snail's pace in growth. We, as adults, operate very unevenly in our daily jobs, be it teaching or whatever. Some days are just great, we have tremendous energy and everything seems to flow —others just don't happen like that. Can't children have the same feelings and frustrations? Some days they want to work and do things to peak capacity; other days may need to be thinking days, or exploring days—or even daydreaming days.

If starting at about the grade four level for the first time, work slowly. Start a "lab session" perhaps once a week for half an hour—maybe pick that last half hour in the day when everything drags. The children need to relax and so does the teacher. Start with some interesting mathematical games like QUINTO and HEX and chip trading, or VECTOR. Maybe cross number puzzles, or the TOWER OF HANOI or the peg puzzle or KALAH—all things that get children thinking from a logic and strategy standpoint, but which don't look like the usual "school" stuff. As they begin to find things to do without suggestions from you, stretch the time a little and start another session on another day. Gradually build up the time you allot to math lab activities to longer and longer periods, and more of them each week. Start collecting ideas that come to you and the children on 5″ by 8″ file cards—things that are fun to do mathematically, and soon you will have a ready reference file all your own. Take particular care to record the things that come from the children; as they work on one thing, it often leads to another. Add materials as ideas pop up: games can be acquired through birthdays that come during the school year. Instead of that "party" with cookies or cupcakes, etc., encourage the children to give a game to the math lab in honor of their birthday, and paste a sticker on the box with their name and birth date. Don't hesitate to let children just read, or even just sit and think—all of this can lead to something quite interesting and profitable.

The boys in my lab have asked to work on social studies projects, reading, researching, making maps both two- and three-dimensional, scale models (what can be more mathematical?)—which has in some small way made the children realize that education is learning about all kinds of things, and that in so very many ways these things correlate. School is not just a bunch of subjects to be thought about for three quarters of an hour and then turned off as the next "subject" comes up. It is learning in all its phases and very much integrated. Art and math correlate beautifully, as do all the subject areas, really. Writing up the results of an experiment or a work-card in math or science becomes a way of communication with others about what you are doing, not just an exercise in English to see if you know a noun from a verb. And trying to find out more about Pythagoras' theorem, and other things he did, often leads to reading extensively in the biographies of other thinkers of the age. As you become more comfortable in this role of observer and guide instead of leader and "teller," gradually expand the time, the topics, and the materials available for use, until both you and the children feel quite at ease in this kind of situation. Be aware that, of course, things are going to be considerably noisier than in a traditional classroom, that children should work together in twos and threes and sometimes larger groups, and that their talking is not wrong. Listen carefully to the chit-chat—many times I have found a child much better able to explain something, or to express a thought, than I; or have even heard a peer group argument, not refereed by me, become a means for a real discovery into the meaning of a concept. How much I wish I had had the tape recorder back a few years ago in grade five, when I had turned the group loose on projects, and two young lads had chosen to work with volume (without knowing that this is what you call it)!

A word of caution about the cards in the Appendix. They are not intended to be used exactly as presented. Nor are they intended to be used, each and every card! Some ways of covering a topic may be more appealing to you than others. Don't hesitate to scrap any cards you don't like. Neither topic nor sequence is that important. Use your own best judgment for your children. Number line work need not precede "other names for numbers," or measuring need not come after work on geoboards. I stuck them in the sequence you find here, for variety and interest and change of pace. The topics are definitely to be used as you see fit with your class. Each topic, however, is divided in the following manner: The yellow card in each set is for the GO GO GO kids, and the green ones are programmed into easier and, I hope, more logical steps for the less secure children. In most cases, there are two or three or more green cards for each yellow card. The yellow cards can be used with all the children after they have caught the idea of a freer situation and have begun to blossom—use them as a sort of "No restrictions now, kids, GO!" type of approach.

Don't hesitate to rewrite or reword or in any way improve the work cards for your bunch of children. These are to be only suggestions, some thoughts to get you and the children started in this open situation.

A word about the format of the cards: you will notice that they are handwritten. My boys seem to prefer this; a bit more of the personal touch than the printed word, I guess. I have tried both ways, with typewritten directions and in my own printing. Surprisingly enough, the handwritten ones go over much better. Perhaps it's also because they know that these can be easily scrapped and written again if something isn't clear—not quite so "final" as printed ones! And it often encourages the children to try writing their own—they do a fine job, believe me, once they see what the game is! Have fun, and good luck!

Now for the work cards. . . .

Appendix

Reproductions of my 8½″ x 11″ work cards follow. Since this book is printed in black and white, we are indicating the yellow cards by the word "yellow." The unmarked cards you are to imagine are green!

Remember: a yellow card starts each new "project" or topic, and the green ones that follow are, in each case, a more directed version of the yellow card.

Notes to Teachers

The notes that follow are intended to be read *after* reading through the series of work cards which go with each topic. (See Appendix.) The set of cards, of course, is arranged in the same order as the notes, so that it is reasonably easy to locate precisely the topic one wishes to pursue.

other names for numbers (Yellow)

Get a roll of adding machine tape. Choose a number & write as many names for that number as you can. You may use the whole roll!

$5 = \frac{10}{2} = 5 \cdot 1 = \frac{.}{.} = 20 =$

other names for numbers — 1

Get a roll of adding machine tape. Choose a number, like "7", & using only +, write as many names for your number as you can!

$7 = 4 + 3 = 8 + 1 = 2 + 5 = 9 + 2 = -3 + 10 =$

other names for numbers — 2

This time use only subtraction — & your number; write as many names as you can!

Can you find a pattern?

other names for numbers — 3

Now try your number with multiplication & division $\times$ & $\div$

Is there a pattern here too?

A yellow card starts each new "project" or topic—whatever you prefer to call it, and the green ones that follow are, in each case, a more directed version of the yellow card.

These are the projects the children themselves have enjoyed working with the most, as well as the ones I have found to be most productive in the formation of concepts I feel are important ones at this level. AGAIN LET ME EMPHASIZE THAT THEY ARE NOT INTENDED TO BE A CURRICULUM for nine-, ten-, and eleven-year-olds, but just some interesting and productive ideas that do work in a mathematics laboratory situation.

Others Names for Numbers

Using adding machine tape to create long strings of "other names for numbers" has proved to be a very profitable game for all upper elementary-age children. Simple as this activity may sound, many of these older children really have very little realization that $9 + 7$ is another name for $8 + 8$ or $6 + 10$ or 4×4 and 2×8 and 4^2, etc. They seem to look upon $9 + 7$ as something to put an answer at the end of, which must be 16 and nothing else! To them $9 + 7 = 3 \times 4 + 4$ looks very strange indeed! Many can write beautiful trains of addition and subtraction but cannot shift over into using all four operations. How many times have your children encountered a page of equations looking like $3 \times 3 = \square - 6$ and filled the frame with 9? Adding machine tape works wonders to clear up this misconception! This activity will often open up a whole new world of numbers and patterns to the children who have been locked up with a single idea. Encouraging the children to use the whole roll of tape usually keeps the motivation going at top speed, and a little contest to see who can create the longest strip (without error, of course!) in a given length of time can add to the excitement IF the children involved in this race are able to cope with competition successfully. This is also an activity that can be done over and over again by the children during the year, each time expanding their concepts and computational skills. My children often work in pairs, taking turns writing and thinking up "other names."

I would suggest using magic markers for the writing, and would encourage the children to write as large as possible on the tape, for when they are finished it is fun to post the tape down the hall, around the room, wherever it can be done impressively to show the quality as well as the quantity of work it took to finish. Written with magic marker, it is visible for quite a distance! And don't worry about checking for errors—as they are spotted, they can be indicated with a notation of "I don't agree" or an arrow or a question mark. Usually the children will catch their own errors when working in pairs or groups, and can usually find a way to fix them so they work.

For the "turned-on" bunch, just give them the tape, magic markers, and the yellow card; for the more timid, suggest a small number to get them started, like 7, and the green cards. It might even help to write a couple of names to give them an idea; $7 = 1 \times 7 = 15 - 8 = 49 \div 7 =$ and let them take over from there. Maybe some child would be better off working with just one operation at a time until he gains confidence. Start with subtraction, maybe, then suggest a move to division, or multiplication, etc. This is a good way to get a child to practice the operation he is weakest in, or at least with which he might need additional practice.

With card one in the green series, if your children haven't played around with negative numbers, they will very quickly reach a limit of possibility with a small number. Go on to the next card. Watch what happens, and perhaps come in with a question like: "Can you find more names with subtraction than you can with addition?" "Why?" Same with multiplication and division; knowledge of negatives extends the possibilities, and so does intuitive knowledge of fractions. Sometimes, if you step in and ask a couple of leading questions like "How many ½'s in 2?" There is a name for 4! "How many ¼'s in 1?" Another name for 4! If they pick up the pattern, they can often continue for quite a spell!

My students have really become fascinated with this game, and several have come up with some most unusual patterns in division and multiplication. Many have learned the principle of halving and doubling the factors to come up with the same products, and what happens when you add zeros to a dividend and a divisor. (There I go using mathematical vocabulary, which I am NOT denying eventually comes in handy to know, but I would not make an issue of it with the children—at this level.) If they refer to "the number I am dividing by" or the "number I am dividing into"—and use them correctly—I am happy.

And in spite of the many times I have gently tried to get the children to realize that 2/4 means nothing more than $2 \div 4$, it took two or three sessions with the adding machine tape for a number of the group to come screaming to me about a discovery! "Hey, Mrs. Charbonneau, did you know that 8/4 is just another way of naming 2?" How about that!

Number Lines

Watching children make number lines can give a teacher considerable insight into the thinking of the children involved. Do they start right in working from the left edge of the strip of paper, and make rather helter-skelter marks along the row, and stick on numbers in sequences as simple as ones only, or twos? How do they mark off the interval between numbers? Let them start exactly as they wish; then as you watch their progress, ask a question here and there and make a suggestion, but *number lines — 1*

Use some adding machine tape to make a number line. Put your starting number at the left end, choose an interval (space), & put on as many points as you can.

number lines (Yellow)

Use some adding machine tape & make some number line segments. Be as tricky as you can!

number lines — 2

Now try it again, but start at the right end of your segment. Choose a new interval & work backwards as far as possible.

number lines — 3

Try something different! Start with numbers at either end & work towards the middle. Try one like

$$10 \rule{3cm}{0.4pt} 50$$

then get tricky!

refrain from giving directions. What you are out to find out first, here, is their idea about a number line, what it means, what it can show, the child's basic understanding of "numberness"—to use a word that probably doesn't even exist! That's a strange phrase, but I really don't know how else to put it—it is an understanding of numbers in sequence carried out in a logical way. What the sequence is matters not at all—it can be by 7's or ½'s or .10, but the spacing and pattern of numbers must be logical.

I do not expect precision of nine-, ten-, and eleven-year-olds: by this I mean that I do not demand that they make these number-line segments with a yardstick and ruler in hand. However, I do suggest that these tools can help if I find that the children are totally unaware of spaces (intervals) between numbers (points on the number line), and their sloppiness is creating more havoc than anything else. If I find that a child has changed the interval between numbers, I will talk to him about a space of one unit, then work on up to the idea of adding unit spaces together to reach whatever other points he might wish to name, and perhaps something like a hand's width or an orange rod or a pencil length might act as a guide for spacing, once he understands why something like

10 11   12 13 14   15   16 17   18   19   20

cannot be logical.

One can get a pretty fair idea of who is ready for lots of work with fractions if they start naming these kinds of points on their number lines. Those who shy off and use only whole numbers might work this way for a while. Then suggest that they might like to try something tricky and work with halves—then extend it a bit and see if they pick up the challenge. Most children will start working from left to right: fine, but encourage them NOT to start with zero or one, but somewhere else up and down the number line.

One of the most creative children I have had takes his adding machine tape, folds it in half, again in half, and again and again until he gets down to about two-inch intervals; opens it up, runs a magic marker line down the center lengthwise to make the "line," and proceeds to use his fold marks (marked over with magic marker) to name his points. Sometimes he works from left to right, always choosing an interesting and tricky interval, and sometimes he works backwards. The most fun was to watch him do one when I suggested he put in the two end points and fill in the points in between, as many as he could.

What you want to come out of this project is a real feel for numbers, for different kinds of sequences, for spacing and intervals, and a logical approach to naming fractional points, and some adventuresomeness in naming numbers; also, you hope, some discovery about such things as

4/2 being another name for 2 or 15/6 being another name for 2½—
which, believe me, is a real revelation for some children despite the fact
that many textbooks have told them this before grade four or five.

Refrain from placing an already made-up number line around the
room—the children come to accept it like the calendar and rarely look
at it; I mean really look at it and try to make something interesting and
useful out of it. Then too, ready-made number lines almost always start
with zero or one—no wonder children are glued to the idea that nothing
exists below zero! Now if the children themselves decide to make a
long number line and either leave space available or work below zero,
great! Put it up, add to it from time to time—that is, encourage the
children to add to it, and see what comes.

For the child who needs more guidance, use the green cards that guide
him from left to right at first and talk about even spacing and logical
intervals. Then when he gets quite good at this approach, go on to the
work from right to left, and finally with only the end points given, but
be careful what interval he ends up with. I can remember giving a child
a strip of tape and telling him his two end points were 1 and 10! The
child had a terrible time with it and I couldn't figure out why it was
taking him so long to figure out a simple ten-space interval, when suddenly as I looked at it, I realized that it WASN'T a simple ten-space
interval—it was a quite difficult nine-space one!

This is a project that can be worked on again and again throughout
the year, with each segment getting progressively more difficult. The
children love to keep their segments and see how much more tricky they
can get each time. Once in a while it can be quite valuable to take a
poorly done number line (with absolutely NO reference to who did it)
and a good one (again anonymously), make overhead projector slides
of them, and get a small group together to discuss them: their good
points and bad ones, why, etc. My approach with the bad ones is usually
"Please help me out with this one. I'm not sure what I'm supposed to be
able to find out about numbers from this." And never hesitate to suggest that the wastebasket might be the best place to file some piece of
work that got messed up—adding machine tape is cheap and starting
over can be so much more helpful than erasing and fixing.

Weighing and Balancing

As the cards indicate, this is a project that can and should continue
all year long, and is one that the children never seem to tire of—they
can always find something interesting to weigh and an interesting way to
record its weight.

Pan balances or balance scales with gram and ounce weights are the
equipment needed, as well as blocks, marbles, or almost anything to

number lines — 5

Try a number line segment with negative (below zero) numbers! If you are not sure of what happens, talk it over with a friend!

weighing and balancing — 1

Use the pan balance to weigh lots of different objects. Balance the "objects" with marbles or the SEE cubes.

number lines — 4

Make up a number line segment starting with zero & ending with 1. Fill in as many fractional parts as you can. Or start with 4 & end with 5, etc.

weighing and balancing (Yellow)

Weigh as much as you can each week! Find different ways to record your work.

weighing and balancing — 2

Make a set of weights from plasticene or blocks or something! Weigh some objects with your weights & write up what you did.

weighing and balancing — 3

Try weighing 1 cup of lots of things (different). Use the small balance scales & the gram weights. Keep a record or graph your answers.

weighing and balancing — 4

Weigh the same cupfuls, but this time with the ounce weights. Can you figure out about how many grams to an ounce?

weighing and balancing — 5

Keep working with the scales & weights throughout the year. Find lots of things to weigh & decide which scales & weights are most appropriate for what you want to weigh. Be sure to record all your work!

balance the scales. Simple pan balances can be made by the children, and this is a great exercise in itself. Nine-, ten-, and eleven-year-olds can accept relatively good balance, so the initial pan balance used need not be perfect. The pan balance can be made from aluminum pie tins, heavy cord, a yard or meter stick, and a stand which is quite simple to make. They can experiment for hours about where to hang the pans, etc., and loads of learning about balance, and even the density of wood, its imperfections, etc., comes into play. We even started with a sand-paper balance before a pan balance. This was nothing more than a block of wood, a piece of two-by-four, sanded semi-round on the top and covered with sand paper to reduce the friction. We used a meter-long board about six inches wide to balance on this "fulcrum," and proceeded to find out what would and would not balance and where. Needless to say, because of the crudeness and heaviness of our "balance board," we could not weigh or balance anything of a delicate nature, but our Base Ten Dienes blocks, and our Cuisenaire Prisms and Cubes, as well as shoes, bottles, books, etc., worked very nicely. One of the major concepts we all learned was whether you marked the balance arm starting from the middle out, or whether you worked from the outside in towards the middle! Hmmmmmm?! *I* was surprised!

Our initial try with a pan balance was not too successful either, but with lots of trial and error, we produced one that works quite well, and a balance beam for use with metal or plastic washers for just straight numerical work as well. I cannot urge you strongly enough to try mak-ing these things; it's great experience for student and teacher alike, and by no means wasted time, even if it doesn't work!

As you can see, the yellow card is very open, and leaves the whole project up to the student to carry on by himself throughout the year. The green cards start the children off with nonstandard units of weight; the first card refers to "SEE cubes." These are the most kinesthetically appealing and visually attractive plastic blocks—clear plexiglass, I guess really—I have ever seen, and I personally HATE plastics and have very little of this material in the lab. (My dislike of plastic comes from several years' experience with it. I find that it does not hold up well under the strains and stresses of child use daily. Wood or metal is much more durable.) But I do have to commend these plexiglass cubes —they are not only appealing, they work magnificently for weighing on the more sensitive balance scales, as well as the very primary pan balances.

With respect to recording with nonstandard weights or not-exact "answers," there are several ways of doing it. One, and the simplest, is to write a statement like "The orange cube weighs more than fifty marbles but less than fifty-one," and this, of course, can be translated into mathematical language quite easily:

$$50 < \text{the orange cube} < 51$$
marbles   marbles

Once standard weights are used, there are many possibilities, including graphing, which is not only fun but very colorful.

I personally like the written-out statements as well as any method: such things as "One measuring cup of dried peas weighs as much as two measuring cups of rice," and "30cc of coffee weighs 14 grams less than 30cc of iron filings," but it is very important that the children learn to use all methods of recording from lengthy, well-written English to short mathematical symbols to pictorial representation, so do encourage them!

Measuring: All Ways

This unit can be used before any of the specific ones on area and/or volume, but just keep in mind that for some children finding lengths does not necessarily have to come first. My experience has indicated that area is sometimes easier, and occasionally volume makes more sense to a child.

Linear measure allows for some of the simplest, yet creative tools to work with: sticks of varied lengths (children on different teams or groups do not need to use the same measuring device), even tongue depressors, pieces of rope, a surveying chain, trundle wheels, steel tapes, cloth tape measure—and other things the children can find. I have given strong direction to finding out "all about our campus" on both the yellow and green cards: perhaps you are not set up to find this useful or productive or even possible. The whole set can be re-done to apply to a school building, a section of a building, the school playground, even to things in the room IF the children must be restricted.

Basically, I want children to experience different kinds of measure with different kinds of tools, and especially not to feel thwarted or as if they must "wait" if someone has just the tool they were planning to use. One of the important lessons to learn in measuring is that it is not the unit you use that is of primary importance, it's how you tell the rest of us what you did so that we understand. And, of course, it is precisely that, communication, which standardized the units we do use today. What helps with this whole project now is that wonderful chart I spoke of in the beginning section of this book which shows in words and pictures the history of measurement. When someone (or several) chooses this card, I leave him alone for several days to see how it develops, and if ideas begin to bog down, out comes the chart to look over and study.

The third green card is concerned with "how big is"—the soccer field, the football field, etc.—deliberately ambiguous. What does "big" mean? What kind of measurement should or could be done here?

measuring all ways — 1

Use the trundle wheel to measure distances around our campus. Be sure to estimate (educated guess) the distance first; then measure accurately. Record both your estimates & your measurements.

measuring all ways — 3

How big is the soccer field?
the football field?
the baseball diamond?
the Lacrosse field?
the gym floor?

measuring all ways (Yellow)

Using different units of measure, let's find out all we can about our campus, the buildings, the classrooms, the playing fields, etc. Estimate first, then measure & see how close you came!

measuring all ways — 2

We're going to put new tiles on the floor of the maths lab. How many will it take? Suppose we retile the whole building: how many should we buy?

measuring all ways — 4

Make a cubic foot. Then
find out how many of
these it would take to
fill the maths lab, or any
classroom. How about
a cubic yard?
Estimate first, then measure

scale drawings — 1

Measure the maths lab
very carefully: floors,
walls, doors, windows,
chalkboard, shelves, &
cupboards. Keep good
records.

COMMUNICATION, again—a mighty important item, and this time, on my part, for it really isn't clear what is meant. And it does seem to generate the kind of conversation and decision-making that I hope for here. The whole set of green cards progresses from linear to area to volume. The yellow card implies it, and usually it happens with the children who use it.

[Note: there are more than 20 additional sets of Math Lab ideas in *Learning to Think in a Math Lab*.]

IV

Science

The science curriculum should nurture children's natural curiosity about the world and help them order their experiences in increasingly coherent ways. The objective should not be to turn children into scientists; it should be to make children scientifically literate, so that they will have the capacity as well as the interest to continue examining, analyzing, and understanding the world about them.

As with math, there should be continuity between children's preschool and school experiences. Children come to school, after all, with all kinds of interests and unanswered questions. They want to know more about living things and how they grow and change. They want to know why the sky is blue, why it rains, where clouds come from, where puddles disappear to after the rain, why lights go on and off. They are fascinated by their own shadows and curious about (and perhaps a little frightened of) the dark. They want to know more about space and rocks and seasons. Any and all of these interests can provide starting points for science instruction.

The teacher cannot simply rely on happenstance, however. Scientific concepts are not just lying around waiting to be discovered automatically; nature has to be stirred up, so to speak, and experiences have to be devised if children are to be led to the necessary understandings. But since science is a humane and even playful as well as rigorous discipline, the experiences that are devised must leave plenty of room for exploration and play.

1. The Aims of Science Education

Over its ten years of active existence, the Elementary Science Study underwent a transformation in which its goals broadened and changed from its initial preoccupation with the content of science to an equal concern with the ways in which children (and teachers) may be helped to learn. What happened was that the ESS staff members, under David Hawkins' direction, gradually reached the conclusion that they could not improve education by improving its content alone. Turning out better curriculum packages—the approach of most curriculum reform efforts— would have little impact unless the prevailing style of teaching and learning was also revised. Hence the ESS staff moved away from the highly structured, carefully sequenced curriculum units toward much more open-ended investigations.

The scientists and the teachers and experts on child development were equally affected. "We who have been involved in this study of science and children have ourselves been changed in the process—in some way not easy to voice, we have been liberated," Professor Hawkins has explained in his Foreword to The ESS Reader. *"Those of us who knew children before science have now seen the former (and ourselves as well) in a new light—as inventors, as analysts, and synthesizers, as homelovers, lovers of the world of nature. Those of us who knew science first and children later have an altered and more childlike view of science—more humane, more playful, more available, and even at its most 'elementary,' full of unexpected delights."*

This selection, taken from Introduction to the Elementary Science Study, *a pamphlet which accompanied the "trial editions" of five ESS units distributed in 1965, provides a graceful and illuminating discussion of both the objectives of science education as ESS came to see them and the strategies the staff devised to try to fulfill these goals.*

Theory: an Approach

OUR GENERAL AIM

Within the Elementary Science Study we have found basic agreement that a major aim of our project must be to encourage children to examine, analyze, and understand the world around them and to stimulate

From *Introduction to the Elementary Science Study,* a booklet accompanying trial editions of the first five ESS units which were distributed in 1965 by Houghton Mifflin. Reprinted in *The ESS Reader* (Newton, Mass.: Education Development Center, 1970).

their desire to continue to do so. We view our task simply as the development of a variety of materials and techniques explicit enough to preclude the need for specialist teachers and diverse enough to awaken the curiosity and desire for understanding in children of many ages, interests, attitudes, skills, and backgrounds. In approaching our task we should not attempt to make all children into scientists, but to promote their scientific literacy and general intellectual curiosity.

THEORIES OF LEARNING

Learning theorists are quick to remind us that they do not yet fully understand which approach, which experiences, in which sequences produce the situation that makes an individual child or group of children respond. Jerome S. Bruner, Professor of Psychology at Harvard, emphasizes two ways of learning, knowing, and acting, which he calls the "right-handed" and "left-handed." The right-handed is rational, deductive, purposeful, straightforward; the left-handed is intuitive, hypothetical, playful, witty, imaginative, and sometimes simply wrong. Both ways are useful.

Confronted by such variables and unknowns, we feel that our approach should follow a mixed strategy—one that does not even pretend to be perfectly planned and leaves occasional decisions to chance and to the opportunities of the moment for a particular child, teacher, and classroom. Our materials therefore provide situations for traditional, rational, "right-handed" learning and situations suited more to the intuitive, playful, "left-handed" approach. They are designed to appeal to all the senses, to the imagination and artistic instincts, and through the wordless experimental equipment as much as through the printed or spoken word.

A DIVERSIFIED CLASSROOM

Accordingly our ideal becomes a classroom in which sometimes the teacher talks, sometimes the student, sometimes no one; a room in which sometimes pencils are busy at each desk, sometimes no paper or book is in sight; a classroom in which plastic sheets and tubes, metal rods, wooden balances, aquaria, leaves, copper wire, clay, mealworms, microscopes, and water are as natural as books and paper; one in which motion is as welcome as stillness; one in which error is accepted as a natural and useful part of learning. In this kind of class the memorization of a few simple if valuable formulae will never adequately express the world's diversity. In such a room we can hope to kindle real interest for each child in some way at some time.

MANAGEABLE COMPLEXITY

Because learning is approached differently by different children and differently by the same child at different times, it is important that the materials of science possess what we call "manageable complexity." Children should be able to work their own way into a subject, going from simple to complex and from complex to simple. There should be a time for detailed guidance, for breaking down what is complex into a series of simple steps; there should also be a time for letting children make their own way, by steps which only they can devise.

The more complex the subject, the more this is likely to be true. Children need to play with a piece of equipment or get a feeling for the habits of living things before they are able to see the point of a more analytical, step-by-step approach. They must watch plants grow, for example, and raise many sorts of questions about them before they will be motivated to keep a record of the growth from day to day or plant to plant. To see the point in making a graph of a plant's growth is more than half the battle; and it takes more than half the time. In the class as in the garden, the seed must be nourished below the surface before its growth can be seen and measured.

The validity of this approach is further emphasized by the analogy of language learning. Young children do not first learn to talk in a logical, "right-handed" way; they do not consciously memorize vocabulary nor analyze grammatical structure. Their approach winds through a more natural context; it is sometimes playful, sometimes earnest, sometimes austere, sometimes facetious. Nevertheless, they learn to communicate well enough to begin more formal study of their language early in the elementary grades.

THE CONCRETE
BEFORE THE ABSTRACT

Similarly active involvement in observing and manipulating phenomena could be the strongest of a child's early experiences in science. Pushing a lever or turning a crank, watching the fall of a column of water, seeing a yeast cell bud, balancing on a swing are experiences which cannot be replaced by verbal formulations even when accompanied by slow-motion film. With the experiences behind him, a child may be able to analyze them, abstract from them, and perhaps even reach a generality he can test in other situations. When the generality works, it becomes more than a few symbols in an abstract language: it helps the child organize a part of the world he had no reason to believe was organized. And this, after all, is what we really mean by understanding.

NEW SLOGANS
OR OLD INSIGHTS

This approach has led us to see the importance of providing laboratory materials for each child and an environment in which each can make his own observations, ask his own questions, perform his own experiments, and draw his own conclusions. Discoveries of many kinds—esthetic as well as scientific—will and should result. Yet in our enthusiasm for this approach we should not reduce it to a simple slogan: "the discovery method." Expectation or insistence that children make preplanned "discoveries" is sterile and unrealistic. Even if we could prepare a comprehensive schedule of scientific phenomena useful for them to discover, we could not expect children to make a significant number of these discoveries in the less than one and a half classroom years available to the science curriculum from kindergarten through the eighth grade.

It does not follow, however, that this limited time should be tightly packed with scientific facts to be memorized and repeated by rote. School, and especially elementary school, should not be a storage time but an insightful time, a time to acquire a taste for learning and the motivation to continue to learn. An approach designed to produce such insights will lead to quite different use of the time available: what any textbook can tersely summarize in a page of results—that life is cellular, cells have water, and cells divide to multiply—our approach hopes to build up with the child's own hands, with his own microscope and his own arithmetic, in about six weeks of classroom activity. Yet we are not disturbed by the slowness of this method, for what is slow can run deep. We believe that in the end it is better to stroll into the detail and the context, to unravel and uncover, to handle and to touch, than to speed past, reading the showy billboards of science, even if the slower journey covers far fewer miles.

We realize that this approach requires patience and confidence on the part of the teacher, since it is not always easy to guide development of the flexible learning situations it calls for nor to evaluate the insights it enables children to acquire. Nevertheless many teachers have shown us that such patience and confidence are amply rewarded, and we would hasten to reassure others that our exhortations are neither original nor new; witness the following passage from the 26th Annual Report by the Superintendent of Public Instruction of the State of Michigan—for the year 1862:

> Leave the pupils mainly to their own spontaneous self-activities. The teacher may awaken and give direction to their curiosity by an occasional adroit question; but he should chiefly rely upon the action of his pupils' own powers for the discovery of new facts. As a general rule, nothing should be told to pupils which they can discover for themselves. The zealous and impatient teacher will often fail here, and the failure is a serious and fatal one.
>
> It is so much easier to tell a child what we wish him to know, rather than wait for him to discover it for himself, that the inexperienced

and careless can rarely resist the temptation. But the babbling teacher will assuredly learn, in the long run, the truth of the maxim, "The more haste, the worse speed."

2. The Importance of Unguided Exploration

In the teaching of science, David Hawkins argues, a substantial amount of time should be devoted to what he calls messing about—free and unguided exploratory work in which children are given concrete materials and are allowed "to construct, test, probe and experiment without superimposed questions or instructions." It is misleading to call this phase unstructured, since there always is some kind of structure in the materials the teacher decides to provide.

"Messing about" is not all there is to science instruction, of course. The teacher needs to provide guidance so that individual children can be helped to go further along the idiosyncratic paths they have chosen in their "messing about." And there is an appropriate time for group discussion and instruction, even lecturing, so that children can move from the concrete to the abstract. Good science instruction requires all three phases, but it is the first that tends to be most neglected.

"Nice? It's the only *thing," said the Water Rat solemnly, as he leant forward for his stroke. "Believe me, my young friend, there is nothing— absolutely nothing—half so much worth doing as simply messing about in boats. Simply messing," he went on dreamily, "messing—about—in— boats—messing—"*

Kenneth Grahame,
The Wind in the Willows

As a college teacher, I have long suspected that my students' difficulties with the intellectual process comes not from the complexity of college work itself, but mainly from their home background and the first years of their formal education. A student who cannot seem to understand the workings of the Ptolemaic astronomy, for example, turns out to have no evident acquaintance with the simple and "obvious" relativity of motion, or the simple geometrical relations of light and shadow. Sometimes for these students a style of laboratory work which might be called "Kinder-

From David Hawkins, "Messing About in Science", *Science and Children,* February 1965, reprinted in *The ESS Reader* (Newton, Mass.: Education Development Center, 1970).

garten Revisited" has dramatically liberated their intellectual powers. Turn on your heel with your head back until you *see* the ceiling—turn the other way—and don't fall over!

In the past two years, working in the Elementary Science Study, I have had the experience, marvelous for a naive college teacher, of studying young children's learning in science. I am now convinced that my earlier suspicions were correct. In writing about these convictions, I must acknowledge the strong influence on me by other staff members in the Study. We came together from a variety of backgrounds—college, high school, and elementary school teachers—and with a variety of dispositions toward science and toward teaching. In the course of trial teaching and of inventing new curricular materials, our shop talks brought us toward some consensus but we still had disagreements.* The outline of ideas I wish to present here is my own, therefore, and not that of the group which has so much influenced my thinking. The formulation I want to make is only a beginning. Even if it is right, it leaves many questions unanswered, and therefore much room for further disagreement. In so complex a matter as education, this is as it should be. What I am going to say applies, I believe, to all aspects of elementary education. However, let me stick to science teaching.

My outline is divided into three patterns or phases of school work in science. These phases are different from each other in the relations they induce between children, materials of study, and teachers. Another way of putting it is that they differ in the way they make a classroom look and sound. My claim is that good science teaching moves from one phase to the other in a pattern which, though it will not follow mechanical rules or ever be twice the same, will evolve according to simple principles. There is no necessary order among these phases, and for this reason, I avoid calling them I, II, and III, and use instead some mnemonic signs which have, perhaps, a certain suggestiveness: O, △, and □.

O Phase. There is a time, much greater in amount than commonly allowed, which should be devoted to free and unguided exploratory work (call it play if you wish; I call it work). Children are given ma-

---

* I would also like to acknowledge the assistance of Frances Hawkins, who has long practiced in preschool what I now wish to generalize over the entire elementary range.

terials and equipment—*things*—and are allowed to construct, test, probe, and experiment without superimposed questions or instructions. I call this O phase "Messing About," honoring the philosophy of the Water Rat, who absentmindedly ran his boat into the bank, picked himself up, and went on without interrupting the joyous train of thought:

> —about in boats—or *with* boats . . . In or out of 'em, it doesn't matter. Nothing seems really to matter, that's the charm of it. Whether you get away, or whether you don't; whether you arrive at your destination or whether you reach somewhere else, or whether you never get anywhere at all, you're always busy, and you never do anything in particular; and when you've done it there's always something else to do, and you can do it if you like, but you'd much better not.

In some jargon, this kind of situation is called "unstructured," which is misleading; some doubters call it chaotic, which it need never be. "Unstructured" is misleading because there is always a kind of structure to *what* is presented in a class, as there was to the world of boats and the river, with its rushes and weeds and mud that smelled like plum-cake. Structure in this sense is of the utmost importance, depending on the children, the teacher, and the backgrounds of all concerned.

Let me cite an example from my own recent experiences. Simple frames, each designed to support two or three weights on strings, were handed out one morning in a fifth-grade class. There was one such frame for each pair of children. In two earlier trial classes, we had introduced the same equipment with a much more "structured" beginning, demonstrating the striking phenomenon of coupled pendula and raising questions about it before the laboratory work was allowed to begin. If there was guidance this time, however, it came only from the apparatus—a pendulum is to swing! In starting this way I, for one, naively assumed that a couple of hours of "Messing About" would suffice. After two hours, instead, we allowed two more and, in the end, a stretch of several weeks. In all this time, there was little or no evidence of boredom or confusion. Most of the questions we might have planned for came up unscheduled.

Why did we permit this length of time? First, because in our previous classes we had noticed that things went well when we veered toward "Messing About" and not as well when we held too tight a rein on what we wanted the children to do. It was clear that these children had had insufficient acquaintance with the sheer phenomena of pendulum motion and needed to build an apperceptive background, against which a more analytical sort of knowledge could take form and make sense. Second, we allowed things to develop this way because we decided we were getting a new kind of feedback from the children and were eager to see where and by what paths their interests would evolve and carry them. We were rewarded with a higher level of involvement and a much greater diversity of experiments. Our role was only to move from spot to spot, being helpful but never consciously prompting or directing. In spite of—because of!—this lack of direction, these fifth-graders became very familiar with pendula. They varied the conditions of motion in many ways, exploring differences of length and amplitude, using different sorts of bobs, bobs in clusters, and strings, etc. And have *you* tried the underwater pendulum? They did! There were many sorts of discoveries made, but we let them slip by without much adult resonance, beyond our spontaneous and manifest enjoyment of the phenomena. So discoveries were made, noted, lost, and made again. I think this is why the slightly pontifical phrase "discovery method" bothers me. When learning is at the most fundamental level, as it is here, with all the abstractions of Newtonian mechanics just around the corner, don't rush! When the mind is evolving the abstractions which will lead to physical comprehension, all of us must cross the line between ignorance and insight many times before we truly understand. Little facts, "discoveries" without the growth of insight, are *not* what we should seek to harvest. Such facts are only seedlings and should sometimes be let alone to grow into. . . .

I have illustrated the phase of "Messing About" with a constrained and inherently very elegant topic from physics. In other fields, the pattern will be different in detail, but the essential justification is the same. "Messing About" with what can be found in pond water looks much more like the Water Rat's own chosen field of study. Here, the implicit structure is that of nature in a very different mood from what is manifest in the austerities of things like pendular motion or planet orbits. And here, the need for sheer acquaintance with the variety of things and phenomena is more obvious, before one can embark on any of the roads toward the big generalizations or the big open questions of biology. Regardless of differences, there is a generic justification of "Messing About" that I would like, briefly, to touch upon.

Preschool Influences

This phase is important, above all, because it carries over into school that which is the source of most of what children have already learned, the roots of their moral, intellectual, and esthetic development. If education were defined, for the moment, to include everything that children have learned since birth, everything that has come to them from living in the natural and the human world, then by any sensible measure what has come before age five or six would outweigh all the rest. When we narrow the scope of education to what goes on in schools, we throw out the method of that early and spectacular progress at our peril. We know that five-year-olds are very unequal in their mastery of this or that. We also know that their histories are responsible for most of this inequality, utterly masking the congenital differences except in special cases. This is the immediate fact confronting us as educators in a society committed, morally and now by sheer economic necessity, to universal education.

To continue the cultivation of earlier ways of learning, therefore; to find *in school* the good beginnings, the liberating involvements that will make the kindergarten seem a garden to the child and not a dry and frightening desert, this is a need that requires much emphasis on the style of work I have called O, or "Messing About." Nor does the garden in this sense end with a child's first school year, or his tenth, as though one could then put away childish things. As time goes on, through a good mixture of this with other phases of work, "Messing About" evolves with the child and thus changes its quality. It becomes a way of working that is no longer childish, though it remains always childlike, the kind of self-disciplined probing and exploring that is the essence of creativity.

The variety of the learning—and of inhibition against learning—that children bring from home when school begins is great, even within the limited range of a common culture with common economic background (or, for that matter, within a single family). Admitting this, then if you cast your mind over the whole range of abilities and backgrounds that children bring to kindergarten, you see the folly of standardized and formalized beginnings. We are profoundly ignorant about the subtleties of learning but one principle ought to be asserted dogmatically: That there must be provided some continuity in the content, direction, and style of learning. Good schools begin with what children have *in fact* mastered, probe next to see what *in fact* they are learning, continue with what *in fact* sustains their involvement.

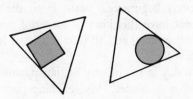

△ Phase. When children are led along a common path, there are always the advanced ones and always the stragglers. Generalized over the years of school routine, this lends apparent support to the still wide-spread belief in some fixed, inherent levels of "ability," and to the curious notions of "under-" and "over-achievement." Now, if you introduce a topic with a good deal of "Messing About," the variance does not decrease, it increases. From a conventional point of view, this means the situation gets worse, not better. But I say it gets better, not worse. If after such a beginning you pull in the reins and "get down to business," some children have happened to go your way already, and you will believe that you are leading these successfully. Others will have begun, however, to travel along quite different paths, and you have to tug hard to get them back on to yours. Through the eyes of these children you will see yourself as a dragger, not a leader. We saw this clearly in the pendulum class I referred to; the pendulum being a thing which seems deceptively simple but which raises many questions in no particular necessary order. So the path which each child chooses is his best path.

The result is obvious, but it took me time to see it. If you once let children evolve their own learning along paths of their choosing, you then must see it through and *maintain* the individuality of their work. You cannot begin that way and then say, in effect, "That was only a teaser," thus using your adult authority to devalue what the children themselves, in the meantime, have found most valuable. So if "Messing About" is to be followed by, or evolve into, a stage where work is more externally guided and disciplined, there must be at hand what I call "Multiply Programmed" material; material that contains written and pictorial guidance of some sort for the student, but which is designed for the greatest possible variety of topics, ordering of topics, etc., so that for almost any given way into a subject that a child may evolve on his own, there is material available which he will recognize as helping him farther along that very way. Heroic teachers have sometimes done this on their own, but it is obviously one of the places where designers of curriculum materials can be of enormous help, designing those materials with a rich variety of choices for teacher and child, and freeing the teacher from the role of "leader-dragger" along a single preconceived path, giving the teacher encouragement and real logistical help in diversifying the activities of a group. Such material includes good equipment, but above all, it suggests many beginnings, paths from the familiar into the unknown. We did not have this kind of material ready for the pendulum class I spoke about earlier, and still do not have it. I intend to work at it and hope others will.

It was a special day in the history of that pendulum class that brought home to me what was needed. My teaching partner was away (I had been the observer, she the teacher). To shift gears for what I saw as a more organized phase of our work, I announced that for a change we were all going to do the same experiment. I said it firmly and the children were, of course, obliging. Yet, I saw the immediate loss of interest in part of the class as soon as my experiment was proposed. It was designed to raise questions about the *length* of a pendulum, when the bob is multiple or odd-shaped. Some had come upon the germ of that question; others had had no reason to. As a college teacher I have tricks, and they worked here as well, so the class went well, in spite of the unequal readiness to look at "length." We hit common ground with rough blackboard pictures, many pendula shown hanging from a common support, differing in length and in the shape and size of bobs. Which ones will "swing together"? Because their eyes were full of real pendula, I think, they could *see* those blackboard pictures swinging! A colloquium evolved which harvested the crop of insights that had been sowed and cultivated in previous weeks. I was left with a hollow feeling, nevertheless. It went well where, and only where, the class found common ground. Whereas in "Messing About" all things had gone uniformly well. In staff discussion afterward, it became clear that we had skipped an essential phase of our work, the one I am now calling △ phase, or Multiply Programmed.

There is a common opinion, floating about, that a rich diversity of classroom work is possible only when a teacher has small classes. "Maybe *you* can do that; but you ought to try it in my class of 43!" I want to be the last person to belittle the importance of small classes. But in this particular case, the statement ought to be made that in a large class one cannot afford *not* to diversify children's work—or rather *not* to allow children to diversify, as they inevitably will, if given the chance. So-called "ability grouping" is a popular answer today, but it is no answer at all to the real questions of motivation. Groups which are lumped as equivalent with respect to the usual measures are just as diverse in their tastes and spontaneous interests as unstratified groups! The complaint that in heterogeneous classes the bright ones are likely to be bored because things go too slow for them ought to be met with another question: Does that mean that the slower students are *not* bored? When children have no autonomy in learning everyone is likely to be bored. In such situations the overworked teachers have to be "leader-draggers" always, playing the role of Fate in the old Roman proverb: "The Fates lead the willing; the unwilling they drag."

A Good Beginning

"Messing About" produces the early and indispensable autonomy and diversity. It is good—indispensable—for the opening game but not for the long middle game, where guidance is needed; needed to lead the willing! To illustrate once more from my example of the pendulum, I want to produce a thick set of cards—illustrated cards in a central file, or single sheets in plastic envelopes—to cover the following topics among others:

1. Relations of amplitude and period.
2. Relations of period and weight of bob.
3. How long is a pendulum (odd-shaped bobs)?
4. Coupled pendula, compound pendula.
5. The decay of the motion (and the idea of half-life).
6. String pendula and stick pendula—comparisons.
7. Underwater pendula.
8. Arms and legs as pendula (dogs, people, and elephants).
9. Pendula of other kinds—springs, etc.
10. Bobs that drop sand for patterns and graphs.
11. Pendulum clocks.
12. Historical materials, with bibliography.
13. Cards relating to filmloops available, in class or library.
14. Cross-index cards to other topics, such as falling bodies, inclined planes, etc.
15.–75. Blank cards to be filled in by classes and teachers for others.

This is only an illustration; each area of elementary science will have its own style of Multiply Programmed materials, of course, the ways of organizing these materials will depend on the subject. There should always be those blank cards, outnumbering the rest.

Careful!

There is one final warning. Such a file is properly a kind of programming —but it is not the base of rote or merely verbal learning, taking a child little step by little step through the adult maze. Each item is simple, pictorial, and it guides by suggesting further explorations, not by replacing them. The cards are only there to relieve the teacher from a heroic task. And they are only there because there are apparatus, film, library, and raw materials from which to improvise.

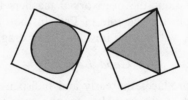

☐ Phase. In the class discussion I referred to, about the meaning of *length* applied to a pendulum, I was reverting back to the college-teacher habit of lecturing; I said it went very well in spite of the lack of Multiply Programmed background, one that would have taken more of the class through more of the basic pendulum topics. It was not, of course, a lecture in the formal sense. It was question-and-answer, with discussion between children as well. But still, I was guiding it and fishing for the good ideas that were ready to be born, and I was telling a few stories, for example, about Galileo. Others could do it better. I was a visitor, and am still only an amateur. I was successful then only because of the long build-up of latent insight, the kind of insight that the Water Rat had stored up from long afternoons of "Messing About" in boats. It was more than he could ever have been told, but it gave him much to tell. This is not all there is to learning, of course; but it is the magical part, and the part most often killed in school. The language is not yet that of the textbook, but with it even a dull-looking textbook can come alive. One boy thinks the length of a pendulum should be measured from the top to what he calls "the center of gravity." If they have not done a lot of work with balance materials, this phase is for most children only the handle of an empty pitcher, or a handle without a pitcher at all. So I did not insist on the term. Incidentally, it is not quite correct physics anyway, as those will discover who work with the stick pendulum. Although different children had specialized differently in the way they worked with pendula, there were common elements, increasing with time, which would sustain a serious and extended class discussion. It is this pattern of discussion I want to emphasize by calling it a separate, □ phase. It includes lecturing, formal or informal. In the above situation, we were all quite ready for a short talk about Galileo, and ready to ponder the question whether there was any relation between the way unequal weights fall together and the way they swing together when hanging on strings of the same length. Here we were approaching a question—a rather deep one, not to be disposed of in fifteen minutes— of theory, going from the concrete perceptual to the abstract conceptual. I do not believe that such questions will come alive either through the early "Messing About" or through the Multiply Programmed work with guiding questions and instructions. I think they come primarily with discussion, argument, the full colloquium of children and teacher. Theorizing in a creative sense needs the content of experience and the logic of experimentation to support it. But these do not automatically lead to conscious abstract thought. Theory is square! □

We of the Elementary Science Study are probably identified in the minds of those acquainted with our work (and sometimes perhaps in our own minds) with the advocacy of laboratory work and a free, fairly ○ style of laboratory work at that. This may be right and justified by the fact that prevailing styles of science teaching are □ most of the time, much too much of the time. But what we criticize for being too much and too early, we must work to re-admit in its proper place.

I have put ○, △, and □ in that order, but I do not advocate any rigid order; such phases may be mixed in many ways and ordered in many ways. Out of the colloquium comes new "Messing About." Halfway along a programmed path, new phenomena are accidentally observed. In an earlier, more structured class, two girls were trying obediently to reproduce some phenomena of coupled pendula I had demonstrated. I heard one say, "Ours isn't working right." Of course, pendula never misbehave; it is not in their nature; they always do what comes naturally, and in this case, they were executing a curious dance of energy transference, promptly christened the "twist." It was a new phenomenon, which I had not seen before, nor had several physicists to whom, in my delight, I later showed it. Needless to say, this led to a good deal of "Messing About," right then and there.

What I have been concerned to say is only that there are, as I see it, three major phases of good science teaching; that no teaching is likely to be optimal which does not mix all three; and that the one most neglected is that which made the Water Rat go dreamy with joy when he talked about it. At a time when the pressures of prestige education are likely to push children to work like hungry laboratory rats in a maze, it is good to remember that their wild, watery cousin, reminiscing about the joys of his life, uttered a profound truth about education.

3. Science As a Social Activity

Human learning, as Molly Brearley and her colleagues at the Froebel Institute write, is a process of building up and internalizing successively more accurate models of the world. Children, like scientists, develop and improve their models through experimentation; the purpose of science education is to help the child order his experiences into a rational unity. To fulfill this function, teachers must understand that scientific knowledge does not exist apart from the methods by which the knowledge is acquired. In particular, they must understand, and convey to their students, that science is a social as well as intellectual activity. This can be done effectively in a classroom in which children are encouraged to submit their methods as well as their results to group scrutiny.

Human learning is a process of building up an internal model of the world. This is a personal experience: but a new-born child has no store of personal experiences upon which to build. There is certainly evidence that he has virtually seen nothing, tasted nothing, heard nothing, smelled nothing and felt nothing. Thus the world has no coherence for him. At

From Molly Brearley, editor, *The Teaching of Young Children* (New York: Schocken Books, 1970), pp. 17–18, 19, 24, 25–27. Copyright © 1969 by Basil Blackwell Publisher. Reprinted by permission of Schocken Books, Inc.

birth the child cannot even be taught, and so has to learn for himself. At first this learning will be derived from chance events, and then from his own experiments. It will be characterized by the relation of his own actions to external events, by which he gradually differentiates patterns of behaviour through which he interprets the world. In so doing, the young baby manifests *purpose*. Although he may explore at random, he is beginning to search for what has happened before and purpose gives a direction to search. However, not all particular, organized sensitivities to the environment are learnt from experience. For example, as a bird inherits in its genetic endowment the ability to build nests, so a baby is equipped with the sucking reflex.

In this technological age, much of our adult information about the world is achieved through the use of technical and scientific apparatus. However delicate and complex this is the scientific investigator shares with all of us the fact that, in the end, what he records enters his mind directly through his senses. Whether it is an ordinary everyday happening, or an investigation conducted with the use of scientific instruments, e.g. a microscope, a galvanometer or an X-ray spectrometer, ultimately the data are interpreted after passing through one or more of our five senses.

But what the senses report does not have meaning in itself, for each message is piecemeal and unstructured. As Bronowski points out, we build up a model of the world only as we learn to link one message with another, to relate what the ear hears with what the hand touches and the eye sees. Smells, tastes, visual patterns, sounds and tactile events are differentiated and organized into a unified whole. Both the ordinary human being and the scientist share similar experiences in this way. The discoveries of science are not there to be picked up. They come into being only by an activity enacted between the scientist and his selected environment. In an analogous manner, the child has to find reality for himself, by building up from simple to more complex experiences.

By learning to co-ordinate his actions, particularly visual and grasping ones, the young child invents space for himself. Like scientists, children make their discoveries through creative activity. They do not record just what they see: they *experiment*. Experimentation is the means by which scientific theories are improved and modified. Similarly a child improves his interpretation of the world. As the child grows, and takes more and more things into account, so the interpretation is refined and elaborated.

A further major discovery by the child is that of the permanent existence of objects. Once a child has learned that even when an object is out of sight it is still somewhere, he starts a new stage in mental awareness. Such a child is beginning to separate the world from himself. Up to this point he has been learning to manipulate objects with his hands and mouth: now he can start to manipulate them in thought. The child begins to be aware of the world as consisting of things and people, of which he is one. He has moved into a world of imagination and reason. This is a basic step, for when the child has learned to be aware of the existence of something which has been put out of sight, out of the immediate field of the senses, thought rests upon the formation of images. Thought and imagination therefore are inseparable.

A child comes to school equipped in some measure with an imaginative curiosity about the world around him. This chapter is concerned with how we, as teachers and educators, help him to order his experiences into a rational unity. Young children should find in the schools a nurturing influence for their natural curiosity. It is to be expected that many of their investigations will be transitory and fleeting, for they are seeking merely to answer specific questions. But as they build up understanding of relationships, so they begin to search for more general statements.

In considering the function of science in the classroom, we must decide initially what we mean when we use the term 'science.' The popular notion is that of a large collection of facts carefully classified and structured, a kind of reservoir of technical know-how. This we might use firstly, in an instrumental way, to solve practical problems and secondly as a source of explanation which reveals to us the nature of the world. From the first point of view we would regard the telephone directory as a fragment of science. But this seems to be far too restrictive a notion. Science, it is true, includes a body of knowledge, but in appreciating its full meaning, it is necessary to include the *methods* by which such knowledge is acquired. When we come to do this we are involved in considering the activities of scientists.

It would seem that knowledge is derived, at least in part, from experience, but no statement by a single person reporting an experience can be incorporated into scientific knowledge, no matter how strong the conviction. It has to undergo a kind of inter-subjective scrutiny. That is to say, it has to be confirmed by others using agreed methods of testing. Only in this way can it be said that the data is objective, and may become incorporated into the body of knowledge. This inter-subjective requirement shows us that the growth of scientific knowledge is a social act. The history of science is set in the solving of human practical problems: an intellectual effort embedded in the changing needs of mankind. Similarly, the growth of understanding by children in the natural scene around them, arises out of practical problems which the teacher has the responsibility of drawing to the children's attention.

In the adult world of science, individuals contribute, but only within a social context. In a classroom providing opportunities for experiment, children will arrive at tentative conclusions and should be encouraged to submit them to the scrutiny of group discussions. As indicated earlier, the judgment is not just on the *results* of experiments, but also upon the *method*. It is the examination of the means by which a statement has been derived that determines whether it is acceptable. One important notion to get across to young children is whether an observation is invariant to individuals, e.g. 'Do you think if John tried our floating and sinking experiment it would happen in a similar way for him?'

Thus only after children have come to see that things behave consistently from individual to individual, providing other conditions are similar, can they challenge a claim on the grounds that the method of acquiring the result is as much a part of the discovery as the so-called discovery itself.

Science is not the only social activity that demands an inter-subjective agreement. Art, too, requires some measure of acceptance. Both being social activities, they need to gain this acceptance before they can be incorporated within the body of artistic or scientific expression. An important distinction between the two, however, is that a work of art is appraised as a finished product—for example, a novel, a painting or a piece of sculpture. Although we may be interested for other reasons in the processes that led up to the finished piece of artistic work, this in no way affects the evaluation of it as a work of art. But a scientific statement, as distinct from an artistic one, requires not only that we scrutinize it as the result of a method, but also that we scrutinize and make a judgment upon the method as well.

A work of science must not only provide a conclusion, but also the means by which it was reached. The statement that there are invisible elephants living on Mars would never gain acceptance scientifically, without an accompanying explanation of how this remarkable conclusion was reached. The method of acquiring the result is bound up with the discovery. It is important to appreciate, therefore, that the criterion of general assent has to be understood in this broader sense. The criterion for science is more social than individual, while the artistic world is by its very nature, less unified.

Yet from the point of view of the individual effort of the artist or scientist, there is little difference in the manner of handling their respective problems. Both manifest imagination handling their respective problems. Both manifest imagination or inspiration. With the research worker in the laboratory this is most obvious: before he decides the detailed nature of his test, he has already jumped ahead of his evidence. For any particular test he sets up is determined solely by the expected result he seeks. Thus verification waits upon action; and the kind of action is determined by expectations. The term 'expectations' is not to be understood as prior knowledge of results, for if this were so there would be no point in setting up the test. An expectation is a derivative from a point of view about a task in hand. The point of view determines what we observe, and we make a discriminatory forecast. Objects can be classified, and can become similar or dissimilar only in this way, by being related to needs and interests. This applies to the inquiring child as well as to the scientist . . .

4. The Need for Sensory Experience

If it is to be taught to maximum advantage in the primary school, the directors of the Nuffield Junior Science Project argue, "science must not be treated as a subject to be studied at a set time on a timetable. Rather, it must be seen as a particular way of working to be employed at any time if it will lead to greater understanding." For many children, to be sure, science ultimately will emerge as a specific discipline, but in the primary school "it is merely one of the ways by which children learn." If they are to use the study of science as a way of deepening and extending children's thinking about and understanding of their environment, teachers need a clear understanding of how children learn. In particular, they must appreciate the importance of direct sensory experience—of "messing about," to use David Hawkins' term.

The best of all cases can be made out for the inclusion of science in the primary school curriculum, for it is essentially a practical investigation of the environment. It makes use of some of the young child's most outstanding characteristics, his natural curiosity and his love of asking questions. What is more, science presents the teacher with a constant challenge to learn and discover for himself, a challenge which can have only a beneficial effect upon his teaching.

Science starts from observable facts and attempts to explain them through accurate observations and carefully planned experiment. The steadily growing and changing body of knowledge which accrues is acceptable only as long as it fits the observed facts. It can be used to predict future events, and any discrepancies will demand further investigation and modification. This is how the model of the universe has changed from that of Ptolemy, via Copernicus and Newton, to that of Einstein.

Science demands critical appraisal of observations made through the senses, or through instruments which are man-made extensions of the senses. But it is not all analysis, for seeking an explanation often de-

From E. R. Wastnedge, ed., *Nuffield Junior Science: Teacher's Guide 1* (London: Collins, 1967 [distributed in the United States by Agathon Press]), pp. 9, 13–15, 24–26, 42–44. Reprinted by permission of Collins Publishers.

mands great imaginative leaps, and devising experiments is an act of great creativity.

Clearly science is not deeply divided from other aspects of the curriculum. It is not the only way of learning and it is interdependent on mathematics, art, language, and history. The child will come through all of these, and not by any one alone, to question his environment, seek answers, gain understanding and control, and break free of the fears which come from superstition and ignorance. Science alone cannot do all this, but it has an important part to play. . . .

Our first principle is that the child should have the widest possible range of practical experience. It is vital that he should *handle* materials, as well as hear, smell, and taste them too, if that is practicable. The value of such experience cannot be over-estimated and *there can be no substitute for it.*

The further removed from first hand the experience is, the more tenuous the quality of understanding. Films, books, radio, television, and verbal explanations can extend, but cannot replace it.

We believe that the child thinks as a result of the vast experience which is constantly flowing in through his senses. When he handles things he talks about them. Mind and body act together, and while this is true at all ages, it is never more so than in the very young. This is traceable in his monologue as he plays.

Even adults confronted by a new object want to handle it. They run their fingers over an interesting new wallpaper, or test the texture and weight of clothing fabrics. They may know by looking that a polished surface will be smooth and slippery, but *only* because they have handled many such surfaces in the past. Even then, they can often be surprised by what they find when they do handle things—as many are surprised by the apparent warmth of expanded polystyrene.

How much greater, then, is the same need in a child who is moving through a world of new things?

Is it fair to expect him to understand the warmth of the body and the texture of the fur of a hamster if he is never allowed to hold one? Can children who have never, or rarely, had the chance to experiment with clay ever appreciate its peculiar plastic qualities?

Most children want to explore a new problem actively with all the appropriate senses—even taste, where that is permissible.

An eleven-year-old boy in a secondary school had to place on his tongue a tiny grain of salt he had recovered from a solution, even though he knew perfectly well that nothing but salt had been dissolved in the water.

The Extent and Kind of Experience

Teachers must also realize that each individual has his own particular needs. Some children come from rich home backgrounds—rich, that is, in terms of experience—others from arid ones. To try to give them all the same experience will be superfluous in some cases and fall far short in others.

In some cases, the school must compensate for the limited experience in the home. In two schools, one serving a new housing estate, the other a multi-racial society, the teachers found that they had to provide even such basic experience as playing with water, sand, and common household materials, over a much longer period than usual. The children became so lively and so curious as a result that parents began to visit the schools to find out what made their children enthuse, and to ask if they could help by buying books, scientific kits, or toys.

Sometimes the response of the children can be moving. One of the Nuffield team took a bunch of flowers to a school in a large seaport and was greeted by a worried and rather frightened child, who said, 'Who's dead?' The child's limited experience of a bunch of flowers is obvious.

We believe that the way to fulfil the different needs of individual children is to offer them the opportunities for as wide a range of experience as possible (by taking children out and by bringing materials into the classroom), and then to encourage them to explore freely and savour what they will. . . .

The Child As a Scientist

The child of five entering the reception class of the infant school spends most of his time observing. To do this, he experiments, in so far as he pushes his finger into a lump of clay, or mixes paints to see what colour they will make. In fact, he often manipulates things in this way in order to learn more about what they are like and what they can do. Occasionally, he will even plan an experiment, although most of the time he is exploring rather than experimenting. But these early observations are still of inestimable value, for through them he builds up a growing body of knowledge about the world.

Thus, after prodding a finger into many lumps of clay, he realizes that it is peculiarly plastic, and he will generalize similarly about other properties of numerous other materials which he investigates. The scientist's way, of course, is not so simple. He has had to learn from long experience to be careful about generalizing on evidence that is not comprehensive. He knows, for example, that if he drastically varies temperature or pressure, he will change properties like consistency and shape.

Thus, before jumping from anything generally found true to an assumed universal rule, the scientist will expressly test it under the conditions most likely to show up any flaw. And even when a probable rule has passed every such test, he will usually put it forward cautiously, since new limits may come to light later.

But the mature scientific attitude can only develop step by step. It is still true that if a child observes, experiments, and tests any idea that comes to him before he accepts it, he is making a genuine start towards science. In fact, as he goes on with this, trial and error will soon guide him to the beginnings of the right method. He will begin to distinguish between the less stable and the more stable characteristics of things. . . .

The exploratory methods used by a child to satisfy his natural curiosity about his environment are essentially scientific. He is, of course, too curious about everything to stay interested in any one thing for long, and he turns quickly from one problem to another, apparently unrelated one. In doing so, he rapidly collects a mass of data, without which it would be impossible for him to form the understanding of the under-lying general principles of science which may come later. General scien-tific ideas, like energy interchange, natural classification, or evolutionary change, can only emerge after a broad survey has been made and as much evidence as possible collected and examined. This is true at all ages and not only in the case of very young children. To expect a young child to appreciate scientific ideas, then, before he has had a chance to experience and examine the evidence would be as foolish as to have expected Linnaeus to devise his system of classification without first ex-amining a multitude of organisms.

Science and the Curriculum

It will be clear by now, that even if it were desirable, it would be quite impossible to isolate science from the remainder of the curriculum. It may even be argued that science occupies a peculiar position, in that it is essentially a practical way of finding out about the environment, and as such can often form the basis for much other activity. Many examples of this have already been quoted—talking, writing, painting, modelling, counting, computation, and graphs.

It is also true that science can, and should, arise from work in other subjects. There was an instance of a five-year-old investigating the possi-bilities of using coffee, orange juice, washing-up liquids, and other ma-terials as paints. There have been cases where a question asked in history has been the start of a scientific investigation, and in mathematics an experiment is frequently needed before a solution can be found to a problem.

There is, of course, more to it than the content of one 'subject' over-lapping that of another. Different approaches to learning and ways of thinking are brought to bear on the same problem. The various disciplines interact and interweave in such an elaborate fashion that it becomes almost impossible to distinguish them. And at the root of all this is the attitude of the children to learning. When a child wants to know something, he will bring to bear on the problem any discipline or technique which is likely to help him find an answer.

Perhaps he finds that his scientific investigation can progress only if he applies a particular mathematical technique, or that his answer will be incomplete until he has read some history. Similarly, he can understand much better what it was like to be a cave painter if he paints on stone, improvising with natural materials as the cavemen did.

Ultimately, for many children the science will emerge as a specific discipline, but for the moment it is merely one of the ways by which children learn and it must take its place alongside mathematics, English, or art, in the child's educational armoury, supporting, as well as being supported by them.

If it is to be seen at its most fruitful, science must not be treated as a subject to be studied at a set time on a timetable. Rather, it must be seen as a particular way of working to be employed at any time if it will lead to greater understanding.

Science at First and Second Hand

So far, great stress has been laid on learning from first-hand experience, but it must be clearly understood that this is not the only way. If it were, then the process would be long and laborious and end in the child knowing only a limited amount, even though what he did know would be thoroughly understood. There are many other things which he would not know because they cannot be investigated directly by this method— usually for reasons of safety, or expense. Children have to learn about these things at second hand, from books, film, radio, television, or any other medium of communication.

Then, too, often as a *result* of direct enquiry, children will want to know more and must turn to information imparted by others. It is important that they should learn where and how to find the information they want, and to make some kind of assessment of its validity and value.

Because the knowledge, in such cases, comes at second hand, it must not be confused with passive learning. It still involves an active search for information and understanding. Compare this search with the child following precise instructions from a card or a book, telling him what to do and what to look for. Although he is carrying out a practical experiment, nevertheless the learning is likely to be completely passive and its quality is not to be compared with that involved, for example, in the *active* seeking of information in a library or, perhaps, from a film strip.

Learning may be at first or second hand. It is the active search for understanding that matters.

5. How to Arrange the Classroom

In this selection, the Nuffield Junior Science Project explains how to arrange the classroom for science learning and lists the kinds of equipment that are desirable.

Arranging the Classroom

In arranging the classroom a teacher tries to create the best possible conditions for learning, and its layout reflects his personal view of the situations in which children learn most effectively.

Our experience is that when children learn by tackling practical problems, they tend to work as individuals or in small groups. Ideally, they will have available to them a wide range of materials, plenty of flat surfaces on which to work, space to move freely, adequate sources of reference, and ample display and storage space. Materials, equipment, and books will be easily accessible so that the children themselves can find whatever they need for their work. This helps them to become self-reliant and reduces their routine demands on the teacher, so giving him more time to concentrate on helping children to learn, that is, to develop in the widest sense.

The General Situation

No classroom is ideal. For most teachers, the problem is how to make the best possible use of the available furniture and facilities. Many begin by examining furniture arrangements, and it is surprising how often a rearrangement can provide a little extra space for movement, greater flexibility, and better surfaces on which to work. Primary school classrooms are used for such a wide range of activities that furniture arrangements should be as flexible as possible.

If the desks are arranged in blocks rather than straight rows, children can work together in groups without disturbing others, while the compactness of the group encourages discussion and sharing of ideas. It also provides large flat surfaces, and this makes it easier for the children to use large pieces of paper, maps, charts, materials of all kinds, and reference books. Apparatus placed in the centre is safer and less likely

From E. R. Wastnedge, ed., *Nuffield Junior Science: Teacher's Guide 1* (London: Collins, 1967 [distributed in the United States by Agathon Press]), pp. 152–158. Reprinted by permission of Collins Publishers.

to be knocked by passers-by. This arrangement also leaves useful floor space so that children can move around the classroom and seek the materials they require.

There are occasions when the teacher may want all the children to listen to a story, or to be able to see the blackboard. For either purpose, it is usually only necessary for the children with their backs to the teacher to turn their chairs round. On the other hand, many teachers prefer to gather the children around them, or around the blackboard, some sitting on the floor, others on chairs. This informal arrangement helps to create a good atmosphere for story telling, and encourages discussion.

It is often rewarding to pay attention to the siting of large pieces of furniture. It is worth trying to make room for one or two tables which provide extra working space for the children and which can be used for displays, or for storing material and unfinished work. Usually they are placed with their long side against a wall, but in some cases it is better to turn the short end to the wall so that children can work at both long sides. When they are used for displays, pieces of pegboard can be used to cover the sides and provide display space. If the pegboard is suspended from cup hooks it can be lifted out of the way when necessary to give access to materials stored under the table.

When space is extremely limited, a teacher may well have to consider whether he can afford the space needed for opening cupboard doors. If not, he can remove the doors, and if the shelves or the inside look dull, their appearance can be improved with self-adhesive plastic.

Sometimes it helps to turn a cupboard sideways, with one end against the wall. The back can then be covered with pinboard and used for displays, or two cupboards may be placed back to back to give a double-sided storage unit with a wide top on which to stand things, and a double end for display. Cupboards turned sideways mean more wall space available for displays or shelving, with the cupboard itself acting as a room divider to cut off a bay for quiet reading, or for accommodating a woodwork bench.

Some teachers arrange their furniture to form a number of bays. . . . Used flexibly, this arrangement has a number of advantages over more conventional ones. By separating different activities it avoids certain kinds of disturbance—for example, the child who is writing is no longer troubled by another child carrying out an experiment at the same table. It reduces the chance of accidents when children carry apparatus and materials across the room to their desks and, since only part of the room is used for material like clay and plaster of Paris, it simplifies the task of clearing up. When furniture is used as a room divider it increases the amount of storage and display space.

Main Services

Ideally, in every classroom there should be a sink with hot and cold water. If this is not provided and the children have to carry water from the taps in the cloakroom, it is useful to keep a supply of water in the classroom. The most satisfactory containers for this purpose are the plastic water carriers used by campers, or plastic jerrycans, depending on the strength of the children who have to use them.

Apparatus and Materials

The apparatus and materials which children use in the course of their investigations fall into four broad categories:

1. scientific apparatus and equipment
2. tools and materials for constructing things
3. materials for recording and communicating
4. books and other reference material

If these are readily available, the children can be encouraged to seek what they require for themselves, and return it to its place after use.

1. SCIENTIFIC APPARATUS AND EQUIPMENT

The following lists indicate the kind of equipment which teachers have found most useful. Further details are available in *Apparatus: a Source Book of Information and Ideas.*

(a) Tools of investigation

Magnifiers—hand lenses, 3D viewers, microscope (such as Bausch & Lomb S.S.M.-15)

Stopclock or stopwatch

Thermometers—10°–110°C, clinical, maximum and minimum

Measuring tapes 1 yd. and 22 yd. plastic clothes line marked in yards and feet

Measuring jugs or measuring cylinders, e.g. 1½ pt showing fluid oz and cc

Measuring spoons—kitchen type, plastic

Weights—for kitchen scales, hanging weights, washers, etc.

Spring balances—0–100 g × 1 g 0–4 lb × 1 oz

Kitchen scales—balance type

Letter balance 0–8 oz × ⅛ oz

Trundle wheel

Spirit level

Protractors, set squares

Magnetic compass

Filter papers—coarse, e.g. Whatman No. 1

Plastic funnels—various sizes

Assorted corks

Set of cork borers

Glass tubing, e.g. 5 and 7 mm external diameter

Capillary tubing

Plastic tubing, e.g. 5 mm and 7 mm bore

Hoffman's screw burette clips
Mohr's spring burette clips

(b) Collecting equipment

Pond-dipping nets
Plastic bowls—yellow or white, for sorting animals, etc.
Polythene bags
Sweep net
Trowel
Sieves and strainers, e.g. household type plastic strainers, soil sieves
Secateurs

(c) Containers

Plastic boxes, transparent, various sizes
Polythene bags
Polythene sheeting—use it to line a box and make temporary aquarium, miniature garden, etc.
Empty plastic detergent bottles
Jam jars, sweet jars, etc.
Aquaria
Petri dishes, or similar ones; plastic containers
Test-tubes and test-tube brush
Plant pots—various sizes in plastic, pottery, etc.
Square plastic washing up bowl
Plastic bucket
Enamel pie-dishes

Paper cups, foil cake cases
Acetate sheets to make insect cages

(d) Support apparatus

Clamp stand and clamp
Tripod stands, wire gauze and asbestos mats, metal tongs
'G' clamps

(e) Sources of heat, light, power

Candles and night lights
Spirit burner
Electric torches—several sizes
Dry batteries—1½ V to 6 V—bulbs, bulb holders, wire, switches

(f) Materials for specific studies

EXAMPLE: magnetism—
horse shoe magnets
bar magnets
rod magnets
disc magnets
pocket compass
magnetic rubber, etc.

EXAMPLE: light and colour—
bicycle lamps and torches
prism, lenses
mirrors, plane, convex, concave
coloured Cellophane or plastic
dyes
kaleidoscope
sunglasses, etc.

2. TOOLS AND MATERIALS FOR CONSTRUCTING THINGS

Children often need to make their own apparatus or models. For this they need a few tools, and suitable materials.

Suggestions are given below. Again, *Apparatus: a Source Book of Information and Ideas* gives fuller details.

Tools
Adjustable spanner—small
Bradawl

Materials
Wood offcuts
Balsa wood

Tools
Cold chisel—small
Drill and bits ⅛ in., ³⁄₁₆ in.,
  and ¼ in. or brace and bits
File 6 in. flat
'G' clamps
Hack-saw
Hammer
Pincers
Pliers
Punch, face ⅛ in.
Screwdrivers
Tinsmith's snips—straight
  bladed, Gilbow safety pattern
Vise, 4–5 in.

Materials
Dowel rod—several sizes
Wood strip, square section, ¼
  in., ⅜ in., flat 1 in. × ¼ in.,
  etc.
Pegboard offcuts, etc.
Nails and screws, assorted
Nuts and bolts, assorted
Adhesives
Wood, plastic, or metal construc-
  tion sets
Adhesive tape
Waverley clips

A stout table or bench for the children to work on is a great advantage.

3. MATERIALS FOR RECORDING AND COMMUNICATION

When children come to record or communicate their findings, it is
particularly important to put at their disposal a wide range of attractive
materials. Not only does this stimulate their desire to communicate, and
increase their pleasure in doing so, but it enables them to learn about
the properties of different materials and gradually, with the teacher's
help, to choose the best means of communicating whatever they have to
say. The teacher may discuss with individuals, or groups, all the possible
ways in which they may do this, e.g. by writing, mathematical representation, painting, or models before leaving them to decide for themselves which it will be.

The following list is not meant to be exhaustive, but simply to indicate the range of materials to which the children might have free access.

(a) Paper

Assorted sizes, colours, and types will be needed.

White drawing paper 7 in. × 11
  in. to ½ Imp.
Black paper ½ Imp.
Sugar paper—assorted colours ½
  Imp.
Manila—assorted colours ½
  Imp.
Tissue paper—assorted colours
Brown paper

Squared paper—several sizes and
  rulings, e.g. ⅛ in., ¹⁄₁₀ in.,
  ¼ in., etc.
Gummed paper squares—as-
  sorted colours
Gummed paper discs—assorted
  colours
Postcards
Newsprint—roll

(*b*) *Colouring and sketching materials*

Poster paint	Charcoal
Powder paint	Felt-tipped pens
Chalks	Brushes—several sizes
Pastels	Coloured inks
Crayons	

(*c*) *Fabrics*

An assortment of colours and textures will be found useful.
Hessian, velvet, corduroy, lace, sewing cotton, wools, tapes, ribbons.

(*d*) *Adhesives*

Balsa cement, gum, cold water paste, all-purpose adhesive, etc.

(*e*) *Junk box materials*

Wood, strings, wires, paper clips, sequins, beads, buttons, raffia, metal
foil, feathers, expanded polystyrene, cardboard cylinders, rubber bands,
milk straws, pipe cleaners, corrugated cardboard, corks, matchboxes,
small cardboard boxes, sea shells, pine cones, pebbles, etc.

(*f*) *Beads and bricks*

Threading beads, Poppit beads, wooden or plastic cubes, structural
materials, etc.

(*g*) *Modelling materials*

Clay, Plasticine.

4. BOOKS AND OTHER REFERENCE MATERIAL

Children need reference material both to identify their finds, and to
provide either general or specific background information.

Keeping plants and animals is an integral part of classroom organization. For information about their housing and care see *Animals and
Plants: a Source Book of Information and Ideas*.

6. How to Begin

*Here, the Nuffield Junior Science Project provides some detailed guid-
ance for ways in which teachers can implement the approach to science
education described above. The discussion is illustrated by the inclusion
of two experiments from the Nuffield Teacher's Guide 2, all of which is
devoted to detailed descriptions of classroom activities.*

The Main Points Arising Out of Chapter 1

1. Understanding science, like understanding other subjects, demands a wide range of practical experience. Children need to be given opportunities for frequent repetition of the same and similar experiences, and although this seems to be especially true of the very young and the slower learners, it applies all through the child's school career and will do so on into adult life.

This need should be reflected in a school environment which is rich in materials and potentialities for practical experience.

2. Children learn effectively by solving practical problems (including simple practical exploration) related to the world around them. Given the opportunity, they will devise practical investigations aimed at finding answers to those problems, often designing and making any apparatus which may be necessary.

It follows that the school should be a place where individuals or small groups of children carry out practical investigations into the problems raised.

3. The problems which have the greatest significance for the child are those he has taken up actively either through his own observations or as the result of discussions with his teacher or classmates.

Clearly our classrooms should be so interesting that children will be moved and encouraged to ask questions.

4. So far as knowledge is concerned, the child's world is more of a whole than a series of subjects. Problems may arise at any time in the school day, perhaps during the study of history, geography, or English, and can be the start of an investigation which may well be classed as scientific.

Consequently, we believe that science should not be isolated from other school work and that it would be desirable to think in terms of a curriculum in which there is little differentiation between subjects.

5. Following discovery, children frequently want to communicate, and scientific exploration provides excellent opportunities for talking, writing, painting, and so on.

6. Although most of the science will be at an observational level, there are children who will want to raise problems of a more abstract or of a theoretical nature and it is important that they should be given a sympathetic and understanding ear.

7. Practical investigation does not replace the use of books. The two are complementary. Children often want to read more about what they have learnt through experiment; and frequently their practical enquiries have a start in their reading.

From E. R. Wastnedge, ed., *Nuffield Junior Science: Teacher's Guide 1* (London: Collins, 1967 [distributed in the United States by Agathon Press]), pp. 113–124. Reprinted by permission of Collins Publishers.

The Teacher's Role

From the foregoing it appears that the teacher's first task is to make sure that the classroom is well equipped to provide a wide range of practical experience for the children.

Thus, a science table can be a constantly changing source of interest, including displays set up by the teacher and later augmented by the children. A collection of carefully selected stones showing a variety of interesting shapes and textures may well inspire children to bring more samples, especially if the teacher has had the foresight to display photographs, drawings, and books about rocks. Even if the children do no more than handle the stones they will discover something of their weight, shape, and roughness, and the display will have served a valuable purpose; but it is quite likely that questions will be asked, say, about relative hardnesses, or how a rough stone can be made smooth by the sea or a river, or perhaps whether stones will dissolve in water. Answers to these questions can be sought through experiments.

It is imperative that children should be allowed to handle the display. One that is set up and guarded by the teacher will lose much of its value if the children are allowed only to look.

Other articles and materials may be displayed in other ways than by a science table. To begin with, a card asking a question or posing a problem may help to encourage the questioning attitude which we hope will build up in the classroom.

Materials which children might find useful in their work—wire, clay, balsa, polystyrene, rubber elastic, springs, and weighing and measuring equipment—all these should be readily available so that children can handle them and learn about their properties and potentialities. Indeed these articles themselves might prompt questions which could initiate investigations.

The teacher should also provide situations which will so interest children that they will be stimulated to ask questions. These situations may be in the form of displays of materials or equipment—such as an electric torch, a rotting log, or a collection of mirrors and lenses. Or it may involve an expedition beyond the classroom, to the school field, a pond, a building site, or a market place (in which case certain precautions need to be taken.

We have found that children quickly adapt themselves to the existing classroom situation and behave accordingly. Those who have been used to sitting quietly, waiting to be told what to do, will not start to ask questions simply because it is suddenly expected of them; they will need time to adjust and to accept the new atmosphere of enquiry, and at first the teacher will probably have to ask many, if not all, of the questions. But after a time (and no one can predict how long this will be), the questions will come more and more from the children.

We have also found that the mere display of materials, however extensive, rarely results in spoken questions. It is usually necessary for the teachers to move amongst the children and discuss with them the materials they are examining. It is then that the ideas begin to flow and the questions to be asked.

As the questions come, whether from the children or for the time being from the teacher, they can be used as a basis for enquiry. This means that the teacher needs to discuss the question with the child or children, collect children's ideas as to how it might be solved, and refine those ideas by further discussion. *It cannot be emphasized too strongly that discussion plays a most important part in the development of the enquiry.*

A teacher brought a rotting log, on which there was a variety of small animals, into the classroom, and one child wondered how fast a snail crawls. The conversation between teacher and child took this form:

'How could we find out how fast it moves?'
'By timing it.'
'What could we time it with?'
'A clock.'
'Which clock? The big one on the wall, or my wrist watch?'
'The one on the wall.'
'Why should we use that one?'
'It is easier to see.'
'How can we measure how fast the snail has moved?'
'See how long it takes to crawl.'
'To crawl how far?' etc., etc.

Finally, the idea emerged that it would be necessary to measure a distance and a time. This child then timed the animal as it moved over a few inches, and calculated how long it would take to crawl along the length of the log.

In this way, the children may arrive at a method of solving the problem, but the teacher plays an important part by throwing back their too general statements to them for refinement. *This is not the same thing as the teacher deciding in advance what will be done and then guiding them into the appropriate channel;* the children often produce quite new and unexpected ideas which are then accepted by the teacher or the other children for discussion. They may well turn out to be impractical but they *must never be ridiculed or summarily dismissed,* otherwise the child is not likely to offer ideas in future.

It should also be remembered that discussion has value only for those children for whom the question has some relevance, and that a so-called class discussion often really involves only two or three children, the majority being bystanders who derive little in the way of learning.

Another important part of the teacher's work is to make sure that the necessary materials are available so that the children can make apparatus and carry out their investigations.

Two things can be done about this. A teacher can build up a collection of material in a cupboard or 'junk box.' This is the kind of material which is likely to be generally useful on many occasions, and advice on it is to be found in *Apparatus: a Source Book of Information and Ideas*. It consists of things like string, wood, screws, wire, 'squeezy' bottles, tin cans, elastic bands, and similar materials which are likely to be useful in making any one of a number of pieces of equipment. In addition, the teacher will have to anticipate the *kind* of problem which might arise, and collect appropriate materials.

Thus, if an electric torch, or the electricity system of a house or classroom is to be studied, it will be necessary to have batteries, bulbs, bulb holders, and wires. After the enquiry has been under way for a little while it may be possible to anticipate new lines which are developing. Someone may be asking about electromagnets and will need plenty of wire and large nails (see *Apparatus: a Source Book of Information and Ideas*). Others may be interested in insulators and will need a varied assortment of objects to test—pottery, rubber, plastics, metals, and so on.

The experienced teacher becomes aware of the possible value of materials and objects which other people throw away as scrap, and snaps them up. Often a walk round a local store reveals useful materials, like wire-pan-scrubbers as a source of copper, steel wool as a source of very fine wire, or hair curlers from which to extract springs.

As the work proceeds there will be constant discussion with the children. The teacher will move round the class offering suggestions, help, and encouragement. The children will have to consider their observations and formulate some idea of what they might mean.

Many problems are raised to which there are no answers in books, and since answers in books may sometimes be inaccurate in any case, it is a good thing to develop the habit of checking conclusions against the actual observations. Children have to learn to ask, 'What exactly do my experimental observations mean? Where do I need more evidence? In what ways is my experiment falling short?' We have found that in this way they can develop independence of thought and a critical attitude of mind.

With experience, teacher and children learn to judge the quality of their answers by this attitude rather than by reference to books. In addition, there is some evidence that children who have been encouraged to work in this way will look critically at their apparatus and techniques and devise new and more precise methods of obtaining more satisfactory answers.

There will come a time when the teacher will have to discuss with the children what they think they should communicate and how they will do it. It is important to realize that not everything will be written about or drawn; many important discoveries will never be mentioned at all, and others will be the subject of a brief conversation with a friend. But much will be communicated in some form or other, so the teacher must be sure that there is a good supply of the necessary materials available and that as far as possible the children have experience in using them. Clearly, this is not always possible, since there must be a first time and that may be when the need to use them is first realized.

There will be times when the teacher finds it appropriate to *teach* an individual or small group. The evidence is that many children—especially older and more able ones—frequently reach a stage where they can make no further progress on their own. At this point the teacher, with his greater experience and wisdom, has to step in and help the pupil over the immediate hurdle *so that he can start again on his own.* This is no excuse for the teacher habitually to lecture at length; his job is to give just enough help through discussion, film strips, pictures, books, etc., for the child to take over again as soon as possible.

How to Prepare

The first task is to choose a starting point for study. This may be decided arbitrarily by the teacher or possibly after a discussion with the class; it may arise in any one of a number of ways, as when a child expresses a strong interest in a subject which is then taken up by the whole class. In fact, many situations are full of possibilities and some have already been tried in schools.

If a general situation is chosen for study—like the classroom, or the staff's cars in the playground—this will be examined by the children, who will probably have a few specific aims in view. Perhaps they will want to start by finding the dimensions of the room or the cars, the materials used, the colour schemes, and so on, all of which will involve them personally in the investigation. *Personal involvement is the first essential.* But as a result of this initial attack, more problems will be raised, and these will each become the particular concern of an individual or small group, so that the class necessarily breaks itself down into small units, each tackling part of the problem. As will be seen from the examples quoted in *Teacher's Guide 2,* the initial problems may lead in any number of different directions, and the study of the classroom or the cars may well bear little relationship to what comes later.

Of course, *the teacher who does not yet feel competent to embark on so independent a course will have to adopt a way of working which is more easily controlled,* and would do best to start by reading through the examples and choosing one of them. Let us suppose that he decides to do a study of sound based on the example in *Teacher's Guide 2* entitled 'Sound II.' (See page 737 below.) How does he organize his work? The following is our advice to the teacher.

First read through the example carefully and get the general picture of the development of the work and then decide how you are going to initiate the study. Perhaps you will decide, like the teacher in that case, to ask the children to bring things to school; perhaps you will decide to set up your own display; or maybe at this stage you will merely want to raise the problem by talking to the class about it.

Next fill in as fully as possible your own background knowledge of the subject. This can best be done through books or discussion with other teachers, or at the teachers' centre if one has been established in your area.

What you will do next will depend largely on the extent of your experience and how much confidence you have. If you feel uncertain, you will do well to decide to work at a restricted number of problems with the whole class rather than to have a large number of small groups working at lots of problems. In this case you will have to decide on a particular area of study. If you would feel happier by doing so, choose one yourself; better still, discuss it with the children first. Let us suppose you decide on 'Sounds and how they are made.' What materials should you have ready so that the work can go on?

In the example quoted, the children who did the work used a tuning fork; sand, a drum, and something for beating the drum; a jar of water; stringed instruments; a board, nails, and wire to make a stringed instrument; a bit of wood to make a bridge and to change the length of the string; rattles; bottles to make a 'xylophone'; a frame and string for suspending the bottles, and water to put in the bottles; a tape recorder.

In addition, you might like to add things of your own. You may like to try making a wine glass vibrate by rubbing a wet finger round the rim, or making tubular bells from bits of brass tubing.

Whatever you decide, collect together some likely materials before the work starts and *give the children plenty of chances to handle them.* The children described in the example were allowed to play with the instruments for more than a week before work in the accepted sense started.

How to Start

The first need is to let the children have the necessary experience to start them talking. If the instruments have been displayed and handled, there will no doubt be plenty of comment. If you are introducing the subject verbally, you will probably have to attack it directly and throw ideas to the children to start them. Some teachers will probably want to collect and consider the facts the children already know, and work from there, eventually arriving at the problem that way.

Your main concern is that the children should have a problem they *want* to solve, in this case connected with producing sounds. The question you decide to tackle will depend largely on the children, your own preference (in turn depending on your own knowledge), and on the materials you have available, but once it has been stated there will have to be a thorough discussion on how to find an answer.

If the question is, 'How do all these various instruments make a sound?', the next move is to collect suggestions from the children. Remember that they should have had plenty of opportunity to experiment with the rattle and the drum and to make sounds if they are to be able to suggest answers to the question.

As answers are given, consider them. The attitude you will be trying to build up in your classroom is one which asks: 'Is it possible that this is the explanation? Can we find out for certain if it is?'

Suppose that a child suggests that all the instruments make sounds because they are hollow. How can we test the veracity of this suggestion? By taking some hollow objects and some solid ones and seeing which can be made to produce a sound? *The suggestion stands or falls on the result of this test.*

Someone else says it is because they are made of wood, or metal, or plastic. Test other materials like a glass bottle, a cork, or a china cup, and find out if they will make a sound. Again, the idea is accepted or rejected on the experimental evidence.

Eventually someone may suggest that the objects have to be struck. But is this true? What about a whistle, or a violin? More experiments.

Finally, something may be said about vibrations. If not, you may be prepared to consider other ideas and abandon your original one (which was to discuss vibration at some point), but if you are not yet sufficiently confident, then perhaps you will continue discussing the strings and percussion and investigate a little further. If the question of vibrations is raised, you will be prepared for this possibility, but you must remember that the children may put forward suggestions for vibration experiments other than those for which you were prepared, or which are usually quoted in textbooks, and these ideas of the children *should* be tried out. For instance, someone may ask if the wind instruments vibrate, and this would provide an interesting problem for investigation.

Performing Experiments

Precisely what is done here must depend on your own experience and confidence. You may wish to keep the class working as one large group (although there is every probability that not all of a large group will be very interested in the same problem), in which case you will have to tackle one problem and one experiment at a time. With more experience you will no doubt feel dissatisfied with this arrangement and allow many things to go on at one and the same time.

Whatever your decision, the problem should be discussed with the children concerned, and *they* must seek an answer. It often helps to let them see the assorted materials which have been brought, for the mere sight of, say, sand or peas and a drum is often enough to put the children on the track of an experiment.

When they have planned the experiment, *they* must perform it, and afterwards they will need to discuss what they have done and observed.

The Development of Freedom

As your confidence and experience grow, you may feel that to work with the whole class is a little restricting both for you and for them, and then you will have to find a more satisfactory way of working. Usually this means breaking the class into small units, and although that may sound frightening, it is not really too difficult and can be achieved by degrees. Group work is only effective if the groups are formed, and work is allocated to them, according to the particular interests the children have shown. Dividing the class into groups in an arbitrary way inevitably results in children working at tasks with which they have little or no concern. The result is a low quality of work and increased disciplinary problems.

Thus, when a child suggests that the objects make sounds because they are hollow, and when the experiment has been planned, it is easy to say to the child, 'Here are some materials, go and work there. You can collect other materials yourself if you need them. When you have found an answer come back and tell us about it.' The other children can then turn their attention to a new idea, although there may be one or two who are anxious to join the first child in his investigation. These children constitute a natural group.

From the break-away of a single child or one small group, it is not a big step to forming a second and third group, until the whole class is involved in solving a number of distinct problems, some of which may well be independent of the general class enquiry.

The Final Drawing Together

Throughout the whole of the investigation there will have been a great deal of communication through discussion and through using the material displayed in the classroom in various stages of investigation and development. All this communication is most important and is to be encouraged.

If the class has been working as one large group, by the end of the investigation the children's communication has all been done, but if they have been divided and involved with different problems they will probably want to communicate their findings to those who do not know them. They will do this by talking and discussing, but also by writing, painting, or making models, all of which can be displayed for the others to see.

For this to be done satisfactorily, the teacher has to talk with the child about what he wants to say and how he wants to say it. The best work comes from a child who has been encouraged to talk about his ideas, to put them in order, and to consider a number of possibilities so that he can choose the most suitable way of saying what he wants.

In this way, the important communication is done *immediately* the discovery has been made, and a display builds up steadily as the work proceeds.

If the class has worked as a whole, the children will no doubt want to display their findings, and it is important that this display should be given some significance, for example, by making it freely available for other children in the school to see.

Children's ideas about display are varied and ingenious and the teacher will have to be sure that there is plenty of paper, charcoal, clay, ink, paint, silk ribbon, and whatever else may be needed. Few things are so frustrating as not having the materials with which to get on with the work in hand.

The Next Step

There are a number of fresh possibilities which may arise. Once they are involved, children have a habit of asking fresh questions about the work they are doing. Sometimes these lead along new and exciting trails which may have little connection with the original work. For example, a child may be very interested in the pigskin of a drum or tambourine, and want to start on a new line of study about animals' skins.

How far you are prepared to let this go must, once again, depend on your experience and confidence. We believe that it is desirable to allow children to follow these lines, but you may feel happier at first to have the situation more carefully controlled.

Whatever you decide, there will almost certainly be a number of questions to which the children now have fairly conclusive answers, together with other questions whose answers are not so certain. Thus, from the sound experiments you may be able to say, 'We *know* that stringed and percussion instruments vibrate to give out a sound, but we only believe (and cannot be sure at this stage) that wind instruments do.'

It is useful to look at the findings in this way, and the problems to which the answers are not conclusive can often open up new lines of enquiry.

The Need to Teach

You will notice in the example we have been considering that at one point the teacher did a piece of teaching about 'frequency.' This situation occurs from time to time and this is when your own background knowledge of the subject is useful. You may only need to talk and give illustrations briefly. It may be only a brief session, *just sufficient to satisfy the immediate need for help and start the children going again.*

The Changing Display

Throughout the enquiry the teacher will have been concerned with displays of pictures, books, materials. At first the display is his, but as the work proceeds his work is steadily replaced by that of the children. Nevertheless, as new interests appear, he will have to look carefully at his display materials. Thus, if children did begin to show a keen interest in the pigskin of a drum, the teacher might add to his display animal skins, pictures of animals, tanneries, and so on, or on the other hand he might decide to display fresh materials which could easily be made into vibrating diaphragms.

The Follow-up

You will find that the interest developed through enquiry will make many children want to know more. This they can find out partly by further experimenting and partly from books, films, and other aids. Books should not be seen as something to replace the experiment but as something to complement the practical work by adding general background knowledge and often raising further problems. Throughout the work, therefore, we would recommend that you have in your classroom a selection of books—in this case about sound—not those which suggest 'experiments to prove that something is true' but to provide general background reading.

A Word About the Infant School

Many teachers will read this chapter and feel that the advice given would lead to more restriction than they are prepared to accept in their classrooms. This is particularly true of the infant and lower junior school where the children do not readily submit to being treated as one large group. All teachers, but especially infant teachers, should remember that much of the science will consist of nothing more than observation, with no experiments—observation is part of the process of learning and is just as important as experiment—and that children have a natural desire to investigate what is interesting to them as individuals. The infant teacher will no doubt find herself working largely with individuals and not with a group. But she can also take comfort from the fact that many of the investigations she has come to regard as a normal part of the children's work are 'scientific' even though she has never realized it before.

* * *

Leaves

Class	*9–10 years. Upper stream in two-stream school; nevertheless, range of ability is wide*
Class number	42 boys and girls
School roll	523
Term	Autumn and spring
Building	A one-storey brick building erected in 1934
Classroom	Cramped conditions for this large class and there is little space for free movement. One wall is used for display. Storage space is completely inadequate.
School environment	Large paved playgrounds, bordered on the roadside with grass verge and shrubs. Classrooms arranged around two pleasant grassed quadrangles with flower borders. Swimming bath as a separate block.
Local setting	North-west England. In the midst of a housing estate about six miles from the centre of a large industrial city, housing a population engaged in a great variety of occupations.

Autumn term

In the first art lesson of the term the children painted 'fantastic' leaves. Real leaves were brought in by the children who seemed surprised at the great variation in shape. They decided it was much more interesting to paint proper leaves than made-up ones and a study of leaves began in earnest.

Some children made collections of leaves for beauty of colour and

From E. R. Wastnedge, ed., *Nuffield Junior Science: Teacher's Guide 2* (London: Collins, 1967 [distributed in the United States by Agathon Press]), pp. 117–120, 135–139. Reprinted by permission of Collins Publishers.

shape; others studied the details of structure of particular leaves, making lists of the words they used to describe texture, margins, colour, and veins. More paintings were done and the children tried matching original colours. Leaf prints and plaster casts were made by some of them and in trying to identify their specimens they asked each other or consulted books from the library. One group of six boys spent hours in a wood at the weekend. Two boys sat on logs with books while the others collected leaves for identification. Fruits, seeds, and branches were brought in by the children and the classroom began to look like a wood!

A visit to look at the trees in the grounds of a nearby private estate was arranged. The children were very excited and obviously enjoyed being out of doors. They decided to join up with friends in small groups to study particular trees. Height and age seemed to be the first queries. Some guesses and estimations were made. These were checked later. Leaves, twigs, and old pieces of bark were taken back to school. Oak apples and willow bean galls had been found by the groups studying these trees. They aroused interest. All available books were consulted for information. Bernard spent over an hour on his own in a field, looking for oak apples with 'no holes in them.' He found five. He opened one and discovered 'a kind of white grub that goes long and short like a caterpillar.' The rest he put in a jar with a perforated lid 'to find out what the grub turns into.' He looked at the grub under the microscope and recorded his discoveries.

The children became interested in the only tree in the school grounds —a poplar. In an English lesson they sat under it, listening, and watching the movements of the leaves. They tried to think of just the right words to describe them. In an art lesson some of them made charcoal sketches of the outline. Comments overheard were: 'It leans over to the left'; 'The branches on the left are larger'; 'Must be the wind.' The class listened to a junior science broadcast about wind (the teacher's comment being 'a good broadcast but far too much in it'). During the next few days the children made and brought to school all kinds of anemometers and wind vanes, all ingenious in design. These were tried out in the playground and their performance appraised. 'It turned round four times in three minutes.' 'Mine turned twelve times in ten minutes.' The need for consistent timing was soon appreciated. Two girls took readings twice daily for a month. They used a stopclock and graphed their results.

A second visit to the estate was made. The children were left free to study anything which interested them. Some chose a 'new' tree, while others found their way to the 'old' tree to discover more about it. There was a noticeable change in their attitude—they were less excited, more businesslike; they worked together on self-chosen jobs. More information was obtained than on the first visit.

They asked questions the whole time of each other and of the teacher when she was near. 'Finds' were put in plastic bags, if they weren't too big! Roy had found a large fungus, another boy was carrying a rotten log: 'What was the white stuff under the bark?' Clarke had a large stone full of holes: 'What had made them?' The teacher's heart sank when she thought of the not very large classroom and forty-two children, each needing space to examine their 'finds.' The next day every available inch of space was in use. A cry of dismay came from Roy when he discovered that his prize fungus had gone 'all soggy.' General conversation sprang up: 'They die quickly,'—'How can we keep them?' The children decided to set up a fungus terrarium in an old sink in the quadrangle.

Interest in fungi captured the whole class and lasted for about two weeks. The children brought in specimens 'from our fence,' 'from the rotten part of our garage,' or 'from the woods,' and books were in great demand for identification. Some children selected interesting clumps or pieces of fungus, and painted them, often in the dinner hours. The teacher was amazed at how careful their observations were.

The microscope came into its own, and pieces of gills were examined and spores seen. Roy stated, 'Mushrooms have sixteen thousand million spores—I read it when I was trying to find out about my fungus. I think it is true, too!' Mark worked out a new technique for making spore prints, using sticky paper. To quote his teacher:

> When Mark came into the class he wrote a composition in which he stated bluntly that he did not like school. In this work he has developed beyond belief. He has experimented at home, spent weekends looking for things, and his research on fungi is remarkable.

A great deal of experimental work on moulds was carried out at home and at school, by individuals and groups, and results were compared. Experiments were devised to find out which things produced the most exciting moulds, and what conditions were best for their growth.

The teacher commented that no story books were being borrowed from the library, but only books on things the children wanted to find out about—rocks, trees, and fungi.

> The children are now taking over, and this is a difficult stage for the teacher. For ages we have been used to being in charge. I have never found difficulty in giving children freedom, but I do tend to direct and suggest. Now I find myself lagging behind them; they are so busy and obsessed that I am only necessary as a provider of tools and materials. My role has definitely changed, and not hold-

ing the centre of the stage is something I shall have to accept, *but* they still need and demand my interest in what they are doing— which is not easy with a class of forty-two.

The interest in trees revived when logs and pieces of wood were brought in. One girl had asked for a thick branch from men who were cutting down trees along the road. The caretaker cut it into logs, and much sandpapering was done until the age rings could be counted. Another girl arrived one morning with a branch taller than she was, from a tree her father had been pruning. The question was where to put it. In desperation, the teacher hung it from a pipe running below the ceiling along one side of the room. Branches from other trees were obtained and hung up. Another surge of interest swept the class. There were detailed studies and drawings of twigs, and much measuring to find out how much the different branches had grown last year.

The children attached pieces of paper and wrote on them the relevant measurements, checking each other's results. Bernard announced: 'This one has grown seven-tenths of an inch.' 'Rubbish,' said Douglas. 'Get the lens, that's just a scar. You must look for more than one scar: they run round the whole twig.' 'Let me see,' said Bernard. 'You're right, it's three and two-tenths of an inch.'

A graph was made of the final findings, after much discussion about an appropriate scale.

IAN: Shall we have one block or two to the inch?
CHRISTOPHER: We'll never get the poplar on. It's grown twenty-five inches.
BRUCE: We'll join the paper.
IAN: We'll use one block to the inch and these [small squares] will have to represent two-tenths of an inch.

In talking about the results, a query arose as to which were the commonest trees in the area. The children decided that during the holidays they would identify and count the trees in the roads where they lived.

Spring term

During the Christmas holidays all but a few of the children went round identifying and recording the trees along the roads in which they lived. When they came back to school they began discussing their findings. The general enthusiasm and the fear of being left out of things encouraged the few who had not done anything to collect information. In a short time the whole class was involved. Questions such as 'Where do you live?' and 'How many beeches in your road?' led some of the children to describe where they lived and to give directions for getting there.

They discussed precise uses of words with the teacher and with each other. Mark drew a plan to show where he lived. Others followed his example. The need for accuracy was emphasized by the teacher and the children paced out the roads and worked out a scale to fit the particular size of paper they had chosen.

This sparked off an interest in scale drawing. They measured the classroom and corridors and checked compass directions. The teacher wrote, 'Quite a lot of real mathematical thinking is going on; the children are discussing freely and the classroom is full of bits of paper covered with figures. Tremendous difference in ability shown here—the girls love the work but the boys are leading them. The boys also seem to have a natural sense of direction; the girls are much slower.'

At this point the teacher produced a map of the area. The roads covered by the children's tree survey were located, and ways of presenting their findings were discussed. In the end they decided to make a large bar graph. Scale was discussed, the size of paper required was estimated, and a long strip of graph paper was pinned along the top frame of the blackboard. The children experienced some of the difficulties involved in collecting and sorting data from a large number of people, but they gained much satisfaction from the graph when they had completed it.

Man's use of wood seemed to be a natural development of the work on trees. A visit to the docks to see the unloading of timber was arranged for January 21st. In spite of a bitterly cold day the children were keenly interested in all they saw. They asked questions continuously, and made jottings in their notebooks of things that interested them. The official guide was quick to respond to the children's interest; forgetting his 'set pieces,' he allowed himself to be 'guided' by the children's questions.

Back in the classroom groups formed according to common interests:

1 Floating and 'dead weight.' (Billy had found out that a collier of 970 tons can carry a cargo of over a thousand tons. 'Why doesn't it sink?' he asked.)
2 Freezing and thawing. Some of the children were interested in the design of the prow of the Russian ship which had passed through ice on its journey.
3 Timber in Canada and Russia. The group considered kinds and uses of imported wood; slow and quick growing trees; hard and soft wood; method of loading. 'Why don't you carry logs?' Ian had asked a Russian sailor.

Other interests centred around:

4 The docks themselves.
5 The machines used.

6 The ships.
7 Coal (which was exported).
8 Cubic capacity in relation to loading cargoes of coal and timber; this
  concerned only one boy.

Sound

Class	9–10 years. Full range of ability
Class number	41 boys and girls
School roll	250
Term	Autumn
Building	19th Century. Soon to be replaced.
Classroom	Large and spacious. Modern desks and furniture.
School environment	Facing an iron foundry. Gas works fifty yards away. Pupils drawn mainly from two new estates.
Local setting	North-east England. Small market town. Local industries clothing, synthetic fibres, agriculture.

The children were asked to bring to school anything which made a
sound. On the following day a violin, a baby's rattle, a tin containing
peas, a gramophone, and other objects were brought. These, together
with a few school musical instruments, a tuning fork, and some books
about sound were set out on a table. The children were interested and
the teacher listened to their comments and questions as they played.

The children talked about their discoveries, then wrote down what
they wanted to know about. This provided the teacher with enough information to draw up a list of topics:

1 Sounds and how they are made.
2 The pitch of sounds.
3 Amplification.
4 Transmitting sounds.
5 Sound insulation.
6 Acuteness of hearing.

There was a good supply of materials freely available to the children
so that they were able not only to plan and perform their experiments,
but also to display their findings.

After a brief discussion, the children chose the topics they wanted to
study and formed groups based on their particular interests. Each group

began by tackling a question, but looking back on this later, the teacher felt that the topics were too formal and, indeed, unnecessary. It would have been better simply to have asked the children to choose questions rather than topics.

Most of the work was done in groups, but there were periodic class discussions and occasional bursts of class activity, for example when an exciting discovery in one group commanded everyone's attention.

This is how the work of the different groups developed.

1 Sounds and How They Are Made

The children began by drawing up a list of as many sounds as possible and saying how each was made. They found that sounds were associated with vibration, for example, by putting sand on a drum, beating it, and watching the grains bouncing as the drumskin vibrated. The teacher also noticed that they were striking the tuning fork and then feeling the vibrating prongs. He left a jar half full of water on the table and soon Graham discovered that if he touched the surface of the water with a vibrating tuning fork, it made tiny waves.

The children were keenly interested in stringed instruments, and began to make their own. This is not surprising, since several of them play the violin, and various stringed instruments were included in the classroom display. They discovered that changing the length or the tension of a string altered the pitch of the sound it made.

While making a large harp from scrap materials, John noticed that the long wires vibrated slowly and made low notes while the short wires vibrated quickly and made high notes. He suggested to the group that the pitch depended upon the speed at which the string vibrated. The teacher introduced the word 'frequency' at this point and explained that the frequency of different notes could be measured. They now looked again at what happened as they tightened a vibrating string, and concluded that it altered the frequency.

This group made and experimented with various percussion instruments including drums, rattles, and a 'bottle xylophone.' They also recorded some common sounds and played them to the rest of the class, who were required to identify them.

2 The Pitch of Sounds

The children began by making stringed instruments and then followed a path very like the first group's. They experimented with strings of different materials and found in every case that the pitch rose as the string was shortened or tightened. Valerie made a simple instrument of a row of nails in a piece of wood with nylon fastened to them. Each string was made a little tighter than its neighbour. Figure on the following page shows how she did this.

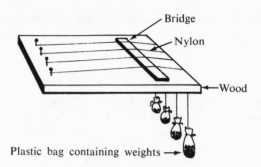

Valerie's stringed instrument.

When one of the group suggested that the thickness of a string might affect the pitch of the note it made, Valerie's instrument was used to test the idea. Different thicknesses of string and nylon fishing line were tried.

The children soon found pictures of xylophones and asked if they could make some. The teacher provided some tubular metal and a few strips of oak, and the children read in a book that the bars should rest on rubber or felt strips. They found strips of balsa wood quite satisfactory. They also made nail xylophones, but considered them unsatisfactory because the nails did not vibrate very well.

The work of the first two groups overlapped to such an extent that they gradually merged.

Paul then brought a whistling kettle to school so that everyone could hear how the pitch of the whistle rose as steam pressure built up, and this prompted two girls to write a booklet on wind instruments explaining how their recorders worked. John also wrote about a cane flute he was making and Valerie added a section about a pedal organ. This booklet was a mixture of first-hand experience and material from books.

3 Amplification

The children pursued two main lines of enquiry. The boys experimented with an old gramophone to find out how they could make the sound as loud as possible. They mounted a needle in a block of balsa and held the point in the groove of an old record on the turntable. Next they fixed the needle in the edge of a circular cheese box, then in the apex of a paper cone, and so on, until they could decide which needle holder made the most efficient amplifier. This was their own experiment which developed out of an idea they had found in a book. They found that their xylophones played louder on desks than on the floor and the teacher suggested that they should try a series of boxes. The girls began to experiment with sounding boards. They compared the sounds of a xylophone bar ring on the floor with those made when it was resting on balsa strips and on a wooden box. A boy who had been watching these experiments touched the box with a tuning fork and found that it amplified the sound. He felt sure that a bigger box would make it even louder and so collected a series of cardboard boxes to test his idea. Finally, he calculated the volume of each box.

The whole group made megaphones of different shapes and sizes and then used them as ear trumpets. Kenneth tried to explain this by saying, 'They brought the sound waves to a focus.'

They concluded their study by using tin cans to test the saying, 'Empty vessels make the most noise.'

4 Transmitting Sound

The group that studied this included some of the most able children in the class. They started by making speaking-tubes from polythene funnels and rubber tubing, and when they had written descriptions of their construction and their uses, they showed them to the teacher. He felt they could take this further, and asked, 'How far will your voice carry along the tube?' They were keen to find out and tried the longest piece of rubber tubing they could find, only to discover that their voices travelled its full length. Then they made string telephones, an idea from a book,

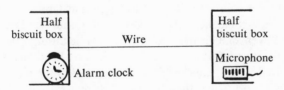

The wire was replaced by twine. The efficiency with which they conduct sound was compared.

instead, and carried out some valuable experiments with different thicknesses of string and different end cups in an attempt to improve transmission.

In the junk box was some fine wire, and two children used this to make a telephone. They tried to compare the efficiency of wire and string but this was difficult until they thought of using the tape recorder. Two halves of biscuit boxes were used with a small hole in the centre of the bottom of each one. They were then placed on their sides about six feet apart and connected by a piece of wire passing through the holes, and the children put an alarm clock in one and the microphone in the other (see figure above). They then replaced the wire by a piece of clothes line, repeating the process until they had recorded the sound transmitted by many different strings. Finally they played the recording several times and decided which connection was best.

From a book, they got the idea of tapping the central heating pipes to see if sound would travel through metal, and it was then that Eric asked if sound travels through water. He asked the teacher for a tube to fill with water, and was given a plastic one about three feet long and an inch in diameter. He looked for corks to put in each end, but as there were none, he brought two table tennis balls and asked if he could use them. He stuck a ball into one end of the tube, using impact adhesive, filled the tube with water, and closed the other end with the second ball. He then clamped the tube horizontally, struck a tuning fork, and put it on the ball at one end. His friend who listened at the other end could hear it clearly.

The teacher said little at this time, but a day or two later he asked whether the sound could have travelled from the tuning fork to his ear without passing through the water. Eric said at once, 'Oh, of course! It could have gone along the plastic tube.'

He was determined to prove that sound could travel through water, so he used a sleigh bell and an aquarium half full of water. He held the bell under water, shook it, and pressed his ear against the glass.

Following a conversation about Red Indians listening for the sound of horses' hoofs, the children decided to find out if sound really did travel through the ground. They found a crack in the concrete playground, put the point of a long nail into it, and tapped the head with a hammer. They could hear the sound seventy-four yards away through the ground even though they could not hear it through the air.

Although most of their work involved first-hand investigation, the children loved reading and they searched in books for more information. It was hardly surprising, therefore, to find that they decided to write a booklet on modern methods of communication. It began with a brief account of the life and work of Marconi and included chapters on Morse code, semaphore, telephones, and radio.

5 Sound Insulation

The group began with the question, 'How can we insulate a room from sound?' To find out what substances were good insulators, they selected a range of materials and used each, in turn, to cover an alarm clock. They measured the distance from the clock at which the sound became inaudible and presented their results as a block graph.

It was generally agreed that the sound of a transistor radio was one of the biggest nuisances in a house, so they decided to see how effectively they could insulate a room against it. They found a large cardboard box and made a compartment inside it just big enough to hold a transistor radio. The space between the compartment and the sides of the box was then packed with materials which had been found to be the most effective insulators. When the children turned on the radio and lowered it into the box, the effect was dramatic. The teacher suggested that they should take the tape recorder to the school gates and record street noises. Later, after listening to their recording, they suggested ways of reducing the noise. Amongst other things, they thought that plastic milk bottles would be a welcome innovation for those who were awakened early in the morning by the milkman.

6 *Acuteness of Hearing*

'How do we hear?' This was the question engaging the attention of the sixth group, and they found themselves working mainly from books. They read about the human ear and drew a diagram showing its structure, then jotted a few notes about acuteness of hearing in animals. They listed the frequencies of sounds made by musical instruments and read about the range of hearing of various creatures, including humans. Some notes on bats, and how they navigate, were included.

When, near the end of term, they asked the teacher to tell them more about sound waves and what they are like, he enlisted the help of a science teacher from a nearby secondary school. He showed them a film about sound waves, and set up an oscilloscope so that they could see the trace made by their own instruments and tuning forks.

The whole class became involved when Linda announced that sound travels at 650 miles an hour. When the teacher asked how it was measured, two boys said that you had to make a sound and see how long it took to travel a mile. During the discussion which followed the teacher asked whether a firework would be of any use, and they thought it would be ideal.

The children chose a long, straight cart track between two fields and measured a quarter of a mile. They tied a firework to the end of a long stick so that it was visible from a distance, and stood it upright. As each firework went off the children at the other end of the cart track timed the interval between seeing the flash and hearing the bang.

An extract from Linda's notes reads:

'My teacher and the boys didn't see the flash and then hear the bang. They saw the flash and heard the bang together. Because they were right under the sound. And it took less time to get to them. But we were a quarter of a mile away and it took time to reach us.

1st time 1½ seconds.
2nd time 1⅕ seconds.
3rd time 1⅕ seconds.
4th time 1⅕ seconds.

I think the first time when I got the result of 1½ I wasn't quite ready. So we took the time as 1⅕.'

The children timed how long it took them to walk back to school, and this was the beginning of an interest in speeds. They found out how fast they could walk, run, cycle, and skip, and then looked up the speeds of animals, birds, and aeroplanes.

Katherine read about the eruption of Krakatoa and then wrote a description of it, drawing a map showing all the places where the sound was heard. Eric rounded it off by working out the time at which the sound reached different places.

V

The Role of the Arts

The arts play a radically different role in the open classroom than in the traditional school. Painting, sculpture, music, dance, crafts—these are not frills to be indulged in if time is left over from the real business of education; they are the business of education as much as reading, writing, math, or science. For the arts are the language of a whole range of human experience; to neglect them is to neglect ourselves and to deny children the full development that education should provide.

To understand the role of the arts in the curriculum, we need to understand how art relates to children's intellectual and emotional development. As we have seen before, education and learning can be defined as the process by which the child builds up successively more sophisticated internal models of the world—conceptual models by which he can organize, understand, and communicate experience. In discussing the role of math and science, we pointed to the gradual development in infancy of the child's understanding that objects which have been removed from his sight or hearing continue to exist. When the child understands this, he is able to form images, which enables him to move on to a new level of intellectual functioning, for it permits him to construct images through which he can evoke the past and anticipate the future. To be able to think, as distinct from the pure sensory-motor activity of infants, the child must be able to evoke what is absent or what has happened to him in the past. In order to be able to do this, the child must construct some kind of symbol to represent what is not immediately present. Representation—the creation of symbols—is thus the means by which the human being organizes his experience in order to understand or communicate it. Language is one way of representing or symbolizing the world; math is another, science another—and the imagery of art is still another. In Susanne Langer's definition, "Every art image is a purified and simplified aspect of the outer world."

What makes art so important is that it embodies and unites affective and cognitive experiences and responses. In a sense, art can be defined as the expression of ideas about feeling. Art thus has an important function in extending human experience: it can deepen and enlarge understanding and refine feeling. Not all children can or should become accomplished artists; all children can and should develop aesthetic sensibility.

Aesthetic sensibility can be manifested in a variety of ways. The science area, for example, lends itself particularly well to a concern for beauty and artistic expression. Teachers who are sensitive to beauty will have attractive arrangements of leaves, pine cones, acorns, rocks, wood bark, driftwood. The reading area also lends itself to the use of color, shape, and form.

But the concern for beauty should not be limited to specific interest areas; it should be manifested in the way the classroom as a whole is arranged and organized. One of the things that distinguish a good open classroom from a poor one is the overall aesthetic appeal; the sense of order and structure is conveyed by the way a room is organized and arranged.

This concern with beauty is also manifested in the ways in which the children's work is displayed. In a good open classroom, there are displays of the children's art everywhere—the freest and most imaginative kinds of paintings, murals, collages, sculpture, and craft objects. And just as reading and writing grow out of art and construction, so art and construction can and should grow out of reading, math, science, and indeed every other activity.

Needless to say, none of this occurs by happenstance; what appears to be spontaneous activity is the result of the most careful preparation and planning and thought on the part of the teacher. Thought is expressed in the first instance in the kinds of materials the teacher provides. Before children can express their ideas and feelings through art, they need experience with the materials of art. They need to explore the qualities of clay, for example, pummeling it, pulling it, squeezing it, bouncing it. They need to explore various kinds and colors and textures of paint and paper and various kinds of brushes, pens, crayons, and pencils. They need to explore the textures, colors, and patterns of the wide variety of materials from which collages can be made. And so it goes. In short, the teacher needs to provide a wide variety of materials for artistic expression and give the children the opportunity to explore and experience all of them before they can develop the capacity to use these materials with some degree of skill, and before they can exercise some choice in deciding which materials they feel comfortable using for different purposes.

Since art is not a mechanical reproduction of experience but rather the reconstruction of experience, the teacher needs to provide experiences that encourage imagery and sensibility. Not only should the experiences cover a broad spectrum of type and intensity; they should be in a sequence which leads to greater and greater depth of understanding. Just as children must have something to talk and to write about if they are not going to become inarticulate or illiterate or forced back into their own fantasies, so they must have something about which to paint, sculpt, dance, and so on. This means reading stories to the children, exploring the outdoors, exploring their immediate neighborhood, going on trips.

It is not enough to provide experiences that can lead to artistic expression. Teachers must also provide opportunities through which children can evaluate and express these experiences. That means, in the first instance, talking about what experiences mean and how they feel. It means providing opportunities for children to express those feelings and meanings through paint, clay, collage, dance, music, construction—whatever medium each child wishes to use. The teacher needs to stimulate the children; she needs to give them an understanding of the potentials of the various art media; and she has to help them select the medium through which different kinds of experiences or feelings can be expressed best. Hence the arts should not be developed in isolation from one another. After hearing the teacher read a story, for example, most children may want to write and perform their own dramatization of the story. Some may prefer to paint a picture illustrating the story as a whole or some particular episode in it; others may wish to dance, and others may wish to compose music for the dance. Each of these activities, moreover, may lead to the others. There should be a constant interflow not only among the various arts but among all subjects and activities, to prevent false distinctions between work and play, the arts and the sciences, thought and feeling.

1. The Language of Human Experience

Because the arts play so minor and isolated a role in most American schools, this section begins with a portrait of some of the ways in which informal English educators' concern with the arts manifests itself in the classroom and a brief explanation of why the arts are given so high a priority.

"Education," Sir Herbert Read has written, "may be defined as the cultivation of modes of expression—it is teaching children and adults how

From Charles E. Silberman, *Crisis in the Classroom* (New York: Random House, 1970), pp. 251–256.

to make sounds, images, movements, tools and utensils." Most informal schools operate on this definition. The emphasis on communication extends beyond reading, writing, and talking to painting, drawing, sculpting, dancing, crafts—to all the forms of nonverbal expression. The arts "are not 'frills' but essentials just as much as the 3 Rs," John Blackie writes in *Inside the Primary School.* "Everything that we know about human beings generally, and children in particular, points to the importance of the arts in education. They are the language of a whole range of human experience and to neglect them is to neglect ourselves. "

The Plowden Committee was even more explicit. "Art is both a form of communication and a means of expression of feeling which ought to permeate the whole curriculum and life of the school," the Committee declared. "A society which neglects or despises it is dangerously sick. It affects, or should affect, all aspects of our life from the design of the commonplace articles of everyday life to the highest forms of individual expression."

And so it does. An American visitor is inevitably struck, for example, by the fact that there are flowers everywhere—in the entrance to the school, in the hall, in the head's office, and in every classroom. ("Every school is a warmer and more congenial place for the presence of flowers," Sir Alec Clegg has written.) There literally was not a school I visited, and this in October and November, that did not have flowers about —something one rarely sees in American schools—as well as attractive arrangements of autumn leaves, pine cones, acorns, and other local flora. Yet the flowers were very much taken for granted. I frequently asked, for example, who was responsible for the arrangements gracing the entrance hall. The question always took people by surprise; no one was "responsible," as such.

The concern for beauty was not limited to the floral arrangements; in the Plowden Committee's phrase, it permeated the life of almost every informal school visited. There are displays of the children's art everywhere—the freest and most imaginative kinds of paintings, murals, collages, illustrated stories, etc.

ITEM: An infant school in Melton Mowbray, a lower-middle-class and upper-working-class neighborhood in Leicestershire County. On a classroom wall is a collage—a piece of white oaktag, attached to the middle of which is a long piece of string, artfully coiled into an ever-widening series of concentric circles. In one corner of the oaktag is the legend, "I am six and I go 34 times along the string"; in another corner, the legend, "the string fits around two sides of the playground"; in another, "we have made string as long as a rocket and it is as long as the school."

ITEM: A primary school in Oxfordshire. In one classroom, there is a large wall mural, called "The Bottom of the Sea"—a collage of fishes made of old pieces of fabric, seaweed, sand, and shells, among other things, with a wide variety of textures and colors. On another wall is a collage of butterflies and fish, made out of multicolored crumpled tissue paper.

ITEM: A classroom in a school in a coal-mining town in Yorkshire. On one wall there is a large and striking mural of dinosaurs, made out of egg crates painted green and studded with little silver foil milk-bottle caps.

It wasn't always thus. Thirty or forty years ago, in fact, art instruction in English primary schools was much the same as it is in American schools today: the arid copying of objects and pictures, with every child drawing nearly identical flowers, trees, fruit, pumpkins, turkeys, Christmas trees, etc. The change began in the 1920s and '30s, under the influence of a few outstanding teachers, who substituted large sheets of kitchen paper and large brushes for the pencils, crayons, and small sheets of drawing paper the children had been using, and who turned the children free to paint whatever and however they wished. The results demonstrated that young children have far greater artistic potential than had been realized, and that it was the schools themselves, with their sterile formalism, that was destroying this native talent.

The most striking example of education as "the cultivation of modes of expression" is an activity that has no counterpart in American schools—something the English call "Movement," with a capital "M." One of the important aspects of the growth of informal education, the Plowden Committee writes, "has been the increasing recognition of the place of expressive movement in primary education. Children have a great capacity to respond to music, stories, and ideas, and there is a close link through movement, whether as dance or drama, with other areas of learning and experience—with speech, language, literature, and art as well as with music."

In its most fundamental sense, Movement is an attempt to educate children in the use of their bodies—to provide them with an ease, grace, and agility of bodily movement that can carry over into sports, crafts, and dance. "How many of us feel awkward, clumsy, self-conscious and embarrassed if we are called upon to perform any movement to which we are not accustomed?" John Blackie writes in *Inside the Primary School,* in a chapter interestingly entitled "Body and Soul." "How many of us have watched with envy the apparently effortless ease with which expert riders, skiers, fencers, divers, dancers, potters, woodcutters, etc., move their bodies and compared it with our own ineptitude?"

The procedure is a fascinating blend of formal and informal instruction. As a rule, an entire class participates under the teacher's direction; but precisely *how* the teacher's directions are carried out is left to each child. There is, after all, no right way or wrong way to move as if you were a snowflake, or a leaf fluttering down from a tree, which are the kinds of things children may be asked to do. The purpose, as the Plowden Committee explains it, is "to develop each child's resources as fully as possible through exploratory stages and actions which will not be the same for any two children. When these ends are pursued successfully," the Committee continues, "the children are able to bring much more to any situation than that which is specifically asked of them; the results transcend the limits of what can be prescribed or 'produced,' and lead to a greater realization of the high potential of young children."

A Movement lesson may be concerned with agility on the physical education apparatus, with skills in handling balls and other athletic apparatus, or with expressive movement of a dramatic and dancelike quality; the latter is what we are concerned with here. Barefoot and stripped to their underwear, the children assemble in the hall to learn to communicate through bodily movement—to express the whole range of feelings and emotions through the use of their hands, arms, heads, legs, torsos, and to do so with agility and ease and without self-consciousness or embarrassment.

ITEM: A junior school in the West Riding of Yorkshire. A class of ten- and eleven-year-old boys and girls, most of them the children of coal miners, are taking a class in Movement. The teacher, with tweed suit and British walking shoes, looking like the American stereotype of a British headmistress, calls out the directions; their execution is left to each child's imagination and ability. "Move about in a small circle, as if your body were very heavy. . . . Move about in a small circle as if your body were very light. . . . Move very quickly. . . . Move very slowly. . . . Now find a partner and make your movements in response to his, so that you are aware of what he or she is doing as well as what you are doing. . . . Speed the movements up. . . . Slow them down. . . . Make them sharp and jerky. . . . Move only your arms and body above the waist; move as if you felt very sad. . . . Move only your fingers, hands and arms, as though they were very sad. . . . Now move them as though they were very happy. . . . Find a partner and move your fingers, hands, and arms as though you were talking to each other. . . . Move about the room as though you were a butterfly. . . . Move about the room as though you were an elephant. . . . Move about in your own space as though you were a snowflake. . . . Stay in the space around you, but try to use all of it, close to the floor, above your head. . . ." All this without music, then repeated with music of various kinds. (This same school, incidentally, has the best rugby team for miles around.)

ITEM: A Movement class in an infant school in Bristol. A class of six- and seven-year-olds is performing a ballet of their own invention about a trip through outer space; they use only their own bodies and a few percussion instruments. One child is the earth, another the moon, several are stars. Several rocket ships go into orbit. A number of children are clouds, which at one point converge in a thunderstorm, which almost, but not quite, downs one of the rocket ships.

And so it goes; the specific approach and teaching technique varies from school district to school district and from school to school, depending on the tastes and talents of the teachers and heads and the influence of the local inspectors and advisors. But almost always, the children, except for an occasional shy or chubby or clumsy youngster, move with a marvelous grace and ease and apparent total lack of self-consciousness. The experience brings to mind Lillian Smith's haunting evocation of Martha Graham dancing:

> Sometimes as I have sat in the audience watching Martha Graham dance, it has seemed to me as if she were unwrapping our body image which has been tied up so long with the barbed wires of fear and guilt and ignorance, and offering it back to us: a thing of honor. Freeing, at last, our concept of Self. Saying to us, The body is not a thing of danger, it is a fine instrument that can express not only today's feeling and act, but subtle, archaic experiences, memories which words are too young in human affairs to know the meaning of.*

The advocates of Movement are persuaded that the activity has a profound effect on other activities. "You don't dance to get rid of something, you dance to be aware of something," Martha Graham says, and the awareness that Movement evokes seems to carry over into the children's writing, painting, and sculpture.

ITEM: An infant school in an impoverished London slum. The visitor admires the sensitivity of the poetry these cockney boys are writing. "A child who has moved like a snowflake or a falling leaf is bound to write more sensitively," the headmistress explains. "He knows how it *feels* to be a snowflake or a leaf." He also knows that sensitivity to feelings and awareness of beauty are neither effeminate nor effete. The visitor wonders what it might mean for the quality of American life if this kind of schooling were widespread in the United States.

---

* Lillian Smith, *The Journey,* New York: W. W. Norton, 1954.

2. Exercising Children's Imaginative Spirit

*"For the scientist as well as the mathematician, for the poet as well as
the sociologist, for the doctor and the archaeologist and the teacher,"
Sybil Marshall writes, "for any human being caught up in the intricacies
of ordinary everyday life, early education must provide the eye that sees,
the mind that comprehends, and the spirit which leaps to respond. Art
teaches and develops them all. That is the real justification of the important place it has in education here today."*

*Art did not always have so large a role in English education. In this
selection, Mrs. Marshall describes the transformation that overtook the
teaching of art in England after the Second World War and the ways
in which this transformation in turn helped liberate the entire curriculum.
Now a member of the faculty of the University of Sussex, Sybil Marshall
played an important role in these changes as teacher, head teacher,
teacher of teachers, and author.*

———————————

The great changes that have overtaken the primary schools of England
in the last twenty-five years began, to a very large extent, in the field of
art. In the 1930s art suddenly became 'free' in every sense of the word.
In doing so, it pointed the way to freedom for the rest of the curriculum.

Until that time, the word 'art' had not been applied to what children
did in the primary school. The rigid timetables of the first quarter of
the century indicated that 'Drawing' took place once or twice a week.
What actually went on in those 'drawing' lessons was very much of the
same nature as what went on in all other lessons—English, arithmetic,
history, or anything else. The lesson consisted of a teacher doggedly
trying to make children accept adult concepts and adult standards, and
to use adult techniques and skills long before they had even come to
terms with infant ones. The poor children were not being asked to run
before they could walk—they were being commanded to fly. The result,
of course, was bewilderment, failure and fear on the part of the pupils,
and resigned frustration on the part of the teacher. In those days, many
an intelligent teacher must have asked himself what purpose it all
served: if he had been bold enough to ask the question out loud, he

Sybil Marshall, "ART," in Geoffrey Howson, ed., *Primary Education in Britain
Today* (London: Heinemann Educational Books, and New York: Teachers College Press, 1969), pp. 120–130.

would have been told that drawing provided a useful exercise in 'discipline' and gave the children a chance to learn manual control.

In fact, the methods of those days completely ignored the children in their own right as living, thinking, feeling human beings. It simply wasted their precious 'growing time'—worse, indeed, for the endless, hopeless attempts at drawing some such object as teacher's chair, or occasionally the meticulous copying of a spray of leaves, set up in the majority of the children feelings of utter ineptitude, combined with resentment and rebellion against the authority that persistently demanded from them such nonsensical irrelevance. Secondly, this boring 'learning to draw' ignored art in its own right as the means by which the human spirit discovers itself, encourages itself, enlarges itself and purifies itself. (Art in this context includes all the arts, of course.)

Then, suddenly, common sense broke through, largely due to the efforts of Marion Richardson and her disciples who tried out in all schools, even the very academic grammar schools of the day, the theories progressive educationists had previously been promulgating for the infant schools. The basis of the new approach was that a child exists, feels and acts as a child. When he meets a new experience, he wants to use it, to make it his own, to do something with it in a child-like way. One of these ways is to depict the experience in some medium or other. What experiences he will choose to depict, out of the many that come his way every hour that he lives, cannot be forecast. That is his own concern. However, in order to be able to satisfy himself when he chooses to depict any experience, he must be in control of the tools he is using, whatever they may be. The tools must therefore be suited to the size of his hands and the state of his muscular control. In addition, as a child reacts to colour instinctively, it is reasonable to suppose that to work in a colour medium instead of black-and-white will have more direct appeal to him.

As soon as the Second World War was over and materials became available again, these new ideas began to spread. Children everywhere began to find delight and release of imaginative power in the freedom of the 'art period' (no longer the 'drawing lesson'!). Large sheets of cheap paper, large, fat brushes of hog-bristle, and containers of bright pigment in powder form which mixed at a touch with water replaced the hard pencils and expensive cartridge paper 'drawing-books' of pre-war days. There was no longer a command to 'draw' a certain object chosen by the teacher; instead, there was an open invitation to symbolize in picture form some experience of their own. The revolution had begun, but it was by no means over, for no one in those early days could have foretold the explosion of freedom from the shackles of past educational practice this breakthrough in the field of art heralded.

In the first place, the work the children produced under the new conditions gave teachers everywhere a great deal to think about. Working with materials they enjoyed, in an atmosphere of relaxing freedom, the children were prolific to an extent that would previously have been considered impossible. Even more startling was the quality of what they produced in such enormous quantity. While not measuring up to those standards of adult representational art that had so far been the criterion, they nevertheless set new standards of their own, throwing new light on the workings of the child's imagination, and giving an entire new range of aesthetic values until then unsuspected and unappreciated. To put it simply, we found that in our adult pride and ignorance we had constantly *underestimated the ability of children,* and because we, the ignorant adults, were in authority, we had actually been holding back their burgeoning ability to learn and to achieve. Moreover, it was soon revealed, contrary to any belief held in the past, that the instinct of children is towards what is aesthetically of high quality. Their basic taste is *good.* Yet for many decades at least, a fifth-rate standard of conformity had been pressed upon them, to the complete exclusion and repression of anything that arose naturally from 'the shaping spirit of their imagination.'

These revelations had far-reaching effects. The children were teaching their educators how to use paint. It was not long before it dawned on the brightest of those educators that what applied to paint probably applied to other things. A few bold spirits introduced into their classrooms other media by which pictures could be made—things like fat wax crayons, pastels, and coloured inks. Others, alarmed at the cost of keeping enthusiastic classes of more than forty little artists supplied with a constant flow of expensive paint, looked around for less expensive media with which to improvise. This was perhaps one of the most significant developments, for it meant that for the first time the teacher had been forced into a situation in which he, too, had to use his imaginative faculties. One of the solutions found was the 'paper mosaic', a method in which colour is supplied by cutting up and sticking on to a sketched background the coloured illustrations of cheap, weekly magazines and journals. The only materials required for this were a pile of old magazines, a pair of scissors (and even the scissors could be dispensed with if necessary, small fingers being adept at tearing), and a pot of some reasonably clean adhesive. Again, once this idea had been thoroughly explored, there were lateral developments. 'Mosaics' are built up of small irregular pieces of glass, or stones, or tiny tiles set into a material, plastic while wet but hard when dry. Imitation mosaics could be built up with materials that could be obtained merely for the trouble of collecting them, particularly natural things like straw, for instance. They could be used in their natural colour, or stained with dye or ink, seeds of all kinds, like those of the sunflower or vegetable marrow, being ideal. Nowadays, there are specially prepared adhesives that will hold even weighty objects like stones and shells securely in place on a background of paper; in the early days of experiment with such things in schools, these wonderful adhesives were simply not available, and substitutes had to be found. The obvious base for mosaics was clay, not the expensive refined potter's clay now common in schools as a medium for pottery and sculpture, but common clay dug direct from the school garden. The disadvantages of this were obvious, the main one being that it dried too quickly and as soon as it did, it cracked, and the art-work just fell to pieces. Did that really matter? Would it matter now? Surely not, for the object of art in schools is not to produce durable works, but to exercise the imaginative spirit of the human child. (It is worth remarking, in passing, that in the Midlands of England, particularly in Derbyshire, there exists an age-old custom of 'dressing the wells' in certain villages. This is done by erecting over the well-head a picture, sometimes of dimensions as large as eight feet by five feet, made up entirely of flower petals and other natural materials like cotton grass and onion skins embedded in clay. The clay is kept moist by the application of water at regular intervals, and these marvellous works of art have, in this way, a life of approximately one week's duration. Their evanescence is part of their charm. That they are worth the effort involved, no one doubts, especially the artists themselves, that is, the men and women of the villages who have handed down this beautiful art from father to son and from mother to daughter, for centuries, probably back to pagan times. And what an extraordinary reflection it is upon 'education' that the children of Derbyshire at the beginning of this century knew how to execute an art form as delightful and unusual as this, while sitting bored and fearful at their desks in the village school attempting to draw teacher's tea-pot or walking-stick with a hard pencil on unsuitable paper!)

'Sticking things on' became a further development, that before long became known to schools, as it is elsewhere in the world of art, as 'collage.'

The basic material used in collage in most English schools is fabric—scraps of dress and furnishing textiles, collected by the children (and teachers) and enhanced and supplemented by such oddments as beads, buttons, sequins, trimmings of lace, braid and ribbon, fur and feathers. But once the idea has taken root, the number of things that can be used for this sort of picture-making is legion—straw and grass, dried leaves, seeds and seedcases; stones, shells, bark and twigs; string and thread, especially such as will easily unravel, wool and cotton; and even more unexpected things like fish-bones (dried and cleaned, of course), iron filings, and a variety of industrial waste materials. What all this really adds up to is that the children are being invited to experiment *in the creative use of whatever materials lie ready to hand.* Most schools do, in fact, still rely heavily on paint and crayon, used on a reasonably tough 'sugar' paper; but the more progressive ones add an infinite variety of materials to their pupils' experience by mosaic and collage, in both cases making as much use of natural and cheap materials from the immediate environment as possible. In the list of such truly progressive schools must be counted the many, small, rural schools whose budgets do not allow them to purchase lavishly art supplies produced commercially, but who nevertheless practise real education through art by improvising imaginatively with the aid of waste and junk material.

Once picture-making has been extended to include collage, it lies very close to the three-dimensional world of craft. Take the question of 'needlework,' for example. It would obviously be easy to draw a parallel between the changes in art and those in needlework, from the days of the tear-and-blood-stained hem of a duster to the gorgeous riot of imaginative work produced with fabric and thread today. The significant thing, however, is not that, but the fact that thirty years ago 'needlework' and 'drawing' bore no relationship whatsoever to each other except for the fact that girls often did the former while boys did the latter. Today they are twins, born of the same creative impulses, fed by the same imaginative response to materials, and mutually dependent. The knowledge of the nature of fabrics and textiles acquired while using them for making pictures is a pre-requisite for true needlecraft: no less so the cutting and shaping, the colour matching and the familiarity with the intricacies of overall patterns and designs. In return, the skilled use of the needle for applying one material to another, for attaching things together and for inventing intricate patterns in fine threads gives generously to the understanding of design and to achievement in art work in general.

The cutting and sticking of materials lead the way also to other crafts like taking rubbings, and the many techniques of low-relief work, such as modelling in papier mâché, balsawood or expanded polystyrene, and in casting in sand and clay.

All this must make it plain that one of the results of the revolution in art teaching has been the closing of the gap between the so-called 'subjects' in the curriculum. This may be a direct consequence of the discovery that it is not necessary to separate from each other the various media used in the course of straight-forward picture-making. The multiplicity of effect one can obtain by mixing media has truly to be tried to be believed—paint with wax-crayon, with pencil, chalk, charcoal, ink, or any permutation of these: mosaic and collage combined, with paint or crayon to fill in the background, and black ink to add the finer details: needle and thread always at hand to add pattern or decora-

tion, even on the flimsiest of paper backgrounds—these are but a few
of the ways that have served to show that 'creative' art is a reality in
more ways than one. (It is worth noting that a flowering in craft almost
equal to that in art has also shown itself lately in our schools, in clay-
work (pottery and sculpture), bookcrafts, modelling in all sorts of
materials, and puppetry, to name but a few crafts to be seen in the
majority of primary schools.)

The new type adhesives have made three-dimensional work easy as
well as popular, and in infant schools the concept of 'art' includes such
activities as modelling with 'junk,' making houses, castles, fairy palaces
or Dyak long houses, large enough to get into for play purposes, from
cardboard boxes and grocery cartons, and the designing and making
up of clothes for proper dramatic play.

Before leaving the subject of creative work for its own sake, and for
the sake of nurturing to the full the creative impulse which every child
in some measure appears to possess, we ought briefly to discuss the
sort of things children choose to depict in their artwork, and the rôle
the teacher plays in helping his pupils to progress.

One could almost make a bald statement that there is nothing children
will not attempt, once they have learned enough control of their materials
to taste achievement and success. It is, however, possible to make three
broad divisions in what they do, and why they do it. There are those
processes chosen simply because the children love the doing of them.
Cutting and sticking come into this category, and so do rubbing and
taking impressions in clay. The results of their efforts may not be
pictures or patterns in the strict sense of these terms. There is a danger
here for the teacher. Obviously, children doing these things for the sake
of doing them are learning while experimenting, and such joyful experimentation must be encouraged, *but recognized for what it is*. If the
children set out to 'make a pattern' by any of these means, well and
good, so long as they possess the basic understanding that patterns
are meant to be used, usually in the decoration of some other object
such as a page of a book, or a pot, or a piece of fabric. There are still
too many schools in which 'making patterns' in paint or crayon, paper
or 'collage from oddments' is a time-filler which never gets anywhere in
its own right, but does become an obstacle to progress in picture-making.
Worse still is the acceptance, day after day, by many teachers, of a
panel composed of a conglomeration of disparate materials stuck
haphazardly together, as 'abstract work.' To the small child, the interest
in such a piece of 'work' has been in the sticking, and as such the work
is valid. For the teacher to pretend it is *art,* by any standards other
than his own purely subjective ones, is dangerous nonsense. Children
are no more able to deal with abstract concepts in art than they are in
mathematics or grammar.

Then again, children will celebrate or 'symbolize' experience of a significant kind to them, personally, in pictures. As these pictures arise in every case from individual experience, it is always difficult for the teacher to assess their value altogether as art. They may, and often do, have considerable merit as art, in which case there is no difficulty. But they may be repetitious attempts by the child to come to terms with some sort of experience, sad experiences such as death, loss, fear, hate, rejection, failure, anger—or conversely the equally repetitious desire to recapture delight or pleasure, even such an 'everyday' pleasure as watching the garage hand fill the tank of a passing car from a petrol pump. As it is the function of the teacher to see that the child progresses, he must be aware when a child becomes 'stuck in a groove' of this kind, apparently unable to extricate himself. If it is plain to the teacher that the child is actually using art, especially as a therapeutic agent, it is well to leave well alone; but if it becomes obvious that he is merely making the same statements again and again without using any imagination it is time for the teacher to exercise some coercion in order to get him to move on.

The third category of what children will do covers most of the true art done in schools. It includes both the other categories, but uses the children's innate good taste, their growing skill and technical ability, and their desire to achieve by creating works that can be enjoyed by others. Teachers have come to regard themselves as promoters of situations that will introduce experiences of a new and stimulating kind. This includes sensory experience and the experience of imagination as well. They take care, therefore, to promote situations which can be explored in as many ways as possible, in language, movement, drama, sound, art and craft. They help the children to select which art will best symbolize which experience, make practical suggestions with regard to choice of materials, and give help and advice when things go wrong. When art is produced in this way, it is truly educational, for the whole set-up is an ideal one from an educational standpoint, the willing child working under the supervision of an interested adult trained to advise and appreciate, but not to interfere.

The new approach to art was not long in spilling over into other subjects, particularly English, where the same experiments in child-freedom met with the same encouraging results. More recently, it has been tried out in the field of music. Gone, with the drawing of the school bell and the everlasting composition about 'What I did at the Weekend,' are the days when children stood in straight lines droning national songs or lugubrious hymns. Instead, they experiment with percussion and melody-making instruments (many of them home-made) creating music as they create pictures or drama.

This broadening of the scope of each subject to the point at which it overlaps other subjects has given rise to a new concept of what the curriculum in its entirety is. As more and more of the divisions between the subjects become blurred and indistinct in practice, progressive educators realize that those divisions, admitted and acted upon though they were for so long, were, in fact, unreal. Experience, the substance of the curriculum, is whole and undivided, though it may be looked at from many different angles, and explored from many different starting points.

Art was one of the first subjects to be correlated deliberately with others. The days of mere 'correlation' are, however, now giving way fast to complete 'integration' of the entire curriculum and of the time at the child's disposal in school. In such conditions, what is the rôle of art in a truly progressive primary school using an integrated curriculum and an integrated time schedule?

First, it exists in its own right as an activity which develops the child's powers of expression with regard to his environment, and as a partner to craft.

Next, it exists as one of several means for the symbolization of experience. Let us suppose the children have spent an afternoon exploring the nearest park, or wood, or seashore, or riverbank, or canal, or farmyard, or building site—or anything else; in the days following, this experience will be assessed, re-lived, re-explored and re-enjoyed in imagination as the children gradually assimilate it, in the same way that food is used when it is ingested. Art will be one of the ways in which it will be used. They may paint straightforward pictures of the expedition as a whole, or select tiny aspects of which they only were conscious, and blow these small things up to large size. They may make imaginative leaps away from the central experience, in which the wood becomes a jungle, the municipal car-park a space-station, the council house under erection a medieval castle, the pet-shop a Noah's Ark. They will employ any technique they choose to portray their idea, and maybe, while out, collect materials for it on the spot. They will also record their trip in language, illustrating their stories as they go along, this time using neater, smaller ways of producing pictorial art; for the days when art always meant fat brushes and powder tempera are, in their turn, at an end. Children can create art using any materials and any tools.

The class may decide to make a co-operative record of their visit, either in book form or by making a large frieze for the classroom wall. If the former, it will be illustrated with individual pictures in any known technique. If the latter, it may be an enormous collage in which the children work together using materials gathered on the site to splendid advantage.

Stories, poems, songs and music all become springboards from which expression in the form of pictorial art can take flight. History and geography, while no longer appearing on the timetable as isolated subjects, are given scope as aspects of any experience, and demand expression and investigation in and through art. Religious education, still compulsory, is both helped and inspired by art, in the same way as religion has always given inspiration to the artist throughout the ages.

Lastly, there remain those aspects of experience covered by mathematics and science. For a long time, these were left outside the circle in which art was a central influence, but this is so no longer. We know now, as never before, that art and mathematics are inseparable, linked by so many strands that it is difficult to pick out one to serve as an example. To take the link at a very simple yet significant level, let us remember that the composition of any picture is an exercise in spatial relationships in which recognition of basic shapes and complete understanding of relative sizes are counters. Taking the concept of symmetry as another example, one crosses another vague and indistinct borderline into the field of science, for the world of natural history supplies examples of symmetry at every turn. In other areas of scientific exploration, pattern and colour, the pillars of art, play no small part. But for the scientist as well as the mathematician, for the poet as well as the sociologist, for the doctor and the archaeologist and the teacher, for any human being caught up in the intricacies of ordinary everyday life, early education must provide the eye that sees, the mind that comprehends, and the spirit which leaps to respond. Art teaches and develops them all. That is the real justification for the important place it has in education here today. It is, as all education everywhere should be, preparation for a happy and satisfying life as an adult, for it engenders in the human spirit an interest in those few things over which economic success or failures can have little, if any, control.

3. The Teacher's Role

The teacher has a complex role to play in art education. On the one hand, he needs to make available the widest range of materials and give children the freedom to explore these materials in their own way: "messing about" plays as important a role in art as in science. On the other hand, the teacher needs to intervene in subtle or not-so-subtle ways if children are to deepen their mastery of artistic materials and media— if they are to learn to express themselves in disciplined ways. While teachers should avoid destroying children's innate artistic drives by teaching them technique before they have a need for it, there are times when technique needs to be taught, since some materials have to be understood before they can be used fully or properly. (Henry Pluckrose, a London primary-school head, has written widely on the role of the arts in the education of young children.)

Children have a way of communicating that is uniquely their own—for they have not been sophisticated by adult standards, and are uncluttered by the cultural conventions of the society in which they are growing up. String and newspaper, feathers and pulses, fir cones and leaves, fabric scraps and packing boxes, tin cans and chipped plates—all are materials which a young child handles with tremendous enthusiasm. They provide an additional outlet for his innate desire to handle and to fashion, to make and to do, 'I'm going to make these pieces of leather say Owl,' one six-year-old announced, 'and he can have these foil bottle tops for eyes because he must see in the dark to fly.' Imagery and fantasy wrapped up in reality!

Discovery and Direction

In the seven years that a child spends at the primary school he is encouraged to undertake a wide range of activities which, for successful completion, depend upon his intuitive response to materials. Moreover, the nature of these materials imposes a discipline upon a child. For example, it is possible to model a boat in clay and in wood. John is making a boat in clay. His response to his material will be utterly different from that of Peter who is working in wood. John's boat will grow from a soft easily shapeable mass, its form slowly changing under his finger tips. Meanwhile Peter is bound by the hardness of the wood, the sharpness of the tools that are available and the degree of control he has over them. Although Peter and John may each end up with something which says 'boat' to the onlooker . . . the problems which they had to overcome (and the skills which they had to employ to do so) were quite different.

It is in such situations that the teacher has an especially significant role to play. One does not want to destroy a child's innate curiosity with technique lessons unrelated to his particular needs and accomplishments. At the same time, some materials have to be understood before they can be used fully and to leave expensive materials out 'to be played with until their properties are discovered' is both unrealistic and foolhardy.

How the balance is achieved between the two contrasting aims of child discovery and adult direction is virtually impossible to describe. It happens if the climate in the classroom is such that the teacher is one who inspires rather than dictates, it happens where discoveries about the nature of materials are discussed so that children learn through each other's experiences as well as from the teacher. A group of ten-year-olds, for example, might discover that wax crayons resist water-based ink. From this starting point (simple wax resists), the gifted teacher will try to create situations in which the process of using wax to repel water is examined in as many contrasting ways as possible. What would happen if we tried to dye a piece of waxed fabric? How could we wax a length of cloth? What would we need? How could we apply the dye? How could we remove the wax? Can we apply more than one colour? The teacher might initiate the discussion but his aim should always be to provoke questions from the children which *they* (not he) will attempt to answer. (The sad thing is that many teachers fell ill-equipped to fulfil this role—to suggest a starting point one has to be aware of the various options available. If teachers have in fact 'played' with materials themselves, they will be far more likely to be able to ask these 'developmental' questions in a sensitive and perceptive way. This might involve regular attendance on courses, and reading professional magazines. The development of new materials surely makes this an absolute necessity!)

Thus, throughout the whole time the child is at primary school, he is learning about materials, the way they behave, and the things for which particular materials are suitable. At the same time, this rich variety of experience is helping the child to discover his own individual gifts. Every child has his own personality and, because of this, particular materials will have a particular appeal to individual children. Mary might find that she can express herself most satisfactorily with size 12 hog brushes on large sheets of paper; for John, scraper board provides the ideal surface for fine line drawings, which for him are an important aspect of visual communication. Peter, on the other hand, prefers modelling and enjoys the discipline imposed by paper sculpture. Iris finds chalk carving far more satisfactory, and Jaki, imaginative and unconventional, is never happier than when building weird constructions from junk material.

Moreover, the variety of materials available not only makes it possible for each child to discover his own gifts but also to deepen his understanding of the ways particular materials behave. That is, he comes to terms with a process (or craft) at a much deeper level than he would ever do if the teacher imposed an identical art situation on every member of the group.

Jennifer, for example, had a penchant for weaving and this interest took her, in two final years at primary school (9+ to 11+), from using cardboard looms, to working on large two-heddle wooden table looms, to carding, spinning, and the use of the warping board, to woven patterns and to a study of the woollen industry in Britain (including a brief historical survey, types of sheep, raw wool imports, textile exports, knitting patterns and folk lore).

Aspects of the Teacher's Role

This development of specific interests does not mean that experiment in other media is discouraged—rather, it means that teachers are prepared to shape their art programme to meet the needs of individuals rather than the supposed needs of a group. There is nothing worse, for example, than to make Stephen paint for seven years in the hope that his pictures will eventually be something more than muddy grey splodges. Usually, after a much shorter period, Stephen discovers that he can't make paint say what he wants it to—and his interest in art atrophies accordingly.

Underlying all that has been written so far, is the assumption that the teacher himself is prepared to continue to learn about materials and the way they behave, for the horizons in art education are not static but continually expanding. The teacher (however expert his professional training) will need to keep abreast of new developments by reading, by attending refresher courses, and, most important of all, by experimenting for himself. To take a typical classroom situation: a teacher is introducing lino block cutting to a group of nine-year-olds. She has prepared the lesson thoughtfully, has all the tools and equipment readily available. Yet is she really in a position to answer all the 'why?' and 'how?' questions if she has not, quite recently, experienced for herself the same sort of 'doing it' situation, laboured under similar difficulties, suffered similar frustrations, and, finally, been elated at the success of her design? The *raison d'être* for art practice lies in personal involvement. John Newick, whose interest in art education took him from a teaching post in an English boarding school to central Africa, and then to London University, makes this point very succinctly: '. . . unless we are mysteriously fortified by the problems of a craft at a level which draws sleepily upon our personal resourcefulness, we have no defence against the intrusion of the commonplace.'

And yet—as in all learning situations—the teacher cannot sit back and just expect 'something' (ie, art) 'to turn up.' Some form of organization is essential. Although, in many British primary schools, the 'art period' (in which all children in any one class 'do' art at the same time) is a thing of the past, let us assume that it is in such a situation that we find ourselves. How can we cope? Firstly it is essential to break down our class of thirty children into much smaller groups—say five groups of six children each. Let us assume that four of these groups are already engaged upon an activity which they can manage without too much adult help (eg, making papier mâché puppet heads, doing wax resist, carving in soapstone or chalk, colour cutting into oil pastel). The fifth group consists of children who have been concerned with fabric decoration (block printing, tie-and-dye). The teacher now wishes to introduce them to batik, and this will require direct teaching. The teacher might begin by explaining the process and the tools, following this by working alongside of the children as they in turn experiment. Such teacher-led discussion as takes place should have the aim of consolidating the children's understanding of the activity.

From time to time the teacher must, of necessity, move to other groups, offering help and advice as and when appropriate, but he will continually return to those children who, for that period are his especial responsibility (the batik workers).

This pattern will be repeated during subsequent lessons. The batik workers will become reasonably conversant with the process, and will then need time to deepen their appreciation by further experimentation. But the puppet heads will be dry, and will need painting and clothing. Is the teacher's main responsibility here, or with the children who seem to have exhausted their interest in wax resist and soapstone? Could these two groups merge for some supportive work on the theatre project from which the puppets grew? Herein lies the teacher's role: a professional know-how, supported by an understanding of the children for whom he works.

Of course, the example developed above does not only apply to art-orientated subjects. One could in the same way have the groups following quite different programmes (eg, maths, science, creative writing, weaving, individual research work). The teacher then becomes rather like a master juggler at a circus, whose aim is to keep thirty plates spinning on thirty poles. This he does by moving to where he is most needed when he is most needed, increasing the momentum of individual poles to prevent the plates falling to the ground.

As the young child learns about materials he is better able to relate them to the particular things he wants to do. He becomes comparatively expert in some, whilst in others his knowledge is sketchy and peripheral. Children with knowledge are able to share ideas and technical know-how with less gifted members of the group. Leaders emerge, and often these include children who in other spheres (for example, games, drama) have much less to offer.

Environmental Studies

Knowledge of materials, however, is of little worth unless it is used purposefully. Environmental studies play an important part in the curricula of British primary schools, and out-of-school visits to places of interest are common. A visit may be linked to a study of the area around the school—its factories, the shopping area, the town hall, the police, fire, and ambulance services. It may take in a local farm, a church, an old building or a museum—or it may be (with small children) nothing more than a visit to a nearby park, to walk through autumn leaves, or to feed the ducks on a pond. Any of these experiences will trigger off discussion, and this will invariably lead to a desire to paint, to write in prose and verse, to model. In other words, to a desire to communicate. 'We went to the museum and this is what we saw . . .'

Each visit will give each child a unique individual experience, and, because it is individual and unique, each member of the group should be given the opportunity to express himself in his own way. It is worth remembering that the impact of any visit depends largely upon the child's previous experiences. A quite commonplace happening for one child can be utterly shattering for another. Barry, a lad of ten, who lived in a downtown slum, was taken to the seaside. Stunned silence was followed by a torrent of questions. 'Look at all that water. Does it go all over the world? Is it cold? Can I touch it? Why does it make that noise? Why does it move?' On returning to school, Barry looked in the library for as many 'sea' books, from atlases to reference books, as he could find, and he made an anthology of 'sea' drawings and 'sea' poetry.

The group experience—written work, pictures and models—is taken by the teacher and displayed so that a variety of viewpoints is presented —each child contributing something of himself to the overall effect. Photographs, maps and diagrams are also added and the final display should be a synopsis of the children's experiences. 'We went to . . . and this display is our way of showing you what we saw, what we learned, how we felt.' . . .

. . . By providing experiences and the means through which these experiences can be expressed, the teacher will have come a long way towards realizing an environment in which creative work will flourish.

There are, however, two other important aspects of the teacher's role which are often ignored. First, the teacher must be prepared to plan his work programme so that the child is given time to assimilate new experiences and then to extend and develop them. An 'art period' which is fixed and immovable rarely allows sufficient time for really creative work to develop. A creative act cannot be bound by time. It is in schools where syllabus and timetable serve to indicate direction, rather than to instruct and command, that creative work flourishes. Thus, in such a school, one might find a group of girls spending a whole morning labouring over a piece of embroidery, while, in the same period of time, three other groups have written poetry, made music, and constructed polyhedra from plastic shapes. Each activity was, in essence, creative. Each required a different amount of time for its consummation.

Secondly, the teacher should provide children with the opportunity to touch. Essentially, art in school is education through the senses, and, in young children, the pleasure gained through tactile experience is immense. In addition to displays of children's work, classrooms should also contain small ever-changing exhibitions of things which children can handle. These could contain man-made objects (carvings, ornaments of glass and clay), or leaves and stones, shells, pieces of bark, and feathers. An Indian's moccasin and a robin's egg provide the young child with essential visual and tactile experience, as well as material for a discussion on colour, pattern and texture. . . .

Art and Life

In addition to art practices which flow from drama, music, poetry, and local studies, some crafts will be undertaken simply for their own sake. What is the point, the cynic might ask, in letting an eight-year-old fashion a pot from green clay when he can buy one which holds water from the local store? Why bother to tie-dye fabric, or pattern it with lino blocks for a school display table, when the supermarket two streets away sells attractive material at a few pence per yard?

Hidden in the answer lies the basic reason for art practice. Man's progress towards civilization has been marked by his ability to discipline materials, to fashion clay, metal and wood, to spin, to weave, to carve, to construct, to build. In an age when individuality is being continually undermined by mass production ('soft sell,' 'built-in obsolescence' and all), our children, born into a technological society, need to have some awareness of the basic processes of mankind, if they are to live fully.

Thus, the majority of British primary schools also include traditional crafts as part of their art programme. Weaving, spinning, cane and raffia work, sewing (embroidery and simple dressmaking), woodcraft, basketry, pottery, and bookcraft continue to be practised. Sometimes, crafts which are found in the local community (for example, corn-dolly making) are also to be found in the neighbourhood schools. At this stage, girls and boys will be found following similar crafts—there is little specialization by sex. Often, boys sew or make collage pictures in fabric and braid, and girls use wood and cane.

In the best of British primary schools, art is not regarded as something unrelated to living and learning. It is seen as an integral part of the life of the school and of the community beyond, providing, as it does, an outlet for the young child's innate desire to explore with hands and eyes, and to express himself freely through an incredible range of materials, both unconventional and traditional.

4. Creating a Proper Human Environment

"For most of their history," the Plowden Committee suggests, "the English people have shown at least as much genius as any other for the

creation of a physical environment suitable for human living." One of the reasons for emphasizing craft work of all sorts in primary schools is to restore the aesthetic sensibilities that have been blunted by industrialization. It is not enough, however, to include crafts and art in the school curriculum; educators must pay equal attention to the invisible art curriculum that grows out of the school environment as a whole. "It should be the object of every school," the Committee urges, "to do all in its power to add to the beauty of its equipment and environment" so that in time, "every school in England is worth visiting, not only for what goes on in it, but for the surroundings it gives to its children and the example it sets for civilised living."

Art is both a form of communication and a means of expression of feeling which ought to permeate the whole curriculum and the whole life of the school. A society which neglects or despises it is dangerously sick. It affects, or should affect, all aspects of our life from the design of the commonplace articles of everyday life to the highest forms of individual expression.

The beginning of the revolt against formalism occurred in the realm of pictorial art. In the late 1920s the influence of Marion Richardson began to be felt and by 1939 a considerable number of schools had broken away from the old tradition and were trying something new. The old tradition consisted of the careful copying of objects—flowers, twigs, fruit, geometrical forms and sometimes pictures—usually in black and white and usually with a hard lead pencil. If colour was introduced, it was to fill in outlines, and crayons were much commoner than paint. If paint was used, it was cheap water colour. There was little in this tradition to commend. It encouraged neither vision nor invention. The close observation and careful recording that might have been its merits were disappointingly absent from the work of the majority of children, for whom the demands made were quite inappropriate. The essence of the new approach was to let children use large sheets of paper and big brushes, requiring larger movements of hand and arm, more suitable to their age than the fine, delicate movement required by the old tradition. Powder colour in plenty and free brush work were introduced from the earliest moment and the children were allowed to paint "what they liked." Little attempt was made to teach them perspective or techniques, but certainly Marion Richardson and those close to her did much to arouse children's powers of observation.

The immediate result of the inter-war approach was the production

From *Children and Their Primary Schools,* "The Plowden Report," Vol. 1, para. 676–685. Reprinted by permission of the Controller of Her Britannic Majesty's Stationery Office.

of vast quantities of childlike pictures, boldly executed, usually aglow with colour, often showing freshness and originality of vision and sometimes a remarkable power of organising two-dimensional space. This stage of almost complete freedom from teaching of techniques was necessary. It was probably the only means of breaking away from the arid formalism of the tradition, but it was only a stage, and good primary school art has developed considerably beyond it in recent years.

There are many more teachers now than there ever were with an appreciation of painting and other arts and an understanding of their value for children. They still do little teaching of techniques, but do much more than those of 30 years ago to stimulate children's vision, to develop the "seeing eye," to multiply the possible sources of inspiration and to enrich the school environment. They supply the better art books and magazines and make use of everyday objects of good design from this country and others, as well as of the resources of the past. The subject matter, the treatment and the media of children's painting show a much greater variety than those of the thirties. The primary schools have, indeed, participated to the full in the more general flourishing of art in the whole community. Some primary schools encourage close observation of the detail and subtleties of colour and texture to be found in bark, stones, shells, plants and seaweed. Many delightful coloured and black and white drawings are acutely observed and lovingly executed. Much that was banished in the thirties, and rightly banished because it was feebly conceived and inadequately provided for, has now returned to its rightful place, infused with life and assisted by the use of better tools and media.

We think, at its best, primary school art is very good indeed. But there is no cause for complacency. Many schools still show too little sign of having moved far from the outlook of the thirties and although this is better than the tradition that preceded it, it is too limited in scope to be acceptable. There is often too little progression, and the work of the ten year olds is less developed than would be expected from what is done by the sixes, sevens and eights. This is partly attributable to a failure on the part of teachers to realise their pupils' possibilities, and partly to teachers' lack of confidence in their power to help. As long ago as 1933 some children in Wiltshire painted large murals in the school and expressed a desire to brighten up in a similar way the local station waiting room, a suggestion in which the railway company took no interest! We are convinced that the artistic capabilities of children are much greater than many primary teachers realise. This underestimate will become more serious if some children remain in the middle school till nearly 13. Too many teachers still believe that after that "first fine careless rapture" children's imaginative powers diminish and wither. Other teachers have proved the reverse. What has to be recognised is that, as children grow, their vision and also their interests and viewpoint change. For example, although not all twelve year olds "see" perspective in the adult sense, many become deeply absorbed in what the adult world calls "drawing." The form and construction of things, both natural and man-made, are of consuming interest to some boys and girls of this age. If the school can feed and satisfy this interest, all should be well. Of course twelve year olds will paint differently from nine year olds; but, if they have a full life, their work will certainly not be empty or derivative: it will be as exploratory and as satisfying to themselves as it ever was. Moreover, the impact of commercial art and the influence of the camera, particularly through television, must be recognised. The school has to manage these forces tactfully. In both there is something stimulating and good as well as bad, and the discerning teacher will know how to guide his children's emerging powers of criticism. A more fundamental obstacle to full development is the lukewarm attitude not only of the public but also of many teachers and many schools, especially grammar schools, to the importance of art in education. If the word "frill" is not now often used of it, the attitude that it implies is still widespread. We shall return to this point later, and will only say here that we are ourselves satisfied that the practice of art by children is a fundamental and indispensable part of their education.

Craft in the elementary school was traditionally separated from art. For the boys it meant woodwork, cardboard models and geometrical drawing and for the girls needlework and knitting. Certain other crafts, notably basket-making, book-binding, weaving, block-printing and occasionally pottery became common in the senior elementary schools in the thirties, but the primary schools were not much affected. Latterly a much greater variety of crafts, including wood-carving, clay-modelling, dyeing and block-cutting, have come into the primary schools and the distinction between what is done by boys and girls has partly disappeared. Except possibly for the oldest children, it is quite artificial and unhelpful; boys enjoy stitchery and girls can benefit from work in wood and metal.

The basis for much of the best work done in the primary school has been the willingness of many infant teachers to make materials and tools of good quality available to young children. There has been a welcome trend away from didactic to natural materials and to those whose use is rooted in our tradition. Clay has replaced Plasticine, the well-kept "piece box" has taken the place of the hessian mate and school knitting cottons, and wood and waste materials have been substituted for paper as a medium for three dimensional models. Children need to experiment with a wide range of materials, natural and man-made.

The connection of art and craft with the rest of the curriculum is of paramount importance. The development of sensitivity and the growth of techniques come partly as the result of play and experiment with materials. But, just as in mathematics, techniques are learnt most easily when they are needed for the purposes children have in mind.

At its best, the craft of English primary schools is outstanding. We have seen work of extraordinary beauty and technical perfection which we could hardly have believed had been produced by young children had we not watched them doing it; but here, equally, there is much still to be done. There is far too much mechanical and repetitive work, especially in needlework, far too much dull and tasteless craft, far too widespread an acceptance of poor standards, far too little integration of the craft into the curriculum as a whole. If children stay in the middle school for an extra year, more account must be taken of their growing concern to know how things work and how to do a job "properly," almost to pursue a technique for its own sake. There must be a more workmanlike and ambitious outlook for the older children. Some girls will certainly wish to make simple outfits for themselves. They should be given opportunity to discriminate between the fabrics which are suitable for their purpose and for their degree of skill, and should be helped by frequent discussion. Guidance should be given in the ways of holding and manipulating tools and materials, and the sewing machine should have a place. Many of the crafts associated with textiles, block printing, tie dyeing, embroidery and weaving appeal to boys and girls alike. An over-academic emphasis in the work of the abler streams in the grammar schools and the neglect of craft in their education has left its mark on the great majority of teachers in primary schools. Some of the colleges of education have done splendid work in the correction of this lopsided education, as also have some of the advisers to local authorities. Exhibitions of children's work have also provided much stimulus, but a considerable upheaval in the educational world and the world in general will be needed before art and craft take their proper place in the education of the young.

For most of their history the English people have shown at least as much genius as any other for the creation of a physical environment suitable for human living—the eighteenth century town, the village, the country house, the parkland, the cottage garden, the farm with all its appurtenances—the ages which produced them could be criticised for their inequality, their poverty, their squalor and their harshness, but not for their taste and craftsmanship. The industrial revolution saw a decline in many things aesthetic, a decline which became steeper as the nineteenth century advanced, though we are beginning to perceive achievement even in the worst period. The results of this decline are about us, above all in our large towns, and the schools of the period are characteristic. Until recently people had become accustomed to the idea that schools were ugly and dark places surrounded by dreary stretches of asphalt without and painted dark brown within, though some teachers worked wonders by the environment they created inside the school. Opinions will differ about contemporary school buildings, but it is generally agreed that they represent an advance in lightness, spaciousness and convenience, and anyhow in aesthetic good intentions. But much of the rest of the environment, rural as well as urban, in which children grow up is all too evidently the product of a crude indifference to aesthetic values and of an insensitiveness to many of the deepest human needs. We should like to see the schools becoming much more than most of them now are, places in which the children are surrounded by many examples, old and new, of taste and discrimination—furniture, clocks, fabrics, ceramics, pictures and books. It should be the object of every school to do all in its power to add to the beauty of its equipment and environment, in exactly the same way as a householder with a sensitive eye for beauty will make such constant additions, improvements and adaptations as his means allow to the house and garden in which he lives. In recent years the public have become familiar with the interiors of many great houses which were once closed to all but a privileged few, and which are now worth seeing because their former owners had taste, thought their own surroundings important and took trouble with them. We should like to see schools set out on the same course, so that in time every school in England is worth visiting, not only for what goes on in it, but for the surroundings it gives to its children and the example it sets of civilised living. Much of the beauty in the school environment should be created by the children themselves and by the care taken in the display of their work. There are schools which already do much and which are showing others the way. Though opportunities and circumstances are very unequal, every school could do something and in the aggregate the schools could become a strong, perhaps a decisive, influence on public taste.

5. Messing About in Music

"Music can be one of the most subjective and intimate expressions of the human personality, and as such has been valued from time immemorial as a life-enhancing medium," John Horton, a leading British music educator has written. "But it is also an art of communication and social coherence, enabling members of a group to establish sympathetic contact with one another with minimal need for the intervention of verbal language. This process can be observed, as it were under laboratory conditions, in the music corners of the modern infant school."

Most American schools (and until recently, most English schools) tend to suppress children's interest in music, in part because schools do not really value music, in part because teachers seem to think that children will learn to appreciate music by listening to it rather than by making it. The reverse is true, according to Benjamin Koenig, a gifted teacher who has conducted music workshops for teachers in a number of parts of the country. The classics "do deserve recognition," Koenig argues, "but not at the expense of active music making." On the contrary, children need the opportunity to "mess about" in music, no less than in art or science or any other part of the curriculum. With help from the teacher, children can learn to express themselves through music.

Music consists of sounds and silences. One goal is to organize these into what will become a musical piece. Because there are many ways to organize sounds, one must keep mind and ears open to any valid attempt. Validity must be left up to the composer, whether child or adult. In the grown-up world, John Cage believes it is valid to compose pieces that leave much to chance happenings, while others, perhaps more traditional, want nothing left to chance. Similarly, children must have the freedom to decide in which manner they will compose. This presupposes a broad definition of music, to be sure, but it will allow for a maximum of discovery and invention in the classroom; and perhaps discovering and inventing often will prove to be more valuable than the end product itself.

Children, let loose in school to experiment with sounds and mix tonal colors and textures, would undoubtedly create a noise level of epic proportions. Perhaps this is why teachers have waited so long to let the children go. Yet it is experimentation (experience) that the child lacks when he comes to confront a musical experience. He needs time and place to "mess about" in music.

As an infant he banged on crib and high chair, babbled, sang, and in other experiments established that sound exists. But what of organized sound? Today this is most often left to TV, radio, and records. "The beat goes on" and is unavoidably plugged into today's child. Department stores, elevators, apartment complexes, even toilets have music piped in. It so surrounds us that we become unaware of its existence. And, worse, we take no active part or pleasure in its production. We have become a mass audience, dimly aware that in order for us to participate in music making we must compete with not only the high technical competence we are constantly exposed to, but the electronic perfection of those performances as well. Couple this with the general oppressiveness of the educational system—fortifying our basic insecurities, as a rule, and

From Benjamin Koenig, "Creative Music for Children: Attitude Not Aptitude," *Outlook,* Autumn 1971, Mountain View Center for Environmental Education.

often convincing us that we are incapable of producing anything worth-while on our own—and we get the result; the temptation to sit back, surround ourselves with the perfection of electronic equipment, and enjoy the show. We certainly will not risk failure again by actually making music.

Unfortunately the schools play right into this situation by deciding that 1) music study requires a knowledge of notation (thereby robbing music of spontaneity and joy), and 2) music appreciation is best gained by *listening* to "good" music. By "good" we usually mean the great classics (Bach, Beethoven, Brahms, and may I add Bartok, Barber, Berg and Boulez?). Of course these do deserve recognition, but not at the expense of active music making. And although music notation is a prerequisite to performing classics, children can be actively involved in music activities and enjoy them before formal, more traditional, lessons begin. As an introductory experience, active involvement is more important than any factual knowledge we can give. The noise level is *high*—but oh what emerges from that momentary chaos!

Creativity, to my mind, is inherently linked with exploring, probing, discovering, inventing and re-creating. A child can be as creative in finding a harmony to a song as in composing an original composition. If he finds new words for an old melody he is being as creative as if he makes up an entirely new melody.

Today one must be aware of the music of Schoenberg, Stravinsky, John Cage, and others. (For example, music in the western world has not been the same since May 29th, 1913, when, in the first strains of the first performance of Stravinsky's *Rite of Spring,* a bassoon ventured into a high range never before played on that instrument.) We must be equally aware of rhythm and blues. At our disposal is African, Indian, Greek, Irish, and all other music of the world's people. There are the avant-garde and classical composers. We are free to move out into the future. (Electronic music has become a viable medium.) The problem now is a choice of what kind of music to make and how to begin. Let me share my experience with you.

The creative music atmosphere in my room is built around an attractive body of instruments with which children cannot fail to make music. Actually I have found them to be as attractive to adults as to children, and that may be a good test. There are drums of many shapes and sizes; gongs with oriental attraction; bells from horse-drawn sleighs, Pakistan, China, and Santa Claus; a homemade marimba with beautiful sound; maracas, a guiro, and the jawbone-of-an-ass, all from South American bands; a stringed psaltery from the Lincoln School of Teachers College; an mbira (thumb piano) from Africa; and finally there are sticks of all shapes and sizes, from bamboo to regulation drum sticks.

To these "real" instruments I have added a sizable body of found sounds, i.e., "junk." (I have become a discriminating junk collector, recycling those articles with good tone quality.) Rhythm bands today have become so standardized that they are boring. A single company will sell you a ready-made set of mediocre instruments for children which have terrible sound quality and will undoubtedly be broken in short order. My way of collecting takes slightly longer, but it's worth it. There is no reason why the kids can't be brought into the search. Combine eye attraction and good sound and you have musical beginnings.

My odd assortment of sound sources has become a bag of tricks which I carry with me. When I enter a classroom I dig directly into my bag and come up with a South American jawbone-of-an-ass, an African zebra-skin drum, or perhaps a pair of spoons bought at the Salvation Army. The kids are visually attracted immediately and, as I demonstrate, they become aurally attracted as well.

If the class is small enough I can merely unpack the instruments, put them in the center, and let the kids start on their own. Excited, they go from instrument to instrument, trying one here, listening to someone there. I allow this freedom—I encourage them to experiment. If I step in too soon they become inhibited.

One of the beauties of this approach is that anyone can participate on his own level. Few of the instruments pose any technical problems. One virtually cannot make a mistake. Both teacher and student have two freedoms; the freedom to experiment, and freedom from worrying about doing something wrong.

Usually this initial period is quite loud. I only step in if the instruments are being mistreated. However, there comes a time when the sound level begins to subside. This is the "teachable moment." The group has lost its first momentum and wants some guidance. Whenever I have stepped in at this time I have found the children ready to respond positively, but if I interrupt sooner, the class usually rebels. They want to experiment. Indeed, how can we put such temptingly beautiful instruments in front of them and expect them to sit quietly and not touch? When they begin to quiet down and look around I usually ask them to find one instrument they want to play. I also now ask for silence.

While they are experimenting I am watching them, helping those who need help, and answering questions. I am dealing with individuals, making personal contact. The information I gain during this period will be stored and used. In one class, for instance, I see from his use of the instruments that Edgar is an emotionally tense person. He has been doing some nice drumming, however. When I get the class quiet I ask Edgar to start us off. He begins to drum—I cue in someone else—and gradually add people until everyone is playing. Then I gradually stop each from playing until the piece ends. As I am cuing in the group I have to deal with an initial shyness on the part of two of the girls in the room, but that soon vanishes as Clara sets up a marvelous rhythm on the maracas and Rose follows with a tambourine, which she plays by using the back part of her palm (near her wrist). Both girls are obviously aware of their Puerto Rican heritage and I shall take that clue to use later in my choice of song material.

Often Helen Lanfer, a New York music specialist, begins her creative music classes with the question, "How many sounds can you make with your hands?" This is later extended to, "How many sounds can you make on *anything?*" And Helen remains quite willing to accept anything as long as the child is truly satisfied with the resulting sounds. The "How many" questions eventually narrow down to "Which sounds do you like best?" And once this is established the most important question still remains: "What shall we do with all the sounds?"

From this point on it is tricky to describe what goes on because literally anything can happen. The class goes its own route. Perhaps all will choose to work together. Maybe small groups will go their separate ways. Often individuals decide to work alone. In this pluralistic way of working, group and individual experiences combine in a vital, living, active outlet for musical creativity. No piece can be graded because each is playing his own creation. "You can't write a wrong composition," Helen has said, and this is basic to the educational rebuilding of musical spirit and strength in the individual.

Another way I begin is to paraphrase Helen Lanfer's question: "How many sounds can you find on your instrument?" I allow a few minutes for exploration and then stress the fact that we must listen sometimes as well as play. We proceed to listen to each person in turn as he demonstrates how many different sounds he has found. This approach has the value of introducing each instrument to the whole group so that they can choose more clearly next time. However, this can only be done with children who already have the inner controls to sit and listen. If it is to become a discipline thing, forget it, and try something which will use the fact that the class is an active one.

With any approach to opening the session I find that I have to encourage even the youngest children to believe in what they are doing. They look to me for guidance or discipline—I only smile, nod, or pat their heads encouragingly. A child hits the side of the drum instead of the head. He looks at me with a mischievous grin. I smile back and tell him it's a nice sound. He soon gets the idea that something else is being stressed here. The one question he will be asked will be, "Do *you* like that sound?" And I will have to be more than careful not to inflict my prejudices onto him. "If you tell me, honestly, that you like that sound, I will believe you."

Often, after I have directed a class through a musical piece, I hand over the direction to a class member. I have found, consistently, that if the class conductor is strong enough the class will undoubtedly respond more readily to him than to me. For instance, in one class Rose accepted my invitation to conduct. In what has become a common experience to me, she directed the group with startling precision. She knew exactly what she wanted to hear and how to get it out of the class.

In a recent teacher workshop three women made up a piece for two cymbals and a bell. They struck all three simultaneously for six times and then paused before repeating. During the pause the cymbal players stopped the sound with their hands, but the bell player let hers go on. I pointed this out to the group and asked them to listen for it. I have grown accustomed to listening and picking out special features of compositions to point out to the group. I was also able to differentiate between a *short sound* on the cymbals and a *long sound* on the bell.

Being able to be consciously aware of long sounds and short sounds is basic to musical composition. It is one of the basic elements of music theory. Other basics are high and low sounds, loud and soft sounds, fast and slow sounds. Silence is the opposite of sound itself. I try to make a class aware of these musical elements because it helps a person to verbalize what he might want in his piece. Using a musical opposite is also a technique which all composers employ to keep up interest in a piece: if it's a slow piece and getting boring, throw in a fast section to liven it up, etc.

Situation: John composes a piece for the drum. I ask him if I can play his piece. Until now I have been stressing the fact that with this "method" one can't make a mistake. But if *I* try to play *his* piece I can indeed play it wrong. He tries to teach it to me but for some reason (purposely on my part) I can't seem to learn it properly. "Why not write it down," I say to him, "in that way I can play it anytime I wish."

John goes off to find a way of writing it down. He doesn't know traditional music notation so he makes up one of his own. There are numerous ways he can do this. Perhaps he uses colors, each one meaning something else. Then again he might make a squiggle which means loud, and a line which means soft, and proceed to notate his piece with squiggles and lines. He might number different parts of the drum, and by writing a number he would be indicating where we were to strike the instrument. Or perhaps the numbers might mean how many times to strike the drum.

At any rate he finds a way, and brings the paper back to me. I sit down with the drum, and begin to play. "Oh no!" says John. "That's not the right way. You have to hold this one longer and make this one a short beat." I go at it again and am stopped again. It seems that I just can't get it right—even from the notated version. "Go back," I say, "and show me on the paper just how long to hold each note." This is a fiendishly difficult task and is designed to further define the purpose of music notation.

Eventually John will be shown some of the traditional ways of notating music. I will show him this not because it is the *only* way to notate music, but rather because it is the best means we have to date. One should be aware of the fact (as most people are not) that our notational system in no way duplicates a composer's wishes exactly, and is in need of much further revision. We have learned to accept it without question. John will understand, through his experience, the true needs and purposes of notation, and will appreciate it that much more. He will learn it, eventually, because he *needs* to know it. And my role as the teacher is to help create that need.

In fact my role as teacher has been to create all kinds of things. I am playing a very active role and this is important to understand. I created an atmosphere which said: Explore, discover, create. But I didn't stop there. I further defined the seriousness with which one should approach any area of study, although I didn't attempt to take the fun out of it. Seriousness of study doesn't necessarily mean relinquishing one's sense of humor, but it does set up an atmosphere in which the product of one's creative energies will be treated with respect. And it also allows me to insist on a high level of active participation. I *expect* a high level and this sets a tone for the class. In other words I am not delving into the arena of musical games. The creation of musical compositions, and perhaps the writing down of these pieces, takes work. My attitude, revealing my belief in the capability of the child, provides an atmosphere in which children can work with the freedom necessary to reveal themselves, to their own satisfaction, through the medium of music.

6. Movement, Drama and Dance

"We had to find some means of bringing color and vitality into this grey world," Bess Bullough writes in recalling her experience in a primary school in a depressed coal-mining town—"ways of making the school an exciting place where there was pride in achievement," as well as of making the children more sensitive to and aware of their environment. "We were eager to do anything that invited the children's involvement as feeling, thinking beings," she continues. "So we concentrated on physical education, drama, music and art."

Although she began her teaching career as a secondary-school specialist in English and drama, Ms. Bullough has become an expert on the Movement approach to what she calls "physical and creative education." Currently head of the department of physical education and drama in a middle school in the West Riding of Yorkshire, she has demonstrated her approach in pre-service and in-service teacher workshops and

*courses and teaching films and video tapes. In this selection, she de-
scribes the approach she takes in teaching primary-school children.*

━━━━━━━━━━

Every movement we make, moving part of the body or all the body,
involves three basic fundamentals—the use of space, weight and time.

SPACE   Use of much space, little space
         Moving at different levels
         Moving directly, moving indirectly
TIME   Moving at various speeds—moving quickly, slowly, coming
         to stillness, being still, leaving stillness
WEIGHT   Control of weight
         Transfer of weight
         Relaxation

Expressive Movement

Expressive movement develops from exploring and experimenting with
these basic fundamentals.

Expressive
   and   Basic movement (Exploring personal and communal space)
 creative   Movement into dramatic and dance situations
 movement   Adaptation to partners and groups
               Recalling of sensory experiences
               Characterization and improvization
               Sounds from movement leading to language flow
               Moving in response to sounds and music
               Dramatic themes

Introducing Movement

The first introduction to basic movement must be approached with
patience and understanding. Instructions must be simple and clear, given
in words the children can easily understand. The children must not be
rushed into situations that are beyond their understanding or control.
The awareness, self-discipline and control at which we are aiming cannot be expected from the start. If the movement experience is to be of
real value, helping a child to become a *feeling* as well as a *thinking* being,

From Bess Bullough, "Basic and Expressive Movement: A World of Action,
Thought and Feeling," Chapter 2 of Pamela Blackie, Bess Bullough, and Doris
Nash, *Drama* (Anglo-American Primary School Project, *Informal Schools in
Britain Today*) (New York: Citation Press, 1972), pp. 26–35, 37, 39. Copyright
© 1972 by School's Council Publication. Used by permission of Citation Press, a
Division of Scholastic Magazines, Inc.

then this must be a gradual process. The teacher must be prepared to accept what the children offer and then, through her observations, present them with situations that invite their interest, capture their imagination, and encourage their exploration, so helping them to become fully involved in what they are doing.

Throughout all the children's movement and dramatic experiences, they should be given frequent opportunities for observing each other's work. If this 'watching each other' is introduced sympathetically by the teacher, the children will accept it readily, and soon will comment on and discuss what they see. This class observation is of great value, for it helps to increase a child's awareness, clarify his movements, and deepen and widen his experience.

Exploration of Personal and Communal Space

When I begin to work with a class of children who have had no previous movement experience, I first ask them to move about the hall in any way they choose. Invariably there is chaos and confusion. So we come to a halt. Then I ask the children each to find a space of his own where he is not touching anyone. Now I draw the children's attention to their own *personal space*. It could be in the following way:

We are each standing in our own space. Let's look at it. How much space have we to move in without touching anyone? Look right up to the ceiling and down to the floor. That space is yours. Stretch out as far as you can in all directions without touching anyone or 'stealing' anyone's space.

Now, move in any way you like in your *own space but take great care that you don't touch anyone else.*

At this stage of exploration, a child's movements will have little control or inner effort—it is just a game, which at this stage is right. But, from this stage, a child should be helped to become more aware of his own movements, to work with increasing control and absorption. Here I find it helpful to narrow the field of movement by directing the child's attention to one part of his body: eg, feet.

Look at your feet. Move them anywhere in your own space. Try standing on your toes, heels, sides of your feet. Watch your feet all the time. See how they move. Feel how they move. Can you move your feet at different speeds? Sometimes quickly, sometimes slowly?

Now try touching the floor lightly with your feet—anywhere in your space. Watch them carefully. Are you using all the space around you?

Can you let your feet sink into the floor . . . hit the floor? Can you feel the difference right from inside when they touch, sink into, or hit the floor?

Now explore your space with your feet, sometimes touching, sometimes sinking into, and sometimes hitting the floor. See how many dif-

ferent ways you can move your feet—but all the time watch how they are moving, feel *how they are moving.*

Here, and throughout all their movement experiences, the children should be given plenty of time to explore, select and consolidate. They will become more and more interested in watching and feeling what their feet can do. Their minds begin to direct their movements with increasing absorption, inner effort and control.

Now, return to further exploration of communal space. Ask the children to move around the hall again, finding for themselves how many different ways they can move on their feet. Remind them that wherever they go they must think of their own individual space, taking care not to touch or 'steal' anyone else's space. Now narrow the field again by giving definite instructions: eg, walking at varying speeds, looking for spaces; running in a straight line, and making a sudden stop (*feeling* the suddenness of the stop); running on a curving path, gradually getting slower until stillness is reached (*feeling* the stillness), and so on. After repeated moving around in this way, awareness of others in the group is increased, and moving with ease and control without invading another's territory becomes a habit.

Now, return to further exploration of personal space, perhaps this time concentrating on *transfer of weight,* aiming at increasing body management and flow. Remind the children that, so far, we have been moving mainly with our weight on our feet. Now we are going to experiment, taking our weight on other parts of our bodies—big parts and little parts: eg, hands, feet, back.

Stand perfectly still, so that you know your weight is on your feet. Think about lying down in your space. Now find out how slowly and smoothly you can get there. Feel the slowness and smoothness from inside as you are moving. Where is your weight now? Can you put your weight onto another part of your body? Think where it is going and then try moving it there quickly. Can you hold it there? Now relax so that every part of you sinks into the floor.

As you are lying there, think of two or three different parts where you could take your weight. Now, find a good starting place and work out each transfer, separately if you like, but somewhere trying to bring in quickness, slowness, and stillness. Now, repeat the same movements, trying to join the three transfers easily and smoothly into one sequence.

Here the children have been concerned mainly with controlling their movements in varying degrees of time. At the same time they will have been working at different spatial levels and in different directions, since it is impossible to isolate the fundamentals. During these movement sequences, without being actively aware of it, the children will have experienced different qualities of movement: eg, curling, stretching, and so on.

Awareness of Movement Qualities

To help the children to become consciously aware of these movement qualities, I introduce them to what I call 'shape-making.' They start by simply moving in their space to make shape patterns. They draw on previous movement experiences, using varying speeds, tensions, levels, and directions. They are invited to think about the movement qualities in the shapes they are making.

They readily make and feel the different movements in changing from a small, curled shape to a big stretching shape, finding different levels and directions within their own space. Other movement shapes can be suggested and explored: eg, a big, flowing movement, followed by a quick, straight movement, or a slow, strong movement, followed by quick, jerky movements. The children will soon begin to experiment on their own, letting their shapes flow from one into another. Through continued exploration and repetition, they begin to appreciate difference in movement qualities. Their work becomes increasingly expressive and, depending on how they feel, their shapes move towards dramatic and dance forms.

And so these practical movement experiences gradually establish a language of movement that is the basis of creative work in drama and dance.

Reasons for Movement Qualities

Simple ideas or reasons for moving in certain ways can now be introduced: for example, ask the children to move, as quietly as they can, anywhere in the hall. When they become really involved in this moving quietly, I should probably continue as follows:

You have been moving quietly because I asked you to. Now can you think of any reason for moving quietly without making a sound? Work out your own ideas and I will watch for the pictures you make.

This could be followed by a sequence of given movements: eg, moving quickly, stopping suddenly, and then moving slowly. Ask the children to repeat this pattern, trying to make clearer to themselves the variations of time; *feeling* from *inside* the sudden stop, the stillness, and the slow moving growing out of the stillness.

As they work with increasing inner effort, the movement sequence will become dramatic, and ideas will emerge. Now, encourage them to let their ideas take over, reminding them that every movement they make should help to build up their picture. They are now becoming more aware and appreciative of the qualities of movement, and simple situations can be given for the children to work out in their own ways: eg, moving through a wood without being seen; using stepping stones to cross a stream; crawling under a fence; looking for a gap in a hedge and forcing a way through; pushing open a heavy door and closing it quietly.

Adaptation to Partners and Groups

During these movement exercises, the children, while being aware of others moving around them, have been working individually. Through her own observations, the teacher will know when the time arrives for the children to work with others.

First let each child work with a partner. Start by asking them to walk together, looking for spaces, sensing changes of direction and speed without touching. Follow this by asking them to share a space with fingers lightly touching, making flowing shapes at different levels. Now they can share a space without touching, each child making his own shapes but being aware of his partner's movements. Now invite them to find different ways of meeting and leaving each other, such as coming together slowly, and leaving each other quickly. Out of these moving patterns, dramatic or dance forms may emerge. If this happens, encourage dramatic and dance development.

Now give them plenty of opportunity to explore definite situations that they can share and work out together: one helping the other across stepping stones; exploring a dark cave together; Bedivere helping the wounded King Arthur down to the lake.

Working in Groups

After working with a partner, sharing a space, responding to another's movements, and sharing ideas, the child can begin to work in similar ways with increasing numbers.

1. Ask five or six children to share a space, weaving in and out at different levels, using varying speeds and movement qualities.
2. Ask them to walk around the hall, following a leader, feeling they are moving as a group, and avoiding contacts with other groups.
3. As their group feeling increases, encourage them to think of movement patterns: eg, making big, flowing movements, followed by a quick, downward movement; quickly forward, sudden stop, slowly backward. Encourage any resulting dramatic or dance form, giving time for development.
4. Let them move around with common feeling in their groups: eg, groups of frightened people, strong people, angry people, happy people. Develop these further by asking why they are moving in these ways. Give them time for discussion within their own groups so that they can work out their own situations.
5. Find out what happens when one group becomes aware of another group: eg, two groups meeting each other slowly; the meeting of two strong groups; the coming together of a weak and a strong group.

Give time for discussion between the groups on resulting situations and working for further development.

6. Now give definite situations in which such groups are involved: eg, a meeting of groups of conspirators in the Gunpowder Plot; King Arthur and his followers facing Mordred and his men.

Recalling of Sensory Experiences

Sensitive observation and awareness give colour, shape and meaning to the world around us. To develop greater depth and feeling in expressive work, frequent opportunity must be given for sensory experiences and recalling of these experiences.

Handling of objects and materials from observation and discovery tables helps to pin-point the child's observation. Ask the children to pick up shells, fossils, pieces of wood, glass, cinders, pebbles; to look at their shape and colour in different lights, to feel and contrast their textures. After giving children time for delight in the handling of an object, ask them to recall their feelings in words or paint. Later, ask them to imagine that they are holding the shell, the piece of glass, etc. Can their eyes and their fingers recall the shape, texture, colour?

Ask them to perform various actions involving vivid sensory recall:

Put your hands into a bowl of sticky dough. Feel them sink in. Feel and watch the pull of the dough as you lift your hands out. Pull and scrape the dough from your fingers.

Think of a holly leaf. Let your fingers feel its smooth, glossy surface. Now touch its sharp, pointed prickles.

Think of snow. Watch the snowflakes falling, see how lightly they move. Feel them falling on your face, your hands. Watch them disappear as they melt on your hand. Let your feet sink into the snow. Can you feel and hear the crunch under your feet? Gather up some snow, feel its coldness. Press it firmly into snowballs. Feel the hardness and the shape.

Lie down. Imagine it is a warm, sunny day and you are lying on grass. Feel the warmth of the sun on your face, arms. Let your fingers touch the grass. Perhaps if you look carefully, you can see a ladybird on a blade of grass. Look at its colour as it moves. Hold out your hands. See if it will move onto your finger. Watch and feel it move on your hand and arm. Watch it disappear between the blades of grass. There is a sound overhead. What is it? A plane streaks across the sky leaving a white trail. Watch it disappear.

Think of King Arthur's sword. See it lying at your feet. Look at the length and strength of it, at the jewel-encrusted handle. Lift it carefully.

Feel its weight. Move it around in different ways, watching the tip of it. Can you see the sparkle of the jewels as they catch the light? Feel the dryness of the rushes as you hide the sword on the edge of the lake. Hear the lapping of the water.

Characterization

During the exploring of personal space, the children will have had countless opportunities of finding out how their own bodies move. When the time is ripe, draw their attention to how other people move, and how the way they move depends on how they feel and on what sort of people they are.

1. Start by directing their attention to parts of their own bodies: eg, feet, hands:

   Feet   *As you look at your feet, try to make them feel like the feet of an old man. How does this make the rest of your body feel? Move about inside this old man's body. Try to think like the old man. How does he speak? What does he talk about?*

   Hands   *Look at your hands. Watch them grow into the greedy, grasping hands of Scrooge. What does this do to the rest of your body? How do you feel inside? What are your thoughts? Count your money, feeling like Scrooge.*

They can be asked to make their shoulders those of a boastful or arrogant person, a timid or weak person; the head that of a proud person, and so on. Explore and experiment as with other parts.

2. Now try developing characterization from shape making.

   In your own space, grow into the sort of person who takes up a lot of space. Change to a person who takes up a little space. Try walking in these shapes.

   Think of a witch shape. Feel this shape from inside. Grow into it. Prepare your spells, keeping this shape. Talk to your cat.

   Make up your own character. Can you move in this shape, think in this shape? Can you meet another character and have a movement conversation, still keeping your shape?

3. Develop group characterization. Invite small groups, after discussion, to grow into the same sort of people, to walk about together, trying to keep the group character.

4. Start improvization. For example, take the theme of a family on the beach. The group discusses this situation. Then talk about the dif-

ferent people in the 'family.' They decide what sort of person each of them will be. They work out the situation.

Sound and Movement Leading to Language Flow

During all movement experiences, feeling is all important. As a child becomes more absorbed in his movements, there is continual searching for the right movements to express his feelings. The time comes when a child feels the need to communicate his experiences still further. Intense movement feeling develops into sounds expressing the same feeling. There is joy and life in this sound since it comes from within and is not imposed. Through further exploration, out of these sounds, come words and phrases leading to language expression, and natural communication that has vitality and flow. . . .

Responding to External Sounds and Music

From an early stage in their movement experiences, children will respond readily to clear and direct sounds such as clapping, the beating of a drum, or the clash of cymbals. As they become more involved in movement qualities, as their sensitivity increases, they will respond to more subtle and varied percussion sounds, weaving patterns of movement that are either dance-like or dramatic.

Again, these movement sequences should develop from working individually to working with a partner and then with a group.

Careful choice of music is essential. From the beginning, children must have plenty of opportunity for listening and should be directly encouraged to listen. . . .

Working Out a Drama Theme

After the children have explored the varied avenues of movement experience, the working out of dramatic themes with the entire class can be attempted. They now have a movement vocabulary, their movements are expressive and controlled, their imagination has been stimulated, and they have a sensitive awareness of individuals and the group.

Sources and materials for themes can be sparked off by some situation already worked out in movement; they may arise from the children's imaginative and creative writing; they may come from stories from literature, history, scripture, etc.

Whatever the source, all the children should be thoroughly immersed in the fabric of the theme and excited by the idea of working something out together.

There should be no definite or set plan to begin with. Gradually this will develop, as individual characterizations are drawn, situations and group reactions are worked out, and creative ideas are introduced through movement experiences.

About the Author

CHARLES E. SILBERMAN's most recent book is *Crisis in the Classroom,* which has sold more than 100,000 copies in its hardcover edition and 240,000 copies in Vintage paperback. That book was the result of a three-and-a-half-year study of American education commissioned by the Carnegie Corporation of New York. Selected by the American Library Association as a Notable Book for 1970 and by *The New York Times Book Review* as one of the twelve outstanding books for that year, *Crisis in the Classroom* received six national educational awards: the John Dewey Award of the National Federation of Teachers, the John Dewey Society Award, the National Fellowship Award, the National Council for the Advancement of Education Writing Award, the 1970 Christopher Award, and the National Conference of Christians and Jews Special Award. In 1971 the National Society for the Study of Education published a collection of critical essays, *Reactions to Silberman's Crisis in the Classroom.*

Mr. Silberman is also the author of *Crisis in Black and White,* which won the Four Freedoms Literary Award and the National Conference of Christians and Jews Superior Merit Award. In 1965 Mr. Silberman was given the Loeb Award for Distinguished Business and Financial Writing for his book *The Myths of Automation.*

Mr. Silberman is currently the Director of the Study of Law and Justice, a Ford Foundation research project, where he is working on a forthcoming book on the law. Married and the father of four sons, he lives in Mount Vernon, New York.